# PERVERSIONS OF JUSTICE
## INDIGENOUS PEOPLES AND ANGLOAMERICAN LAW
### by WARD CHURCHILL

**CITY LIGHTS**
**SAN FRANCISCO**

Cover design by Rex Ray
Book design by Elaine Katzenberger
Typography by Harvest Graphics

Library of Congress Cataloging-in-Publication Data

Churchill, Ward.
    Perversions of justice : indigenous peoples and angloamerican law / by Ward Churchill.
        p.    cm.
    Includes bibliographical references and index.
    ISBN 0-87286-416-2 (cloth) – ISBN 0-87286-411-1 (pbk.)
    1. Indians of North America-Legal status, laws, etc.-United States-History.
2. International law-United States-History.   3. North America-Colonization.   I. Title.
KF8205 .C49 2003
342.73'0872—dc21                                                    2002073869

**Visit our web site: www.citylights.com**

CITY LIGHTS BOOKS are edited by Lawrence Ferlinghetti and Nancy J. Peters and published
at the City Lights Bookstore, 261 Columbus Avenue, San Francisco, CA 94133

# ACKNOWLEDGMENTS

My views on "The Law" as it applies to indigenous peoples has been influenced over the years by the writing of a number of other scholars, often in ways that may seem strange or mysterious to them. These include, most notably, Milner Ball, Francis Anthony Boyle, Noam Chomsky, the late Felix S. Cohen, Richard Delgado, Vine Deloria, Jr., Jimmie Durham, Richard Falk, the late Raphaël Lemkin, Barbara Alice Mann, Bernard Nietschmann, Bertrand Russell, Natsu Taylor Saito, Jean-Paul Sartre, Robert K. Thomas, Robert A. Williams, Jr., and the late Quincy Wright. More "in the trenches" sorts of effects have accrued as the result of conversation/interaction with S. James Anaya, Kathleen Neal Cleaver, Bruce Ellison, Don Grinde, the late Lew Gurwitz, Lilikala Kameʻeleihiwa, Jim Kimball, the late William Kunstler, John Mohawk, Glenn T. Morris, Simon J. Ortiz, Jim Page, Brooklyn Rivera, David Stannard, George Tinker, Haunani-Kay and Mililani Trask, J.J. Vander Wall and Sharon Helen Venne. To each of them, thanks is due, as well as release from responsibility for whatever errors I may have committed, whether of fact or of a more theoretical nature.

My writing is of course both formed and tempered by my activism, and here it has benefited from associations far too numerous to list. Particularly important have been the insights borne of struggle conveyed by Faith Attaguille, the late Nilak Butler, Bobby Castillo, the late Mark Clark, Roxanne Dunbar Ortiz, Corky Gonzales and his daughter Nita, Mike James, Geronimo ji Jaga (Pratt), Russ Means, Bernard Ominiyak, Leonard Peltier, Bob Robideau, Susan Rosenberg, Mike Ryan, Madonna Thunderhawk, John Trudell and Phyllis Young. As well, the elders who have shaped my perceptions, not only of history, but regarding the very essence of right and wrong. These include not only those who have now passed—among them Chief Frank Fools Crow and his assistant, Matthew King (Noble Red Man), and Philip Deer, Grampa David So Happy, and my adoptive auntie, Roberta Blackgoat—but many who remain among us: Uncle Joe Locust and Aunt Fifi, as examples, and the Kelly boys, John, Peter and Fred. To each, I owe a debt of gratitude, as I do to the many others who've gone unnamed.

Finally, appreciation must also be expressed to my publishers at City Lights, especially my editor/friend, Elaine Katzenberger, not only for believing in the merits of my work, but for investing the time, energy and resources necessary to ensure that it appears with the quality of design and production evident herein. Again, whatever mistakes may be made in the book are mine, not theirs.

in memory of Nilak Butler

# CONTENTS

Foreward   *by James Wm. Chichetto*                                        xi
  "From Emily Dickenson and Sitting Bull on *Dakota*"

Introduction   *by Sharon Helen Venne*                                    xiii
  "The Creator Knows Their Lies and So Should We"
    Ward Churchill's Pursuit of Juridical Truth

Essays
  Perversions of Justice:                                                   1
    Examining U.S. Rights to Occupancy in North America

  Rights of Conquest:                                                      33
    The Devolution of a Myth in International Law

  Stolen Kingdom:                                                          73
    The Right of Hawai'i to Decolonization

  Charades, Anyone?                                                       125
    The Indian Claims Commission in Context

  A Breach of Trust:                                                      153
    The Radioactive Colonization of Native North America

  The Crucible of American Indian Identity:                               201
    Native Tradition versus Colonial Imposition in
    Postconquest North America

  Forbidding the "G-Word":                                                247
    Holocaust Denial as Judicial Doctrine in Canada

  The Bloody Wake of Alcatraz:                                            263
    Repression of the American Indian Movement
    During the 1970s

  "To Judge Them by the Standards of Their Time":                         303
    America's Indian Fighters, the Laws of War and the
    Question of International Order

# Appendices

A. United Nations Declaration on the Granting of Independence    405
to Colonial Countries and Peoples
December 14, 1960

B. Congressional Apology to Native Hawaiians    408
November 23, 1993

C. Draft United Nations Declaration on the Rights of Indigenous Peoples  414
August 26, 1994

D. National Security Council Memorandum on the Rights of    427
Indigenous Peoples
January 18, 2001

# Index

433

## FORWARD

                . . . Emily Dickenson sings
                        of Ward Churchill

                "Kathleen Norris is fine
                But Ward Churchill is better,
                I love his Sabbath sounds
                Hooped together.
                He sits in an ancient tree,
                Talking like God with hair
                    —A forbidden voice
                            in our Hills,
                Hidden from eyesight there.
                O Churchill of sun-
                        flecked questions
                Sown with a jointed hand,
                Behind Wakan's eclipse
                And watchful land,
                You arrived with Delphic gold
                Not vanquished by
                        the birds.
                I love your Sabbath mind
                In the half-light of
                        God's Word."


                        —James Wm. Chichetto
                        1999

---

Excerpted from the fragment of a play entitled "Emily Dickenson and Sitting Bull on *Dakota*," published in *The Connecticut Poetry Review,* Vol. 18, No. 1, 1999.

# "The Creator Knows Their Lies and So Must We"
## Ward Churchill's Pursuit of Truth and Justice

> Colonialism by any other name is still colonialism, a crime against nature, peace and humanity.
>
> —John Trudell
> 1988

This continent has not entered a "postcolonial era." Native North America remains occupied by invaders from abroad, settlers who have appropriated our land and resources for their own benefit. Indigenous peoples who conducted themselves as sovereign nations since time immemorial continue to be forcibly subordinated to the self-assigned "governing authority" of recently established settler states both north and south of an arbitrary boundary separating the United States and Canada. It is thus patently obvious that we, the indigenous nations of North America, have not been decolonized. Until we are, the idea of "postcolonialism" has no relevance to us. Indeed, the very term, now quite fashionable in academic discourse, serves only to render us invisible, masking the reality of our circumstance.

This is in keeping with a broader colonialist enterprise of deception. It is in this sense that Cree singer Buffy Sainte Marie has observed how history has been written in "a liar's scrawl." The versions of history penned by the colonizer always and invariably defend the colonial order, either by denying that the process of colonization has "really" been colonizing, or, to the extent that the opposite is sometimes acknowledged, by carefully applying the spin necessary to make the whole thing appear to have been of benefit to all concerned, victims as well as victimizers.

As Adolf Hitler contended in *Mein Kampf*, the bigger and more frequently a lie is repeated, the more likely it is to be received as "truth" (especially when it is convenient for the audience to believe it anyway).[1] The nazi führer was hardly unique in subscribing to such views. Noam Chomsky,

Edward S. Herman, Michael Parenti, and numerous others have abundantly demonstrated that the "Big Lie," constantly repeated, is every bit as ubiquitous in North America today as it was in the Third Reich a half-century ago.[2] Whether one prefers to follow Gramsci in describing the resulting tissue of falsity as "hegemony," or to adopt a postmodernist vernacular in which it is referred as "the metanarrative," the purpose served is to reinforce the existing order, making it seem natural, inevitable, and therefore inherently "just."[3]

Nowhere is such distortion more prominently displayed than in the corpus of European and Euroamerican law by which the colonizers have sought to rationalize, disguise, or deny the character of their relationship to indigenous America. This seems especially true, at least at present, with respect to Angloamerican law and, as a consequence, to North America. The object here, even more than in other quarters, is, as it has been all along, to create a pervasive misimpression that, whatever the defects of the extant system, "TINA." TINA is a catchy acronym coined by former British prime minister Margaret Thatcher to convey the message to the colonized and otherwise oppressed that "There Is No Alternative" to our present situation.[4]

Into this intricately crafted conceptual morass wades Keetoowah Cherokee scholar Ward Churchill (Kizhiinaabe). Fortunately, he is a tall man, because the muck is truly deep. Fortunate, too, is the fact that he has over the years acquired considerable experience in confronting and debunking the web of interconnected falsehoods which comprise Euroamerica's historical, political and anthropological metanarratives. In previous books—*A Little Matter of Genocide*, for example, and *Struggle for the Land*[5]—Churchill has often used history quite effectively as a means of illuminating the fallacies of Angloamerican law. In the present volume, *Perversions of Justice*, he reverses polarity, employing examples drawn from the same body of law as windows through which to examine history. The results are equally satisfying.

**Perversions of Justice**
In the title essay, beginning with the so-called "Doctrine of Discovery," Churchill traces the entire five-century sweep of "innovations" by which Europe and its derivatives have presumed, unilaterally and typically by force, to extend their jurisdiction over indigenous peoples the world over. Insofar as he focuses upon North America, particular attention is paid to the often preposterous but nonetheless pivotal theories produced by Chief Justice of the U.S. Supreme Court John Marshall during the early nineteenth century,

and how the "reasoning" embodied therein has served to shape the subsequent evolution of federal "Indian law," not only in the United States but Canada as well (yes, Canadian courts cite U.S. judicial precedent in this connection, and it should be noted that the U.S. is currently attempting to establish its own juridical/statutory posture as a model for replication by every settler-state government on the planet).[6]

From there, the author turns his gaze full-force upon a particular legal construction, the "Right of Conquest," upon which Euroamericans frequently rely, at least rhetorically, in an effort to justify their assertion of colonial prerogatives over indigenous lands and lives. Compellingly, he demonstrates that the notion of conquest rights has always amounted to a logical fallacy, that it has never been considered so acceptable within the framework of international law as contemporary U.S. and Canadian commentators would have us believe, and that, in any event, such "rights" evidence no applicability at all to the North American context.

A related fable concerns the imagined right of the U.S. to possess Hawai'i. In his next essay, "Stolen Kingdom," Churchill takes as his frame of reference the 1993 apology officially extended by the U.S. to the Kanaka Maoli (indigenous Hawaiians) for its role in the illegal overthrow of their nation's constitutional monarchy a century earlier, and points out that any such acknowledgement of a criminal act triggers a clearly defined legal obligation on the part of the perpetrator to make restitution (i.e., restoring the situation as nearly as possible to its original condition). Given the nature of the offense in the Hawaiian case, such redress would necessarily entail the U.S. (re)placing Hawai'i on the United Nations Secretariat's list of "non-self-governing territories" subject to timely decolonization. The same principle applies, of course, with respect to every indigenous nation in North America.

The fourth essay—"Charades, Anyone?"—addresses the manner in which, having never relinquished resort to them as a fallback position, the U.S. has attempted to distance itself from at least the more blatant crudities entailed in assertions of conquest rights. The topic in this instance is a fiction, fostered through the functioning of the Indian Claims Commission from 1946-1978, that "just compensation" has been provided to those indigenous nations from which territory was illegally expropriated by the United States at earlier points in its history. Both the invalidity of the terms under which such transactions were conducted and the magnitude of the ensuing fraud are detailed.

Next comes "A Breach of Trust," dissecting the manner in which the United States has abused its self-assigned and intendedly perpetual "plenary power" over the mineral assets endowing indigenous nations. As illustration, Churchill explores the various ways an assortment of federal agencies have utilized internally colonized native territories to develop U.S. nuclear capacity, enriching and strengthening the colonizing power while systematically displacing catestrophic levels of environmental contamination and corresponding health impacts onto the colonized. Noting that the government itself has actively entertained the idea of declaring the locales in which it conducts nuclear mining, processing, testing and disposal to be "national sacrifice areas," and that this necessarily means the sacrifice of the people residing therein, the author concludes that "the radioactive colonization of Native North America" is both ecocidal and genocidal in its implications.

There follows an essay—"The Crucible of American Indian Identity"— analyzing the ways in which the U.S. has usurped the ability of indigenous peoples to exercise the most fundamental right of any nation: that of determining for themselves who their members/constituents are. "Crucible" is devoted primarily to describing the means by which such decisions were made within the parameters of traditional indigenous law, and contrasting them to the methods employed by colonial officials to supplant self-determining indigenous procedures with their own explicitly racial nomenclature. Churchill singles out for analysis the latest variation on the federal theme: the 1990 Act for the Protection of American Indian Arts and Crafts, a statute making it a criminal offense for anyone to identify him/herself as an indigenous person without express permission from the colonial régime. Overall, it is observed that the settler state government has thereby positioned itself to engage in a bizarre form of definitional/statistical genocide of native people.

To respond constructively to any phenomenon, one must first be able to make out what it is with a considerable degree of accuracy. In "Forbidding the G-Word," Churchill points out, as he does throughout the book, that in North America the purpose of judicial interpretation is more often to obfuscate than to clarify, at least where indigenous issues are concerned. Using the recent *Friends of the Lubicon* case as an example, he first offers a precise delineation of the legal meaning of the word "genocide," then lays bare the manner in which Canadian courts and parliamentarians have contrived to suppress both understanding and proper usage of the term. As is plainly implied in the essay, although the particulars are somewhat different, the resulting analysis and conclusions are as appropriate to the U.S. as to the Canadian context.

Having thus sketched out what he sees as the contours of the problem, the author turns to the question of what happens when an indigenous nation sets out to free itself from colonial subjugation. In "The Bloody Wake of Alcatraz," he provides a blow-by-blow recounting of the lethal counterinsurgency campaign mounted by the FBI and other federal agencies against the American Indian Movement (AIM) on the Pine Ridge Sioux Reservation in South Dakota during the mid-1970s. Special emphasis is placed on the extralegality of such operations, a matter reflecting the extent to which the sometimes noble-sounding principles of Angloamerican legalism are situational, put to use or jettisoned on the basis of élite perceptions of interest and expediency.

Churchill also underscores the fact that, although it was orchestrated by FBI personnel, much of the violence directed against AIM on Pine Ridge was actually carried out by other native people. This, he attributes to the effects of the 1934 Indian Reorganization Act, a statute designed in classic colonialist fashion to create puppet governments on reservations across the U.S. (through its succession of Indian Acts, Canada has done very much the same[7]). It was from this Quisling apparatus,[8] and the comprador class which swarms about all such entities like flies around a dung heap, that the anti-AIM death squads were assembled. Viewed in this way, one can detect little difference between the methods with which the U.S. administers internally colonized indigenous nations on the one hand, and, on the other, those it employs to "maintain stability" in the countries it dominates abroad, in the Third World.[9]

This is hardly the first time Churchill has pointed out the role played by collaborationist elements within indigenous societies in reinforcing the U.S./Canadian colonial order. Elsewhere, he has likened the pathology afflicting those involved to that described by Frantz Fanon in *Black Skin, White Masks*[10] (or manifested by Rudyard Kipling's "good Indian" in "Gunga Din"[11]). In the present volume, he further develops such analyses in "Crucible" and in "The Bloody Wake of Alcatraz" he offers an explicit comparison of the "Vichy" governments installed throughout North America's Indian Country to the raft of treasonous régimes set up by the nazis to administer the occupied countries of Europe during World War II.[12]

Rounding out the collection, the author turns his gaze full force upon the most patently criminal dimension of all the wrongs Angloamerica has done unto others. In "To Judge Them by the Standards of Their Time," he thoroughly debunks the tired cliché most often advanced by champions of the status quo—that critics are guilty of projecting modern legal principles "backwards" into historical contexts where they are surely inapplicable—by relying upon the customary law extant in the mid-nineteenth century as well as the U.S. Army's own 1863 codification of the Laws of War as lenses through which to assess the military's performance during its so-called Indian Wars. The relevance of this exercise to the world is then demonstrated when Churchill traces the conflicting evolutionary tracks of law and U.S. aggression forward in time, from the Wounded Knee Massacre of 1890 to the present preparations for an invasion of Iraq, displaying the costs and consequences to humanity at every step along the way. In the end, his call for "law enforcement" vis-à-vis the U.S. thus becomes a call for survival itself.

## In the Spirit of Big Bear and Crazy Horse

When the peoples indigenous to this continent we call Great Turtle Island were first placed here by the Creator, we were given the laws necessary to govern our relationships with one another, with our nonhuman relatives, and with the land itself. While each people has evolved its own particular articulation of these laws, and its own unique way of applying them, it is safe to observe that every indigenous "legal code" devolves upon an identical set of requirements that humans shoulder an individual/collective responsibility to preserve the balance of the natural order into which we have been introduced, and that we do so in the only way possible: by conducting our affairs on the basis of mutual respect, not only among and between peoples, but between people and the world in which we reside. Hence, in indigenous law, we humans have but one true right, that of fulfilling our responsibilities to the Creator.[14]

At the most fundamental level, it is precisely the fulfillment of these responsibilities that the European invasion, subsequent Euroamerican colonization, and the legalistic sophistries attending both, has served first and foremost to prevent. By the same token, it is the right to such fulfillment that indigenous people have all along fought hardest to protect. The struggle has always and more than anything represented a confrontation of worldviews: on one side a synthetic and predatory culture bent upon standing apart from, dominating and ultimately consuming nature;[15] on the other, a multiplicity of organic cultures, each seeing itself as being integral to and entirely dependent upon the natural order for its very survival. A conflict between more diametrically opposed antagonists is inconceivable.

Much of what has transpired since the European invasion of Turtle Island commenced can be understood in terms of the sort of sheer physical combat perhaps best symbolized by the nineteenth-century Lakota patriot, Crazy Horse. Concomitantly, and in some ways even more substantively, however, indigenous people have fought back by way of our steadfast refusal to abandon the values, priorities and understandings that are foundational to our traditional ways of life. This posture is exemplified by many people in the course of our history, quite notably by the Cree leader, Big Bear.

Things were never so dichotomized, of course. Big Bear engaged in physical resistance when necessary, and, for his part, Crazy Horse spent far more of his time living in a traditional Lakota way than he did defeating Crook at the Rosebud and Custer at the Little Big Horn. Taken together as symbols, however, the lives of the two men can be seen as representing the main currents in an unending stream of indigenous resistance.[16] Taken together, they also demonstrate as little else can the degree to which questions of resistance and repression reduce in the end to matters of consciousness; that is, whether truth will continue to be perceived, spoken and acted upon—irrespective of consequences—or whether it is to be twisted by increasingly sophisticated elaborations of falsehood, employed in its deformity as a tool of oppression rather than of liberation.

It is squarely within the stream of traditional indigenous resistance that Ward Churchill has elected to swim. In the spirit of both Big Bear and Crazy Horse, he has committed himself to a life's work of finding and speaking truth, not so much "to power" as to *us*, the people in whom responsibility to the Creator is and has always been invested. He does so boldly, without hesitation, equivocation or apology. Yet he also does so carefully, allowing precision to guide the anger informing his words. "The Creator knows their lies," he says of those subscribing to the prevailing paradigms of domination, "and so must we. We've got to understand such things clearly, for what they are rather than what they're purported to be, if we're going be able to free ourselves from colonialism rather than continuing to pass it along from generation to generation in an ever more perfected form."

Churchill's purpose is thus to challenge Eurosupremacist hegemony in its own terms, debunking the master narratives that support and give it form, enabling us thereby to see in sharp relief the combination of physical intimidation and intellectual mystification with which the colonizer endeavors to preclude us from meeting our most basic obligations as human beings. The goal, as he's put it in his usual straightforward fashion, is help forge the consciousness necessary to achieve "nothing less than the complete decolonization of Native North America."[17] In effect, Ward seeks creation of a genuine rather than merely theoretical postcolonial reality on Great Turtle Island.

Nor is this all. Those hoping to discount Ward's contribution to the struggle for indigenous liberation as consisting *only* of words would do well to bear in mind that he doesn't just "talk the talk," he "walks the walk" as well. A veteran activist, he has been beaten, shot at, defamed, "disemployed," arrested more than thirty times, and not infrequently jailed over the past three decades, always in defense of native rights.[18] His intellectuality has been harnessed rather consistently to more concrete dimensions of resistance.

Although Ward and his work have been much disparaged in the more sold-out quarters of indigenous society, there is nothing about either that might offend the likes of Big Bear or Crazy Horse. On the contrary, by launching assaults on the conceptual structures of our oppression as forcefully as he does, and by so regularly putting his body where his mind is, he honors their memory in ways of which each would heartily approve. In turn, he is himself honored by those among us, especially our elders, who maintain the greatest allegiance to our traditions.[19] There is much to be learned from any man who fights so well, so hard, and so long to fulfill his responsibilities. Read this book and you will understand why I am proud to call him "Brother."

Sharon H. Venne (Old Woman Bear)
School of Law, University of Saskatchewan
October 2000

# Notes

1. Adolf Hitler, *Mein Kampf* (Boston: Sentry Editions, 1962) esp. pp. 184, 467.

2. Noam Chomsky, *Necessary Illusions: Thought Control in Democratic Societies* (Boston: South End Press, 1989); Edward S. Herman and Noam Chomsky, *Manufacturing Consent: The Political Economy of the Mass Media* (New York: Pantheon, 1988); Michael Parenti, *Inventing Reality: The Politics of the News Media* (New York: St. Martin's Press, 1993).

3. On Gramsci, see Walter L. Adamson, *Hegemony and Revolution: A Study of Antonio Gramsci's Political and Cultural Theory* (Berkeley: University of California Press, 1980) pp. 170-9. On the notion of the "metanarrative"—also referred to as the "Master" or "Grand Narrative"—see Jean-François Lyotard, *The Postmodern Condition: A Report on Knowledge* (Minneapolis: University of Minnesota Press, 1993) esp. pp. xii, xix, 32-9.

4. Quoted in Noam Chomsky, *Rogue States: The Role of Force in World Affairs* (Cambridge, MA: South End Press, 2000) pp. 204-6.

5. Ward Churchill, *A Little Matter of Genocide: Holocaust and Denial in the Americas, 1492 to the Present* (San Francisco: City Lights, 1997); *Struggle for the Land: Native North American Resistance to Genocide, Ecocide and Colonization* (San Francisco: City Lights, [2nd ed.] 2002).

6. Witness, for example, the Canadian Supreme Court's citation of Marshall's 1822 *McIntosh* opinion as "the *locus classicus* of the principles governing aboriginal title" in its own 1973 *Calder* opinion (SCR 313 at 380). More broadly, see John Hurley, "Aboriginal Rights, the Constitution and the Marshall Court," *Revue Juridique Themis*, No. 17, 1983.

7. David C. Hawkes, *Aboriginal Self-Government: What Does It Mean?* (Kingston, Ont.: Institute for Intergovernmental Relations, Queen's University, 1983) p. 9.

8. Quisling, a Norwegian, served as head of the puppet government installed in his country by the nazis after it was occupied in 1940. His very name thereupon became synonymous with "traitor"; Paul M. Hayes, *Quisling: The Career and Political Ideas of Vikdun Quisling, 1887-1945* (Bloomington: Indiana University Press, 1972).

9. See, e.g., Edward S. Herman, *The Real Terror Network: Terrorism in Fact and Propaganda* (Boston: South End Press, 1982).

10. Ward Churchill, "White Studies: The Intellectual Imperialism of U.S. Higher Education," in his *From a Native Son: Essays in Indigenism, 1985-1995* (Boston: South End Press, 1996) p. 277.

11. Ward Churchill, "Hi-Ho, Hillerman . . . (Away): The Role of Detective Fiction in Indian Country," in his *Fantasies of the Master Race: Literature, Cinema and the Colonization of American Indians* (San Francisco: City Lights, [2nd ed.] 1999) pp. 83-4.

12. "Vichy" was capitol of the collaborationist régime in France during the nazi occupation. The term carries the same connotation as "Quisling"; Geoffrey Warner, *Pierre Laval and the Eclipse of France* (London: Macmillan, 1978).

13. Like that of the United States, the Canadian government has lately adopted a cosmetic practice of issuing formal apologies for some of its more egregious crimes against indigenous peoples. Most notably, an apology was offered with respect to damages accruing from the culturally genocidal system of residential schools Canada imposed upon indigenous children until the 1980s. Also like its U.S. counterpart, Canada has actively sought to constrain understanding of the implications of what it has admitted, and, where possible, to displace the onus of responsibility onto religious and other institutions that operated under its sanction; see, e.g., James Brooke, "Indian Lawsuits on School Abuse May Bankrupt Canadian Churches," *New York Times*, Nov. 2, 2000.

14. William Andrew Shutkin, "International Human Rights Law and the Earth: Protection of Indigenous Peoples and the Environment, *Virginia Journal of International Law*, No. 479, 1991.

15. See Winona LaDuke, "Natural to Synthetic and Back Again," in Ward Churchill, ed., *Marxism and Native Americans* (Boston: South End Press, 1983) pp. i-viii; Ward Churchill, *Since Predator Came: Notes from the Struggle for American Indian Liberation* (Littleton, CO: Aigis, 1995).

16. For further information on Crazy Horse and Big Bear, see Mari Sandoz, *Crazy Horse: Strange Man of the Oglalas* (Lincoln: University of Nebraska Press, 1961).

17. See, e.g., Churchill's "I Am Indigenist: Notes on the Ideology of the Fourth World," in *Struggle for the Land*.

18. Some of Churchill's "battle ribbons" are mentioned in AIM leader Russell Means' autobiography, *Where White Men Fear to Tread* (New York: St. Martin's Press, 1995).

19. Sharon Helen Venne, *Our Elders Understand Our Rights: Evolving International Law Regarding Indigenous Rights* (Pinticton, B.C.: Theytus Books, 1998).

# Perversions of Justice

## Examining the Doctrine of U.S. Rights to Occupancy in North America

It's a travesty of a mockery of a sham.

— Groucho Marx

Recognition of the legal and moral rights by which it occupies whatever landbase it calls its own is one of the most fundamental issues confronting any nation. Typically, such claims to sovereign and proprietary interest in national territorialities devolve, at least in considerable part, upon supportable contentions that the citizenry is preponderantly composed of persons directly descended from peoples who have dwelt within the geographical area claimed since "time immemorial."[1] The matter becomes infinitely more complex in situations where the dominant—or dominating—population is comprised either of the representatives of a foreign power, or of immigrants ("settlers") who can offer no such assertion of "aboriginal" lineage to justify their presence or ownership of property in the usual sense.[2]

History is replete with instances in which various peoples have advanced philosophical, theological and juridical arguments concerning their alleged entitlement to the homelands of others, only to have them rebuffed by the community of nations as lacking both moral force and sound legal principle. In such cases, the trend has been that international rejection of "imperial" pretensions has led to the inability of the nations extending such claims to sustain them.[3] Modern illustrations of this tendency include the dissolution of the classic European empires—those of France, Netherlands, Portugal and Great Britain in particular—during the post-World War II period, as well as the resounding defeat of the Axis powers' territorial ambitions during the war itself. Even more recent examples may be found in the breakup of the Soviet (Great Russian) and Yugoslavian (Serbian) states, and in the extreme controversy attending maintenance of such settler states as Northern Ireland, Israel and South Africa.

The purpose of this essay is to examine the basis upon which another contemporary settler state, the United States of America, contends that it possesses legitimate—indeed, inviolate—rights to approximately two and a quarter-billion acres of territory in North America.[4] Through such scrutiny, the philosophical validity of U.S. legal claims to territorial integrity can be understood and tested against the standards of both logic and morality. This, in turn, is intended to provide a firm foundation from which readers may assess the substance of that image generated by the sweeping pronouncements so frequently offered by official America and its adherents over the years: that this is a country so essentially "peaceful," so uniquely enlightened in its commitments to the rule of law and concept of liberty, that it has inevitably emerged as the natural leader of a global drive to consolidate a "New World Order" in which the conquest and occupation of the territoriality of any nation by another "cannot and will not stand."[5]

## Rights to Territorial Acquisition in International Law

From the outset of the "Age of Discovery" precipitated by the Columbian voyages, the European powers, eager to obtain uncontested title to at least some portion of the lands their emissaries were encountering, quickly recognized the need to establish a formal code of juridical standards to legitimate what they acquired.[6] To some extent, this was meant to lend a patina of "civilized"—and therefore, it was imagined, inherently superior—legality to the actions of the European Crowns in their relations with the peoples indigenous to the desired geography. More importantly, however, the system was envisioned as a necessary means of resolving disputes between the Crowns themselves, each of which was vying with the others in a rapacious battle over the prerogative to benefit from wealth accruing through ownership of given regions in the "New World."[7] In order for any such regulatory code to be considered effectively binding by all Old World parties, it was vital that it be sanctioned by the Church.[8]

Hence, the mechanism deployed for this purpose was a theme embodied in a series of Papal Bulls begun by Pope Innocent IV during the Crusades of the late thirteenth-century.[9] The Bulls were intended to define the proper ("lawful") relationship between Christians and "Infidels" in all such worldly matters as property rights. Beginning in the early sixteenth century, Spanish jurists in particular did much to develop this theory into what have come to be known as the "Doctrine of Discovery" and an attendant dogma, the "Right of Conquest."[10] Through the efforts of legal scholars such as Franciscus de Vitoria and Matías de la Paz, Spanish articulations of Discovery Doctrine, endorsed by the Pope, rapidly evolved to hold the following as primary tenets of international law:[11]

1) Outright ownership of land accrued to the Crown represented by a given Christian (European) discoverer only when the land discovered proved to be uninhabited (*territorium res nullius*).[12]

2) Title to inhabited lands discovered by Crown representatives was recognized as belonging inherently to the indigenous people thereby encountered, but rights to acquire land from, and to trade with, the natives of the region accrued exclusively to the discovering Crown vis-à-vis other European powers. In exchange for this right, the discovering power committed itself to proselytizing the Christian gospel among the natives.[13]

3) Acquisition of land title from indigenous peoples could occur only by their consent—that is, by an agreement usually involving purchase—rather than through force of arms, so long as the natives did not arbitrarily decline to trade with Crown representatives, refuse to admit missionaries among them, or inflict gratuitous violence upon citizens of the Crown.

4) Absent these last three conditions, utilization of armed force to acquire aboriginally owned territory was considered unjust and claims to land title accruing therefrom to be correspondingly invalid.

5) Should one or more of the three conditions be present, then it was held that the Crown had a legal right to use whatever force was required to subdue native resistance and impound their property as compensation. Land title gained by prosecution of such "Just Wars" was considered valid.[14]

Although this legal perspective was hotly debated at the time (it still is, in certain quarters), and saw considerable violation by European colonists, it was generally acknowledged as the standard against which international conduct would be weighed.[15] By the early seventeenth century, the requirements of Discovery Doctrine had led the European states, England in particular, to adopt a policy of entering into formal treaties—full-fledged international compacts in which the sovereignty of the indigenous parties were, by definition, officially recognized as equivalent to that of the respective Crowns—as an expedient to obtaining legally valid land titles from American Indian peoples, first in what is now the state of Virginia, and then in areas further north. Treaties concerning trade, professions of peace and friendship, and to consummate military alliances were also quite common.[16]

Undeniably, there is a certain arrogance imbedded in the proposition that Europeans were somehow self-imbued with an authority to restrict the prerogatives of native people to sell their property to whomsoever they chose, assuming they wished to sell it at all. Nonetheless, in its recognition that indigenous peoples constituted bona fide nations holding essentially the same rights to land and sovereignty as any other, the legal posture of early European colonialism seems rather advanced and refined in retrospect. In these respects, the Doctrine of Discovery is widely viewed as one of the more important cornerstones of modern international law and diplomacy.[17]

With its adoption of Protestantism, however, Britain had already begun to mark its independence from papal regulation by adding an element of its own to the doctrine. Usually termed the "Norman Yoke," this concept asserted that land rights devolve in the main upon the extent to which owners demonstrate a willingness and ability to "develop" their properties in accordance with a scriptural obligation to exercise "dominium" over nature. In other words, a person or a people is ultimately entitled to only that quantity of real estate which s/he/they convert from "wilderness" to a "domesticated" state.[18] By this criterion, English settlers were seen as possessing an inherent right to dispossess native people of all land other than that which the latter might be "reasonably expected" to put to such "proper" usage as cultivation.[19] By the same token, this doctrinal innovation automatically placed the British Crown on a legal footing from which it could contest the discovery rights of any European power not adhering to the requirement of "overcoming the wilderness."

This last allowed England to simultaneously "abide by the law" *and* directly confront Catholic France for ascendancy in the Atlantic regions of North America. After a series of "French and Indian Wars" beginning in the

4

late 1600s and lasting nearly a century, the English were victorious, but at a cost more than negating the expected financial benefits that had led the Crown to launch its colonial venture in the first place. As one major consequence, King George III, in a move intended to preclude further warfare with indigenous nations, issued the Proclamation of 1763. This royal edict stipulated that all settlement or other forms of land acquisition by his subjects west of a line running along the Allegheny and Appalachian Mountains from Canada to the Spanish colony of Florida would be suspended indefinitely, and perhaps permanently. English expansion on the North American continent was thereby brought to an abrupt halt.[20]

### Enter the U.S.

The new policy conflicted sharply with the desires for personal gain evident among a voracious élite which had been growing within England's seaboard colonial population. Most of the colonies held some pretense of title to "western" lands, much of it conveyed by earlier Crown grant, and had planned to use it as a means of bolstering their respective economic positions. Similarly, members of the landed gentry such as George Washington, Thomas Jefferson, John Adams, James Madison and Anthony Wayne all possessed considerable speculative interests in land parcels on the far side of the 1763 demarcation line. The only way in which these could be converted into profit was for the parcels to be settled and developed. Vociferous contestation and frequent violation of the Proclamation became commonplace.[21] All in all, this dynamic was a powerful precipitating factor in the American War of Independence, during which many rank-and-file rebels were convinced to fight against the Crown by promises of western land grants "for services rendered" in the event the revolt was successful.[22]

There was, however, a catch. The United States emerged from its decolonization struggle against England—perhaps the most grievous offense which could be perpetrated by any subject people under then-prevailing law—as a pariah, an outlaw state that was shunned as an utterly illegitimate entity by most other countries. Desperate to establish itself as a legitimate nation, and lacking other viable alternatives through which to demonstrate its aptitude for complying with international legality, the new government was compelled to observe the strictest of protocols in its dealings with Indians. Indeed, what the Continental Congress needed more than anything at the time was for indigenous nations, already recognized as respectable sovereignties in their treaties with the European states, to bestow a comparable recognition upon the fledgling U.S. by entering into treaties with *it*.[23] The urgency of the matter was compounded by the fact that the Indians maintained military parity with, and in some cases superiority to, the U.S. Army all along the frontier.

As a result, both the Articles of Confederation and subsequent Constitution of the United States contained clauses explicitly and exclusively restricting relations with indigenous nations to the federal government, insofar as the former were recognized as enjoying the same politico-legal status as any other foreign power.[24] The U.S. also officially renounced, in the 1787 Northwest Ordinance and elsewhere, any aggressive intent concerning indigenous nations, especially with regard to their respective landbases:

> The utmost good faith shall always be observed towards the Indians; their land and property shall never be taken from them without their consent; and in their property, rights, and liberty, they shall never be disturbed . . . but laws founded in justice and humanity shall from time to time be made, for wrongs done to them, and for peace and friendship with them.[25]

This rhetorical stance, reflecting an impeccable observance of international legality, was also incorporated into such compacts with European states as the U.S. was able to obtain during its formative years. In the 1803 Louisiana Purchase of much of North America west of the Mississippi from France, for instance, the federal government solemnly pledged itself to protect "the inhabitants of the ceded territory . . . in the free enjoyment of their liberty, property and the religion they profess."[26] Other phraseology in the purchase agreement makes it clear that federal authorities understood they were acquiring from the French, not the land itself, but France's monopolistic trade rights and prerogative to buy any acreage within the area its indigenous owners wished to sell.

The same understanding certainly pertained to all unceded Indian Country east of the Mississippi River, once England's discovery rights were quitclaimed by George III in the Treaty of Paris (by which the American independence struggle was concluded). Even if English rights somehow "passed" to the new republic by virtue of this royal action, an extremely dubious premise in itself, there still remained the matter of obtaining native consent to literal U.S. ownership of any area beyond the 1763 proclamation line.[27] Hence, the securing of indigenous agreement to land cessions must be added to the impressive list of diplomatic and military reasons why treatymaking with Indians comprised the main current of American diplomacy throughout the immediate postrevolutionary period. The need to acquire valid land title from native people through treaties far outlasted the motivations of military necessity, moreover, this having been of greatly diminished importance after U.S. victories over Tecumseh's alliance in 1794 and 1811, Britain in the War of 1812, and the Muscogee Red Sticks in 1814.[28] The treaties were and remain, in substance, the basic real estate documents anchoring U.S. claims to land title—and thus to rights of occupancy—in North America.

What was most problematic in this situation for early federal policy-makers was the fact that in gaining diplomatic recognition and land cessions from indigenous nations through treaties, the U.S. was simultaneously admitting not only that Indians owned virtually all of the territory coveted by the U.S., but that they were really under no obligation to part with it. As William Wirt, an early attorney general, put it in 1821: "[Legally speaking,] so long as a tribe exists and remains in possession of its lands, its title and possession are sovereign and exclusive. We treat with them as separate sovereignties, and while an Indian nation continues to exist within its acknowledged limits, we have no more right to enter upon their territory than we have to enter upon the territory of a foreign prince."[29] A few years later, he further elaborated this same understanding:

> The point, once conceded, that the Indians are independent to the purpose of treating, their independence is to that purpose as absolute as any other nation. Being competent to bind themselves by treaty, they are equally competent to bind the party that treats with them. Such party cannot take benefit of [a] treaty with the Indians, and then deny them the reciprocal benefits of the treaty on the grounds that they are not independent nations to all intents and purposes. . . Nor can it be conceded that their independence as a nation is a limited independence. Like all other independent nations, they have the absolute power of war and peace. Like all other independent nations, their territories are inviolate by any other sovereignty. . . They are entirely self-governed, self-directed. They treat, or refuse to treat, at their pleasure; and there is no human power that can rightly control them in the exercise of their discretion in this respect.[30]

Such enjoyment of genuine sovereign rights and status by indigenous nations served, during the twenty years following the revolution (roughly 1790-1810), to considerably retard the assumption of lawful possession of their land grants by revolutionary soldiers, as well as consummation of the plans of the élite caste of western land speculators. Over the next two decades (1810-1830), the issue assumed an ever-increasing policy importance as the matter of native sovereignty came to replace Crown policy in being construed as *the* preeminent barrier to U.S. territorial consolidation east of the Mississippi.[31] Worse, as Chief Justice of the Supreme Court John Marshall pointed out in 1822, any real adherence to the rule of law in regard to native rights would not only block U.S. expansion, but—since not all the territory therein had been secured through Crown treaties—cloud title to significant portions of the original thirteen states as well.[32] Perhaps predictably, it was perceived in juridical circles that the only means of circumventing this dilemma was through construction of a legal theory—a subterfuge, as it were—by which the more inconvenient implications of international law might be nullified even while the republic maintained an appearance of holding to its doctrinal requirements.

**Emergence of the Marshall Doctrine**

Not unnaturally, the task of forging the required "interpretation" of existing law fell to John Marshall, widely considered one of the great legal minds of his time. Whatever his scholarly qualifications, the Chief Justice can hardly be said to have been a disinterested party, given not only his vociferous ideological advocacy of the rebel cause before and during the revolution, but the fact that both he and his father were consequent recipients of 10,000-acre grants west of the Appalachians, in what is now the state of West Virginia.[33] His first serious foray into land rights law thus centered in devising a conceptual basis to secure title for his own and similar grants. In the 1810 *Fletcher v. Peck* case, he invoked the Norman Yoke tradition in a manner which far exceeded previous English applications, advancing the patently absurd contention that the areas involved were effectively "vacant" even though very much occupied—and in many instances stoutly defended—by indigenous inhabitants. On this basis, he declared individual Euroamerican deeds within recognized Indian territories might be considered valid whether or not native consent was obtained.[34]

While *Peck* was obviously useful from the U.S. point of view, resolving as it did a number of shortrun difficulties in meeting obligations already incurred by the government to individual citizens, it was a tactical opinion, falling far short of accommodating the country's overall territorial goals and objectives. In the 1823 *Johnson v. McIntosh* case, however, Marshall followed up with a more clearly strategic enunciation, reaching for something much closer to the core of what he had in mind. Here, he opined that, because Discovery Rights purportedly constricted native discretion in disposing of property, the sovereignty of discoverers was to that extent inherently superior to that of indigenous nations. From this point of departure, he then proceeded to invert all conventional understandings of Discovery Doctrine, ultimately asserting that native people occupied land within discovered regions at the sufferance of their discoverers rather than the other way around. A preliminary rationalization was thus contrived by which to explain the fact that the U.S. had already begun depicting its borders as encompassing rather vast quantities of unceded Indian territory.[35]

Undoubtedly aware that neither *Peck* nor *McIntosh* was likely to withstand the gaze of international scrutiny, Marshall next moved to bolster the logic undergirding his position. In the two so-called "*Cherokee* Opinions" of the early 1830s, he hammered out the thesis that native peoples within North America comprised "nations like any other" in the sense that we possessed both territories we were capable of ceding, and recognizable governmental bodies empowered to cede these areas through treaties.[36] On the other hand, he argued on the basis of the reasoning deployed in *McIntosh*, we were nations of a "peculiar type," both "domestic to" and "dependent upon" the United States, and therefore possessed of a degree of sovereignty subordinate to that enjoyed by the U.S.[37] The idea boils down to an assertion that, while native peoples are entitled to exercise some range of autonomy in managing our affairs within our own territories, both the limits of that autonomy and the extent of the territories involved can be "naturally" and unilaterally established by the U.S. At base, this is little more than a judicial description of the classic relationship between colonizer and colonized,[38] but worded so as to seem at first glance to be the opposite.

While it might be contended (and has been, routinely enough) that Marshall's framing of the circumstances pertaining to the Cherokee Nation, already completely surrounded by U.S. territory by 1830, bore some genuine relationship to then-prevailing reality,[39] it must be reiterated that the Chief Justice did not confine his observations to the situation of Cherokees, or even to native nations east of the Mississippi. Rather, he purported to articulate the legal status of *all* indigenous nations, including those west of the Mississippi which had not yet encountered the U.S. in any appreciable way. Obviously, the latter could not have been described with the faintest accuracy as being either domestic to or dependent upon the United States. The clear intent thereby revealed in Marshall's formulation was that they were to be *made* so in the future. The doctrine completed with enunciation of the *Cherokee* opinions was thus the pivotal official attempt to rationalize and legitimate a vast campaign of conquest and colonization upon which the U.S. was planning to embark in the years ahead.[40]

A final inversion of accepted international legal norms and definitions stems from Marshall's opinions, that being an outright reversal of what was meant by "Just" and "Unjust" warfare.[41] Within his convoluted and falsely premised reasoning, it became arguable that indigenous nations acted unlawfully whenever and wherever they attempted to prevent exercise of the U.S. "right" to expropriate our property. Put another way, Indians could be construed as committing "aggression" against the United States at any point we attempted to resist the invasion of our homelands by American citizens. In this sense, the U.S. could declare itself to be waging a "Just"—and therefore lawful—war against native people on virtually any occasion where force of arms was required to realize its territorial ambitions. Ipso facto, all efforts of native people to defend ourselves against systematic dispossession and subordination could thereby be categorized as "unjust"—and thus unlawful—by the United States.[42]

In sum, the Marshall Doctrine shredded significant elements of the existing Law of Nations. Given the understandings of these very same legal requirements placed on record by federal judicial officials such as Attorney General Wirt and Marshall himself, not to mention the embodiment of such understandings in the Constitution and formative federal statutes, this cannot be said to have been unintentional or inadvertent. Instead, the Chief Justice engaged in a calculated exercise in juridical cynicism, quite deliberately confusing and deforming accepted legal principles as an expedient to "justifying" his country's pursuit of a thoroughly illegitimate course of territorial acquisition. Insofar as federal courts and policymakers elected to adopt his doctrine as the predicate to all subsequent relations with American Indians, it may be said that he not only replicated the initial posture of the U.S. as an outlaw state, but rendered it permanent.

### Evolution of the Marshall Doctrine

The *Cherokee* opinions were followed by a half-century hiatus in important judicial determinations regarding American Indians. On the foundation provided by the Marshall Doctrine, the government felt confident in entering into the great bulk of the 400-odd treaties with indigenous nations by which it professed to have gained the consent of native people in ceding huge portions of the indigenous landbase, assured that its self-anointed position of superior sovereignty burdened it with "no legal obligation" to live up to its end of the various bargains struck.[43] Well before the end of the nineteenth century, the United States stood in default on virtually every treaty it had made with native people, and there is considerable evidence that this was intended from the outset.[44] Aside from the fraudulent nature of U.S. participation in the treaty process, there is an ample record that many of the instruments of cession were militarily coerced while the government implemented Marshall's version of Just Wars against Indians. As the U.S. Census Bureau put it in 1894:

> The Indian wars under the United States government have been about 40 in number [most of them occurring after 1835]. They have cost the lives of . . . about 30,000 Indians [at a minimum]. . . The actual number of killed and wounded Indians must be very much greater than the number given, as they conceal, where possible, their actual loss in battle. . . Fifty percent additional would be a safe number to add to the numbers given.[45]

The same report noted that some number "very much more" than 8,500 Indians were known to have been killed by government-sanctioned "private citizen action"—often dubbed "individual affairs"—during the course of U.S./Indian warfare.[46] In reality, such citizen action is known to have been primarily responsible for the reduction of the native population of Texas from about 100,000 in 1828 to less than 10,000 in 1880.[47] Similarly, in California, an aggregate indigenous population which still numbered approximately 300,000 in 1849 had been reduced to fewer than 35,000 by 1860, mainly because of "the cruelties and wholesale massacres perpetrated by [American] miners and early settlers."[48] Either of these illustrations offers a death toll several times that officially acknowledged as having accrued through individual affairs within the whole of the forty-eight contiguous states.

Even while this slaughter was occurring, the Army was conducting what it described as a "policy of extermination" in its wars against those indigenous nations which proved "recalcitrant" about giving up their land and liberty.[49] This manifested itself in a lengthy series of wholesale massacres of native people—men, women, children, and old people alike—at the hands of U.S. troops. Among the worst were those at Blue River (Nebraska, 1854), Bear River (Idaho, 1863), Sand Creek (Colorado, 1864), Washita River (Oklahoma, 1868), Marias River (Montana, 1870), Sappa Creek (Kansas, 1875), Camp Robinson (Nebraska, 1878), and Wounded Knee (South Dakota, 1890).[50]

Somewhat different, but comparable, methods of destroying indigenous peoples were evidenced in the forced march of the entire Cherokee Nation along the "Trail of Tears" to Oklahoma during the 1830s (roughly 55 percent attrition),[51] and the internment of the bulk of the Navajo Nation under abysmal conditions at the Bosque Redondo from 1864 to 1868 (50 percent attrition).[52] Such atrocities against humans were coupled with an equally systematic extermination of an entire species, the North American Bison ("buffalo"), as part of a strategy to starve resistant Indians into submission by "destroying their commissary."[53]

All told, it is probable that more than a quarter-million Indians perished as a direct result of the exterminatory campaigns directed against us.[54] By the turn of the century, only 237,196 native people were recorded by census as still alive within the United States,[55] perhaps 2 percent of the total indigenous population of the U.S. portion of North America at the outset of the European invasion.[56] Correlating rather precisely with this genocidal reduction in the number of native inhabitants was an erosion of Indian landholdings to approximately 2.5 percent of the "lower forty-eight" states.[57]

Small wonder that, barely thirty years later, Adolf Hitler would explicitly anchor his concept of *Lebensraumpolitik* ("politics of living space") upon U.S. practice against American Indians.[58] Meanwhile, even as the census figures were being tallied, the U.S. had already moved beyond the "Manifest Destiny" embodied in the conquest phase of its continental expansion, and was emphasizing the development of colonial administration over residual indigenous territories through the Bureau of Indian Affairs (BIA), a subpart of the War Department which had been reassigned for this purpose to the Department of Interior.

This was begun as early as 1871, when Congress—having determined that the military capacity of native peoples had been sufficiently reduced by incessant wars of attrition—elected to consecrate Marshall's description of their "domestic" status by suspending further treatymaking with them.[59] In 1885, the U.S. moved for the first time to directly extend its internal jurisdiction over reserved Indian territories through passage of the Major Crimes Act.[60] When this was challenged as a violation of international standards, Supreme Court Justice Samuel F. Miller rendered an opinion which consolidated and extended Marshall's earlier assertion of federal plenary power over indigenous nations, contending that the government held an "incontrovertible right" to exercise authority over Indians as it saw fit and "for their own good."[61] Miller also concluded that Indians lacked any legal recourse in matters of federal interest, their sovereignty being defined as whatever Congress did not remove from us through specific legislation. This decision opened the door to enactment of more than 5,000 U.S. statutes regulating affairs in Indian Country.[62]

One of the first of these was the General Allotment Act of 1887, "which unilaterally negated Indian control over land tenure patterns within the reservations, forcibly replacing the traditional mode of collective use and occupancy with the Anglo-Saxon system of individual property owner-ship."[63] The Act also imposed for the first time a formal race code — dubbed "blood quantum" — by which native identity would be federally defined on racial grounds rather than in accordance with the traditional means of iden-tification/group membership employed by indigenous peoples.[64]

> The Allotment Act set forth that each American Indian recognized as such by the fed-eral government would receive an allotment of land according to the following for-mula: 160 acres for family heads, eighty acres for single persons over eighteen years of age and orphans under eighteen, and forty acres for [non-orphan] children under eigh-teen. "Mixed blood" Indians received title by fee simple patent; "full bloods" were issued "trust patents," meaning they had no control over their property for a period of twenty-five years. Once each person recognized by the government as belonging to a given Indian nation had received his or her allotment, the "surplus" acreage was "opened" to non-Indian homesteading or conversion into the emerging system of national parks, forests, and grasslands.[65]

Needless to say, there proved to be far fewer Indians identifiable as such under federal racial criteria than there were individual parcels available within the reserved land areas of the 1890s. Hence, "not only was the cohe-sion of indigenous society dramatically disrupted by allotment, and tradi-tional government prerogatives preempted, but it led to the loss of some two-thirds of all the acreage [about 100 million of 150 million acres] still held by native people at the time it was passed."[66] Moreover, the land assigned to individual Indians during the allotment process fell overwhelm-ingly within arid and semiarid locales considered to be the least productive in North America; uniformly, the best-watered and otherwise useful portions of the reservations were declared surplus and quickly stripped away.[67] This, of course, greatly reinforced the "dependency" aspect of the Marshall thesis, and led U.S. Indian Commissioner Francis Leupp to conclude approvingly that allotment should be considered "a mighty pulverizing engine for break-ing up [the last vestiges of] the tribal mass" which stood as a final barrier to complete Euroamerican hegemony on the continent.[68]

As with the Major Crimes Act, native people attempted to utilize their treatied standing in federal courts to block the allotment process and corresponding erosion of the reservation landbase. In the 1903 *Lone Wolf v. Hitchcock* case, however, Justice Edward D. White extended the concept of federal plenary power to hold that the government possessed a right to unilaterally abrogate whatever portion of any treaty with Indians it found inconvenient while continuing to consider the remaining terms and provisions binding upon the Indians.[69]

In essence, this meant that the U.S. could point to the treaties as being the instruments which legally validated much of its North American land title while simultaneously avoiding whatever reciprocal obligations it had incurred by way of payment. White also opined that the government's plenary power over Indians lent it a "trust responsibility" with respect to residual native property such that it might opt to "change the form" of this property—from land, say, to cash or "services"—whenever and however it chose to do so. This final consolidation of the Marshall Doctrine effectively left native people with *no* true national rights under U.S. law while voiding the remaining pittance of conformity to international standards the United States had exhibited with regard to its Indian treaties.[70]

### The Open Veins of Native America

A little-discussed aspect of the Allotment Act is that it required each Indian, as a condition of receiving the deed to his or her land parcel, to accept U.S. citizenship. By the early 1920s, when most of the allotment the U.S. wished to accomplish had been completed, there were a significant number of native people who were still not "naturalized," either because they'd been left out of the process for one reason or another, or because they'd refused to participate. Consequently, in 1924 the Congress passed a "clean-up bill" entitled the Indian Citizenship Act which imposed citizenship upon all remaining indigenous people within U.S. borders whether they desired it or not.[71]

> The Indian Citizenship Act greatly confused the circumstances even of many of the blooded and federally certified Indians insofar as it was held to bear legal force, and to carry legal obligations, whether or not any given Indian or group of Indians wished to be U.S. citizens. As for the host of non-certified, mixed-blood people residing in the U.S., their status was finally "clarified"; they had been definitionally absorbed into the American mainstream at the stroke of the congressional pen. And, despite the fact that the act technically left certified Indians occupying the status of citizenship within their

14

own indigenous nation as well as the U.S. (a "dual form" of citizenship so awkward as to be sublime), the juridical door had been opened by which the weight of Indian obligations would begin to accrue more to the U.S. than to themselves.[72]

All of this—suspension of treatymaking, extension of federal jurisdiction, plenary power and "trust" prerogatives, blood quantum and allotment, and the imposition of citizenship—was bound up in a policy officially designated as being the compulsory assimilation of American Indians into the dominant (Euroamerican) society.[73] Put another way, U.S. Indian policy was carefully (and openly) designed to bring about the disappearance of all recognizable native groups, as such.[74] The methods used included the general proscription of indigenous languages[75] and spiritual practices,[76] the systematic and massive transfer of native children into non-Indian settings via mandatory attendance at boarding schools remote from their communities,[77] and the deliberate suppression of reservation economic structures.[78] As Indian Commissioner Charles Burke put it at the time, "It is not consistent with the general welfare to promote [American Indian national] characteristics and organization."[79]

The assimilationist policy trajectory culminated during the 1950s with the passage of House Concurrent Resolution 108, otherwise known as the "Termination Act of 1953," a measure through which the U.S. moved to unilaterally dissolve 109 indigenous nations within its borders.[80] Termination was coupled to the "Relocation Act," a statute passed in 1956 and designed to coerce reservation residents to disperse to various urban centers around the country.[81] The ensuing programmatic emphasis upon creating an American Indian diaspora had resulted, by 1990, in over half of all Indians inside the U.S. being severed from our respective landbases and generally acculturated to non-Indian morés.[82] Meanwhile, the enactment of Public Law 280, placed many reservations under state jurisdiction, thereby reducing the level of native sovereignty to that of counties or municipalities and eliminating the last vestige of U.S. acknowledgement that indigenous peoples retain "certain characteristics of sovereign nations."[83]

The question arises of course as to why, given the contours of this aspect of federal policy, the final obliteration of the indigenous nations of North America has not long since occurred. The answer resides within something of a supreme irony: unbeknownst to the policymakers who implemented the allotment policy during the late nineteenth century, much of the ostensibly useless land to which native people were consigned has turned out to be some of the most mineral-rich on earth. It is presently esti-

15

mated that two-thirds of all U.S. "domestic" uranium deposits lie beneath reservation lands, as well as a quarter of the readily accessible low sulfur coal, and about a fifth of the oil and natural gas. In addition, the reservations are now known to be endowed with substantial quantities of copper, zinc, iron, nickel, molybdenum, bauxite, zeolites and gold, among other mineral assets.[84]

By the early 1920s, federal economic planners had discerned a distinct advantage in retaining these abundant resources within the framework of governmental trust control, an expedient to awarding mining licenses to preferred corporations in ways which might have proven impossible had the reservations been liquidated altogether.[85] Hence, beginning in 1921, it was determined that at least some indigenous nations should be maintained in some semblance of existence, and Washington began to experiment with the creation of "tribal governments" intended to administer what was left of Indian Country on behalf of an emerging complex of interlocking federal/corporate interests.[86] This resulted, in 1934, in passage of the Indian Reorganization Act (IRA), a statute serving to usurp virtually every remaining traditional native government, supplanting them with federally designed "Tribal Councils" structured along the lines of corporate boards and empowered primarily to sign off on mineral leases and the like.[87]

The arrangement led to a recapitulation of the Marshall Doctrine's principle of indigenous "quasi-sovereignty" in slightly revised form: now, native nations were cast as always being sovereign enough to legitimate Euroamerican mineral exploitation on their reservations, never sovereign enough to prevent it. Predictably, under such circumstances the BIA negotiated extractive leases, duly endorsed by the puppet governments it had installed, "in behalf of" its "Indian wards" which have typically paid native people fifteen percent or less of market royalty rates on minerals taken from their lands.[88]

The "superprofits" thus generated for major corporations have had a significant positive effect on U.S. economic growth since 1950, a matter amplified by the fact that the BIA also "neglected" to include worker safety, land rehabilitation and other environmental protection clauses into contracts pertaining to reservation land (currently, Indians are always construed as being sovereign enough to waive such things as environmental protection regulations, never sovereign enough to enforce them).[89] One consequence of this trend is that, on reservations where uranium mining has occurred, Indian Country has become so contaminated by radioactive substances that the government has actively considered designating them as "National Sacrifice Areas" unfit for human habitation.[90] At this juncture, several reservations are also being used as dumpsites for high-level nuclear wastes and toxic chemicals which cannot be otherwise easily disposed of.[91]

Further indication of the extent and virulence of the colonial system by which the United States has come to rule Native North America is not difficult to find. Dividing the fifty million-odd acres of land still nominally reserved for Indian use and occupancy in the U.S. by the approximately 1.8 million Indians the government recognized as such in its 1990 census, reveals that native people—on paper, at least—remain the largest landholders on a per capita basis of any population sector on the continent.[92] This, in combination with the resources known to lie within our land and the increasingly intensive "development" of these resources over the past fifty years, simple arithmetic strongly suggests that we should also be the wealthiest of all aggregate groups.[93]

Instead, according to the federal government's own data, we are far and away the poorest in terms of both annual and lifetime per capita income. Correspondingly, we suffer all the standard indices of dire poverty: North America's highest rates of infant mortality and teen suicide, death from malnutrition, exposure, and plague disease.[94] Overall, we consistently experience the highest rate of unemployment, lowest level of educational attainment, and one of the highest rates of incarceration of any group. The average life expectancy of a reservation-based American Indian male is less than forty-five years; that of a reservation-based female, barely over forty-seven.[95]

In Iberoamerica, there is a core postulation guiding understandings of the interactive dynamics between the northern and southern continents of the Western Hemisphere. "Your wealth," latino analysts point out to their yanqui counterparts, "is our poverty."[96] Plainly, the structure of the relationship forged by the United States vis-à-vis the indigenous nations of the northern continent follows exactly the same pattern of parasitic domination. The economic veins of the prostrate Native North American indigenous host have been carefully opened, their contents providing lifeblood to the predatory creature which applied the knife. Such are the fruits of John Marshall's doctrine after a century and a half of continuous application and evolution.

### International Sleight of Hand

It's not that the U.S. has failed to attempt to mask the face of this reality. Indeed, in the wake of World War II, even as the United States was engaged in setting a "moral example" to all of humanity by assuming a lead role in prosecuting former nazi leaders for having ventured down much the same road of continental conquest that the U.S. itself had pioneered,[97] Congress passed what it called the Indian Claims Commission Act.[98] The premise of the law was that all nonconsensual—and therefore illegal—takings of native property which had transpired during the course of American history had been "errors," sometimes "tragic" ones.[99]

As a means, at least figuratively, of separating U.S. historical performance and expansionist philosophy from the more immediate undertakings of the nazis, the Act established a commission empowered to review the basis of U.S. title in every quarter of the country, and to award retroactive monetary compensation to indigenous nations shown to have been unlawfully deprived of their lands. Tellingly, the commission was authorized to set compensation amounts at the estimated per-acre value of indigenous property *at the time it was taken* (often a century or more before), and was specifically disempowered from restoring land to Indian control, no matter *how* the land was taken or *what* the desires of the impacted native people might be.[100]

Although the life of the commission was originally envisioned as being only ten years, the magnitude of the issues it encountered, and the urgency with which its mission to "quiet title" to aboriginal lands came to be viewed by the Euroamerican status quo, caused it to be repeatedly extended.[101] When it was finally disbanded on September 30, 1978, it still had sixty-eight cases docketed for review, despite having heard and ostensibly "disposed of" several hundred others over a period of three decades.[102] In the end, while its intent had been the exact opposite, it had accomplished nothing so much as to establish with graphic clarity how little of North America the United States could be said to legally own.

> The fact is that about half the land area of the country was purchased by treaty or agreement at an average price of less than a dollar an acre; another third of a [billion] acres, mainly in the West, were confiscated without compensation; another two-thirds of a [billion] acres were claimed by the United States without pretense of even a unilateral action extinguishing native title.[103]

This summary, of course, says nothing at all about the approximately forty-four million acres of land recently taken from the Indians, Aleuts and Inuits of the Arctic North under provision of the 1971 Alaska Native Claims Settlement Act,[104] or the several million acres of Hawai'i stripped away from the natives of those islands.[105] Similarly, it ignores the situation in such U.S.

"possessions" as Guam, Puerto Rico, the "U.S." Virgin Islands, "American" Samoa, and the Marshall Islands.[106]

Serious challenges to commission findings have been mounted in federal courts, based largely in the cumulative contradictions inherent to federal Indian law. As a consequence, the Supreme Court has been compelled to resort to ever more convoluted and logically untenable argumentation as a means of upholding certain U.S. assertions of "legitimate" land title. In its 1980 opinion in the Black Hills Land Claim case, for example, the high court was forced to extend the Marshall Doctrine's indigenous domesticity thesis to a ludicrous extreme, holding that the U.S. had merely exercised its rightful internal power of "eminent domain" over the territory of the Lakota Nation when it expropriated 90 percent of the latter's land a century earlier, in direct violation of the 1868 Treaty of Fort Laramie.[107] Similarly, in the Western Shoshone Land Claim case, where the government could show no documentation that it had ever even pretended to assume title to the land at issue, the Supreme Court let stand the Claims Commission's assignment of an arbitrary date on which a transfer supposedly took place.[108]

During the 1970s, the American Indian Movement (AIM), an organization militantly devoted to the national liberation of Native North America, emerged in the United States. In part, the group attempted the physical decolonization of the Pine Ridge (Oglala Lakota) Reservation in South Dakota, but was met with a counterinsurgency war waged by federal agencies such as the FBI and U.S. Marshals Service, and surrogates associated with the reservation's IRA Council.[109] Although unsuccessful in achieving a resumption of indigenous self-determination at Pine Ridge, the tenacity of AIM's struggle (and the ferocity of the government's repression of it) attracted considerable international attention. This led, in 1981, to the establishment, under auspices of the U.N. Economic and Social Council (ECOSOC), of a United Nations Working Group on Indigenous Populations to assess the situation of native peoples globally and produce a universal declaration of their rights as a binding element of international law.[110]

Within this arena, the United States, joined by Canada, has consistently sought to defend its relations with indigenous nations by trotting out the Marshall Doctrine's rationalization that the U.S. has assumed a trust responsibility towards rather than outright colonial domination over Native North America.[111] Native delegates have countered, correctly, that trust prerogatives, in order to be valid under international law, must be tied to some clearly articulated point at which the trust territories resume independent existence. This requirement has been contrasted to the U.S./Canadian governments' claims that they enjoy a permanent trust authority over indigenous nations; the assumption by any nation of such authority over another's affairs and property is the essential definition of colonialism, and is thus illegal under a number of international covenants.[112]

The U.S. and Canada have responded with prevarication, contending that their relationship to Native North America cannot be one of colonialism insofar as United Nations Resolution 1541 (XV), the so-called "Blue Water Thesis," specifies that in order to be defined as a colony a nation must be separated from its colonizer by at least thirty miles of open ocean.[113] The representatives of both countries have also done everything in their power to delay or prevent completion of the Declaration of the Rights of Indigenous Peoples, arguing, among other things, that the term "peoples," when applied to native populations, should not carry the force of law implied by its use in such international legal instruments as the Universal Declaration of Human Rights, the Convention on the Elimination of All Forms of Racial Discrimination the International Covenant on Economic, Social and Cultural Rights and the International Covenant on Civil and Political Rights.[114] The United States in particular has implied that it will not abide by any declaration of indigenous rights which runs counter to what it perceives as its own interests, a matter which would replicate its posture with regard to the authority of the International Court of Justice (the "World Court")[115] and elements of international law such as the 1948 Convention on Prevention and Punishment of the Crime of Genocide.[116]

Meanwhile, the U.S. set out to "resolve things internally" through what may be intended as a capstone extrapolation of the Marshall Doctrine. This assumed the form of a drive to convince Indians to accept the premise that, rather than struggling to regain our self-determining rights to separate sovereign existence embodied in our national histories and treaty relationships, we should voluntarily merge ourselves with the U.S. polity.[117] In this scenario, the IRA administrative apparatus created during the 1930s would assume a position as a "third level of the federal government," finally making indigenous rights within the U.S. inseparable from those of the citizenry as a whole. This final assimilation of native people into the "American sociopolitical mainstream" would obviously void most (or perhaps all) potential utility for Indian rights which exist or might emerge from international law in the years ahead. The idea has therefore been seriously pursued by the Senate Select Committee on Indian Affairs, chaired by Hawai'i's Senator Daniel Inouye (who has already done much to undermine the rights of native people of his own state).[118]

## U.S. Out of North America

During the fall of 1990, President George Bush stepped onto the world stage beating the drums for what he termed a "Just War" to roll back the "naked aggression" of Iraq's invasion and occupation of neighboring Kuwait. Claiming to articulate "universal principles of international relations and human decency," Bush stated that such aggression "cannot stand," that "occupied territory must be liberated, legitimate governments must be reinstated, the benefits of their aggression must be denied to aggressive powers."[119] Given the tone and tenor of this Bushian rhetoric — and the undeniable fact that Iraq had a far better claim to Kuwait (its nineteenth province, separated from the Iraqis by the British as an administrative measure in 1916), than the U.S. has to virtually any part of North America[120] — one could only wait with baited breath for the American president to call airstrikes in upon his own capitol as a means of forcing his own government to withdraw from Indian Country. Insofar as he did not, the nature of the "New World Order" his war in the Persian Gulf harkened tends to speak for itself.[121]

The United States does not now possess, nor has it ever possessed, a legitimate right to occupancy in at least half the territory it claims as its own. It began its existence as an outlaw state and, given the nature of its expansion to its present size, it has adamantly remained so through the present moment. In order to make things appear otherwise, its legal scholars and its legislators have persistently and often grotesquely manipulated and deformed sound and accepted legal principles, both internationally and domestically. They have done so in precisely the same fashion, and on the same basis, as the nazi leaders they stood at the forefront in condemning for Crimes Against Peace and Humanity at Nuremberg.[122]

In no small part because of its success in consolidating its position on other peoples' land in North America, the United States may well continue to succeed where the nazis failed. With the collapse of the Soviet Union, it emerged as *the* ascendant military power during the late twentieth century. As the sheer margin of its victory over Iraq revealed, it now possesses the capacity to extend essentially the same sort of relationships it has imposed

21

upon American Indians to the remainder of the world. And, given the experience it has acquired in Indian Affairs over the years, it is undoubtedly capable of cloaking this process of planetary subordination in a legalistic attire symbolizing its deep-seated concern with international freedom and dignity, the sovereignty of other nations, and the human rights of all peoples. At a number of levels, the Marshall Doctrine reckons to become truly globalized in the years ahead.[123]

This is likely to remain the case, unless and until significant numbers of people, within the United States as well as without, come to recognize the danger and the philosophical system which underpins it, for what they are. More importantly, any genuine alternative to a consummation of the Bushian vision of world order is predicated upon these same people acting upon their insights, opposing the order implicit to the U.S. status quo both at home and abroad. Ultimately, the dynamic represented by the Marshall Doctrine must be reversed, the structure it fostered dismantled, within the territorial corpus of the United States itself. In this, nothing can be more central than the restoration of indigenous land and national rights in the fullest sense of the term. The U.S., at least as it has come to be known, and in the sense that it knows itself, must be driven from North America. In its stead resides the possibility, likely the *only* possibility, of a genuinely just and liberatory future for all humanity.

# Notes

1. This, in essence, is the legal concept of "aboriginal" land rights. One of the strongest and clearest articulations of the doctrine may be found in Gaston Jeze, *Etud Theoretique et Pratique Sur L'occupation Comme Mode d'Acquerir les Territoires en Droit International* (Paris, 1896).

2. For a very solid analysis of the various problems at issue in this regard, see Robert Taylor, *International Public Law* (London: Metheun, 1901). Also see Mark Frank Lindley, *The Acquisition and Government of Backward Country in International Law: A Treatise on the Law and Practice Relating to Colonial Expansion* (London: Longman, Green, 1926).

3. This principle is most plainly embodied in the United Nations Charter (59 Stat. 1031, T.S. No. 993, 3 Bevans 1153, 1976 Y.B.U.N. (24 Oct. 1945)) and the subsequent U.N. Declaration on the Granting of Independence to Colonial Countries and Peoples (U.N.G.A. Res. 1514 (XV), 15 U.N. GAOR, Supp. (No. 16) 66, U.N. Doc. A/4684 (14 Dec. 1960)). For texts, see Burns H. Weston, Richard A. Falk and Anthony D'Amato, *Basic Documents in International Law and World Order* (Minneapolis: West Publishing, 1990) pp. 16-32, 343-4.

4. A comprehensive elaboration of the U.S. position may be found in Felix S. Cohen, *Handbook on Federal Indian Law* (Albuquerque: University of New Mexico Press, (reprint of 1942 ed., 1981).

5. Broad analysis of such rhetoric by President George Bush during the 1990-91 Gulf War may be found in Cynthia Peters, ed., *Collateral Damage: The "New World Order" at Home and Abroad* (Boston: South End Press, 1992).

6. Antonio Truyol y Serra, "The Discovery of the New World and International Law," *Toledo Law Review*, No. 43, 1971.

7. Probably the best delineation of these issues may be found in Robert A. Williams, Jr., *The American Indian in Western Legal Thought: The Discourses of Conquest* (New York: Oxford University Press, 1990).

8. The first solid evidence that the Church had become engaged in this process comes on May 3 and May 5, 1493, with the signing of Bulls by Pope Alexander VI endorsing the rights of the sovereigns of Castille and Aragon to acquire the lands of newly discovered portions of America while spreading Christianity among the natives thereof; Paul Gottschalk, *The Earliest Diplomatic Documents of America* (Albany: New York State Historical Society, 1978) p. 21.

9. On the Bulls of Innocent IV (Sinibaldo Fiesco), see Ernest Nys, *Les Origins du Droit International* (Brussels/Paris, 1984) esp. Chapter Seven. It is worth noting that Innocent himself was heavily influenced by the treatise of Thomas Aquinas in *Summa Theologica Secunda Secundae*, written around 1250; Herbert Andrew Deane, *The Political and Social Ideals of St. Augustine* (New York: Columbia University Press, 1963).

10. Alfred Nussbaum, *A Concise History of the Laws of Nations* (New York: Macmillan, [rev. ed.] 1954); Lewis Hanke, *The Spanish Struggle for Justice in the Conquest of America* (Philadelphia: University of Pennsylvania Press, 1949).

11. Vitoria's formulation of the doctrine is available under the title *De Indis et De Jure Belli Reflectiones*, published by the Carnegie Institution in 1917. The pivotal international legal theorist Emmerich de Vattel drew heavily on Vitoria's discourse when drafting his *The Laws of Nations* (Philadelphia: T. & J.W. Johnson Publishers, 1855). Overall, see John Horace Parry, *The Spanish Theory of Empire in the Sixteenth Century* (Cambridge, MA: Cambridge University Press, 1940).

12. This principle derives directly from Roman law promulgated at least a century before Christ; see Henry Maine, ed., *Ancient Law* (London, [13th ed.] 1850).

13. This thinking is embodied in the Bull *Inter Caetera* of May 4, 1493: Gottschalk, *Diplomatic Documents*, p. 21. The matter is also taken up about thirty years later by the renowned jurist John Mair, in his *Commentary on the Sentences of Pater Lombard*; Truyol y Serra, "Discovery," p. 313.

14. See "Rights of Conquest," in this volume.

15. Lewis Hanke, *All Mankind Is One: A Study of the Disputation Between Bartolomé de Las Casas and Juan Ginés de Sepúlveda in 1550 on the Intellectual and Religious Capacity of American Indians* (DeKalb: Northern Illinois University, 1950). On general acceptance of the doctrine, see Howard Peckham and Charles Gibson, eds., *Attitudes of the Colonial Powers Towards American Indians* (Salt Lake City: University of Utah Press, 1969). An excellent textual source in the latter regard is Francis Gardiner Davenport, ed., *European Treaties Bearing on the History of the United States and Its Dependencies*, 2 vols. (Washington, D.C.: Carnegie Institution, 1917).

16. See generally, David Beers Quinn, *England and the Discovery of America, 1481-1620* (New York: Alfred A. Knopf, 1974); Harry Culverwell Porter, *The Inconstant Savage: England and the American Indian, 1500-1600* (London: Duckworth, 1979); John Horace Parry, *The Establishment of European Hegemony, 1415-1713* (New York: Harper & Row, [rev. ed.] 1966). For a selection of relevant texts with regard to England, see Alden T. Vaughn, *Early American Indian Documents: Treaties and Laws, 1607-1789* (Washington, D.C.: University Publications of America, 1979).

17. James Brown Scott, *The Spanish Origin of International Law* (Oxford: Clarendon Press, 1934); Lassa Oppenheim, *International Law, Vol. I* (London: Longman, Green, 1955). That these principles were not unknown to or misunderstood by early U.S. jurists is conclusively demonstrated by Felix S. Cohen in his essay, "The Spanish Origin of Indian Rights in the Law of the United States," *Georgetown Law Review*, Vol. 31, No. 1, Winter 1942.

18. The concept of the Norman Yoke emerged from the idea of "Natural Law"; Friedrich von Gierke, *Natural Law and the Theory of Society, 1500-1800* (Cambridge, MA: Cambridge University Press, 1934). For application in the New World setting, see Klaus E. Knorr, *British Colonial Theories, 1570-1850* (Toronto: University of Toronto Press, 1944); Wilbur R. Jacobs, *Dispossessing the American Indian: Indians and Whites on the Colonial Frontier* (New York: Charles Scribner, 1972), and Williams, *American Indian in Western Legal Thought*.

19. The seeds of the subsequent "reservation" systems developed by the U.S. and Canada are imbedded in this construction. The motivations underlying nearly three centuries of endemic falsification of indigenous American demographic and agricultural realities by Angloamerican "scholars" can also be discerned within the theory of the Norman Yoke. In order to justify, or at least rationalize, the sorts of territorial acquisition undertaken by Britain and its U.S. descendants, it was necessary that North America would have been very sparsely populated by peoples subsisting primarily on the basis of hunting and gathering. A good job of debunking such patent nonsense is found in Francis Jennings' *The Invasion of America: Indians, Colonialism, and the Cant of Conquest* (New York: W.W. Norton, 1976).

20. For a good overview and contextualization of the French and Indian Wars, as well as the 1763 Proclamation, see Douglas Edward Leach, *The Northern Colonial Frontier, 1607-1763*, (New York: Histories of the American Frontier, 1966). A focus on the last, and decisive, of these wars will be found in Wilbur R. Jacobs, *Diplomacy and Indian Gifts: Anglo-French Rivalry Along the Ohio and Northwest Frontiers, 1748-1763* (Stanford, CA: Stanford University Press, 1950). Also see Randolph C. Downes, *Council Fires on the Upper Ohio* (Pittsburgh: University of Pittsburgh Press, 1940).

21. Merrill Jensen, *Founding of a Nation: A History of the American Revolution, 1763-1776* (London: Oxford University Press, 1979).

22. Thomas Perkins Abernathy, *Western Lands and the American Revolution* (New York: Russell and Russell, 1959); Gordon Wood, *Creation of the American Republic, 1776-1787* (Chapel Hill: University of North Carolina Press, 1969).

23. Vine Deloria, Jr., "Self-Determination and the Concept of Sovereignty," in Roxanne Dunbar Ortiz and Larry Emerson, eds., *Economic Development in American Indian Reservations* (Albuquerque: Native American Studies Center, University of New Mexico, 1979). Also see Walter Harrison Mohr, *Federal Indian Relations, 1774-1788* (Philadelphia: University of Pennsylvania Press, 1933).

24. For an assessment of the centrality of Indian relations in congressional deliberations concerning the treatymaking provisions found in Article IX of the Articles of Confederation, and Articles I and VI of the Constitution (as well as its so-called "Commerce Clause"), Merrill Jensen, *The Articles of Confederation: An Interpretation of the Socio-Constitutional History of the American Revolution, 1774-1788* (Madison: University of Wisconsin Press, 1940) esp. pp. 154-62, 190-232.

25. 1 Stat. 50, 1789.

26. Quoted in Edward Lazarus, *Black Hills, White Justice: The Sioux Nation versus the United States, 1775 to the Present* (New York: HarperCollins, 1991) p. 158.

27. U.S. contentions that it gained "Discovery Rights" by virtue of the English capitulation are strained at best. Such rights, under both English and Spanish legal understandings, attached themselves solely to monarchs under the doctrine of "Divine Right." In other words, it is dubious that George III could have conveyed such rights upon the rebels, even had he desired to do so (and there is no language in the treaty suggesting that he did). At most, then, the U.S. could claim bona fide rights to only that

territory—all of it east of the 1763 demarcation line—which the British Crown could be said to have acquired by prior treaties with indigenous nations. On the relationship between Divine Rights and Discovery Rights, see Walter Ullman, *The Church and Laws in the Early Middle Ages* (London: Metheun, 1975).

28. On Tecumseh, see R. David Edmunds, *Tecumseh and the Quest for American Indian Leadership* (Boston: Little, Brown, 1984). On the Red Sticks, see Joel W. Martin, *Sacred Revolt: The Muskogees' Struggle for a New World* Boston: Beacon Press, 1991).

29. Opinion rendered by the Attorney General (Op. Atty. Gen.), Apr. 26, 1821, p. 345.

30. Op. Atty. Gen., 1828, pp. 623-3. For further background, see Howard Berman, "The Concept of Aboriginal Rights in the Early Legal History of the United States," *Buffalo Law Review*, No. 28, 1978, pp. 637-67; Felix S. Cohen, "Original Indian Land Title," *Minnesota Law Review*, No. 32, 1947, pp. 28-59.

31. For context, see Reginald Horsman's, *Expansion and American Policy, 1783-1812* (East Lansing: Michigan State University Press, 1967).

32. *Johnson v. McIntosh,* (21 U.S. (8 Wheat.) 543 (1832)).

33. Leonard Baker, *John Marshall: A Life in Law* (New York: Macmillan, 1974) p. 80.

34. *Fletcher v. Peck,* (10 U.S. 87 (1810)).

35. *Johnson v. McIntosh.*

36. The cases are *Cherokee Nation v. Georgia* (30 U.S. (5 Pet.) 1 (1831)) and *Worcester v. Georgia* (31 U.S. (6 Pet.) 551 (1832)). In effect, Marshall held that indigenous nations should always be considered sovereign enough to transfer legal title to their lands to the United States, but never sovereign enough to possess a right to prevent U.S. assumption of ownership of those lands. Simultaneously, he denied comparable rights over Indian property to the various states, reserving them exclusively to the federal government. Oddly, this last has led to Marshall being generally considered a "champion" of native rights; John Hurley, "Aboriginal Rights, the Constitution and the Marshall Court," *Revue Juridique Themis*, No. 17, 1983.

37. This is a constitutional absurdity. The sort of limited sovereignty implied in Marshall's "domestic dependent nation" theory places indigenous nations in essentially the same "quasi-sovereign" status of subordination to the federal government as is manifested by the states of the union or Canadian provinces. Article 1, Section 10, of the U.S. Constitution specifically prohibits the states from entering into treaty relationships. Conversely, the federal government is prohibited from entering into a treaty relationship with states or provinces (or any entity other than another *fully* sovereign nation). The unprecedented (and untenable) politicolegal status invented by Marshall to describe the "partial sovereignty" he needed native nations to fulfill has been compared to "the biological impossibility of a woman's being part-pregnant."

38. For penetrating insights into the power relations involved, see Albert Memmi, *The Colonizer and the Colonized* (Boston: Beacon Press, 1965).

39. This is the basic argument advanced by Charles F. Wilkinson in his *Indians, Time and Law* (New Haven: Yale University Press, 1987).

40. It is interesting to note that the U.S., without renouncing its own doctrine, took a leading role in defining as criminal the assertion of an exactly similar juridical/philosophical rationalization of expansionist intent by nazi Germany; Bradley F. Smith, *The Road to Nuremberg* (New York: Basic Books, 1981). Also see Frank Parrella, *Lebensraum and Manifest Destiny: A Comparative Study in the Justification of Expansionism* (Washington, D.C.: MA thesis, Dept. of Political Science, Georgetown University, 1950).

41. Michael Walzer, *Just and Unjust Wars: A Moral Argument with Historical Illustrations* (New York: Basic Books, 1977).

42. One indicator of the pervasiveness with which this outlook has been implanted is that armed conflicts between the U.S. and indigenous nations are inevitably described as "Indian Wars" despite the fact that each one was demonstrably initiated by the invasion by American citizens of territory belonging to one or more native peoples. The so-called Indian Wars would thus be accurately depicted as "Settlers' Wars," or, more appropriately yet, "Wars of Aggression by the United States."

43. The texts of 371 ratified treaties are reproduced verbatim in Charles J. Kappler, comp., *Indian Treaties, 1778-1883* (New York: Interland, 1973). The texts of these and several additional ratified treaties, as well as those of numerous unratified instruments, will be found in Vine Deloria, Jr., and Raymond J.

DeMallie, *Documents of American Indian Diplomacy: Treaties, Agreements and Conventions, 1775-1979*, 2 vols. (Norman: University of Oklahoma Press, 1999) pp. 249-513, 1237-1473.

44. There are a number of indicators of this. One of the more salient was a tendency of the Senate to alter the terms and conditions of treaties negotiated with indigenous nations *after* the native leadership had signed. The modified treaty instruments were then passed into U.S. law, and said to be binding upon the Indians involved, even though they'd never agreed to—or in some cases even been notified of—the new terms. The 1861 Treaty with the Cheyennes and Arapahos, otherwise known as the Treaty of Fort Wise, is a good example; Stan Hoig, *The Sand Creek Massacre* (Norman: University of Oklahoma Press, 1961) pp. 13-7.

45. U.S. Bureau of the Census, *Report on Indians Taxed and Indians Not Taxed in the United States (except Alaska) at the Eleventh U.S. Census: 1890* (Washington, D.C.: U.S. Government Printing Office, 1894) pp. 637-8.

46. Ibid.

47. Lenore A. Stiffarm and Phil Lane, Jr., "The Demography of Native North America: A Question of American Indian Survival," in M. Annette Jaimes, ed., *The State of Native America: Genocide, Colonization and Resistance* (Boston: South End Press, 1992) pp. 35-6. The State of Texas maintained a bounty on Indian—*any* Indian—scalps until well into the 1870s; see my *A Little Matter of Genocide: Holocaust and Denial in the Americas, 1492 to the Present* (San Francisco: City Lights, 1998) pp. 178-88.

48. James M. Mooney, "Population," in Frederick W. Dodge, ed., *Handbook of the Indians North of Mexico*, 2 vols. (Washington, D.C.: Bureau of American Ethnology Bulletin No. 30, Smithsonian Institution, 1910) pp. 286-7. Also see Sherburn F. Cook, *The Conflict Between the California Indian and White Civilization* (Berkeley: University of California Press, 1976).

49. See " 'To Judge Them by the Standards of Their Time'," in this volume.

50. Stiffarm and Lane, "Demography," p. 34.

51. Russell Thornton, "Cherokee Population Losses During the Trail of Tears: A New Perspective and Estimate," *Ethnohistory*, No. 31, 1984, pp. 289-300.

52. Ryan S. Johansson and S.H. Preston, "Tribal Demography: The Navajo and Hopi Populations as Seen Through Manuscripts from the 1900 Census," *Social Science History*, No. 3, 1978, p. 26.

53. Paul Andrew Hutton, *Phil Sheridan and His Army* (Lincoln: University of Nebraska Press, 1985) p. 246.

54. Scholarly estimates of the actual total run as high as a half-million; Russell Thornton, *American Indian Holocaust and Survival: A Population History Since 1492* (Norman: University of Oklahoma Press, 1987) p. 49.

55. U.S. Bureau of the Census, *Fifteenth Census of the United States, 1930: The Indian Population of the United States and Alaska* (Washington, D.C.: U.S. Government Printing Office, 1937). Barely 101,000 Canadian Indians were estimated as surviving in the same year.

56. Estimating native population figures at the point of first contact is, at best, a slippery business. Recent demographic work has, however, produced a broad consensus that the standard anthropological estimates of "about one million north of the Río Grande" fashioned by James Mooney and Alfred Kroeber, as well as Harold Driver's subsequent upward revision of their calculations to "approximately two million," are *far* too low. Others, using more appropriate methods, have computed a "maximal" precontact North American Indian population of 18.5 million, about fifteen million of them within present U.S. borders; Henry F. Dobyns, *Their Numbers Become Thinned: Native American Population Dynamics in Eastern North America* (Knoxville: University of Tennessee Press, 1983). More conservative estimates put the figure at about 12.5 million, perhaps 9.5 million of them within the U.S.; Thornton, *American Indian Holocaust and Survival*. Splitting the difference leaves one with an approximate fifteen million North American population total, about 12.5 million in the U.S. Interestingly, no matter which set of the newer estimates one uses, the overall attrition by 1890 is in the upper 90th percentile.

57. The figure is arrived by relying upon Charles C. Royce, *Indian Land Cessions in the United States*, 2 vols. (Washington, D.C.: Bureau of American Ethnography, 18th Annual Report, 1896-97, Smithsonian Institution, 1899).

58. The idea was to destroy the *untermensch* ("subhuman") populations—Slavs, Jews and Gypsies among them—of eastern Europe, replacing them on the lands thus vacated with "superior" Germanic "settlers," and thereby establishing Germany as a first-class world power. Hitler expressed this rather

consistently during his career, beginning with *Mein Kampf*. For instance, after outlining the necessity of a large continental land base for any country seeking a "world historical" role, he observed that, "Today many European states are like pyramids stood on their heads. Their European area is absurdly small in comparison to their weight of colonies, foreign trade, etc. We may say: summit in Europe, base in the whole world; contrasting with the American Union which possesses its base in its own continent and touches the rest of the earth only with its summit. And from this comes the immense inner strength of this state and the weakness of most European colonial powers. . . Nor is England any proof to the contrary, since in consideration of the British empire we forget too easily the Anglo-Saxon world as such. The position of England, if only because of her linguistic and cultural bond with the American Union, can be compared to no other state in Europe. . . For Germany, consequently, the only possibility for carrying out a healthy territorial policy [lies] in the acquisition of new land in Europe itself . . . suited for settlement by [Germans] . . . [S]uch a colonial policy [must be] carried out by means of a hard struggle . . . not for territories outside of Europe, but for land on the home continent itself. . . If land [is] desired in Europe, it [can] be obtained by and large only at the expense of Russia, and this [means] that the new Reich must again set itself on the march along the road of the Teutonic Knights of old, to obtain by the German sword sod for the German plow and daily bread for the nation"; Adolf Hitler, *Mein Kampf* (New York: Sentry Editions, 1962) pp. 139-40.

59. Ch. 120, 16 Stat. 544, 566, now codified at 25 U.S.C. 71. According to its authors, the suspension did nothing to impair the standing of existing treaties between the U.S. and native nations.

60. Ch. 341, 24 Stat. 362, 385, now codified at 18 U.S.C. 1153; on context and implementation of the act, see Sidney L. Harring, *Crow Dog's Case: American Indian Sovereignty, Tribal Law, and United States Law in the Nineteenth Century* (New York: Cambridge University Press, 1994) esp. pp. 100-41.

61. *United States v. Kagama,* (118 U.S. 375 (1886)).

62. Deloria and Lytle, *American Indians, American Justice.*

63. Ch. 119, 24 Stat. 388, now codified as amended at 25 U.S.C. 331 *et seq.*, better known as the "Dawes Act," after its primary sponsor, Massachusetts Senator Henry Dawes.

64. See "The Crucible of American Indian Identity," in this volume.

65. Janet A. McDonnell, *The Dispossession of the American Indian, 1887-1934* (Bloomington: Indiana University Press, 1991).

66. Kirk Kicking Bird and Karen Ducheneaux, *One Hundred Million Acres* (New York: Macmillan, 1973).

67. D.S. Otis, *The Dawes Act and the Allotment of Indian Land* (Norman: University of Oklahoma Press, 1973).

68. Francis E. Leupp, *The Indian and His Problem* (New York: Scribner's, 1910) p. 93.

69. 187 U.S. 553 (1903).

70. Customary international law (*jus cogens*) with regard to treaty relations was not formally codified until the Vienna Convention on the Law of Treaties (U.N. Doc. A/CONF.39/27 at 289 (1969), 115 U.N.T.S. 331, *reprinted in* 8 I.L.M. 679 (1969)). However, all parties—including the United States, which has yet to ratify it—concur that its major provisions have been in practical effect for two centuries or more. Article 27 of the Convention states categorically that no state can invoke its own internal laws (including its constitution) as a basis to avoid meeting its treaty obligations. *Lone Wolf* plainly defies this principle. On the Vienna Convention, see Sir Ian Sinclair, *The Vienna Convention on the Law of Treaties* (Manchester, UK: Manchester University Press, [2nd ed.] 1984). On U.S. acknowledgement that its terms are valid and legally binding, see U.S. Senate, Committee on the Judiciary, Subcommittee on the Constitution, *Hearing on Constitutional Issues Relating to the Proposed Genocide Convention Before the Subcommittee on the Constitution of the Senate Committee on the Judiciary* (Washington, D.C.: 99th Cong., 1st Sess., 1985).

71. Ch. 233, 43 Stat. 25.

72. M. Annette Jaimes, "Federal Indian Identification Policy: A Usurpation of Indigenous Sovereignty in the United States," in Jaimes, *State of Native America*, pp. 127-8.

73. For the origins of this policy, see Henry E. Fritz, *The Movement for Indian Assimilation, 1860-1890* (Philadelphia: University of Pennsylvania Press, 1963).

74. This is a clinically genocidal posture within the meaning of the term offered by Raphaël Lemkin, the man who coined it: "Generally speaking, genocide does not necessarily mean the immediate

destruction of a nation, *except when* accomplished by mass killing of all the members of a nation. It is intended rather to signify a coordinated plan of different actions aimed at destruction of the essential foundations of the life of national groups, with the aim of annihilating the groups themselves. The objective of such a plan would be disintegration of the political and social institutions, of culture, language, national feelings, religion, and the economic existence of national groups, and the destruction of personal security, liberty, health, dignity, and the lives of individuals belonging to such groups. Genocide is the destruction of the national group as an entity, and the actions involved are directed against individuals, not in their individual capacity but as members of the national group [emphasis added]"; Raphaël Lemkin, *Axis Rule in Occupied Europe* (Washington, D.C.: Carnegie Endowment for International Peace, 1944) p. 79.

75. As the Commissioner of Indian Affairs put it in his 1886 *Annual Report* (pp. xxiii–iv): "I [have] expressed very decidedly the idea that Indians should be taught the English language *only*. . . There is not an Indian pupil whose tuition is paid for by the United States Government who is permitted to study *any* other language than our own vernacular—the language of the greatest, most powerful, and enterprising nationalities under the sun. The English language as taught in America is good enough for all her people of all races [emphasis added]."

76. Central Indian spiritual practices such as the Potlatch of the nations of the Pacific Northwest and the Sundance of the Lakota were prohibited under pain of criminal law. See Douglas Cole and Ira Chaikan, *An Iron Hand Upon the People: The Law Against Potlatch on the Northwest Coast* (Seattle: University of Washington Press, 1990); Curtis E. Jackson and Marcia J. Galli, *A History of the Bureau of Indian Affairs and Its Activities Among Indians* (San Francisco: R&E Research Associates, 1977) pp. 189–93.

77. David Wallace Adams, *Education for Extinction: American Indians and the Boarding School Experience, 1875-1928* (Lawrence: University Press of Kansas, 1995). It should be noted that such systematic transfer of the children of a targeted racial or ethnic group to the targeting group is defined as a genocidal act under Article II(e) of the United Nations Convention on the Prevention and Punishment of the Crime of Genocide (U.S.T._____, T.I.A.S. No. _____, 78 U.N.T.S. 277 (1948)); Weston, Falk and D'Amato, *Basic Documents*, p. 297.

78. The Lakota, for example, rapidly developed a basis for reservation self-sufficiency predicated in livestock during the quarter-century following the 1890 Wounded Knee Massacre. During World War I, however, the U.S. appealed to Lakota "patriotism" to engage in a near-total and cut-rate sell-off of their cattle to provide rations for American troops fighting in France. After the war, when the Lakota requested assistance in replenishing their herds, the government declined. Lakota grazing lands were then leased by the BIA to non-Indian ranchers, while the Indians assumed a position of permanent destitution; Lazarus, *Black Hills, White Justice*, pp. 150–2.

79. Letter, Charles Burke to William Williamson, September 16, 1921; William Williamson Papers, Box 2, File—Indian Matters, Miscellaneous, I.D. Weeks Library, University of South Dakota, Vermilion. Such articulation of official sensibility was hardly isolated; see Robert M. Kvasnicka and Herman J. Viola, eds., *The Commissioners of Indian Affairs, 1824-1977* (Lincoln: University of Nebraska Press, 1979).

80. The method was to withdraw federal recognition of the existence of specific indigenous nations, converting large reservations into counties, or incorporating smaller reservations into existing counties. Examples of legislation enacted pursuant to House Resolution 108 which authorized such practices include the Menominee Termination Act (ch. 303, 68 Stat. 250 (June 17, 1954)), Klamath Termination Act (ch. 732, 68 Stat. 718 (August 13, 1954), codified at 25 U.S.C. 564 *et seq.*), and the Act Terminating the Tribes of Western Oregon (ch. 733, 68 Stat. 724 (August 13, 1954), codified at 25 U.S.C. 691 *et seq.*).

81. Public Law 959. On implementation, see Donald L. Fixico, *Termination and Relocation: Federal Indian Policy, 1945-1960* (Albuquerque: University of New Mexico Press, 1986).

82. The U.S. Census of 1900 reported almost no Indians (0.4 percent of the native population) living in cities. The 1950 Census showed that proportion had grown to only 13.4 percent. With implementation of coherent federal relocation programs, however, the number mushroomed to 44.5 percent by 1970. Although relocation was geared down during the 1970s, and finally suspended during the 1980s, it continues to have a lingering effect, with the result that the proportion of urban Indians grew to 49 percent in 1980 and about 52 percent in 1990; Stiffarm and Lane, "Demography," p. 42.

83. Ch. 505, 67 Stat. 588 (August 14, 1954), codified in part at 18 U.S.C. 1162 and 28 U.S.C. 1360. On implementation, see Carol E. Goldberg, "Public Law 280: The Limits of State Law over Indian Reservations," *UCLA Law Review*, No. 22, Feb. 1975.

84. On resource distribution, see Ronald L. Trosper, "Appendix I: Indian Minerals," in American Indian Policy Review Commission, *Task Force 7 Final Report: Reservation and Resource Development and Protection* (Washington, D.C.: U.S. Government Printing Office, 1977); U.S. Department of Interior, Bureau of Indian Affairs, *Indian Lands Map: Oil, Gas and Minerals on Indian Reservations* (Washington, D.C.: U.S. Government Printing Office, 1978).

85. Louis R. Moore, *Mineral Development on Indian Lands: Cooperation and Conflict* (Denver: Rocky Mountain Mineral Law Foundation, 1983); Michael Garrity, "The U.S. Colonial Empire is as Close as the Nearest Reservation," in Holly Sklar, ed., *Trilateralism: The Trilateral Commission and Elite Planning for World Government* (Boston: South End Press, 1980) pp. 238-68.

86. The IRA was implemented by referenda, reservation by reservation. In instances where traditionals such as the Hopi manifested their resistance to it through the time-honored means of boycotting the proceedings, however, Indian Commissioner John Collier counted their abstentions as "aye" votes. The same method was used with regard to the Lakota Nation, as well as the inclusion of "aye" votes allegedly cast by long-dead voters. Such fraud permeated implementation of reorganization throughout Indian Country; see the testimony of Rupert Costo in Kenneth R. Philp, ed., *Indian Self-Rule: First-Hand Accounts of Indian-White Relations from Roosevelt to Reagan* (Salt Lake City: Howe Bros., 1986). Also see Graham D. Taylor, *The New Deal and American Indian Tribalism: The Administration of the Indian Reorganization Act, 1934-45* (Lincoln: University of Nebraska Press, 1980).

87. See generally, Vine Deloria, Jr., and Clifford M. Lytle, *The Nations Within: The Past and Future of American Indian Sovereignty* (New York: Pantheon, 1984).

88. Jimmie Durham, "Native Americans and Colonialism," *The Guardian*, Mar. 28, 1979.

89. For official acknowledgement of this situation, see U.S. Commission on Civil Rights, *The Navajo Nation: An American Colony* (Washington, D.C.: U.S. Dept. of Justice, 1976).

90. See "A Breach of Trust," in this volume.

91. This idea has been increasingly fronted during the 1980s by the Council of Energy Resource Tribes (CERT), a federally supported consortium of representatives from IRA Tribal Councils; Marjane Ambler, *Breaking the Iron Bonds: Indian Control of Energy Development* (Lawrence: University Press of Kansas, 1990) pp. 117, 234. Also see Philip S. Deloria, "CERT: It's Time for an Evaluation," *American Indian Law Newsletter*, Sept. 1982.

92. U.S. Bureau of the Census, *1980 Census of the Population, Supplementary Reports, Race of the Population by States, 1980* (Washington, D.C.: U.S. Government Printing Office, 1981); *Ancestry of the Population by State, 1980* (Washington, D.C.: U.S. Government Printing Office, 1983).

93. This argument was advanced rather well by Gerald F. Seib in his "Indians Awaken to their Lands' Energy Riches and Seek to Wrest Development from Companies," *Wall Street Journal*, Sept. 20, 1979.

94. U.S. Bureau of the Census, *General Population Characteristics: United States Summary* (Washington, D.C.: U.S. Government Printing Office, 1983); *General Social and Economic Characteristics: United States Summary* (Washington, D.C.: U.S. Government Printing Office, 1983); *1980 Census of the Population, Supplementary Report: American Indian Areas and Alaska Native Villages* (Washington, D.C.: U.S. Government Printing Office, 1984).

95. U.S. Bureau of the Census, Population Division, Racial Statistics Branch, *A Statistical Profile of the American Indian Population* (Washington, D.C.: U.S. Government Printing Office, 1984); U.S. Public Health Service, *Chart Series Book* (Washington, D.C.: Department of Health and Human Series, 1988).

96. The quote is taken from Eduardo Galeano, *The Open Veins of Latin America: Five Centuries of the Pillage of a Continent* (New York: Monthly Review Press, 1973).

97. For analysis of the U.S. role in formulating the so-called Nuremberg Principles under which the nazi leadership was tried for violating "customary international law"; Smith, *Road to Nuremberg*.

98. 60 Stat. 1049 (1946).

99. Harvey D. Rosenthal, *Their Day in Court: A History of the Indian Claims Commission* (New York: Garland, 1990). Also see "Charades, Anyone?", in this volume.

100. Russel Barsh, "Indian Land Claims Policy in the United States," *North Dakota Law Review*, No. 58, 1982, pp. 1-82; "Behind the Land Claims: Rationalizing Dispossession," *Law and Anthropology*, No. 1, 1986, pp. 15-50. Also see "Charades, Anyone?", in this volume.

101. In 1956, the original ten year lifespan of the commission was extended for five years. The process was repeated in 1961, 1967, 1972, and 1976; U.S. Congress, Joint Committee on Appropriations, *Hearings on Appropriations for the Department of Interior and Related Agencies for 1977* (Washington, D.C.: 94th Cong., 1st Sess., 1976).

102. Indian Claims Commission, *Final Report* (Washington, D.C.: U.S. Department of Interior, 1978).

103. Imre Sutton, "Prologomena," in Imre Sutton, ed., *Irredeemable America: The Indians Estate and Land Tenure* (Albuquerque: University of New Mexico Press, 1985) p. 7; citing Barsh, "Land Claims Policy," p. 1.

104. 85 Stat. 688, codified at 43 U.S.C. 1601 *et seq*. For background, see M.C. Berry, *The Alaska Pipeline: The Politics of Oil and Native Land Claims* (Bloomington: Indiana University Press, 1975).

105. Haunani-Kay Trask, *From a Native Daughter: Sovereignty and Colonialism in Hawai'i* (Honolulu: University of Hawai'i Press, [2nd ed.] 1999). For "official" data, see L. Cannelora, *The Origin of Hawaiian Land Titles and the Rights of Native Tenants* (Honolulu: Security Title Corporation, 1974). Also see "Stolen Kingdom," in this volume.

106. See generally, David Robie, *Blood on the Their Banner: Nationalist Struggles in the South Pacific* (London: Zed Books, 1989); Ronald Fernandez, *Prisoners of Colonialism: The Struggle for Justice in Puerto Rico* (Monroe, ME: Common Courage Press, 1994).

107. Sioux Nation of Indians v. United States, 448 U.S. 371 (1980). For analysis, see Steven C. Hanson, "*United States v. Sioux Nation*: Political Questions, Moral Imperative and National Honor," *American Indian Law Review*, Vol. 8, No. 2, 1980, pp. 459-84.

108. Western Shoshone Identifiable Group v. United States, 40 Ind. Cl. Comm. 311 (1977); *United States v. Dann*, 706 F.2d 919, 926 (1983). For background, see Glenn T. Morris, "The Battle for Newe Segobia: The Western Shoshone Land Rights Struggle," in Ward Churchill, ed., *Critical Issues in Native North America, Vol. II* (Copenhagen: International Work Group on Indigenous Affairs, 1991) pp. 86-98.

109. See "The Bloody Wake of Alcatraz," in this volume.

110. The global study has been completed; see José R. Martinez Cobo, *Study of the Problem of Discrimination Against Indigenous Populations, Final Report: Conclusions, Proposals and Recommendations* (U.N./ID # E/CN.4/Sub.2/1983/21/Add.83, Sept. 1983). At present, an enhancing study covering the extent and nature of treaty relations between indigenous peoples and various states around the world is being completed by the Cuban representative to the Working Group, Miguel Alfonso Martinez. Meanwhile, a draft Declaration of the Rights of Indigenous Peoples has been prepared, but has been stalled by the U.S. prior to its submission to the General Assembly; Isabelle Schulte-Tenckhoff, "The Irresistible Ascension of the UN Draft Declaration on the Rights of Indigenous Peoples: Stopped Dead in Its Tracks?" *European Review of Native American Studies*, Vol. 9, No. 2, 1995; Glenn T. Morris, "Further Motion by the State Department to Railroad Indigenous Rights," *Fourth World Bulletin*, No. 6, Summer 1998, pp. 1-9. Also see Appendix D.

111. As the U.S. Department of State put it in its presentation to the Working Group in 1980 (at p. 13): "Actually, the U.S. Government entered into a trust relationship with the separate tribes in acknowledgement . . . of their political status as sovereign nations"; quoted in Roxanne Dunbar Ortiz, "Protection of American Indian Territories in the United States: Applicability of International Law," in Sutton, *Irredeemable America*, pp. 247-70.

112. This jockeying is well summarized in S. James Anaya, "The Rights of Indigenous Peoples and International Law in Historical and Contemporary Perspective," in Robert N. Clinton, Nell Jessup Newton and Monroe E. Price, eds., *American Indian Law: Cases and Materials* (Charlottesville, VA: Michie Co., 1991) pp. 1257-76.

113. For analysis, see Dunbar Ortiz, "Protection," pp. 260-1.

114. Universal Declaration of Human Rights (U.N.G.A. Res 217 A (III), U.N. Doc A/180, at 71 (1948)); Convention on the Elimination of All Forms of Racial Discrimination (660 U.N.T.S. 195, *reprinted in* 5 I.L.M. 352 (1966); International Covenant on Economic, Social and Cultural Rights

(U.N.G.A. Res 2200 (XXI), 21 U.N. GAOR, Supp. (No. 16) 49, U.N. Doc. A/6316 (1967), *reprinted in* 6 I.L.M. 360 (1967)); International Covenant on Civil and Political Rights (U.N.G.A. Res. 2200 (XXI), 21 U.N. GAOR, Supp. (No. 16) 52, U.N. Doc A/6316 (1967), *reprinted in* 6 I.L.M. 368 (1967)). The texts of these instruments may be found in Weston, Falk and D'Amato, *Basic Documents*, pp. 298-301, 364-8, 371-5, 376-85.

115. In October 1985, President Ronald Reagan withdrew a 1946 U.S. declaration accepting ICJ jurisdiction in all matters of "international dispute." The withdrawal took effect in April 1986. This was in response to the ICJ determination in *Nicaragua v. United States*, the first substantive case ever brought before it to which the U.S. was a party. The ICJ ruled the U.S. action of mining Nicaraguan harbors in times of peace to be unlawful. The Reagan Administration formally rejected the authority of the ICJ to decide the matter (but removed the mines). It is undoubtedly significant that the Reagan instrument contained a clause accepting continued ICJ jurisdiction over matters pertaining to "international commercial relationships," thus attempting to convert the world court into a mechanism for mere trade arbitration; *U.S. Terminates Acceptance of ICJ Compulsory Jurisdiction* (Washington, D.C.: Department of State Bulletin No. 86, Jan. 1986).

116. The United States declined to ratify the Genocide Convention until 1988, forty years after it became international law (and after more than 100 other nations had ratified it), and then only with an attached "Sovereignty Package" purporting to subordinate the convention to the U.S. Constitution (thereby seeking to protect certain aspects of genocidal conduct). The U.S. stipulation in this regard is of course invalid under Article 27 of the 1969 Vienna Convention on the Law of Treaties, and has been protested as such by such countries as Britain, Denmark and the Netherlands. Further, the Genocide Convention is now customary international law, meaning—according to the Nuremberg Doctrine—that it is binding upon the U.S., whether Congress ratifies its terms or not; Lawrence J. LeBlanc, *The United States and the Genocide Convention* (Durham, N.C.: Duke University Press, 1991).

117. On the nature of self-determining rights as articulated in international rather than U.S. domestic law, see Lee C. Buckheit, *Secession: The Legitimacy of Self-Determination* (New Have, CT: Yale University Press, 1978); Michla Pomerance, *Self-Determination in Law and Practice* (The Hague: Marinus Nijhoff, 1982).

118. The Inouye Committee relied on the groundwork laid for such a maneuver by such earlier incorporating legislation as the Indian Civil Rights Act of 1968 (Public Law 90-284; 82 Stat. 77, codified in part at 25 U.S.C. 1301 *et seq.*) and the Indian Self-Determination and Educational Assistance Act of 1975 (Public Law 93-638; 88 Stat. 2203, codified at 25 U.S.C. 450a and elsewhere in Titles 25, 42, and 50, U.S.C.A.). It should be noted that the latter completely inverts international definitions of "self-determination," providing instead for an Indian preference in the hiring of individuals to fill positions within the federal system of administering Indian Country. Critics such as AIM leader Russell Means have therefore dubbed it the "Indian Self-Administration Act." For details on the committee itself, see U.S. Senate, Select Committee on Indian Affairs, *Final Report and Legislative Recommendations: A Report of the Special Committee on Investigations* (Washington, D.C.: 101st Cong. 2d Sess.,1989).

119. For context, see Noam Chomsky, " 'What We Say Goes': The Middle East in the New World Order," in Peters, *Collateral Damage*, pp. 49-92.

120. Noam Chomsky and Eqbal Ahmed, "The Gulf Crisis: How We Got There," in Gregg Bates, ed., *Mobilizing Democracy: Changing the U.S. Role in the Middle East* (Monroe, ME: Common Courage Press, 1991) pp. 3-24.

121. See the essay entitled "On Gaining 'Moral High Ground': An Ode to George Bush and the 'New World Order'," in my *From a Native Son: Selected Essay in Indigenism, 1985-1995* (Boston: South End Press, 1996) pp. 297-310.

122. The same point has been made in other connections; see, e.g., Quincy Wright, "Legal Aspects of the Viet-Nam Situation," in Richard A. Falk, ed., *The Vietnam War and International Law* (Princeton, NJ: Princeton University Press, 1969) pp. 271-91.

123. See, e.g., Ralph Miliband and Leo Panitch, eds., *Socialist Register 1992: New World Order?* (London: Merlin Press, 1992); Christopher D. Merrett, *Free Trade: Neither Free Nor About Trade* (Montréal: Black Rose, 1996).

Earlier versions of this essay have been published in the first edition of my *Struggle for the Land* (Monroe, ME: Common Courage Press, 1993); Steven Jay Gold, ed., *Moral Controversies: Race, Class, and Gender in Applied Ethics* (New York: Wadsworth, 1993); David S. Caudill and Steven Jay Gold, eds., *The Radical Philosophy of Law: Contemporary Challenges to Mainstream Legal Theory* (Atlantic Highlands, NJ: Humanities Press, 1995); James P. Sterba, ed., *Social and Political Philosophy: Classical Western Texts in Feminist and Multicultural Perspectives* (Belmont, CA: Wadsworth, 1995); and James P. Sterba, ed., *Ethics: Classical Western Texts in Feminist and Multicultural Perspectives* (New York: Oxford University Press, 2000).

# The Right of Conquest
## The Devolution of a Myth in International Law

> It is clear from the facts of this century's history that states did not renounce conquest as a means of gaining territory: only conquest as a *lawful* means of doing so.
>
> — Sharon Korman
> *The Right of Conquest* (1996)

While channel-surfing late one February evening in 1999, I happened to land momentarily on C-Span 2. Seeing there the familiar face of LaDonna Harris, the Comanche wife of former progressive Senator Fred Harris, herself a one-time Citizens' Party vice presidential candidate behind Barry Commoner, and longtime head of Americans for Indian Opportunity, a lobbying enterprise based in the U.S. capitol,[1] I decided to stop browsing long enough to find out what was happening. As it happened, the segment was a replay of a panel convened by Harris to "dialogue" on questions of native rights. Interest piqued, I opted to watch it through.

Prominent among the ostensible "Indian experts" assembled for the event was Leonard Garment, a personality whose main claim to fame in this connection is to have served, along with future CIA Director Frank Carlucci, as Richard Nixon's bag man in November 1972, delivering some $66,650 in illegally obtained funds to facilitate the speedy departure of a couple-hundred American Indian Movement members who'd occupied the Interior Department's Bureau of Indian Affairs Building in the government quarter of Washington, D.C., garnering considerable press attention in the process.[2] Nixon, embarrassed by their presence, wanted them quickly gone; AIM wanted to negotiate with the administration about establishing mechanisms to ensure U.S. compliance with the terms and provisions of its 400-odd ratified treaties with indigenous nations; Garment played a not insignificant role in achieving the first agenda item while subverting the latter.[3] But that's another story.

33

As the panel's discussion evolved, it became increasingly apparent—even within the self-imposed parameters of liberal discourse employed by the participants—that resolution of most of the issues raised—"economic development," for instance—was effectively precluded by the nature of federal Indian policy, or, more accurately, by the nature of the authority over their assets and affairs the United States has unilaterally assigned itself vis-à-vis every indigenous people trapped within its claimed boundaries.[4] Although such words were never used, the panel began to display a certain visible discomfort as they floundered about, realizing no doubt that what they were inadvertently describing was the relationship between colonizer and colonized, the sorts of policies typically attending administration of a colonial order, and the "problems" for the colonized inevitably accruing therefrom.[5]

The problem with calling things by their right names, of course, was that colonialism is a crime, prohibited under international law since implementation of the United Nations Charter in 1945.[6] Eager to leave their audience an impression that even the more glaring transgressions entailed in the U.S. posture might somehow be reconciled to the requisites of propriety, the panelists turned hopefully and en bloc to Garment, awaiting his concluding remarks. And, for his part, adopting the fugitive pose of sage council—that is, something between befuddlement and a smirk—Lenny did his level best, dissembling in a manner worthy of Henry Kissinger,[7] or even Madeline Albright.[8]

The international legal requirement, he began—accurately enough—is that all peoples be afforded an opportunity to exercise the right to determine for themselves the form of their relationships to other peoples and countries.[9] Then, in a sly but total departure from reality, he opined that American Indians had long since been accorded their rights in this regard, a "fact" statutorily enshrined in the American Indian Self-Determination and Educational Assistance Act of 1975 (a measure doing little more than extending a hiring preference to Indians willing to impose federal policies upon themselves, and to train them for such purposes).[10] More to the point, he continued, native people in the U.S. had been self-governing since implementation of the 1934 Indian Reorganization Act (a measure designed to usurp traditional governments, replacing them with administrative structures more useful to the United States).[11] In sum, all appearances to the contrary notwithstanding, things here are as they should be, he seemed to conclude.

But Garment was not as yet quite finished. There would always be those, he observed, who might wish to "quibble" about whether the U.S.

configurations of self-determination and self-government really conform to either the letter or spirit of international legal definition. Such critics, he informed listeners, should bear in mind that "the rights of conquest are also recognized in international law."[12] In other words, the niceties of international legality are ultimately irrelevant. Those indigenous nations whose lands have been forcibly incorporated into the U.S. "home territory" are subject only to the domestic legalisms of the occupying power.[13] We have, or should have, no recourse to the international arena, and would thus do well to be grateful that our conquerors have proven so benevolent and enlightened as to recognize that we possess any semblance of rights at all.

With that, each of them appearing immensely relieved that the bullet had been dodged, with the illusion of U.S.-dispensed oppression equaling humanitarianism once again quite neatly fostered, the panelists ended their session, smiling vacuously and indulging in hearty handshakes for a job well done. That the whole spiel was untrue was something they knew perfectly well—or were obliged to know—given their status as intellectual minions of the status quo in a country where the Nuremberg Doctrine was quite literally invented.[14] Moreover, recognizing the magnitude of Garment's falsehood didn't even require any particular knowledge of the law. History alone might have done.

The U.S. presently recognizes the existence of nearly 500 "indigenous groups" within its borders.[15] Yet, by its own count, America waged fewer than fifty "Indian Wars" in the course of its expansion.[16] That leaves well over 400 now-subordinated peoples with whom the U.S. never exchanged a blow. One can only marvel at a definition of "conquest" allowing it to have occurred without a shot being fired. Preoccupation with the "details" of mere factual consistency has never figured very highly among those articulating America's triumphalist narratives of self-legitimation, however. On the contrary, as Sartre once observed, "concealing, deceiving and lying" is perceived as "a duty" among those whose minds are mortgaged to rationalizing whatever benefits and privileges they might obtain from colonial order.[17]

### The Right of Conquest

Legally speaking, the notion that a right of possession attends the taking of territory by armed force has always been strained at best. Although, as Lassa Oppenheim observed at the dawn of the twentieth century, "as long as a Law of Nations has been in existence, the states as well as the vast majority of writers have recognized subjugation as a mode of acquiring terri-tory,"[18] the evidence is clear that even legal theorists who endorsed the idea considered it problematic. Emmerich de Vattel, for example, conceded that conquest confers a certain territorial title and consequent jurisdiction to conquering powers, but declined to treat these as being either permanent or binding upon the conquered.

> [W]ar does not decide the question: victory only compels the vanquished to subscribe to the treaty which terminates the difference. It is an error, no less absurd than perni-cious, to say that war is to decide controversies between those who acknowledge no superior judge — as is the case with nations. Victory usually favours the cause of strength and prudence, rather than of right or justice. It would be a bad rule of decision.[19]

In effect, as Yoram Dinstein has noted, the entire concept of a "right of conquest" created "an egregious anomaly" in international law,[20] the pre-dominating thrust of which has from its inception been to affirm and pro-tect the sovereignty of all nations (or at least states).

> It does not make much sense for the international legal system to be based on respect for the sovereignty of States, while each State has a sovereign right to destroy the sov-ereignty of others. On the one hand, it is incumbent on every State to defer to a plethora of rights accorded to other States under both customary and conventional international law. On the other hand, each State was at liberty to attack any other State whenever it pleased.[21]

Leaving aside Europe's heritage of mystic mumbo-jumbo concerning the supposed "Divine Rights of Kings" and similar claptrap, the concept that conquest implied any rights at all appears to have arisen during the sixteenth century from pragmatic concerns over how best to constrain warfare between the continent's emergent states. As the matter was framed by "the father of modern international law, Hugo Grotius, power disparities between these countries had already generated interminable struggles for "territorial adjustment." Confirming the results in as rapid and orderly a manner as pos-sible seemed the most effective means of constraining the duration of these conflicts. "Unless this rule was adopted," Grotius wrote in his landmark 1625 study, *De Jure Belli ac Pacis*, "no limit or termination could have been fixed for such wars, which are extremely frequent."[22]

One difficulty with the expediency embodied in Grotius' formulation was that it flatly contradicted the bedrock juridical principle of *ex injuria jus non obitur*—that rights cannot arise from a wrong or unjust act—in a man-ner which "equated law to power," rewarding violators for their violations in a way creating strong disincentives to generalized legal compliance.[23] The problem had been recognized as early as 1539 by the Spanish legal philosopher Franciscus de Vitoria, who'd sought to resolve it through the stipulation that conquest rights might be enjoyed only by those acquiring territory during prosecution of a "Just War."[24] Those seizing territory by the waging of "unjust," "unprovoked" or "aggressive" wars—Vitoria carefully delineated the criteria by which the just should be distinguished from the unjust[25]—would incur no such benefits.[26]

Beginning in the early 1670s,[27] Samuel Pufendorf not only elaborated upon Vitoria's position, but explicitly rejected the Grotian premise that conquest rights applied as much to territory seized through aggression as that acquired justly, questioning whether the idea was even rooted in law: "Grotius [argues that] the custom has become the law of nations . . . yet what has been extorted by an unjust war cannot be kept with good conscience . . . so it does not appear clear that there is any law of nations which [legitimates the acquisitions] of an unjust victor."[28]

> And even if such a law were to be found, it does not seem that to neglect it would mean any great loss for the peace of mankind. For, according to Grotius, the effect of formal war, whatever the nature of the justifying cause, is this: that external domination, to use his phrase, is secured over the possessions of one's enemies. Therefore, if a man later wage a war on his former victor, even though he have no justifying cause beyond [the fact of being conquered], he will still, when fortune smiles upon him, not only get back what he lost in an unjust war, but also acquire all his enemy's property.[29]

In other words, by inverting legal logic to facilitate a "realpolitik" approach to the curtailment of warfare, Grotius had accomplished the opposite, contriving instead a recipe that all but guaranteed perpetual bloodletting. If limiting frequency and duration of armed conflicts was the object, as Pufendorf agreed it should be, the best means would be to foreclose the possibility that fruits of aggression might ever in any sense be legitimated. Not only would this conform with the broader demands of legal coherence in the international arena, it would ultimately remove the motive forces generating many if not most wars. In substance, Pufendorf argued that the shortest possible war would be no war at all, and that the Law of Nations should therefore be consciously designed to attain precisely that result.[30]

He was hardly alone. By the nineteenth century, a number of prominent jurists and legal scholars had taken up the theme that "conquest is force, and force is antithetical to law . . . therefore, conquest cannot give legal title" to territorial acquisitions.[31] Among those taking this position were Montluc, Pasquale Fiore, Pierre Pradier-Fodére, Henry Bonfils and Frantz Despagnet.[32] The political philosopher Jean-Jacques Rousseau had also joined in the chorus of condemnation, observing that it would be absurd to argue seriously "that one can at one's pleasure transfer peoples from master to master, like herds of cattle, without consulting their interests or their wishes."[33]

Such positions might well have eclipsed the Grotian tradition altogether, save for a question of law enforcement. As Vattel put it in 1758, in a manner more reminiscent of Vitoria than of Grotius: "the conditions necessary for rendering an acquisition, made by arms, just and irreproachable before God and our conscience are these—justice in the cause, and equity in the measure of satisfaction."[34] He then went on to frame what he saw as the decisive problem confronting proponents of such legal niceties, however.

> [I]n the contests of nations and sovereigns who live together in a state of nature, how can this rule be judged? They acknowledge no superior. Who then shall judge between them, to assign each his right and obligations—to say to the one, "you have a right to take up arms, to attack your enemy and subdue him by force";—and to the other, "Every act of hostility you commit will be an act of injustice; your victories will be so many murders, your conquests, rapines and robberies?"[35]

Sharon Korman states Vattel's conclusion with alacrity: "In the absence of a supranational body above states which might legally establish, in the event of a war, which side has the just cause and which is the aggressor, which victories are lawful and which conquests unlawful, and in the absence of an international police force with the power to ensure that all conquests illegally acquired are returned to their rightful owner, the law of nations has had instead to insist that provided the laws of war themselves are observed, all victories are lawful, and every conquest provides just title."[36] Thus, through the end of the nineteenth century, the Grotian view remained normative, official defiance of legality rather than legality itself setting the tone.[37]

In actuality, the situation was anything but uniform. The major states of Europe seem to have pursued something more-or-less Pufendorfian in their relations among themselves following the Napoleonic wars—that is, by roughly 1820—a reality manifested in what is generally referred to as the "Continental balance of power system."[38] As Oppenheim summarized the practice:

[T]the conqueror has not in fact an unlimited possibility of annexation of territory of the vanquished State. When the balance of power is endangered or when other vital interests are at stake, third Powers can and will intervene, and history records many instances of such interventions.[39]

While such geopolitical considerations—as opposed to legality, per se—tended with certain notable exceptions to preclude the so-called Great Powers from asserting conquest rights vis-à-vis one another,[40] Europe's "peripheral" peoples, whom the main players tended to view as cultural and sometimes even "racial" inferiors, fared less well. Poland, to offer a classic illustration, was partitioned three times during the last quarter of the eighteen century, remaining completely occupied and subordinated until its reconstitution in 1918.[41] The Irish and Balkan examples are even more extreme,[42] as are those of the Scots, Welsh and other Celts,[43] in addition to the Basques and Catalans.[44] In such cases it was obvious that, mere legality notwithstanding, the conquerors simply refused to acknowledge the conquered as vested with rights they were in any way bound to respect.[45]

The implications of this highly ethnocentric outlook were defined still more sharply, and in more starkly racialist terms, outside Europe itself, in what Mao Zedong would later call the "Third World."[46] There, in the fastnesses of Africa, Asia, the Americas and the Pacific Basin, the resident populations—peoples of color, one and all—were seen as something altogether other and less than human.[47] It followed that, in their own minds, European peoples held "a self-evident right to settle in territories they found agreeable and to subjugate any native inhabitants as might offer resistance."[48] That such sentiments and the policies attending them ran directly counter to long-articulated international legal principles like the Doctrine of Discovery made no difference.[49]

Their imperial dominions swelling to truly global proportions, the colonizing powers of Europe busily crafted pseudoscientific pretexts by which to create the chimera that their aggressions were vindicated, even glorious,[50] and a set of corresponding philosophical subterfuges through which to claim more formal justification.[51] One result was the emergence of a contradictory and thereby unsustainable duality in the body of international law, one code applying to colonizers, another to the colonized.[52] As Sartre has explained:

Colonialism denies human rights to people it has subjugated by violence, and whom it keeps in poverty and ignorance by force, therefore, as Marx would say, in a state of "subhumanity." Racism is inscribed in the events themselves, in the institutions, in the nature of exchanges and production. The political and social statuses reinforce one another: since the natives are subhuman, the [very concept of rights] does not apply to them.[53]

Nowhere was this more apparent than in North America, where, during the early 1830s, Chief Justice of the U.S. Supreme Court John Marshall penned what even otherwise antagonistic foreign jurists continue to describe as the "magisterial" statements of why indigenous nations should be considered "inherently subordinate" to European/euroderivative states, with whatever property remaining to us retained not by right but sheerly at the sufferance of our white "betters."[54] In American law, it would be another half-century before Indians were declared legally human,[55] a century after that before we would be accorded the same standing as our colonizers in even the most technical sense.[56] By then, the entirety of our landbase had long since been impounded, the pittance reserved for our own nominal use and occupancy—about 2.5 percent of the total[57]—administered under the perpetual "trust authority" of the United States.[58]

## Repudiation of the "Right"

Given Garment's assertion nearly a hundred years after the fact, as well as the nature of its own record, it seems paradoxical that the United States should have assumed a lead role in formally repudiating presumptive rights of conquest and colonization during the early decades of the twentieth century. The country's entire history, after all, had to that point been devoted to expansionism on a continental scale,[59] so much so and with such success that its enterprise would be adopted as *the* model for emulation by Adolf Hitler barely a quarter-century later.[60] As recently as 1898, moreover, it had surged outward, into the Caribbean[61] and across the Pacific to Guam and the Philippines,[62] annexing Hawai'i along the way.[63] Suffice to note that America's abrupt conversion to a more enlightened posture was never as it appeared on the surface.

In general, the impetus to shift from condoning assertions of conquest rights by major powers to the enshrinement of the right to self-determination for all peoples as a centerpiece of international legalism was precipitated by World War I. In the first instance, this resulted from the assassination, on June 28, 1914, of Austria's Archduke Franz Ferdinand at the hands of Serbian nationalists bent upon safeguarding their small country's territorial integrity against the annexationist designs of the adjoining Austrohungarian Empire.[64] Within weeks, like dominoes falling, Europe's intricate web of power balancing compacts plunged first the subcontinent, then the majority of the planet into a four-year conflagration that would forever change the international order.[65] The "Sarajevo Incident" and its consequences demonstrated as little else could the extent to which the arrogance of Grotian pragmatism could splash back to the detriment of those employing it.

In some ways most significant were the collapse of Great Russia's Romanov Empire during the course of the war, and the resulting Bolshevik ascent of 1917.[66] This established for the first time a bona fide "Second World" (socialist, "Asiatic") polarity to counterbalance the theretofore unchallenged global hegemony of the "First World" (capitalist, European or euroderivative) states.[67] The new régime, although it was already rigging referenda in nations previously conquered and colonized by the Romanovs as an expedient to retaining them within the newly proclaimed Union of Soviet Socialist Republics,[68] was quick to appreciate that its greatest base of external support would likely be found among peoples suffering the burden of colonialism elsewhere in the world.[69] One of its first moves in terms of foreign policy was thus to take the moral high ground, issuing a call for renunciation of the prerogative of any country to appropriate by force the territory of another.[70]

On December 25, 1917, Germany fostered an appearance that it had adopted the same lofty principle by announcing that it was entering into a treaty of peace on that basis with the USSR.[71] Upstaged, the countries allied against the Germans—including such notable imperial powers as Great Britain and France, as well as the United States—were forced into making comparable statements of purpose.[72] In large part, this consisted of their public renunciation of any intent to claim territorial indemnities in the wake of the war, and endorsement of a Fourteen-Point Program advanced by U.S. President Woodrow Wilson to rearrange global power relations in a manner meant to prevent recurrence.[73] As this last has been elsewhere and rather glowingly described:

> Wilson's overriding ambition, as he conceived it, was not national but international. After securing the defeat of Germany in co-operation with the Allies, he intended to exploit the latter's dependence [on the U.S., which had entered the war at a late and convenient date, and was therefore relatively unscathed by it] to carry through his grand design for the reform of the international order, the principle ingredient of which was a post-war association of democratic nations that would punish violations of territorial integrity. It was clear that the liberal programme which Wilson personified repudiated the right to acquire territory by force [or] without the inhabitants' consent.[74]

As Wilson himself, echoing Lenin's November 1917 "Decree of Peace,"[75] put it in a speech shortly thereafter, "There shall be no annexations, no contributions, no punitive damages" levied in the wake of an allied victory. Borrowing from Rousseau, he went on to announce that, "Peoples are not to be handed about from one sovereignty to another by an international conference or an understanding between rivals and antagonists. National aspirations must be respected: peoples may now be dominated and governed only by their own consent."[76] Creation of a "League of Nations" through which to regularize diplomatic rather than military resolutions of territorial and related issues was the centerpiece of the Wilsonian scheme of world order.[77] Addressing Vattel's concerns, the entity would be equipped with a "World Court" to properly adjudicate disputes, the member-states themselves serving as the requisite "international police force" needed to bring violators into line.[78]

The ultimate failure of Wilson's "progressive vision" is customarily attributed to "conservative" or "isolationist members of the Senate" who refused either to allow the U.S. to join the League of Nations or to accept World Court jurisdiction over the country's foreign affairs (thus confirming Vattel's irony about the lawlessness of states comprising a de facto "rule of law").[79] Thus gutted before it started, the League proved utterly ineffectual in coping with German, Italian and Japanese expansionism during the mid-1930s, and thereupon collapsed, a circumstance figuring heavily in the outbreak of World War II.[80]

Be that as it may, there is considerable evidence that Woodrow Wilson, an inveterate white supremacist,[81] never really intended anything quite as noble as his posturing suggested. One powerful indication was his failure to so much as mention that application to North America of his vaunted "principles" would have required divestiture of indigenous homelands forcibly incorporated into U.S. and Canadian territorialities.[82] That this was no "oversight" became abundantly clear when Deskaheh, a Cayuga statesman representing the Haudenosaunee (Iroquois Six Nations Confederation of upstate New York/southern Québec), sought to bring his people's case before the League in 1923. U.S. diplomats supported those of Great Britain in blocking his appearance.[83]

The double standard involved was rendered still more explicit in December 1918—that is, while Wilson was still in office, and before the U.S. declined to join—when the incipient League accepted without objection a "practical suggestion" from South Africa's General J.C. Smuts that Third World peoples should be denied the rights accorded whites on the basis that the "colonies in the Pacific and Africa are inhabited by barbarians, who not only cannot possibly govern themselves, but to whom it would be impracticable to apply any idea of political self-determination in the European sense."[84] Exactly how the "barbarians" had gone about governing themselves for millennia prior to being invaded by Europeans, or why, as noneuropeans, they should be legally required to conduct themselves in a manner mimicking Europe, was left unstated. It was simply taken as a given that they hadn't, but should, even that they would "aspire" to do so, given the "opportunity."[85]

As a compromise with Wilson's—and the Soviets'—proclamations that "peoples should not be handed about as if they were property," the Allies carved up the colonial holdings of their vanquished foes—primarily those of Germany and the Ottoman Empire[86]—not through outright annexation, but by assigning them to one another as "Mandates."[87] The deeper purpose underlying the maneuver has been spelled out elsewhere:

> European conflict over colonies ought to be eliminated in the future; hence Allied nonannexation pledges should be respected, so as to avoid providing a pretext for a new war to reconquer lost colonies, and to establish the precedent that war should not be used as an instrument of colonial rivalry.[88]

In effect, "the principle of self-determination [was] applied . . . only where the interests of national and imperial policy permitted, but not when the principle came in conflict with those interests."[89] While this was undoubtedly far less than Wilson had in hoped to achieve—a more sweeping repudiation of classic (external) colonial pretension might have served to accelerate U.S. neocolonial penetration of the Third World[90]—it set things in motion. As Korman has pointed out, the "proclamation of Wilsonian [and leninist] principles may not have served to *abolish* title by conquest, but public opinion was undoubtedly moving in that direction" by the mid-1920s.[91] And, tellingly, the rationalization by which both ends were played against the middle in this regard was couched in language essentially paraphrasing that employed by Chief Justice Marshall in 1831.[92]

## Outlawing Conquest

Because of its adamancy in rejecting propositions that there might be a source of authority on the planet superior to that vested in itself, "the overall objectives and dilemmas of U.S. foreign policy during the interwar period became how to advance the nation's perceived vital security interest in promoting international law . . . without participating in the League of Nations."[93] Thinking along the same line had led the United States to use the First International American Conference (1899) as a platform upon which to instigate a treaty requiring the compulsory arbitration of disputes rather than resort to armed conflict throughout the hemisphere, a position it was still building upon during the fifth such conference in 1923.[94] The treaty included a provision, originally proposed jointly by Argentina and Brazil, "that acts of conquest should thereafter be considered a violation of the public law of America."[95] In its final form, the treaty held that:

- the principle of conquest shall not . . . be recognized as admissible under American public law;

- all cessions [of territory] shall be void if made under threats of war or the presence of armed force;

- any nation from which such cessions shall be exacted may demand that the validity of the cessions . . . be submitted to arbitration;

- any renunciation of the right to arbitration made under threats of war or presence of armed force . . . be null and void. [96]

This was followed, in 1928, by negotiation and ratification of the U.S./French sponsored Kellogg-Briand Pact—otherwise known as the General Treaty for the Renunciation of War, or the Pact of Paris—Article I of which stated that the "High Contracting Parties solemnly declare in the names of their respective peoples that they condemn recourse to war for resolution of international controversies, and renounce it as an instrument of national policy in their relations with one another."[97] That this provision of the Pact served for all intents and purposes to outlaw conquest remains a matter of juridical consensus, the first practical evidence coming four years later, when the U.S. announced a new foreign policy doctrine crafted by Secretary of State Henry Stimson.

The U.S. . . . sought to effectuate the Kellogg-Briand Pact proclaiming the illegality of conquest with reference to the Japanese invasion of Manchuria by means of promulgating the so-called Stimson Doctrine on January 7, 1932. Pursuant thereto, the U.S. government would not recognize as valid any legal effects flowing from a violation of the Kellogg-Briand Pact. The Stimson Doctrine was unanimously adopted [other than by Japan] by the Assembly of the League of Nations on March 11, 1932. According to this resolution, the Assembly declared it "incumbent upon the Members of the League of

Nations not to recognize any situation, treaty or agreement which may be brought about by means contrary to the Covenant of the League of Nations or the Pact of Paris.[98]

On August 3, 1932, the Stimson Doctrine was manifested once again in the Chaco Declaration, which stated in part that nineteen countries in the Americas would "not recognize any territorial arrangement . . . which has not been obtained by peaceful means nor the validity of territorial acquisitions which may be obtained through occupation or conquest by force of arms."[99] Then, on October 10, 1933, eleven European countries joined all twenty-one of their American counterparts in consolidating the principle through the Saavedra Lamas Pact.

> [B]etween the high contracting parties territorial questions must not be settled by violence, and . . . they will not recognize any territorial arrangement which is not obtained by pacific means, nor the validity of the occupation or acquisition of territories that may be brought about by force of arms.[100]

The Montevideo Convention on the Rights and Duties of States effected during the Seventh Pan-American Conference (1933) was still more forceful, declaring in its eleventh article that:

> The contracting States definitely establish as the rule of their conduct the precise obligation not to recognize territorial acquisitions or special advantages obtained by force. . . . The territory of a State is inviolable and may not be the object of military occupation nor other measures of force imposed by another State directly or indirectly or for any motive whatever even temporarily.[101]

At the 1936 Inter-American Conference for the Promotion of Peace, the law was refined still further, a declaration being issued that entered a flat "proscription of territorial conquest."[102] The Eighth Pan-American Conference (1938) then adopted a Declaration on Non-Recognition of the Acquisition of Territory by Force, noting that "the geographical, historical and political conditions of the American nations preclude . . . all territorial acquisitions by force."[103] In sum, the Declaration reiterated that:

> [A]s a matter of the fundamental Public Law of America . . . the occupation or acquisition of territory or any modification of territorial or boundary arrangement obtained through conquest by force or non-pacific means shall not be valid or have legal effect.[104]

While the United States had plainly been at the cutting edge in establishing clear legal prohibitions against contemporary conquests during the 1920s and '30s—the legacy of conquests past being another matter altogether[105]—its own refusal to subordinate itself to either the jurisdiction of the World Court or the diplomatic régime of the League of Nations undermined such gains. Although the League imposed economic sanctions on Italy as a result of its conquest of Abyssinia (Ethiopia) in 1936, they failed, largely as a result of U.S. nonparticipation (America refused recognition of Italian title in Africa, but continued trading merrily away).[106] Absent the surety of American participation in whatever military response they might offer, League members were also forced to acquiesce in the German seizures of Austria and Czechoslovakia in 1938 and 1939 (although it is generally agreed that a credible threat of intervention might still have deterred nazi aggression at that point).[107] The U.S. did come around to imposing an embargo upon Japan in 1941, but by then it was far too late.[108]

Under such circumstances, enforcement of the laws the United States had stood at the forefront in promulgating ultimately required the waging of what has been described as "a war of sanction" designed to "extirpate the source of aggression and impose measures intended to prevent further breaches of the peace by . . . aggressor states" bent upon conquest.[109] In this second world war, as it had in the first, the U.S. entered belatedly, compelling the countries with which it was allied—especially the Soviet Union[110]—to bear the entire initial brunt of the fighting for two full years, and to carry a disproportionate share of the weight for the remaining three.[111] One result was that the war ended with America in an unparalleled, and in many ways unprecedented, position of global ascendancy, both militarily and economically.[112]

It was on the basis of this postwar hegemony that the U.S. reversed its position with respect to organizations like the League of Nations, itself taking the initiative in 1945 to establish the League's successor, the United Nations (which, to all appearances, it expected from the outset to wield as an instrument in working its will upon the rest of the world).[113] Article 2(3) of the UN Charter was written as a restatement of the Kellogg-Briand Pact's guiding premise that only "pacific means" are legitimate in the resolution of international disputes, while Article 2(4) specifically obliges all member-states to "refrain in their international relations from the threat or use of force against the territorial integrity or political independence of any state."[114] Jurisdiction of a newly created International Court of Justice, successor to the by-then defunct World Court, was also made compulsory for all UN member-states.[115]

Similar statements of principle were incorporated into Articles 3 and 18-21 of the Charter of the Organization of American States—the U.S.-sponsored outgrowth of the Inter-American Conferences mentioned above—when it was effected on April 30, 1948.[116] Indeed, Article 20 of the OAS Charter follows the Montevideo Convention in proclaiming that the "territory of a State is inviolable" while Article 3(e) announces unequivocally that military "victory does not give rights" of territorial acquisition. The OAS Charter thereby surpasses in clarity the corresponding language in its UN counterpart.[117]

Meanwhile, punctuating its purported point concerning the place of conquest under the rule of law, the U.S. also took the lead in assembling an international tribunal to prosecute surviving leaders of the vanquished Axis Powers for, most saliently, the illegality of the policies bound up in their territorial aggressions.[118] While Japanese and, to a much lesser extent, Italians were taken to trial and convicted of such charges,[119] by far the most precedential proceeding was conducted in 1945-46 with respect to twenty-two members of the nazi hierarchy in Nuremberg, Germany.[120] There, the provisions of the Kellogg-Briand Pact were declared to constitute customary international law (*jus cogens*), binding upon all the governments of all countries, whether or not they were signatories to it (in this sense, the Stimson Doctrine was also declared to embody customary law).[121] Those found guilty of violations were sentenced to execution or imprisonment.[122]

An Affirmation of the Principles of International Law Recognized by the Charter of the Nuremberg Tribunal was unanimously adopted by the United Nations General Assembly on December 11, 1946,[123] in the most resounding imaginable repudiation of the tradition of legal compromise and expediency represented by Grotius and Vattel. Conversely, to say that the line of reasoning embodied by Vitoria, Pufendorf and Rousseau was validated at that point is to seriously understate the case. This was underscored yet again in the General Assembly's 1970 Declaration on Principles of International Law.[124] And, since matters of customary law were plainly brought to the fore at Nuremberg, it is fair to argue that the thinking of Pufendorf, not Grotius, must be taken as the lens through which the validity of claims to conquest rights are assessed at points as far removed in time as the early sixteenth century.[125]

## On the Matter of Decolonialization

At some levels, the U.S. posture with regard to the UN amounted to little other than a rather retarded actualization of Woodrow Wilson's design to use the League of Nations and international law to undermine the extant structure of European imperialism, thus paving the way for America's preferred and more sophisticated mode of neocolonial domination in the Third World. Hence, Chapter XI of the United Nations Charter sets forth the requirement that member-states presiding over "territories whose peoples have not yet attained a full measure of self-government"—otherwise referred to as "non-self-governing territories"—ensure their "progressive development towards self-government or independence [according to] the freely expressed wishes of the peoples concerned.[126] Chapters XII and XIII establish the mechanism(s) by which this is to be accomplished.[127]

In 1960, these provisions were further clarified and strongly reinforced by the UN's Declaration of the Granting of Independence to Colonial Countries which asserted as a matter of law that "all peoples have an inalienable right to freedom, the exercise of their sovereignty and the integrity of their national territory" and that "an end must [therefore] be put to colonialism . . . in all its manifestations."[128]

1. The subjection of peoples to alien subjugation, domination and exploitation constitutes a denial of fundamental human rights, is contrary to the Charter of the United Nations and is an impediment to the promotion of world peace and cooperation.

2. All peoples have the right to self-determination; by virtue of that right they freely determine their political status and freely pursue their economic, social and cultural development.

3. Inadequacy of political, economic, social or educational preparedness should never serve as a pretext for delaying independence.

4. All armed action or repressive measures of all kinds directed against dependent peoples shall cease in order to enable them to exercise peacefully and freely their right to complete independence, and the integrity of their national territory shall be respected.

5. Immediate steps shall be taken, in Trust and Non-Self-Governing Territories or all other territories that have not yet gained independence, to transfer all powers to the peoples of those territories, without any conditions or reservations, in accordance with their freely expressed will and desire, without any distinction as to race, creed, or colour, in order to enable them to enjoy complete independence and freedom.[129]

The primary target of the U.S. initiative was originally the British Empire, by far the world's most expansive,[130] although the colonies of France, Belgium, the Netherlands, Portugal and what remained of Spain's were also at issue.[131] America was always playing a double-game in this regard, however. Even as it was making the exemplary gesture of relinquishing its own hold upon the Philippines in 1946,[132] for example, it was asserting what amounted to conquest rights over the Marshalls, Carolines, Marianas and other Pacific island groups previously mandated to Japan.[133] Although these archipelagos were subsequently referred to as "protectorates" rather than as mandates—much less colonies—the fact that the U.S. conducted most of its early postwar nuclear testing in the Marshalls should give some indication as to how much emphasis was placed on the expressed wishes of the islanders (and how much "protection" they actually received, for that matter).[134]

The problems attending U.S. possession of two other non–self-governing territories, Alaska and Hawai'i, were "resolved" during the late 1950s; in both instances, settler majorities were enfranchised and thus empowered to determine for colonized native populations that their territories should become integral components of the United States itself.[135] Variations on the procedure, albeit concerning statuses well short of statehood, were employed in Puerto Rico, Guam and elsewhere.[136] That the United States was fully aware such maneuvers violated black letter law was evident in its refusal to acknowledge the legitimacy of French resorts to almost identical subterfuges in Algeria and New Caledonia (Kanaky) during the same period.[137]

Other contradictory outcomes accrued from growing U.S. geopolitical concerns that Lenin had been right: alignment with the "Soviet Bloc"—a descriptor encompassing China as well as the USSR, for nearly two decades after the maoist revolution of 1949—was in many cases proving more attractive to Third World peoples than new forms of subordination to the "Free World."[138] The result was a thoroughly situational and legally erratic foreign policy in which the U.S. pushed vigorously for decolonization in some instances (where it was confident a strongly anticommunist régime could be installed), and opposed it just as vigorously in others (where it appeared "communism" would ensue).[139] Probably the most striking illustration of the latter was in Vietnam, where the U.S. provided substantial military aid to the French in their effort to sustain colonial dominion over a people who had fought alongside Americans against the Japanese during World War II.[140] When the French nonetheless failed, the U.S. of course assumed the full burden the "ten thousand day war" to prevent the Vietnamese from exercising their right to determine for themselves whether or not they wished to "go communist."[141]

A still deeper problem, perhaps, can be located in the fact that any generalized policy of decolonization implied a repeal of purported conquest rights dating back to the early 1800s, and in some cases earlier still. The French conquest of Algeria, for instance, had occurred in 1830.[142] That of India by Britain not later than 1817.[143] That of Timor by Portugal in 1646.[144] That of Java by the Dutch in 1609.[145] In challenging the legitimacy of such "ancient" titles, it ran a discernable risk of having the validity of its own claims to territorial integrity drawn into question — by the Soviets, for example — a matter that remained true despite transparencies like the Indian Claims Commission by which it pretended to have separated itself from the pack.[146] The situation often required a certain circumspection, even in cases where broader U.S. interests and the law were otherwise clear.

It was Belgians who eventually brought the issue to a head, in the process of relinquishing the Congo, when they quite accurately pointed out that the boundaries of the "country" they were decolonizing had been created, not by the colonized Africans therein, but wholly by Belgium, acting in concert with other colonizing powers of Europe.[147] Within what was called the Congo, they observed, were numerous African peoples who had been first subjugated, then arbitrarily lumped together in a single "territorial compartment" for purposes of efficiency in colonial administration. Were the principle of equal rights to self-determination for all peoples enunciated in the UN Charter to be genuinely adhered to, it would have to be acknowledged that each people within the Congo was as entitled to independence from any "postcolonial" Congolese government as that government was from Belgium. In other words, it was likely that true decolonization would entail outright dissolution of the Congo as a geographical-political entity, with several smaller countries (re)emerging in its stead.[148]

Insofar as its implications extended far beyond the question of postcolonial order in the Congo itself, the "Belgian Thesis" sent shock waves through the Third World anti-imperialist movement everywhere. The boundaries of every country in Africa had been established by the colonizers during the Berlin Conference of 1884-85.[149] In Nigeria alone, the territories of some two hundred indigenous peoples had been consolidated by the British into a single administrative bloc.[150] In Ghana, another hundred.[151] Even in Madagascar, there are twenty.[152] To accord each of these peoples the right to self-determination would have served to preclude postcolonial nation-state development of the sort deemed "civilizing" and "progressive" by those of the marxian persuasion no less than their capitalist opponents.[153] Nor were things much different outside Africa. There are twenty different peoples within the area British colonizers called Malaya (now Malaysia), 380 in India, 670 in Indonesia.[154] In Iberoamerica, the numbers range from thirty-five in Ecuador to 210 in Brazil.[155]

One response from the Third World anti-imperialists was Kwame Nkrumah's articulation of a "Pan-Africanist vision" which designated "tribalism" as the "greatest danger confronting the whole of Africa."[156] A second was an initiative undertaken by the Organization of African Unity and supported by Third World anti-imperialists more generally to legally restrict application of the term "colony" to countries or peoples separated from their colonizers by at least thirty miles of open ocean.[157] Instructively, the United States, Great Britain and several other powers which were traditionally seen as being pitted against the Third Worlders suddenly proved quite cooperative, adopting the OAU's "Blue Water Thesis"—alternately known as the "Salt Water Thesis"—without argument or modification. It was thereby rendered definitive for purposes of interpreting the decolonization requirements embodied in both the UN Charter and the 1960 Declaration.[158]

The definition is absurd, of course, requiring as it does that the nazi occupation policies in eastern Europe, to offer but one recent and notorious illustration, be legally construed as something other than colonizing in nature. It obviously served the purposes of newly independent Third World states, however, as well as those of their First and Second World counterparts. The interest of the First World in accepting it will be found among the hundreds of indigenous peoples encapsulated within the megastates of North America, the roughly 250 in Australia, and so on.[159] With respect to the Second World, one need only look to the more than a hundred "national minorities" recognized as such by the former Soviet Union or the 150-odd non-Han peoples still forcibly incorporated into the territorial corpus claimed by China to get the idea.[160] There are some 5,000 indigenous peoples in the world today, and only 199 states.[161]

## The Fourth World

This reality bespeaks the existence of a Fourth World, an indigenous or "host" world, atop which each of the other three—capitalist, socialist and "developing"—sit.[162] It follows that the others each owe their existence to the appropriation of the Fourth World landbase, to expropriation of natural resources rightly belonging to those indigenous to that landbase, and to other usurpations of our rights, both collective and individual.[163] The relationship, all disclaimers about open blue salt water to the contrary notwithstanding, remains explicitly colonial. This is the nature of the modern—we will *not* arrive at anything approximating "postmodern" until an actual rather than merely symbolic or rhetorical postcolonial condition has been achieved—world order.[164] That such facts have gone for the most part unacknowledged—*dis*acknowledged might be a better term—has precipitated a variety of rather dire consequences.

Much of the ongoing warfare in "postcolonial" Africa—the bloody struggle of Katanga against the Congo (*cum* Zaire) during the mid-'60s, for example,[165] or that of the Biafran Ibos against Nigeria a few years later[166]—resulted from the attempts of one or more indigenous peoples to secede from the states to which they'd been consigned without consent, and within which they were subordinated. The sustained struggle for independence waged by the Nagas in India fits much the same mold,[167] as do those of the Karens in Myanmar (Burma),[168] the so-called Montagnards of upland Vietnam,[169] the Kurds in Iraq and Turkey,[170] the Hmongs in Laos,[171] the Miskito, Sumu and Rama in Nicaragua,[172] the Berbers of the western Sahara,[173] the Chechens of the former USSR,[174] the Mayas of Chiapas,[175] and a host of others. Much the same can be said about the Indonesian slaughter of Timorese,[176] that of the Mayas by Guatemala,[177] the Achés by Paraguay,[178] and, most recently, of the Tutsis by Hutus in Rwanda.[179] The lists could be extended to great length.[180]

Of the 122 armed conflicts recorded by cultural geographer Bernard Nietschmann as occurring on the planet in 1993, only one was between states, while 97 involved efforts by indigenous peoples to free themselves from domination by states and military operations aimed at (re)subjugating them.[181] Some 20 million native people had been turned into refugees by statist encroachments upon their dwindling homelands since 1945, another 73.5 million killed during the wars and outright extermination campaigns by the time of Nietschmann's study.[182] The death toll would be far higher if those attributable to the degraded living standards imposed as a matter of course under any colonial system were factored in; worldwide, indigenous peoples comprise far and away the most impoverished of all "population groups," experiencing correspondingly truncated lifespans.[183] A more eloquent confirmation of Sartre's "controversial" equation of colonialism to genocide is difficult to conceive.[184]

Given the magnitude of this mostly silent holocaust, Fourth Worlders have no practical alternative but to resist by all available means. As the

Peruvian Qechua Hugo Blanco framed it nearly thirty years ago, the choice is one of "land or death."[185] The result is a quietly ongoing form of planetary combat that Nietschmann aptly described as a "Third World War,"[186] a situation entirely contrary to the United Nations' self-proclaimed mandate, announced in the Statute of its International Law Commission, to employ "the progressive development of international law" as a means to "save succeeding generations from the scourge of war" by reaffirming "fundamental human rights, the dignity and worth of the human person, in the equal rights of men and women and of nations large and small."[187] Self-evidently, the UN's adoption of and continuing adherence to the Blue Water Thesis leads in precisely the opposite direction.

There are other effects as well. The preoccupation with (dis)economies of scale inherent to protecting the "integrity" of large states,[188] irrespective of how they were consolidated (conquest) and are now maintained (internal colonization of the conquered), reflects the essential psychointellectual ingredient fueling the present drive to achieve a whole new level of corporate "globalization" (i.e., domination).[189] The kind of hegemony that stands to emanate from the fulfillment of these "neoliberal" ambitions would have the effect of placing even the now relatively privileged citizens of First World states in the position of colonial subjects, a fact to which the Canadians, to take but one example, are already beginning to attest.[190] Those of the U.S. and western Europe are sure to follow,[191] while, for inhabitants of the "decolonized" Third World states restoration of de facto colonization has long since been accomplished (if, indeed, it ever ended).[192]

In that questions of scale figure so centrally in this gloomy prognosis, it can be said with assurance that the reverse holds true as well. Dismantlement of the statist structures which are foundational to projections of both military and corporate power is key to thwarting the fate now in store for the great bulk of the world's population.[193] This, in turn, requires a categorical rejection of contentions that states possess any sort of "inherent" right to territorial cohesion. Their claims to title and consequent jurisdiction over their purported interior geographies are no less logically accountable to standards of legality than are their assertions of sovereignty over external holdings.[194] The conquest and colonization or "absorption" of contiguous nations is, as the Nuremberg precedent clearly established, no more justified or legitimate than crossing a body of water to do so.[195] Arguments to the contrary are, as they've always been, duplicitous or delusional, merging effortlessly with the long and tortuous stream of self-serving prevarications by which interested parties have promoted ambiguity, inconsistency and hierarchy in the praxis of juridical legitimation.[196]

(Re)articulating the existing body of international law concerning conquest and colonialism in terms that are at last completely consistent with themselves—that is, through unequivocal recognition that native peoples hold the same self-determining rights as any others—thus serves not only the interests of Fourth Worlders, but of nearly everyone else as well.[197] The extent to which indigenous nations are able to reassert direct control over our lands and lives—and receive generalized popular support in doing so—is *exactly* the extent to which the present statist structure of domination can be rendered incapable of sustaining itself, either physically or conceptually. Where monolithic state sovereignties now prevail, a multiplicity of interactively independent Fourth World sovereignties would result.[198] This transformation of relations to "human scale" is a scenario utterly antithetical to the requirements of globalization.[199]

Such considerations, important everywhere, are especially acute with respect to territorial monstrosities like the United States, Canada, Russia, China, Australia, Mexico and Brazil. Of these, the U.S. is head and shoulders above the rest in terms of its significance to the globalizing dynamic.[200] Its UN and OAS delegations have also been the most insistent of any country's in advancing a legal formulation that would permanently constrain the rights of indigenous peoples to those of "internal self-determination" (i.e., "legitimating" of our internally colonized status; see Appendix D).[201] On both counts, the U.S. should be the focal point of Fourth World liberation efforts. Were such initiatives successfully pursued, "the world's only remaining superpower," to borrow a phrase from its own hyperinflated rhetoric of official self-congratulation, could be shorn of Guam, Hawai'i, at least a third of its continental landbase, all of its uranium deposits, at least half of its readily accessible low-sulfur coal, the bulk of its oil and natural gas, and much else.[202] That this would serve to radically and favorably alter global power relations—not only between states, but between people and states—should go without saying. It is all the more true, however, in that the same devolutionary process would be occurring on a planetary basis.

Were the U.S. to refuse literal implementation of a legal instrument requiring decolonization of Fourth World nations within its "domestic" sphere, which is more than likely at the outset, its very refusal would serve to *de*legitimate it even among significant sectors of its own constituents.[203] A very important element of the mythic narrative by which U.S. élites have manufactured the requisite degree of popular consent to their posture and attendant policies has, after all, been that they represent "a nation of laws, not men."[204] Their rejection of the law in so glaring a fashion can thus serve only to precipitate a substantial erosion of the internal consensus necessary to them to function with their customary order and efficiency "at home" while exacerbating their already problematic circumstances abroad.[205] This, too, points to a fundamental reconfiguration of power relations both within and without the U.S. Either way, the liberatory potential embodied in legally proclaiming and asserting the self-determining rights of the Fourth World is extraordinary.[206]

### Seceding Into Native North America

Things have thus come full circle, back to Leonard Garment's bland assertion that the right of conquest is applicable to settler state ownership of indigenous national territories in North America. In rebuttal—and rebut it we must, if we are either to alleviate the suffering or avail ourselves of the opportunities sketched in the preceding section—it should be noted that the common sense query posed in the opening section of this essay has a firm grounding in law. Even in the days when Grotius and Vattel were deemed credible authorities on such questions—from the 1648 Treaty of Westpahalia until the beginning of World War I—it was clearly understood that conquest rights pertain only in instances where territory has been seized by direct military action.[207] As the World Court put it in 1933:

> Conquest [has] only operated as a cause of loss of sovereignty when there is a war between two States and by reason of the defeat of one of them sovereignty over territory passes from the loser to the victor.[208]

Hence, there has *never* been an arguable *legal* basis, under *any* doctrine, for claims that the U.S. holds "title by conquest" to the territories of native peoples against whom it never waged a war. In Canada, where "Indian Wars," as such, were never fought at all, the notion of conquest rights holds not even the most passing relevance.[209]

Where wars against indigenous nations *were* fought by the United States, the preconditions for contentions that the resulting conquest title possessed legal validity were always—or at least since the days of Emmerich de

Vattel—not only that the wars themselves be demonstrably "Just," but that the Laws of War be otherwise observed by the victor during the course of the conflict.[210] As the most cursory review of U.S. warfare against Indians will reveal—and as will be brought out in detail in the next chapter—neither of these requirements was ever met by the U.S. in even the remotest sense.[211] Correspondingly, the official pretense voiced by Garment, that Euroamerican rights of conquest over Native North America "are recognized in international law," exhibits not a scintilla of truth or accuracy. No such right is now recognized, nor was it ever.

What has all along been recognized in law are the voluntary cessions of land made by native peoples to the settler states by treaty and agreement. There are significant stipulations here, too, however. To be binding on indigenous nations, it is incumbent upon the U.S. and Canadian settler states, wherever they are relying upon a given treaty as the basis of their sovereignty in a particular area, to show that native consent to its terms and provisions was neither fraudulent nor coercively obtained.[212] As to the terms and provisions themselves, virtually all of which are reciprocal, with native people exchanging territory for specified goods, services and other commitments, often in perpetuity, it is equally incumbent upon the states to demonstrate that they have lived up to both the letter and the spirit of the bargains made.[213] In the event either that a treaty is revealed to have been fraudulent or coerced, or that the state party has failed to meet its obligations as delineated therein, both it and whatever title stems from it must be considered nullified by the offending state.[214]

This is not only a matter of the customary interpretation set forth in the Vienna Convention on the Law of Treaties.[215] The fact that the responsibilities incurred by the North American settler states in exchange for land were often perpetual raises serious questions as to whether the territorial transfers involved in the treaties can even be properly viewed as cessions or "sales." Insofar as the states committed themselves to doing certain things for so long as they continue to use and occupy the property in question—to pay "rent," in other words—the treaty instruments more nearly resemble longterm or open-ended leases than actual transfers of title. To the extent that this is so, the U.S. and Canada would be in the position, not of ownership, but of enjoying certain use rights in vast swaths of their purported territoriality, while indigenous nations continue to hold underlying legal title.[216]

Each of the more than 400 hundred treaties with Fourth World peoples ratified by the Senate between 1778 and 1871—each of which imparted formal recognition by the U.S. under its own constitution as well as custom-ary law that these peoples comprised fully sovereign nations in their own right[217]—will have to been scrutinized in this light.[218] Only where both the treaties and U.S. compliance with them meet international legal standards can it be said that they convey rights to the United States in terms either of land ownership or of rental prerogatives. Where they do not, the native peo-ple coerced or defrauded into "ceding" our homelands have every legal enti-tlement to recover our property and to secede from a jurisdiction which was never legitimately extended over us in the first place.[219] The situation in Canada is no different on its face.[220]

There is no real legal basis for either settler state to prevent such processes from taking place. Their most time-honored defense, that a "fun-damental change of circumstances" warrants their noncompliance with treaty obligations to indigenous nations, entitling them to unilaterally abrogate inconvenient articles or clauses while insisting the treaties nonetheless remain in force and native peoples are bound by them, is flatly disallowed by the Vienna Convention.[221] Nor is it consistent with the Vienna Convention to argue, as have both the U.S. and Canada, that treaty obligations are in any way subordinate to or alterable by their domestic legislation. As this is framed in the Convention's 27th Article, "A party may not invoke the provisions of its internal law as justification for its failure to perform a treaty" obligation.[222] As seems clear enough in Article 46, this principle applies as much at the constitutional as the statutory level.[223]

All that is left, then, is the Vattelian question of how the law will be enforced. Here, the thinking of Supreme Court Justice Robert H. Jackson, during his stint as lead U.S. prosecutor at Nuremberg, is surely germane. To the extent that the citizenry of any country supports—or acquiesces in—the criminal comportment of its leaders, Jackson reasoned, is precisely the extent to which they are implicated in the crimes.[224] Conversely, not only the right but the obligation inheres in each citizen to do whatever is required to ensure that the policies of his/her government conforms to the rule of law. Thus were ordinary Germans indicted for what the nazis had done,[225] the "traitors" and "conspirators" who sought to assassinate Hitler glorified.[226] On that precedential formulation, it can be stated without hesitancy or equivocation that there are no valid legal limits constraining the actions of citizens in enforcing the law.[227] As Malcolm X once put it, "any means nec-essary" are appropriate.[228]

The conceptual tools needed for the task are thus in our hands, and have been for the past half-century and more. The only question before us is whether enough of us will be willing to shoulder the responsibility of using them, or whether we will, like the "Good Germans" before us, merely add the chorus of our own mendacity to that of Leonard Garment and the order he represents. Either we make the fate of First Nations our collective first priority, seceding and thereby "succeeding" into the Fourth World of Native North America,[229] or, irrespective of how the alternative is packaged or "spun," we simply pass along the endless night of conquest, colonization and genocide to coming generations. The choice is ours to make.

# Notes

1. For more on Harris, see Gretchen M. Bataille and Laurie Lisa, eds., *Native American Women: A Biographical Dictionary* (New York: Routledge, [2nd ed.] 2001).

2. Paul Chaat Smith and Robert Allen Warrior, *Like a Hurricane: The American Indian Movement from Alcatraz to Wounded Knee* (New York: Free Press, 1996) pp. 164-5.

3. Ibid., p. 174. Also see generally, Vine Deloria, Jr., *Behind the Trail of Broken Treaties: An Indian Declaration of Independence* (Austin: University of Texas Press, [2nd ed.] 1984).

4. This includes not only the continental U.S. and Alaska, but, of course, the Hawaiian Archipelago; Haunani-Kay Trask, *From a Native Daughter: Colonialism and Sovereignty in Hawai'i* (Honolulu: University of Hawai'i Press, [2nd ed.] 1999). The imperial reach also extends beyond the boundaries, as in Guam and "American" Samoa; Robert F. Rogers, *Destiny's Landfall: A History of Guam* (Honolulu: University of Hawai'i Press, 1995) esp. pp. 265-90. As well, it extends over certain nonindigenous peoples, like those of Puerto Rico and the "U.S." Virgin Islands; Ronald Fernandez, *Prisoners of Colonialism: The Struggle for Justice in Puerto Rico* (Monroe, ME: Common Courage Press, 1994).

5. See, e.g., Albert Memmi, *The Colonizer and the Colonized* (Boston: Beacon Press, [2nd ed.] 1991); Jean-Paul Sartre, "Colonialism is a System," in his *Colonialism and Neocolonialism* (New York: Routledge, 2001) pp. 30-47.

6. Chapter XI, Article 73, Charter of the United Nations, (59 Stat. 1031, T.S. No. 993, 3 Bevans 1153, 1976 Y.B.U.N. 1043 (June 26, 1945)). For text, see Burns H. Weston, Richard A. Falk and Anthony D'Amato, eds., *Basic Documents in International Law and World Order* (St, Paul, MN: West, 1990) p. 27.

7. Christopher Hitchens, "The Case Against Henry Kissinger, Parts 1&2," *Harper's*, Feb.-Mar. 2001.

8. For a telling selection of Albrightianisms, see Phyllis Bennis, *Calling the Shots: How Washington Dominates Today's UN* (Brooklyn, NY: Olive Branch Press, 2000) esp. pp. 97-8, 104, 138, 164, 225-8, 256, 295-9.

9. Aside from the United Nations Charter (note 6), the principle is affirmed in a number of international covenants, and quite forcefully reaffirmed in the UN's 1960 Declaration on the Granting of Independence to Colonial Countries and Peoples (U.N.G.A. Res. 1514 (XV), 15 U.N. GAOR, Supp. (No. 16) 66, U.N. Doc. A/4684 (1961)). For text, see Weston, Falk and D'Amato, *Basic Documents*, pp. 343-4. For explication, see A. Rigo Sureda, *The Evolution of the Right to Self-Determination: A Study of United Nations Practice* (Leiden, Netherlands: A.W. Sijhoff, 1973); ) Michla Pomerance, *Self-Determination in Law and Practice* (The Hague: Marinus Nijhoff, 1982); Hurst Hannum, *Autonomy, Sovereignty and Self-Determination* (Philadelphia: University of Pennsylvania Press, 1990).

10. P.L. 93-638; 88 Stat. 2203, codified at 25 U.S.C. 450a and elsewhere in titles 25, 42 and 50, U.S.C.A. For further breakdowns, see Michael P. Gross, "Indian Self-Determination and Tribal Sovereignty: An Analysis of Recent Federal Indian Policy," *Texas Law Review*, No. 56, 1978; Rebecca L. Robbins, "American Indian Self-Determination: Comparative Analysis and Rhetorical Criticism," *New Studies on the Left*, Vol. XIII, Nos. 3-4, 1988.

11. Graham D. Taylor, *The New Deal and American Indian Tribalism: The Administration of the Indian Reorganization Act, 1934-45* (Lincoln: University of Nebraska Press, 1980); Kenneth R. Philp, ed., *Indian Self-Rule: First-Hand Accounts of Indian-White Relations from Roosevelt to Reagan* (Salt Lake City: Howe Bros., 1986).

12. At issue here is a deformed interpretation of a principle enunciated in the UN Charter, Chapter I, Article 2(4), guaranteeing the territorial integrity of all member-states against dissolution by armed force; Weston, Falk and D'Amato, *Basic Documents*, p. 17. While the provision was actually designed to preclude conquest, it has been routinely inverted, quoted by historically aggressive powers like the U.S. in framing arguments that they are entitled to the territorial integrity ensuing from the legitimation of their past takings. See Djura Nincic, *The Problem of Sovereignty in the Charter and Practice of the United Nations* (The Hague: Marinus Nijhoff, 1979).

13. Rationalization of this travesty of juridical logic has long been a preoccupation of mainstream specialists in federal Indian law; see, e.g., Charles F. Wilkinson, *American Indians, Time, and Law: Native Societies in a Modern Constitutional Democracy* (New Haven, CT: Yale University Press, 1987). Unfortunately, a similar orientation seems lately to have emerged among native legal scholars; see, e.g.,

Vine Deloria, Jr., and David E. Wilkins, *Tribes, Treaties and Constitutional Tribulations* (Austin: University of Texas Press, 1999).

14. For the best overview of the U.S. role in this regard, see Bradley F. Smith, *The Road to Nuremberg* (New York: Basic Books, 1981) esp. Chaps. 2-3.

15. See, e.g., Vine Deloria, Jr., "The Size and Status of Nations," in Susan Lobo and Steve Talbot, eds., *Native American Voices: A Reader* (New York: Longman, 1998) pp. 457-65.

16. U.S. Bureau of the Census, *Report on Indians Taxed and Not Taxed in the United States (except Alaska) of the Eleventh U.S. Census: 1890* (Washington, D.C.: U.S. Government Printing Office, 1894) pp. 637-8.

17. Jean-Paul Sartre, "You Are Wonderful," in *Colonialism and Neocolonialism*, pp. 55-6.

18. Lassa Oppenheim, *International Law* (London: Longmans, Green, 1905-6) p. 288.

19. Emmerich de Vattel, *The Law of Nations* (Philadelphia: T. & J.W. Johnson, 1863 translation of 1758 original) Bk. III, Ch. 3, Sect. 38.

20. Yoram Dinstein, *War, Aggression and Self-Defense* (Cambridge, UK: Grotius, 1988) p. 73.

21. Ibid.

22. Hugo Grotius, *De Jure Belli ac Pacis* (Oxford, UK: Clarendon Press, 1925 translation of 1625 original) Bk. III, Ch. 19, Sect. 11.

23. Robert W. Tucker, *The Inequality of Nations* (London: Martin Robinson, 1977) p. 12.

24. Franciscus de Vitoria, *De Indis et de Jure Belli Relectiones* (Washington, D.C.: Carnegie Institution of Washington, 1917 translation of 1539 original) p. 128.

25. See "Perversions of Justice," in this volume, for a summary of Vitoria's criteria for Just War. For broader explication of the concepts involved, see Michael Walzer, *Just and Unjust Wars: A Moral Argument with Historical Illustrations* (New York: Basic Books, 1977).

26. Matthew M. MacMahon, *Conquest and Modern International Law: The Legal Limitations on the Acquisition of Territory by Conquest* (Washington, D.C.: Catholic University of America Press, 1940) p. 35.

27. See, e.g., Samuel Pufendorf, *Elementorum Jurisprudentiae Universalis* (Oxford, UK: Clarendon Press, 1931 translation of 1672 original).

28. Samuel Pufendorf, *De Jure Naturae et Gentium* (Oxford, UK: Clarendon Press, 1934 translation of 1688 original) Bk. III, Ch. 8, Sect. 1.

29. Ibid. Also see Samuel Pufendorf, *De Officio Hominis et Civis Juxta Legem Naturalum* (New York: Oxford University Press, 1927 translation of 1682 original).

30. For an unfriendly analysis of Pufendorf leading to essentially the same conclusion, see Sharon Korman, *The Right of Conquest: The Acquisition of Territory by Force in International Law and Practice* (New York: Oxford University Press, 1996) pp. 21-5.

31. Ibid. p. 94.

32. L.A. de Montluc, "Le Droit de conquête," *Revue de droit international et législation comparée*, No. 3, 1871; Pasquale Fiore, *Nouveau Droit international public* (Paris, 1880) Sects. 863, 1693, 1696; Pierre Pradier-Fodéré, *Traité de droit international public* (Paris, 1885-1906) Vol. 2, p. 833; Henry Bonfils, *Manuel de droit international public* (Paris, 1905) p. 535; Frantz C. R. Despagnet, *Cours de droit international public* (Paris, 1910) Sects. 387-90.

33. Quoted in Alfred Cobban, *The Nation State and National Self-Determination* (London: Collins, 1969) p. 32.

34. Vattel, *Law of Nations*, Bk. III, Ch. 13, Sec. 195.

35. Ibid., Ch. 12, Sect. 188.

36. Korman, *Right of Conquest*, p. 28.

37. Hedley Bull takes up this theme in his essay, "Society and Anarchy in International Relations," in Herbert Butterfield and Martin Wright, eds., *Diplomatic Investigations* (London: Allen and Unwin, 1966) pp. 35-50.

38. For background, see Derek McKay and H.M. Scott, *The Rise of the Great Powers, 1648-1813* (London: Longman, 1983); F.R. Bridge and Roger Bullen, *The Great Powers and the European States System, 1815-1914* (London: Longman, 1980).

39. Oppenheim, *International Law*, p. 292.

40. A prime example of such exceptions is Prussia's annexation of the French Alsace-Lorraine

region in 1871. Interestingly, the military seizure was broadly condemned, not only as a disturbance of the balance of power, but as "an open flouting of that public law upon which Europe was beginning to pride itself"; Michael Howard, *The Franco-Prussian War* (Oxford, UK: Oxford University Press, 1961) p. 449.

41. One eminent nineteenth-century American jurist went so far as to describe the Polish partitions by Russia, Austria and Prussia as "the most flagrant violation of natural justice and international law which has occurred in Europe since it emerged from barbarism"; Henry Wheaton, *History of the Law of Nations in Europe and America* (New York: Garland, 1973 reprint of the 1842 original) p. 269. For further background, see Norman Davies, *God's Playground: A History of Poland* (Oxford, UK: Clarendon Press, 1981).

42. Ciaran Brady, "The Decline of the Irish Kingdom," in Mark Greengrass, ed., *Conquest and Coalescence: The Shaping of the State in Early Modern Europe* (London: Edward Arnold, 1991) pp. 94–115; E. Garrison Walters, *The Other Europe: Eastern Europe to 1945* (New York: Dorset Press, 1988) pp. 24–31.

43. Michael Hecter, *Internal Colonialism: The Celtic Fringe in British National Politics, 1536-1966* (Berkeley: University of California Press, 1975); Peter Berresford Ellis, *The Celtic Revolution: A Study in Anti-Imperialism* (Talybont, Wales: Y Lolfa Press, 1985).

44. See generally, Joseba Zulaika, *Basque Violence: Metaphor and Sacrament* (Reno: University of Nevada Press, 1988) esp. pp. 1-102; Kenneth Medhurst, *The Basques and Catalans* (Minority Rights Group Rept. No 9., 1977).

45. The attitude is of course paralleled by that contemporaneously enunciated by U.S. Chief Justice of the Supreme Court Roger Taney at about the same time: "A black man holds no right a white man is bound to respect"; *Dred Scott v. Sandford* (60 U.S. (19 How.) 393 (1857)). For analysis, see Don Fehrenbacher, *The Dred Scott Case: Its Significance in American Law and Politics* (New York: Oxford University Press, 1978).

46. Mao surfaced the term during the 1955 Bandung Conference; Robert Young, *White Mythologies: Writing History and the West* (New York: Routledge, 1990) p. 11. For context, see Peter Worsely, *The Third World* (London: Weidenfeld & Nicholson, [2nd. ed.] 1967).

47. See Gayatari Chakravorty Spivak, "The Rani of Samir," in Francis Barker, et al., eds., *Europe and Its Others* (Colchester, UK: University of Essex, 1985) esp. p. 128.

48. Michael Howard, *The Lessons of History* (Oxford, UK: Clarendon Press, 1991) p. 42.

49. Discovery Doctrine dates back to a series of Bulls promulgated by Pope Innocent IV (Sinibaldo Fiesco) at the time of the Third Crusade. Innocent himself was heavily influenced by the treatise of Thomas Aquinas in *Summa Theologica Secunda Secundae*, written around 1250. The ideas were subsequently developed by Spanish jurists like Vitoria and Matías de Paz in a form endorsed by the Vatican during the mid-fifteenth century; Robert A. Williams, Jr., *The American Indian in Western Legal Thought: The Discourses of Conquest* (New York: Oxford University Press, 1990). Also see "Perversions of Justice," in this volume.

50. For a range of insights into the misconstructions of reality attending the rise of 19th century "scientific racism," see William Stanton, *The Leopard's Spots: Scientific Attitudes Towards Race in America, 1815-1859* (Chicago: University of Chicago Press, 1960); Stephen Jay Gould, *The Mismeasure of Man* (New York: W.W. Norton, 1981); Sven Lindquist, *The Skull Measurer's Mistake* (New York: New Press, 1997).

51. Numerous readings present themselves in this connection. Among the most useful are A.P. Thornton, *Doctrines of Imperialism* (New York: John Wiley, 1965); Gerrit W. Gong, *The Standard of "Civilization" in International Society* (Oxford, UK: Clarendon Press, 1984); Frederick Merk, *Manifest Destiny and Mission in American History: A Reinterpretation* (New York: Alfred A. Knopf, 1963); Reginald Horsman, *Race and Manifest Destiny: The Origins of American Racial Anglo-Saxonism* (Cambridge, MA: Harvard University Press, 1981).

52. The best overall study remains Mark Frank Lindley's *The Acquisition and Government of Backward Country in International Law: A Treatise on the Law and Practice Relating to Colonial Expansion* (London: Longman, Green, 1926).

53. Sartre, "Colonialism is a System," p. 50.

54. *Cherokee Nation v. Georgia* (30 U.S. (5 Pet.) 1 (1831)); *Worcester v. Georgia* (31 U.S. (6 Pet.) 551 (1832)). As to reference in foreign courts, see the 1867 Québec case *Connolly v. Woolrich* (11 LCJ 197) in

which a lengthy passage from *Worcester* is quoted verbatim. Use of the word "magisterial" to describe the *Cherokee* opinion will be found in *Attorney General of Ontario v. Bear Island Foundation* (49 OR 353 (HC), affirmed (1989) 68 OR 394 (CA). For a comprehensive overview of this phenomenon, see Bruce Clark, *Indian Land Title in Canada* (Toronto: Carswell, 1987); *Native Liberty, Crown Sovereignty: The Existing Aboriginal Right of Self-Government in Canada* (Montréal: McGill-Queens University Press, 1990).

55. *United States ex rel. Standing Bear v. Crook* (25 Fed. Cas. 695 (C.C.D. Neb., 1879)). *Standing Bear* is covered in Sidney L. Haring, *Crow Dog's Case: American Indian Sovereignty, Tribal Law, and United States Law in the Nineteenth Century* (Cambridge, UK: Cambridge University Press, 1994) pp. 192-7.

56. Indian Civil Rights Act of 1968 (P.L. 90-284, 82 Stat. 77, 25 U.S.C.A. §§ 1302-1303). For analysis, see Vine Deloria, Jr., and Clifford M. Lytle, *American Indians, American Justice* (Austin: University of Texas Press, 1983) esp. p. 129; David E. Wilkins, *American Indian Sovereignty and the Supreme Court: The Masking of Justice* (Austin: University of Texas Press, 1997) pp. 26, 201.

57. Excellent statistical breakdowns will be found in Russel Barsh, "Indian Land Claims Policy in the United States," *North Dakota Law Review*, No. 58, 1982; "Behind Land Claims: Rationalizing Dispossession in Anglo-American Law," *Law and Anthropology*, No. 1, 1986.

58. The contention that the U.S. holds indigenous assets in perpetual trust, deriving from its self-assigned "plenary power" over our affairs, was articulated most clearly and forcefully in *Lone Wolf v. Hitchcock* (187 U.S. 553 (1903)). For analysis, see Ann Laquer Estin, "*Lone Wolf v. Hitchcock*: The Long Shadow," in Sandra L. Cadwalader and Vine Deloria, Jr., eds., *The Aggressions of Civilization: Federal Indian Policy Since the 1880s* (Philadelphia: Temple University Press, 1984); Carter Blue Clark, *Lone Wolf v. Hitchcock: Treaty Rights and Indian Law at the End of the Nineteenth Century* (Lincoln: University of Nebraska Press, 1994).

59. Although such terminology as "conquest," "colonization" and "empire" is no longer fashionable among the great majority of "responsible" American historians when describing U.S. internal development, it must be recalled that this was by no means always the case. For a sample of the triumphalist fare available during the period under discussion, see Hugh Latimer Burleson, *The Conquest of the Continent* (New York: Domestic and Foreign Missionary Society, 1911). For a more balanced view offered at midcentury, see Bernard DeVoto, *The Course of Empire* (Lincoln: University of Nebraska Press, 1955). A more current apologia will be found in Patricia Nelson Limerick's *The Legacy of Conquest: The Unbroken Past of the American West* (New York: W.W. Norton, 1987).

60. Norman Rich, *Hitler's War Aims: Ideology, the Nazi State, and the Course of Expansion* (New York: W.W. Norton, 1973) p. 8; citing the 2-volume 1939 English language edition of *Mein Kampf* at pp. 403, 591. Also see *Hitler's Secret Book* (New York: Grove Press, 1961) pp. 106-8.

61. David Healy, *Drive to Hegemony: The United States in the Caribbean, 1898-1917* (Madison: University of Wisconsin Press, 1988).

62. On Guam, see Rogers, *Destiny's Landfall*, pp. 108-26. On the Philippines, see Stuart Creighton Miller, *"Benevolent Assimilation": The American Conquest of the Philippines, 1899-1903* (New Haven, CT: Yale University Press, 1982). Also see "By the Standards of Their Times," in this volume.

63. Hawai'i's constitutional monarchy had been overthrown by a group of American missionaries and settler-planters, supported by U.S. Marines, in 1893. Although the U.S. had ratified several treaties with the legitimate Hawaiian government, it quickly recognized the "Republic" proclaimed by the conspirators, annexing the entire archipelago five years later; Michael Dougherty, *To Steal a Kingdom: Probing Hawaiian History* (Waimanalo, HI: Island Style Press, 1992); William Adam Russ, Jr., *The Hawaiian Republic (1894-1898) and Its Struggle to Win Annexation* (Cranbury, NJ: Associated University Presses, 1992).

64. Walters, *Other Europe*, pp. 135-6; Michael B. Petrovich, *History of Serbia*, 2 vols. (New York: Harcourt, Brace, Jovanovich, 1972) Vol. 2, pp. 618-20.

65. On the "domino effect," see Barbara W. Tuchman, *The Guns of August* (New York: Macmillan, 1962); George F. Kennan, *The Fateful Alliance: France, Russia and the Coming of the First World War* (New York: Pantheon, 1984). On the resulting rearrangements to world order, see generally, David Stevenson, *The First World War and International Politics* (New York: Oxford University Press, 1988).

66. Although there are a number of more detailed books available on the Bolshevik Revolution, I still enjoy John Reed's *Ten Days That Shook the World* (New York: Boni and Liveright, 1919) as well as any.

67. This is figuratively but not literally true. One simply has to look back far enough in time to discover that the world did quite well before the "benefits" of eurodomination were bestowed upon it; Janet L. Abu-Lughod, *Before European Hegemony: The World System, A.D. 1250-1350* (New York: Oxford University Press, 1989).

68. An excellent summary of these maneuvers will be found in Walker Connor, *The National Question in Marxist-Leninist Theory and Strategy* (Princeton, NJ: Princeton University Press, 1984) pp. 45-66.

69. See, as examples, V.I. Lenin, *Imperialism: The Highest Stage of Capitalism* (Peking: Foreign Language Press, 1973 translation of 1917 original); Joseph Stalin, *Marxism and the National-Colonial Question* (San Francisco: Proletarian, 1975 translation of 1934 original); Institute of Marxism–Leninism, CC CPSU, *Leninism and the National Question* (Moscow: Progress, 1977).

70. Quoted in Arno J. Mayer, *Political Origins of the New Diplomacy, 1917-1918* (New Haven, CT: Yale University Press, 1959) p. 77.

71. Korman, *Right of Conquest*, p. 137.

72. See, e.g., the text of the speech delivered by British Prime Minister Lloyd George in his *War Memoirs* (London: Ivor Nicholson and Watson, 1933-6) Vol. 5, pp. 2515-27.

73. In calling upon Congress to declare war against Germany on April 2, 1917, Wilson had made America the first of the Allies to take this position, announcing that the U.S. sought "no conquest, no dominion; we seek no indemnity for ourselves"; quoted in George F. Kennan, *Russia and the West under Lenin and Stalin* (Boston: Little, Brown, 1961) p. 34. In a speech to the Senate on January 22, the president had already observed, in perfectly Pufendorfian fashion, that "no right exists anywhere to hand peoples about from sovereignty to sovereignty as if they were property"; Ray Stannard Baker and William E. Dodd, eds., *The Public Papers of Woodrow Wilson*, 2 vols. (New York: Harper, 1926) Vol. 2, pp. 407-14.

74. Korman, *Right of Conquest*, pp. 136-7. The 14 Points are analyzed in considerable depth in W.W.V. Temperley, ed., *A History of the Peace Conference of Paris* (London: Frowde, Hodder, and Stoughton, 1920-4).

75. "Any incorporation into a large or powerful state of a small or weak people without the precise, clear and voluntary expressed concurrence and desire of that people" shall be considered invalid (Nov. 11, 1917); text in George F. Kennan, *Soviet Foreign Policy, 1917-1941* (Westport, CT: Greenwood Press, 1960) pp. 116-9, quote at p. 117.

76. Feb. 11, 1918; for complete text, see Temperley *History of the Peace Conference*, pp. 437-9.

77. See generally, F.P. Walters, *A History of the League of Nations* (New York: Oxford University Press, 1960).

78. The League's Permanent Court of International Justice ("World Court") was a logical extension of the Permanent Court of Arbitration, established through the 1899 Hague Convention; Francis Anthony Boyle, *Foundations of World Order: The Legalist Approach to International Relations, 1898-1922* (Durham, NC: Duke University Press, 1999) pp. 28-48.

79. Ibid., pp. 53-4. Also see Quincy Wright, "The United States and the Permanent International Court of Justice," *American Journal of International Law*, Vol. 21, No. 1, 1927.

80. Boyle, *Foundations of World Order*, pp. 149-51.

81. Before becoming president, Wilson, a Johns Hopkins graduate, had been a history professor at Princeton, and was author of the influential *History of the American People* (New York: Harper, 1902) in which he'd extolled the virtues of the Ku Klux Klan. After taking up residency in the White House, he arranged for a private showing of D.W. Griffith's notorious cinematic glorification of the Klan, *Birth of a Nation*, afterwards lauding it as a fair and accurate portrayal of fact, that it was indeed the "writing [of] history in lightning"; Wyn Craig Wade, *The Fiery Cross: The Ku Klux Klan in America* (New York: Simon and Schuster, 1987) pp. 115, 125-7.

82. More broadly, while the fifth of Wilson's Fourteen Points did make reference to the interests of native inhabitants in colonial settings, it carefully overbalanced these with the "legitimate interests" of the colonizers; Temperley, *History of the Peace Conference*, p. 295.

83. Editors, *Deskaheh: Iroquois Statesman and Patriot* (Rooseveltown, NY: Akwesasne Notes, Six Nations Museum Series, n.d.).

84. Quoted in David Hunter Miller, *The Drafting of the Covenant* (New York: Putnam, 1928) p. 28.

85. Article 22 of the Covenant of the League of Nations contains much flowery language about

promoting "the wellbeing and development" of native peoples until they'd reached a point at which they could "stand by themselves in the strenuous conditions of the modern world"; Lindley, *Acquisition of Backward Territory*, pp. 247-8.

86. While stripped of their colonial possessions, both Germany and Turkey (Ottoman Empire) continued to exist. The Austrohungarian (Hapsburg) Empire, on the other hand, was dissolved into the independent countries of Austria, Hungary and Czechoslovakia, as well as a doubling of the size of Rumania. Along with Germany, it was also forced to relinquish the great bulk of the territory necessary to reconstitute Poland; see generally, Temperley, *History of the Peace Conference*; Michael L. Dockrill and J. Douglas Goold, *Peace without Promise: England and the Peace Conferences, 1919-23* (London: Bratsford, 1981).

87. Quincy Wright, *Mandates Under the League of Nations* (Chicago: University of Chicago Press, 1930).

88. Inis L. Claude, *Swords Into Plowshares: The Problems and Progress of International Organization* (London: University of London Press, 1964) p. 328.

89. Korman, *Right of Conquest*, p. 140.

90. In simplest terms, neocolonialism involves domination of one country's economy by another, without the latter asserting title, either de facto or de jure, to the territory of the former. In fact, for a neocolonial system to function, it is necessary that the crude territorial claims asserted under the classic, externalized mode of colonialism be relinquished; Jack Woodis, *Introduction to Neo-Colonialism* (New York: International, 1967); Kwame Nkrumah, *Neo-Colonialism: The Last Stage of Imperialism* (New York: International, 1965). Internal and settler-state modes of colonialism are related to but very different from the classic form, and are not incompatible with neocolonialism; Hugh Seton-Watson, *Nations and States: An Inquiry into the Origins of Nations and the Politics of Nationalism* (Boulder, CO: Westview Press, 1977); James M. Blaut, *The National Question: Decolonizing the Theory of Nationalism* (London: Zed Press, 1987); Bernard Nietschmann, "The Fourth World: Nations versus States," in George J. Demko and William B. Wood, *Reordering the World: Geopolitical Perspectives on the Twenty-First Century* (Boulder, CO: Westview Press, 1994) pp. 225-42.

91. Korman, *Right of Conquest*, p. 161.

92. In *Cherokee v. Georgia*, Marshall had pronounced Indians to be in "a state of pupilage" vis-à-vis the United States. Article 22 of the League Covenant held that "the advanced nations" of Europe should exercise "tutelage" over mandated colonial subjects; Korman, *Right of Conquest*, p. 152; Lindley, *Acquisition of Backward Territory*, pp. 247-8; Rudolf von Albertini, *Decolonization* (New York: Africana, 1982) p. 7.

93. Boyle, *Foundations of World Order*, p. 144.

94. See generally, J. Scott, ed., *The International Conferences of American States, 1889-1928* (Washington, D.C.: Carnegie Endowment for International Peace, 1933).

95. Boyle, *Foundations of World Order*, pp. 104-6.

96. Scott, *International Conferences of America States*, p. 1147-8. The signatories included Bolivia, Brazil, Ecuador, El Salvador, Guatemala, Haiti, Honduras, Nicaragua, Uruguay and Venezuela, in addition to the U.S.

97. Kellogg-Briand Pact, 46 Stat. 2343, 2345-46 (Pt. 2), Aug. 27, 1928. For text and analysis of this provision, see Ian Brownlie, *International Law and the Use of Force by States* (Oxford, UK: Clarendon Press, 1963) pp. 90-1.

98. Boyle, *Foundations of World Order*, p. 107. For contemporaneous analysis, see Charles Cheney Hyde, "Conquest Today," *American Journal of International Law*, No. 30, 1936.

99. U.S. Dept. of State Press Release (Aug. 6, 1932); quoted in Herbert W. Briggs, "Non-Recognition of Title by Conquest and Limitations on the Doctrine," *Pan-American Studies in International Law*, No. 34, 1940, p. 74.

100. Quoted in Korman, *Right of Conquest*, p. 240. The European countries were Bulgaria, Czechoslovakia, Finland, Greece, Italy, Norway, Portugal, Rumania, Spain, Turkey and Yugoslavia.

101. Quoted in ibid., p. 241.

102. Quoted in Robert Langer, *The Seizure of Territory: The Stimson Doctrine and Related Principles in Legal Theory and Diplomatic Practice* (Princeton, NJ: Princeton University Press, 1947) p. 78.

103. *American Journal of International Law* (Supp.), No. 23, 1940, p. 197.

104. Ibid.

105. Although moves to formally outlaw resorts to conquest in the hemisphere dated back to the First Inter-American Conference (1826), and a clause repudiating "the so-called right of conquest" appeared in the 1883 Caracas Protocol before the U.S. itself sponsored a proposal to abolish such rights during the Pan-American Conference of 1890, there is much evidence that the country's legal scholars were carefully attempting to separate its own history of territorial seizures from contemporary aggressions while formulating prohibitionist instruments during the first half of the twentieth century. In its 1925 "Draft on the Problem of Conquest," for example, the American Institute on International Law offered a declaration condemning as "unlawful [all] future territorial acquisitions obtained by means of war or under the menace of war or in the presence of armed force . . . without criticizing territorial acquisitions effected in the past"; Langer, *Seizure of Territory*, pp. 34–8.

106. Brownlie, *International Law and the Use of Force*, pp. 240-1; Denis Mack Smith, *Mussolini: A Biography* (New York: Alfred A. Knopf, 1982) pp. 174-5, 197-8. For contemporaneous analysis, see Alfred Zimmern, *The League of Nations and the Rule of Law, 1918-1935* (New York: Macmillan, 1936).

107. D.P. O'Connell, *International Law* (London: Stevens, [2nd ed.] 1970) p. 145. With Germany, U.S. corporations continued to do business even while American troops were fighting the German Army during World War II; Charles Higham, *Trading with the Enemy: The Nazi-American Money Plot, 1933-1949* (New York: Barnes & Noble, 1995 reprint of 1983 original). Concerning the tenuousness of the nazi annexation of Austria, see Ian Kershaw, *Hitler, 1936-1945: Nemesis* (New York: W.W. Norton, 2000) pp. 73-6. Had Hitler failed in Austria, of course, Czechoslovakia would have been a moot point.

108. David Bergamini, *Japan's Imperial Conspiracy*, 2 vols. (New York: Morrow, 1971) Vol. 2, pp. 1004-6.

109. Brownlie, *International Law and the Use of Force*, pp. 332-3, 443. Also see Walters, *History of the League of Nations*, p. 385.

110. One measure will be found in the fact that while the U.S. suffered fewer than a half-million fatalities in all theaters of fighting during World War II, Soviet deaths numbered approximately 27 million. Another is that of the 8 million German war dead, well over 5 million were lost fighting the USSR. See generally, James Lucas, *War on the Eastern Front, 1941-1945: The German Soldier in Russia* (London: Jane's, 1979); Alexander Werth, *Russia at War, 1941-1945* (New York: Carroll & Graf, [2nd ed.] 1984).

111. This truth peeks through even in popular illustrated histories designed to instill a sense of triumphalism in the American public. See, as examples, Lt. Col. Eddy Bauer, *The History of World War II* (New York: Garland, [rev. ed.] 1979); Editors, *WW II: Time-Life Books History of the Second World War* (New York: Prentice-Hall, 1989).

112. A good interpretation will be found in the introduction to Noam Chomsky's *Towards a New Cold War: Essays on the Current Crisis and How We Got There* (New York: Pantheon, 1982) pp. 1-59. For an opposing view, see John Lewis Gaddis, *The United States and the Origins of the Cold War, 1941-1947* (New York: Columbia University Press, 1972). Also see Thomas H. Etzold and John Lewis Gaddis, eds., *Containment: Documents on U.S. Foreign Policy and Strategy, 1945-1950* (New York: Columbia University Press, 1978).

113. See Bennis, *Calling the Shots*, pp. 2-8.

114. Weston, Falk and D'Amato, *Basic Documents*, pp. 16-32, cites at pp. 16-7.

115. Ibid., p. 30. For the specific statute by which the U.S. accepted ICJ jurisdiction—59 Stat. 1031, T.S. No. 993, 3 Bevans 1153, 1976 Y.N.U.N. (Oct. 24, 1945)—see pp.33-8.

116. On the OAS, see Boyle, *Foundations of World Order*, pp. 119-22.

117. 2 U.S.T. 2394, T.I.A.S. No. 2361, 119 U.N.T.S. 3 (Apr. 30, 1948), amended as 21 U.S.T. 607, T.I.A.S. No 6847 (Feb. 27, 1967); for text, see Weston, Falk and D'Amato, *Basic Documents*, pp. 50-61, cites at pp. 50-2.

118. On the primacy of the U.S. in this regard, see Bradley F. Smith, *The Road to Nuremberg* (New York: Basic Books, 1981).

119. Arnold C. Brackman, *The Other Nuremberg: The Untold Story of the Tokyo War Crimes Trials* (New York: Quill, 1987); Roy Palmer Domenico, *Italian Fascists on Trial, 1943-1948* (Chapel Hill, NC: University of North Carolina Press, 1991).

120. Perhaps the best overall study is Eugene Davidson's *The Trial of the Germans: Nuremberg, 1945-*

*1946* (New York: Macmillan, 1966). Davidson has also raised some of the more pointed queries with respect to whether the trial can really be considered precedential; *The Nuremberg Fallacy* (Columbia: University of Missouri Press, 1998 reprint of 1973 original). Also see "By the Standards of Their Times," in this volume.

121. Boyle, *Foundations of World Order*, p. 107.

122. Eleven men were hanged, two committed suicide prior to execution, and another was sentenced to death in absentia. Only three of the 22 were acquitted; Robert H. Jackson, *The Nürnberg Case* (New York: Alfred A. Knopf, 1947) pp. xii-xiii.

123. U.N.G.A. Res. 95(I), U.N. Doc. A/236 (1946), at 1144; for text, see Weston, Falk and D'Amato, *Basic Documents*, p. 140.

124. U.N.G.A. Res. 2625 (XXV), 25 U.N. GAOR, Supp. (No. 28) 121, U.N. Doc. A/8028 (1971), *reprinted in* 9 I.L.M. (1970). For text, see Weston, Falk and D'Amato, *Basic Documents*, p. 108.

125. This is actually standard practice in terms of international legal interpretation; see Adam Roberts and Richard Guelff, eds., *Documents on the Laws of War* (Oxford, UK: Clarendon Press, 1982) pp. 4-6.

126. Weston, Falk and D'Amato, *Basic Documents*, p. 27.

127. Ibid. pp. 27-30. Also see "Stolen Kingdom," in this volume.

128. U.N.G.A. Res. 1514 (XV), 15 U.N. GAOR, Supp. (No. 16) 66, U.N. Doc. A/4684 (1961); for text, see Weston, Falk and D'Amato, *Basic Documents*, pp. 343-4, quotes at p. 343.

129. Ibid., pp. 343-4.

130. For background, see William Roger Louis, *Imperialism at Bay, 1941-1945: The United States and the Decolonization of the British Empire* (Oxford, UK: Clarendon Press, 1977).

131. Most of these were already tottering. For a broad overview, see Franz Anspringer, *The Dissolution of Colonial Empires* (New York: Routledge, 1989).

132. Philippine "independence" was granted with considerable strings attached. Not only did the U.S. retain substantial areas for use as military bases, but Filipino agreement to the terms of the Bell Trade Act was required as a quid pro quo. The latter virtually guaranteed American domination of the local economy, and a counterinsurgency war against the islands' Huk guerrillas fought until well into the 1950s; Daniel B. Schirmer and Stephen Rosskamm Shalom, *The Philippines Reader: A History of Colonialism, Neocolonialism, Dictatorship and Resistance* (Boston: South End Press, 1987) pp. 87-124.

133. Christopher Thorne, *Allies of a Kind: The United States, Britain and the War Against Japan, 1941-1945* (London: Hamish Hamilton, 1978) pp. 664-5. Also see Huntington Gilchrist, "The Japanese Islands: Annexation or Trusteeship?" *Foreign Affairs*, No. 22, 1944.

134. Giff Johnson, "Nuclear Legacy: Islands Laid Waste," *Oceans*, Jan. 1980.

135. Trask, *Native Daughter*, pp. 88-9. Also see Noel J. Kent, *Hawai'i: Islands Under the Influence* (Honolulu: University of Hawaii Press, [2nd ed.] 1993); "Stolen Kingdom," in this volume.

136. "As an unincorporated Territory, Guam like Puerto Rico and the Virgin Islands is appurtenant to the United States and belongs to the United States, but is not part of the United States, as distinguished from Alaska and Hawaii, which are incorporated territories. Unincorporated areas are not integral parts of the United States and no promise of statehood or a status approaching statehood is held out to them"; 1950 Organic Act of Guam (H.R. 7273), quoted in Rogers, *Destiny's Landfall*, p. 222. As to Puerto Rico, which was subject to a bill "granting" it "Commonwealth Status" on June 30, 1950, the words of New York Senator Jacob Javits should prove instructive: "This bill does restrict, and let us have that very clear, the people of Puerto Rico to a constitution that is within the limits of the [1917] Organic Act for Puerto Rico. Their fundamental status is unchanged"; quoted in Fernandez, *Prisoners of Colonialism*, p. 77.

137. As then-Interior Minister François Mitterand put it on Nov. 13, 1954, "Algeria is France, because Algerian departments are departments of the French Republic"; quoted in Phillip C. Naylor, *France and Algeria: A History of Decolonization and Transformation* (Gainesville: University Press of Florida, 2000) p. 18. On New Caledonia, see Michla Pomerance, *Self-Determination in Law and Practice* (The Hague: Marinus Nijhoff, 1982) p. 30; David Robie, *Blood on Their Banner: Nationalist Struggles in the South Pacific* (London: Zed Press, 1989) pp. 82-140, 256-69, 275-82.

138. See Albertini, *Decolonization*. Also see John Gerassi, *The Coming of the New International* (New

York: World, 1971); Richard J. Barnet, *Intervention and Revolution: America's Confrontations with Insurgent Movements Around the World* (New York: New American Library, [2nd ed.] 1972).

139. Such cynicism could generate truly bizarre tangles. One example: In order to prevent the country from "going communist," the U.S. quietly provided material support to Angolan nationalists seeking to expel their Portuguese colonizers by armed struggle. The Portuguese, catching wind of what was going on, threatened to withdraw from NATO and deny it use of strategically important military bases in the Azores. Deciding the latter installations were more important than the rights of Angolans in the anticommunist scheme of things, the U.S. quickly terminated its aid to the guerrillas, who thereupon turned to the Soviets, Chinese and Cubans for munitions, equipage and, eventually, troops. This last resulted in the U.S. committing personnel to fight the very people it had been arming in the first place; Thomas Pakenham, *The Scramble for Africa: The White Man's Conquest of the Dark Continent, 1876-1912* (New York: Random House, 1991) p. 679. Also see John Stockwell, *In Search of Enemies: A CIA Story* (New York: W.W. Norton, 1978).

140. At one point immediately following Japan's surrender, U.S. Office of Strategic Services personnel were actually instructed to assist where possible in disarming their Vietnamese allies while at least 5,000 Japanese troops were rearmed to "keep order" until French military units arrived in sufficient strength to prevent the independence of Indochina; John T. McAlister, Jr., *Viet Nam: The Origins of a Revolution* (New York: Alfred A. Knopf, 1969) pp. 198, 210-1; R. Harris Smith, *OSS: The Secret History of America's First Central Intelligence Agency* (Berkeley: University of California Press, 1972) p. 358.

141. Michael MacClear, *The Ten Thousand Day War: Vietnam, 1945-1975* (New York: St Martin's Press, 1981). Also see "By the Standards of Their Time," in this volume.

142. V.G. Kiernan, *European Empires from Conquest to Collapse, 1815-1960* (Leicester, UK: Leicester University Press, 1982) pp. 73-4.

143. Ibid., p. 37. There was to be sure almost continuous insurgency within this huge possession thereafter, but the conquest itself was complete; Byron Farwell, *Queen Victoria's Little Wars* (New York: W.W. Norton, 1972).

144. Sanjay Subrahmanyam, *The Portuguese Empire in Asia, 1500-1700* (London: Longman, 1993) p. 209.

145. C.R. Boxer, *The Dutch Seaborne Empire, 1600-1800* (New York: Penguin, 1988) p. 105.

146. H.D. Rosenthal, *Their Day in Court: A History of the Indian Claims Commission* (New York: Garland, 1990). Also see "Charades Anyone?" in this volume.

147. For background, see Adam Hothschild, *King Leopold's Ghost: A Story of Greed, Terror and Heroism in Colonial Africa* (New York: Houghton Mifflin, 1998) esp. pp. 61-74.

148. Government of Belgium, *The Belgian Thesis: The Sacred Mission of Civilization, To Which Peoples Should the Benefit be Extended?* (New York: Belgian Government Information Center, 1953). For analysis, see Gordon Bennett, "Aboriginal Title in the Common Law: A Stony Path through a Feudal Doctrine," *Buffalo Law Review*, Vol. 27, No. 4, 1978.

149. Pakenham, *Scramble for Africa*, esp. pp. 239-55; J.M. McKenzie, *The Partition of Africa, 1880-1900* (London: Metheun, 1983).

150. Pakenham, *Scramble for Africa*, p. 675.

151. Alan Thein Durning, "Guardians of the Land: Indigenous Peoples and the Health of the Earth," *Worldwatch Paper No. 12* (Washington, DC: Worldwatch Institute, 1992); quoted in Nietschmann, "Fourth World," p. 240.

152. Ibid.

153. For the theoretical bases of this commonality, see Connor, *National Question*, pp. 5-27.

154. Neitschmann, "Fourth World," p. 240. For insights concerning the left outlook on such matters in South Asia, see Partha Chatterjee, *Nationalist Thought and the Colonial World: A Derivative Discourse* (London: Zed Press, 1986).

155. Neitschmann, "Fourth World," p. 240. For background, see Greg Urban and Joel Sherzer, *Nation States and Indians in Latin America* (Austin: University of Texas Press, 1991).

156. For context, see Elenga M'buyinga, *Pan Africanism or Neo-Colonialism: The Bankruptcy of the O.A.U.* (London: Zed Press, 1975).

157. As it is put in UN General Assembly Resolution 1541 (XV), a colony "is *geographically separate*

from and . . . distinct ethnically/culturally from the country administering it [emphasis added]"; quoted in Roxanne Dunbar Ortiz, "Protection of American Indian Territories in the United States: Applicability of International Law," in Imre Sutton, ed., *Irredeemable America: The Indians' Estate and Land Tenure* (Albuquerque: University of New Mexico Press, 1985) p. 260.

158. Bennett, "Aboriginal Title"; Mathew Snipp, "The Changing Economic and Political Status of American Indians: From Captive Nations to Internal Colonies," *American Journal of Economics and Sociology*, No. 45, 1986.

159. Nietschmann, "Fourth World," p. 240. For background reading in this connection, see Leopold Kohr, *The Breakdown of Nations* (New York: E.P. Dutton, 1957).

160. Nietschmann, "Fourth World," p. 240. For details, see Connor, *National Question*, pp. 45-61, 67-92.

161. Nietschmann, "Fourth World," p. 226. Also see Seton-Watson, *Nations and States*; Richard Falk, *Human Rights and State Sovereignty* (New York: Holmes & Meier, 1984).

162. Nietschmann. "Fourth World"; Ben Whitaker, ed., *The Fourth World: Victims of Group Oppression* (London: Sidgwick & Jackson, 1972); George Manuel and Michael Posluns, *The Fourth World: An Indian Reality* (New York: Free Press, 1974). For use of the term "Host World," see Winona LaDuke, "Natural to Synthetic and Back Again," in my *Marxism and Native Americans* (Boston: South End Press, 1983) pp. i–viii.

163. For broad surveys of conditions, see Sadruddin Aga Khan and Hassan bin Talal, *Indigenous Peoples: A Global Quest for Justice* (London: Zed Press, 1987); Julian Burger, *Report from the Frontier: The State of the World's Indigenous Peoples* (London: Zed Press, 1987).

164. It is seldom that I find myself much in agreement with those of a marxian bent. I do, however, concur with many of the points advanced by Alex Callincos in his *Against Postmodernism: A Marxist Critique* (New York: St. Martin's Press, 1989). On the other hand, I also refuse much of what Callincos seemingly accepts; see, e.g., the essay "False Promises: An Indigenist Perspective on Marxist Theory and Practice," in my *From a Native Son: Selected Essays in Indigenism, 1985-1995* (Boston: South End Press, 1996) pp. 461–82.

165. Jules Gerard-Libois, *Katanga Secession* (Madison: University of Wisconsin Press, 1966).

166. Peter Schwab, ed. *Biafra* (New York: Facts on File, 1971).

167. Isak Chisi Swu and Th. Muivah, *Free Nagaland Manifesto* (Oking: National Socialist Council of Nagaland, [2nd ed.] 1993).

168. Khan and Talal, *Indigenous Peoples*, pp. 131-4.

169. Connor, *National Question*, pp. 101-27.

170. Gerald Chaliand, ed., *People Without A Country: The Kurds and Kurdistan* (London: Zed Press, 1980).

171. Fred Branfman, "Presidential War in Laos, 1964-1970," in Nina S. Adams and Alfred W. McCoy, eds., *Laos: War and Revolution* (New York: Harper Torchbooks, 1970) esp. pp. 244-55.

172. See my and Glenn T. Morris' essay, "Between a Rock and a Hard Place: Left-Wing Revolution, Right-Wing Reaction, and the Destruction of Indigenous Peoples," in my *Since Predator Came: Notes on the Struggle for American Indian Liberation* (Littleton, CO: Aigis, 1995) pp. 329-48.

173. Tony Hodges, *Western Sahara: The Roots of a Desert War* (Westport, CT: Lawrence Hill, 1983).

174. Juan Goytisolo, *Landscapes of War from Sarajevo to Chechnya* (San Francisco: City Lights, 2000) pp. 155-202..

175. Elaine Katzenberger, ed., *First World, Ha-Ha-Ha! The Zapatista Challenge* (San Francisco: City Lights, 1995).

176. John G. Taylor, *Indonesia's Forgotten War: The Hidden History of East Timor* (London: Zed Press, 1991).

177. C.W. Nelson and K. Taylor, *Witness to Genocide: The Present Situation of the Indians in Guatemala* (London: Survival International, 1983); Robert M. Carmack, *Harvest of Violence: The Mayan Indians and the Guatemala Crisis* (Norman: University of Oklahoma Press, 1988).

178. Richard Arens, ed., *Genocide in Paraguay* (Philadelphia: Temple University Press, 1976).

179. Alain Destexhe, *Rwanda and Genocide in the Twentieth Century* (New York: New York University Press, 1995); Gérard Prunier, *The Rwanda Crisis: History of a Genocide* (New York: Columbia University Press, 1995).

180. Broader surveys will be found in R. Brian Ferguson and Neil Lancelot Whitehead, eds., *War in the Tribal Zone: Expanding States and Indigenous Warfare* (Seattle: School of American Research and University of Washington Press, 1992); Ted Robert Gurr, *Minorities at Risk:A Global Survey of Ethnopolitical Conflicts* (Washington, DC: State Institute of Peace Press, 1993).

181. Nietschmann, "Fourth World," p. 237. Of the remaining 24 conflicts, 23 are classified as state responses to "insurgencies," usually by leftist guerrillas. Several of these, such as that of the Sendero Luminoso in Peru, are composed at the grassroots level primarily of native people; Simon Strong, *Shining Path:Terror and Revolution in Peru* (New York: Times Books, 1992). More broadly, see Lisa Gross, *Handbook of Leftist Guerrilla Groups in Latin America and the Caribbean* (Boulder, CO: Westview Press, 1995). It should also be noted that the U.S. conducted a counterinsurgency campaign against the American Indian Movement during the mid-1970s; see Smith and Warrior, *Like a Hurricane*; also see "The Bloody Wake of Alcatraz," in this volume.

182. Nietschmann, "Fourth World," p. 237.

183. See generally, Berger, *Report from the Frontier*; José Martinez Cobo, *Study of the Problem of Discrimination Against Indigenous Populations, Vol. 5: Conclusions, Proposals and Recommendations* (U.N. Doc. E/CN.4/Sub.2/1986/Add.4 (1987)).

184. Jean-Paul Sartre and Arlette El Kaim-Sartre, *On Genocide and a Summary of the Evidence and Judgements of the International War Crimes Tribunal* (Boston: Beacon Press, 1968) pp. 62-3. For an example of the criticism directed against the Sartrian equation, see Leo Kuper, *Genocide: Its Political Use in the Twentieth Century* (New Haven, CT: Yale University Press, 1981) pp. 44-6.

185. Hugo Blanco, *Land or Death: The Peasant Struggle in Peru* (New York: Pathfinder, 1972). "Peasant," incidentally, is the standard marxian euphemism throughout Iberoamerica for Indians who have been dislodged from their traditional territories/ways of life.

186. Bernard Nietschmann, "Militarization and Indigenous Peoples: The Third World War," *Cultural Survival Quarterly*, Vol. 11, No. 3, 1987.

187. Weston, Falk and D'Amato, *Basic Documents*, p. 16; "Memorandum for Encouraging the Progressive Development of International Law and Its Eventual Codification," A/AC.10/7 (May 6, 1947).

188. Leopold Kohr, *The Overdeveloped Nations: The Diseconomies of Scale* (New York: Schocken Books, 1978).

189. See, e.g., Leo Panitch, "Rethinking the Role of the State," in James H. Mittelman, ed., *Globalization: Critical Reflections* (Boulder, CO: Lynne Rienner, 1996) pp. 83-116.

190. The case is made well in Stephen McBride and John Shields, *Dismantling a Nation: The Transition to Corporate Rule in Canada* (Halifax, NS: Fernwood, 1997).

191. See, e.g., Maude Barlow and Tony Clark, *MIA and the Threat to American Freedom* (New York: Stoddard, 1998); Noam Chomsky, *Profit Over People: Neoliberalism and the Global Order* (New York: Seven Stories Press, 1999).

192. See, e.g., Louis Turner, *Multinational Companies and the Third World* (New York: Hill and Wang, 1973); Richard J. Barnet and Ronald Müller, *Global Reach:The Power of Multinational Corporations* (New York: Simon and Schuster, 1974); Krishna Kumar, ed., *Transnational Enterprises:Their Impact on Third World Societies and Cultures* (Boulder, CO: Westview Press, 1980). For a useful update, see James H. Mittelman, "How Does Globalization Really Work?" in Mittelman, *Globalization*, pp. 229-41.

193. This is essentially the argument made by Kohr in *Breakdown of Nations*. It is made still more sharply by a number of other anarchist theorists; for an overview, see Richard Falk, "Anarchism and World Order," in his *The End of World Order: Essays on Normative International Relations* (New York: Holmes & Meier, 1983) pp. 277-98. Also see Barry Buzan, Charles Jones and Richard Little, *The Logic of Anarchy: Neorealism to Structural Realism* (New York: Columbia University Press, 1993) esp. pp. 155-68.

194. The case is well-made by Ved Nanda in his "Self-Determination in International Law: The Validity of Claims to Secede," *Case Western Reserve Journal of International Law*, No. 13, 1981. Also see Lee Buchheit, *Secession: The Legitimacy of Self-Determination* (New Haven: Yale University Press, 1978).

195. This was in fact conceded in 1990, when, "in its last days, [the Soviet Union] admitted the illegality of its conquest of the Baltic states" of Lithuania, Latvia and Estonia in 1940, and restored their independence; Korman, *Right of Conquest*, p. 304.

196. An interesting discussion of precisely these points will be found in Eyal Benvenisti, *The International Law of Occupation* (Princeton, NJ: Princeton University Press, 1993).

197. Such thinking has in fact been increasingly a part of the international legal discourse over the past quarter-century; Douglas Sanders, "The Re-Emergence of Indigenous Questions in International Law," *Canadian Human Rights Yearbook*, No. 3, 1983; Russel Lawrence Barsh, "Indigenous Peoples: An Emerging Object of International Law," *American Journal of International Law*, No. 80, 1986; S. James Anaya, "The Rights of Indigenous Peoples and International Law in Historical and Contemporary Perspective," in Robert N. Clinton, Nell Jessup Newton and Monroe E. Price, eds., *American Indian Law: Cases and Materials* (Charlottesville, VA: Michie, 1991).

198. I have elsewhere sketched out the basis for and possible configuration of such a "Union of North American Indigenous Nations" within the lower-48 portion of the U.S.; see "I Am Indigenist: Notes on the Ideology of the Fourth World," in my *Struggle for the Land: Native North American Resistance to Genocide, Ecocide and Colonization* (San Francisco: City Lights, 2002) pp. 367-402.

199. Kirkpatrick Sale, *Human Scale* (New York: Coward, McCann & Geoghegan, 1980).

200. This has been so since the inception of the current phase; see Holly Sklar, ed., *Trilateralism: The Trilateral Commission and Elite Planning for World Management* (Boston: South End Press, 1980).

201. Glenn T. Morris, "Further Motion by the State Department to Railroad Indigenous Rights," *Fourth World Bulletin*, No. 6, Summer 1998.

202. These estimates are extrapolated on the basis of the Indian Claims Commission data on the extent of unceded native land in combination with Bureau of Indian Affairs data on reservation assets. See Indian Claims Commission, *Final Report* (Washington, D.C.: U.S. Government Printing Office, 1978); U.S. Dept. of Interior, Bureau of Indian Affairs, *Indian Lands Map: Oil, Gas and Minerals on Indian Reservations* (Washington, DC: U.S. Government Printing Office, 1978). Also see "Charades Anyone?" and "A Breach of Trust," in this volume.

203. For discussion of the process, albeit with regard to a different set of issues, see Jürgen Habermas, *Legitimation Crisis* (Boston: Beacon Press, 1975).

204. There are a number of studies that move in this direction. Two of the better are Edward S. Herman and Noam Chomsky, *Manufacturing Consent: The Political Economy of the Mass Media* (New York: Pantheon, 1988); Noam Chomsky, *Necessary Illusions: Thought Control in Democratic Societies* (Boston: South End Press, 1989).

205. This is not so far-fetched as it may sound to younger readers. Something not so dissimilar actually happened in the U.S. barely a third of a century ago, and for not entirely dissimilar reasons; see William L. O'Neill, *Coming Apart: An Informal History of America in the 1960s* (Chicago: Quadrangle, 1971); Paul Joseph, *Cracks in the Empire: State Politics in the Vietnam War* (Boston: South End Press, 1981). One measure of the current estrangement of the U.S. from its traditional allies in the UN can be judged by their recent expulsion of its representative on the Human Rights Commission; for background, see Bennis, *Calling the Shots*.

206. For an appreciation of the flux that can be generated by such processes, see George Katsiaficas, *The Imagination of the New Left: A Global Analysis of 1968* (Boston: South End Press, 1987).

207. Oppenheim, *International Law*, p. 295. Also see Robert E. Osgood and Robert W. Tucker, *Force, Order and Justice: A Study in the History of Thought* (Baltimore: Johns Hopkins University Press, 1967).

208. *Legal Status of Eastern Greenland (Denmark v. Norway)* (1933), Perm. Ct. Int. Jus., ser. A/B, no. 53, at 47.

209. This is aside from the pair of "Métis Rebellions" in Manitoba (1868) and Saskatchewan (1885), neither of which were "Indian Wars," per se; see Joseph Howard, *Strange Empire: Louis Riel and the Métis People* (Toronto: James Lewis & Samuel, 1974).

210. See note 36 and accompanying text.

211. For overviews independent of my own, see Ralph K. Andrist, *The Long Death: The Last Days of the Plains Indian* (New York: Macmillan, 1964); Dee Brown, *Bury My Heart at Wounded Knee: An Indian History of the American West* (New York: Holt, Rinehart and Winston, 1970); Alan Axelrod, *Chronicle of the Indian Wars from Colonial Times to Wounded Knee* (New York: Prentice Hall, 1993).

212. This is true under the UN and OAS Charters, already cited. It is true as well under Article 49 (Fraud) and Articles 50-51 (Coercion) of the Vienna Convention on the Law of Treaties, (U.N. Doc. A/CONF.39/27 at 289 (1969), 1155 U.N.T.S. 331, *reprinted in* 8 I.L.M. 679 (1969)). For text, see Weston, Falk and D'Amato, *Basic Documents*, pp. 93-113, cites at p. 102. Also see the *Icelandic Fisheries Jurisdiction*

case, in which the International Court of Justice held that "an agreement concluded under threat or use of force is void" (*ICJ Report*, 1973, p. 14).

213. Both the U.S. and Canada have argued that there is a "supervening impossibility of performance" preventing their meeting their treaty commitments to indigenous nations. Under Article 61 of the Vienna Convention, however, "impossibility" cannot be invoked by any party to a treaty as a defense against meeting its responsibilities, "if the impossibility is the result of a breach by that party . . . of an obligation under the treaty"; Weston, Falk and D'Amato, *Basic Documents*, p. 104.

214. Treaty "nullity may be invoked . . . by a state which has been the victim of error, fraud or corruption or [other] manifest violation of international law"; Jimenez de Arechaga, "International Law in the Last Third of a Century," *Recueil des Cours*, No. 159, 1978, p. 68.

215. "It was generally agreed that most of the contents of the present Convention were merely expressive of rules which existed in customary international law. The rules obviously could be invoked as custom without any reference to the present Convention"; United Nations Conference on the Law of Treaties, Official Records: Second Session (A/Conf.39/11 Add. 1 (1966)); quoted in Ian Sinclair, *The Vienna Convention on the Law of Treaties* (Manchester, UK: Manchester University Press, [2nd ed.] 1984) p. 8. Or, as the International Court of Arbitration has put it, "The traditional canons of treaty interpretation [are] now enshrined in the Vienna Convention on the Law of Treaties"; *Beagle Channel Arbitration* (52 ILR 93 (1981)) at p. 1.

216. Deloria and Wilkins, *Tribes, Treaties and Constitutional Tribulations*, p. 29.

217. U.S. Constitution, Art. 1 § 10; Vienna Convention, Art. 2(1)(a). Also see Ti-Chiang Chen, *The International Law of Recognition* (London: Stevens, 1951).

218. By far the best compilation of relevant texts will be found in Vine Deloria, Jr., and Raymond J. DeMallie, *Documents of American Indian Diplomacy: Treaties, Agreements and Conventions, 1775-1979*, 2 vols. (Norman: University of Oklahoma Press, 1999).

219. Pomerance, *Self-Determination*; Buchheit, *Secession*; Henry Reynolds, *Aboriginal Sovereignty: Reflections on Race, State and Nation* (London: Allen & Unwin, 1996).

220. The Canadian counterpart to Deloria and DeMallie (note 218) is *Canada: Indian Treaties and Surrenders from 1680 to 1890*, 3 vols. (Ottawa: Queen's Printer, 1891; reprinted by Coles [Toronto], 1971; reprinted by Fifth House [Saskatoon], 1992).

221. The "diminished capacity" of indigenous nations of course results from a series of illegal actions by the U.S. and Canada. Under Article 62 § 2 of the Vienna Convention, "a fundamental change of circumstances may not be invoked . . . if the fundamental change is the result of a breach by the party invoking it either of an obligation under the treaty or of any other international obligation owed to any other party under the treaty." Entire treaties are abrogated, moreover, not certain sections of it (the abrogation process does not resemble a "line item veto"). Under Article 69, when a valid abrogation occurs, "each party may require any other party to establish as far as possible in their mutual relations the position that would have existed" had the treaty not been effected; Weston, Falk and D'Amato, *Basic Documents*, pp. 105, 106. In other words, if the U.S. and/or Canada wish to abrogate treaties with Indians, they can do so, but they are required as a concomitant to relinquish their claims to all territory accruing therefrom; voiding the treaties voids their title and jurisdiction.

222. Weston, Falk and D'Amato, *Basic Documents*, p. 98.

223. Ibid., p. 103; Sinclair, *Vienna Convention*, p. 19.

224. Jackson observed in his opening statement that the prosecution had "no purpose of incriminating the whole German people" although he seemingly contradicted himself later, when he addressed the question of "vicarious liability"; Jackson, *Nürnberg Case*, pp. 35, 89. "In effect, despite the disclaimers, the indictments were directed against the German people. . . Collective guilt clung to millions of Germans"; Davidson, *Trial of the Germans*, p. 7. Also see Elezar Barkman, *The Guilt of Nations: Restitution and Negotiating Historical Injustices* (New York: W.W. Norton, 2000) pp. 3-29.

225. An extreme formulation will be found in Daniel Jonah Goldhagen's *Hitler's Willing Executioners: Ordinary Germans and the Holocaust* (New York: Alfred A. Knopf, 1996). For critique, see Norman G. Finkelstein and Ruth Bettina Birn, *A Nation on Trial: The Goldhagen Thesis and Historical Truth* (New York: Holt, Rinehart, 1998); Geoff Eley, ed., *The "Goldhagen Effect": History, Memory, Nazism—Facing the German Past* (Ann Arbor: University of Michigan Press, 2000).

226. Robert Weldon Whaley, *Assassinating Hitler: Ethics and Resistance in Germany* (London, Ont.: McGill University Press, 1993); Michael Baigent and Richard Leigh, *Secret Germany: Stauffenberg and the Mystical Crusade Against Hitler* (London: Allen & Unwin, 1994). Other resistance groups have also acquired a certain luster; see, e.g., Inge Scholl, *The White Rose: Munich, 1942-1943* (Middletown, CT: Wesleyan University Press, [2nd ed.] 1983).

227. For related discussion, see Heather A. Wilson, *International Law and the Use of Force by National Liberation Movements* (Oxford, UK: Clarendon Press, 1988).

228. See, e.g., "Whatever is Necessary to Protect Ourselves," in Bruce Perry, ed., *Malcolm X: The Last Speeches* (New York: Pathfinder, 1989) esp. pp. 87-8.

229. Winona LaDuke, "Succeeding Into Native North America: A Secessionist View," in my *Struggle for the Land*, pp. 11-13.

# Stolen Kingdom
## The Right of Hawai'i to Decolonization

> It may be assumed that the colonizer will resort to any subterfuge to main-
> tain the order of his domination of the colonized.
>
> — Frantz Fanon
> *A Dying Colonialism*

On November 23, 1993, President Bill Clinton placed his signature on Public Law 103-150, thereby conveying a formal apology by the United States to the Polynesians native to Hawai'i for the tangibly criminal "act of war" through which the U.S. had forcibly abolished their government a century earlier (the full text is included herein as Appendix A).[1] By implication, P.L. 103-150 also expressed certain "regrets" for America's behavior, both official and quasiofficial, and occurring both before and since the 1893 coup, which has resulted in the near-total dispossession of the Kanaka Maoli (indigenous Hawaiians) within their homeland, and the subsuming of Hawai'i itself, first as a U.S. "possession" held in perpetual "trust" (i.e., an outright colony), and, since 1959, as a "State of the Union" (that is, as an integral component of what the U.S. claims as its own "home territory").

To quote the Apology itself, although "between 1826 and 1893 the United States recognized the independence of the Kingdom of Hawaii, extended full and complete recognition of the Hawaiian Government, and entered into treaties and conventions with the Hawaiian monarchs...the United States Minister and the naval representatives of the United States caused naval armed forces of the United States to invade the sovereign Hawaiian nation on January 16, 1893, and to position themselves near Hawaiian Government buildings...to intimidate [the Hawaiian] government."

[The] United States Minister thereupon extended diplomatic recognition of the Provisional Government that was formed by [a cabal of Euroamerican] conspirators without the consent of the Native Hawaiian people or the lawful Government of Hawaii and *in violation of treaties between the two nations and of international law* [emphasis added].

P.L. 103-150 thereby officially admits that the U.S. violated two cardinal principles of international legal custom and convention: first, that all nations must refrain from the unprovoked use of force in international affairs;[2] second, that all countries must observe the primacy of treaties — *"pacta sunt servanda,"* or "treaties are to be observed" — in their interactions with other nations.[3] It is worth mentioning as well that America's breach of its treaties with the Hawaiian Kingdom in 1893 was also undertaken in flagrant violation of Article VI(2) of the U.S. Constitution: "This Constitution, and the Laws of the United States made in pursuance thereof; and all the *Treaties made…under authority of the United States, shall be the Supreme Law of the land*; and the judges in every State shall be bound thereby, any thing in the Constitution or Laws of any State to the contrary notwithstanding [emphasis added]."[4]

In international law no less than in U.S. domestic jurisprudence, it is well-established that when the commission of an illegal act causing material damage is conceded (or proven), apologies and/or professions of regret are in themselves insufficient to constitute a remedy.[5] Instead, leaving aside issues concerning the punishment of criminal conduct, per se, it is understood that the offending party is obliged to effect restitution, reparation and/or adequate compensation to the victims.[6] Such obligation is in no way contingent upon its being convenient to the offender. Rather, in cases where the offending party proves unwilling to do everything possible to "make things right," procedures exist — usually by recourse to tort law — through which the courts are empowered to order fulfillment of this basic responsibility.[7] Should such a decree be itself defied, the use of coercive means, including the employment of whatever degree of armed force may prove necessary, is legally warranted to ensure compliance.[8]

Such principles have an obvious bearing on the present context of U.S./Hawaiian affairs insofar as America's admission that its "ownership" of Hawai'i was attained through illegal means has been accompanied neither by a willingness to substantively alter the resulting relationship between itself and the Kanaka Maoli nor by even an offer of the most token compensation to them. On the contrary, and despite an unambiguous acknowledgement earlier in the text that "the indigenous Hawaiian people *never* directly relin-

74

quished their...inherent sovereignty as a people [emphasis added]," the concluding sentence of P.L. 103-150 asserts that the Apology is meant to provide "nothing" by way of "a settlement of any claims against the United States." In effect, while recognizing that the Kanaka Maoli continue to hold a *de jure* (primary and innate) right to the undisturbed exercise of sovereignty within their homeland, the U.S. has used the Apology itself to assert its intention of maintaining *de facto* rule—that is, imposition of the "fact" of governing prerogatives without establishment of a genuine legal basis for them—over the entire archipelago.[9]

The "bond" thus described is explicitly colonial in nature. Accordingly, it must be noted that colonialism, no less than treaty violations and the forcible usurpation of legitimate governments, has since 1945 been cast as an illegality under provision of the United Nations Charter and other elements of black letter international law.[10] The ongoing U.S. posture vis-à-vis Hawai'i consequently serves to amplify rather than rectify the very pattern of criminal comportment for which the United States has purported to apologize. In this sense, P.L. 103-150 reveals itself as being no more than a cosmetic gesture, or, more accurately, a stratagem by which the U.S.—most likely hopeful of peddling an illusion that the situation is actually the opposite of itself—has sought once again, as it has for more than a century, to confuse the issue of Hawai'i's right to resume a self-determining existence, thereby retarding or perhaps precluding its fulfillment.[11]

Under such circumstances, the international community, employing the vehicle embodied in the United Nations, is unequivocally invested with a range of obligations to actively intervene in behalf of the Kanaka Maoli.[12] The primary purpose of this essay is to spell these out, citing both precedent and legal postulation in the process. It will, however, be useful to first recount the U.S. record with respect to Hawai'i in somewhat greater detail. This is so, not simply because of the monumental ignorance of their country's history with which most Americans are notoriously afflicted,[13] but because the reality is far worse than anything the relative few who've troubled to try and acquaint themselves with the facts have by and large been led by the shills of orthodox historiography to believe.[14]

## To Steal a Kingdom

On January 15, 1893, a group of about 100 U.S. nationals calling themselves the "Committee for Public Safety" seized the government quarter of

Honolulu, capitol of the Kingdom of Hawai'i.[15] Itself armed to the teeth, the Committee was backed by a much larger paramilitary formation, the Honolulu Rifles, ostensibly organized as a "citizens' militia" but composed exclusively of Euroamerican immigrants.[16] A day later, at the request of U.S. Minister J.L. Stevens, a contingent of Marines was put ashore from a warship, the *U.S.S. Boston*, anchored in Pearl Harbor. Although the Marines were purportedly landed to "assist in preserving public order," they did nothing to interfere as the insurgents deposed the Kingdom's legitimate government, personified in Queen Lili'uokalani, occupied its buildings, and installed eighteen of their number as a provisional junta.[17] Rather, the deployment of U.S. forces was plainly designed to forestall any effective response by Hawaiian police and military units, the combined strength of which would otherwise have been quite sufficient to crush the rebellion.[18] That those on the scene were well satisfied with the results of their handiwork is readily evidenced in the observation of Lt. Lucien Young, who commanded the Marine detachment, that his men's presence had allowed "the best citizens and nine-tenths of the property-owners of the country"—i.e., whites—to assume complete control over the islands.[19]

In the aftermath, although President Grover Cleveland heatedly regaled the whole affair as an "unprovoked act of war" and a gross violation of "international morality,"[20] he adamantly refused Lili'uokalani's repeated requests that he enforce the rule of law by reinstating her authority.[21] Instead, with what can only be described as utter duplicity, Cleveland bestowed approval on the result of what he'd condemned with a letter recognizing the usurpers' new "Republic of Hawaii" as a "lawful State."[22] In July 1898—"coincidental" to America's openly expansionist war with Spain—Congress followed up with the Newlands Resolution, thereby "acceding to a desire expressed by the government of Hawaii" that the islands be annexed as a "permanent trust territory [colony] of the United States."[23] "The Gibraltar of the Pacific," as Commodore George Melville described it, was thus officially added to "the Philippines, Guam, the Carolines [and] Samoa...to complete the chain" or "bridge" upon which U.S. policymakers were then loudly proclaiming their intent to realize their country's "imperial destiny" in Asia.[24] Few Americans, needless to say, asked—or apparently cared in the least—how the Kanaks felt about their homeland's being incorporated into the growing galaxy of U.S. "territorial possessions."[25]

The illegal and aggressive pattern of "*haole*"[26] behavior in Hawai'i during the last decade of the nineteenth century did not emerge from a vacuum, of course. Rather, in the words of Lorrin Thurston, a key figure in both the 1893 coup and the Republic's subsequent drive to annexation, it was "not a change, [but] a consummation...of seventy years" of steadily increasing Euroamerican belligerence and subversion in the islands.[27] More accurately still, the process culminating in the Newlands Resolution can be said to have begun in 1788, when the English naval captain *cum* explorer James Cook reputedly became the first European to happen upon what he dubbed the "Sandwich Islands."[28] Within a few years, England had set about building the archipelago into a rapidly developing military/commercial linkage between its Australian and Canadian colonies.[29] In no small part, this initiative involved direct intervention in the internal affairs of the Kanaka Maoli, as when, in 1795, Captain George Vancouver provided artillery and other such support to Chief Kamehameha during a dispute between the latter and rivals on the islands of Mau'i and Kaua'i. The result was establishment of a more-or-less European-style kingdom presided over by Kamehameha and heavily indebted to Great Britain.[30] As analyst Noel Kent has observed, such "cooptation of the Hawaiian elite was the essential prerequisite for integration of the Hawaiian economy into the emerging global economy."[31]

By 1810, Hawai'i's utility as a base for whaling operations and its lush sandalwood forests—the brief but immensely profitable trade in this commodity was then in full swing—had combined to make control of the islands attractive to the U.S. as well as Britain.[32] While their relationship with Kamehameha afforded the British a distinct advantage at the outset, the Americans adopted a longer range and ultimately far more insidious approach. In 1820, a group of Congregationalist missionaries arrived from the U.S. and, playing upon insecurities engendered by a precipitous drop in the Kanaka Maoli population size brought on by the introduction of Old World diseases, made rapid progress in converting grassroots Hawaiians.[33] Their efforts were significantly enhanced by a concomitant undermining of the islands' traditional economic system resulting not only from the population decline, but from the environmental ravages of wholesale sandalwood "harvesting" and a steadily accelerating influx of western "development" capital.[34] Also at issue were the effects of American "gunboat diplomacy," beginning in 1826, when Captain Thomas ap Gatesby Jones anchored a sloop of war, the *U.S.S. Peacock*, in Pearl Harbor for several days to press the point that the U.S. would abide nothing but its own version of "free trade" (the message was punctuated three years later through a "visit" by Captain William Bolton Finch, commanding the *U.S.S. Vincennes*).[35]

Under such circumstances, the missionaries were able to rapidly expand their influence, becoming by the late 1830s the closest advisers to Hawai'i's royal family, not only in spiritual matters, but with respect to political and economic affairs as well. By the early 1840s, Richard Armstrong, pastor of Honolulu's Kawaihae Church, was in charge of the Hawaiian school system, missionary and former Maine congressman Elisha Allen had become minister of finance, and "all executive prerogatives and functions [had] been assumed by [missionaries and merchants] constituting themselves as a Privy Council."[36] As one observer remarked at the time, "Missionaries now have everything in their hands."[37] As a result, the Kingdom's first written constitution, promulgated in October 1840, was drafted by two prominent clergymen *cum* planters, Gerrit Judd and John Ricord. The instrument, which posited Christianity as Hawai'i's veritable state religion and guaranteed "all men"—a phrase specifically meaning whites—"equity" in the islands' civil life, was amended by the same pair in 1852 to greatly increase the ability of *haoles* to own land outright.[38]

This last occurred in the context of what Judd himself viewed as his greatest accomplishment: the "Great Mahele" (Division of Lands) of 1848, through which the entire structure of Hawaiian land tenure was redefined.[39]

> Under provisions of the Great Mahele, 60 percent of the land in the Hawaiian archipelago (2,479,000 acres) was allotted to the crown and the government, 39 percent (1,619,000 acres) to 208 chiefs, and less than 1 percent to the 11,000 [surviving] commoners. Additional laws conferred the right of ownership to foreigners, and through the Kuleana Act (1850) granted fee-simple rights to tenants on land they already occupied [their *kuleanas*, or home sites].[40]

Imposition of an alien system of individuated property titles and taxes upon the Kanaks, who had always held land in common, generated the entirely predictable result—as it would on a much larger scale with the "General Allotment" of American Indian reservations a generation later[41]— of dispossessing commoners on an almost across-the-board basis.

> The new system required personal applications for land deeds, proof of occupancy and of having "really cultivated" the land (particularly serious obstacles), and a relatively sizeable cash fee for surveying and registering the land title. Some commoners simply ignored the new legislation and tried to continue the old ways. Western concepts like "land title," "land tax," and even the conception of land as a marketable commodity, lay

outside the realm of ordinary Hawaiian experience. Only 28,000 acres were ultimately awarded to commoners, and many of these were subsequently alienated for nonpayment of taxes or noncompliance with some other facet of the law... [O]pportunistic [whites] loitered around tax and land offices eagerly snapping up land declared legally vacated. Land baronies were created instantaneously.[42]

The *alii* (Hawaiian royalty), moreover, was quickly conned into selling off vast tracts of its holdings in an effort to acquire the accoutrements of western "civilization," or to pay off sometimes imaginary "debts" to its advisers.[43] In 1856, only 209 of 15,514 land titles issued in Hawai'i were held by foreigners; by 1886, *haoles* possessed two-thirds of the total.[44] This dramatic transformation in the distribution of real property gave rise to a plantation system, owned exclusively by whites and devoted to the manufacture of sugar for consumption in the U.S., and, by 1870, had resulted in the domination of the islands' economy by a handful of major sugar-producing corporations—Hackfield (Amfac), C. Brewer, Theo Davies, Castle and Cooke, and Alexander and Baldwin—known as the "Big Five."[45] Divested of the land upon which their traditional "tarot roots" subsistence depended, the Kanaks were by and large reduced to laboring in the cane fields at pittance wages, and, after 1875, increasingly displaced even from that pursuit, as the sugar growers imported hundreds of thousands of Chinese and Japanese laborers— later, Filipinos as well—radically altering Hawai'i's demography.[46]

Both officially and otherwise, the U.S. had done much to facilitate what was happening. The message delivered at gunpoint by Captain Gatesby Jones in 1826 was codified in a "Treaty of Friendship, Commerce and Navigation, between the United States and the Sandwich Islands" on December 23 of the same year.[47] With the Kingdom thus "legally-bound" to open itself to the ravages of U.S. economic penetration, American pundits and policymakers alike were soon remarking upon the desirability of simply annexing the islands.[48] In 1842, President John Tyler went part way by enunciating a corollary to the Monroe Doctrine in which Hawai'i, while recognized as constituting an "independent state," was proclaimed part of the U.S. sphere of "intercourse," and a "decided remonstrance"—i.e., use of military force— threatened against any third power "interfering" with America's commercial hegemony there.[49] Nonetheless, a much more bellicose policy was continuously advocated by "business leaders,"[50] civilian authorities like Secretary of State William Seward,[51] and naval officers like Admiral A.E. DuPont.[52]

Although the ambition of officials like Seward and DuPont to simply seize the archipelago were not immediately actualized, the U.S. moved in 1849 to expand its commercial advantages in Hawai'i via a substantial reworking of the 1826 treaty.[53] To all intents and purposes, the U.S. negotiated the new compact with itself, at least to the extent that the Kingdom was represented by a Euroamerican "special envoy," James Jackson Jarvis, and all discussions were conducted in Washington rather than Honolulu.[54] In any event, along with the Mahele, the 1849 treaty went far towards consolidating *haole* power in the islands, and thus laid the groundwork for enactment of Hawai'i's 1852 constitution. This, in turn, paved the way in 1875 for a still more thoroughgoing Treaty of Commercial Reciprocity, negotiated "in behalf of" the Crown by Elisha Allen and another *haole* planter, Henry Carter,[55] and revised in 1884 to provide the U.S. an exclusive right to establish naval facilities in "the harbor at the mouth of the Pearl River."[56] At this point, as Charles Harris, the Kingdom's Euroamerican foreign minister put it, Hawai'i had been bound "to the interests of the United States [by] hooks of steel."[57]

By the early 1870s, serious resistance among the Kanaka Maoli had begun to emerge. The question of who was to succeed King Lunalilo when he died in 1873 brought things to something of a head for the first time. On the one hand was his wife, Queen Emma, who enjoyed considerable popularity among her own people; on the other was David Kalakaua, a member of the *alii* strongly preferred by the *haole* planter élite.[58] When it became apparent that Kalakaua was to be installed over the objections of the Kanaks themselves, a revolt broke out. A force of about 150 sailors and Marines was then landed from the U.S. warships *Tuscarora* and *Portsmouth*, sent to Pearl Harbor to ensure that the travesty was successfully carried out, and "marched up Fort Street, dispersing demonstrators and arresting key leaders. Government buildings were occupied by marine detachments" until the rebellion was completely quelled.[59] With that, Kalakaua was seated, and "the façade of Hawaiian sovereignty...irrevocably shattered."[60]

In the aftermath, "half-caste" patriots Robert W. Wilcox and Robert Boyd set about building a much better organized nationalist movement among the Kanaks, while the whites, led by men like Sanford Dole (of Dole fruit) and planter/banker/lawyer/government minister Charles Reed Bishop, founded what they called the "Hawaiian League" and began importing large quantities of arms and munitions with which to retain their position of dominance.[61] In July 1887, this weaponry was used to impose a

"Bayonet Constitution" on Kalakaua, formalizing the figurehead status to which the Crown had long since been reduced and concretizing *haole* control over every aspect of the Kingdom's functioning.[62] Two years later, almost to the day, Wilcox, Boyd and their followers responded with an insurrection intended to depose Kalakaua and replace him with his sister, Lili'uokalani.[63] Only the deployment of a contingent of Marines from the *U.S.S. Adams* temporarily averted this outcome.[64] The *U.S.S. Pensacola*—later, the *Boston*—was thereafter placed on "permanent station" at Pearl Harbor for such purposes.[65]

The death of Kalakaua on January 20, 1891, nonetheless propelled Lili'uokalani onto the throne, and, as was anticipated by Wilcox and other nationalists, she quickly undertook initiatives designed to reassert Kanaka rights in civil affairs.[66] By late 1892, she'd begun to raise serious questions with regard to land distribution,[67] taken steps to ensure that governmental revenues would be rendered independent of the planters,[68] and had initiated preliminary discussions with U.S. officials aimed at an overhaul of the Reciprocity Treaty (which had been partially abrogated by the U.S. in 1890, and was at any rate shortly due to expire).[69] Against this backdrop, tension mounted steadily, plots and counterplots abounding.

> The long-awaited crisis erupted on January 14, 1893, when Liliuokalani, in the wake of a series of cabinet shakeups, mounted the throne and read a declaration promulgating a new constitution. It asserted the power of the monarchy over the government and declared that all cabinet members would henceforth serve at her pleasure. This was nothing less than a blunt repudiation of the plantation bourgeoisie and the institutions it had established in the half-century since the [first] constitution.[70]

With that, U.S. Minister Stevens concluded that "intelligent and responsible men here [meaning whites], unaided by outside support, are too few in numbers to control political affairs and serve good government," and inquired of Secretary of State James Blaine whether, "in such contingencies [he would] be justified in responding affirmatively to the call of the members of the removed Government to restore them to power?"[71] In other words, Stevens wanted to know whether it might "be justifiable to use the United States forces here to restore the Government buildings here to the possession of the displaced officials," and, if so, "how far [he should] deviate from established international rules and precedents" in doing so?[72] A few months later, he apparently determined the latter issue to be irrelevant, announcing in a letter to Blaine's successor, John Foster, that, legal niceties notwithstanding, since the "value of the Hawaiian Islands to the United States for commercial and naval purposes has been well understood by American statesmen for more than half-a-century," the "golden hour is at hand" to completely "Americanize the islands" and "assume control over 'crown lands.' "[73]

Although there is no record of Stevens receiving an official go-ahead, it is instructive that he was neither replaced in his position nor instructed *not* to proceed with what was by late 1892 an open collaboration with the conspirators plotting to overthrow the Hawaiian government.[74] Instead, additional naval forces were posted to Pearl Harbor, and there is considerable evidence that Captain G.C. Wiltse, commander of the *Boston* and ranking U.S. military officer at the facility, also entered directly into the planning. Well before the fact, then, both the coup and the role American forces would play in it were already foregone conclusions.[75] Indeed, as Secretary of the Navy B.G. Tracy explained to Admiral Joseph Skerritt in December 1892, "the wishes of the [U.S.] government have changed over the past twenty years. They will [now] be very glad to annex Hawai'i."[76]

**Islands Under the Influence**

There can be no question but that those formulating and implementing U.S. policy vis-à-vis the "Hawaiian Revolution" were from the outset aware of the illegality marking their performance. Within weeks of the coup, former Georgia Congressman James Blount was dispatched to the islands by President Cleveland, charged with the "paramount responsibility" of investigating and documenting what had happened, as well as America's role in it. On July 17, 1893, Blount submitted a 700-page report, as excruciating in its detail as it was blistering in its assessment.[77] Both the Senate and the House compiled equally lengthy studies—the Senate document, usually referred to as the "Morgan Report," runs 809 pages—avoiding the sharp edge of Blount's conclusions, but replicating most of the record he'd compiled.[78] While much has been made of the fact that both Stevens and Wiltse were "sacked" on the basis of these findings, it should be noted that neither was criminally prosecuted and that both were already of retirement age.[79] Their being cashiered must thus be seen as amounting to no more than a sop designed to allay international protests expressed on Lili'uokalani's behalf.[80]

Such obfuscation notwithstanding, the meat of U.S. policy can be discerned in a backhanded confirmation of Stevens' "unauthorized" extension of "protectorate" status over the Kingdom by Secretary of State Foster on February 11, 1893,[81] and Cleveland's bestowal of recognition upon the conspirators' "provisional government" a few months later.[82] An even stronger indication will be found in the solid military and diplomatic support rendered by the U.S. to the Republic of Hawaii when, on January 16, 1895, Robert Wilcox led an attempt to physically remove the *haole* junta and reinstate Lili'uokalani.[83] Nor was the least official protest was raised when, once American arms had been used to crush the revolt, the queen herself was charged with "treason" and incarcerated for two years,[84] or the death penalty imposed upon Wilcox and other Kanaka Maoli nationalists (the sentences were ultimately commuted to 35 years imprisonment as part of a public relations gambit to demonstrate the junta's "humanitarian" characteristics).[85]

In substance, the official practice of saying one thing—as with Cleveland's earlier-mentioned denunciation of the "unprovoked act of war" embodied in the unseating of Lili'uokalani—while consciously steering a reverse course, allowed the U.S. to enjoy many of the benefits of seizing Hawai'i outright while evading the onus that would likely have accrued to such a maneuver.[86] Given the composition of the "revolutionary" junta itself, moreover—it consisted of fourteen Americans like Dole, Thurston and William R. Castle (of Castle and Cooke), as well as a German, an Englishman and a Scotsman, all "major business leaders" and decisively proannexationist[87]—American policymakers could be sure that a formalized takeover would be possible whenever it became convenient to the United States (i.e., at such time as international indignation over the 1893 coup had sufficiently subsided to make the transition a diplomatically uncomplicated affair).[88]

The matter was brought to a head more rapidly than anticipated, however, mainly because of the possibility that the junta might formally declare their "republic" neutral during America's 1898 war with Spain.[89] Since the U.S. fleet could not be legally operate from a neutral port—and it very much needed its Pearl Harbor facility as a base from which to proceed against the Philippines and other Spanish targets in the Pacific—annexation, despite considerable domestic opposition and irrespective of international opinion, was swiftly accomplished.[90] Two years later, on April 30, 1900, President William McKinley signed an Organic Act under which a territorial government was established, all traditionally-based laws nullified, and direct U.S. title asserted over all lands not already deeded to individuals or corporations (i.e., land owned by the Crown or government, per se; more than forty percent of the islands' total surface area).[91] Hawai'i was thus defined as an American jurisdiction, its property, like that of Puerto Rico and Guam, "domestic in a foreign sense" and therefore, like the indigenous nations of North America itself, subject to the plenary authority of the federal government.[92]

Freed of their "governmental responsibilities," and finally occupying the integral trade relationship to the U.S. they'd so long desired, Dole, Castle and other former junta members, along with the rest of the *haole* planter/merchant élite, were quick to capitalize.[93] "Annexation incited a burst of economic expansion. Thirteen spanking new plantations appeared, fueled by $40 million in new capital investment, the bulk of which continued to be locally generated. Land in sugarcane increased by 128,000 acres between 1900 and 1913."[94]

> Although sugar profits varied with the ups and downs of the market price (which were sometimes disturbingly low), there were sufficient years of plenty to offset the lean. In 1925, a bountiful year, Island sugar interests realized a $25 million profit on a $100 million crop. The Hawaiian Agricultural Company made a 30 percent profit in 1915, 67 percent in 1920, and 17 percent in 1925. An even larger Big Five Firm, Maui's Hawaiian Sugar and Commercial Company, sprawling over 35,000 acres and housing 3,200 workers, regularly returned a 20 percent profit to its stockholders. From 1894 through 1923 Castle and Cooke profits amounted to over $12 million, out of which over $6 million was paid as dividends—average yearly dividends being a most substantial 36.2 percent.[95]

There is simply no way to overstate the dominance exercised by the Big Five within the postannexation economy of Hawai'i. In 1914, "sugar accounted for $33.2 million in exports, followed by pineapples at $4.5 million; all remaining items taken together…did not come close to equaling the figure for pineapple."[96] By 1935, "sugar and pineapple exports…were $89.9 million out of a total figure of $94.5 million."[97] The degree to which U.S. rather than Hawaiian interests deformed the local economy was equally overwhelming.

> In 1914 the United States provided the market for over $40.6 million of a grand total of $42.5 million of Hawaiian exports. Two decades later, in fiscal 1935, Hawaiian exports to the United States had climbed to over $94.5 million, against exports to all foreign nations of $1.3 million. In return Hawaii's imports were almost entirely from the United States: using 1914 figures again…Hawaii imported $32.1 million worth of goods, $25.8 million of which was from the United States; in 1915 the figures were $69.2 million and $63.5 million… In 1913-14, breadstuffs, cotton clothing, oil, automobiles and parts, nails-pipes-spikes, lumber, tobacco, fertilizers, and dairy and hog products were (in that order) Hawaii's leading imports by dollar volume. The figures

reveal a society unable to feed itself or even to produce the basic capital goods necessary for its agro-industrial life.[98]

This combination of factors, indicative as they are of colonialism in its classic form,[99] served to radically inflate commodity prices in the islands, and thence profits accruing to the Big Five monopolists. In 1930, bread cost 10¢ per pound, butter 58¢ per pound, eggs 78¢ per dozen and milk 20¢ per quart in Honolulu, more than twice the price of identical foodstuffs in San Francisco.[100] Lumber, which in 1940 wholesaled for $15 per thousand board feet in California was wholesale-priced at $28.50 in Honolulu, and consumers ultimately paid $78.[101] Meanwhile, wages were driven through the floor, with adult plantation laborers paid $31 on average per month (children received on $6), cannery workers $21, construction workers $20, and longshoremen as little as $12.[102] Those at the bottom struggled to alter their situation, of course, but were met head-on with tactics drawn from the bloody "labor wars" unique to the United States.[103]

> In the 1930s, a time when Territorial delegate Joseph Farrington stood on the floor of the U.S. Congress eulogizing Hawaii as the "lighthouse of democracy in the Pacific," union organizers on the Hawaiian docks were beaten up and deported by thugs personally hired by Big Five lawyer Frank Thompson, and the Honolulu police (besides protecting these thugs) operated as crews to break a 1936 Honolulu-Hilo Inland Boatmen's strike, reporting to Castle and Cooke managers for orders.[104]

Such things were standard. In 1924, for example, planters on Kaua'i had utilized National Guard machinegunners to break a strike by Filipino field workers, killing six and wounding scores of others; the courts were then employed to send sixty strike leaders to prison for four years apiece.[105] On August 31, 1938, in another stunning example of state/corporate solidarity, police used gunfire and grenades to break up a peaceful strike of longshoremen on the Hilo docks, wounding 51.[106] At the legislative level, the U.S. model was also followed, as is witnessed by a "Criminal Syndicalism Act" passed in 1919, a 1921 law banning "anarchistic publications," and a 1923 "Anti-Picketing Act." In effect, labor was "denied by these laws the right of organizing publicly, of presenting its case before the public and of demonstrating its solidarity in times of crisis."[107] Any confusion on the matter was quickly dispelled by judges drawn exclusively from the *haole* élite. By 1937, things had reached such a pass that, as a member of the American Labor Relations Board observed, "If there is a truer picture of fascism in the world today than in the Hawaiian Islands, I do not know a definition of it."[108]

As for the Kanaks, dispossession was virtually complete, utter destitution ubiquitous. To be sure, the U.S. had put a cheery face on the situation for international consumption. The Hawaiian Homes Commission Act of 1920 supposedly guaranteed the indigenous people "homesteads" within the vast area impounded by the federal government as by-product of annexation.[109] Although some 194,000 acres were quickly — and with much fanfare — distributed by a commission established for this purpose, most of the parcels were in the highlands and, without irrigation and other costly improvements, entirely unsuited for agriculture. The law contained no provision for the kind of subsidy plainly necessary for the Kanaks to make use of their allotments.[110] A provision *was* included, however, allowing the commissioners to "re-lease" huge blocks of "Hawaiian Homes Land" to *haole* planters for as little as 2¢ per acre annually — Castle and Cooke alone gobbled up 95,000 acres in this fashion — as the native allottees predictably failed in their efforts to eke a living from their tiny plots.[111] Under these circumstances, "almost half the total land area in Hawaii was in the hands of 80 private owners" by 1940, while the "landless Hawaiians occupied shanties and hovels around Honolulu," their population plummeting to fewer than 25,000.[112]

Meanwhile, the U.S. was busily militarizing the portion of Hawai'i's landmass it had retained for its own usage. Aside from the Navy's Pearl Harbor facility, the first step in this process came with the establishment of the Army's Camp McKinley, near Diamond Head, in 1898. This was followed, in 1905, by the establishment of Fort DeRussy, also on O'ahu, and a year later, by Fort Ruger. In 1907 came Forts Armstrong and Shafter, in then, in 1908, the Schofield Barracks. 1913 saw the establishment of Fort Kamehameha, and 1933 Bellows Air Field. In 1934, the Pearl Harbor complex was expanded to accommodate the Lualualei Naval Magazine, and in 1937 the Army established Wheeler Air Field. In 1938, Hickham Air Field was added. During World War II, the Barber's Point Naval Air Station was established, while two entire valleys on O'ahu — Makua and Waikane — were converted into a bombing practice range and a live-fire training area for the Army and Marine Corps, respectively. After the war, in 1953, an entire island, Kaho'olawe, sacred to Kanaks, was "condemned" for use by the Navy as a gunnery range. By the time all was said and done, there were 46 major military installations encompassing approximately 500,000 acres in the archipelago.[113]

## The Statehood Scam

If anything, America's emergence at the end of the Second World War in a position of incipient global primacy dramatically increased Hawai'i's strategic importance to the United States. Although, even after the U.S. granted those islands their independence in 1946, Subic Bay and the Clark Air Station, in the Philippines,[114] continued to serve along with Guam, in the northern Marianas, as the key forward bases in what would soon be known as the "Pacific Rim Strategy" for first "containing," then "rolling back...the spread of communism in Asia," Hawai'i constituted *the* geographic hub for the entire Far Eastern theater of operations.[115] The military's doctrinal emphasis upon retaining its massive facilities there, and the magnitude of its investment in expanding and refining the capacity of these bases for both communications and "force projection" purposes, therefore increased steadily during the 1940s and '50s.[116]

Economically, too, the former Kingdom's significance was amplified tremendously. Arguably, the military dimension of U.S. containment/rollback policy was itself harnessed to the aspirations of U.S. business leaders to realize a collective vision of converting all the Pacific into an "American lake" from which profits would accrue at previously unheard of levels.

> After 1945, a capitalism undergoing an unprecedented expansion in its productive and distributive capacity, and consequently in dire need of huge new resource inputs and markets, found it imperative to integrate the Pacific Basin into the world economy to an extent unimaginable before the war... Although exploitation of Pacific resources had occurred for half a millennium, and had intensified with the development of the world capitalist system, it still lacked the comprehensive and systematic character it took on after World War II. Now Pacific Basin oil, rubber, hardwoods, copper, tin, uranium, etc., together with factory girls assembling electrical components in Panang and Taiwan and hundreds of millions of eager consumers from Seoul to Sumatra [beckoned]... U.S. corporations...recognizing the commercial opportunities presented by an area of 14.1 million square miles [and] containing two-thirds of the world's population...formed the leading wedge of international capital into the Pacific.[117]

In 1950, U.S. corporate investment in Asia was only $1 billion. The figure in 1970 was $5.56 billion, not counting $3.49 billion plowed into infrastructural development in Oceania, and in 1976, $11.4 billion. By the latter year, overall return on investments in the Far East reached 25.5 percent, a matter prompting an even greater and more rapid infusion of capital into the region.[118] Once again, Hawai'i's geographic location, aptly symbolized in the "East-West Center" situated within its university,[119] served to make it a natural hub for broader U.S. operations in the Pacific. Hence, beginning with a $70 million outlay by Henry J. Kaiser (founder of the Permanente Corp.) in 1954, American banks and corporations began to invest heavily in Hawaiian enterprises.[120] By the end of the decade, U.S. firms had acquired many of the assets previously owned by the Big Five—the pattern would be repeated during the early-60s with Dilco, another major local player[121]—while the sugar and pineapple interests employed the resulting liquidity to buy themselves a place at the transnational table.

Castle and Cooke, for example, while selling off many of its local holdings, and transferring much of it pineapple production to the cheaper terrain of the Philippines, used the proceeds—along with considerable international financing—to buy up agribusiness concerns in Central America, Brazil and California, as well as more diversified enterprises (e.g., a pipe manufacturing company in Thailand). The resulting multinationalized corporation, whose antecedent generated about $10 million in revenues in 1947, was by 1973 an amalgam worth about $1 billion.[122] The success of Amfac—once the Big Five company, Hackfield—has been even more spectacular. Still only a $100 million plantation complex in 1967, it had grown into a multinational conglomerate with $1.4 billion in sales a decade later. Between 1968 and 1973 it indulged in a frenzied buying spree in which it acquired upwards of *fifty* smaller corporations, mostly in the U.S., and shortly numbered its subsidiaries at over a hundred.[123]

> Even the two smallest Big Five corporations have expanded overseas... Theo Davies holds a myriad of appliance and light manufacturing companies in the Philippines, while Alexander and Baldwin owns the largest processing company for tropical hardwoods in Southeast Asia, with 250,000 acres of timber in Indonesia and factories in Taiwan, Singapore, Hong Kong, and Malaysia.[124]

The islands' two major financial institutions, First Hawaiian Bank and Bank of Hawaii (shortly renamed Bank of the Pacific), followed a more or less parallel trajectory. Bringing in high-powered executives like future Bank of America president Rudolph Peterson, Bank of Hawaii utilized its new capital along with a range of third country financing schemes to underwrite a series of investments throughout the Pacific Basin, doubling its earnings between 1954 and '59.[125] First Hawaiian had done the same, meanwhile establishing branch offices in Guam, Tonga, Micronesia, and a number of other locations.[126] Both banks simultaneously plunged substantial amounts into acquiring state-of-the-art computer systems and other automated banking technology.[127] So swift was the transition from the relaxed atmosphere of plantation banking to the frenetic environment of international finance that by the early–60s Hawai'i was already being referred to as "the Switzerland of the Pacific."[128]

Thus, by the mid-to-late 1950s, the process was well underway by which the "traditional" *haole* economy of Hawai'i was completely subsumed and redeployed as a component in preliminary U.S. globalization initiatives, the archipelago itself redefined as a meeting place/playground for the world's corporate élite doubling as world class tourist destination.[129] The only real fly in the ointment concerned the illegitimate nature of America's purported ownership of/jurisdiction over the islands, a problem deriving not simply from the specifics of America's historical interaction with the Hawaiian Kingdom but, somewhat paradoxically, from the broader design through which U.S. strategists had set out to fulfill their dream of placing the United States in a position of unfettered planetary ascendancy.[130]

At the founding meeting of the United Nations it sponsored in San Francisco in 1945, the U.S. had, in the name of preventing "the scourge of war" and "reaffirm[ing] faith in fundamental human rights…the dignity and worth of the human person…the equal rights of men and women, and of nations large and small [while] promot[ing] social progress and better standards of life in larger freedom," endeavored to concretize elements of international law which would serve to preclude reconstruction of the old European empires with which it might otherwise have to compete in the postwar environment.[131] This took the form, as articulated in Article 1(2) and 55 of the U.N. Charter, of guaranteeing the right of self-determination to *all* peoples.[132] Consequently, Chapters XI (applying to overt colonies like "French" Indochina and the "Belgian" Congo) and XII (applying to somewhat more ambiguously administered "mandate" or "trust" territories) of the Charter were explicitly framed to "bring the Colonial world generally within the sphere of international responsibility."[133]

Procedurally, as explained in Chapter XI of the Charter, it was legally required that all such "non-self-governing territories" (colonies) be inscribed by the administering power (colonizer) on a list maintained by the U.N. Secretariat, which would then receive regular reports concerning the progress made towards the "timely realization of self-government" in each case.[134] Self-government, construed as being in many respects synonymous with the exercise of self-determination, was interpreted as the attainment of full and complete independence by each country/people inscribed on the

Secretariat's list from the country administering it.[135] In cases where arrangements other than complete independence were proposed as the outcome of the "self-determining process," the Secretariat was charged with the responsibility of ensuring that it was the colonized rather than the "administering authority" who proposed it, and that the latter had neither coerced nor manipulated the result.[136] Finally, in cases where colonizers openly refused to grant independence to their colonial subjects, the Secretariat incurred the responsibility of undertaking such measures as were necessary to compel compliance with the law.[137]

Placing such emphasis upon the right of self-determination in its Charter has been rightly described as "one of the most significant, and in a sense also the most revolutionary, steps accomplished" in the entire history of the United Nations.[138] Certainly, this is true with respect to the decolonization of much of Africa, South/Southeast Asia and other parts of the Third World.[139] On the other hand, it afforded the U.S. an extraordinarily lucrative opportunity to move into the power vacuums created thereby, asserting a more indirect and for the most part more efficient neocolonial form of economic hegemony over Europe's former colonies.[140] Given the role Hawai'i was envisioned as playing in America's gambit along the Pacific Rim, however, such relatively defused means of asserting dominance were plainly insufficient. In those islands, it was essential that U.S. control continued to be quite direct. The question was how, given the lofty principles enshrined at the behest of U.S. statesmen in international law, to cast an aura of legality over the situation.[141]

The answer, seriously proposed as early as 1947, and again in both 1950 and 1953, was to make Hawai'i a State of the Union.[142] The means of doing so, finally undertaken in 1958, was to conduct an islands-wide referendum in which the only alternatives posed were whether voters desired statehood or a continuation of trust status.[143] No option of returning to the pre-1893 reality of constitutional monarchy or assuming some other form of independent Kanaka Maoli existence was presented.[144] Still more to the point, the electorate casting ballots was defined to include not only the Kanaks, but the *haole* settler population and a significant segment of the imported Asian population as well.[145] Unsurprisingly, under the circumstances, statehood was approved at the polls on June 27, 1959. Hawai'i was thereupon declared to be the fiftieth U.S. state and withdrawn from the Secretariat's list of non–self-governing territories (on which it had appeared since 1946).[146]

Although, so long as it remained unscrutinized, the "Hawaiian Plebiscite" was enough to provide the desired patina of legitimation over U.S. retention, it had actually been conducted in flagrant violation of the requirements posited in the UN Charter. Most conspicuously, this involved the inclusion of non-Kanaka voters in the referendum despite the stipulation under Chapter XI of the Charter that "*only* the indigenous population [emphasis added]" was eligible to decide such matters.[147] By virtue of the interpretation of Chapter XI advanced in General Assembly Resolution 742 (VIII),[148] moreover, "selection of an alternative to independence, especially if that alternative is a union or association with the former 'colonial parent,' [should have been] viewed with a jaundiced eye."[149]

> The insistence on independence "without any conditions or reservations" is also based on the rejection of the concept of trusteeship, and the unwillingness of the majority of the states to, as it were, consent to the fruits of assimilationist policies implemented under the guise of the trusteeship principle. There was a general suspicion on the part of the most ardent supporters of decolonization that the choice of a dependent people for any stakes other than independence was not genuine but rather the result of colonial machination.[150]

Since any such outcome as that obtaining in Hawai'i was/is, by law, "deemed to be inherently reversible rather than final," the UN itself was obligated to defer removal of Hawai'i from the Secretariat's list until a full investigation of the referendum procedure had been completed.[151] The extent to which this was so is revealed in the General Assembly's rejection of the attempt by France, using a referendum procedure not dissimilar to that employed by the U.S. in Hawai'i, to incorporate Algeria into its "home compartment" in 1954.[152] So, too, the argument put forth by Portugal from 1955 onward that, since Portuguese law applied as much to its colonial subjects as to its citizens, the peoples indigenous to colonies like Angola and Mozambique should be considered "assimilado," their territories "integral parts of the nation," and the colonies themselves thus sharing "in the independence" of the Portuguese state.[153] Instructively, both Algeria and the Portuguese colonies remained inscribed on the Secretariat's list until genuine decolonization occurred.

**"Focal Point of the Pacific"**

With the stability attending statehood in hand, the islands' new Democratic governor, John Burns, moved rapidly to fulfill the a campaign pledge his Republican predecessor, William Quinn, had made in 1957 to realize Hawai'i's "destiny as the focal point of the Pacific."[154] Following up on the $260 million expended by Quinn on projects like the Kona Airport over the preceding two years, Burns announced on the day he took office that he planned a $490 million "civic improvement program," to be funded primarily by bond sales, with an "emphasis on communications, transportation, and recreational facilities, [as well as] the opening of the windward side of O'ahu to intensive suburban development."[155] Within months, banks like Chase Manhattan and Wells Fargo were snapping up the bond issues in $10 million increments, thereby acquiring a controlling interest in the fiftieth state's evolving "infrastructure."[156] The trend continued for the rest of the decade.

> In October 1963, for instance, a Bank of America consortium purchased $39.6 million worth of state bonds, while a Chase Manhattan syndicate snapped up $15 million of a subsequent issue. Between 1958 and 1968, the state's outstanding public bonds increased sharply, from $212 million to $528.9 million, while an average of $48 million in bonds was sold annually between 1960 and 1967.[157]

Revenues were of course increasingly accruing from other sources as well. In late 1959—that is, the moment much of the Hawaiian Crown Land held by the federal government was transferred to the state—Quinn had proclaimed a "Second Mahele," opening 175,000 acres to sale for as much as $1,000 per acre (obviously pricing the impoverished Kanaks out of the market from the outset).[158] Taken in combination with the sell-off of Big Five plantation property occurring at the same time, this maneuver precipitated something of a land rush by U.S. financial institutions: "by the end of 1963 giants like Equitable (with $46 million invested in Hawaii), Prudential ($44 million), New York Life ($25 million), and Occidental Life ($25 million) had substantial holdings in the tourism-land development sector."[159] During the early-70s, hotel chains—primarily Sheraton, Hyatt, Inter-Continental, Holiday Inns, Western International and Ramada Inns—teamed up with the financiers to launch a blitz of hotel, resort and "leisure community" construction throughout the islands, spending nearly $1 billion to more than quadruple the number of rooms available while assuming control over about 75 percent of the "visitor industry."[160] By 1980, another eleven "tourist destination" schemes were in the works, involving the construction of a further 18,000 rooms and 33,000 "timeshare" residential units.[161] All this, in turn, caused an almost vertical climb in real estate prices, paralleled rather closely by an influx to state coffers of monies from land sales and property taxes.

Intense speculation pushed the price of Kaanapali Whaler one-bedroom condominium units up from $86,000 in 1975 to $534,000 four years later. At Kapalua Bay Villas, condominium apartments increased from $135,000 to $500,000 between 1976 and 1979… As one realtor summed up at the time, "Condominiums are running wild. It's like the Alaska Gold Rush… Prices have escalated so fast it's impossible to keep up with the market" … Alex Napier, a member of the State Land Use Commission [rezoned his own land to accommodate resort construction] increasing its value *116 times* [emphasis original].[162]

Adding tremendously to the state treasury was a massive and steadily increasing gush of funds from sales and room taxes, airport fees and the like attending the burgeoning flow of tourists (less than 250,000 in 1958, over 429,000 in 1963, 2,630,000 a decade later, and *seven million* two decades after that).[163] Revenues from income tax also became increasingly significant as the corporate investors' luxury housing sprawls attracted a new and highly affluent "resident population" of *haoles*. During the 1980s, the population of Moloka'i, which had been just over 5,000 in 1975, swelled by 30,000; Castle and Cooke's "development" project on Lana'i tripled that island's population during the same period; the situation elsewhere was similar, if somewhat less pronounced.[164] Among other things, this served to drive the price of even the most basic commodities through the roof; by 1980, the cost-of-living in Hawai'i was running 20-25 percent higher than the U.S. average (homes by then cost $169,107; *triple* the U.S. average; by 1990, the average price of a single family dwelling on O'ahu had swollen to $352,000).[165]

Of those who'd lived in prestatehood Hawai'i, native and non-native alike, fully 95 percent found themselves unable to buy or retain a house by 1981; in the same year, on O'ahu, one-third of all such families were paying out more than 35 percent of their monthly income to rent whatever might be available.[166] One reason for this was that a large segment of the population at issue was unable to find gainful employment of any sort. In 1966, Governor Burns had trumpeted—as is always the case with those promoting corporate "development"—that that the official policy of using massive public outlays to "stimulate capital investment" would in short order "assure a job to every citizen willing and able to work."[167] The reality was that, between 1947 and 1974, unemployment in Hawai'i *quadrupled*.[168] Of those who could find any sort of work by the latter year, a lopsided majority— forty percent of all employed Kanaks, for instance—had been forced into the most menial and low-paid service jobs (hotel workers earned an average of $73.58 per week in 1967, workers in laundries even less).[169] Even fulltime workers—and most hotel jobs were/are part-time (a handy corporate expedient to avoiding the costs of health insurance, etc.)—often received wages falling well below the poverty line.[170]

Then, in 1975, the bubble of Hawai'i's much-leveraged "economic miracle" abruptly burst. By then, the state had amassed more than $900 million in debt because of its unending "infrastructural improvements," the service on which was expanding rapidly—from $35 million in 1971 to $92 million in 1976—as many of its earlier bond issues began to come due.[171] The official unemployment rate stood at nine percent—every week, 2,000 workers exhausted their benefits—and the annual bill in this connection had risen to $78.2 million.[172] From there, welfare took over, to the tune of $190 million (at least fifteen percent of Hawai'i's population had no other income by that point).[173] While returns accruing to the banks and corporations that had taken over the islands' economy remained quite handsome—in 1973, the profit rate associated with tourism was 17.45 percent, real estate a staggering 105 percent[174]—the financial position of the state government that had so lavishly subsidized their doing so quickly reached the brink of insolvency.

In 1975, a banking cartel assembled for the purpose by First Hawaiian Bank president John Bellinger loaned the state $235 million to see it through its crisis, but, adhering to the model established by the World Bank and International Monetary Fund for application to the Third World, did so only on the basis of a quid pro quo in which the government would exercise "fiscal responsibility" by adhering to a "budget ceiling."[175] The mechanics of just such an "austerity program" had already been worked out by Governor George Ariyoshi, who'd succeeded Burns when he'd fallen gravely ill a year earlier. In 1974, Ariyoshi prevailed upon the legislature to pass laws denying unemployment benefits to any worker who quit or was fired from his/her job, regardless of mitigating circumstances.[176] A partial flat grant statute was also effected, reducing welfare benefits to two-thirds of the state's recipients, while other legislation converted much of the remainder into "workfare." By 1976, "2,976 recipients found themselves working in parks, schools, and other state facilities with none of the monetary or fringe benefits of unionized state workers doing the same jobs, and without any job security."[177] Funding was also cut to the point that Hawai'i dropped to forty-sixth among the fifty states in terms of proportional revenues devoted to higher education.[178]

Meanwhile, the tax burden on working people, already one of the heaviest in the U.S., was also increased through extraordinarily retrogressive measures which left people earning less than $3,000 per year paying an average of 15.85 percent in income tax while for those bringing in $25,000 or more the average was only 11.26 percent.[179] Well before the end of the decade, such circumstances had prompted a marked outflow of Hawai'i's prestatehood *haole* residents and their offspring, as "regular folks" fled the islands for the continental U.S. in search of jobs and a lower cost of living.[180] The Kanaks, whose numbers were officially estimated to have declined to 7,186 by 1980,[181] and the depths of whose impoverishment had long generated some of the worst health and longevity data among "U.S. population groups,"[182] were in large part forced to try and live in parks and along the beaches (from which they were often driven by police on the premise that they constituted an "unsightly nuisance," disturbing to tourists).[183]

To be sure, such austerity did not apply to programs mainly of use to the tourism establishment. Even as the legislature was taking out huge loans, slashing social service and education programs, and burying Hawai'i's poorest citizens under a load of new taxes, it was spending $80 million to build another runway at Honolulu International Airport, another $30 on the Hilo Airport, and approving construction of the TH-3 highway on O'ahu.[184] Simultaneously, it was offering "tax incentives"—that is, exemption from taxes—as well as rent-free use of state lands and waivers of environmental protection standards as "enticements" to a whole new wave of corporate profiteering.[185] With American capital increasingly flowing into the development of tourism complexes in the Caribbean and southern Mexico, as well as Tahiti, Fiji and Guam,[186] Ariyoshi and his colleagues turned more and more to "foreign" investors, primarily Japanese firms, to launch new projects.[187]

By the early-80s, the influx of such capital totaled some $3 billion, as Kokusai Osana bought out Sheraton's Hawaiian holdings and once again "reconfigured" Waikiki, while the Asahi Development Corp. plunged heavily into the construction of new tourist centers on Mau'i, Kaua'i and the Big Island of Hawai'i.[188] All the while, the number of Japanese electing to "visit" Hawai'i climbed precipitously: in 1970, there were 120,000; in 1972, 235,000; in 1975, 455,000; by 1990, nearly 2.5 million.[189] Given the degree of vertical integration evident in Japanese business enterprises and the Ariyoshi administration's "investment incentive packages," however, most of this contributed very little to the state's economy, per se.

> The vast majority of Japanese tourists (81 percent in 1971) come to Hawaii on prepaid package tours of four-to-six or six-to-eight days, arrive and depart via Japan Airlines,

stay in Japanese-owned hotels, and tour Hawaii with Kintetsu International, a Japanese tour operator. A fair proportion of retail trade is carried on in Japanese-owned department stores [since] investments in tourism are only the most obvious of the Japanese holdings, which include banks, automobile [dealerships and rental agencies], camera dealerships, the market for polyester fibers, and large retail and shopping centers.[190]

Very much the same is true for more upscale operations.

For the new monied class of Japanese corporate executives, there is a range of luxury amenities, including a half-dozen Japanese-owned golf courses, the most luxurious of which is the Honolulu International Country Club, "an exclusive club with plush facilities and an immaculately manicured 18-hole golf course," complete with thick English carpets and Italian stained glass ceilings. Memberships sell for $12,000 each. And for those affluent enough to afford a "piece of the rock," Asahi Development Corporation offers its Waikiki condominium units on the Tokyo market for a quarter of a million dollars each.[191]

As was observed in a 1977 issue of *Economic World*, the Japanese system extends to construction. "When Kenji Osana decided to expand his two hotels, he brought in a close corporate ally, the Ohbayashi Construction Company. Seibu, another Japanese conglomerate, [used] one of its subsidiaries, the largest landscaping firm in Japan, to landscape its huge residential-resort complex at Makena, Maui, and...another to build the hotel."[192] Self-evidently, then, for all the "incentives" underwritten by Hawaiian taxpayers, "Japanese tourism operations [like their U.S. counterparts vis-à-vis the continental United States] have contributed only to the development of the Japanese economy and to the profits of Japanese corporations, along with a few local allies" like John Bellinger's First Hawaiian Bank and the fat cats infesting the state legislature.[193]

By the 1990s, Hawai'i had, just as William Quinn and other proponents of statehood predicted, become "the focal point of the Pacific." Not only does it remain the centerpiece of America's military presence throughout the region, its economy, in which "every enterprise...from the department stores to the hotels to the paper company to the utilities to the bakery, is controlled by overseas capital" has become a preeminent generator of the profits used to replicate the "miracle" it embodies elsewhere in the Pacific and beyond.[194] The islands have become, as well, the locale of choice for the world's corporate élites—not just American and Japanese executives, but their associates from other quarters—to congregate informally, relaxing and socializing in true colonial opulence while plotting their latest imperial undertakings. All supposed "benefits of statehood" to the contrary notwithstanding, the situation in Hawai'i thus remains essentially what it's been all along, the conditions evident there far more akin to those typically associated with "a Third World nation than a state of the United States."[195]

## Ka Lahui Hawai'i

By the mid–70s, there were signs that the Kanaka Maoli had had enough. Probably the first overt indication that an organized resistance was once again beginning to congeal came in February 1973, when Charles Maxwell, head of a newly-formed Hawaiian rights group called the Aloha Association, advanced an agenda centering on recovery of the sacred island of Kaho'olawe from the Navy.[196] On January 3, 1976, the Aloha's demands were for the first time punctuated by the physical occupation of Kaho'olawe by a group of Kanaks, a pattern of action that continued and gained intensity over the next several years despite—or because of—the loss at sea on March 6, 1977 of two of the group's major leaders, George Helm and James Kimo Mitchell, while they were trying to reach the island during a storm.[197] By 1980, moreover, the Aloha had both broadened its outlook to include a wide range of indigenous issues and spun off several organizations committed to confronting such things as the TH-3 highway construction project and new resort development head on.[198]

As a National Institutes of Health team studying "ethnic Hawaiians" discovered to its surprise in 1980, these "New Hawaiians" were as a rule quite "serious about their struggle over the absorption of their land. They expressed a willingness to fight by any means necessary. There is definitely a strong potential for violence."[199] In actuality, however—although they were well aware of their legal prerogative as "a people forcibly deprived of the right of self-determination, freedom and independence by a…colonial and racist regime [involving] foreign occupation" to employ armed force, including methods otherwise proscribed under the rubric of "terrorism," to liberate themselves from their circumstances[200]—the Kanaka activists were moving in an altogether different direction. This was heralded in 1977, when in August a young Hawaiian Studies professor, Haunani-Kay Trask, already a leading figure in the struggle for Kanaka self-determination, participated in the so-called Indian Summer in Geneva, a conference at which representatives of ninety-eight indigenous nations made preliminary presentations concerning their peoples' circumstances to the United Nations Subcommittee on Racism and Decolonization (a component of the UN Commission on Human Rights).[201]

In 1981, as a follow-up to the 1977 conference, the UN formed the Working Group on Indigenous Populations as a subpart of its Economic and Social Council (ECOSOC) and mandated it both to make global studies of the conditions prevailing among indigenous peoples—an aspect of which process was to conduct biannual meetings at which native delegations could report on developments within their territories, make recommendations concerning remedies, and, under certain circumstances, request direct UN intervention—and to draft a Universal Declaration on the Rights of Indigenous Peoples (see Appendix C).[202] While Trask and other Kanaka activists continued to serve as delegates to the UN proceedings,[203] her sister, Mililani, took the lead in forging a viable nationalist organization. This resulted, in 1987, in the founding of Ka Lahui Hawai'i, by far the most broadly based and politically effective such entity in more than a century.[204]

With Mililani Trask serving as *kia'aina* (governor), Ka Lahui, moved swiftly to galvanize Kanaka Maoli throughout the islands as citizens of their own polity, employing traditional genealogical criteria rather than *haole*-imposed "blood quantum standards" in determining the composition of its con-stituency.[205] This move compelled recognition in the 1990 U.S. Census of the fact that there were actually 138,742 Native Hawaiians rather than the fewer than 10,000 officially recorded only a decade earlier.[206] Casting off the shack-les of governmental "low counting" allowed the Kanaks to develop a certain critical mass in their own right, forging alliances on an equal footing with local environmental and antidevelopment organizations for the first time and thereby gaining an ability to strategically engage in a bit of electoral muscle-flexing.

> The hugely successful campaign to save Oahu's Sandy Beach from unsightly develop-ment was one straw in the wind. The intense debate (and 1992 rejection of) a waste-ful and unneeded fixed rail system in Honolulu marked the first setback for unlimited growth on Oahu. On Maui, Kauai, and the Big Island, proponents of limited growth and environmental concerns...challenged airport-road expansion, gained popular sup-port, and captured public offices. Lanaians for Sensible Growth have emerged to chal-lenge...enclave resort plans there. Running on an antidevelopment-grassroots democracy-community-based economics platform, Hawaii's fledgling Greens Party did surprisingly well in the 1992 election.[207]

On January 17, 1993—the 100th anniversary of Queen Lili'uokalani's overthrow—a truly massive "sovereignty march" by Ka Lahui and its supporters was conducted through downtown Honolulu, ending in a rally of over 15,000 people at the Iolani Palace.[208] It was under these circumstances that the U.S. "apology" to the Kanaka Maoli was issued. By then, Ka Lahui had joined with a smaller sovereigntist organization, Ka Pakaukau, headed by Dr. Kekuni Blaisdell, to convene an International People's Tribunal composed of prominent legal scholars and human rights activists from around the world to receive evidence and hear testimony on-site in Hawai'i.[209] The hearing/investigation process, carried out under provision of UN Resolution 1503 (XLVIII) in July 1993, resulted in an interim report summarizing the pattern of U.S. illegality in the islands and unequivocally affirming the right of the Kanaks to resume a fully self-determining existence.[210] A much more comprehensive and detailed Report of Findings and Recommendations was transmitted to the Working Group a year later.[211]

In 1995, responding to an islands-wide poll indicating that well over half of all Kanaks actively favored a such an initiative—and that almost none opposed it—Ka Lahui crafted a Master Plan for the resumption of outright Kanaka Maoli sovereignty (*Ho'okupu a Ka Lahui Hawai'i*).[212] While accepting the 1993 Congressional Apology on its face, the plan clarified the ingredients of the "reconciliation" called for by U.S. legislators as a matter of public law.

1. Final resolution of the historic claims relating to the overthrow; to state and federal misuse of Native trust lands and resources; to violations of human and civil rights; and to federally held lands and resources.
2. Termination of the U.S. policy of nonrecognition of Native Hawaiian self-determination, including repudiation of the policy of wardship.
3. Federal recognition of Ka Lahui Hawai'i as the indigenous sovereign Hawaiian Nation, including recognition of the jurisdiction of Ka Lahui Hawai'i over its national assets, lands, and natural recourses.
4. A commitment to decolonize Hawai'i through the United Nations process for non-self-governing territories.
5. Restoration of traditional lands, natural resources, ocean and energy resources to the Ka Lahui National Land Trust. These lands include the Hawaiian home lands, the ceded lands, and federally held lands. These lands shall be segregated from other public lands. [213]

In substance, the Ka Lahui Master Plan demands restoration of the Kanaka right to function as a "nation within a nation" exercising sovereign jurisdiction over some 1.6 million acres—including the 200,000 acres of Hawaiian Homes Land they were supposed to have retained all along—all of it subject to reparation of damages done during the years of the Kanaks' dispossession, and with adequate compensation for damage that proves irreparable.[214] Among the many specific parcels at issue is Kaho'olawe, "the most shot-at island in the Pacific," which, under a 1980 consent decree resulting from litigation undertaken by native activist Noa Emmett Aluli, is in the process of environmental restoration and is scheduled to be "returned" to the State of Hawaii (which has never for a moment possessed it).[215]

Predictably, the U.S. has made no official response to the *Ho'okupu*, opting instead to try and divert attention to the "self-determining" functions of the state's own Office of Hawaiian Affairs (OHA), and a blatantly cooptive "Hawaiian Autonomy Act" put forth by the state legislature in the form of a 1998 referendum.[216] Ka Lahui responded with a "tarot-roots organizing campaign" of such effectiveness that not only was the Act itself overwhelmingly voted down, but the state was forced, in 2001, to appoint Mililani Trask herself to the board overseeing the OHA.[217] Ka Lahui, meanwhile, has set about actualizing aspects of its "Four Arenas of Sovereignty" program,[218] primarily by pursuing reestablishment of the bases for Kanaka Maoli self-sufficiency: by once again placing hundreds of acres in tarot and breadfruit cultivation,[218] for example, and resurrecting some of the traditional fish ponds that had long fallen into disuse and disrepair.[219] Community control has been asserted over several schools, making instruction in the Hawaiian language a priority,[220] and revitalization of traditional spiritual/health care practices is well underway.[221] In some instances, entire communities have been reconstituted on their customary sites, with or without permission of *haole* "authorities."[222]

### The Responsibility of the United Nations to Native Hawaiians

To date, despite the clarity of the 1993 U.S. admission of culpability and the sovereigntists' submission of a corroborating report prepared by a legally authorized tribunal in 1995, the Kanaks have received even less response to their demands for justice from the United Nations than they have from the United States. The UN's silence in the matter is peculiar, to say the least — "inexcusable," might well be a better word choice — given its many reiterations of the guarantee of self-determination to *all* peoples as a cardinal principle of international law, adherence to which is essential if international peace and security are to be maintained.[223] As has been mentioned, and as is abundantly confirmed in the tribunal report, there can be no question but that the conferral of statehood upon Hawai'i in 1959 involved "conduct of a [colonizing power] which does not promote, but which hinders, the process towards independent [nation]hood, or is expressly aimed at its obstruction," and was thus in 1959 "qualified already [even before the vote was taken] as being contrary to the rules of international law."[224] The obligation of the United Nations to take corrective action is thus manifest.

It must be borne in mind when considering the situation that, as was also mentioned earlier, the "self" in "self-determination" refers to "colonized peoples and countries," the victims of "colonial exploitation [as well as] colonial and alien domination," *not* the settler populations of alien colonizers who have exploited them.[225] The principle applies not only to such glaring examples as those the French attempted in Algeria and the Portuguese in Angola and Mozambique.[226] It was on this basis that the UN rejected self-government by the settler population of the former British colony of Rhodesia (now Zimbabwe).[227] Similarly, in 1986, when it was discovered that a settler population outnumbering the indigenous population of New Caledonia (Kanaky) had dominated the "the process of self-determination" in that French colony to keep it in a subordinate relationship with France, it was reinscribed on the list of non–self-governing territories.[228] In each instance, the "assumption is patent that expatriates' [settlers'] wishes should be accorded relatively little weight."[229]

It might be argued that these are improper analogies, that the U.S. "resolution" of its "Hawaiian Problem" had far more in common with that of Great Britain in its former colonies of Bermuda and Ceylon (Sri Lanka), where UN oversight bodies approved participation of settler populations in the processes of self-determination. In Bermuda, however, the UN's Special Committee on Decolonization effected extraordinary measures to prevent the "expatriate vote" from having a decisive influence on determining the island's political destiny.[230] In Sri Lanka, where the settlers were not even British, but Tamils relocated there from southern India by the colonizers, a special arrangement was nonetheless effected to leave the island's indigenous people with the decisive voice in the outcome (after independence, the Sri Lankans disenfranchised the "Estate Tamils" altogether).[231] In neither example, unlike Hawai'i, were settlers allowed to ignore or override the preferences of the native population.

Actually, the closest parallel to Hawai'i might turn out to be Malta, where, prompted by the same sorts of strategic considerations as the U.S.,

Britain attempted to claim that it had legally integrated a remote colony into itself after World War II. Although Malta was consequently removed from the Secretariat's list of non-self-governing territories in 1949, a 1959 constitutional crisis exposed the nature of the manipulation by which island's process of self-determination had been subverted, and it was therefore reinscribed by the United Nations. Ultimately, in 1964, the Maltese opted for complete independence from the British Empire.[232] This outcome should prove instructive with respect to Hawai'i (it might in fact serve as a template).

In any event, the U.S. can plead no "mitigating circumstances" in the fact that the United Nations failed to exercise meaningful oversight authority during the run-up to Hawaiian statehood. Although the UN may indeed have been remiss in not directly supervising the application of proper decolonization procedures during the Hawaiian plebiscite, the examples of Malta and New Caledonia plainly demonstrate that this in no sense confirms the results of such travesties. Absent direct United Nations oversight, administering states are themselves required to observe the "strictest" standards in implementing the process of self-determination within the territories they administer.[234] Failure of the administering state to uphold such standards, as was patently the case in Hawai'i, serves to invalidate both the process and its outcome.[235]

There really are no legitimate counterarguments the U.S. can advance. Certainly, it cannot pretend that its retention of Hawai'i falls within the Charter's protection of "the territorial integrity of all states," a premise with which the federal government has sought to nullify the self-determining claims of American Indian peoples encapsulated within its continental boundaries, both because the very word "integrity" presupposes that the territory protected was in some sense legitimately acquired in the first place, and because Hawai'i is self-evidently *not* integral to the U.S. territorial corpus (real or pretended).[236] Rather the archipelago is separated from North America by far more than the thirty miles of "open blue water" required under UN Resolution 1514 (XV)—the "Declaration on the Granting of Independence to Colonial Countries and Peoples" enunciated by the General Assembly in 1960—to qualify as a colony by even the strictest (or most arbitrary) definition.[237]

Nor can the issue be fudged by postulations that since "the world has changed a lot over the past 110 years," the U.S. has "naturally" come to enjoy the option of redefining its relationship to the Kanaka Maoli in terms more "realistic" than those implied in its repeated recognition, through treaty ratifications, that they were a sovereign *national* entity.[238] It has long been a matter of settled law that no nation, having duly recognized the sovereignty of another, holds the prerogative of unilaterally withdrawing that recognition.[239] Similarly settled in law are the principles that an illegal occupation can never be legitimated by the unilateral decrees of the occupying power, and that the mere duration of such an occupation, no matter how longterm, serves neither to legitimate it nor to nullify the *de jure* sovereignty of the occupied country.[240] In this sense, the U.S. presence in Hawai'i resembles nothing so much as the "permanent aggression" displayed by Portugal in its 450-year occupation of Goa.[241]

Hence, both because of the illegalities embodied in its behavior during the 1893 coup d'etat in and subsequent annexation of Hawai'i, to which it has openly admitted, and with respect to the illegalities involved in its manipulation of the process by which Hawai'i became a state, to which it has not owned up, the U.S. is liable under international tort law.[242] Since commission of an international tort involves a clear duty to make restitution[243]— both *restitutio integrum* (restoration of the former legal situation) and *restitutio in natura* (returning of something wrongfully taken to its original owner)[244]—the Kanaka Maoli are plainly entitled to relief of the sort specified in the Ka Lahui Hawai'i Master Plan.[245] Since no such remedies can be expected to obtain through the workings of U.S. domestic courts—to the contrary, as was recently demonstrated by the Supreme Court decision in *Rice v. Cayetano*, a precisely opposite result may be invariably anticipated[246]— it is incumbent upon the UN to meet its obligation, expressed in its own Charter, to intervene for purposes of effecting a just resolution.

The place to begin in this regard would of course be for the Secretariat to follow the precedent set in 1986 with regard to New Caledonia, reinscribing Hawai'i on the list of non–self-governing territories.[247] This would afford the United States an opportunity to finally discharge its legal responsibilities to the Kanaka Maoli in a manner consistent with its station as an administering state, or "obligatee," as such entities are sometimes described. Here, it must be borne in mind that the U.S. will in no sense be making disposition of "a part of itself."

> The territory of a colony or other Non-Self-Governing Territory has, under the Charter, a status separate and distinct from the territory of the State administering it; and such separate and distinct status under the Charter shall exist until the people of the

colony of Non-Self-Governing Territory have exercised their right of self-determination in accordance with the Charter, and particularly its purposes and principles.[248]

Obligatees are required to prepare non-self-governing territories under their administration for nothing less than the resumption of complete independence, with the UN serving as "guarantor" that they've fulfilled their obligations in this connection.

> [The] existence of a dependent or subject people under the right of self-determination calls for an "active obligatee." This "obligatee" is the perpetrator of the act of subjugation. Specifically, its obligation is to restore the subjugated community to full self-government in a manner consistent with the norms of international society. The relationship between the "obligatee" and the beneficiary, which often lacks the capacity to remedy its situation, is such that "the protection of beneficiary rights and interests requires…the interpolation of a guarantor."[249]

In cases, such as Hawai'i, where the obligatee can be shown to have already subverted the process, rendering the UN's normal guarantor role ineffectual, the UN is required not only to invalidate the outcome, but, through its Special Committee on the Situation with Regard to Implementation of the Declaration on the Granting of Independence to Colonial Countries and Peoples—the so-called Committee of Twenty-Four, established in 1961 by General Assembly Resolution 1654 (XVI)—to adopt an active role as an "Agent of Protection" ensuring the rights of the colonized.[250] As the General Assembly framed the matter in Resolution 35/118, the UN categorically "rejects any agreement, arrangement or unilateral action by colonial and racist Powers which ignores, violates, denies or conflicts with the inalienable right of peoples under colonial domination to self-determination and independence."[251]

> The Special Committee shall continue to examine the full compliance of all states with the Declaration and with other relevant resolutions on the question of decolonization… Where General Assembly Resolution 1514 (XV) has not been fully implemented with regard to a given Territory, the Assembly shall continue to bear responsibility for that Territory until all powers are transferred to the people of the Territory without any reservations and the people concerned have had an opportunity to exercise freely their right to self-determination and independence… The Special Committee is directed…to continue to examine the view expressed, orally or in writing by the peoples of the colonial Territories as well as by representatives of non-governmental organizations and individuals with knowledge of the conditions in those Territories. Particular consideration shall be given to oral petitions and written communications regarding the Territories on which information is not being transmitted [e.g., the report of the 1994 international tribunal regarding Hawai'i].[252]

Under provision of General Assembly Resolution 2625(VIII), *all* UN member states are required to support the measures recommended by the Special Committee to enforce Chapter XI of the Charter.

> Every State has the duty to promote, through joint and separate action, realization of the principle of equal rights and self-determination of peoples, in accordance with the provisions of the Charter, and to render assistance to the United Nations in carrying on the responsibilities entrusted to it by the Charter regarding the implementation of the principle, in order to… (a) bring a speedy end to colonialism, having due regard to the freely expressed will of the peoples concerned; and bearing in mind that the subjugation, domination and exploitation constitutes a violation of the principles, as well as a denial of fundamental human rights, and is contrary to the Charter.[253]

The means by which the international community might ultimately go about enforcing the rule of law against "the world's sole remaining superpower," especially when that superpower has exhibited an ever-increasing tendency to conduct itself in the manner of a "rogue state" and its own citizenry not the least inclination to correct the situation, is, to say the least, problematic.[254] Such circumstances neither negate nor qualify the obligation of the United Nations to try, however. Indeed, it is arguable that it is under precisely such conditions that the UN's obligation is greatest.[255] Reinscribing Hawai'i on the list of non-self-governing territories, and assembling an appropriate plebiscite to implement the archipelago's actual decolonization, are therefore imperatives, both legally and morally.[256] Even though the U.S. will likely reject such an intervention in its purported "domestic affairs," the statement thus made would be a potent one, likely to generate a tangible enhancement of the Kanaka Maoli negotiating position vis-à-vis their colonizers, and lending a sorely needed credence to the tattered image of international law (and the UN itself).[257] It would also expose as little else could the truth lurking behind the shopworn U.S. façade of being "a nation of laws."[258]

The benefits of such a precedent speak for themselves, not only with regard to the instant case, but many others. The long-suffering people of Puerto Rico and the Chamorros of Guam,[259] present ready examples, as do the several hundred internal colonies of Native North America.[260] So, too, the literally thousands of indigenous nations comprising a planetary "Fourth World,"[261] most of them outside the immediate sphere of U.S. domination, but none free of colonization by similarly-minded statist overlords,[262] and all of their situations steadily worsened by the U.S.-driven onslaught of corporate "globalization."[263] By these terms, what has happened in Hawai'i represents in microcosm the very worst "the system" has in store, not just for the proverbial "natives," but—as the Kanaks' erstwhile working-class *haole* neighbors have long since been able to attest—virtually *everyone*.[264]

Reinscription of Hawai'i as a non-self-governing territory and advancement by the community of nations of the formal demand that they be genuinely decolonized could thus serve as what Marcuse once described as "the Archimedean point [from which] a larger emancipation" can occur.[265] Shorn of its *de facto* colonial authority—which is to say, obliged to conform to the fundamental requirements of international human rights law—the U.S. would be unable to consummate the imposition of its envisioned "New World Order."[266] Ultimately, the United States, no more than its one-time arch rival, the Soviet Union, would be unable to sustain itself, geographically or otherwise, in the "continental bloc" or "megastate" form to which it has grown accustomed.[267] From this emerges the possibility of a "break-down of [states]" more generally, the "reordering of the world" on something more nearly resembling a "human scale," and much more.[268]

If, on the other hand, the UN remains mute with regard to Hawai'i, its default can only be construed as a tacit endorsement of what it is the U.S. has done there and, thence, a license for it to do the same to anyone and everyone, anywhere and everywhere. The UN, and international law in the bargain, will forfeit thereby all potential of serving as anything other than "tools of American foreign policy" (to borrow a phrase from such noteworthy U.S. spokespersons as Jesse Helms and Madeline Albright),[269] together constituting "the perfect companion to empire" (following Antonio de Nebrija's famous 1492 observation on language).[270] In that case, those like the Kanaka Maoli who are correspondingly consigned like so much refuse to "the rubbish-can of history" will have no alternative but to adopt other means of asserting their rights (or at least of making those who privilege themselves to deny those rights pay for the denial).[271] That events such as that of September 11, 2001 will under such circumstances recur, and perhaps become commonplace, is inevitable.[272]

The stakes are thus—and unmistakably—*very* high. There are choices to be made and no place for "bystanders" to the consequences of their making. For individuals, as for the UN, the acquiescence implied by silence serves as endorsement of the crimes of state at issue, and thereby of complicity in their perpetration.[273] We are, all of us, as Eldridge Cleaver once put it, either "part of the solution, or part of the problem."[274] For the Kanaka Maoli, and for the host of other peoples sharing the essentials of their circumstance, there can be no serious question as to the road that must be traveled in the years ahead. They owe it, not only to themselves but to their future generations to move in that direction. And they have every right—nay, duty—to demand that all persons of good conscience join them in their journey.

# Notes

1. For complete text of this and many of the other documents referenced herein, see my and Sharon H. Venne's coedited *Islands in Captivity: The Record of the International People's Tribunal on the Rights of Indigenous Hawaiians*, 3 vols. (Cambridge, MA: South End Press E-Books, 2002) Vol. 3, *Official Documents*.

2. On the relevant customary law (*jus cogens*), see Adam Roberts and Richard Guelff, *Documents on the Laws of War* (Oxford, UK: Clarendon Press, 1982) pp. 4-6, 10, 16.

3. On the relevant customary law, see Ian Sinclair, *The Vienna Convention on the Law of Treaties* (Manchester, UK: Manchester University Press, [2nd ed.] 1984) pp. 2-21.

4. Burns H. Weston, Richard A. Falk and Anthony D'Amato, eds., *Basic Documents in International Law and World Order* (St. Paul, MN: West, 1990) p. 3.

5. Although the question of Hawai'i is left conspicuously unaddressed in the book, the issue is framed reasonably well in Roy L. Brooks' "The Age of Apology," in his edited volume, *When Sorry Isn't Enough: The Controversy Over Apologies and Reparations for Human Injustice* (New York: New York University Press, 1999) pp. 3-11. Also see Elazar Barkman, *The Guilt of Nations: Restitution and Negotiating Historical Injustices* (New York: W.W. Norton, 2000) pp. xxix, xxxvi,164, 188, 216-31, 321.

6. "A State discharges the responsibility incumbent upon it for breach of an international obligation by making reparation for the injury caused"; Jiménez de Aréchaga, "Reparations for the Breach of an International Obligation," in Louis Henkin, Richard Crawford Pugh, Oscar Schachter and Hans Smit, eds., *International Law: Cases and Materials* (St. Paul, MN: West, [3rd ed.] 1993) p. 583. For recognition of the principle in U.S. courts, see, e.g., *Rodriguez-Fernandez v. Wilkinson* (505 F.Supp. 787, 798 (D. Kan. 1980), *aff'd*, 654 F.2d 1382 (10th Cir. 1981)). Overall, see Dinah Shelton, *Remedies in International Human Rights Law* (New York: Oxford University Press, 1999) esp. the chapter entitled "Remedies in National Law," pp. 57-92.

7. On the matter of international torts, see Eduardo Jiménez de Aréchaga, "International Responsibility," in M. Sorenson, ed., *Manual of Public International Law* (New York: St. Martin's Press, 1968) pp. 564-72.

8. This is certainly true with regard to the range of prerogatives vested in the United Nations Security Council under the organization's charter; see, e.g., Phyllis Bennis, *Calling the Shots: How Washington Dominates Today's UN* (Brooklyn, NY: Olive Branch Press, 2000) pp. 3-4, 10-1. Under provision of UN Resolution 42/159 (1987), moreover, "the right to self-determination, freedom, and independence, as derived from the Charter of the United Nations, of people forcibly deprived of that right…particularly peoples under colonial and racist regimes and foreign occupation" may be legitimately pursued by means otherwise construed as amounting to "terrorism."

9. For an excellent framing of the distinction between *de jure* and *de facto* sovereignty, see Eyal Benvenisti, *The International Law of Occupation* (Princeton: Princeton University Press, 1993) pp. 5-6.

10. United Nations Charter (59 Stat. 1031, T.S. No. 993, 3 Bevans 1153, 1976 Y.B.U.N. 1043 (June 26, 1945)), Chapter XI: Declaration Regarding Non-Self-Governing Territories; for text, see Weston, Falk and D'Amato, *Basic Documents*, pp. 27-9. Also particularly at issue are the United Nations Declaration on the Granting of Independence to Colonial Countries and Peoples (U.N.G.A. Res. 1514 (XV), 15 U.N. GAOR, Supp. (No. 16) 66, U.N. Doc. A/4684 (1961)), the International Covenant on Economic, Social and Cultural Rights (U.N.G.A. Res. 2200 (XXI), 21 U.N. GAOR, Supp. (No. 16) 49, U.N. Doc. A/6316 (1967), *reprinted in* 6 I.L.M. 360 (1967)), the International Covenant on Civil and Political Rights (U.N.G.A. Res. 2200 (XXI), 21 U.N. GAOR, Supp. (No. 16) 52, U.N. Doc. A/6316 (1967), *reprinted in* 6 I.L.M. 368 (1967)), and the U.N. Declaration on the Right to Development (U.N.G.A. Res. 41/128, 41 U.N. GAOR, Supp. (No. 53), U.N. Doc. A/41/925 (1986)); Weston, Falk and D'Amato, *Basic Documents,* pp. 343-4, 371-5, 376-85, 485-8.

11. For analysis of the principle involved, see Noam Chomsky, *Necessary Illusions: Thought Control in Democratic Societies* (Boston: South End Press, 1989).

12. "Apart from tribunals established pursuant to human rights treaties, other international courts and decision-makers exercise jurisdiction over matters that may include human rights issues. [These include] global and regional administrative tribunals, and various ad hoc tribunals, [each of which has] contributed to the law of remedies for human rights violations"; Shelton, *Remedies*, p. 14. For background,

see Samuel Benjamin Crandall, *Treaties: Their Making and Enforcement* (New York: Columbia University Press, [2nd ed.] 1916).

13. See, e.g., Kenneth C. Davis' rather presumptuously titled *Don't Know Much About History: Everything You Need to Know About American History but Never Learned* (New York: Avon, 1990).

14. A good read in this connection will be found in James W. Loewen's *Lies My Teacher Told Me: Everything Your American History Textbook Got Wrong* (New York: Touchstone, 1996). A more refined thematic treatment will be found in Michel-Rolph Trouillot's *Silencing the Past: Power and the Production of History* (Boston: Beacon Press, 1995).

15. For an extremely chauvinistic but nonetheless detailed overview, see William Adam Russ, Jr., *The Hawaiian Revolution (1893-1894)* (London/Toronto: Associated University Presses, [2nd ed.] 1992).

16. The Honolulu Rifles was a very well-armed "all-Caucasian...paramilitary organization led by the militant-radical, Volney Ashford," himself a member of a secret organization, the Hawaiian League, from which members of the Committee for Public Safety were drawn; Rich Budnick, *Stolen Kingdom: An American Conspiracy* (Honolulu: Aloha Press, 1992) p. 63.

17. As Admiral J.S. Skerritt observed in *Foreign Relations* a year later, the Marines were "very improperly located...if they were landed to protect American citizens in their person and property." However, "if they were landed to support the Provisional Government troops it was a wise choice"; quoted in Michael Dougherty, *To Steal a Kingdom: Probing Hawaiian History* (Waimanalo, HI: Island Style Press, 1992) p. 169.

18. On the effect of the Marine deployment in tipping the balance of force from the Hawaiian authorities to the insurgents, see Noel J. Kent, *Hawaii: Islands Under the Influence* (Honolulu: University of Hawaii Press, [2nd ed.] 1993) p. 63. Also see the superb video documentary, *Act of War: The Overthrow of the Hawaiian Nation* (Honolulu: Na Maka o ka Aina in association with the Ctr. For Hawaiian Studies, University of Hawai'i at Manoa, 1993).

19. Lucien Young, *The Boston of Hawaii* (Washington, D.C.: Gibson Bros., 1898) p. 182.

20. "Message of President Grover Cleveland to the Congress (Dec. 18, 1893)," in Michael Kioni Dudley and Keoni Kealoha Agard, eds., *A Call for Hawaiian Sovereignty* (Waipahu, HI: Na Kane O Ka Malo Press, 1990) pp. 25-46. Also see the quote in Samuel Weaver, *Hawaii, USA* (New York: Pageant Press, 1959) p. 103.

21. See generally, Helena Allen, *The Betrayal of Queen Lili'uokalani: Last Queen of Hawaii, 1838-1917* (Honolulu: Mutual, 1982).

22. Cleveland's letter was received by the Republic on Aug, 27, 1894; William Adam Russ, Jr. *The Hawaiian Republic and Its Struggle to Win Annexation (1894-98)* (London/Toronto: Associated University Presses, [2nd ed.] 1992) p. 37.

23. President William McKinley — an "eager imperialist," according to a complimentary editorial in the *New York Times* — signed the Joint Resolution to Provide for the Annexing of the Hawaiian Islands to the United States (Public Resolution No. 51, 30 Stat. 750), which had earlier passed in the Senate by a vote of 42 to 21 (with 26 abstentions), on July 7, 1898; ibid., p. 353. For text, see Churchill and Venne, *Islands in Captivity*, Vol. 3.

24. Both Melville and "Bridge the Pacific," a July 1898 *Philadelphia Press* editorial in which the "chain" rhetoric appears, are quoted in Julius W. Pratt, *The Expansionists of 1898* (Baltimore: Johns Hopkins University Press, 1936) p. 274. The notion of a U.S. "imperial destiny" of course evolved from the country's earlier belief that it was imbued with a "manifest destiny" to possess all of the North American landmass, "from sea to shining sea"; Frederick Merk, *Manifest Destiny and Mission in American History: A Reinterpretation* (New York: Alfred A, Knopf, 1963); Sidney Lens, *Forging the American Empire* (New York: Thomas Y. Crowell, 1971) esp. pp. 169-94.

25. An amendment to the Newlands Resolution introduced by Georgia Senator A.O. Bacon, which would have made annexation contingent upon a referendum enfranchising "all Hawaiians over 21 years of age," was rejected by a 20 to 42 vote (with 27 abstentions); Russ, *Hawaiian Republic*, p. 352.

26. "Haole," a term literally meaning "foreigner," is applied by the Kanaks to all whites, including those born in Hawai'i. The premise, that invaders/colonizers are *never* entitled to declare themselves "native," is quite apt.

27. Quoted in Theon Wright, *The Disenchanted Islands* (New York: Dial Press, 1972) pp. 17-9. On Thurston, see his *Memoirs of the Hawaiian Revolution* (Honolulu: Advertiser Publishing Co., 1936).

28. See generally, *The Voyages of Captain Cook Around the World* (London: John Tallis, *circa* 1800).

29. This initial phase is summarized in the first chapters of Theodore Morgan's *A Century of Economic Change* (Cambridge, MA: Harvard University Press, 1948) esp. p. 48.

30. See the assessments offered by Kekuaolani, one of the more insightful of Kamehameha's contemporaneous critics, in Ralph S. Kuykendall, *The Hawaiian Kingdom, 1778-1854* (Honolulu: University of Hawaii Press, 1938) pp. 65, 47. Also see the chapters entitled "Kamehameha Wins All Hawaii" and "The Last Days of Ka-Hekili" in S.M. Kamakau, *Ruling Chiefs of Hawaii* (Honolulu: Kamehameha Schools Press, [rev. ed.] 1992) pp. 142-58, 159-67.

31. Kent, *Hawaii*, p. 15.

32. In 1810, sandalwood cost 1¢ per pound in Hawai'i and sold for 34¢ per pound in China; Richard O'Connor, *Pacific Destiny* (Boston: Little, Brown, 1969) p. 43; also see Dorothy Shineberg, *They Came for Sandalwood* (London: Melbourne University Press, 1967). On the overwhelming significance of whaling in the "Hawaiian" economy, circa 1830, see Morgan, *Economic Change*, p. 51.

33. See the population trajectories displayed in David E. Stannard, *Before the Horror: The Population of Hawai'i on the Eve of Western Contact* (Honolulu: Social Science Institute, University of Hawaii, 1989) p. 51. Although there is no concrete evidence that either the British or their Euroamerican counterparts deliberately unleashed pathogens for purposes of reducing the native Hawaiian population, both are known to have done so vis-à-vis Native North Americans; R.G. Robertson, *Rotting Face: Smallpox and the American Indian* (Caldwell, ID: Caxton, 2001) p. 301. For broader views of the effects of disease in facilitating western expansionism, see Alfred W. Crosby, *Ecological Imperialism: The Biological Expansion of Europe, 900-1900* (Cambridge, UK: Cambridge University Press, 1986); Jared Diamond, *Guns, Germs, and Steel: The Fates of Human Societies* (New York: W.W. Norton, 1997).

34. As R.C. Wyllie, "one of the most influential of the many *haole* ministers and advisers to the Hawaiian government," put it in 1844, the "prosperity of these islands [now] depends mainly on the whale ships that annually flock to their ports. Were the whale fishing to fall off, the islands' " economy would collapse; quoted in Kent, *Hawaii*, p. 23. Also see the early chapters of Robert Heller's *The Economic and Social Impact of Foreign Investment in Hawaii* (Honolulu: University of Hawaii Economic Research Center, 1973).

35. "Report upon the Relations of the United States with the Hawaiian Islands from the First Appointment of a Consular Officer There by This Government," in *Executive Documents of the House of Representatives* (Washington, D.C.: 53rd Cong., 3rd Sess., 1894-95) p. 8; Kuykendall, *Hawaiian Kingdom*, p. 90. Subsequent noteworthy "visits" by American warships included that of the sloop of war *Dolphin* in 1831, and a frigate, the *U.S.S. Constitution*, which anchored near Pearl Harbor for several weeks in 1845; Budnick, *Stolen Kingdom*, pp. 61, 139.

36. Editorial in an 1847 issue of *The Sandwich Islands*; quoted in Wright, *Disenchanted Islands*, p. xiii. Overall, see Marion Kelly, *Early Mission Impact on Hawaiians and Their Culture* (Honolulu: Church at the Crossroads, 1988).

37. Harold W. Bradley, *The American Frontier in Hawaii* (Glouchester, MA: Peter Smith, 1968) p. 415. For the most comprehensive range of information on the individuals involved, see Albert Judd, ed., *Missionary Album: Portraits and Biographical Sketches of the American Protestant Missionaries in the Hawaiian Islands* (Honolulu: Hawaiian Missionary Children's Society, 1969).

38. For the texts of the 1840 constitution and the 1852 amendments, see Churchill and Venne, *Islands in Captivity*, Vol. 3. On Judd's and Ricord's roles as drafters, see Kent, *Hawaii*, p. 27.

39. For an overview of Judd's role in effecting the Mahele, and a good selection of quotes indicating his sense of achievement in this connection, see Lilikala Kame'eleihiwa, *Native Land and Foreign Desires: Pahea La E Pono Ai?* (Honolulu: Bishop Museum Press, 1992) pp. 221-5. Also see the chapter entitled "Gerrit Parmele Judd, 1845," in Dougherty, *To Steal a Kingdom*, pp. 97-117; and Judd's own *Dr. Judd: Hawaii's Friend* (Honolulu: University of Hawaii Press, 1960).

40. Kent, *Hawaii*, p. 31. For more comprehensive treatments, see J.J. Chinen, *The Great Mahele* (Honolulu: University of Hawaii Press, 1958); Kame'eleihiwa, *Native Land*, 227-86. On the Kuleana Act, see Maivân Clech Lâm, "The Kuleana Act Revisited: The Survival of Traditional Hawaiian Commoner Rights in Land," *Washington Law Review*, Vol. 64, No. 2, 1989.

41. For comparison of the two processes, see Linda S. Parker, *Native American Estate: The Struggle Over Indian and Hawaiian Lands* (Honolulu: University of Hawaii Press, 1989).

42. Kent, *Hawaii*, p. 32.

43. In 1850, the Congregationalists' American Missionary Board began releasing its cadres in Hawai'i from further obligation. Meanwhile, under provision of Judd's legislation, the Kingdom adopted a policy of selling land to mission members "at a fraction of its customary price." It thus comes as no surprise to find that, by 1860, many former missionaries—Samuel Alexander and Henry Baldwin, for example, as well as Henry Diamond and Walter Rice—had assumed positions within the islands' landed business élite; ibid., pp. 36-7.

44. Morgan, *Economic Change*, p. 178. Also see Kame'eleihiwa, *Native Land*, pp. 298-306

45. Excellent overviews of the consolidation process will be found in two self-published studies, John Anthony Mollett's *Capital in Hawaiian Sugar: Its Formation and Relation to Labor and Output* (Honolulu, 1961), and John Kelly's *Hawaii: Showcase of Imperialism, Land Alienation, and Foreign Control* (Honolulu, 1974). Also see Heller, *Foreign Investment in Hawaii*, and Morgan, *Economic Change*.

46. While the Kanaks numbered fewer than 55,000 in 1850, approximately 200,000 Japanese alone were brought to the islands as laborers during the second half of the $19^{th}$ century; Kent, *Hawaii*, p. 39.

47. The treaty text is appended to "Relations of the United States with the Hawaiian Islands" at pp. 35-6.

48. The first such statement seems to have appeared in an editorial published by the *Pacific Commercial Advertiser* in 1837; quoted in Merze Tate, *Hawaii: Reciprocity or Annexation* (East Lansing: Michigan State University Press, 1968) p. 4.

49. Tyler's "Message to the Congress on the Sandwich Islands and China (Dec. 31, 1842)" is appended to "Relations of the United States with the Hawaiian Islands" at pp. 39-41. The purpose of this policy was both to curtail the extent of England's residual influence in Hawai'i and, increasingly, to prevent France from making significant inroads. Although the Kingdom entered into treaties with both countries in 1846, as well as Denmark in 1847 and Hamburg (Germany) in 1848, the U.S. was well positioned to shape the commercial terms of these compacts to its own advantage, and to prevent their containing a military dimension; ibid., pp. 12-3. Also see Sylvester Stevens, *American Expansion in Hawaii, 1842-1898* (New York: Russell and Russell, 1945).

50. These included representatives of business concerns in both the U.S. and Hawai'i itself. In 1853, an ad hoc amalgam of commercial interests in New York actually proposed to buy the islands for $5 million. At the same time, a statement signed by "nineteen prominent merchants and planters"—including the ex-missionary Samuel Castle, a partner in the Big Five corporation Castle and Cooke—argued that annexation would generate "prosperity and security"; Kuykendall, *Hawaiian Kingdom*, p. 387.

51. Seward's position was that the U.S. should endeavor to "build an empire such as the world has never seen," and that, therefore, "annexation of the Sandwich Islands is deemed desirable"; quoted in O'Connor, *Pacific Destiny*, p. 104; Kuykendall, *Hawaiian Kingdom*, p. 208.

52. In an 1851 statement, DuPont proclaimed it "impossible to estimate too highly the value and importance of the Hawaiian Islands, whether in a commercial or a military sense"; quoted in Kent, *Hawaii*, p. 41.

53. The 1849 treaty is appended to "Relations of the United States with the Hawaiian Islands" at pp. 79-87.

54. "Relations of the United States with the Hawaiian Islands," p. 13. For insight into Jarvis' loyalties and values, see his *History of the Hawaiian Islands* (Honolulu: Henry M. Whitney, 1872).

55. The 1875 treaty text is appended to "Relations of the United States with the Hawaiian Islands" at pp. 164-7.

56. For the text of the supplemental convention by which this was accomplished, see ibid., pp. 170-2.

57. Quoted in Tate, *Hawaii*, p. 118. The 1887 Parcel Post Convention is appended to "Relations of the United States with the Hawaiian Islands" at pp. 172-8.

58. On alignments, see Russ, *Hawaiian Revolution*, pp. 17-21.

59. Kent, *Hawaii*, p. 45; "Relations of the United States with the Hawaiian Islands," p. 20.

60. Kent, *Hawaii*, p. 45.

61. On the principals mentioned, see *Sanford Ballard Dole and His Hawaii* (Honolulu: Hawaiian

Historical Society, 1957); Harold Kent, *Charles Reed Bishop: Man of Hawaii* (Honolulu: Kamehameha Schools Press, 1966).

62. On the imposition, see Russ, *Hawaiian Revolution*, pp. 19-22; Kent, *Hawaii*, pp. 54-5. For the text of the 1887 constitution, see Churchill and Venne, *Islands in Captivity*, Vol. 3. The descriptor, "Bayonet Constitution," was coined by Lili'uokalani in her memoir, *Hawai'i's Story by Hawai'i's Queen* (Boston: Charles E. Tuttle, 1898).

63. Ironically, some of the best material on the revolt and the politics attending it will be found in a pair of unsigned manuscripts entitled "Biography of R.W. Wilcox" and "Wilcox Insurrection of 1889" in the Lorrin A. Thurston Papers, Archives of Hawaii, Honolulu.

64. "Relations of the United States with the Hawaiian Islands," p. 20.

65. Kuykendall, *Hawaiian Kingdom*, p. 487.

66. Most significantly, Lili'uokalani rejected a provision in the Bayonet Constitution by which noncitizen (white) foreigners were allowed to vote; Kame'eleihiwa, *Native Land*, p. 315; Dougherty, *To Steal a Kingdom*, p. 162.

67. Kame'eleihiwa, *Native Land*, p. 315.

68. The most prominent measures consisted of approving a national lottery and imposing a tax on opium, consumption of which had grown considerably after Chinese laborers had begun to be imported in significant numbers; Budnick, *Stolen Kingdom*, pp. 84-5; Russ, *Hawaiian Revolution*, pp. 63-4.

69. On the reciprocity negotiations—which at one point involved the Hawaiian legislature unsuccessfully ordering the U.S. fleet to leave Pearl Harbor, see Dougherty, *To Steal a Kingdom*, pp. 162-4, 167-8.

70. Kent, *Hawaii*, p. 62.

71. Stevens to Blaine, Feb. 8 and Mar. 8, 1892; included in U.S. House of Representatives, "Executive Document: Report to Secretary of State W.Q. Gresham on Recent Events Transpiring in the Hawaiian Islands, July 17, 1893" (Washington, D.C.: 53rd Cong., 2nd Sess., 1895) at pp. 353-4, 182. The document was prepared by former Georgia congressman James Blount, after completing an on-site investigation in Hawai'i undertaken at the behest of President Cleveland. It is hereinafter referred to as the "Blount Report."

72. Stevens to Blaine, Mar. 8, 1892; "Blount Report," p. 182.

73. Stevens to Foster, Nov. 20, 1892; "Blount Report," pp. 377-84.

74. On the contrary, Foster informed Stevens that his reports and suggestions were being received "with interest" and instructed that they be routed under the heading "Strictly Reserved and Confidential"; "Relations of the United States with the Hawaiian Islands," p. 384. For his part, Stevens informed the Committee of Public Safety that "United States troops on board the *Boston* will be ready to land at any moment...and they of course will recognize [your] government"; quoted in Kuykendall, *Hawaiian Kingdom*, p. 788.

75. Evidence of preplanning is abundant. For example, although, "technically, the marines couldn't land without direct orders from Stevens...at 10 A.M., five hours before Stevens requested the troops go ashore, Captain Wiltse began making preparations... By the time Stevens boarded the *U.S.S. Boston* that afternoon, the soldiers were armed [and] Wiltse's written order...had [already] been issued"; Budnick, *Stolen Kingdom*, pp. 112-3. Wiltse also received a letter of gratitude from the provisional government established as a result of the coup; Russ, *Hawaiian Revolution*, pp. 157-8.

76. Quoted in "Blount Report," p. 476.

77. Cleveland's "Message to Congress" was based directly upon the preliminary findings arrived at by Blount.

78. On the House document, see note 35. The Senate report—Exec. Doc. 227 (Washington, D.C.: 53rd Cong., 2nd Sess., 1894)—derives its more common designation from Senator John T. Morgan, who chaired the committee investigating what had transpired in Hawai'i. Although, like its House counterpart, the "Morgan Report" is far more ambiguous in it conclusions than Blount's, it straightforwardly denounced Stevens' "officious and unbecoming participation in the events which led to the revolution" (pp. 35-6).

79. Stevens was recalled from Hawai'i on May 24, 1893. On Feb. 7, 1894, he was subjected to a formal vote of censure by the House of Representatives; Russ, *Hawaiian Revolution*, pp. 189, 314-5. It

should be noted that before being appointed U.S. Minister to Hawai'i, Stevens had held similar positions in Uruguay/Paraguay (1870-74) and Norway/Sweden (1877-83). He was removed from both posts for "meddling in the internal affairs" of the host countries; Helena G. Allen, *The Betrayal of Queen Lili'uokalani: Last Queen of Hawaii, 1838-1917* (Honolulu: Mutual, 1982) p. 218.

80. An identical ploy was shortly adopted with regard to General Jacob "Hell Roaring Jake" Smith, who presided over the genocidal U.S. campaign in the Philippines at the turn of the century; Stuart Creighton Miller, *"Benevolent Assimilation": The American Conquest of the Philippines, 1899-1903* (New Haven, CT: Yale University Press, 1982) pp. 236-8; Richard Drinnon, *Facing West: The Metaphysics of Indian-Hating and Empire-Building* (Minneapolis: University of Minnesota Press, 1980) p. 328; Richard Slotkin, *Gunfighter Nation: The Myth of the Frontier in Twentieth-Century America* (Norman: University of Oklahoma Press, [2nd ed.] 1998) p. 121.

81. Stevens informed Foster that he'd unilaterally declared Hawai'i to be a U.S. "military protectorate" via his Dispatch No. 79, Feb. 1, 1893 (Wiltse sent a similar dispatch to Secretary of the Navy Tracy on the same day). On Feb. 11, Foster "reprimanded" Stevens for exceeding his authority in this regard, and "correcting" Stevens' articulation of U.S. policy by noting that the conspirators' provisional government should be considered sovereign in its own right (a matter which Stevens had never denied). In effect, as was observed in an editorial published by the *St. Louis Republic* on Feb. 23, "Secretary of State Foster's pretended rebuke to Minister Stevens for exceeding his authority in establishing a Protectorate over Hawaii is equivalent to the verdict of 'Guilty, but go on doing it.'"

82. See note 22.

83. Ed Touse, *The Rebellion of 1895* (Honolulu: Advertiser Publishing Co., 1895).

84. Lili'uokalani was sentenced to 5 years in prison, reduced to two years of house arrest; Allen, *Betrayal*, p. 341.

85. Russ, Hawaiian *Republic*, pp. 83-5.

86. This was rather well understood at the time; see, as examples, James Schouler, "A Review of the Hawaii Controversy," *The Forum*, XVI, Feb. 1894; Albert Shaw, "Do We Own Pearl Harbor?" *The Forum*, XV, June 1897; Stephen M. White, "The Proposed Annexation of Hawaii," *The Forum*, XXIII, Aug. 1897; James Bryce, "The Policy of Annexation for America," *The Forum*, XXIV, Dec. 1897.

87. See the roster included in Budnick, *Stolen Kingdom*, p. 118. On Dole, see note 61; on Thurston, note 27. On Castle, see William A. Russ, Jr., "The Role of Sugar in Hawaiian Annexation," *Pacific Historical Review*, XII, 1943.

88. This, again, was rather well understood at the time; see, e.g., J. Franklin Jameson, "Typical Steps of American Expansion," *History Teacher's Magazine*, V, Feb. 1914.

89. This backdrop is well presented in the chapter entitled "Annexation to Help Conquer the Philippines," in Russ, *Hawaiian Republic*, pp. 280-92. Also see Lorrin Thurston, *Annexation to the United States* (Washington, D.C.: Hawaiian Friends League, 1898).

90. On annexation, see note 23. It's worth noting that those opposed, the so-called anti-imperialists, were by and large motivated by no lofty sentiments. Rather, they were mostly virulent racists, seeking to prevent the introduction of Hawai'i's "disease-ridden" population of color into the U.S. polity; Burnside Foster, "Leprosy and Hawaiian Annexation," *North American Review*, CLXVII, Sept. 1898; Fred H. Harrington, "The Anti-Imperialist Movement in the United States, 1898-1900," *Mississippi Valley Historical Review*, XXII, Sept. 1935.

91. An Act to Provide Government for the Territory of Hawaii (31 Stat. 141 (1900)); for text, see Churchill and Venne, *Islands in Captivity*, Vol. 3. On the proportion of land impounded, see George Cooper and Gavan Daws, *Land and Power in Hawaii* (Honolulu: University of Hawaii Press, 1990) p. 2.

92. Christina Duffy Burnett and Burke Marshall, eds., *Foreign in a Domestic Sense: Puerto Rico, American Expansion, and the Constitution* (Durham, NC: Duke University Press, 2001); Natsu Taylor Saito, "Asserting Plenary Power Over the 'Other': Indians, Immigrants, Colonial Subjects, and Why U.S. Jurisprudence Needs to Incorporate International Law," *Yale Law & Policy Review*, Vol. 20, No. 2, 2002.

93. For another study of a representative figure, see Jacob Adler, *Claus Spreckels: The Sugar King of Hawaii* (Honolulu: University of Hawaii Press, 1966). Also see Mollett, *Capital in Hawaiian Sugar*; Kelly, *Hawaii*; John W. Vandercook, *King Cane* (New York: Harper Bros., 1939).

94. Kent, *Hawaii*, p. 69.

95. Ibid., p. 75. Also see Samuel Weinman, *Hawaii: A Case of Imperialist Plunder* (Honolulu: n.p., 1934) p. 33; Frank J. Taylor, *From Land and Sea* (San Francisco: Chronicle Books, 1976) p. 143.

96. Kent, *Hawaii*, p. 89, relying on *Thrumm's Hawaiian Almanac and Annual, 1916* (Honolulu: Thomas G. Thrumm, 1915) p.26.

97. Kent, *Hawaii*, p. 89, relying on *Thrumm's Hawaiian Almanac and Annual, 1936* (Honolulu: Thomas G. Thrumm, 1935) pp. 25–6.

98. Kent, *Hawaii*, p. 89, relying on *Thrumm's, 1916*, p.27; *Thrumm's, 1936*, pp. 26, 23.

99. See Samir Amin, *Imperialism and Unequal Development* (New York: Monthly Review Press, 1977); Albert Szymanski, *The Logic of Imperialism* (New York: Praeger, 1981).

100. Weinman, *Hawaii*, p. 2.

101. Barber, *Hawaii: The Restless Rampart* (Indianapolis: Bobbs–Merrill, 1940) p. 46.

102. Weinman, *Hawaii*, p. 3.

103. Sidney Lens, *The Labor Wars: From the Molly Maguires to the Sitdowns* (New York: Anchor Books, 1974). According two preeminent chroniclers of the topic, the U.S. has the "bloodiest and most violent labor history of any industrial nation in the world"; Philip Taft and Philip Ross, "American Labor Violence: Its Causes, Character and Outcome," in Hugh D. Graham and Ted R. Gurr, eds., *Violence in America* (New York: Bantam Books, 1969) p. 281.

104. Kent, *Hawaii*, p. 87.

105. Alexander MacDonald, *Revolt in Paradise* (New York: S. Daye & Co., 1944) p. 130.

106. Ibid., p. 138.

107. Richard Alan Liebes, *Labor Organization in Hawaii* (Honolulu: MA Thesis, University of Hawaii, 1938) p. 81. Also see Edward L. Johanessen, *The Hawaiian Labor Movement: A Brief History* (Boston: Bryce Humphries, 1956).

108. Quoted in Barber, *Hawaii*, p. 87.

109. 42 Stat. 108 (1921). The measure was described as a "triumph of justice for the Hawaiians"; Wright, *Disenchanted Isles*, p. 31. Also see Marilyn Vause, *The Hawaiian Homes Commission Act of 1920* (Honolulu: MA Thesis, University of Hawaii, 1962); Frederick Simpich, *Anatomy of Hawaii* (New York: Avon Books, 1973).

110. Lawrence Fuchs, *Hawaii Pono: A Social History* (New York: Harcourt, Brace and World, 1968) p. 174.

111. Kent, *Hawaii*, p. 76. Also see Diana Hansen, *The Homestead Papers: A Critical Analysis of the Management of the Hawaiian Home Lands* (Honolulu: University of Hawaii Press, 1971); Susan Falaudi, "Broken Promise: How Everybody Got the Hawaiians' Homelands Except the Hawaiians," *Wall Street Journal*, Sept. 9, 1990. This is again similar to the effects of the 1887 General Allotment Act on American Indians; see ref., note 41.

112. Cooper and Daws, *Land and Power*, p. 3; Kent, *Hawaii*, p. 76; Parker, *Native American Estate*, p. 153.

113. See generally, Kathy Ferguson, Phyllis Turnbull and Mehmed Ali, "Rethinking the Military in Hawai'i," in Ulla Hasager and Jonathan Friedman, eds., *Hawai'i: Return to Nationhood* (Copenhagen: IWGIA Doc. 75, 1994) pp. 183–93. Also see Patricia Tummons, "From Fertile Fields to No-Man's Land: The Transformation of Waikane Valley," in Churchill and Venne, *Islands in Captivity*, Vol. 2 (the essay results from combining two articles published in *Environment Hawai'i*, Vol. 3, No. 2, Aug. 1992); Hannibal M. Taveres, Noa Emmett Aluli, A. Frenchy DeSoto, James A. Kelly and H. Howard Stephenson, *Kaho'olawe Island: Restoring a Cultural Treasure* (Honolulu: Kaho'olawe Island Conveyance Commission, 1993).

114. The Philippines became formally independent on July 4, 1946. However, under the Military Bases Agreement, formalized on March 14, 1947, the U.S. retained rights to Subic Bay and the 130,000 acre Clark complex for 99 years, while the Philippines government foreswore the granting of military basing rights to any other country; U.S. Senate, *A Decade of American Foreign Policy: Basic Documents, 1941-49* (Washington, D.C.: 81st Cong., 1st Sess., 1950) pp. 869–81.

115. Overall, the strategy was—and to some extent remains—contingent upon the U.S. maintaining "a Pacific-wide security zone consisting of thirty-three bases in twenty-two locations, from the Aleutians to Australia," with intermediate stops in Japan, South Korea and Taiwan; Kent, *Hawaii*, p.

99. On the centrality of Hawai'i to all this, see Ian Lind, "Ring of Steel: The Militarization of Hawaii," *Social Forces in Hawaii,* No. 31, 1984.

116. Haunani-Kay Trask, *From a Native Daughter: Colonialism and Sovereignty in Hawai'i* (Honolulu: University of Hawai'i Press, [2nd ed.] 1999) p. 17.

117. Kent, *Hawaii,* p. 99. For historical background, see Immanuel Wallerstein, *The Modern World System II: Mercantilism and the Consolidation of the European World-Economy, 1600-1750* (New York: Academic Press, 1980). A comprehensive view of the more immediate context will be found in Richard J. Barnet and Ronald E. Müller, *Global Reach: The Power of Multinational Corporations* (New York: Touchstone, 1974).

118. Gabriel Kolko, *Main Currents in Modern American History* (New York: Harper and Row, 1976) p. 159.

119. John Witeck, "The East-West Center: An Intercult of Colonialism," *Hawai'i Pono Journal,* May 1971.

120. Kaiser's initial expenditure went into resort development, building the Hawaiian Village hotel, acquisition of radio and television stations, the construction of a cement plant and a 6,000 acre southern California-style housing sprawl near the Koko Head Crater; Kent, *Hawaii,* p. 105.

121. On Dilco—the Dillingham Corp., founded by Walter Dillingham, probably the last don of the old planter élite—see Laura Brown and Walter Cohen, "Hawaii Faces the Pacific," *Pacific Studies Center Bulletin,* Jan.-Feb. 1975.

122. Simpich, *Anatomy of Hawaii,* p. 110.

123. See the Jan. 1978 issue of *Hawaii Business.*

124. Kent, *Hawaii,* p. 114, relying mainly on *Hawaii Business,* Feb. 1976.

125. *Honolulu Star-Bulletin and Advertiser,* Apr. 17, 1966.

126. *Economic Salon,* Mar. 1972, esp. p. 34.

127. Kent, *Hawaii,* p. 109.

128. *Honolulu Advertiser,* Jan. 15, 1964. For an overview of what had come before, see Cecil Tilton, *A History of Banking in Hawaii* (Honolulu: University of Hawaii Press, 1927).

129. Good background in the latter connection will be found in Francisco Quesada, *The Mechanisms and Economics of Tourism* (Manila: Manila Book Store, 1976).

130. For a fine overview of implications, see the chapter entitled "Economics of Human Rights," in Sandy Vogelgesang, *American Dream, Global Nightmare: The Dilemma of U.S. Human Rights Policy* (New York: W.W. Norton: 1977) pp. 181-240.

131. For background on the founding and the language quoted, see Bennis, *Calling the Shots,* pp. 1-8.

132. Weston, Falk and D'Amato, *Basic Documents,* pp. 16, 24.

133. Hans Kelsen, *The Law of the United Nations* (London: Stevens & Son, 1951) pp. 27-9; Rigo Sureda, *Right to Self-Determination,* p. 102.

134. Djura Nincic, *The Problem of Sovereignty in the Charter and Practice of the United Nations* (The Hague: Marinus Nijhoff, 1979) p. 228.

135. Ibid., p. 227; Kelsen, *Law of the United Nations,* p. 559.

136. The term "'people'…includes *only* the indigenous population [emphasis added]" of a colonial or trust territory; Kelsen, *Law of the United Nations,* p. 559.

137. For examples of such "extraordinary measures," see A. Rigo-Sureda, *The Evolution of the Right to Self-Determination: A Study of United Nations Practice* (Leiden, Netherlands: A.W. Sijhoff, 1973) p. 181.

138. Nincic, *Problem of Sovereignty,* p. 222.

139. See, Stewart C. Easton, *The Rise and Fall of Western Colonialism: An Historical Survey from the Early Nineteenth Century to the Present* (New York: Praeger, 1964); Franz Ansprenger, *The Dissolution of Colonial Empires* (New York: Routledge, 1989).

140. The breakthrough analysis concerning this new mode of domination will be found in Kwame Nkrumah's *Neocolonialism: The Last Stage of Imperialism* (New York: International, 1965). For a more recent explication, see David D. Newsom, *The Imperial Mantle: The United States and the Third World* (Bloomington: Indiana University Press, 2001).

141. The sorts of issues with which the U.S. was concerned are summarized very well in the

opening section of Eyal Benvenisti's *The International Law of Occupation* (Princeton, NJ: Princeton University Press, 1993) esp. pp. 5-6.

142. Actually the idea had been discussed as early as 1854.On the 1947 proposal and its successors, see Gavan Daws, *Shoal of Time: A History of the Hawaiian Islands* (New York: Macmillan, 1969) pp. 382, 389.

143. Hawaiian Sovereignty Advisory Commission, *Final Report* (Honolulu: State of Hawaii, 1994) p. 45.

144. This was true not only of the ballot itself, but of the officially-conducted debates and other "educational activities" leading up to their being cast; Daws, *Shoal of Time*, p. 385; Dudley and Agard, *Call for Hawaiian Sovereignty*, p. 74.

145. Niihau, the only precinct in which Kanaks comprised a majority, was also the only precinct in which the vote was solidly against statehood; Daws, *Shoal of Time*, p. 391.

146. Hawaii Statehood Act of 1959 (73 Stat. 4). Also see "Summary of Information Transmitted by the Government of the United States to the United Nations on the Territory of Hawaii (July 25, 1947)," in Churchill and Venne, *Islands in Captivity*, Vol. 3. For analysis of the implications attending the U.S. having conducted the plebiscite absent UN supervision, see Hurst Hannum, *Autonomy, Sovereignty and Self-Determination* (Philadelphia: University of Pennsylvania Press, 1990) p. 40; W. Ofuatey-Kodjoe, *The Principle of Self-Determination in International Law* (Hamden, CT: Archon Books, 1972) p. 118.

147. Kelsen, *Law of the United Nations*, p. 559.

148. Resolution 742 (VIII) was effected on Nov. 27, 1953. Also see "Factors Which Should Be Taken Into Account in Deciding Whether a Territory Is or Is Not a Territory Whose People Have Not Yet Attained A Full Measure of Self-Government," General Assembly Resolution 741(VIII), which went into effect the same day.

149. Michla Pomerance, *Self-Determination in Law and Practice* (The Hague: Marinus Nijhoff, 1982) p. 25.

150. Ibid., p. 121.

151. Ibid., p. 25.

152. Rigo Sureda, *Right to Self-Determination*, p. 107. For background, see Philip C. Naylor, *France and Algeria: A History of Decolonization and Transformation* (Gainesville: University Press of Florida, 2000) pp. 18-21. It should be noted that Great Britain attempted a reverse approach to the same deception by declaring that its colony of Oman had "always retained its independence"(and had thus, presumably, "freely chosen" its subjugation to the British). The UN was not fooled by this ruse, and inscribed Oman on the list of non-self-governing territories over Britain's vociferous objections; Rigo Sureda, *Right to Self-Determination*, p. 63.

153. Ofuatey-Kodjoe, *Principle of Self-Determination*, p. 136. For background, see Ernest Harsch and Tony Thomas, *Angola: The Hidden History of Washington's War* (New York: Pathfinder Press, 1976) pp. 25-48; Courtland Cox, "Western Strategy in Southern Africa," Western Massachusetts Association of Concerned Scholars, *U.S. Military Involvement in Southern Africa* (Boston: South End Press, 1978) pp. 41-4.

154. Quoted in the *Honolulu Advertiser*, Sept. 3, 1957.

155. Kent, *Hawaii*, pp. 123, 141. For the official view, see Governor's Advisory Committee on the Tourism Industry, *The Role of Government in the Development of Hawaii's Visitor Industry* (Honolulu: State of Hawaii, 1957).

156."An infrastructure means more than transportation, ports, power supplies and the like. It also means an economic environment, a framework of fiscal and monetary policies conducive to 'development' along unquestioned and preconceived paths"; Joyce Kolko, *America and the Crisis of World Capitalism* (Boston: Beacon Press, 1974) p. 120.

157. Kent, *Hawaii*, p. 142, relying on *Pacific Business News*, Oct. 20, 1969.

158. Thomas Creighton, *The Lands of Hawaii: Their Use and Misuse* (Honolulu: University of Hawaii Press, 1978) p. 66. Also see Legislative Reference Bureau, *Public Land Use in Hawaii: An Historical Analysis* (Honolulu: University of Hawaii Press, 1969).

159. Kent, *Hawaii*, p. 124.

160. The process involved not only a dramatic increase in the number of rooms available, but replacement of existing units with larger and far more lavish facilities. A classic example concerns Hyatt's

demolition of the landmark Biltmore Hotel in Waikiki—large, at 10 stories, by 1950s standards—to replace it with a $67 million, 40-story, twin tower, 1260 room Regency complex containing 5 restaurants, 5 lounges and more than 70 shops. The most grandiose undertaking during the 1970s, at least in terms of sheer scale, was probably Signal Oil's construction of an 2400 room monstrosity surrounded by 800 "ranchettes" in an 8,000 acre compound of the Big Island of Hawai'i; *Pacific Business News*, Dec. 23, 1976; *Hawaii Business*, Apr. 1978.

161. The largest of these, financed in large part by Boise-Cascade, was a 32,000 acre complex on the Big Island involving 3,000 hotel rooms, four 18-hole golf courses, and 11,000 residential units. Another "development" project, undertaken by the Louisiana Land Corp. on Moloka'i, involved 3,600 hotel rooms, 3,400 villa and cottage units, and more than 6,600 townhouses and condominiums; Kent, *Hawaii*, pp. 167-8; Dept. of Planning and Economic Development, *Growth Policies Plan, 1974-1984* (Honolulu: State of Hawaii, 1978).

162. Napier was by no means alone in abusing public office to personally profit from the officially-contrived boom. Among numerous other examples, State Land Commission member *cum* Amfac vice president C.E. Burns did exactly the same (albeit, in behalf of his corporation), as did a third commission member, Shiro Nishimura; Kent, *Hawaii*, pp. 143, 168. Also see the *Honolulu Star-Bulletin*, Oct. 11, 1970.

163. *Honolulu Star-Bulletin*, Apr. 10, 1960; Dept. of Planning and Economic Development, *State of Hawaii Data Book, 1977* (Honolulu: State of Hawaii, 1977); *Honolulu Star-Bulletin*, Jan. 22, 1993.

164. Kent, *Hawaii*, p. 169. Also see Louis Crampon, *Hawaii's Visitor Industry: Its Growth and Development* (Honolulu: University of Hawaii School of Tourism Industry Management, 1976).

165. Kent, *Hawaii*, pp. 147, 168; Lou Rose, "Speculators," in Randall W. Roth, ed., *The Price of Paradise: Lucky We Live in Hawaii* (Honolulu: Mutual, 1992) pp. 18-21.

166. Kent, *Hawaii*, p. 168.

167. Quoted in *Pacific News*, May 1, 1972.

168. Kelly, *Hawaii*, p. 24. The stubbornness with which proponents insist upon this theme is astonishing. In early 1977, long after Burns' "development brings employment" scenario had proven itself to produce a precisely opposite result, state Representative Richard Wakatsuki, to name just one prominent example, was arguing in the House that, "We must ...provide cheaper money to [corporations] who wish to extend their operations through investments in capital goods and facilities, thereby creating jobs"; quoted in the *Honolulu Star-Bulletin*, Feb. 10, 1977.

169. Tom Coffman, "Hawaii's High-Priced Politics," *Honolulu Advertiser*, Feb. 13, 1973.

170. While overall unemployment among the Kanaks averaged well over 30 percent during this period, 39.9 percent of those with jobs worked, usually part-time, in the hotel industry; R. Merrill, *Hotel Employment and the Community in Hawaii* (Honolulu: pamphlet, n.d.).

171. *Hawaii Observer*, Jan. 20, 1976; Feb. 3, 1976.

172. Commission on Manpower and Unemployment, *Unemployment and Welfare in Hawaii* (Honolulu: State of Hawaii, 1977) pp. 1-3.

173. Ibid.

174. Department of Taxation, *Hawaii Income Patterns, 1973* (Honolulu: State of Hawaii, 1974). Even in 1977, an "off" year for tourism, the industry generated $1.845 billion in gross revenues; Department of Planning and Economic Development, *Hawaii Data Book, 1978* (Honolulu: State of Hawaii, 1978) p. 190.

175. *Honolulu Star-Bulletin*, Feb. 10, 1977. On the World Bank and IMF, see Kevin Danahar, ed., *Fifty Years is Enough: The Case Against the World Bank and the International Monetary Fund* (Boston: South End Press, 1994).

176. Kent, *Hawaii*, p. 158, relying on Committee on Unemployment and Welfare, *Unemployment and Welfare*, p. 31.

177. Ibid.

178. This was a striking turnabout. Between 1959 and 1969, the University of Hawai'i's annual operating budget rose from $4 million to $41 million—a 742.5 percent increase—as two-dozen new departments were added to the 34 already existing. By 1976, this trend had been completely reversed; *East Meets West* (Honolulu: Club 15, 1965) pp. 1-3; *Honolulu Star-Bulletin*, Feb. 26, 1976.

179. *Hawaii Observer*, Mar. 20, 1976.

180. By the mid-70s, this out-migration by working class whites was in fact "strongly encouraged" as a matter of state policy; Dept. of General Planning, *The Interim Report on the Future of Oahu's Economy* (Honolulu: City and County of Honolulu, 1976) p. 5. Also see Walter Miklius, "Outmigration" and "Too Many Are Moving Away," *Honolulu Star-Bulletin and Advertiser*, Oct. 11, 1992.

181. The figure, which conforms to the then-prevailing state identification policy, is wildly inaccurate, including as it does only those documentably of "full blood"; Dougherty, *Stolen Kingdom*, p. 234.

182. U.S. Congress, Office of Technology Assessment, *Current Health Status and Population Projections of Native Hawaiians Living in Hawaii* (Washington, D.C. 100th Cong., 1st Sess., 1987); Dept. of Health, *Research and Statistics Report No. 47: Life Tables by Ethnic Group for Hawaii* (Honolulu: State of Hawaii, 1984). Also see K. Ikeda, *Demographic Profile of Native Hawaiians, 1980-1986* (Honolulu: Dept. of Sociology, University of Hawaii, 1987); Jo Ann Umilani Tsark, "Native Hawaiian Health Data: Contours of a Hidden Holocaust," in Churchill and Venne, *Islands in Captivity*, Vol. 2.

183. See generally, *The Homeless in Hawai'i: An Interim Report* (Honolulu: Homeless Aloha, 1990).

184. Kent, *Hawaii*, p. 160.

185. The legislative spearhead on such initiatives was hotel owner cum state Senator Francis Wong, who argued that, "We must find new ways to attract new equity and mortgage capital... We must eliminate government red tape and make Hawaii more attractive for investment capital"; quoted in *Pacific Business News*, Mar. 14, 1977; *Honolulu Star-Bulletin*, Aug. 28, 1977.

186. This shift is analyzed very well in Jafar Jafari's *The Role of Tourism in the Socioeconomic Transformation of Developing Countries* (Ithaca, NY: MA Thesis, Cornell University, 1974; self-published in 1975).

187. About a third of the venture capital channeled into Hawai'i during the late-70s and early-80s came from Canada, Australia and Hong Kong, the other two-thirds from Japan; Kent, *Hawaii*, p. 174.

188. Heller, *Foreign Investment in Hawaii*, pp. 56-62. Also see John Kelly/Maka'ainana Media, "Look What Happened to Waikiki," in Hasager and Friedman, *Hawai'i*, pp. 254-5.

189. Ibid., p. 50; "Whither the Mighty Yen?" *Hawaii Business*, Mar. 1991. Also see Quesada, *Mechanism and Economics of Tourism*, p. 4.

190. Kent, *Hawaii*, pp. 175-6.

191. Ibid., quoting *Economic World*, June 1977, p. 22.

192. Kent, *Hawaii*, p. 176, citing *Economic World*, Nov. 1977, p. 13.

193. Kent, *Hawaii*, p. 176.

194. Ibid., p. 186.

195. Ibid., p. 187.

196. Taveres, et al., *Kaho'olawe*, p. 26. Another possible "incept date" coincides with the 1971 mass refusal of Kanaka "squatters" to accept evictions from their homes in O'ahu's Kalama Valley; Kent, *Hawaii*, p. 194.

197. The first action was undertaken by the "Kaho'olawe Nine": George Helm, Kimo Mitchell, Noa Emmett Aluli, Ian Lind, Ellen Miles, Walter Ritt, Jr., Kawaipuna Prejean, Steve Morris and Karla Villalba. There were eight more landings by members of the original group: Jan, 12, 1976; Jan. 30, 1977; Feb. 6, 1977; Feb. 13, 1977; Feb. 20, 1977; Feb. 26, 1977; Mar. 5, 1977; and July 17, 1977; Taveres, et al. *Kaho'olawe*. On the missing men, see Rodney Morales, ed., *Ho'iho'i Hou: A Tribute to George Helm and Kim Mitchell* (Honolulu: Bamboo Ridge Press, 1984).

198. See, e.g., the overview presented in *The Valley Isle*, Aug. 10-23, 1977.

199. Quoted in Kent, *Hawaii*, pp. 168-9.

200. "Armed conflicts in which people are fighting against colonial domination and alien occupation and against racist regimes in exercise of their right to self-determination"—i.e., "Wars of National Liberation"—are protected under the 1977 Protocol Additional to the Geneva Conventions of 12 August 1949 (Protocol I, Art. 1, Para. 4); for text, see Adam Roberts and Richard Guelff, eds., *Documents on the Laws of War* (Oxford, UK: Clarendon Press, 1982) p. 390. By definition, such wars involve "the calculated...use of violence or threat of violence to attain goals that are political, religious, or ideological in nature" otherwise defined as "terrorism" in U.N.G.A. Res. 42/159 (1987); for a succinct framing, see Noam Chomsky, "Terror and Just Response," in Milan Rai, *War Plan Iraq: Ten Reasons Against War on Iraq* (London: Verso, 2002) p. 23.

201. On the "Indian Summer," see Jimmie Durham's "The United Nations Conference on Indians" and "An Open Letter on Recent Developments in the American Indian Movement/International Indian Treaty Council," in his *A Certain Lack of Coherence: Writings on Art and Cultural Politics* (London: Kala Press, 1993) pp.30-2, 46-56.

202. The first objective was in fact reached; see José R. Martinez Cobo, *Study of the Problem of Discrimination Against Indigenous Populations* (U.N. Doc. E/CN.4/Sub.2/1983/21/Ass.83, Sept. 1983). For context and amplification, see Sadruddin Aga Khan and Hassan bin Talal, *Indigenous Peoples: A Global Quest for Justice* (London: Zed Books, 1987). As to the draft declaration, which was originally scheduled for completion in 1992, but met with persistent obstruction by the U.S. and Canada, see Isabelle Schulte-Tenckhoff, "The Irresistible Ascension of the UN Draft Declaration on the Rights of Indigenous Peoples: Stopped Dead in Its Tracks?" *European Review of Native American Studies*, Vol. 9, No. 2, 1995. For further background, see Douglas Sanders, "The Re-Emergence of Indigenous Questions in International Law," *Canadian Human Rights Yearbook*, No. 3., 1983; "The U.N. Working Group on Indigenous Peoples," *Human Rights Quarterly*, No. 11, 1989.

203. Another key player at the UN during this period was Poka Laenu (Hayden Burgess), representing the World Council of Indigenous Peoples; Kent, *Hawaii*, pp. 199-200. More broadly, see Nakoa Prejean, "Kanaka Maoli and the United Nations," in Hasager and Friedman, *Hawai'i*, pp. 276-85.

204. On the founding of Ka Lahui Hawai'i, see Haunani-Kay Trask, "Hawaiians and Human Rights," in her *From a Native Daughter*, pp. 37-8. Also see the video documentary *Faces of the Nation* (Honolulu: Na Maka O Ka Aina, 1989).

205. On "blood quantum" and its effects, see "The Crucible of American Indian Identity," herein.

206. Dougherty, *To Steal a Kingdom*, pp. 233-4.

207. Kent, *Hawaii*, p. 198.

208. Photos of the event appear in Trask, *From a Native Daughter*.

209. The tribunal consisted of Milner S. Ball (Caldwell Professor of Constitutional Law at the University of Georgia), Hyun-Kyung Chung (Professor of Theology at Ewha Women's University in Seoul, Korea), Richard Falk (Albert G. Milbank Professor of International Law and Practice at Princeton University), Lennox Hinds (Professor of Criminal Law at Rutgers University), Te Moana Nui A Kiwa Jackson (Director of Maori Legal Service, Wellington, Aotearoa ["New Zealand"]), Asma Khader (attorney for the Palestinian Rights Society in Amman, Jordan), Oda Makoto (noted novelist and member of the Rome-based Permanent People's Tribunal) and Sharon H. Venne (United Nations advocate and then attorney for the Lubicon Lake Cree in Canada). The present author served as rapporteur. Professor Glenn T. Morris, of the Political Science Dept. at the University of Colorado/Denver, served as advocate/prosecutor. For the history and legal background of such tribunals, see Richard Falk, "Keeping Nuremberg Alive," in his *Human Rights and State Sovereignty* (New York: Holmes & Meier, 1981) pp. 195-201.

210. The interim report will be found in Hasager and Friedman, *Hawaii*, pp. 288-96.

211. The complete record of the tribunal will be found in Churchill and Venne, *Islands in Captivity*; the full (45 page) report is included in Vol. 1.

212. The complete text of the Ho'okupu is appended in Trask, *From a Native Daughter*, at pp. 211-36. On the poll, see the *Honolulu Star-Bulletin*, Jan. 6, 1977.

213. Trask, *From a Native Daughter*, p. 77.

214. Ibid., 74-7; Kent, *Hawaii*, p.199; Haunani-Kay Trask, "Money Cannot Substitute for Hawaiian Land Base," *Honolulu Star-Bulletin and Advertiser*, Jan. 17, 1993. It should be noted that Blaisdell has indicated that he disagrees with Ka Lahui on its "nation within a nation" formulation. His Ka Pakaukau calls for complete separation from the U.S. and a resumption of sovereign indigenous "control over our lands and natural resources" everywhere in the archipelago; quoted in *Hawaii Business*, Jan. 1992, p. 71.

215. *Aluli v. Rumsfeld* (Civ. No. 76-0380, U.S. Dist. For Hawaii (Oct. 13, 1976)). On the outcome described, see Taveres, et al., *Kaho'olawe*, pp. 2-3; Bruce Dunford, "Waihe'e Bill Gives Kahoolawe to Hawaiian Nation," *Honolulu Star-Bulletin*, Feb. 4, 1993.

216. House Bill 2340—otherwise known as the "Case Act," after its sponsor, Representative Ed Case, then chair of the state's Hawaiian Affairs Committee—is analyzed in Task, *From a Native Daughter*, pp. 78-9. The OHA is analyzed at pp. 72-4.

217. Only 27 percent of eligible Kanaka voters endorsed the state's plan; conversation with Mililani Trask, June 14, 2001 (notes on file).

218. The program text is appended in Trask, *From a Native Daughter*, at pp. 237-44.

218. A good overview is provided in Linda Hosek, "Traditional Diet: The Case for a Taro Economy," in Churchill and Venne, *Islands in Captivity*, Vol. 2.

219. See Kajsa Ekholm-Friedman and Jonathan Friedman, "Big Business in Small Places," in Hasager and Friedman, *Hawai'i*, pp. 222-53.

220. Ku Kuhakalau, "Preferred Education: Learning from the Past to Survive in the Future," in Hasager and Friedman, *Hawai'i*, pp. 218-21. Inroads have also been made in higher education; see Haunani-Kay Trask, "Native Student Organizing: The Case of the University of Hawai'i," in her *From a Native Daughter*, pp. 185-92.

221. L. Ku'umeaaloha Gomes, "Malama i Kekahi i Kekaha: Take Care of One, Take Care of All," in Hasager and Friedman, *Hawai'i*, pp. 68-70. Also see Alu Like, *Principles to Improve Health Care for Native Hawaiians* (Honolulu: E Ola Mau, 1990); H. Apoliona, A. Nahulu, H. Chang, N. Minton and K. Isaacs, *Native Hawaiian Traditional Practitioners' Forum* (Honolulu: E Ola Mau, 1990).

222. The early phase of this land recovery effort is covered in John Foster Dulles II, *A Broken Trust: Seventy Years of Failure of the State and Federal Governments to Protect the Civil Rights of Native Hawaiians* (Washington, D.C.: U.S. Department of Justice, Commission on Civil Rights, Hawaii Advisory Committee, 1991). Also see Haunani-Kay Trask, "The Birth of a Modern Hawaiian Movement: Kalama Valley, O'ahu," *Journal of Hawaiian History*, No. 21, 1987); Sondra Field Grace, "Anahola—Taro-Roots Practice of Self-Determination," in Hasager and Friedman, *Hawai'i*, pp. 210-3.

223. That "all peoples have the right to self-determination" is a phrase common to such important elements of international law as the United Nations Declaration on the Granting of Independence to Colonial Countries and Peoples (U.N.G.A. Res. 1514 (XV), 15 U.N. GAOR, Supp. (No. 16) 66, U.N. Doc. A/4684 (1961)), the International Covenant on Economic, Social, and Cultural Rights (U.N.G.A. Res. 2200 (XXI), 21 U.N. GAOR, Supp. (No.16) 49, U.N. Doc. A/6316 (1967); *reprinted in* 6 I.L.M. 360 (1967)), the International Covenant on Civil and Political Rights (U.N.G.A. Res. 2200 (XXI), 21 U.N. GAOR, Supp. (No. 16) 52, U.N. Doc. A/6316 (1967); *reprinted in* 6 I.L.M. 368 (1967)), and the United Nations Declaration on the Right to Development (U.N.G.A. Res. 41/128, 41 U.N. GAOR, Supp. (No. 53) U.N. Doc. A/41/925 (1986); see Weston, Falk and D'Amato, *Basic Documents*, pp. 343, 371, 376, 485.

224. Hanna Bokor-Szeggo, *New States and International Law* (Budapest: Academiai Kiado, 1970) p. 50.

225. Pomerance, *Self-Determination*, p. 89; Rigo Sureda, *Right to Self-Determination*, p. 106.

226. See notes 152, 153 and accompanying text.

227. U.N.G.A. Res. 41/41A UN GAOR Supp. (No. 53), UN Doc. A/41/53 (1986) at 49. Also see "Report of the Special Committee on the Situation with regard to the Implementation of the Declaration on the Granting of Independence to Colonial Countries and Peoples" (41 UN GAOR (No. 23), UN Doc A/41/23 (1986)); Vera Gowlland-Debbas, *Collective Responses to Illegal Acts in International Law: United Nations Actions in the Question of Southern Rhodesia* (Hague: Marinus Nijhoff, 1990).

228. Pomerance, *Self-Determination*, p. 30.

229. Ibid.

230. Rigo Sureda, *Right to Self-Determination*, p. 181.

231. James Crawford, *The Creation of States in International Law* (Oxford: Clarendon Press, 1979) p. 432.

232. Pomerance, *Self-Determination*, p. 32.

234. Lee Buchheit, *Secession: The Legitimacy of Self-Determination* (Hew Haven, CT: Yale University Press, 1978) p. 33.

235. Pomerance, *Self-Determination*, pp. 30-1.

236. Art. 1(4) of the UN Charter states that "All Members shall refrain in their international relations from the threat or use of force against the territorial integrity or political independence of any state"; Weston, Falk and D'Amato, *Basic Documents*, p. 17. Obviously, this is what the U.S. did to the Kanaka Maoli, not the other way around. American arguments against the independence of Hawai'i on the basis of 1(4) are thus roughly on par with German arguments that the liberation of Poland and the Ukraine after it had invaded and occupied them during World War II disturbed *its* "territorial integrity."

237. On the "Blue Water Thesis" and its implications for American Indians, see Roxanne Dunbar Ortiz, "Protection of Indian Territories in the United States: Applicability of International Law," in Imre Sutton, ed., *Irredeemable America: The Indians' Estate and Land Claims* (Albuquerque: University of New Mexico Press, 1985) pp. 247-66. Also see Appendix C, herein.

238. This is so under Art. 1, Sec. 10 of the U.S. Constitution; it is also a matter of international customary law, as stated in Art. 1 of the Vienna Convention on the Law of Treaties (U.N. Doc. A/CONF.39/27 at 289 (1969), 1155 U.N.T.S. 331, reprinted in 8 I.L.M. 679 (1969)); Weston, Falk and D'Amato, *Basic Documents*, pp. 2, 93. For background, see Ian Sinclair, *The Vienna Convention on the Law of Treaties* (Manchester, UK: Manchester University Press, [2nd ed.] 1984).

239. Lassa Oppenheim, *International Law* (London: Longman, Green, [8th ed.] 1955) p. 120. It should also be noted that in terms of the sovereignty inherent to any nation, "the recognition of [another] state is not constitutive, but merely declaratory... The status of a [nation] 'subject to international law' is [therefore] independent of recognition." That the right to sovereign expression on the part of any nation derives at base, not from its recognition by other nations, but from its "continued existence" within its own borders is a principle committed to black letter law in the 1919 Treaty of Saint-Germain; Crawford, *Creation of States*, pp. 21, 24, 50.

240. Ian Brownlie, *Principles of Public International Law* (Oxford: Clarendon Press, 1973) p. 82.

241. Pomerance, *Self-Determination*, p. 49;

242. The breach of any international obligation constitutes an "illegal act of tort"; George Schwarzenberger, *A Manual of International Law* (London: Stevens & Sons, 1967) p. 173. At p. 175, an international tort is further defined as being any "act or omission which is unjustified, uncondoned, attributable to a subject of international law and voluntary."

243. Ibid., p. 173. As concerns the matter of "legal interest" which the plaintiffs—in this instance the Kanaka Maoli—are required to demonstrate as a predication for a tort action, it is understood that if "an international tort has been committed directly against a subject of international law as, for instance by an invasion of the territory of another State, it is not necessary for the claimant to prove actual damage. The illegal act itself—and even a mere threat of such action—constitutes a sufficient legal interest"; ibid., p. 175. The Kanaks, nonetheless would plainly have no difficulty in demonstrating legal interest by way of tangible damages to both their lands and their lives.

244. Istvan Vasarhelyi, *Restitution in International Law* (Budapest: Hungary Academy of Science, 1964) p. 74.

245. Roy L. Brooks, "What Form Redress?" in Brooks, *When Sorry Isn't Enough*, pp. 87-91.

246. *Rice v. Cayetano* (528 U.S. 495 (2000)). In this case, the high court opined that it would be a matter of "reverse racism," and thus legally impermissible, for *haoles* to be barred from making disposition of Hawaiian Homes Land. For details, see Chris K. Iijima, "Race Over Rice: Binary Analytical Boxes and a Twenty-First Century Endorsement of Nineteenth Century Imperialism in *Rice v. Cayetano*," *Rutgers Law Review*, No. 91, Fall 2000; J. Kehaulani Kauanui, "The Politics of Blood and Sovereignty in *Rice v. Cayetano*," *Political and Legal Anthropology Review*, Vol. 25, No. 1, 2002.

247. Stephan Bates, *The South Pacific Island Countries and France: A Study of Inter-State Relations* (Canberra: Australian National University, 1990) p. 77.

248. General Assembly Resolution 2625 (XXV).

249. Ofuatey-Kodjoe, *Principle of Self-Determination*, pp. 177, 179.

250. There were several precursors to the Committee of Twenty-Four. An ad hoc committee was created in 1946 to receive reports from administering states. In 1948, this was redesignated the Special Committee of Information, and, in 1952, as the Special Committee of Information from Non-Self-Governing Territories. None of these earlier versions were imbued with any sort of enforcement power; Pomerance, *Self-Determination*, p. 35. Reinscription of a supposedly decolonized entity on the Secretariat's list automatically attends invocation of Committee powers; Ofuatey-Kodjoe, *Principle of Self-Determination*, p. 178-9.

251. Quoted in John Dugard, *The South West Africa/Namibia Dispute* (Berkeley: University of California Press, 1983) p. 481. The resolution was passed in opposition to South Africa's asserted right to administer Namibia.

252. Ibid., pp. 481-2.

253. The reinscription of New Caledonia was in fact one of first initiatives undertaken under provision of Res. 2625; Stephen Hemmingham, *France and the South Pacific* (Honolulu: University of Hawaii Press, 1992) p. 197.

254. William Blum, *Rogue State: A Guide to the World's Only Superpower* (Monroe, ME: Common Courage Press, 2000); Noam Chomsky, *Rogue States: The Rule of Force in World Affairs* (Cambridge, MA: South End Press, 2000).

255. Such a view is implicit to most of the material contained in Richard Falk's *Human Rights and State Sovereignty*, for example, esp. the essay entitled "The Algiers Declaration of the Rights of Peoples and the Struggle for Human Rights," pp. 195-94. The Universal Declaration on the Rights of Peoples ("Algiers Declaration") of July 4, 1976 is appended at pp. 225-8.

256. A relatively "gentle" initial framing could even be placed upon such initiatives by recalling that when it approved Surinam's supposedly self-determining decision to maintain its position of subordination to the Netherlands in 1954, the General Assembly "reserved its position as regard[ed] these territories with respect to Resolution 742." In effect, the right of the people of Surinam to alter their relationship to the Netherlands at such time and in such fashion as they themselves desired was reserved for them by the UN, and finally exercised in 1975, when Surinam opted for full independence. Arguably, given the binding effect of Resolution 742 (see note 148), the contingent aspect of the 1954 approval instrument (UNGA Res. 946) could be considered implicit to all other such approvals, including the instrument by which Hawaiian statehood was approved (UNGA Res. 1469). It follows that the Kanaka Maoli retain the right to alter their relationship to the U.S. at such time as they choose, absent the least misconduct on the part of the United States. In this way, the U.S. could be offered the opportunity to accept Hawaiian independence without concomitantly accepting censure for its record of illegalities. On the Surinam arrangement, see Rigo Sureda, *Right to Self-Determination*, p. 63; Easton, *Western Colonialism*, p. 110; Ansprenger, *Colonial Empires*, pp. 106-8.

257. This is entirely consistent with the sorts of initiatives called for by Phyllis Bennis in the chapter entitled "Democratizing the UN," in her *Calling the Shots*, pp. 233-44.

258. The famous phrase was penned by John Marshall, third Chief Justice of the U.S. Supreme Court, in *Marbury v. Madison* (1 Cranch 137 (1803)). For analysis, see Jean Edward Smith, *John Marshall: Defender of a Nation* (New York: Henry Holt, 1996) pp. 309-26, quote at p. 325.

259. See Robert Underwood and Laura Souder, eds. *Chamorro Self-Determination* (Agana, Guam: Micronesia Area Research Ctr., 1986). The situation in Puerto Rico is more complex. Although the island was removed by the U.S. from the List of Non-Self-Governing Territories in 1953, persistent reports of discrimination against, and outright persecution of, Puerto Rican nationalists caused the committee to investigate the situation during the early 1980s. The findings were significant enough that it was decided in 1986 that the committee should take the "Puerto Rican Question" under continuing review; "Special Committee Decision of 14 August 1986 Concerning Puerto Rico" (UN Doc. A/AC.109/25, 11 Aug. 1987). In 1993, the colonized population of Puerto Rico was finally given an opportunity to vote upon their status, with the result that the majority appear to have opted to continue in their "commonwealth" relationship to the U.S. (statehood polled a close second, with independence coming in a distant third). The background of the plebiscite is covered, but the outcome avoided, in Ronald Fernandez, *Prisoners of Colonialism: The Struggle for Justice in Puerto Rico* (Monroe, ME: Common Courage Press, 1994) pp. 321-8. This outcome seems challengeable on its face, however, insofar as the U.S. allowed no direct UN supervision over the "self-determining" process leading to decision by the colonized to elect a status other than full independence. It was on precisely these grounds that the General Assembly rejected the results of a French administered plebiscite in Somaliland in 1967; Rigo Sureda, *Right to Self-Determination*, p. 314. Indeed, the mandate of the Committee of 24 has been construed as "refus[ing] to endorse the results of [referenda on status] in which the [U.N.] was not officially represented"; Pomerance, *Self-Determination*, pp. 35-6.

260. Aside from the present volume, see my *Struggle for the Land: Native North American Resistance to Genocide, Ecocide and Colonization* (San Francisco: City Lights, [2nd ed.] 2002).

261. See George Manuel and Michael Posluns, *The Fourth World: An Indian Reality* (New York: Free Press, 1974).

262. For explication of the point at issue, see Bernard Nietschmann, "The Fourth World: Nations

versus States," in George J. Demko and William B. Wood, eds., *Reordering the World: Geopolitical Perspectives for the Twenty-First Century* (Boulder, CO: Westview Press, 1994) pp. 225-42.

263. See Noam Chomsky, *Profit Over People: Neoliberalism and the Global Order* (New York: Seven Stories Press, 1999); Richard Falk, *Predatory Globalization: A Critique* (Oxford, UK: Polity Press, 1999).

264. This is quite in line with Felix S. Cohen's observation, made a half-century ago, that the fate of indigenous peoples serves as a sort of "miner's canary" providing early warning of what lies ahead for the "broader" society; see his "The Erosion of Indian Rights, 1950-53: A Case-Study in Bureaucracy," *Yale Law Journal*, No. 62, 1953, p. 390.

265. Herbert Marcuse, "Repressive Tolerance," in Robert Paul Wolf, Barrington Moore, Jr., and Herbert Marcuse, *A Critique of Pure Tolerance* (Boston: Beacon Press, [2nd ed.] 1970) p. 111.

266. See, e.g., Holly Sklar, "Brave New World Order," and Noam Chomsky, " 'What We Say Goes': The Middle East in the New World Order," in Cynthia Peters, ed., *Collateral Damage: The "New World Order" at Home and Abroad* (Boston: South End Press, 1992) pp. 3-46, 49-92.

267. Alexander J. Motyl, ed., *The Post-Soviet Nations: Perspectives on the Demise of the USSR* (New York: Columbia University Press, 1992).

268. See the 1941 essay entitled "Disunion Now: A Plea for a Society Based on Small Autonomous Units," in Leopold Kohr's *The Breakdown of Nations* (London: Routledge & Kegan Paul, 1957; reprinted by Green Books, 2001) pp. 73-86; Winona LaDuke's preface, "Succeeding into Native North America: A Secessionist View," and my own essay, "I Am Indigenist: Notes on the Ideology of the Fourth World," in my *Struggle for the Land*, pp. 10-3, 367-402; Alexander R. Murphy, "International Law and the Sovereign State: Challenges to the Status Quo," in Demko and Wood, *Reordering the World*, pp. 209-24. Also see Kirkpatrick Sale, *Human Scale* (New York: Coward, McCann & Geoghegan, 1980).

269. Quoted in Bennis, *Calling the Shots*, p. 319.

270. Quoted in Patricia Seed, *Ceremonies of Possession in Europe's Conquest of the New World, 1492-1640* (Cambridge, UK: Cambridge University Press, 1995) p. 8.

271. For the phrase used, see Léon Trotsky, *History of the Russian Revolution* (New York: Pathfinder Press, 2001) p. 1157. On the "dynamic of violence" suggested, see my and Mike Ryan's *Pacifism as Pathology: Reflections on the Role of Armed Struggle in North America* (Winnipeg: Arbeiter Ring, 1998).

272. For a preliminary analysis leading in very much the same direction, see Noam Chomsky, *9-11* (New York: Seven Stories Press, 2001). Also see Nafeez Mosaddeq Ahmed, *The War on Freedom: How and Why America was Attacked on September 11, 2001* (Joshua Tree, CA: Media Messenger Books, 2002).

273. Ample elaboration of this principle will be found in John Duffet, ed., *Against the Crime of Silence: Proceedings of the International War Crimes Tribunal* (New York: Clarion Books, 1970). Also see Jeffrey Ross, ed., *Controlling State Crime* (New York: Garland, 1995).

274. Cleaver's formulation, which he actually attributed to his wife, Kathleen, was first articulated in a speech at Syracuse University during the fall of 1968, an excerpt from which was collected on an obscure spoken word LP entitled *Dig!* the following year. By then, it had also been adopted as the masthead slogan of *New Left Notes*, the organizational newspaper of Students for a Democratic Society.

# Charades, Anyone?
## The Indian Claims Commission in Context

> For the nation, there is an unrequited account of sin and injustice that sooner
> or later will call for national retribution.
>
> —George Catlin
> 1844

One of the more pernicious myths shrouding the realities of Indian/white relations in the United States is that the U.S. has historically comported itself according to uniquely lofty legal and moral principles when interacting with "its" indigenous peoples. The idea has been around in the form of official rhetoric since at least as early as 1787, when the Congress, already pursuing a practical policy going in exactly the opposite direction, used its enactment of the Northwest Ordinance as an opportunity to pledge itself to conducting its Indian affairs in "utmost good faith."[1] As President Harry S. Truman would put it 159 years later, it should be "perfectly clear...that in our transactions with Indian tribes we have...set for ourselves the standard of fair and honorable dealings, pledging respect for all Indian property rights."[2]

In 1985, the late Wilcomb E. Washburn, then preeminent "American Indianist" historian for the federal government's Smithsonian Institution, waxed a bit more expansive when he observed that "[b]ecause U.S. Indian policy is...supportive of Indian values and aspirations, questions that in other countries would not arise are the subject of intense debate in the United States...[Hence,] in broad, general perspective, one is impressed with the extraordinary recognition to the now powerless Indian tribes of this country not only to maintain a secure trust-guaranteed and tax-free land base, but to exercise aspects of sovereignty that normally derive from the control of territory held by a powerful sovereign."[3]

Lest it be argued that views like Truman's and Washburn's represent little at this point beyond quaintly jingoistic anachronisms, note should be taken that the United States is presently engaged at the United Nations in pushing its own version of Indian law as *the* model upon which the U.N.'s incipient Universal Declaration on the Rights of Indigenous Peoples should be based, its own Indian policy as that most worthy of emulation by the rest of the world. Conversely, the U.S. has threatened to block any codification of native rights in international law which fails to conform to its own purportedly exalted standards of enlightened humanitarianism.[4]

The expression of such sentiments is by no means a uniquely conservative vice. They are continually voiced by more moderate commentators. "Few great powers," observed liberal policy analyst Harvey D. Rosenthal in 1990, "have acknowledged such fundamental moral or legal debts, especially from a small, powerless minority in their midst," as has the United States with respect to American Indians.[5] Nor, by and large, will one encounter much of an alternative among what are ostensibly the more radical sectors of the Euroamerican populace, a matter abundantly evidenced in the recent tirades of Bob Black, Lawrence Jarach and other prominent "antiauthoritarians" in the pages of *Anarchy* magazine.[6]

From start to finish, then, and irrespective of ideological cant, the U.S. settler society's interpretation of itself is all but invariably adorned in "that protective cloak of righteousness which is the inevitable garment of the Anglo-Philistine."[7] As Rosenthal himself admits, the resulting hegemony — that the U.S. has always been "well-intentioned" in its relations with Indians and that, while less than perfect, the process of interaction has ultimately "worked out for the best" for all concerned — is one "that [has] long comforted whites and afflicted Indians" in the most grotesque manner imaginable.[8]

This last is not difficult to discern, at least for anyone willing to look at the matter honestly. Despite Washburn's glowing description of Native North America's "trust-guaranteed and tax-free land base," the fact is that reservation-based American Indians are the poorest people on the continent, receiving by far the lowest annual and lifetime incomes of any census group. Overall unemployment on most reservations hovers around 60 percent, while on some it has been in the ninetieth percentile for decades.[9] The most impoverished area of the U.S. for the past forty years has been Shannon County, on the Pine Ridge Sioux Reservation, in South Dakota.[10]

The indices of poverty in Indian Country are now, as they have been throughout the twentieth century, of a sort more commonly associated with

Third World locales than with those inside the earth's mightiest economic superpower.

> The Indian health level is the lowest and the disease rate the highest of all major population groups in the United States. The incidence of tuberculosis is over 400 percent higher than the national average. Similar statistics show that the incidence of strep infections is 1,000 percent, meningitis is 2,000 percent higher, and dysentery is 10,000 percent higher. Death rates from disease are shocking when Indian and non-Indian populations are compared. Influenza and pneumonia are 300 percent greater killers among Indians. Diseases such as hepatitis are at epidemic proportions, with an 800 percent higher chance of death. Diabetes is almost a plague.[11]

Malnutrition claims Indians at twelve times the U.S. national rate, while infant mortality runs as high as 1,400 percent of the norm.[12] In addition, "between fifty thousand and fifty-seven thousand Indian homes are [officially] considered uninhabitable. Many of these are beyond repair. For example, over 88 percent of the homes of the Sioux in Pine Ridge have been classified as substandard dwellings."[13] Consequently, Indians die from exposure at five times the national rate.[14] Under such conditions, despair is endemic, a circumstance engendering massive rates of alcoholism and other forms of substance abuse, as well as attendant social/familial violence, each of which takes its toll. The suicide rate among native teenagers runs up to 10,000 percent that of non-Indian youth.[15]

All told, in a country where male life expectancy averages 71.8 years, a reservation-based American Indian man can expect to live only 44.6. Although his female counterpart lives about 36 months longer than he, her general-population sister has an average life expectancy of 78.8 years.[16] Thus, each time an American Indian dies—or is born—on a reservation in the U.S., a third of a lifetime is lost. To put it another way, one-third of each succeeding generation of American Indians has been annihilated in a quiet holocaust which has continued unabated since the "Indian Wars" supposedly ended in 1890.

The reason underlying this altogether dismal situation is also strikingly apparent. It will be found in the very trust status—about which Washburn professes such pride—in which indigenous property is held by the United States. Asserted most clearly in the Supreme Court's 1903 *Lone Wolf* opinion, the federal government's self-assigned and perpetual "fiduciary authority" over Indians has afforded it the "plenary power" to dispose of native assets in whatever manner it sees fit.[17] Hence, the abundance of minerals and other resources which grace many reservations have been exploited with increasing intensity over the past half-century at prices deeply discounted to corporate "developers" by the Secretary of Interior (acting in his "trustee" capacity).[18] Both resources and profits have correspondingly flowed into the U.S. economy while Indians have been left destitute.

The term by which such relations between nations or peoples are customarily described is "colonialism," albeit in this case of a sort in which the colonized are encapsulated within the claimed domestic territoriality of the colonizer rather than of the more classical overseas variety.[19] Internal colonialism is colonialism nonetheless, and it has been prohibited under international law since the U.N. Charter was effected in 1945.[20] In no small part, this is because to be colonized, whether externally or internally, is to be denied that range of self-determining prerogatives which, as a matter of law, comprise the most fundamental rights of any nation.[21] Colonialism is thus the very obverse of the sovereignty Washburn and his colleagues contend is exercised by indigenous nations in the United States. Moreover, given the nature of its impact upon native people over the past hundred years, it is fair to say that the U.S. internal colonial model offers ample confirmation of Jean-Paul Sartre's famous dictum that "colonialism equals genocide."[22]

**Necessary Illusions**

One would think that the astonishing gulf separating Washburnian descriptions of U.S. benevolence towards native peoples from the unremitting squalor to which those same peoples continue to be subjected at the hands of the United States might provoke what the sociologist C. Wright Mills once termed "cognitive dissonance" among the public at large.[23] This, in turn, might be expected to generate the sort of outrage which would compel a constructive alteration in the relationship between the U.S. and those indigenous nations upon whose traditional territories it has constituted itself.

As Vine Deloria, Jr., long ago observed, however, it is a characteristic aspect of contemporary North American society that "no significant number of people will be stirred from their inertia to accomplish anything. They will not think. They will not question. And, most importantly, they will not object to whatever happens until it directly affects the manner in which they view their own personal survival."[24] More charitably, Imre Sutton has remarked that "other factors [also] inhibit our fullest perception of tribal grievances. Perhaps apathy or indifference prevails. Yet I am inclined to think that most Americans too readily believe that [American Indians have been] properly compensated" for whatever evils may have befallen them in the past, and that things really *are* "better" now.[25]

There are a number of reasons why this (mis)impression has come to be so deeply rooted in the mainstream American mind, beginning with the relentless drumbeat of official pronouncements such as Truman's and extending through the matrices of news packaging, media depiction and the spin so carefully put to truth by the myriad "responsible scholars" like Washburn and Rosenthal who infest the academic milieu.[26] The cornerstone upon which the whole proposition's credibility may be said to rest, however, assumes a much more concrete form, that of the federal government's Indian Claims Commission (ICC), an entity maintained from 1946 to 1978 for the express purpose of "resolving" outstanding grievances accumulated by native people against the United States during the course of the latter's expansion and consolidation over the preceding two centuries.[27]

The prevailing view is that the Commission represented not only "the greatest submission ever made by a sovereign state to moral and legal claims," as one federal jurist put it at the time,[28] but that its purpose was "to do justice for its own sake" where American Indians were/are concerned.[29] Over the past three generations, it has thus become a veritable truism among members of the dominant settler society that "no stronger motive than conscience has compelled this nation . . . to grant its indigenous minority the right to seek redress" through such a mechanism.[30]

The most cursory examination of the record reveals the magnitude of untruth embedded in such postulations. Had the United States ever actually been motivated by its collective "conscience" to dispense justice to Indians, it might all along, or at any point, have simply elected to comply with the extant requirements of international law rather than ignoring them and/or seeking to pervert them to its own ends (a stance it still displays).[31]

Even within the framework of its own judicial structure, the U.S. might easily have provided the native people whose land it was so systematically expropriating some measure of redress at least as early as 1855, when it created a special court to "hear and determine all claims founded upon any law of Congress, or upon any contract, express or implied, with the government of the United States."[32] Instead, in 1863, Indians were specifically denied access to the Court of Claims by an Act of Congress.[33]

[Moreover, at] the same time the right to redress claims was being circumscribed *for* the Indian it was being expanded for the white man *against* the red man. The claims of whites for "depredations" committed against them by Indians under treaty were first recognized in an act of 1796. This act and ones following it in 1834 and 1859 provided for indemnification of losses from Indian depredations to be paid out of Indian annuities or "out of any money in the Treasury not otherwise appropriated." Thus, though the Indian could not sue the government, he could be "sued" by it (and denied counsel) in the name of its citizens and be subject to forced payment of claims from his treaty funds. By 1872 (the depredation legislation was renewed in 1870, 1872, 1885, 1886 and 1891) close to 300 claims were settled against the Indians for over $434,000. This amount was 55 percent of what was claimed.[34]

Indeed, although they were obviously considered human enough to convey land title by treaty and to compensate Euroamericans for losses (real or invented), U.S. courts never formally conceded that Indians were actually "persons" capable of legal standing in their own right until the *Standing Bear* case of 1879.[35] This led, in 1881, to an act permitting native people to sue in the Court of Claims, but only in the event that they obtained specific legislative authorization whenever they sought to do so.[36] The expensive and time-consuming burden of acquiring a predicating Act of Congress each time they desired access to the claims court had the entirely predictable, and undoubtedly intended, effect of constraining Indians' ability to avail themselves of it. Hence, from 1881 to 1923, only 39 native claims were filed.[37]

A further complication was that in considering claims prior to authorizing them for adjudication, Congress was positioned to alter them substantially. This it did with consistent abandon, invariably rejecting attempts to recover unceded land.[38] Legislators habitually deleted provisions for payment of interest, even on matters dating back a century or more.[39] And, with equal frequency, they introduced provisions requiring that judicial awards forthcoming to the native plaintiffs, if any, be subject to "gratuitous offsets" equal to whatever monies the government could be said to have already expended "in their behalf."[40]

The gratuitous offsets constituted an especially onerous imposition insofar as they placed Indians in the position of retroactively subsidizing "services" they'd never wanted and, in many cases, vociferously opposed. "Gratuities allowed," Rosenthal notes, "included the payment of [federal] Indian agents [and] police, judges, interpreters, maintenance and repair of agency buildings, teachers, and prorated expenses for education of Indian children at various institutions."[41] He concludes, with typical understatement, that most "of these 'gratuities' were more for the benefit of the government than the Indians."[42]

For its part, the U.S. Department of Justice devoted itself to delaying and otherwise obstructing Indian claims cases by all possible means. Years, often decades, passed while federal attorneys "prepared themselves," not to see to it that the government's self-assigned fiduciary responsibility to Indians was fulfilled, but to ensure that native claimants received nothing, or at least as little as possible, in court.[43] As was observed in 1940, it "cannot be shown that the [U.S. Attorneys] in a single case investigated the complaints. . .of the Indians with a view towards doing justice to them."[44]

On the contrary, the energy of Justice Department personnel was spent prodding the General Accounting Office (GAO) to dig up offsets with which to diminish or nullify awards expected to accrue from claims they *knew* to be valid (if offsets could be advanced in an amount equal to or exceeding the amount of the potential award in any case, the claims court could be expected to dismiss it out-of-hand).[45] The fruits of such tactics are altogether unsurprising.

> The Wichita of Oklahoma first gained the right to sue in an act of 1895 but were stalled until a jurisdictional act of 1924 led to a final dismissal in 1939. The Klamath in Oregon gained their act in 1920 [but] were dismissed in 1938. . . . The Northwestern Band of Shoshone of Utah and Idaho [having begun their efforts in 1879] received their act in 1926, and saw dismissal in 1942. The Osage of Oklahoma [after spending 48 years in the process] gained a jurisdictional act 1921, and were dismissed in 1928.[46]

And so it went. By the latter year, Senator Linn Frazier of North Dakota, a member of the Committee on Indian Affairs, was estimating that at the then current rate it would take another 172 years to wade through the 86 pending cases he believed would eventually go to trial.[47] In the sixteen instances where awards had actually been made at that point, the court had allowed a mere $13.6 million against claims totaling $346 million. Offsets amounting to $11 million were then deducted, leaving Indians with a paltry $2.65 million overall.[48]

All told, by 1946, the Attorney General was able to report that Indians had been awarded only $49.4 million—well under 10 percent of the gross amount claimed in the cases involved—offset by $29.4 million in gratuity deductions.[49] This afforded those indigenous nations filing the suits an aggregate pay-out of only $20 million, from which they had to absorb legal costs, the expense of lobbying Congress to gain authorization, and so on. At best, the federal government's vaunted "due process" was for Indians essentially a break-even endeavor, while a number of people lost large chunks of their lives and appreciable sums attempting it.[50]

Truly, the U.S. proved itself an "unsympathetic foe" of indigenous nations, a "tough and clever opponent" when using its own courts to defend against the claims of its native "wards," no matter how legitimate.[51] It can be argued—and has been often enough—that this is exactly as it should be in an adversarial system of justice like that of the United States.[52] Perhaps so, but the blatant systemic conflict of interest with which the process was riddled from top to bottom should really suggest something else.[53] In any event, the portrait thus presented is anything but that of a government/society committed by its conscience to doing the right thing, either morally or legally.

### Footdragging in the First Degree

It's not that the government lacked alternatives to the courts in dealing with Indian land claims, even within its own politicojudicial structure and experience. During the nineteenth century, sixteen separate commissions were created by the United States under various treaties, conventions and agreements, to dispense settlements from foreign nations and/or to resolve mutual claims.[54] The last of these, convened in 1901, had barely completed its work when, in 1910, former Indian Commissioner Francis E. Leupp recommended establishing something like a claims commission to expedite the processing of Indian claims cases.[55]

In 1913, Assistant Commissioner of Indian Affairs Edgar B. Merritt went further, testifying before the House of Representatives that an "investigatory commission . . . or comparable body" should be created to prepare reports and recommendations allowing Congress rather than the Court of Claims to "make some permanent disposition" of native claims. This approach, he argued, would not only be more "prompt and efficient" than the judicial process, but produce more "equitable" outcomes.[56]

Such proposals were met with yawns by legislators, not least because Leupp and Merritt were both avid proponents of assimilation, a national policy then in full force and designed to bring about the disappearance of the last traces of indigenous culture within the U.S.[57] Since it was generally believed that what was left of the Indians were rapidly "vanishing" anyway, and would likely "die off" long before their claims ever came to trial, there seemed no pressing need for improvement in the mechanisms for dealing with them.[58]

It was not until the 1920s, with the increasingly proliferate discovery of mineral deposits on Indian reservations, that attitudes began to change.[59] Loath to recreate the irrational squandering of resources that had occurred in Oklahoma when reservations were abolished and underlying oil deposits opened to the ravages of "free enterprise" at the turn of the century,[60] at least some policymakers began to cast about for ways of retaining these new finds under a central planning authority. The most logical route to this end resided in continuing the government's administration of the reservations "in trust" for an indefinite period, a matter requiring the abrupt abandonment of assimilation policy as it had been configured up till then.[61]

In 1928, the Meriam Commission, a body of one hundred prominent business and civic leaders assembled by Secretary of Interior Hubert Work to consider the "Indian Question," recommended exactly that.[62] The group, echoing Leupp's earlier suggestion, also urged that a "special commission" be created, separate from the courts, to investigate and draft legislation by which Congress could resolve whatever Indian claims were deemed "meritorious."[63] The idea was seconded a year later by Nathan R. Margold, a New York attorney specializing in Indian law and policy, who had been retained by the Institute for Government Research to study the situation.[64]

Although Congress was relatively quick to "reorganize" the reservations for longterm existence, passing an act for this purpose in 1934, it consistently balked at addressing the claims issue.[65] To a significant extent, this was due to an outright hostility expressed by the Justice Department to any measure which might serve to accomplish such objectives. As Attorney General Francis Biddle eventually summed up the Department's position, it would cost "huge sums"—he estimated $3 billion or more—to achieve anything resembling an equitable and comprehensive disposition of native claims. Since it would be "inordinately expensive" for the United States to actually pay for what it had taken from Indians, he reasoned, it would be better to do nothing at all.[66]

Such thinking was restated, endlessly and with discernible vehemence, by legislators like Missouri's John J. Cochrane, who noted with pride in 1937 that he'd personally prevented "dozens" of native claims from being paid over the preceding three years. Congress, he said, could "disregard millions and think of billions if the Indian claims ever got in the hands of [a] commission" designed to treat such cases on their merits.[67] Thomas O'Malley of Wisconsin described the whole idea of native people being compensated for the taking of their property—or anything else, apparently—as "the biggest racket in the country."[68]

Others, plainly ignorant of, or choosing to ignore, the government's historical policy of denying Indians access to U.S. courts, now opined that native claims cases were too "ancient" to be considered. William M. Colmer of Mississippi argued that while "a great injury [had undoubtedly been] done to Indians in the past," it would be unfair to "some 130,000,000 American citizens who are taxpayers" to make any serious contemporary effort to set things right.[69] O'Malley chimed in that it was absolutely necessary for Congress to prevent "some shyster lawyer" from "dig[ging] up a descendant of some blanket Indian and make a million dollar claim against the government" over Manhattan Island.[70]

Perspectives of this sort, which were ubiquitous, received substantial reinforcement from the Supreme Court. As late as 1945, Justice Robert H. Jackson, writing for the majority in the *Northwest Bands of Shoshone* case, held that the ongoing expropriation of native land was not compensable because any injuries done to Indians were "committed by our forefathers in the distant past against remote ancestors of the present claimants."[71] Moreover, Jackson asserted, such claims as a general rule should not be considered legally actionable, since Indians, unlike whites, had traditionally possessed "no true conception" of property ownership.[72]

In arriving at the latter conclusion—which, if applied consistently rather than being trotted out only when convenient to nullify a native claim, would have served to void the legitimacy of all transfers of property from indigenous peoples to the U.S. (leaving the United States without so much as a pretense of valid title to most of its claimed territoriality)—Jackson and his colleagues resorted to what has been called "The Menagerie Theory." At base, this is the notion that Indians "are less than human and that their relations to their lands is not the human relation of ownership but rather something similar to the relation that animals bear to the areas in which they may be temporarily confined."[73]

President Franklin D. Roosevelt also made it clear on several occasions that he was "unsympathetic" to creation of a commission or comparable mechanism by which Indian claims might be resolved in an equitable manner. Purporting to be more preoccupied with the future than with the past, he announced in 1936 that he would be unlikely to sign any bill which might lead to the government's "paying out monies on account of wrongs done to the dead."[74]

Given the negative consensus dominant in all three branches of the federal government, proposals to establish a claims commission went nowhere for more than a third of a century after Francis Leupp's initial recommendation. From 1930 to 1945, at least seventeen bills offering variations on the theme were rejected by Congress, most of them dying in committee before they ever reached the floor of either the House or Senate.[75] On the other hand, legislation *was* passed in 1935 to further entrench the practice of deducting gratuitous offsets from awards achieved through the Court of Claims.[76]

### In the Matter of Self-Interest

Recitation of its background raises the obvious question of why, the Senate having already done so on July 17, the U.S. House of Representatives unanimously approved creation of the ICC on August 2, 1946.[77] The answers here are two, neither of them having the least to do with "good conscience" or a legislative desire "to see justice done" to indigenous peoples encapsulated within the United States. Quite the opposite, since Congress as a whole was demonstrably motivated by the crassest sort of national self-interest.

One track along which things moved concerned a U.S. ambition to assert itself as a planetary moral authority by way of organizing an international tribunal to oversee the punishment of Germany's nazi government in the aftermath of World War II.[78] First publicly articulated in 1944 over the strong objections of America's wartime allies, this precedential concept actually dated from 1943.[79] Eventually, U.S. diplomats were able to negotiate the London Charter of August 8, 1945, setting in motion the Nuremberg Trials.[80]

A problem for the Americans all along, however, resided in their intent to prosecute the nazi leadership for the waging of aggressive war(s) for purposes of acquiring *Lebensraum* (living space) at the expense of peoples they considered *untermenschen* (subhumans) in eastern Europe.[81] The sticking point was that, from at least as early as the publication of *Mein Kampf* in 1925, Adolf Hitler himself had been at pains to explain that he was basing the nazi *Lebensraumpolitik* (policy of territorial expansion) directly on the U.S. design of militarily dispossessing American Indians during the nineteenth century.[82]

As historian Norman Rich has summarized the thesis openly proclaimed therein:

> Neither Spain nor Britain should be the models for German expansion, but the Nordics of North America, who had ruthlessly pushed aside an inferior race to win for themselves soil and territory for the future. To undertake this essential task, sometimes difficult, always cruel—this was Hitler's version of the White Man's Burden.[83]

So well known was the correlation between U.S. and nazi expansionist policies by war's end that graduate students were embarking upon studies of it.[84] Plainly, if it were to assume the moral high ground at Nuremberg and appear to be dispensing anything more than mere "victor's justice," it was vital for the United States to do something concrete to distinguish the contours of its own process of expansion from that pursued by the men in the defendants' dock.[85] In essence, it was understood that the whole historical pattern of U.S. territorial growth needed to be placed, post hoc, on a footing that could be projected as consisting of "acquisition by purchase" rather than by conquest, and the sooner the better.

Not coincidentally, in late 1943—at just the moment the United States first became interested in staging a postwar trial of the nazi hierarchy—Congress quietly convened a select committee both to revive the long dormant and much reviled idea of a claims commission, and to hammer out the details of how it would work.[86] Over the next year and a half, other sectors of the government were brought to accept that establishment of the ICC would be necessary to putting a proper gloss on the U.S. image internationally.

Hence, by 1945 even Attorney General Biddle, preparing as he was to don the judicial robes in which he would sit in judgment at Nuremberg, entered a grudging endorsement of claims commission proposals (albeit, he couldn't resist leaving behind suggestions as to how the final bill might be prevented from compensating Indians too "liberally").[87] The same can be said for Justice Jackson, the ink not yet dry on his description of Indians as a "menagerie" in *Northwestern Bands*, who was in the process of temporarily reversing roles with Biddle by taking leave of the Supreme Court to serve as lead U.S. prosecutor in the cases brought, among others, against Julius Streicher, a nazi publisher charged with depicting Jews as less than human.[88]

The extent to which Congress' belated creation of the ICC was intended not just as a measure fulfilling U.S. domestic requirements, but as a PR gesture meant to resonate favorably at Nuremberg and elsewhere within the international community, was quite evident in the way South Dakota

Representative Karl Mundt introduced the bill authorizing it to the House. The commission, he said, would stand as "an example for all the world to follow in its treatment of minorities."[89]

Such posturing was amplified when President Truman, upon signing it, acquainted the public with the Indian Claims Commission Act on August 13, 1946. "This bill," he intoned with a straight face, "makes perfectly clear what many men and women, here *and abroad*, have failed to recognize, that . . . [i]nstead of confiscating Indian lands, we have purchased from the tribes that once owned this continent more than 90 percent of our public domain (emphasis added)."[90] No mention was made, of course, of which party it was that had set—and was continuing to set—the "sales" price, or whether the native owners had wanted to sell their homelands.

## A Final Solution, American-Style

If the stench of hypocrisy can be said to have emanated from the first of the U.S. motivations in bringing the ICC into being, the second was even more malodorous. This had to do with a desire on the part of such unabashed foes of indigenous rights as Karl Mundt to impose what he called a "permanent solution to the Indian problem."[91] A "final settlement" of outstanding claims, it was argued, would position the government to terminate all further expenditures on behalf of Indians,[92] and to withdraw from its trust relationship with/recognition of the existence of selected peoples,[93] effectively bringing about their speedy dissolution and disappearance as identifiable human groups.[94]

The key for many legislators was how to accomplish the objective in the cheapest manner possible. "Our only real interest," said Representative, later Senator, Henry M. "Scoop" Jackson of Washington, "is to try and economize in this matter."[95] Given that Jackson chaired the House committee responsible for drafting the bill ultimately enacted as law, it is not difficult to discern the reasoning underlying a number of its principle elements. For instance, although the Act mandated the ICC to investigate and "resolve" all claims alleging "wrongful takings" of native land, under no circumstances were Indians permitted to recover their property.[96]

Nor were native people to be compensated at a rate equivalent to the contemporary value of what they'd lost, or, as a rule, allowed to collect interest against whatever amount the Commission concluded they should have received when their land was taken.[97] Moreover, the old practice of deducting gratuitous offsets from any monies awarded was carried over from the Court of Claims to the ICC.[98] With things thus stacked against them, as Oklahoma Senator Elmer Thomas had earlier remarked, Indians "would be lucky [if] in the final adjudication they should get [even] a few dollars."[99]

Cynical as it was, Thomas' insight was more than borne out when, after a full decade of its operational existence, Chief Commissioner Edgar E. Witt reported to Congress in 1956 that the ICC had by then awarded a pay-out of less than $10 million against aggregate claims exceeding $800 million.[100] A decade later, from the grand total of $194 million awarded by the ICC against nearly $2 billion in claims, "compromise settlements" had resulted in net pay-outs of only $87 million (including the $10 million reported by Witt).[101] Such puny awards were expressly construed under the 1946 Act as precluding "any further claims or demand against the United States."[102]

Unquestionably, "Congress could take some fiscal satisfaction [in having] got the better of the Indian once more," even as the ICC averred to have "cleared title" to millions of acres of contested territory.[103] But this was not the worst of it. Since "the goals of Termination and the Claims Commission were seen as parallel for the first twenty years,"[104] a native people's acceptance of even a pittance—which the Justice Department continued to insist was awarded only "as a matter of grace, not as a matter of right"[105]—often served as a pretext upon which it could be declared it "extinct."[106]

Nowhere was this "alliance of the Commission and termination legislation" more blatant than in the appointment of former Utah Senator Arthur V. Watkins as Chief Commissioner in 1959.[107] A proverbial architect of U.S. termination policy in the 1940s and early '50s, Watkins was responsible to a degree probably greater than any other individual for the formal nullification of more than a hundred targeted peoples over the following decade.[108] These ranged from the populous and relatively solvent Menominees and Klamaths in Wisconsin and Oregon to the tiny "Mission Bands" of southern California. They did not, however, include a single nation whose reserved landbase was endowed with mineral deposits federal planners wished to retain in trust.[109]

As head of the ICC, Watkins' stated objective was, as it had been in the Senate, to "get the government out of the Indian business." His method was to accelerate the pace of awards to/termination of "superfluous" peoples as much as possible.[110] This, in a stunning Orwellianism, he described as "emancipation" (he himself was often referred to during the Eisenhower years as

"The Great Emancipator").[111] In his *Red Man's Land, White Man's Law*, even Wilcomb Washburn was forced to choke on this one, outlining the whole minuet orchestrated by Watkins and his colleagues in terms of "Congress cloaking its own interests in a rhetoric of generosity toward the Indian."[112]

More to the point, while until the end of the Second World War native peoples "were thought of as defeated nations and were so treated and so held captive," after the war the resulting relationship "between prisoner and jailer" more frequently became that between condemned and executioner as many of them were liquidated altogether.[113] The ICC was created and maintained largely to mask this ugly reality, sometimes making it appear as the opposite of itself. But it did nothing to change it.

### Charades, Anyone?

When Congress established the ICC in 1946, it anticipated that the new body would be responsible for handling perhaps two hundred cases—a figure roughly corresponding to the backlog piled up in the Court of Claims—and that the task could be accomplished in five years.[114] By the end of 1951, the number of claims had reached 852, "more than ever contemplated by anyone in the process."[115] The lifespan of the Commission was therefore extended for another five years, a procedure which would be repeated several times before the ICC was finally phased out in 1978.

The protracted nature of the proceedings were not due simply to the unexpectedly large number of claims filed. Nor, it should be noted in fairness to the Commission itself, were they typically a result of its own many faults. Rather, applying its usual perverse twist to the dictum that justice delayed is justice denied (always a desirable outcome in Indian claims cases), the Justice Department asked for not less than 5,000 extensions of time in which to file its pleadings between 1951 and 1955 alone.[116] By 1960, Chief Commissioner Watkins—who, after all, wanted to speed things up for his own reasons—was complaining that U.S. Attorneys had received as many as 35 continuances in a single case.[117] A decade later, things were no better: in 1971, Watkins' successor, Jerome Kuykendall, observed that the Justice Department had requested some 6,451 days worth of extensions in active cases over the preceding eighteen months.[118]

Thus, despite having outlived its original charter six-fold, and notwithstanding its increasingly strenuous efforts to do so as time wore on, the Commission was never able to complete its calendar. When it finally expired on September 30, 1978, the commissioners reported that the ICC had over three decades disposed of 547 of the 615 dockets into which the original 852 claims had been consolidated. The remaining 68 dockets were passed along, still unresolved, to the Court of Claims. Of the combined claims in which the ICC was said to have reached a final determination, about 45 percent had been dismissed without award.[119]

> The end result was that the Indian [nations] via a commission that cost the government only $15 million to operate for thirty-two years . . . paid $100 million in legal fees to pry loose some $800 million properly owed them. For thirty years most of this sum remained in the U.S. Treasury, interest free, at a benefit to the government.[120]

At the same time, the Department of Justice and its collaborators in the GAO expended approximately $200 million—an amount equal to one-quarter of total awards—on efforts to block or minimize each and every settlement.[121] So obstinately did they pursue these ends that when in 1955 the Otoes actually won a significant concession in legal principle from the ICC, federal attorneys stalled the resulting award for some months while lobbying Congress to rewrite the law in their favor.[122]

Such data cast in bold relief the contradictions inherent to the kind of subterfuge in which, as a matter of policy, any government sets out to play both (or several) ends against the middle. They do not, however, begin to address the real magnitude of the stakes involved in the ICC process. Aside from the sheer volume of claims which emerged, a development which seems to have genuinely taken all official parties by surprise, there is the matter of the scope of questions raised with respect to U.S. territorial legitimacy.[123]

As early as 1956, the Justice Department warned Congress that the country's legal ownership of about half the area of the lower 48 states was subject to serious challenge.[124] By the mid-1960s, based in large part on research undertaken by the ICC in its struggles to document the basis for U.S. assertion of title to each area within its putative domain, informed observers were reckoning that the United States had never acquired a valid proprietary interest in some 750 million acres.[125] In other words, "one third of the nation's land," as the Interior Department put it in 1970, still legally belonged—and belongs—to native people.[126]

If the ICC accomplished anything of positive utility, it was, according to Vine Deloria, Jr., to "update the legal parity" of Indian land rights by "clear[ing] out the underbrush" which had obscured an accurate view of who actually owns which parts of the United States.[127] Thereby, it can be said to have set the stage for the resolution of title questions, but not in any defensible legal, moral or ethical sense to have "settled" them.[128] As things stand, such monetary awards as were made by the ICC—or the Court of Claims, for that matter—serve only as payment against "back rent" accrued through usage of native property to which the United States has never held title.[129]

This has led many observers to conclude, along with American Indian Movement leader Russell Means, that the U.S. portion of Native North America continues to be "illegally occupied in exactly the same way France and Poland were illegally occupied by Germany during the Second World War." In Means' view, post hoc U.S. awards of cash compensation for the expropriation of native territory "no more puts things right than if the nazis had issued a check to the Vichy government in exchange for France after the fall of Paris." Anyone suggesting otherwise "is either ignorant of the facts, delusional or playing an elaborate game of charades to try and hide the truth."[130]

Far from being unrepresentatively "extreme," Means' position, or something closely akin to it, has been repeatedly manifested in the reactions of indigenous nations to contentions that ICC awards might serve to "uncloud" title to their lands.[131]

> The Suquamish, Puyallup, and Stillaquamish refused their judgments on the grounds that *their* claims were never adjudicated, only those pushed upon them by their attorneys and the Commission. At a tribal council, the [Western Shoshones] voted to reject their settlement, claiming preference for land rather than money. The Oneida Indians of New York filed strong land claims for nearly six million acres of that state.[132]

Under the premise that the "Black Hills Are Not For Sale," Means' own Oglala Lakota people have adamantly refused to accept any part of an award which now totals well over $130 million, insisting that recovery of their treaty-guaranteed landbase rather than monetary compensation is and always was the basis of their claim.[133] Hopi traditionals have taken an even harder line, observing that their land was already theirs "long before Columbus' great-great-grandmother was born" and that they would not dignify an upstart entity like the ICC by petitioning it for "a piece of land that is already ours."[134]

It follows that even if the U.S. were suddenly to evince a willingness to pay something like a fair price for the native property upon which it has constituted, expanded and consolidated itself—something it has never shown the least interest in doing—it is unlikely that title questions would be much affected. To borrow from Richard A. Nielson, "land, not money, is the *only* remedy" to many Indian claims.[135] As the sentiment was expressed in the Declaration of Purpose of the 1961 American Indian Chicago Conference:

> [E]ach remaining acre is a promise that we will still be here tomorrow. Were we paid a thousand times the market value of our lost holdings, still the payment would not suffice. Money never mothered the Indian people, as the land has mothered them, nor has any people become more attached to the land, religiously or traditionally.[136]

The only real question is whether the "preposterous" idea of restoring unceded native land to its rightful owners is in any way feasible and, if so, to what extent.[137] With deadening predictability, nay-sayers argue that to attempt such "extraordinary" restitution would require a concomitant, massive and wholly unwarranted dispossession of non-Indian property owners. Such notions, often advanced in highly sensationalized terms, have gone far towards keeping public opinion four-square against accommodation of indigenous land rights in any tangible form.[138]

The facts of the matter are, however, that, in addition to the roughly fifty million acres it presently "holds in trust" for Indians (about 2 percent of the 48 states), the federal government possesses some 770 million acres of parklands, national forests, wildlife preserves, military reservations, and so on. Collectively, the individual states hold yet another 78 million acres of unpopulated or sparsely populated land.[139] Clearly, it would be possible to return all 700 million acres indigenous peoples are now "short" from governmental holdings, without revoking title to the individual holdings of a single non-Indian.

Some native leaders have suggested that as little as fifty million acres—that is, a doubling of the existing reservation landbase—might be enough to stabilize indigenous nations, providing them the resources needed to, among other things, alleviate the dire conditions sketched in the opening section of this essay.[140] Far from responding favorably to such invitations to compromise, however, the government has elected not only to ignore them, but to continue whittling away at what little remains of Indian Country (during the first ten years of the ICC, the native land base was actually reduced from 54.6 million to 52.5 million acres).[141]

Merely putting a stop to this trend will not be enough. If the United States is ever to resemble in any fashion the resplendent characterizations of it put forth by its promoters and apologists, the attitudes and policies underlying the ongoing erosion of indigenous property rights must be reversed, and native people afforded the sort of territorial restitution to which we are entitled under international law.[142]

This, in turn, could serve as the pivot from which to get at an entire range of claims—everything from damages accruing through the government's sustained and systematic suppression of native languages and religions to those resulting from the supplanting of traditional governments and economies—which the ICC refused even to consider.[143] Each of these is legally/morally compensable, and compensation might in such connections go a long way towards healing the gaping cultural and psychic wounds inflicted upon indigenous societies by the nature of U.S. Indian policy.[144]

In the alternative, if the travesty of justice embodied in the ICC continues to be employed as "proof" that the United States has conducted itself "in good conscience" and "in accordance with a standard of fair and honorable dealings" with Indians, or that native claims have been reasonably well "settled," then Russell Means' harsh remarks about nazis, charades and illegal occupations may come to be seen as restrained in comparison to what follows. "There are," as Harvey Rosenthal has acknowledged, "much harder payments to be made" before the debts the U.S. owes indigenous nations can ever honestly be marked "paid in full."[145]

# Notes

1. 1 Stat. 50 (1787). The more practical policy was suggested in a written plan submitted to the Continental Congress by George Washington, shortly before he became president. In it, the "Father of his Country" recommended using treaties with Indians in much the same fashion Adolf Hitler would employ them against his adversaries at München and elsewhere a century-and-a-half later (i.e., to lull them into a false sense of security or complacency which placed them at a distinct military disadvantage when it came time to confront them with a war of aggression). "Apart from the fact that it was immoral, unethical and actually criminal, this plan placed before Congress by Washington was so logical and well laid out that it was immediately accepted practically without opposition and immediately put into action. There might be — certainly *would* be — further strife with the Indians, new battles and new wars, but the end result was, with the adoption of Washington's plan, inevitable: Without even realizing it had occurred, the fate of all the Indians in the country was sealed. They had lost virtually everything"; Allan W. Eckert, *That Dark and Bloody River: Chronicles of the Ohio River Valley* (New York: Bantam, 1995) p. 440.

2. *Public Papers of the Presidents of the United States: Harry S. Truman, 1946* (Washington, D.C.: U.S. Government Printing Office, 1962) p. 414.

3. Wilcomb E. Washburn, "Land Claims in the Mainstream of Indian/White Relations," in Imre Sutton, ed., *Irredeemable America: The Indians' Estate and Land Claims* (Albuquerque: University of New Mexico Press, 1985) pp. 26, 30-1. One is left unsure exactly which "powerful sovereigns" Washburn considers "normal" in this instance. Certainly, the governments of such obviously weak states as Monaco, Liechtenstein and San Marino enjoy a far greater degree of practical sovereignty than does any American Indian government in the U.S., even though the latter are often territorially larger and, in many cases, more resource-rich; Vine Deloria, Jr., "The Size and Status of Nations," in Susan Lobo and Steve Talbot, eds., *Native American Voices: A Reader* (New York: Longman, 1998) pp. 457-65.

4. Glenn T. Morris, "Further Motion by the State Department to Railroad Indigenous Rights," *Fourth World Bulletin*, No. 6, Summer 1998, pp. 1-9.

5. H.D. Rosenthal, *Their Day in Court: A History of the Indian Claims Commission* (New York: Garland, 1990) pp. 49-50.

6. See the commentaries of Black in particular in the "Letters" section of *Anarchy*, 1997-99, inclusive.

7. William H. Harnell, *Man-Made Morals: Four Philosophies That Shaped America* (New York: Anchor, 1969) p. 238.

8. Rosenthal, *Day in Court*, p. 49.

9. See, e.g., U.S. Senate, Committee on Labor and Human Resources, Subcommittee on Employment and Productivity, *Guaranteed Job Opportunity Act: Hearing on S.777* (Washington, D.C.: 100th Cong., 1st Sess., 1980).

10. For a good profile midway through the period, see Cheryl McCall, "Life on Pine Ridge Bleak," *Colorado Daily*, May 16, 1975.

11. Rennard Strickland, *Tonto's Revenge: Reflections on American Indian Culture and Policy* (Albuquerque: University of New Mexico Press, 1998) p. 53. Also see U.S. Congress, Office of Technology Assessment, *Indian Health Care* (Washington, D.C.: U.S. Government Printing Office, 1996).

12. See generally, U.S. Department of Education, Office of Research and Improvement, National Institute of Education, *Conference on the Educational and Occupational Needs of American Indian Women* (Washington, D.C.: U.S. Government Printing Office, 1980).

13. Strickland, *Tonto's Revenge*, p. 53.

14. U.S. Department of Health and Human Services, Public Health Service, *Chart Series Book* (Washington, D.C.: U.S. Government Printing Office, 1988).

15. Strickland, *Tonto's Revenge*, p. 53.

16. U.S. Bureau of the Census, *U.S. Census of the Population: General Population Characteristics* (Washington, D.C.: U.S. Dept. of Commerce, Economics and Statistics Div., 1990) p. 3.

17. *Lone Wolf v. Hitchcock* (187 U.S. 553 (1903)). There have of course been modifications to the *Lone Wolf* doctrine over the years. Nevertheless, it continues to represent the essential framework within which U.S. Indian policy is formulated and implemented; Ann Laquer Estin, "*Lone Wolf v. Hitchcock*: The Long Shadow," in Sandra L. Cadwalader and Vine Deloria, Jr., eds., *The Aggressions of Civilization: Federal Indian Policy Since the 1880s* (Philadelphia: Temple University Press, 1984).

18. Ronald L. Trosper, "Appendix I: Indian Minerals," in American Indian Policy Review Commission, *Task Force 7 Final Report: Reservation and Resource Development and Protection* (Washington, D.C.: U.S. Government Printing Office, 1977); U.S. Department of Interior, Bureau of Indian Affairs, *Indian Lands Map: Oil, Gas and Minerals on Indian Reservations* (Washington, D.C.: U.S. Government Printing Office, 1978); Louis R. Moore, *Mineral Development on Indian Lands: Cooperation and Conflict* (Denver: Rocky Mountain Mineral Law Foundation, 1983); Presidential Commission on Indian Reservation Economies, *Report and Recommendation to the President of the United States* (Washington, D.C.: U.S. Government Printing Office, Nov. 1984).

19. Robert K. Thomas, "Colonialism: Classic and Internal," *New University Thought*, Vol. 4, No. 4, Winter 1966-67.

20. 59 Stat. 1031, T.S. No. 993, 3 Bevans 1153, 1976 Y.B.U.N. 1043 (entered into force, Oct. 24, 1945). For text, see Burns H. Weston, Richard A. Falk and Anthony D'Amato, eds., *Basic Documents in International Law and World Order* (Minneapolis, West, [2nd ed.] 1990) pp. 16-32, esp. pp. 27-30.

21. "All peoples have the right to self-determination; by virtue of that right they freely determine their political status and freely pursue their economic, social and cultural development"; United Nations Declaration on the Granting of Independence to Colonial Countries and Peoples (U.N.G.A. Res. 1514 (XV), 15 U.N. GAOR, Supp. (No. 16) 66, U.N. Doc. A/4684 (1961)). The same language is repeated in the International Covenant on Economic, Social and Cultural Rights (U.N.G.A. Res. 2200 (XXI), 21 U.N. GAOR, Supp. (No. 16) 49, U.N. Doc. A/6316 (1967; entered into force, Jan. 3, 1976)) and the International Covenant on Civil and Political Rights (U.N.G.A. Res. 2200 (XXI), 21 U.M. GAOR, Supp. (No. 16) 52, U.N. Doc. A/6316 (1967; entered into force, Mar. 23, 1976)). See Weston, Falk and D'Amato, *Basic Documents*, pp. 344, 371, 376.

22. Jean-Paul Sartre, "On Genocide," *Ramparts*, Feb. 1968. This, at least in part, may be why the U.S., virtually alone among U.N. member states, refused to ratify the 1948 Convention on Prevention and Punishment of the Crime of Genocide (U.N.T.S. 277; entered into force, Jan. 12, 1951) for more than forty years, and then attempted to do so by way of attaching a "sovereignty package" which would have allowed it to exempt itself from any and all provisions it might find inconvenient. See generally, Lawrence J. LeBlanc, *The United States and the Genocide Convention* (Durham, N.C.: Duke University Press, 1991).

23. C. Wright Mills, *The Power Elite* (New York: Oxford University Press, 1959).

24. Vine Deloria, Jr., "Non-Violence in American Society," *Katallegete*, Vol. 5, No. 2, 1974; reprinted in James Treat, ed., *For This Land: Writings on Religion in America* (New York: Routledge, 1999) pp. 44-50, quote at p. 45.

25. Imre Sutton, "Prolegomena," in Sutton, *Irredeemable America*, p. 6.

26. This is hardly the only connection in which such things are true. For an excellent overview of the same process at work in other dimensions, see Noam Chomsky, *Necessary Illusions: Thought Control in Democratic Societies* (Boston: South End Press, 1989).

27. See generally, John T. Vance, "The Congressional Mandate and the Indian Claims Commission," *North Dakota Law Review*, No. 45, Spring 1969, pp. 325-36.

28. Quoted in John Kobler, "These Indians Struck It Rich: The Utes' Treaty Land," *Saturday Evening Post*, Sept. 6, 1972, p. 132.

29. Rosenthal, *Day in Court*, p. 49.

30. Sutton, "Prolegomena," p. 5. Not least among the problems of such formulations is the unanswered question of exactly how American Indians, formally recognized by the United States through a lengthy series of eighteenth- and nineteenth-century treaties as constituting separate and distinct nations of people, have come to be construed as "a minority" group *within* the U.S. during the twentieth. Did the Indians at some point agree to such a radical and across the board alteration of their status? If so, when and by what means? The issue is fundamental, because, under international law, it has long been the case that a nation, having once recognized the sovereignty of another, has no legal authority whatsoever to unilaterally "demote" it at some later point. Alteration of the sovereign status of any nation can legitimately occur only on the basis of their voluntary consent to the change; L. Oppenheim, *International Law: A Treatise* (London: Longman's, Green, [5th ed.] 1955) p. 120. Also see Robert T. Coulter, "Contemporary Indian Sovereignty," in National Lawyers Guild, *Rethinking Indian Law* (New Haven, CT: Advocate Press, 1982) pp. 109-20, esp. 118.

31. See notes 4, 20, 21 and 22, above. Also see my, "Perversions of Justice: Examining the Doctrine of U.S. Rights to Occupancy in North America," in this collection.

32. 10 Stat. 612, Feb. 24, 1855.

33. 12 Stat. 765, Mar. 3, 1863. Section 9 specifies that the Court of Claims "shall not extend to or include any claim against the Government . . . growing out of or dependent on, any treaty stipulation entered into with . . . the Indian tribes."

34. Rosenthal, *Day in Court*, pp. 9-10.

35. *United States ex rel. Standing Bear v. Crook*, 25 Fed. Cas. 695 (C.C.D. Nebraska, 1879). For context, see Thomas Henry Tibbles, *The Ponca Chiefs: An Account of the Trial of Standing Bear* (Lincoln: University of Nebraska Press, 1972).

36. 21 Stat. 504, Chap. 139, Mar. 3,1881. See generally, E.B. Smith, *Indian Tribal Claims Decided in the U.S. Court of Claims* (Washington, D.C.: University Publications of America, 1976).

37. U.S. House of Representatives. Committee on Interior and Insular Affairs, *Indirect Services and Expenditures by the Federal Government for the American Indian* (Washington, D.C.: 86th Cong., 1st Sess., 1959) pp. 11-14.

38. Richard A. Nielson, "American Indian Land Claims: Land versus Money as a Remedy," *University of Florida Law Review*, No. 25, Winter 1972, p. 308. Also see Smith, *Tribal Claims*; Glen A. Wilkenson, "Indian Tribal Claims Before the Court of Claims," *Georgetown Law Journal*, No. 55, Dec. 1966, pp. 511-28.

39. Howard Friedman, "Interest on Indian Land Claims: Judicial Protection of the Fisc," *Valparaiso University Law Review*, No. 5, Fall 1970. Also see Smith, *Tribal Claims*; Wilkenson, "Tribal Claims."

40. John R. White, "Barmecide Revisited: The Gratuitous Offset in Indian Claims Cases," *Ethnohistory*, No. 25, Spring 1978, pp. 179-92. Also see Smith, *Tribal Claims*; Wilkenson, "Tribal Claims."

41. Rosenthal, *Day in Court*, p. 30. For a good overview of native resistance to the government's imposition of compulsory schooling—to take but one example—see David Wallace Adams, *Education for Extinction: American Indians and the Boarding School Experience, 1875-1928* (Lawrence: University Press of Kansas, 1995).

42. Rosenthal, *Day in Court*, p. 30-1.

43. It was officially estimated during the mid-1930s that it took, on average, a full ten years from the time an Indian claims case was authorized by Congress to the point it actually came to trial; U.S. House of Representatives, Committee on Indian Affairs, *Hearing on H.R. 7838 to Create an Indian Claims Commission* (Washington, D.C.: 74th Cong., 1st Sess., 1935) p. 10.

44. U.S. Senate, Subcommittee of the Senate Committee on the Judiciary, *Hearing on S. 3083* (Washington, D.C., 76th Cong., 3rd Sess., Feb. 1940) p. 139.

45. "The General Accounting Office estimated, in 1935, that it had [by that point] spent one million dollars examining some 1.38 million 'claim instances' and over 83,000 accounts for reports" to U.S. Attorneys working on the nullification of Indian claims cases; Rosenthal, *Day in Court*, p. 30.

46. Ibid., p. 20.

47. Quoted in Walter Hart Blumenthal, *American Indians Dispossessed: Fraud in Land Cessions Forced Upon the Tribes* (Philadelphia: G.S. McManus, 1955) p. 174.

48. Rosenthal, *Day in Court*, p. 30.

49. *Hearings on S. 3083*, p. 20. In *Their Day in Court* (p. 24), Rosenthal contends that, "From 1881 to 1946, 219 claims were filed with the Court of Claims. Of these cases only thirty-five won awards which totaled $77.3 million or an average of $1.2 million per year in net recoveries."

50. The brunt of this, of course, fell on already impoverished native peoples, but it also included more than a few of the white attorneys who represented them. For example, Francis A. Goodwin, a lawyer in Washington state who took on the case of the Nez Perce, lost twelve years and $5,000 of his own funds in a losing effort. See generally, U.S. House of Representatives, Committee on Indian Affairs, *Hearings on H.R. 1198 and 1341 to Create an Indian Claims Commission* (Washington, D.C.: 79th Cong., 1st Sess., March and June 1945) pp. 81-4.

51. Rosenthal, *Day in Court*, pp. 23, 32.

52. The position has been taken in a number of works. See, e.g., Charles F. Wilkinson, *American Indians, Time, and the Law* (New Haven, CT: Yale University Press, 1987).

53. Such bias is likely inherent to any process of this sort; Richard B. Lillich, *International Claims: Their Adjudication by National Commissions* (Syracuse, NY: Syracuse University Press, 1962).

54. Ibid., p. 6.

55. Francis E. Leupp, *The Indian and His Problem* (New York: Scribner's, 1910) pp. 194-6.

56. U.S. House of Representatives, Subcommittee of the Committee on Indian Affairs, *Hearings on the Appropriations Bill of 1914* (Washington, D.C.: 64th Cong., 2nd Sess., 1913) p. 99.

57. See generally, Henry E. Fritz, *The Movement for Indian Assimilation, 1860-1890* (Philadelphia: University of Pennsylvania Press, 1963); Frederick E. Hoxie, *A Final Promise: The Campaign to Assimilate the Indians, 1880-1920* (Lincoln: University of Nebraska Press, 1984).

58. Overall, see Brian W. Dippie, *The Vanishing American: White Attitudes and U.S. Indian Policy* (Middletown, CT: Wesleyan University Press, 1982); Christopher M. Lyman, *The Vanishing Race and Other Illusions* (New York: Pantheon, 1982).

59. The kick-off came with Standard Oil's preliminary exploration of the Navajo Reservation in 1919-21, under provision of the 1918 Multiferous Minerals Act; Lorraine Turner Ruffing, "Navajo Mineral Development," *American Indian Journal*, No. 4, Sept. 1978, pp. 2-15.

60. See generally, Terry P. Wilson, *The Underground Reservation: Osage Oil* (Lincoln: University of Nebraska Press, 1985).

61. An interesting take on this is provided by Hollis Whitson and Martha Roberge in their "Moving Those Indians Into the Twentieth Century," *Technology Review*, No. 9, July 1986.

62. Lewis Meriam, et al., *The Problems of Indian Administration* (Baltimore: Johns Hopkins University Press, 1928).

63. Ibid., p. 48.

64. U.S. Senate, Subcommittee of the Committee on Indian Affairs, *Hearings on the Survey of Conditions of Indians in the United States* (Washington, D.C.: 70th-71st Cong., 1928-29) pp. 13670-7.

65. Indian Reorganization Act (ch. 5776, 48 Stat. 948, now codified at 25 U.S.C. 461-279)). For background, see Laurence C. Kelly, *Assault on Assimilation: John Collier and the Origins of Indian Policy Reform* (Albuquerque: University of New Mexico Press, 1983); Vine Deloria, Jr., and Clifford M. Lytle, *The Nations Within: The Past and Future of American Indian Sovereignty* (New York: Pantheon, 1984).

66. U.S. House of Representatives, Committee on Indian Affairs, *Creating an Indian Claims Commission*, (Washington, D.C.: 79th Cong., 1st Sess., 1945) p. 1466.

67. *Congressional Record*, June 21, 1937, p. 6058.

68. Ibid., p. 6246.

69. Ibid., p. 6241.

70. Ibid., p. 6261.

71. *Northwest Bands of Shoshone Indians v. United States* (324 U.S. 335 (1945)); quoted in Felix S. Cohen, *The Legal Conscience: Selected Papers* (New Haven, CT: Yale University Press, 1960) p. 264. The takings in question were only 60-70 years old at the time Jackson wrote, meaning that the "ancestors" involved were the parents and grandparents and of the Shoshone claimants. How "remote" a degree of ancestry Jackson considered his own parents was left unstated.

72. Ibid., p. 302.

73. Ibid., p. 303.

74. For an overall description of Roosevelt's attitude, including the statement quoted, see John Collier, *From Every Zenith: A Memoir* (Denver: Sage Books, 1963) pp. 294-9.

75. These included H.R. 7963 (1930), which was never reported out of the House Judiciary Committee; S. 3444 (1934) and S. 1465 (1935), both of which died in committee; H.R. 6655 (1935), which suffered the same fate; S. 2731 (1935) and H.R. 7837 (1935), both of which were reported out — S..2731 was actually approved by the full Senate — but passed over and tabled in the House until the congressional session expired; S.1902 (1937), which was again passed by the Senate, but, despite being considerably amended in committee, was voted down by the full House (176 to 73); S. 3083 (1939), which died in committee; S. 4206 (1940), killed in committee; S. 4234 (1940), killed in committee; S. 4349 (1940), on which the congressional session expired before a vote was taken; S. 1111 and H.R. 4693 (both 1941), which were hashed about interminably and then tabled; H.R. 4593 and H.R. 5569 (1944), both of which died in committee; H.R. 1198 and H.R. 1341 (both 1945), both of

which were killed before reaching the floor. These are summarized in Rosenthal, *Day in Court*, pp. 53-84.

76. Act of Aug, 12, 1935 ("Gratuities Act"; 49 Stat. 596)).

77. Indian Claims Commission Act (60 Stat. 1049 (1946)).

78. For the best overview of U.S. insistence on this idea in the face of staunch allied opposition to it, see Bradley F. Smith, *The Road to Nuremberg* (New York: Basic Books, 1981) esp. Chaps. 2-3.

79. Bradley F. Smith, *The American Road to Nuremberg: The Documentary Record* (Stanford, CA: Hoover Institution Press, 1982) p. 6.

80. Agreement for the Prosecution and Punishment of the Major War Criminals of the European Axis Powers and Charter of the International Military Tribunal (59 Stat. 1544, 82 U.N.T.S. 279)); Weston, Falk and D'Amato, *Basic Documents*, pp. 138-9. On the ensuing prosecution of primary nazi leaders, see Eugene Davidson, *The Trial of the Germans, 1945-1946* (New York: Macmillan, 1966). Concerning the subsequent series of prosecutions of lesser nazi defendants, see John Alan Appleman, *Military Tribunals and Military Crimes* (Westport, CT: Greenwood Press, 1954). With respect to related prosecutions of Japanese, see Arnold C. Brackman, *The Other Nuremberg: The Untold Story of the Tokyo War Crimes Trials* (New York: William Morrow, 1987).

81. As formulated in a July 25, 1945, "Memorandum to All Legal Personnel" prepared by Col. Murray C. Bernays, a key figure in U.S. war crimes policy development, the four overarching categories of activity for which the top nazis should be tried were "the 'Nazi master plan' (aggressive war conspiracy); 'preparatory measures' (preparations for aggression); 'occupying neighboring German areas'; and 'military conquest' (acts of aggression and war crimes, covering the period 1939-45)." In only slightly revised form, this was the schematic actually adopted for the Nuremberg prosecutions; Bradley F. Smith, *Reaching Judgment at Nuremberg* (New York: Basic Books, 1977) p. 65.

82. Adolf Hitler, *Mein Kampf* (New York: Reynal and Hitchcock, 1939) pp. 403, 591; *Hitler's Secret Book* (New York: Grove Press, 1961) pp. 46-52. Another iteration will be found in a memorandum prepared by an aide, Col. Freidrich Hössbach, summarizing Hitler's statements during a high-level "Führer Conference" conducted shortly before Germany's 1939 invasion of Poland; *Trial of the Major Nazi War Criminals Before the International Military Tribunal*, 42 vols (Nuremberg: International Military Tribunal, 1947-49) Vol. 25, pp. 402-13.

83. Norman Rich, *Hitler's War Aims: Ideology, the Nazi State, and the Course of Expansion* (New York: W.W. Norton, 1973) p. 8. Also see John Toland, *Adolf Hitler* (New York: Doubleday, 1976) p. 802.

84. See, e.g., Frank Parella, *Lebensraum and Manifest Destiny: A Comparative Study in the Justification of Expansionism* (Washington, D.C.: Dissertation, School of International Relations, Georgetown University, 1950).

85. Since it is now fashionable to view the North American Indian Wars and the crimes of nazism as belonging to entirely different epochs, it is important to remember that the Wounded Knee Massacre—generally considered to be the last round of the former—occurred in 1890, and that the latter commenced when Hitler came to power only 42 years later. Predictably, under the circumstances, claims of "victor's justice" being visited upon the nazis were raised rather forcefully by German defense counsel Hermann Jahrreiss in his opening statement to the Nuremberg Tribunal; less expectedly, by individuals like Senator Robert A. Taft in the United States itself. See Jay W. Baird, ed., *From Nuremberg to My Lai* (Lexington, MA: D.C. Heath, 1972) pp. 84-90, 107-13.

86. U.S. House of Representatives, Select Committee of the Committee of Indian Affairs, *An Investigation to Determine Whether the Changed Status of the Indian Requires a Revision of the Laws and Regulations Affecting the Indian* (Washington, D.C.: 78th Cong., 2nd Sess., Dec. 23, 1944).

87. The effect of the Justice Department's recommended changes to the Claims Commission Act would have been to "cut many 'identifiable groups' of Indians from the scope of the bill, to strike from the list of claims those based on fraud, duress, mistake and the taking of lands without compensation (the most common kind), to disallow the commission discretion on offsets, to ban transfer of suits from the Court of Claims, to remove the [commission's] investigation division, to limit the commission's access to records . . . to the judicial character of the commission, to prevent compromise settlements, to deny the [commission's] power of final decision, and to close the Court of Claims to post-1946 claims"; Rosenthal, *Day in Court*, p. 87.

88. See the essay "In the Matter of Julius Streicher: Applying Nuremberg Standards to the United States," in my *From a Native Son: Selected Essays in Indigenism, 1985-1995* (Boston: South End Press, 1996) pp. 445-54. Also see Robert H. Jackson, *The Nürnberg Case as Presented by Robert H. Jackson, Chief of Counsel for the United States* (New York: Alfred A. Knopf, 1947).

89. *Congressional Record*, July 30, 1946, p. A. 4923.

90. Truman, *Papers*, p. 414.

91. *Congressional Record*, May 20, 1946, p. 5319.

92. U.S. Dept. of Interior report to the House, 1945; quoted in Rosenthal, *Day in Court*, pp. 86-7.

93. U.S. withdrawal from its trust relations with indigenous nations would have been fine, had it been attended by a simultaneous relinquishment of its claim to title and jurisdiction over their territories. Since it was not, however, it amounted to a final and illegal absorption of them into the U.S. territorial corpus; see, e.g., Eyal Benvenisti, *The International Law of Occupation* (Princeton: Princeton University Press, 1993) pp. 5-6.

94. See, e.g., the statement of Indian Commissioner William A. Brophy; U.S. Senate, Committee on Indian Affairs, *Hearings on H.R. 4497 to Create an Indian Claims Commission* (Washington, D.C.: 79th Cong., 2nd Sess., 1946) p. 15. It should be noted that such goals are entirely consistent with the definition of genocide advanced by Raphaël Lemkin when he coined the term in his *Axis Rule in Occupied Europe* (Washington, D.C.: Carnegie Endowment for the Promotion of World Peace, 1944) p. 78.

95. *Congressional Record*, May 20, 1946, p. 5312.

96. The sole exception was the case of *Pueblo de Taos v. U.S.* (Doc. No. 357, Ind. Cl. Comm. (1965)), in which 48,000 acres in the Blue Lake area were actually restored at the request of President Richard M. Nixon. This outcome was, however, explicitly predicated on a 1926 arrangement negotiated by the Pueblo Lands Board in which the Indians agreed to drop a suit for $300,000 in compensation for reserved land onto which the town of Taos, New Mexico, had been steadily expanding. The case was therefore defined as "unique," and found to hold no precedential value in other land claims settlements; Nielson, "Land Claims," pp. 320-3.

97. The ICC rationalized its "judicial fiscal responsibility" in denying awards of interest against unpaid principal in perfectly circular fashion. In the case of *Loyal Creeks v. U.S.* (1 Ind. Cl. Comm. 22 (1951)) it held that since the taking of Creek land during the 1830s had been extraconstitutional, it lacked a legal authority on which to award interest against unpaid principal. Of course, if the taking were extraconstitutional, principal should never have been at issue in the first place since no valid transfer of title to the U.S. had ever occurred. This meant that the land remained Creek property, subject to recovery. But here the commissioners argued that the 1946 Act itself afforded them a legal authority upon which to deny any such remedy. This juridical conundrum is discussed at some length in Thomas LeDuc's "The Work of the Indian Claims Commission Under the Act of 1946," *Pacific Historical Review*, Vol. 26, No. 1, Feb. 1957, pp. 1-16.

98. Rosenthal, *Day in Court*, p. 138.

99. *Congressional Record*, July 29, 1935, p. 11975.

100. U.S. Senate, Subcommittee of the Committee on Appropriations, *Hearings on H.R. 9390 for Appropriations for Interior and Related Agencies for 1957* (Washington, D.C.: 84th Cong., 2nd Sess., 1956) pp. 552-8.

101. U.S. Senate, Subcommittee on Indian Affairs of the Committee on Interior and Insular Affairs, *Hearings on S. 307, A Bill to amend the Indian Claims Commission Act of 1946* (Washington, D.C.: 90th Cong., 1st Sess., 1967) p. 74.

102. General Rules of the Indian Claims Commission, ch. 3, 25 U.S.C. 503 (1968).

103. Rosenthal, *Day in Court*, p. 123.

104. Ibid., p. 178.

105. *Hearing on S. 4497*, p. 16.

106. In the so-called "Pit River Land Claims Settlement" of the mid-1960s, for example, an award of $29.1 million—approximately 47¢ per acre—was authorized as retroactive payment for virtually the entire state of California. Checks were then issued as per capita payments to individuals identified as members of "California Indian Bands." As each check was cashed, the signature on it was tallied as a "vote for termination" (the only way an Indian could vote *not* to be terminated was thus to refuse his/her

portion of the settlement). On this basis, it was claimed that the termination of the Juaneños and a number of other "Mission Bands" in the Los Angeles/San Diego area had been "voluntary"; see generally, Florence Connolly Shipeck,, *Pushed into the Rocks: Southern California Indian Land Tenure, 1769-1986* (Lincoln: University of Nebraska Press, 1988).

107. Rosenthal, *Day in Court*, pp. 166, 178.

108. All told, 109 peoples, or portions of peoples, were terminated under a series of specific statutes accruing from H.C.R. 108 between 1953 and 1962, the great bulk of them by 1958 (one group, the Poncas of Oklahoma, was terminated in 1966). A handful, such as the Menominees in Wisconsin and Siletz in Oregon, were "reinstated" during the 1970s; see generally, Donald L. Fixico, *Termination and Relocation: Federal Indian Policy, 1945-1960* (Albuquerque: University of New Mexico Press, 1986).

109. U.S. House of Representatives, *Present Relations of the Federal Government to the American Indians* (Washington, D.C.: 85th Cong., 2nd Sess., Dec. 1958).

110. Rosenthal, *Day in Court*, pp. 175-98.

111. Richard Drinnon, *Keeper of Concentration Camps: Dillon S. Myer and American Racism* (Berkeley: University of California Press, 1987) pp. 208-9.

112. Wilcomb E. Washburn, *Red Man's Land, White Man's Law* (New York: Scribner's, 1971) pp. 81-6, 103-4.

113. Stan Steiner, *The New Indians* (New York: Harper & Row, 1967) p. 83.

114. Chief Claims Commissioner Witt estimated in early 1951 that the number might ultimately run as high as 300 by the time the filing period expired at the end of that year; U.S. House of Representatives, Subcommittee of the Committee on Appropriations, *Hearings on the Independent Office Appropriations for 1952* (Washington, D.C.: 82nd Cong., 1st Sess., 1951) pp. 28-37.

115. Rosenthal, *Day in Court*, p. 115.

116. *Hearings on H.R. 9390*, pp. 552-8.

117. *Hearings on S. 307*, p. 20.

118. U.S. Senate, Committee on Appropriations, *Hearings on H.R. 9417 for Appropriations for the Department of Interior and Related Agencies for 1972* (Washington, D.C.: 92nd Cong., 1st Sess., 1971) pp. 1433-50; Committee on Interior and Insular Affairs, *Amending the Indian Claims Commission Act of 1946 as Amended* (Washington, D.C.: 92nd Cong., 2nd Sess., Rpt. 682, Mar. 2, 1972).

119. Indian Claims Commission, *Final Report* (Washington, D.C.: U.S. Government Printing Office, 1978). Through 1962—the termination era—there were 105 dismissals versus 37 awards. The ratio improved thereafter, although the average award amount obviously remained quite small.

120. Rosenthal, *Day in Court*, p. 255.

121. During the late 1950s, the ICC was funded at the level of $178,000 annually. At the same time, the Justice Department was spending upwards of $600,000 and the GAO about $500,000 per year "defending" the United States from having to pay its debts; *Indirect Services and Expenditures 1959*, pp. 5-8. Also see U.S. Senate, Subcommittee of the Committee on Appropriations, *Hearings on H.R. 10802 on Appropriations for Interior Department and Related Agencies for 1963* (Washington, D.C.: 87th Cong., 2nd Sess., 1962) pp. 773-88.

122. *Otoe and Missouria Tribe of Indians v. United States* (131 Ct. Cl. 593 (1955)). The size of the award, which was small, was not itself at issue. Rather, it was the ICC's decision to base it on "aboriginal title" per se, rather than on some earlier recognition of that title. When the Court of Claims upheld the ICC position on appeal, and the Supreme Court declined to review the matter, the Justice Department set out to change the law itself, renewing Francis Biddle's absurd contention that it would cost taxpayers $3 billion in awards if Congress failed to comply with the Attorney General's wishes; U.S. Senate, *Terminating the Existence of the Indian Claims Commission* (Washington, D.C.: 84th Cong., 2nd Sess., Rpt. 1727, Apr. 11, 1956). In the face of this—not to mention the pattern of behavior described in association with notes 116, 117 and 118—the contention advanced by Rosenthal (*Day in Court*, p. 197) that it would be "biased" to suggest the Justice Department was objectively "anti-Indian and purposefully obstructionist" in its handling of Indian claims cases is simply laughable.

123. It is true that the United Nations Charter provides that exercise of the right of self-determination by all peoples be balanced against the need to preserve the territorial integrity of U.N. member states. It is presumptive, however, that the territory in question have been in some sense

legitimately acquired; see, e.g., Lee C. Buchheit, *Secession: The Legitimacy of Self-Determination* (New Haven: Yale University Press, 1978).

124. Rosenthal, *Day in Court*, p. 151.

125. This includes land title "secured" by fraudulent treaties or agreements, lands appropriated by a unilateral Act of Congress, and lands confiscated without even the latter pretense of legal justification. These are issues entirely separate from that of lands for which some arguably legitimate form of native consent to cession was obtained, but for which they were uncompensated or uncompensated at the time. This last is all the ICC was authorized to adjudicate, although, as with the Western Shoshone Land Claim, it often attempted to "create title where none had previously existed" whenever it came upon any of the first three situations; Jack D. Forbes, "The 'Public Domain' of Nevada and Its Relationship to Indian Property Rights," *Nevada State Bar Journal*, Vol. 30, 1965, pp. 16-47; Russel L. Barsh, "Indian Land Claims Policy in the United States," *North Dakota Law Review*, No. 58, pp. 1-82;

126. Public Lands Law Review Commission, *One Third of the Nation's Land* (Washington, D.C.: U.S. Department of Interior, 1970).

127. Vine Deloria, Jr., *Behind the Trail of Broken Treaties: An Indian Declaration of Independence* (New York: Delacourt Press, 1974) p. 227.

128. Robert T. Coulter and Steven M. Tullburg, "Indian Land Rights," in *Aggressions of Civilization*, p. 204.

129. See the 1967 statement by National Indian Youth Council representative Hank Adams to the U.S. Senate; *Hearings on S. 307*, p. 91.

130. Videotaped interview, April 1982; tape on file.

131. The term accrues from Scoop Jackson's assertion, made during his advocacy of the Claims Commission Act in 1946, that failure to dispose of native claims would "perpetuate clouds upon white men's title that interfere with development of our public domain"; *Congressional Record*, May 20, 1946, p. 5312.

132. Rosenthal, *Day in Court*, p. 250. On the Suquamish, Puyallup and Stillaquamish, see U.S. Senate, Subcommittee on Indian Affairs of the Committee on Interior and Insular Affairs, *Hearing on S. 721, A Bill to Authorize Appropriations for the Indian Claims Commission for Fiscal Year 1974 and Other Purposes* (Washington, D.C.: 93d Cong., 1st Sess., Feb. 16, 1973) p. 118. On the Shoshones, see Elmer R. Rusco, "Historic Change in Western Shoshone Country: The Establishment of the Western Shoshone National Council and Traditionalist Land Claims, *American Indian Quarterly*, Summer 1992, pp. 337-60. On the Oneidas, see Arlinda Locklear, "The Oneida Land Claims: A Legal Overview," in Christopher Vescey and William A. Starna, eds., *Iroquois Land Claims* (Syracuse, NY: Syracuse University Press, 1988) pp. 141-53.

133. At issue is the Black Hills area of South Dakota, guaranteed by the 1868 Fort Laramie Treaty but taken by the U.S. in 1877. The original award was for $17.5 million, interest free; *Sioux Nation v. U.S.*, 220 Ct. Cl. 442, 601 F.2d 1157 (1975). On appeal, the Supreme Court, deeming the matter compensable under the 5th Amendment, added 5 percent simple interest, making the gross amount awarded $122.5 million. By referendum, the Lakotas declined to accept; *Sioux Nation v. U.S.*, 488 U.S. 371 (1980). During the 1980s, New Jersey Senator Bill Bradley attempted to resolve the issue by introducing a bill in which the award would have been paid as an indemnity, certain lands would have been restored, and a split jurisdiction effected over the rest. The plan was opposed by South Dakota's congressional delegation and therefore withdrawn; see "The Black Hills Are Not For Sale: The Lakota Struggle for the 1868 Treaty Territory," in my *Struggle for the Land: Native North American Resistance to Genocide, Ecocide and Colonization* (San Francisco: City Lights, [2nd ed.] 2002).

134. Richard O. Clemmer, *Roads in the Sky: The Hopi Indians in a Century of Change* (Boulder: Westview Press, 1995) p. 187.

135. Nielson, "Indian Land Claims," p. 308.

136. Quoted in Fred Eggan, *The American Indian: Perspectives for the Study of Social Change* (Chicago: Aldine, 1966) p. 166.

137. As legal scholar Morton E. Price opined, "It was preposterous to recognize fully such extraordinary claims of a handful of poor people, even if they were based on legitimate entitlement"; quoted in Harold Fey and D'arcy McNickle, *Indians and Other Americans: Two Ways of Life Meet* (New York: Harper & Row, 1970) p. 123. No indication is offered, of course, as to why it would have been—or be—

any more "preposterous" to recognize these particular claims than to recognize the extraordinary claims of, say, the richest 3 percent of Americans to ownership or control of about a third of the nation's wealth (Bill Gates alone being "worth" an estimated $46-69 *billion*).

138. See, e.g., the examples of such disinformation discussed by Paul Brodeur in his *Restitution: The Land Claims of the Mashpee, Passamaquoddy, and Penobscot Indians of New England* (Boston: Northeastern University Press, 1985). Also see Alan Van Gestel, "When Fictions Take Hostages," in James E. Clifton, ed., *The Invented Indian: Cultural Fictions and Government Policies* (New Brunswick, NJ: Transaction Books, 1990) pp. 291–312.

139. For breakouts of this acreage, see *One Third of the Nation's Land*. For analysis, see Barsh, "Land Claims Policy."

140. Rosenthal, *Day in Court*, p. 253.

141. Memo of the Chairman to the Committee on Interior and Insular Affairs, U.S. Senate, *An Analysis of the Problem and Effects of Our Diminishing Indian Land Base, 1948-1957* (Washington, D.C.: 85th Cong., 2nd Sess., Dec. 1959) p. 101.

142. In international law, there are two primary principles of restitution: (a) "*restitutio integrum*" (restoration of the former legal situation) and, (b) "*restitutio in natura*" (returning of something wrongfully taken to its original owner). Acts of compensation or reparation are considered only if the former legal situation cannot be restored. Istvan Vasarhelyi, *Restitution in International Law* (Budapest: Hungary Academy of Science, 1964) p. 74.

143. Deloria, *Trail of Broken Treaties*, pp. 223-6.

144. Consider as analogs the compensation customarily awarded for such things as "mental anguish," "pain and suffering," and "discrimination" in U.S. civil law.

145. Rosenthal, *Day in Court*, p. 257.


This essay was originally published in *American Indian Culture and Research Journal*, Vol. 24, No. 1, Spring 2000.

# A Breach of Trust

## The Radioactive Colonization of Native North America

> There are whole disciplines, institutions, rubrics in our culture which serve
> as categories of denial.
>
> —Susan Griffin
> *A Chorus of Stones*

In 1903, the United States Supreme Court opined that, as a racial group, American Indians, like minor children and those deemed mentally deficient or deranged, should be viewed as legally incompetent to manage our own assets and affairs. Indians were therefore to be understood as perpetual "wards" of the federal government, the government our permanent "trustee." With a deft circularity of reasoning, the justices then proceeded to assert that, since it was Indians' intrinsic incompetence which had led to our being placed under trust supervision, we should by the same definition be construed as having no standing from which to challenge the exercise of our trustee's authority over us.[1]

Thus did the U.S. formally and unilaterally assign itself "plenary"—that is, absolute and unchallengeable—power over all native lands, lives and natural resources within the forty-eight conterminous states of North America, as well as Alaska, Hawai'i and other external possessions such as Guam and "American" Samoa. The only curb upon the imagined prerogatives of the United States in this regard was/is an equally self-appointed fiduciary responsibility to act, or at least claim to act, in the "best interests" of those it had subjugated both physically and juridically.[2] Although the basic proposition at issue has undergone almost continuous modification and perfection over the years, it remains very much in effect at present.[3]

The scale and implications of the situation are in some ways staggering. In its 1978 final report, the government's own Indian Claims Commission conceded that after more than thirty years' intensive investigation, it had been unable to find evidence that the U.S. had ever acquired anything resembling legitimate title to about a third of its claimed territoriality, all of which therefore remains native property in a legal sense.[4] The approximately 2.5 percent of U.S. territory currently reserved for Indian use and occupancy—most of it still held in federal trust status—is also extraordinarily rich in mineral resources.[5] As much as two-thirds of the uranium ore the U.S. claims as its own is situated within reservation boundaries, as is about a quarter of the readily accessible low sulfur coal, up to 20 percent of the oil and natural gas, and substantial deposits of molybdenum, copper, bauxite and zeolites.[6]

The Bureau of Indian Affairs (BIA), a component of the U.S. Department of Interior, presently administers trust relations with several hundred indigenous peoples and communities encompassing, by official count, some two million individuals.[7] Simple arithmetic reveals that when the fifty million-odd acres of reserved land is divided by the federal tally of Indians, we end up as the largest landholding group in North America on a per capita basis. Divide the estimated dollar value of the mineral assets within the land by the number of Indians and you end up with native people as the wealthiest population aggregate on the continent (again, on a per capita basis).

All of this is, unfortunately, on paper. The practical reality is that American Indians, far from being well-off, are today the most impoverished sector of the U.S. population.[8] We experience by far the lowest average annual and lifetime incomes of any group. The poorest locality in the United States for 23 of the past 25 years has been Shannon County, on the Pine Ridge Sioux Reservation in South Dakota, where a recent study found 88 percent of the available housing to be substandard, much of it to the point of virtual uninhabitability. The annual per capita income in Shannon County was barely over $2,000 in 1995, while unemployment hovered in the 90th percentile.[9]

Bad as conditions are on Pine Ridge, they are only marginally worse than those on the adjoining Rosebud Sioux Reservation and a host of others. In many ways, health data convey the costs and consequences of such deep and chronic poverty far better than their financial counterparts. These begin with the facts that, overall, American Indians suffer far and away the highest rates of malnutrition, death from exposure and infant mortality (14.5 times the national average on some reservations).[10]

> The Indian health level is the lowest and the disease rate the highest of all major population groups in the United States. The incidence of tuberculosis is over 400 percent

the national average. Similar statistics show the incidence of strep infections is 1,000 percent, meningitis is 2,000 percent higher, and dysentery is 10,000 percent higher. Death rates from disease are shocking when Indian and non–Indian populations are compared. Influenza and pneumonia are 300 percent greater killers among Indians. Diseases such as hepatitis are at epidemic proportions, with an 800 percent higher chance of death. Diabetes is almost a plague [6.8 times the general population rate].[11]

It should come as no surprise, given the ubiquitousness of such circumstances, that alcoholism and other addictions take an inordinate toll. Although fewer Indians drink than do non–Indians, the rate of alcohol-related accidental deaths among native people is ten times that of the general population, while the rate of Fetal Alcohol Syndrome (FAS) among the newborn is 33 times greater.[12] The suicide rate among Indians is ten times the national norm, while, among native youth, it is 10,000 percent higher than among our non–Indian counterparts.[13]

All told, the current life expectancy of a reservation–based American Indian male is less than fifty years in a society where the average man lives 71.8 years. Reservation-based Indian women live approximately three years longer than their male counterparts, but general population women enjoy an average life expectancy seven years longer than non–Indian men.[14] Hence, every time an American Indian dies on a reservation—or, conversely, every time a child is born—it can be argued that about one-third of a lifetime is lost. This 30th percentile attrition of the native population has prevailed throughout the twentieth century, a situation clearly smacking of genocide.[15]

This last is, of course, a policy-driven phenomenon, not something inadvertent or merely "unfortunate." Here, the BIA's exercise of trust authority over native assets comes into play. While it has orchestrated the increasingly intensive "development" of reservation lands since 1945, a matter which might logically have been expected to alleviate at least the worst of the symptoms sketched above, the Bureau's role in setting the rates at which land was/is leased and royalties for extracted minerals were/are paid by major corporations has precluded any such result.[16]

Instances in which the BIA has opted to rent out the more productive areas on reservations to non–Indian ranchers or agribusiness interests for as little as $1 per acre per year, and for as long as 99 years, are legion and notorious.[17] As to mineral royalties, the Bureau has consistently structured contracts "in behalf of" Indians which require payment of as little as 10 percent of market rates while releasing participating corporations from such normal overhead expenses as the maintenance of minimum standards for worker/community safety and environmental safeguards. In fact, most such arrangements have not even provided for a semblance of post–operational clean–up of mining and processing sites.[18]

Such "savings" accrue to U.S. corporations in the form of superprofits indistinguishable from those gleaned through their enterprises in the Third World, a matter which has unquestionably facilitated the emergence of the United States as the world's dominant economic power in the post-World War II context.[19] Minerals such as uranium, molybdenum and zeolite, moreover, are not only commercially valuable but strategically crucial, an important factor in understanding America's present global military ascendancy.[20]

All of this has been obtained, as a matter of policy, at the direct expense of Native North America as well as other underdeveloped regions of the world. As Eduardo Galeano once explained to mainstream Americans, with respect to the impact of their lifestyle(s) on Latin America: "Your wealth is our poverty."[21] The correlation is no less true on American Indian reservations. It holds up even in such superficially more redeemable connections as U.S. efforts to curtail acid rain and other collateral effects of electrical power generation through reliance upon low–sulfur bituminous rather than high–sulfur anthracite coal.

The largest and most easily extracted deposit of bituminous coal in North America is located at Black Mesa, in northern Arizona, an area occupied almost exclusively by Navajos. Beginning in 1974, the federal government undertook a program of compulsory relocation to remove some 13,000 resident Navajos from the intended mining area, dispersing them into primarily urban areas and completely obliterating their sociocultural existence (until then, they had comprised the largest remaining enclave of traditionally oriented Indians in the lower forty-eight states). The land upon which their subsistence economy was based is itself to be destroyed, a circumstance barring even the possibility of their reconstitution as a viable human group at some future date.[22]

The coal, once mined, is slurried to the Four Corners Power Plant and other generating facilities where it is burned to produce electricity. This "product" is then transported over massive power grids to meet such socially vital needs as keeping the air conditioners humming in the Phoenix Valley and the neon lights lit 24–hours–a–day at Las Vegas casinos. Meanwhile, 46 percent of the homes on the Navajo Reservation have no electricity at all

156

(54 percent have no indoor plumbing, 82 percent no phone).[23] No more fitting illustration of Galeano's equation seems conceivable.

### Internal Colonialism

Historically, the term "colonialism" has been employed to describe this sort of relationship between nations. Since ratification of the United Nations Charter in 1945, however, such structural domination/exploitation of any nation or people by another, even (or especially) when it is disguised as the exercise of a perpetual "trust," has been deemed illegal within the canons of international jurisprudence. The principle has been clarified, and has received considerable amplification, in subsequent instruments, most unequivocally in United Nations General Assembly Resolution 1514 (XV), also known as the "Declaration on the Granting of Independence to Colonial Countries and Peoples, 1960."[24]

1. The subjection of peoples to alien subjugation, domination and exploitation constitutes a denial of fundamental human rights, is contrary to the Charter of the United Nations and is an impediment to the promotion of world peace and co-operation.

2. All peoples have the right to self-determination; by virtue of that right they freely determine their political status and freely pursue their economic, social and cultural development.

3. Inadequacy of political, economic, social or educational preparedness should never serve as a pretext for delaying independence.

4. All armed action or repressive measures directed against dependent peoples shall cease in order to enable them to exercise peacefully and freely their right to complete independence, and the integrity of their national territory shall be respected.

5. Immediate steps shall be taken in Trust or Non-Self-Governing Territories or all other territories which have not yet attained independence, to transfer all powers to the peoples of those territories, without any conditions or reservations, in accordance with their freely expressed will and desire, without any distinction as to race, creed or colour, in order to enable them to enjoy complete independence and freedom.

6. Any attempt aimed at the partial or total disruption of the national unity and the territorial integrity of a country is incompatible with the purpose and principles of the Charter of United Nations.

7. All States shall observe faithfully and strictly the provisions in the Charter of the United Nations, the Universal Declaration of Human Rights and the present Declaration on the basis of equality, non-interference in the internal affairs of all

States, and respect for the sovereign rights of all peoples and their territorial integrity. [25]

While this would seem straightforward enough, the Declaration's universality was muddied by a follow-up provision—General Assembly Resolution 1541 (XV)—which effectively constrained its applicability to peoples/territories separated from colonizing powers by at least thirty miles of open ocean.[26] This "overseas requirement" has seriously undermined assertions of the right to self-determination by American Indians and other indigenous peoples.[27]

> There are decolonization issues in the international system which are not so easily defined, such as the Palestine Question or that of South Africa, while the formation of Pakistan out of greater India and the separation of Bangladesh from Pakistan did not relate to legalisms but to political realities. On the other hand, separation by water is no guarantee of independence, as in the case of Puerto Rico, which is officially the "colony" of the United States under United Nations Trusteeship.[28]

This last could as easily be said of Hawai'i, or such "protectorates" as Guam, "American" Samoa or the "U.S." Virgin Islands.[29] In any event, the "Blue Water Thesis" institutionalized in Resolution 1541 has afforded the U.S., Canada and other U.N. member-states a useful pretext upon which to construct the pretense that their ongoing colonization of indigenous nations/peoples is not really colonialism at all. Rather, they contend, they are merely exercising the prerogative, provided in the U.N. Charter, of preserving the integrity of their own respective territories.[30] At present, the U.S. in particular is endeavoring to have native rights (re)defined in international law in a manner conforming to its own practice of maintaining American Indians in a condition of "domestic" subjugation.[31]

While it is true that the "internal" variety of colonialism visited upon native peoples by modern settler states differs in many respects from the "classic" models of external colonization developed by European empires over the past several centuries, it is colonialism nonetheless.[32] Moreover, it is no less genocidal in its implications and effects than were the forms of overseas colonialism analyzed by Jean-Paul Sartre in his famous 1968 essay on the topic.[33] Indeed, given how seamlessly it has been imposed, how imperfectly its existence and functioning are reflected in even the most ostensibly liberatory political discourses, and how committed to attaining its formal legitimation the great majority of states have lately proven themselves, internal colonialism may well prove to be more so.[34]

Predictably, there are a number of ways in which the Sartrian equation of colonialism to genocide can be brought to bear when examining the situation of contemporary Native North America. Several of these were suggested in the preceding section. Probably the clearest representation will be found, however, in the sorry history of how the United States has wielded its self-assigned trust authority over Indian lands and lives in pursuit of global nuclear supremacy over the past half-century.

## Radioactive Colonization

The origins of the U.S. nuclear policy obviously lie in its quest to develop an atomic bomb during World War II. The "Manhattan Project" was conducted mainly at the Los Alamos National Scientific Laboratory, a huge fortified compound created in 1942 on the Pajarito Plateau, northwest of Santa Fe, New Mexico, on land supposedly reserved for the exclusive use and occupancy of the San Ildefonso Pueblo.[35] Uranium, the key material used in the lab's experiments and eventual fabrication of prototype nuclear weapons, was mined and milled exclusively in the Monument Valley area of the nearby Navajo Reservation.[36] Hanford, a uranium enrichment/plutonium manufacturing facility, was added in 1944, near the town of Richland, on Yakima land in eastern Washington.[37] When the first bomb was detonated on July 16, 1945, it was on the Alamogordo Bombing and Gunnery Range, now the White Sands Test Range, adjoining the Mescalero Apache Reservation.[38]

While the official rationale for these site selections has always been that their remoteness from major urban centers was/is essential to protecting the secrecy of the research and production to which they were devoted, this in itself does not account for why they were not situated in such sparsely populated areas as western Kansas.[39] A better explanation would seem to reside in the fact that planners were concerned from the outset that the nuclear program embodied substantial risks to anyone living in proximity to it.[40] Such people as resided in the central plains region by the 1940s were mostly members of the settler society; those at San Ildefonso, Mescalero and Yakima were almost entirely native. For U.S. policymakers, there appears to have been no real question as to which group was the more readily expendable.

That such an assessment is none too harsh is borne out by even the most cursory review of federal comportment in the immediate postwar period. Already possessed of a nuclear weapons monopoly which it believed would allow it to dictate terms to the planet, the U.S. was unsure exactly how much more uranium it needed to acquire.[41] In such circumstances, it was impossible to entice American corporations to engage in uranium extraction. Beginning in 1947, the government's newly formed Atomic Energy Commission (AEC, now the Department of Energy; DoE) "solved" the problem by arranging for several hundred otherwise destitute Navajos to be underwritten by the Small Business Administration (SBA) in starting up tiny mining operations of their own.[42]

Although it has since been claimed that the AEC was unaware of the dangers attending this occupation, there is ample reason to believe authorities were in possession of sufficient information to realize they were consigning every Navajo they coaxed to go underground to a veritable death sentence.

> It is important to realize that uranium mining is unlike most other kinds of mining in that during the course of blasting and digging for ore, radioactive radon-222 gas is released. Radon-222 is a natural decay product of uranium with a half-life of about three and one-half days. Radon gas by itself poses no real danger: as a noble gas, it is chemically inert and is simply exhaled. But its radioactive "daughter products," can settle in the lungs and injure the tissues. The primary hazard comes from polonium-218 and 214, alpha-emitting radionuclides that lodge in the lining of the lung. Uranium miners are also bombarded by gamma radiation, but the primary danger, again, stems from the ingestion and inhalation of alpha emitters. . . Robert J. Roscoe of the National Institute for Occupational Safety and Health has shown that nonsmoking uranium miners followed from 1950 to 1984 were thirteen times more likely to die from lung cancer than a comparable group of nonsmoking U.S. veterans.[43]

Dr. Roscoe's test group included a significant proportion of miners who had worked in relatively large, well-ventilated shafts and even open-air uranium stripping operations. The initial group of Navajos worked in tiny, unventilated shafts where radon concentrations were often hundreds of times higher than average. As a consequence, *all* the AEC/SBA miners were dead or dying of lung cancer and/or other respiratory ailments by the mid-1980s (in a preview of what by the 1990s would become national policy—and a yuppie fad—an attempt was made to blame cigarette-smoking and other personal behaviors for this health catastrophe).[44]

As early as 1556, Austrian physician Georgius Agricola had described the extraordinary incidence of death by "consumption of the lungs" among Carpathian silver miners digging ores laced with radium.[45] In 1879, F.H. Härting and W. Hesse correctly diagnosed what had by then become known as *Bergkrankheit* (mountain sickness) as lung cancer, and demonstrated that approximately three-quarters of all miners in the Schneeberg region of Saxony died of the disease within twenty years of entering the shafts.[46] By 1924, German researchers P. Ludewig and S. Lorenser had linked the Schneeberg miners' cancers to radon inhalation,[47] a connection explored more fully by American physician Wilhelm C. Hueper, founding director of the American Cancer Institute's Environmental Cancer Section, in his seminal 1942 book, *Occupational Tumors and Allied Diseases*.[48]

Nor was Hueper's study the only one readily available to the AEC. In 1944, Egon Lorenz published an article in the *Journal of the National Cancer Institute* which concluded that "the radioactivity of the ore and the radon content of the air of the mines are generally considered to be the primary cause" of lung cancer among uranium miners.[49] Occupational cancer expert Fred W. Stewart went further in a 1947 issue of the *Bulletin of the New York Academy of Medicine*, predicting that there would likely be epidemic "cases of cancer and leukemia in our newest group of industrialists, workers in the field of fissionable materials."[50] Even Bernard Wolf and Merril Eisenbud, directors of the AEC's own medical division, were warning their superiors of such dangers.[51]

The Navajos, of course, were told none of this. On the contrary, when Wolf and Eisenbud tried to establish minimum safety standards for miners in 1948, they were "told by Washington that the health problems of the mines were not the responsibility of the AEC, and . . . should be left to the jurisdiction of the local authorities."[52]

> The AEC had been assigned by Congress the responsibility for radiation safety in the nuclear program but, according to a bizarre interpretation of the 1946 Atomic Energy Act, the commission was bound only to regulate exposures after the ore had been mined. Responsibility for the health and safety of uranium miners was left up to individual states, a situation that Merril Eisenbud rightly recognized as "absurd," given their lack of equipment and expertise to deal with the expected health problems [not to mention the fact that the states lacked jurisdiction on Indian reservations in any event].[53]

Be that as it may, the AEC plainly went to great lengths to ensure that the general public remained equally uninformed. This was accomplished through a regulation requiring that all scientific papers dealing with radiation prepared under auspices of the National Institutes of Health (NIH) be cleared by the commission prior to presentation/publication. Thus, when Hueper sought to present a paper at a 1952 meeting of the Colorado State

Medical Society, he was instructed by Shields Warren, the AEC's Director of Biology and Medicine, to "delete all references . . . to the hazards of uranium mining."[54]

> Hueper . . . refused on the grounds that he had not joined the [National Cancer Institute; NCI] to become a "scientific liar". . . When word got around that he was not silently accepting his censorship, Warren again wrote the director of the NCI, this time asking for Hueper's dismissal. Hueper stayed on but was soon barred from all epidemiological work on occupational cancer. The order came from the surgeon general. Hueper was henceforth allowed to do only experimental work on animals, and was prohibited from further investigations into the causation of cancer in man related to environmental exposure to carcinogenic chemical, physical, or parasitic agents.[55]

Similarly, in 1955 the AEC managed to prevent Nobel laureate H.J. Muller, a geneticist, from speaking at the International Symposium on the Peaceful Uses of Atomic Energy in Geneva because he had concluded that radiation induced mutagenic effects in human organisms.[56] During the early 1960s, the commission was also able to marginalize the work of Ernest J. Sternglass, whose groundbreaking research demonstrated that the proliferation of radioactive contaminants would lead to increased rates of miscarriage, stillbirth, childhood leukemia and other cancers.[57] A few years later it brought about the dismissal of John W. Gofman, the discoverer of both uranium-233 and plutonium isolation process, from his position at the Lawrence Livermore Laboratories. Gofman's "offense" was determining that, contrary to the AEC's official posture, there was/is really no "safe" level of exposure to radioactive substances.[58]

While the commission's ability to silence such voices diminished over the years, it never really disappeared altogether. When AEC researcher Thomas F. Mancuso set out in 1977 to publish findings that radiation exposure was causing inordinate rates of cancer among workers at the Hanford military complex, he was terminated and his research materials impounded.[59] Much the same fate was bestowed upon Dr. Rosalie Bertell, albeit indirectly, through the National Cancer Institute, when she began to publish the results of epidemiological research on the effects of nuclear contamination during the late 1970s.[60] And so it went for more than forty years.

Unsurprisingly, given the context, the official stance vis-à-vis uranium miners amounted to little more than quietly tallying up the death toll. Even the Public Health Service (PHS), which called in 1957 for "immediate application of corrective measures" to avert an "impending public health disaster" spawned by radon inhalation among miners, was shortly subordinated to the AEC's demand that the truth be hidden.[61] Victor E. Archer, an epidemiologist with the PHS's National Institute for Occupational Safety and Health (NIOSH), spelled this out in 1977, during testimony entered in a suit brought by a group of terminally ill Navajo miners and survivors of those already dead.

> Archer testified that he and his colleagues had caved in to AEC and PHS pressures not to publicize the [radon] hazard: "We did not want to rock the boat. . . [W]e had to take the position that we were neutral scientists trying to find out what the facts were, that we were not going to make any public announcements until the results of our scientific study were completed. Official pressures to "monitor" the disaster without informing those at risk or forcing [mining] companies to reduce the hazard led PHS scientists to characterize their study as a "death watch" or "dead body approach." A federal judge [Aldon Anderson] involved in the Navajo case charged that U.S. atomic authorities had failed to warn the miners in order to guarantee a "constant, uninterrupted and reliable flow" of uranium ore "for national security purposes."[62]

An efficient system for delivering huge quantities of uranium had become an especially high priority for the U.S. military when the Soviet Union, years ahead of expectations, tested a nuclear device of its own on September 23, 1949. This set in motion a mad scramble to amass ever greater numbers of increasingly more powerful and sophisticated atomic weapons, as well as a burgeoning number of nuclear reactors, on both sides of the Atlantic.[63] Thus guaranteed the sustained profitability of such enterprises, and shortly immunized against any liabilities they might entail, America's major corporations entered with a vengeance into uranium mining, milling and related activities, completely supplanting the first generation of Navajo miners' "mom and pop" operations by the end of 1951.[64]

This sudden and massive corporate tie-in to the expansion of U.S. uranium production did not, however, signal a shifting of the burden of supplying it from the shoulders of Native North America. Rather, such weight was increased dramatically. Although only about 60 percent of uranium deposits in the United States were/are situated on American Indian reservations—most of it in the so-called "Grants Uranium Belt" of northern New Mexico and Arizona—well over 90 percent of all the uranium ever mined in the U.S. had been taken from such sources by the time the AEC's "domestic" ore-buying program was phased out in 1982.[65]

Hence, while the USSR and its satellites relied on slave labor provided by hundreds of thousands of political prisoners in meeting their production quotas, the U.S. utilized its internal, indigenous colonies for the same purpose.[66] Not only did the workforce harnessed to the tasks of uranium mining and milling remain disproportionately native, but the vast majority of extraction and processing facilities were situated in Indian Country as well, conveniently out of sight and mind of the general public, their collateral health impacts concentrated among indigenous populations. Much the same can be said with respect to weapons research, testing and, all along, the disposal of radioactive waste by-products. We will examine each of these components of the nuclear process in turn.

## Mining

The first largescale uranium mine in the United States was opened under AEC/BIA sanction by the Kerr-McGee Nuclear Corporation in 1952, on the Navajo Reservation, outside the town of Shiprock, New Mexico. A hundred Navajos were hired to perform the underground labor—at about two-thirds the prevailing off-reservation payscale for comparable work—in what was ostensibly a ventilated mine shaft.[67] When a federal inspector visited the mine a few months after it opened, however, he discovered the ventilator fans were not functioning. When he returned three years later, in 1955, they were still idle.[68] By 1959, radon levels in the mine shaft were routinely testing at 90–100 times maximum "safe" levels, a circumstance which remained essentially unchanged until the ore played out and Kerr-McGee closed the mine in 1970.[69]

Of the 150-odd Navajo miners who worked below ground at Shiprock over the years, eighteen had died of radiation-induced lung cancer by 1975; five years later, another twenty were dead of the same disease, while the bulk of the rest had been diagnosed with serious respiratory ailments.[70] Much the same situation pertained with regard to native employees working in the shaft at Kerr-McGee's second mining operation on Navajo, opened at Red Rock in 1953. By 1979, fifteen were dead of lung cancer and dozens of others had been diagnosed with that malady and/or respiratory fibrosis.[71] The same rates prevail among the well over 700 men who worked underground for Kerr-McGee at Grants, New Mexico, the largest uranium shaft mining operation in the world.[72] Of the original 6,000 or so miners of all races employed below ground in the Grants Belt, Victor Archer has estimated 1,000 will eventually die of lung cancer.[73]

Nonetheless, such mines proliferated on the reservation throughout the remainder of the 1950s, as the AEC, with the active complicity of the BIA, entered into a host of additional contracts, not only with Kerr-McGee, but with corporations like Atlantic-Richfield (ARCO), AMEX, Foote Mineral, Utah International, Climax Uranium, United Nuclear, Union Carbide (a chameleon which was formerly known as the Vanadium Corporation of America, and is now called Umetco Minerals Corporation), Gulf, Conoco, Mobil, Exxon, Getty, Sun Oil, Standard Oil of Ohio (Sohio), and Rockwell International.[74] As of 1958, "the Bureau of Indian Affairs reported that over 900,000 acres of tribal land were leased for uranium exploration and development."[75] From 1946 to 1968, well over 13 million tons of uranium ore were mined on Navajo—some 2.5 million tons at Shiprock alone—and still the rate of increase grew.[76] By late 1976, the year which turned out to have represented the very peak of the "uranium frenzy" afflicting the Colorado Plateau, the BIA had approved a total of 303 leases encumbering a quarter-million acres of Navajo land for corporate mining and milling purposes.[77]

Aside from the effects of all this upon those working underground, the shaft mining on Navajo had an increasingly negative impact upon the physical wellbeing of their families and communities on the surface. One indication of this resides in the fact that, once real ventilation of the mines began to occur during the mid-'60s, the vents were often situated right in the middle of residential areas, the inhabitants of which were then forced to breathe the same potent mixtures of radon, thoron and other toxic substances which were plaguing their husbands, fathers and neighbors below.[78] Then there was the matter of pumping out the groundwater which seeped constantly into scores of the deeper shafts—a process called "dewatering"—all of it heavily contaminated. To appreciate the volume of this outpouring, it should be considered that just one site, Kerr-McGee's Church Rock No. 1 Mine, was pumping more than 80,000 gallons of irradiated effluents per day into the local supply of surface water in 1980.[79]

> The millions of gallons of radioactive water [released in this fashion] carry deadly selenium, cadmium, and lead that are easily absorbed into the local food chain, as well as emitting alpha and beta particles and gamma rays. Human ingestion of radioactive water can result in alpha particles recurrently bombarding human tissue and eventually tearing apart the cells comprising that tissue . . . causing cancer [and/or genetic mutation in offspring].[80]

Small wonder that, by 1981, the Navajo Health Authority (NHA) had documented increasing rates of birth defects—notably cleft palate and

Down's Syndrome—among babies born after 1965 in mine-adjacent reservation communities like Shiprock, Red Rock and Church Rock.[81] At the same time, it was determined that children living in such localities were suffering bone cancers at a rate five times the national average, ovarian cancers at an astonishing seventeen times the norm.[82] Yet another study concluded that, overall, there was "a twofold excess of miscarriages, infant deaths, congenital or genetic abnormalities, and learning disabilities among uranium-area families (compared with Navajo families in non-uranium areas)."[83] Although funding was requested from the Department of Health, Education and Welfare (DHEW) with which to conduct more extensive epidemiological studies throughout the Grants Belt, the request was promptly denied.

> In fact, in 1983, one agency, the Indian Health Services [ a subpart of DHEW, which was by then redesignated the Department of Health and Human Services] sent a report to congress . . . stating that there was "no evidence of adverse health effects on Indians in uranium development areas and there is no need for additional studies or funding for such studies."[84]

Meanwhile, beginning in 1952, an ARCO subsidiary, the Anaconda Copper Corporation, had been operating under AEC/BIA authority on the nearby Laguna Reservation, near Albuquerque. By the early 1970s, the approximately 2,800 acres of Anaconda's Jackpile-Paguate complex at Laguna—from which 22 million tons of ore and more than 44 million tons of other minerals were removed—was the largest open-pit uranium mine in the world.[85] Ultimately, the excavation went so deep that groundwater seepage became as much an issue as in a shaft mine.

> [Anaconda's] mining techniques require "dewatering," i.e., the pumping of water contaminated by radioactive materials to facilitate ore extraction. Since 1972, the Jackpile Mine has wasted more than 119 gallons per minute through this dewatering procedure. Altogether more than 500 million gallons of radioactive water have been discharged [into] a 260-acre tailings pond [from which it] either sinks back into the aquifer, evaporates, or seeps out into the arroyos and drainage channels of the tiny Rio Mequino stream that is fed by a natural spring near the tailings dam.[86]

In 1972, and again in 1977, the Environmental Protection Agency (EPA) notified the Laguna tribal council that both the Río Molino and the nearby Río Paguate, both of which run through the Anaconda leasing area, and which together comprise the pueblo's only source of surface water, were badly contaminated with radium 226 and other heavy metals.[87] This was followed, in 1979, by a General Accounting Office announcement that the aquifer underlying the entire Grants Belt, from which Laguna draws its groundwater, was similarly polluted.[88] The trade-off was, of course, "jobs." But, while most able-bodied Lagunas, and a considerable proportion of neighboring Acomas, were employed by the corporation—a matter touted by the BIA as a "miracle of modernization"—most received poverty-level incomes.[89] And, although the adverse health effects of open-pit uranium mining seem somewhat less pronounced than those associated with shaft mining, disproportionately high rates of cancer among longterm miners were being noted by the early 1980s.[90]

All told, about 3,200 underground and 900 open-pit miners were employed in uranium operations by 1977, and Kerr-McGee was running a multimillion dollar U.S. Department of Labor-funded job training program in the Navajo community of Church Rock, Arizona, to recruit more.[91] The stated governmental/corporate objective was to create a workforce of 18,400 underground and 4,000 open-pit miners to extract ore from approximately 3.5 million acres along the Grants Belt by 1990.[92] Only the collapse of the market for U.S. "domestic" uranium production after 1980—the AEC met its stockpiling quotas in that year, and it quickly became cheaper to acquire commercially designated supplies abroad, first from Namibia, then from Australia, and finally from the native territories of northern Saskatchewan, in Canada—averted realization of this grand plan.[93]

As the dust settled around the Four Corners, the real outcomes of uranium mining began to emerge. The AEC's constellation of corporations had profited mightily as a result, and not just because of their refusal to meet the expense of providing even the most rudimentary forms of worker safety or their having to pay only the artificially depressed wages prevailing within the reservations' colonial economies. The BIA, exercising the government's self-assigned "trust" prerogatives, had written contracts requiring the corporations to pay royalties pegged at an average of only 3.4 percent of market price in an environment where 15 percent was the normative standard.[94] Moreover, the contracts often included no clauses requiring postmining cleanup of any sort, thus sparing Kerr-McGee and its cohorts what would have been automatic and substantial costs of doing business in off-reservation settings. When lucrative mining was completed, the corporations were thus in a position to simply close up shop and walk away.[95]

The already much-impoverished indigenous nations upon which the uranium extraction enterprise had been imposed in the first place, which seldom if ever made money from the process, and whose prior economies had been demolished in the bargain, were then left holding the bag.[96] On Navajo, this involves the necessity of dealing with hundreds of abandoned mine shafts ranging from fifty to several hundred feet in depth, some subject to caving in and all of them steadily emitting radon and thoron from their gaping maws.[97] At Laguna, conditions are even worse.[98] As Dr. Joseph Wagoner, Director of Epidemiological Research for NIOSH, would later put it, with conspicuous understatement, the situation presents "serious medical and ethical questions about the responsibility [not just of the corporations, but] of the federal government, which was the sole purchaser of uranium during [much of] the period."[99]

## Milling

Milling, the separation of pure uranium from its ore, is the first stage of the production process. Ore pockets across the Grants Belt range from .4 to 3 percent uranium content, yielding an average of about four pounds of "yellowcake" per ton.[100] The remaining 1,996 pounds per ton of waste—reduced to the consistency of course sand called "tailings" during milling—invariably accumulates in huge piles alongside the mills, which, for reasons of cost efficiency, tend to be situated in close proximity to mines. Tailings retain approximately 85 percent of the radioactivity of the original ore, have a half-life estimated at 10,000 years, and are a source of continuous radon and thoron gas emissions. They are also subject to wind dispersal and constitute an obvious source of groundwater contamination through leaching.[101]

As with uranium mining, over 90 percent of all milling done in the U.S. occurred on or just outside the boundaries of American Indian reservations.[102] Also as was the case in the mines, "conditions in the mills were deplorable."[103] Even the most elementary precautions to assure worker protection were ignored as an "unnecessary expense." As Laguna poet Simon J. Ortiz, who was employed in a Kerr-McGee mill during the early 1960s, would later reflect:

> Right out of high school I worked in the mining and milling region of Ambrosia Lake. I was nineteen years old. . . At the mill, I worked in crushing, leaching, and yellowcake, usually at various labor positions. . . I had a job, and for poor people with low education and no skills and high unemployment, that was the important thing: a job. . . In 1960, there was no information about the dangers of radiation from yellowcake with which I worked. . . In the milling operation at the end of the leaching and settling process, the yellow liquid was drawn into dryers that took the water out. The dryers

were screen constructions which revolved slowly in hot air; yellow pellets were extruded and crushed into fine powder. The workers were to keep the machinery operating, which was never smooth, and most of the work was to keep it in free operation; i.e., frequently having to unclog it by hand. There was always a haze of yellow dust flying around, and even though filtered masks were used, the workers breathed in the fine dust. It got in the hair and cuts and scratches and in their eyes. I was nineteen then, and twenty years later I worried about it.[104]

The situation was so acute at Kerr-McGee's first mill on the Navajo Reservation, established at Shiprock in 1953, that after it was abandoned in 1974 inspectors discovered more than $100,000 in uranium dust had settled between two layers of roofing and former workers recalled having been routinely instructed by their supervisors to stir yellowcake by hand in open, steam-heated floorpans.[105] Needless to say, by 1980, those who'd been lured into the mills with the promise of a small but steady paycheck during the 1950s and '60s were suffering rates of lung cancer and other serious respiratory illnesses rivaling those of their counterparts in the mines.[106]

By far the greater impact of milling, however, has been upon the broader Navajo, Laguna and Acoma communities. The environmental degradation inflicted by a single mill, the Kerr-McGee plant at Grants—once again, the largest such facility in the world—may equal that of all the shaft mines along the uranium belt combined. At its peak, the monstrosity processed 7,000 tons of ore per day, piling up 23 million tons of tailings in a hundred-foot-high mound which covers 265 acres.[107] And this is just one of more than forty mills, several of them not much smaller, operating simultaneously on and around Navajo during the late 1970s.[108] A similar situation prevailed at plants established by Kerr-McGee, Sohio-Reserve, Bokum Minerals and several other corporations in the immediate vicinity of Laguna and Acoma.[109]

> At the Bluewater Mill, eighteen miles west of the Laguna Reservation [on the western boundary of Acoma, a thirty mile trip by rail from the Jackpile-Paguate complex, with raw ore hauled in open gondolas] near the bed of the San Jose River, Anaconda has added a 107-acre pond and a 159-acre pile comprising 13,500,000 tons of "active" tailings and 765,033 tons of "inactive" residues.[110]

In August 1978, it was discovered that Anaconda, as a means of "holding down costs," had also made massive use of tailings at Laguna as fill in its "improvement" of the reservation road network. At the same time, it was revealed that tailings had constituted the "sand and gravel mix" of concrete with which the corporation had—with much fanfare about the "civic benefits" it was thereby bestowing upon its indigenous "partners"—poured footings for a new tribal council building, community center and housing complex.[111] All were seriously irradiated as a result, a matter which may well be playing into increasing rates of cancer and birth defects, even among the non-miner sectors of Laguna's population.[112]

Probably the worst single example of mill-related contamination occurred about a year later, on July 16, 1979, at the United Nuclear plant in Church Rock, New Mexico, when a tailings dam gave way, releasing more than a hundred million gallons of highly radioactive water into the nearby Río Puerco.[113] About 1,700 Navajos living downstream were immediately effected, as were their sheep and other livestock, all of whom depended on the river for drinking water.[114] Shortly thereafter, with spill-area cattle exhibiting unacceptably high levels of lead 210, polonium 210, thorium 230, radium 236 and similar substances in their tissues, all commercial sales of meat from such animals was indefinitely prohibited.[115]

Still, even as the ban went into effect, IHS Area Director William Moehler—rather than calling for allocation of federal funds with which to provide emergency rations to those most directly at risk—approved consumption of the very same mutton and beef by local Navajos.[116] At about the same time, a request by downstream Navajos for United Nuclear to provide them with trucked-in water, at least in quantities sufficient to meet the immediate needs of the afflicted human population, was met with flat refusal.[117] The corporation stonewalled for another five years—until it was revealed by the Southwest Research and Information Center, an Albuquerque-based environmental organization, that it had known about cracks in the dam at least two months before it broke and had failed to repair it—before agreeing to a minimal, state-facilitated "settlement" of $525,000.[118]

By and large, however, it was not outright disasters such as the Church Rock spill, but the huge and rapidly proliferating accumulation of mill tailings throughout the Four Corners region—more than a half-billion tons in 200 locations by 1979, figures which were projected to double by the end of the century—which provoked a team of Los Alamos experts, utterly at a loss as to what to do with such vast quantities of radioactive waste, to recommend the "zon[ing] of uranium mining and milling districts so as to forbid human habitation."[119]

The idea dovetailed perfectly with the conclusions drawn in a contemporaneous study undertaken by the National Academy of Sciences (NAS), that desert lands subjected to stripmining can never be reclaimed.[120] Since the Peabody Coal Company, among others, was/is engaged in ever-more-massive coal stripping operations on Navajo,[121] the logical outcome of the Los Alamos and NAS studies was formulation of a secret federal "policy option" declaring the Four Corners, and the Black Hills region of the northern plains as well,[122] "national sacrifice areas in the interests of energy development."[123]

Not coincidentally, the pair of localities selected contained the largest and second-largest concentrations of reservation-based Indians remaining in the United States: Navajo, with over 120,000 residents in 1980, is by far the biggest reservation both by size and by population in the U.S. Also sacrificed in the Four Corners region would be—at a minimum—the Hopi, Zuni, Laguna, Acoma, Isleta, Ramah Navajo, Cañoncito Navajo, Ute Mountain and Southern Ute reservations. The 50,000-odd residents of the "Sioux Complex" of reservations in North and South Dakota—Pine Ridge, Rosebud, Crow Creek, Cheyenne River and Standing Rock in particular—make up the second most substantial concentration. Also sacrificed in the Black Hills region would be the Crow and Northern Cheyenne reservations in Montana, and possibly the Wind River Reservation in Wyoming.[124]

As American Indian Movement leader Russell Means observed in 1980, shortly after existence of the plan had been disclosed, to sacrifice the landbase of landbased peoples is tantamount to sacrificing the peoples themselves, a prospect he aptly described as genocide while calling for appropriate modes of resistance.[125]

Although a policy of deliberately creating national sacrifice areas out of American Indian reservations was never formally implemented, the more indirect effect may well be the same. With windblown tailings spread over wide tracts of Navajo, ground and surface water alike contaminated with all manner of radioactive substances, and Navajo children literally using abandoned mounds of tailings as sand piles, it is not unreasonable to suspect that both the land and the people have already been sacrificed on the altar of U.S. armaments development.[126] If so, they and their counterparts at Laguna, Acoma and elsewhere will have become victims of what may be, to date, history's subtlest form of physical extermination.[127]

The Los Alamos lab might well have extended its zoning recommendations to include not just uranium mining and milling districts but localities in which nuclear weapons research and production have been carried out, beginning with itself. Here again, although the sites at which yellowcake is enriched and/or transformed into plutonium have been scattered across the country in localities not typically associated with indigenous people, the great weight of contamination in this connection has been off-loaded by the dominant society onto Indian Country.[128]

The extent of radioactive contamination at Los Alamos itself is astonishing. A half-century of nuclear weapons research on the 43-square-mile "campus"—which adjoins not only San Ildefonso, but the Santa Clara, San Juan, Jemez and Zia reservations—has produced some 2,400 irradiated pollution sites containing "plutonium, uranium, strontium-90, tritium, lead, mercury, nitrates, cyanides, pesticides and other lethal leftovers."[129] A single 1950 experiment in which "simulated nuclear devices" were exploded in order to track radioactive fallout patterns was not only kept secret for decades, but left nearby Bayo Canyon heavily contaminated with strontium.[130] The facility also has a long history of secretly and illegally incinerating irradiated wastes—a practice producing significant atmospheric contamination—as was acknowledged by the EPA in 1991.[131]

The greatest concentration of hazardous materials in the Los Alamos compound is situated in what is called "Area G," which "began taking radioactive waste in 1957. Since 1971, 381,000 cubic feet of [lab]-generated transuranic [plutonium-contaminated] waste has been stored there; no one knows how much went in before 1971, since records are scanty. Wastes were interred without liners or caps, in bulldozed pits" from which they may be presumed to be leaking.[132]

This, in combination with the lab's chronic release of radioactive substances into the atmosphere is thought to be correlated to dramatic increases in cancers and birth defects among local native populations over the past twenty years.[133] Plutonium contamination of surface water has been found downstream at least as far as the Cochiti Reservation, thirty miles away.[134] At present, Area G is slated for considerable expansion.[135] In the new plan, strongly opposed by area Indians, it "would be able to contain 475,000 cubic yards of mixed-waste in pits 2,000 feet long and divided into 25,000 cubic yard segments."[136]

An even worse situation prevails at Hanford, which was closed in 1990. Despite frequent official denials that it presented any sort of public health hazard during the span of its operation, the complex exhibits an unparalleled record of deliberate environmental contamination, beginning with a secret experimental release of radioactive iodides in 1945, the first of seven, which equaled or surpassed the total quantity of pollutants emitted during the disastrous 1986 Soviet reactor meltdown at Chernobyl.[137] Also in 1945, Hanford officials secretly instructed staff to begin "disposing" of irradiated effluents by the simple expedient of pouring them into unlined "sumps" from which they leached into the underlying aquifer. All told, before the plant was closed something in excess of 440 *billion* gallons of water laced with everything from plutonium to tritium to ruthenium had been dumped in this "cost efficient" manner.[138]

Another 900,000 gallons of even more highly radioactive fluids were stored in a 117-unit underground "tank farm" maintained under contract by ARCO, several components of which were found to be leaking badly.[139] Not only has regional groundwater been severely contaminated, but wastes have been found to have passed into the nearby Columbia River in quantities sufficient to irradiate shellfish at the river's mouth, more than 200 miles distant.[140]

> Not only has the Hanford plant been discharging and leaking radiation into the river for forty-five years, but serious accidents have occurred at the reactors. One could perhaps excuse the accidental release of radiation [if not its cover-up], but on several occasions huge clouds of isotopes were created knowingly and willingly. In December [1952, to provide another example,] about 7,800 curies of radioactive Iodine 131 were deliberately [and secretly] released in an experiment designed to detect military reactors in the Soviet Union (only 15 to 24 curies of Iodine 131 escaped at Three Mile Island in 1979).[141]

The true extent of the ecological holocaust perpetrated at and around Hanford is unknown, and is likely to remain so over the foreseeable future, given that most information about the facility is permanently sealed as a matter of "national security," and DoE/Pentagon/corporate officials claim to have "lost" much of what is supposedly accessible.[142] Such information as has come out, however, tends to speak for itself.

> Abnormally high incidence of thyroid tumors and cancers have been observed in populations living downstream from Hanford. Strontium 90, Cesium 137, and Plutonium 239 have been released in large quantities, as was, between 1952 and 1967, Ruthenium 106. People in adjacent neighborhoods [notably, the Yakimas and nearby Spokanes] were kept uninformed about these releases—before, during and after—and none were

warned that they were at risk for subsequent development of cancer. (Some experts have estimated that downwind farms and families received radiation doses ten times higher than those that reached soviet people living near Chernobyl in 1986).[143]

In sum, the probability is that Los Alamos, Hanford and surrounding areas should be added to the extensive geographical sacrifices already discussed with respect to uranium mining and milling. To the extent that this is true—and it is almost certainly the case at Hanford—several more colonized indigenous nations must be added to the roster of those implicitly but officially placed among those peoples whose sacrifice is deemed necessary, useful, or at least acceptable, in the interests of U.S. nuclear development.

### Weapons Testing

Nuclear weapons, once designed, must be tested. During the period immediately following World War II, the U.S. asserted its "trust" authority over the Marshall Islands, gained by its defeat of Japan, for purposes of conducting more than a hundred such tests on the natives' mid-Pacific atolls by 1958.[144] Meanwhile, the search for a more "suitable" continental locality, code-named "Nutmeg," began as early as 1948. Two years later, the AEC/Pentagon combo finally settled on the Las Vegas/Tonopah Bombing and Gunnery Range in Nevada (now called the Nellis Range), an area which it had already decided "really wasn't much good for anything but gunnery practice—you could bomb it into oblivion and never notice the difference."[145]

Of course, nobody bothered to ask the Western Shoshone people, within whose unceded territory the facility was established, whether they felt this was an acceptable use of their land, or whether they were even willing to have it designated as part of the U.S. "public domain" for *any* purpose.[146] Instead, in 1952, having designated 435,000 acres in the Yucca Flats area of Nellis as a "Nevada Test Site"—another 318,000 acres were added in 1961, bringing the total to 753,000—the AEC and its military partners undertook the first of what by now add up to nearly a thousand atmospheric and underground test detonations.[147] In the process, it converted the peaceful and pastoral Shoshones, who had never engaged in an armed conflict with the U.S., into what, by any estimation, is far and away "the most bombed nation on earth."[148]

> The deadly atomic sunburst over Hiroshima, in 1945, produced 13 kilotons of murderous heat and radioactive fallout. At least 27 of the 96 above ground bombs detonated between 1951 and 1958 at the Nevada Test Site produced a total of over 620

kilotons of radioactive debris that fell on downwinders. The radioactive isotopes mixed with the scooped-up rocks and earth of the southwestern desert lands and "lay down a swath of radioactive fallout" over Utah, Arizona, and Nevada. In light of the fact that scientific research has now confirmed that *any* radiation exposure is dangerous, the "virtual inhabitants" (more than 100,000 people) residing in the small towns east and south of the test site were placed in . . . jeopardy by the AEC atomic test program (emphasis added).[149]

Those most effected by the estimated 12 billion curies of radioactivity released into the atmosphere over the past 45 years have undoubtedly been the native communities scattered along the periphery of Nellis.[150] These include not only three Shoshone reservations—Duckwater, Yomba and Timbisha—but the Las Vegas Paiute Colony and the Pahrump Paiute, Goshute, and Moapa reservations as well. Their circumstances have been greatly compounded by the approximately 900 underground test detonations which have, in a region where surface water sources are all but nonexistent, resulted in contamination of groundwater with plutonium, tritium and other radioactive substances at levels up to 3,000 times maximum "safe" limits.[151]

Radionuclides released to groundwater include: antimony-125, barium-140, beryllium-7, cadmium-109, cerium-141, cesium-137, cobalt-60, europium-155, iodine-131, iridium-192, krypton, lanthaum-140, plutonium-238, plutonium-239, plutonium-240, rhodium-106, ruthenium-103, sodium-22, strontium-90, and tritium.[152]

Although the government has been steadfast in its refusal to conduct relevant epidemiology studies in Nevada, especially with respect to indigenous peoples, it has been credibly estimated that several hundred people had already died of radiation-induced cancers by 1981.[153] Rather than admit to any aspect of what it was doing, the military simply gobbled up increasingly gigantic chunks of Shoshone land, pushing everyone off and creating ever-larger "security areas" that rendered its activities less-and-less susceptible to any sort of genuine public scrutiny.[154]

Today, in the state of Nevada, in addition to Nellis Air Force Base and Nevada Test Site, we can add the following military reservations: Fallon Navy Training Range Complex with its airspace; the Hawthorne Army Ammunition Depot, with its restricted airspace; the Reno Military Operations Area Airspace; the Hart Military Operations Area Airspace; the Paradise Military Operations Area Airspace; and parts of the Utah Training Range Complex with its airspace. Military ranges in Nevada alone amount to four million acres. Approximately 40 percent of Nevada's airspace is designated for military use.[155]

Across the state line in California—it is separated from the gargantuan sprawl of military facilities in Nevada only by the width of the interposed Death Valley National Monument—lies the million-acre China Lake Naval Weapons Center.[156] Butted up against the Army's equally sized estate at Fort Irwin, and close to both the half-million acre Edwards Air Force Base and the 800,000 acre Marine Corps Base at Twentynine Palms, China Lake—an oddly named facility in that it incorporates no lake at all—uses its share of the Mojave Desert in the same manner as White Sands, only more so.[157] Established in November 1943 and expanded steadily thereafter, it was crediting itself by 1968 with being the location in which "over 75% of the airborne weapons of the free world [and] 40% of the world's conventional weapons" had been tested and perfected.[158] As in Nevada, local indigenous communities, both Shoshone and Paiute, have been pushed out while their lands, including sacred sites, have been bombed, strafed and shelled relentlessly for more than fifty years.[159]

Probably the only "concession" made to native peoples in the region during this entire period has been that the three largest nuclear devices ever detonated underground, culminating in a monstrous five-megaton blast in 1971, were exploded, not at the Nevada Test Site, but on Amchitka Island, off Alaska. The reason for this change in procedure had nothing to do with concern for the wellbeing of human beings, however. Rather, it was brought on by fears among AEC officials that the shock waves from such large blasts might cause serious damage to casinos and other expensive buildings in downtown Las Vegas, thereby provoking a backlash from segments of the regional "business community."[160] Hence, the brunt of the environmental/biological consequences wrought by the three biggest "bangs" was shifted from the Indians of Nevada to the Aleuts indigenous to the Aleutian Archipelago.[161]

Exactly how large an area has been sacrificed to nuclear testing and related activities is unknown, but it most certainly includes the bulk of southern Nevada and contiguous portions of California.[162] Indications are that it may encompass northern Nevada as well, given the insistence of Reagan era Defense Secretary Casper Weinberger—selected for this position, appropriately enough, on the basis of his credentials as a senior vice president of the Bechtel Corporation, the second largest U.S. nuclear engineering contractor—that the railmounted MX missile system should be sited there, a move which would have effectively precluded human habitation.[163] Given prevailing wind patterns, the sacrifice area likely encompasses northwestern Arizona as well, including three indigenous nations—Hualapi, Havasupi and the Kaibab Reservation—located there.[164] Also at issue are the more westerly reaches of Utah, a region which includes the small Goshute and Skull Valley reservations in addition to another huge complex of military bases and proving grounds.[165]

### Waste "Disposal"

Plutonium, an inevitable byproduct of most reactors and the essential ingredient in nearly all nuclear weapons, has been aptly described as being "the most toxic substance in the universe."[166] Only ten micrograms, a microscopic quantity, is an amount "almost certain to induce cancer, and several grams . . . dispersed in a ventilation system, are enough to cause the death of thousands."[167] Indeed, it has been estimated that a single pound of plutonium, if evenly distributed throughout the earth's atmosphere, would be sufficient to kill every human being on the planet.[168] Viewed from this perspective, the quantity of this material created by the United States during the course of its arms race with the Soviet Union—as of 1989, the U.S. alone had amassed some 21,000 nuclear weapons—is virtually incomprehensible.[169]

> By 1995, military weapons-grade plutonium, in the form of active and dismantled bombs, amounted to 270 metric *tons*. The commercial stockpile of plutonium in nuclear-reactor wastes and isolates from spent fuel amounts to 930 metric tons and will double to 2,130 tons by 2005, only ten years from now. "Every four or five years we're [now] making about as much plutonium in the civil sector as we did during the whole Cold War." And this is only plutonium. Fission reactors create eighty radionuclides that are releasing "ionizing radiation," which causes harm to human beings in the form of genetic mutations, cancer, and birth defects.[170]

Leaving aside the proliferation of commercial reactors and other such facilities, as well as the mining and milling zones, there are 132 sites in thirty states where one or another facet of nuclear weapons production has left radioactive contamination of varying orders of magnitude, all of them unacceptable.[171] The DoE currently estimates that it will cost about $500 billion to return these to habitable condition, an absurdly low figure when it is considered that the department elsewhere admits neither concepts nor technologies presently exist with which even to begin cleaning up "large contaminated river systems like the Columbia, Clinch, and Savannah rivers, most groundwater [and] nuclear test areas on the Nevada Test Site."[172]

It is also conceded that there is no known method of actually "dispos-ing" of—i.e., decontaminating—plutonium and other radioactive wastes after they've been cleaned from the broader environment.[173] Instead, such materials, once collected, can only be sealed under the dubious premise that they can be somehow safely stored for the next 250,000 years.[174] The sheer volume is staggering: "Hanford [alone] stores 8,200,000 cubic feet of high-level waste and 500,000 cubic feet of transuranic waste. Hanford buried 18,000,000 cubic feet of "low-level" waste and 3,900,000 cubic feet of transuranic waste."[175] And, daunting as they are, these numbers—associated exclusively with weapons, weapons production and commercial reactors—don't begin to include the millions of tons of accumulated mill tailings and similar byproducts of "front end" nuclear processing.[176]

Such facilities as now exist to accommodate warhead and reactor wastes are all temporary installations designed to last a century or less, even under ideal sets of conditions which seem never to prevail.[177] The steadily escalat-ing rate of waste proliferation has led to the burning of plutonium and other substances—a practice which certainly reduces the bulk of the offending materials, but also risks sending clouds of radioactivity into the atmos-phere[178]—and an increasingly urgent quest for safer interim facilities, called "monitored retrievable storage" (MRS) sites, and permanent "repositories" into which their contents could eventually be moved.[179] Here, as always, emphasis has been on off-loading the problem onto captive indigenous nations.[180]

The reason, predictably enough, is that despite a chorus of official assur-ances that neither an MRS nor a repository would present a health hazard, the precise opposite is true. John Gofman has calculated that if only 0.01 per-cent of the plutonium now in storage were to escape into the environ-ment—a record of efficiency never remotely approximated by the nuclear establishment—some 25 million people could be expected to die of result-ing cancers over the following half-century.[181] Those most proximate to any dump site can of course expect to suffer the worst impact. Consequently, only one county in the United States has proven amenable to accepting an MRS within its boundaries, and its willingness to do so was quickly over-ridden by the state.[182]

Federal authorities have therefore concentrated all but exclusively on siting the dumps in Indian Country. As longtime indigenous rights activist Grace Thorpe has observed:

The U.S. government targeted Native Americans for several reasons: their lands are some of the most isolated in North America, they are some of the most impoverished and, consequently, most politically vulnerable and, perhaps most important, tribal sovereignty can be used to bypass state environmental laws. . . How ironic that, after centuries of attempting to destroy it, the U.S. government is suddenly interested in promoting Native American sovereignty—just to dump its lethal garbage.[183]

There can be little doubt that during the early 1990s DoE negotiators played heavily upon the colonially imposed destitution of indigenous peoples in peddling their wares.

16 tribes initially applied for $100,000 grants from DoE to study the MRS option on Native lands. The lucrative DoE offer included up to $3 million to actually identify a site for an MRS and as much as $5 million per year for any tribe to accept the deal. The government also offered to build roads, hospitals, schools, railroads, airports and recreation facilities [most of which the Indians should have been receiving anyway].[184]

Another $100,000 was passed along in 1992 to the federally oriented National Congress of American Indians (NCAI) to garner its assistance in selling the proposition to its constituents, while a whopping $1.2 million— 80 percent of the DoE's budget for such purposes—was lavished on the Council of Energy Resource Tribes (CERT), a federally/corporately funded entity created for the sole purpose of systematizing the wholesale brokering of native mineral rights.[185] Despite the best efforts of both organizations— CERT in particular went beyond the MRS concept to promote acceptance of a repository at Hanford by the Yakimas, Nez Perce and Umatillas—the campaign was largely a failure.[186] By 1995, only three reservations—Mescalero, Skull Valley, and Ft. McDermitt in northern Nevada—indicated varying degrees of willingness to accept a dump, regardless of the material incentives offered.

The reasoning which led to this result is instructive. At Skull Valley, the feeling expressed by many residents is that they and their land may already have been sacrificed, in part to radiation blown in over the years from the not far distant Nevada Test Site, in part to a host of nuclear, chemical and bacteriological contaminants emanating from military bases closer to home. Even the specific area committed as an MRS site has long been leased to several corporations as a rocket testing range.[187] As tribal member Leon Bear observes:

People need to understand that this whole area has already been deemed a waste zone by the federal government, the state of Utah, and the country. . . Tooele Depot, a military site, stores 40 percent of the nation's nerve gas and other hazardous gas only 40 miles away from us. Dugway Proving Grounds, an experimental life sciences center, is only 14 miles away, and it experiments with viruses like plague and tuberculosis. Within a 40-mile radius there are three hazardous waste dumps and a "low-level" radioactive waste dump. From all directions, north, south, east, and west we're surrounded by the waste of Tooele County, the state of Utah, and U.S. society.[188]

The sentiment at Skull Valley, that it is better to at least charge for one's demise than endure the suffering free of charge, is shared by an appreciable segment of the Mescalero population. As one reservation resident noted, the feeling of many people is that "since they are getting impacted by nuclear waste [anyway] they should have a chance to benefit economically."[189] Or, as another put it, "The federal government has forced us to choose between being environmentally conscious [and] starving."[190] Such perspectives notwithstanding, local activists like Rufina Laws were able to engineer a "no-acceptance" vote on an MRS proposal at Mescalero during the winter of 1995. It seems that only a policy of outright bribery by pro-nuclear Tribal Chairman Wendell Chino—reputedly the payment of $2,000 per "yes" vote—was sufficient to reverse the outcome by a narrow margin in a second referendum conducted a few months later.[191]

More important than such subsidies, however, may be the fact that many Mescaleros are now experiencing an overwhelming sense of hopelessness, based in the knowledge that not only are they just downwind from White Sands, but that—over their strong objections—the first U.S. nuclear repository has been sited in the Carlsbad Caverns area, immediately to their east.[192] This is the so-called "Waste Isolation Pilot Plant" (WIPP), a plan to store virtually all military transuranics produced after 1970—57,359 cubic meters of it—in a subsurface salt bed already scored by an underground nuclear detonation.[193]

> The disposal area will exceed 100 acres, although the site's surface area covers more than 10,000 acres. . . The repository's design calls for "creeping" salt to seal the wastes [2,150 feet below ground]—a process that is supposed to isolate the substances for tens of thousands of years. Controversy over the WIPP focuses on potential ground water contamination, gases which would be generated by the decomposing wastes, and the hazards posed by transporting approximately 30,000 truckloads of waste to the site, among other things.[194]

It now appears that the deep salt beds below Carlsbad are not so dry as was once believe by the National Academy of Sciences, a matter which could lead to relatively rapid corrosion of the storage canisters in which the repository's plutonium is to be contained and correspondingly massive contamination of the underlying Rustler Aquifer.[195] Serious questions have also arisen as to whether the mass of materials stored in such close quarters—after accommodating its present allocation of transuranics, the WIPP will still retain some 70 percent of its space availability to meet "future requirements," official shorthand for continuing nuclear weapons production—might not "go critical" and thereby set off an incalculably large atomic explosion.[196]

Even worse problems are evident at Yucca Mountain, located on the southwestern boundary of the Nevada Test Site, where a $15 billion repository to accommodate 70,000 tons of mostly civilian high-level waste is being imposed on the long-suffering Western Shoshones and Paiutes.[197] Not only is "spontaneous detonation" just as much a threat as at the WIPP, but Yucca Mountain, located in a volcanically active region, is undercut by no less than 32 geological fault lines.[198] Needless to say, no amount of engineering brilliance can ensure the repository's contents will remain undisturbed through a quarter-million years of earthquakes interspersed with volcanic eruptions. Once again, however, the project is being moved forward as rapidly as possible.

As if this were not enough, it was announced in 1993 by the Southwestern Compact, a consortium of state governments, that it had "decided to keep the option" of siting a huge low-level waste dump in the Mojave Desert's Ward Valley, near the small town of Needles on the California/Arizona boundary.[199] Envisioned as being large enough to accept the contents of all six existing—and failed—low-level facilities in the U.S. with room to spare for the next thirty years, the proposed site is less than eighteen miles from the Colorado River and directly above an aquifer.[200] It is also very close to the Fort Mojave, Chemehuavi Valley and Colorado River Indian Tribes reservations, and upstream from those of the Cocopahs and Quechanis around Yuma, Arizona.

Taken as a whole, the pattern of using "deserts as dumps" which has emerged in nuclear waste disposal practices over the past decade serves to confirm suspicions, already well founded, that creation of sacrificial geographies within the U.S. has been an integral aspect of Cold War policies and planning for nearly fifty years.[201] In many ways, the siting of repositories in particular, since they are explicitly intended to remain in place "forever," may be seen as a sort of capstone gesture in this regard. The collateral genocide of those indigenous peoples whose lands lie within the boundaries of the sacrifice zones, nations whose ultimate negation has always been implicitly bound up in the very nature and depth of their colonization, is thus, finally and irrevocably, to be consummated.[202]

## Freeing the Miner's Canary

The radioactive colonization of Native North America has involved fundamental miscalculations at a number of levels. In retrospect, the very idea that environmental contamination and consequent epidemiologies could be contained within U.S. internal colonies, hidden from polite society and afflicting only those deemed most expendable by federal policymakers, seems ludicrous. Windblown uranium tailings have never known that they were supposed to end their ongoing dispersal at reservation boundaries, no more than irradiated surface water has realized it was meant to stop flowing before it reached the domain of settler society, or polluted groundwater that it was intended to concentrate itself exclusively beneath Indian wellheads. Still less have clouds of radioactive iodides- and strontium-impregnated fallout been aware that they were scripted to remain exclusively within Yakima or Shoshone or Puebloan territories.

As Felix S. Cohen once observed, American Indians serve as the proverbial "miner's canary" of U.S. social, political and economic policies. Whatever is done to Indians, he said, invariably serves as a prototype for things intended by America's élites for application to others, often to society as a whole. The effects of policy implementation upon Indians can thus be viewed as an "early warning" device for the costs and consequences of policy formation upon the broader society. In paying attention to what is happening to Indians, Cohen concluded, non-Indians equip themselves to act in their own self-interest; in the alternative, they will inevitably find themselves sharing the Indians' fate.[203]

Cohen's premise plainly holds in the present connection, and not simply in the more obvious ways. If the citizens of Troy, New York, which became an unanticipated "hot spot" for fallout from atmospheric testing during the early 1950s, can now make the same claims concerning its impacts as can the residents of Nevada,[204] so too can everyone within a fifty-mile radius of any of the more than one hundred nuclear reactors in the United States, all of them made possible by the uranium mined and milled on native land.[205] And there are the scores of nuclear weapons storage facilities, manufacturing centers, and the more than four *tons* of plutonium and comparable materials missing from U.S. inventories by 1977.[206]

If the disposal of mountainous accumulations of transuranic and other wastes has become a problem admitting to no easy solution, its existence essentially accrues from the fact that even the most progressive and enlightened sectors of the settler society have busied themselves for forty years with the protesting of nuclear proliferation at its tail-end rather than at its point(s) of origin. For all the mass actions they have organized at reactors and missile bases over the years, not one has ever been conducted at a mining/milling site like Church Rock, Shiprock or Laguna.[207] Had things been otherwise, it might have been possible to choke off the flow of fissionable materials at their source rather than attempting to combat them in their most proliferate and dispersed state(s).

In the end, however, the opposition has for the most part proven itself as willing to relegate native people to stations of marginality, even irrelevancy, as has the order it ostensibly opposes. And here, to borrow from Malcolm X, it can be said that the chickens have truly come home to roost.[208] This takes the form of the increasingly ubiquitous cancers that have made their appearance across the spectrum of American society since World War II, the spiraling rates of congenital birth defects and suppressed immune systems evident among those whose lives began during the 1940s or later.[209]

These and myriad other radiation-induced maladies are things upon which plastering "no smoking" signs on every flat surface in North America will have absolutely no effect in curing.[210] Wherein lies the cure? In a technical sense, it must be admitted that no one knows. We are very far down the road. The wages of radioactive colonialism are by-and-large being visited upon the colonizing society itself, and will likely continue to be so in what is, in human terms, a permanent fashion. Such effects as have already obtained may well prove irreversible.[211]

Whether or not this is true, one thing is clear: any viable effort to counter the effects of nuclear contamination must begin by halting its continuing proliferation. Here, unavoidably, success devolves first and foremost upon devising ways and means of preventing still more uranium from coming out of the ground. Until that is accomplished, struggles to shut down individual reactors, to clean up specific mill sites and production facilities, to reduce the number of nuclear warheads in military inventories or even to figure out how to dispose of the existing accumulation of wastes will ultimately prove futile.[212]

The principle of course is as time-honored as it is true: to correct a problem it is necessary to confront its source rather than its symptoms. In and of itself, however, uranium mining is not the source of the affliction at hand. Underlying the mining process is the nature of the relationship imposed by the United States upon indigenous peoples within its borders, that of internal colonization, without which such things could never have happened in the first place. And underlying *that* is a mentality shared by the North American settler population as a veritable whole: a core belief that it is somehow inherently, singularly, even mystically, entitled to dominate all it encounters, possessing or at least benefiting from that which belongs to others regardless of the costs and consequences visited upon those thereby subjugated and dispossessed.[213]

It can thus be said with certainty that if the dominant society is to have the least prospect of addressing the steadily mounting nuclear contamination of itself it has no real option but to end the radioactive colonization of Native North America. This can happen only if U.S. élites are forced to abandon their ongoing pretense of holding legitimate and perpetual "trust authority" over native peoples, thus facilitating the genuine exercise of indigenous self-determination and our more general decolonization.[214] In turn, this can happen only to the extent that there is a wholesale alteration in the "genocidal mentality" by which the settler population has presumed to conduct itself as it has.[215]

Key to this last is a breaking down of the codes of denial, both individual and institutional, by which the settler society has always shielded itself from the implications of its own values and resulting actions.[216] The process is in part simply a matter of insisting that things be called by their right names rather than the noble-sounding euphemisms behind which reality has been so carefully hidden: terms like "discovery" and "settlement" do not reflect the actualities of invasion and conquest they are used to disguise; colonialism is not a matter of "trust," it is colonialism, a crime under international law; genocide isn't an "inadvertent" outcome of "progress," it is genocide, an *always* avoidable crime against humanity; ecocide is not "development," it is ecocide, the most blatant and irremediable form of environmental destruction; mere possession constitutes "nine-tenths of the law" only among thugs devoted to enjoying the fruits of an organized system of theft.[217]

Thus accurately described, many of the measures heretofore accepted by the American public in the name of forging and defending its "way of life" become viscerally repulsive, to average Americans no less than to anyone else. Unlike a society based on discovery and settlement, progress and trust, there are few who would queue up to argue the defensibility of a way of life predicated in/sustained by invasion, conquest, genocide, ecocide, colonization and other modes of systemic theft. This is all the more true when it can be demonstrated, as it can in the present connection, that the process of intergroup victimization is bound to subject victims and victimizers alike to an identically ugly destiny. In sum, it is not unreasonable to expect an increasing proportion of the settler population to move towards the position sketched above, if not from a sense of altruism (i.e., "doing the right thing"), then on the basis of newly perceived self-interest.[218]

It is worth observing that the ensuing decolonization of Native North America would offer benefits to humanity extending far beyond itself. Every inch of territory and attendant resources withdrawn from U.S. "domestic" hegemony diminishes the relative capacity of America's corporate managers to project themselves outward via multilateral trade agreements and the like, consummating a "New World Order" in which most of the globe is to be subordinated and exploited in accordance with models already developed, tested and refined through their applications to Indian Country.[219] Overall, elimination of this threat yields the promise of an across-the-board recasting of relations between human beings, and of humans with the rest of nature, which is infinitely more equitable and balanced than anything witnessed since the beginnings of European expansionism more than 500 years ago.[220]

In the alternative, if the current psychopolitical/socioeconomic status quo prevails, things are bound to run their deadly course. Felix Cohen's figurative miners will inevitably share the fate of their canary, the genocide they so smugly allow as an "acceptable cost of doing business" blending perfectly into their own autogenocide until the grim prospect of species extinction has at last been realized. There is, to be sure, a certain unmistakable justice attending the symmetry of this scenario ("What goes around, comes around," as Charlie Manson liked to say).[221] But, surely, we—all of us, settlers as well as natives—owe more to our future generations than to bequeath them a planet so thoroughly irradiated as to deny them the possibility of life itself.

# Notes

1. *Lone Wolf v. Hitchcock* (187 U.S. 553, 557 (1903)). For context and analysis, see Carter Blue Clark, *Lone Wolf v. Hitchcock: Treaty Rights and Indian Law at the End of the Nineteenth Century* (Lincoln: University of Nebraska Press, 1994).

2. See generally, C. Harvey, "Congressional Plenary Power Over Indians: A Doctrine Rooted in Prejudice," *American Indian Law Review*, No. 10, 1982.

3. See generally, Ann Laquer Estin, *Lone Wolf v. Hitchcock*: The Long Shadow," in Sandra L. Cadwalader and Vine Deloria, Jr., eds., *The Aggressions of Civilization: Federal Indian Policy Since the 1880s* (Philadelphia: Temple University Press, 1984).

4. U.S. Department of Interior, Indian Claims Commission, *Final Report* (Washington, D.C.: U.S. Government Printing Office, 1979). For analysis, see Russel L. Barsh, "Indian Land Claims Policy in the United States," *North Dakota Law Review*, No. 58, 1982. On the notion of ownership reversion, see Felix S. Cohen, "Original Indian Title," *Minnesota Law Review*, No. 32, 1947.

5. The aggregate of reserved landholdings totals some 50 million acres (78,000 square miles), an area equivalent in size to the state of South Dakota. Of this, some 44 million acres are held in trust; Roxanne Dunbar Ortiz, "Sources of Underdevelopment," in Roxanne Dunbar Ortiz and Larry Emerson, eds., *Economic Development on American Indian Reservations* (Albuquerque: Institute for Native American Development, University of New Mexico, 1979) p. 61; "Native American Statistics—United States," in Susan Lobo and Steve Talbot, *Native American Voices: A Reader* (New York: Longman, 1998) p. 39.

6. See, e.g., Ronald L. Trosper, "Appendix I: Indian Minerals," in American Indian Policy Review Commission, *Task Force 7 Final Report: Reservation and Resource Development and Protection* (Washington, D.C.: U.S. Government Printing Office, 1977); U.S. Department of Interior, Bureau of Indian Affairs, *Indian Lands Map: Oil, Gas and Minerals on Indian Reservations* (Washington, D.C.: U.S. Government Printing Office, 1978).

7. The 1990 Census tallied 1.96 million American Indians. The count of indigenous peoples exceeds two million when Inuits, Aleuts and Native Hawaiians are added in. This population is subdivided into some 500 federally recognized tribes and nations, including 200 native villages in Alaska; Lobo and Talbot, "Native American Statistics," p. 38. It should be noted that many analysts believe that the baseline indigenous population has been deliberately undercounted by approximately 60 percent, and that serious estimates of the total number of native people in the U.S. run as high as 15 million. See Jack D. Forbes, "Undercounting Native Americans: The 1980 Census and Manipulation of Racial Identity in the United States," *Wicazo Sa Review*, Vol. VI, No. 1, 1990; John Anner, "To the U.S. Census Bureau, Native Americans are Practically Invisible," *Minority Trendsetter*, Vol. 4, No. 1, Winter 1990–91.

8. U.S. Bureau of the Census, Population Division, Racial Statistics Branch, *A Statistical Profile of the American Indian Population* (Washington, D.C.: U.S. Government Printing Office, 1988). These data may be usefully compared to those found in U.S. Bureau of the Census, *General Social and Economic Characteristics: United States Summary* (Washington, D.C.: U.S. Government Printing Office, 1983). For updated information, see *American Indian Digest: Contemporary Demographics of the American Indian* (Phoenix, AZ: Thunderbird Enterprises, 1995).

9. Rennard Strickland, *Tonto's Revenge: Reflections on American Indian Culture and Policy* (Albuquerque: University of New Mexico Press, 1997) p. 53.

10. See, e.g., U.S. Department of Health and Human Services, Public Health Service, *Chart Series Book* (Washington, D.C.: U.S. Government Printing Office, 1988); Karen D. Harvey and Lisa D. Harjo, *Indian Country: A History of Native People in America* (Golden, CO: North American Press, 1994) Appendix L.

11. Strickland, *Tonto's Revenge*, p. 53.

12. Lobo and Talbot, "Native American Statistics," p. 40.

13. Strickland, *Tonto's Revenge*, p. 53.

14. American Indian life expectancy on reservations during the 1990s is thus virtually identical to that of the U.S. general population a century earlier (46.3 years for men; 48.3 for women); Harold Evans, *The American Century* (New York: Alfred A. Knopf, 1998) p. xx.

15. Under Article II (b) of the United Nations Convention on the Prevention and Punishment of the Crime of Genocide (1948), any policy which intentionally causes "serious bodily or mental harm to members" of a targeted "national, ethnical, racial or religious group, as such" can be considered

genocidal. Similarly, under Article II (c), acts or policies "deliberately inflicting on the group conditions of life calculated to bring about its physical destruction in whole or in part" constitute the crime of genocide; Ian Brownlie, *Basic Documents on Human Rights* (Oxford, UK: Clarendon Press, [3rd ed.] 1992) p. 31. Questions are habitually raised in some quarters as to whether the impacts of federal policy on American Indians are "really" intentional and deliberate. Let it be said in response that policies generating such catastrophic results over five successive generations cannot be reasonably understood in any other fashion.

16. Marjane Ambler, *Breaking the Iron Bonds: Indian Control of Energy Development* (Lawrence: University Press of Kansas, 1990) pp. 56, 66, 78, 140–41.

17. This is touched upon in connection with the so-called "heirship problem" by Wilcomb E. Washburn in his *Red Man's Land/White Man's Law: A Study of the Past and Present Status of the American Indian* (New York: Scribner's, 1971).

18. Lorraine Turner Ruffing, "The Role of Policy in American Indian Mineral Development," in Roxanne Dunbar Ortiz, ed., *American Indian Energy Resources and Development* (Albuquerque: Institute for Native American Development, University of New Mexico, 1980).

19. Michael Garrity, "The U.S. Colonial Empire is as Close as the Nearest Reservation," in Holly Sklar, eds., *Trilateralism: The Trilateral Commission and Elite Planning for Global Development* (Boston: South End Press, 1980).

20. It has been argued, persuasively, that without its domination of indigenous land and resources the U.S. military could never have achieved its present posture of global ascendancy; Valerie L. Kuletz, *The Tainted Desert: Environmental and Social Ruin in the American West* (New York: Routledge, 1998).

21. Eduardo Galeano, *The Open Veins of Latin America: Five Centuries of the Pillage of a Continent* (New York: Monthly Review Press, 1973) p. 12.

22. Anita Parlow, *Cry, Sacred Ground: Big Mountain, USA* (Washington, DC: Christic Institute, 1988).

23. Lobo and Talbot, "Native American Statistics," p. 40.

24. See generally, A. Rigo Sureda, *The Evolution of the Right to Self-Determination: A Study of United Nations Practice* (Leyden, Netherlands: A.W. Sijhoff, 1973).

25. Brownlie, *Basic Documents*, pp. 29-30.

26. Roxanne Dunbar Ortiz, "Protection of Indian Territories in the United States: Applicability of International Law," in Imre Sutton, ed., *Irredeemable America: The Indians' Estate and Land Claims* (Albuquerque: University of New Mexico Press, 1985) p. 260. More broadly, see Michla Pomerance, *Self-Determination in Law and Practice* (The Hague: Marinus Nijhoff, 1982).

27. Noteworthy examples are legion. Consider, as illustrations, the situations of the Scots and Welsh on the primary British isle, the Basques in Spain, and the Kurds in Turkey and northern Iraq; Peter Berresford Ellis, *The Celtic Revolution: A Study in Anti-Imperialism* (Talybont, Ceredigion: Y Lolfa, 1985); Robert P. Clark, *Negotiating with ETA: Obstacles to Peace in the Basque Country, 1975-1988* (Reno: University of Nevada Press, 1990); Gerard Chaliand, ed., *People Without A Country: The Kurds and Kurdistan* (London: Zed Press, 1980). For a good overview of legal/political issues, see Gudmunder Alfredsson, "International Law, International Organizations, and Indigenous Peoples," *Journal of International Affairs*, Vol. 36, No. 1, 1982.

28. Dunbar Ortiz, "Protection," p. 261. Also see Ronald Fernandez, *Prisoners of Colonialism: The Struggle for Justice in Puerto Rico* (Monroe, ME: Common Courage Press, 1994); Edward Said, *The Question of Palestine* (New York: Vintage, [2nd ed.] 1992).

29. See generally, Haunani-Kay Trask, *From a Native Daughter: Colonialism and Sovereignty in Hawai'i* (Honolulu: University of Hawai'i Press, [2nd ed.] 1999).

30. A presumption underlying articulation of this principle in the Charter is, of course, that such territory have been legitimately acquired in the first place. With respect to the U.S., this is patently not the case. Leaving aside issues devolving upon coerced or fraudulent land cessions, the federal government's own Indian Claims Commission concluded in its 1978 final report that the U.S. possessed no basis at all for its assertion of title to/jurisdiction over approximately 35 percent of its claimed gross territoriality; Russel L. Barsh, "Indian Land Claims Policy in the United States," *North Dakota Law Review*, No. 58, 1982.

31. See especially the statement of U.S. State Department official Seth Waxman quoted in Glenn T. Morris, "Further Motion by State Department to Railroad Indigenous Rights," *Fourth World Bulletin*, No. 6, Summer 1998, p. 3.

32. Probably the best explication of the concept will be found in Michael Hector's *Internal Colonialism: The Celtic Fringe in British National Politics, 1536-1966* (Berkeley: University of California Press, 1975). For applications to the Native North American context, see, e.g., Robert K. Thomas, "Colonialism: Classic and Internal," *New University Thought*, Winter 1966-67; Menno Bolt, "Social Correlates of Nationalism: A Study of Native Indian Leaders in a Canadian Internal Colony," *Comparative Political Studies*, Vol. 14, No. 2, Summer 1981); my own "Indigenous Peoples of the U.S.: A Struggle Against Internal Colonialism," *Black Scholar*, Vol. 16, No. 1, Feb. 1985; and Matthew Snipp's "The Changing Political and Economic Status of American Indians: From Captive Nations to Internal Colonies," *American Journal of Economics and Sociology*, Vol. 45, No. 2, Apr. 1986.

33. Jean-Paul Sartre, "On Genocide," *Ramparts*, Feb. 1968.

34. It should be noted that this prognosis pertains as much to leftist states as it does to those oriented to the right; Walker Connor, *The National Question in Marxist-Leninist Theory and Strategy* (Princeton, NJ: Princeton University Press, 1984).

35. Kuletz, *Tainted Desert*, pp. 15-6.

36. A single defense contractor, the Vanadium Corporation of America, delivered all 11,000 tons of uranium consumed by the Manhattan Project; Hosteen Kinlicheel, "An Overview of Uranium and Nuclear Development on Indian Lands in the Southwest," *Southwest Indigenous Uranium Forum Newsletter*, Sept. 1993, p. 5.

37. Gerald D. Nash, *The American West Transformed: The Impact of the Second World War* (Bloomington: Indiana University Press, 1985) p. 177.

38. Richard Miller, *Under the Cloud: The Decades of Nuclear Testing* (New York: Free Press, 1986) p. 13.

39. Site selection procedures are reviewed in Richard Rhodes, *The Making of the Atomic Bomb* (New York: Simon & Schuster, 1986). Also see Henry DeWolf Smith, *Atomic Energy for Military Uses: The Official Report on the Development of the Atomic Bomb Under Auspices of the United States Government, 1940-1945* (Princeton, NJ: Princeton University Press, 1945).

40. As is now well-known, there was even a fear among some participating scientists that the initial nuclear detonation might set off a chain reaction that would engulf the entire planet; Stephane Groueff, *The Manhattan Project* (Boston: Little, Brown, 1967) p. 19.

41. David Alan Rosenberg, "The U.S. Nuclear Stockpile, 1945-1950," *Bulletin of Atomic Scientists*, Mar. 1980.

42. The SBA risked little or nothing in funding these small-scale mining startups, since sale of all ore produced was guaranteed at a fixed rate by the AEC; Winona LaDuke, "The History of Uranium Mining: Who Are These Companies and Where Did They Come From?" *Black Hills/Paha Sapa Report*, Vol. 1, No. 1, 1979.

43. Robert N. Procter, "Censorship of American Uranium Mine Epidemiology in the 1950s," in Marjorie Garber and Rebecca L. Walkowitz, eds., *Secret Agents: The Rosenberg Case, McCarthyism and 1950s America* (New York: Routledge, 1995) p. 60. He is citing Robert J. Roscoe, et al., "Lung Cancer Mortality Among Nonsmoking Uranium Miners Exposed to Radon Daughters," *JAMA*, No. 262, 1989.

44. On death rates among this almost entirely nonsmoking population, see Michael Garrity, "The Pending Energy Wars: America's Final Act of Genocide," *Akwesasne Notes*, Early Spring 1980. On attempts by Union Carbide representative Bob Beverly and others to nonetheless displace blame for the disaster onto cigarettes, see Jack Cox, "Studies Show Radon Guidelines May Be Weak," *Denver Post*, Sept. 4, 1979. Also see the quotations from Dr. Joseph Wagoner's unpublished paper, "Uranium Mining and Milling: The Human Costs," included in Leslie J. Freeman's *Nuclear Witnesses: Insiders Speak Out* (New York: W.W. Norton, 1982) p. 142.

45. In the Carpathians, "women are found who have married seven husbands, all of whom this terrible consumption has carried off to a premature death"; Georgius Agricola, *De Re Metallica* (London: Dover, 1912 translation of 1556 original) p. 214.

46. They also suggested that the death rate from lung cancer would have actually been far higher,

were it not that numerous miners died from accidents—cave-ins and the like—before being diagnosed with the disease; F.H. Härting and W. Hesse, "Der Lungenskrebs, die Bergkrankheit in den Schneeberger Gruben," *Vierteljahrsschrift für gerichtliche Medizin*, No. 30, 1879.

47. P. Ludewig and S. Lorenser, "Untersuchung der Grubenluft in den Schneeberger Gruben auf den Gehalt an Radiumemanation," *Zeitschrift für Physik*, No. 22, 1924.

48. A shaft in Saxony with inordinately high radon levels was even known among miners as the *Todesschact* (death mine); Wilhelm C. Hueper, Occupational Tumors and Allied Diseases (Springfield, IL: Charles C. Thomas, 1942) p. 441.

49. Egon Lorenz, "Radioactivity and Lung Cancer: A Critical Review of Lung Cancer in Miners of Schneeberg and Joachimsthal," *Journal of the National Cancer Institute*, No. 5, 1944.

50. Fred W. Stewart, "Occupational and Post-Traumatic Cancer," *Bulletin of the New York Academy of Medicine*, No. 23, 1947. Also see Angela Nugent, "The Power to Define a New Disease: Epidemiological Politics and Radium Poisoning," in Radid Rosner and Gerald Markowitz, eds., *Dying to Work* (Bloomington: Indiana University Press, 1986).

51. Proctor, "Censorship," p. 62.

52. Merril Eisenbud, *An Environmental Odyssey* (Seattle: University of Washington Press, 1990) p. 60.

53. Proctor, "Censorship," pp. 62-3.

54. Ibid., p. 64.

55. Ibid. Hueper was also branded a "security risk," accused alternately of being a "Nazi sympathizer" and a "communist," and prohibited for a time from traveling anywhere west of the Mississippi River.

56. Elof A. Carlson, *Genes, Radiation, and Society* (Ithaca: Cornell University Press, 1981) pp. 356-67.

57. For an overview of Sternglass' findings and suppression for over a decade, see his *Low Level Radiation* (New York: Ballantine, 1972). Also see Freeman, *Nuclear Witnesses*, pp. 50-77.

58. Gofman's AEC funding was revoked and the National Cancer Institute declined to replace it, effectively ending his research career; John W. Gofman and Arthur R. Tamplin, *Population Control Through Nuclear Pollution* (Chicago: Nelson-Hall, 1970); *Poisoned Power: The Case Against Nuclear Power Plants* (Emmaus, PA: Rodale Press, 1971; revised and rereleased in 1979 with a new subtitle, *The Case Before and After Three Mile Island*). Also see Freeman, *Nuclear Witnesses*, pp. 78-114.

59. Thomas F. Mancuso, et al., "Radiation Exposures of Hanford Workers Dying of Various Causes," *Health Physics*, No 33, 1977. William Hines, "Cancer Risk at Nuclear Plant? Government Hushes Up Alarming Study," *Chicago Sun-Times*, Nov. 13, 1977.

60. Rosalie Bertell, *No Immediate Danger?* (London: Women's Press, 1985) pp. 83-8. Also see Freeman, *Nuclear Witnesses*, pp. 22-49.

61. Duncan A. Holaday, et al., *Control of Radon and Daughters in Uranium Mines and Calculations of Biologic Effects* (Washington, D.C.: U.S. Public Health Service, 1957) p. 4. Overall, see Howard Ball, *Cancer Factories: America's Tragic Quest for Uranium Self-Sufficiency* (Westport, CT: Greenwood, 1993) esp. pp. 49-51.

62. Proctor, "Censorship," p. 66. Archer is quoted in Ball, *Cancer Factories*, at pp. 46, 59-60; the judge is quoted at pp. 11-2, 49. Also see the legal analysis offered by George J. Annas in his "The Nuremberg Code in U.S. Courts: Ethics vs. Expediency," in George J. Annas and Michael A. Grodin, eds., *The Nazi Doctors and the Nuremberg Code* (New York: Oxford University Press, 1992) pp. 209-10.

63. On weaponry, see Debra Rosenthal, *At the Heart of the Bomb: The Dangerous Allure of Weapons Work* (Menlo Park, CA: Addison-Wesley, 1990). With regard to reactors, of which there were only thirteen in 1952, all of them government-owned and weapons production-related, see David Dietz, *Atomic Science, Bombs and Power* (New York: Collier, 1962). In 1954, the 1946 Atomic Energy Act was revised to allow private ownership of reactors, all of which were publicly subsidized on a massive scale, an arrangement which brought corporate heavies into the game with a vengeance; Ralph Nader and John Abbott, *The Menace of Nuclear Power* (New York: W.W. Norton, 1977) pp. 275-6. Consequently, more than a hundred additional facilities were built over the next thirty years; John L. Berger, *Nuclear Power: The Unviable Option* (Palo Alto, CA: Ramparts Press, 1976); Amory B. Lovins and L. Hunter Lovins, *Brittle Power: Energy Strategy for National Security* (Andover, MA: Brickhouse, 1982).

64. On profitability—35 corporations secured some $60 billion in federal contracts (over $200

billion in today's dollars) under the Eisenhower administration alone — see William F. Barber and C. Neale Ronning, *Internal Security and Military Power* (Columbus: Ohio State University Press, 1966) p. 13. More or less complete immunity from liability was provided under the 1957 Price-Anderson Indemnity Act; Jim Falk, *Global Fission: The Battle Over Nuclear Power* (New York: Oxford University Press, 1982) pp. 78–81.

65. Richard Hoppe, "A Stretch of Desert along Route 66 — the Grants Belt — Is Chief Locale for U.S. Uranium," *Engineering and Mining Journal*, Vol. 79, No. 11, 1978; Sandra E. Bergman, "Uranium Mining on Indian Lands," *Environment*, Sept. 1982.

66. "In the Soviet Union and in other parts of Eastern Europe, prisoners were literally worked to death in mines, apparently as part of a deliberate plan to kill them. Outside North America, the largest single producer of uranium in the world was the German Democratic Republic, where, from 1945 to the end of the 1980s half a million workers produced some two hundred thousand tons of enriched uranium for Soviet bombs and reactors. . . A somewhat smaller program existed in Czechoslovakia, on the southern slopes of the Erzgebirge. Tens of thousands of political prisoners were forced to work in seventeen uranium "concentration camps" from the late 1940s through the early 1960s; epidemiological studies were conducted, but the State Security Police barred their publication"; Proctor, "Censorship," pp. 74–5. Also see Patricia Kahn, "A Grisly Archive of Key Cancer Data," *Science*, No. 259, 1993; Robert N. Proctor, "The Oberrothenbach Catastrophe," *Science*, No. 260, 1993.

67. J.B. Sorenson, *Radiation Issues: Government Decision Making and Uranium Expansion in Northern New Mexico* (Albuquerque: San Juan Regional Uranium Study Working Paper No. 14, 1978) p. 9.

68. Ibid. Also see Harold Tso and Lora Mangum Shields, "Early Navajo Mining Operations: Early Hazards and Recent Innovations," *New Mexico Journal of Science*, Vol. 12, No. 1, 1980.

69. Jessica S. Pearson, *A Sociological Analysis of the Reduction of Hazardous Radiation in Uranium Mines* (Washington, D.C.: National Institute for Occupational Safety and Health, 1975).

70. V. E. Archer, J.D. Gillan and J.K. Wagoner, "Respiratory Disease Mortality Among Uranium Miners," *Annals of the New York Academy of Sciences*, No. 271, 1976; M.J. Samet, et al., "Uranium Mining and Lung Cancer Among Navajo Men," *New England Journal of Medicine*, No. 310, 1984, pp. 1481-4.

71. Tom Barry, "Bury My Lungs at Red Rock: Uranium Mining Brings New Peril to the Reservation," *The Progressive*, Oct. 1976; Chris Shuey, "The Widows of Red Rock," *Scottsdale Daily Progress Saturday Magazine*, June 2, 1979; Reed Madsden, "Cancer Deaths Linked to Uranium Mining," *Deseret News*, June 4, 1979; Susan Pearce and Karen Navarro, "The Legacy of Uranium Mining for Nuclear Weapons," *Earth Island Journal*, Summer 1993.

72. Garrity, "Energy Wars," p. 10.

73. Quoted in Shuey, "Widows," p. 4; Archer "conservatively" places the lung cancer rate among Navajo miners at 1,000 percent of the national average. Also see Robert O. Pohl, "Health Effects of Radon-222 from Uranium Mining," *Science*, Aug. 1979.

74. Norman Medvin, *The Energy Cartel* (New York: Vintage, 1974); Bruce E. Johansen, "The Great Uranium Rush," *Baltimore Sun*, May 13, 1979.

75. Kinlicheel, "Overview," p. 6.

76. Kuletz, *Tainted Desert*, p. 31; Phil Reno, *Navajo Resources and Economic Development* (Albuquerque: University of New Mexico Press, 1981) p. 138.

77. Marjane Ambler, *Breaking the Iron Bonds: Indian Control Over Energy Development* (Lawrence: University Press of Kansas, 1990) p. 152. For use of the term employed, see Raye C. Ringholz, *Uranium Frenzy: Boom and Bust on the Colorado Plateau* (Albuquerque: University of New Mexico Press, 1989).

78. The vents of one mine run by the Gulf Oil Company at San Mateo, New Mexico, for example, were located so close to the town's school that the State Department of Education ordered closure of the institution — but not the mine — because of the obvious health risk to the children attending it. Meanwhile, the local groundwater was found to have become so contaminated by the corporation's activities that the National Guard was forced to truck in drinking water (at taxpayer expense); Richard O. Clemmer, "The Energy Economy and Pueblo Peoples," in Joseph Jorgenson, ed., *Native Americans and Energy Development, II* (Cambridge, MA: Anthropological Resource Center/Seventh Generation Fund, 1984) p. 98.

79. Although the entire procedure of dewatering was/is in gross violation of both the Clean Water Act of 1972 (P.L. 92-500; 86 Stat. 816) and the Safe Drinking Water Act of 1974 (P.L. 93-523; 88 Stat.

1660), no charges have ever been brought against Kerr-McGee or any other corporation involved in uranium mining; Ambler, *Iron Bonds*, p. 175; "Mine Dewatering Operation in New Mexico Seen Violating Arizona Water Standards," *Nuclear Fuel*, Mar. 1, 1982; Christopher McCleod, "Kerr-McGee's Last Stand," *Mother Jones*, Dec. 1980.

80. Clemmer, "Energy Economy," pp. 101-2.

81. Lora Mangum Shields and Alan B. Goodman, "Outcome of 13,300 Navajo Births from 1964-1981 in the Shiprock Uranium Mining Area" (New York: unpublished paper presented at the American Association of Atomic Scientists Symposium, May 25, 1984); Christopher McCleod, "Uranium Mines and Mills May Have Caused Birth Defects among Navajo Indians," *High Country News*, Feb. 4, 1985.

82. "Neoplasms Among Navajo Children" (Window Rock, AZ: Navajo Health Authority, Feb. 24, 1981).

83. Lora Mangum Shields, et al., "Navajo Birth Outcomes in the Shiprock Uranium Mining Area," *Health Physics*, Vol. 63, No. 5, 1992.

84. Kuletz, *Tainted Desert*, pp. 36, 40; quoting from U.S. Department of Health and Human Services, Indian Health Services, *Health Hazards Related to Nuclear Resources Development on Indian Land* (Washington, D.C.: 97th Cong. 2d. Sess, U.S. Government Printing Office, 1983).

85. It has been estimated that it would require some 400 million tons of earth—enough to cover the entire District of Columbia 43 feet deep—to fill in the Jackpile-Paguate complex; Dan Jackson, "Mine Development on U.S. Indian Lands," *Engineering and Mining Journal*, Jan. 1980. Overall, see U.S. Department of Interior, Bureau of Land Management, *Final Environmental Impact Statement for the Jackpile-Paguate Uranium Mine Reclamation Project*, 2 vols. (Albuquerque: BLM New Mexico Area Office, 1986) vol. 2, p. A-35.

86. Clemmer, "Energy Economy," p. 99.

87. Hope Aldrich, "The Politics of Uranium," *Santa Fe Reporter*, Dec. 7, 1978.

88. U.S. Comptroller General, "EPA Needs to Improve the Navajo Safe Drinking Water Program" (Washington, D.C.: U.S. Government Printing Office, Sept. 10, 1980) p. 5.

89. About 450 Lagunas, some three-quarters of the pueblo's labor force, as well as 160 Acomas worked for Anaconda at any given moment. Another 15–20 percent of the Lagunas worked for the BIA or other federal agencies. Yet, even under such "full-employment" conditions, the median income on the reservation was only $2,661 per year (about $50 per week). This was less than half what a non-Indian open pit miner was earning in an off-reservation locale during the same period; Clemmer, "Energy Economy," p. 99; Kuletz, *Tainted Desert*, p. 35.

90. R. Smith, "Radon Emissions: Open Pit Uranium Mines Said to be Big Contributor," *Nucleonics Week*, May 25, 1978; Linda Taylor, "Uranium Legacy," *The Workbook*, Vol. VIII, No. 6, Nov./Dec. 1983.

91. "Manpower Gap in the Uranium Mines," *Business Week*, Nov. 1, 1977. It should be noted that among the things the Labor Department was spending $2 million per year in tax monies to have Kerr-McGee train native workers to believe was that "if they [did] not smoke, they [would] not develop lung cancer from exposure to radiation in the mines"; Dr. Joseph Wagoner, quoted in Denise Tessier, "Uranium Mine Gas Causes Lung Cancer, UNM Group Told," *Albuquerque Journal*, Mar. 11, 1980. There seem to have been no howls of protest from the surgeon general at the peddling of such quasiofficial falsehoods. Instead, the country's "chief doctor" endorsed a battery of studies over the next several years, each of them reinforcing the credibility of such lies by purporting to prove that the "number one cause" of lung cancer even among *non*smokers was the inhalation of "secondhand" cigarette smoke, even in the most minute quantities, rather than exposure to comparatively massive doses of military-industrial pollutants.

92. Ambler, *Iron Bonds*, p. 152.

93. The 1972 price of U.S.-produced uranium was $6 per pound. By 1979, the figure had risen to $42, a hugely illegal mark-up which contributed greatly to the accrual of U.S. taxpayer-provided corporate superprofits during the final years of the AEC's ore-buying program (as well as the almost instantaneous bust of the domestic market when the program was phased out); David Burnham, "Gulf Aides Admit Cartel Increased Price of Uranium," *New York Times*, June 17, 1977. Shortly after its closure in 1982, Anaconda's Jackpile-Paguate complex was replaced as the world's largest open-pit uranium mine by Rio Tinto Zinc's Rossing Mine, opened in 1976 in Namibia. Uranium from this de facto South

African colony, comprising about one-sixth of the "Free World" supply, was sold at a rate of less than $10 per pound not only to the U.S. and other NATO countries—a factor which drove the highly inflated price of U.S.-mined yellowcake back down to $15, thereby "busting" the profitability of production—but to Israel, supplying that country's secret production of nuclear weapons. It was also used to underpin South Africa's own illicit nuclear weapons development program; Richard Leonard, *South Africa at War: White Power and Crisis in Southern Africa* (Westport, CT; Lawrence Hill, 1983) pp. 60-9. On Australian uranium mining, and the resistance to it spearheaded by aboriginal peoples, see Falk, *Global Fission*, pp. 256-84. On northern Saskatchewan, see Miles Goldstick, *Wollaston: People Resisting Genocide* (Montréal: Black Rose Books, 1987). Overall, see A.D. Owen, "The World Uranium Industry," *Raw Materials Report*, Vol. 2, No. 1, Spring 1983.

94. W.D. Armstrong, *A Report on Mineral Revenues and the Tribal Economy* (Window Rock, AZ: Navajo Office of Mineral Development, June 1976); Joseph G. Jorgenson, "The Political Economy of the Native American Energy Business," in his *Native Americans and Energy Development, II*, pp. 9-20.

95. For a good summary of such practices, see Richard Nafziger, "Uranium Profits and Perils," in LaDonna Harris, ed., *Red Paper* (Albuquerque: Americans for Indian Opportunity, 1976). Also see Molly Ivins, "Uranium Mines in West Leave Deadly Legacy," *New York Times*, May 20, 1979; Bill Freudenberg, "Addictive Economies: Extractive Industries and Vulnerable Localities in a Changing World Economy," *Rural Sociology*, Vol. 57, No. 3, Fall 1992.

96. The federal program to undermine the Navajo self-sufficiency economy devolved upon wholesale impoundment of livestock during the 1930s and '40s; George A. Boyce, *"When the Navajos Had Too Many Sheep": The 1940s* (San Francisco: Indian Historian Press, 1974); Ruth Roessel, ed., *Navajo Livestock Reduction* (Chinle, AZ: Navajo Community College Press, 1975). At Laguna, which had enjoyed an agricultural economy since time immemorial, Anaconda's massive stripmining and related activities—which yielded an estimated $600 million in corporate revenues over thirty years—obliterated much of the arable landbase and irradiated most of the rest; Clemmer, "Energy Economy," pp. 97-8. More broadly, see Nancy J. Owens, "The Effects of Reservation Bordertowns and Energy Exploitation on American Indian Economic Development," *Research in Economic Anthropology*, No. 2, 1979.

97. Kinlicheel, "Overview," p. 6.

98. Laguna has been described as the "single most radioactively contaminated area in North America outside of the military reservations in Nevada where nuclear bombs are tested"; Winona LaDuke, interview on radio station KGNU, Boulder, CO., Apr. 15, 1986. Nevertheless, during 1986 "hearings for the environmental impact draft statement for the Jackpile-Paguate mine's reclamation project began with no less than ten Ph.D.'s and other 'technical' experts in a variety of scientific disciplines, including a mining engineer, a plant ecologist, a radiation ecologist, an expert in biomedicine, and others. All testified in obfuscating language that America's largest uranium mine could be safely unreclaimed. All were under contract to the Anaconda Corporation"; Marjane Ambler, "Lagunas Face Fifth Delay in Uranium Cleanup," *Navajo Times*, Feb. 5, 1986.

99. Quoted in Tom Barry, "The Deaths Still Go On: New Agencies Ignored Uranium Danger," *Navajo Times*, Aug. 31, 1978.

100. Freeman, *Nuclear Witnesses*, p. 140.

101. "Uranium-bearing tailings are constantly decaying into more stable elements and therefore emit radiation, as do particles of dust that blow in the wind and truck travel on dirt roads"; Clemmer, "Energy Economy," p. 102. Also see David Densmore Comey, "The Legacy of Uranium Tailings," *Bulletin of Atomic Scientists*, Sept. 1975.

102. Hoppe, "Grants Belt"; LaDuke, "History of Uranium Mining." In instances where milling was done in areas populated by "mainstream citizens," it was sometimes disguised as something else. For example, the AEC hid a milling operation, beginning in 1951, in Fernald, Ohio, near Cincinnati, behind the front that it was a "pet food factory." The ruse worked for 37 years; Helen Caldicott, *If You Love This Planet: A Plan to Heal the Earth* (New York: W.W. Norton, 1992) p. 90.

103. Lynn A. Robbins, "Energy Development and the Navajo Nation: An Update," in Jorgenson, *Energy Development*, p. 121.

104. Simon J. Ortiz, "Our Homeland: A National Sacrifice Area," in his *Woven Stone* (Tucson: University of Arizona Press, 1992) pp. 356-8.

105. Robbins, "Energy Development," p. 121. It should also be noted that the mill's tailings pile is located only about sixty feet from the San Juan River, Shiprock's only source of surface water, and less than a mile from a daycare center, the public schools and the local business district. The closest residence is less than a hundred yards away; Tso and Shields, "Early Navajo Mining."

106. In 1979, several former mill workers with terminal lung cancer joined with eleven similarly afflicted Red Rock miners and the families of fifteen who'd already died in suing the AEC and Kerr-McGee for what had been done to them; "Claims Filed for Red Rock Miners," *Navajo Times*, July 26, 1979; Marjane Ambler, "Uranium Millworkers Seek Compensation," *APF Reporter*, Sept. 1980.

107. Luther J. Carter, "Uranium Mill Tailings: Congress Addresses a Long Neglected Problem," *Science*, Oct. 13, 1978.

108. See the map by Janet Steele entitled "Uranium Development in the San Juan Basin," in Freeman, *Nuclear Witnesses*, p. 139.

109. For example, the Sohio-Reserve mill at Cebolleta, a mile from the Laguna boundary, processed about 1,500 tons of ore per day during the late 1970s. Its tailings pond covers fifty acres, and the adjoining pile reached a record 350 feet; Clemmer, "Energy Economy," p. 98. Also see Hope Aldrich, "Problems Pile Up at the Uranium Mills," *Santa Fe Reporter*, Nov. 13, 1980.

110. Clemmer, "Energy Economy," pp. 97-8.

111. Report by Johnny Sanders (head of Environmental Health Services Branch of the Indian Health Service), T.J. Hardwood (IHS Albuquerque area director) and Mala L. Beard (the district sanitarian) to Laguna Pueblo Governor Floyd Corea, August 11, 1978; copy on file with the Southwest Research and Information Center, Albuquerque. To be "fair" about it, other communities made similar use of tailings in several backwater non-Indian communities on the Colorado Plateau during this period. These included Moab, Utah, and both Grand Junction and Durango, Colorado.

112. *Jackpile-Paguate Uranium Mine Reclamation Project*, pp. A-62-3.

113. The quantitative release of radioactive substances during the Church Rock spill was several times that of the much more publicized partial meltdown of a reactor at Three Mile Island, near Harrisburg, Pennsylvania, a few months earlier (March 28, 1979); Ambler, *Iron Bonds*, pp. 175-6; Mark Alan Pinsky, "New Mexico Spill Ruins a River: The Worst Radiation Accident in History Gets Little Attention," *Critical Mass*, Dec. 1979.

114. In the immediate aftermath, the Río Puerco was testing at over 100,000 picocuries of radioactivity per liter. The maximum "safe" limit is *fifteen* picocuries; Janet Siskind, "A Beautiful River That Turned Sour," *Mine Talk*, Summer/Fall 1982; Steve Hinschman, "Rebottling the Nuclear Genie," *High Country News*, Jan. 19, 1987. Although the July 16 "incident" was the seventh spill from this single dam in five years, United Nuclear had already applied for, and would receive, federal permission to resume use of its tailings pond within two months; Editors, "The Native American Connection," *Up Against the Wall Street Journal*, Oct. 29, 1979.

115. Report of the New Mexico Environmental Improvement Division (EID), dated Sept. 9, 1979, on file with the Southwest Research and Information Center, Albuquerque.

116. J.W. Schomish, "EID Lifts Ban on Eating Church Rock Cattle," *Gallup Independent*, May 22, 1980.

117. One company spokesperson reportedly informed community representatives that, "This is not a free lunch"; quoted in Dan Liefgree, "Church Rock Chapter Upset at UNC," *Navajo Times*, May 8, 1980. Such behavior is neither unique nor restricted to corporations. When, in 1979, it was discovered that well water in the Red Shirt Table area of the Pine Ridge Reservation in South Dakota was irradiated at a level fourteen times the EPA maximum — apparently as the result of the 3.5 million tons of tailings produced by an isolated AEC mining/milling operation begun in 1954 at Igloo, a nearby army ordnance depot — Tribal President Stanley Looking Elk requested $200,000 in BIA emergency funding to supply potable water to local Oglala Lakota residents. The Bureau approved Looking Elk's request in the amount of $175,000, but stipulated that the water be used *only for cattle*; Madonna Gilbert, "Radioactive Water Contamination on the Redshirt Table, Pine Ridge Reservation, South Dakota" (Porcupine, SD: WARN Reports, Mar. 1980); Women of All Red Nations, "Radiation: Dangerous to Pine Ridge Women" *Akwesasne Notes*, Spring 1980; Patricia J. Winthrop and J. Rothblat, "Radiation Pollution in the Environment," *Bulletin of Atomic Scientists*, Sept. 1981, esp. p. 18.

118. On the cracks, see Chris Huey, "The Río Puerco River: Where Did the Water Go?" *The Workbook*, No. 11, 1988. On the settlement, see Frank Pitman, "Navajos-UNC Settle Tailings Spill Lawsuits," *Navajo Times*, Apr. 22, 1985. On state facilitation, which took the form of discounting the extent and degree of damage done, see "EID Finds that Church Rock Dam Break had Little or No Effect on Residents," *Nuclear Fuel*, Mar. 14, 1983. The questions, of course, are why, if there were "no effect," at least one Navajo woman and an untold number of sheep sickened and died in 1979 after wading in the Río Puerco, why several other people died under similar circumstances over the next few years, and why the EID itself prohibited use of the river as a drinking water source until 1990, more than a decade after the spill; Loretta Schwarz, "Uranium Deaths at Crown Point," *Ms. Magazine*, Oct. 1979; Molly Ivins, "100 Navajo Families Sue on Radioactive Waste Spill," *New York Times*, Aug. 15, 1980.

119. D.R. Dreeson, "Uranium Mill Tailings: Environmental Implication*s*," *Los Alamos Scientific Laboratory Mini-Report*, Feb. 1978.

120. Thadias Box, et al., *Rehabilitation Potential for Western Coal Lands* (Cambridge, MA: Ballinger, 1974).

121. On the extent of Peabody's coal stripping operations on Navajo at the time of the NAS study, see Alvin M. Josephy, Jr., "The Murder of the Southwest," *Audubon Magazine*, July 1971.

122. Although little uranium mining or milling had occurred in this region (with the exception of that at Igloo, which ended in 1972; see note 117, above), it contains substantial deposits of uranium, low-sulfur coal and a wealth of other minerals. As was noted by one contemporaneous observer, overall, "the plans for the hills are staggering. They include a giant energy park featuring more than a score of 10,000 megawatt coal-fired plants, a dozen nuclear reactors, huge coal slurry pipelines designed to use millions of gallons of water to move crushed coal thousands of miles, and at least fourteen major uranium mines"; Harvey Wasserman, "The Sioux's Last Fight for the Black Hills," *Rocky Mountain News*, Aug. 24, 1980. Also see Amelia Irvin, "Energy Development and the Effects of Mining on the Lakota Nation," *Journal of Ethnic Studies*, Vol. 10, No. 2, Spring 1982.

123. The Nixon administration reputedly used this vernacular during discussions from 1972 onward. For the first known official print articulation, see U.S. Department of Energy, Federal Energy Administration, Office of Strategic Analysis, *Project Independence: A Summary* (Washington, D.C.: U.S. Government Printing Office, 1974).

124. Nick Meinhart, "The Four Corners Today, the Black Hills Tomorrow?" *Black Hills/Paha Sapa Report*, Aug. 1979.

125. Means' statements were made during a speech delivered at the Black Hills International Survival Gathering, near Rapid City, South Dakota, June 12, 1980; included in my *Marxism and Native Americans* (South End Press, 1983) referenced material at p. 25.

126. All told, the official count is "approximately 1,000 significant nuclear waste sites" on Navajo alone; U.S. Department of Interior, Environmental Protection Agency, *Potential Health and Environmental Hazards of Nuclear Mine Wastes* (Washington, D.C.: U.S. Government Printing Office, 1983) pp. 1-23. During the National Citizens' Hearings on Radiation Victims in 1980, former uranium miner Kee Begay, dying of lung cancer, testified that he had "lost a son, in 1961. He was one of the many children that used to play in the uranium piles during those years. We had a lot of uranium piles near our homes—just about fifty or a hundred feet away or so—a lot of tailings. Can you imagine? Kids go out and play on those piles!"; Freeman, *Nuclear Witnesses*, pp. 143-4.

127. While Grants Belt mining and milling accounted for all but about 10 percent of U.S. uranium production between 1941 and 1982, small amounts were done elsewhere in Indian Country. The AEC facility at Igloo has already been mentioned (see note 117, above). Other examples include the Dawn Mining Company's mine and mill which operated at Blue Creek, on the Spokane Reservation in Washington State, from 1964 to 1982, and Western Nuclear's Sherwood facility in the same locale, which operated briefly, from 1978 to 1982. The Blue Creek site in particular has generated contamination of local groundwater at levels forty times the EPA's maximum permissible limit for human consumption (4,000 times the area's natural level); Ambler, *Iron Bonds*, p. 176. Another illustration is the Susquehannah-Western Riverton mill site on the Wind River Reservation in Wyoming. Although it ceased operation in 1967, the corporations followed the usual practice of simply walking off and leaving the results for the local Indians, in this case Shoshones and Arapahos, to deal with; Marjane Ambler, "Wyoming to Study Tailings Issue," *Denver Post*, Feb. 5, 1984.

128. See generally, Anna Gyorgy, et al., *No Nukes: Everybody's Guide to Nuclear Power* (Boston: South End Press, 1979) p. 49.

129. Suzanne Ruta, "Fear and Silence at Los Alamos," *The Nation*, Jan. 11, 1993.

130. Concerned Citizens for Nuclear Safety, "LANL [Los Alamos National Laboratory] deliberately, secretly released radiation on at least three separate occasions in 1950," *The Nuclear Reactor*, Vol. 3, No. 1, Feb.-Mar. 1994.

131. It appears that legal prohibitions against such "disposal" of nuclear wastes are being circumvented by shipping materials from other DoE facilities to Los Alamos, where they can be secretly burned in the lab's controlled air incinerator. Currently, it is estimated that 1,236 cubic feet of plutonium-contaminated substances are being dispersed in this way each year; Mary Risely, "LANCL Gropes to Find a New Way," *Enchanted Times*, Fall/Winter 1993, p. 6.

132. Ibid.

133. Since 1980, "physicians at the Santa Fe Indian Hospital have noticed an unusual number of thyroid cancer cases [associated with the atmospheric release of radioactive iodides] at the Santa Clara Pueblo, just north of Los Alamos"; Kuletz, *Tainted Desert*, p. 53. The rate of thyroid cancer at Santa Clara is triple the national average.

134. Ibid.

135. Risely, "New Way."

136. Kuletz, *Tainted Desert*, p. 53.

137. The Chernobyl explosion released, at a minimum, 185 million curies of atmospheric radiation during the first ten days. It has claimed 125,000 dead during the first decade, a rate which is not expected to peak for another ten years; Blanche Wiesen Cook, "Cold War Fallout," *The Nation*, Dec. 9, 1996, p. 32.

138. Elouise Schumacher, "440 Billion Gallons: Hanford wastes could fill 900 King Domes, *Seattle Times*, Apr. 13, 1991.

139. There were at least eleven tank failures at Hanford by 1970. Another, reputedly the worst, was discovered on June 8, 1973; Kenneth B. Noble, "The U.S. for Decades Let Uranium Leak at Weapons Plant," *New York Times*, Oct. 15, 1988.

140. Concerning shellfish as an indicator of the extent the Columbia River has been contaminated, it should been noted that a Hanford worker who dined on oysters harvested near the river's mouth in 1962 reportedly ingested sufficient radioactivity in the process that he triggered the plant's radiation alarm upon returning to work; Caldicott, *Planet*, p. 89.

141. Ibid. Also see Susan Wyndham, "Death in the Air," *Australian Magazine*, Sept. 29-30, 1990; Matthew L. Wald, "Wider Peril Seen in Nuclear Waste from Bomb Making," *New York Times*, Mar. 28, 1991.

142. Larry Lang, "Missing Hanford Documents Probed by Energy Department," *Seattle Post-Intelligencer*, Sept. 20, 1991.

143. Caldicott, *Planet*, p. 90.

144. The U.S. detonated a total of 106 nuclear devices in the Pacific between 1946 and 1958, 101 of them after 1950. Two atolls in the Marshall Islands, Bikini and Enewetak—occupied by the U.S. in 1943—were subjected to 66 blasts of up to fifteen megatons each, beginning in 1946. Among the tests conducted on Enewetak was that of the first hydrogen bomb in 1952. The local populations were forcibly relocated to Kili Island, where they were held against their will until 1968. The Bikinians were then told, falsely, that it was safe to return to their homes, which were saturated with the radiation of 23 bombs. A decade later, the Enewetakans were also encouraged to return to their homes, despite the fact that a 1979 General Accounting Office study concluded they would be exposed to dangerously high radiation levels accruing from the 43 tests conducted there prior to 1958; Giff Johnson, "Nuclear Legacy: Islands Laid Waste," *Oceans*, January 1980. The Bikinians were removed from their island again in 1978—at about the same time the people of Enewetak were going home—because cancers, birth defects and other maladies had become endemic. It is likely that they'd been returned in the first place to serve as a test group upon which the effects of plutonium ingestion could be observed; Giff Johnson, "Bikinians Facing Radiation Horrors Once More," *Micronesia Support Committee Bulletin*, May-June 1978. Quite probably, the Enewetakans were slated to serve the same purpose.

145. David Loomis, *Combat Zoning: Military Land-Use Planning in Nevada* (Las Vegas: University of Nevada Press, 1994) p. 10; citing Michael Skinner, *Red Flag* (Novato, CA: Presidio Press) p. 52. For a more comprehensive overview of how all this evolved, see Gerald D. Nash, *The American West Transformed: The Impact of the Second World War* (Bloomington: University of Indiana Press, 1985).

146. The area was permanently reserved by the Shoshones in the 1863 Treaty of Ruby Valley; Dagmar Thorpe, *Newe Segobia: The Western Shoshone People* (Lee, NV: Western Shoshone Sacred Lands Association, 1982). Also see the map in Kuletz, *Tainted Desert*, p. 68.

147. On acreage, see Loomis, *Combat Zoning*, p. 31. With respect to the number of test detonations—five of which actually occurred north of the test site, on the Nellis bombing range—the official count was 702 U.S. and 23 British as of early 1992; U.S. Department of Energy, *Announced United States Nuclear Tests July 1945 through December 1991* (Washington, D.C.: U.S. Government Printing Office, 1992). On Dec. 8, 1992, however, the *New York Times* reported that there had been 204 *unannounced* U.S. tests conducted at the Nevada facility between 1952 and 1990; Anthony Robbins, Arjun Makhijani and Katherine Yih, *Radioactive Heaven and Earth: The Health and Environmental Effects of Nuclear Weapons Testing In, On, and Above the Earth* (New York/London: Apex Press/Zed Books, 1991) p. 91. Adding the six tests approved by the Clinton administration during 1992, yields a total of 953 nuclear bombings of Western Shoshone territory by that point.

148. See the subsection entitled "The Most Bombed Nation in the World," in Bernard Neitschmann and William Le Bon, "Nuclear Weapons States and Fourth World Nations," *Cultural Survival Quarterly*, Vol. 11, No. 4, 1987, pp. 5-7.

149. Howard Ball, *Justice Downwind: America's Atomic Testing Program in the 1950s* (New York: Oxford University Press) p. 85. Also see Richard Miller, *Under the Cloud: The Decades of Nuclear Testing* (New York: Free Press, 1986).

150. For estimates of atmospheric releases, see Carole Gallegher, *America Ground Zero: The Secret Nuclear War* (New York: Random House, 1993).

151. Kuletz, *Tainted Desert*, p. 72.

152. U.S. Congress, Office of Technology Assessment, *Complex Cleanup: The Environmental Legacy of Nuclear Weapons Production* (Washington, D.C.: U.S. Government Printing Office, 1991) pp. 158-9. The half-life of several of these materials—e.g., plutonium—is estimated as being a quarter-million years.

153. "Report: Fed snub tribe's radiation exposure," *Reno Gazette-Journal*, June 7, 1994. On estimate of deaths, see James W. Hulse, *Forty Years in the Wilderness* (Reno: University of Nevada Press, 1986) p. 61.

154. During a 1956 effort by Nevada residents to enjoin further atmospheric detonations, a battery of the AEC's selected "scientific experts" perjured themselves by uniformly insisting, contrary to all logic and the results of their own classified studies, that nuclear weapons testing entailed "no public health hazard." Although the AEC later conceded that its witnesses had systematically lied under oath, no one was ever prosecuted in the matter, Kuletz, *Tainted Desert*, p. 73. Also see Bill Curry, "A-Test Officials Feared Outcry After Health Study," *Washington Post*, Apr. 14, 1979; Randall Smith, "Charge Ike Mislead Public on N-Tests," *New York Daily News*, Apr. 20, 1979.

155. Kuletz, *Tainted Desert*, pp. 69-70.

156. China Lake, which encompasses 38 percent of the Navy's total land holdings, supports about 1,000 military personnel and over 5,000 civilian scientists, engineers and technicians in more than 1,100 buildings on an annual budget of nearly $1 billion; ibid., pp. 62-3

157. China Lake commands some 20,000 square miles of air space, as do each of the other three facilities. Quite literally, the sky over the entire Mojave has been appropriated by the military; Loomis, *Combat Zoning*, p. 70.

158. U.S. Navy, *Naval Weapons Center Silver Anniversary* (China Lake Naval Weapons Center: Technical Information Dept. Publishing Division, Oct. 1968).

159. One such group of Timbisha Shoshones have more-or-less established themselves as "squatters" in a Death Valley visitor's center. Others are clustered to the north and west, in the Owens Valley, the Tehachapi Mountains and the Lake Isabella area. One of their areas of particularly sacred geography, the Coso Range, is now "officially called the Military Target Range, [and] constitutes some 70 square miles of mountainous area . . . with various targets—bridges, tunnels, vehicles, SAM sites—emplaced in a natural forested environment for tactics development and pilot training under realistic conditions"; R.E. Kistler and

R.M. Glen, *Notable Achievements of the Naval Weapons Center* (China Lake Naval Weapons Center: Technical Information Dept. Publishing Division, 1990) p. 17. For further details, see William Thomas, *Scorched Earth: The Military Assault on the Environment* (Philadelphia: New society, 1995).

160. Aside from the 1971 megablast—dubbed "Cannikan," it was about 350 times as powerful as the Hiroshima bomb, but carrying only one-third the force of the "Bravo" device exploded above ground on Bikini in 1954—the other two Amchitka detonations were "Long Shot" in 1965 (eighty kilotons) and "Milrow" in 1969 (one megaton); Robbins, Makhijani and Yih, *Radioactive Heaven and Earth* p. 66.

161. David Hulen, "After the Bombs: Questions linger about Amchitka nuclear tests," *Anchorage Daily News*, Feb. 7, 1994.

162. Kristen Ostling and Joanna Miller, *Taking Stock: The Impact of Militarism on the Environment* (New York: Science for Peace, 1992).

163. Construction of the MX system—an entirely offensive weapon which was, of course, dubbed the "Peacekeeper"—promised to generate an estimated half-billion in profits for Weinberger's parent corporation; Tristan Coffin, "The MX: America's $100 Billion 'Edsel'," *Washington Spectator*, Oct. 15, 1980. It would also have eliminated the remaining habitable landbase of the Shoshones; Martha C. Knack, "MX Issues for Native American Communities," in Francis Hartigan, ed., *MX in Nevada: A Humanistic Perspective* (Reno: Nevada Humanities Press, 1980). Another fine study is to be found in Rebecca Solnit's *Savage Dreams: A Journey Into the Hidden Wars of the American West* (San Francisco: Sierra Club, 1994).

164. Southwestern Arizona also includes another pair of huge military complexes, the half-million acre Yuma Proving Grounds and adjoining million-acre Luke Air Force Base; see generally, Ostling and Miller, *Taking Stock*. The three native peoples in question are thus completely encircled by these facilities to their south, southern California's constellation of bases and test ranges to their west, the Nevada Test Site and related areas to their north, and the Navajo sacrifice zone to their east.

165. The latter include the 600,000-acre Hill Air Force Training Range, about thirty miles north of the somewhat larger Wendover Range. Adjoining Wendover to the south, is the equally sized Deseret Test Center (containing the Tooele Arms Depot), below which is a much smaller parcel, the Fish Springs Nuclear Weapons Range, Abutting both Wendover and Deseret to the east is another equally sized compound, the Dugway Proving Grounds. No public access is allowed on *any* of these approximately 2,750,000 acres, the combined controlled air space of which exceeds 20,000 square miles; see generally, Ostling and Miller, *Taking Stock*.

166. Karl Grossman, *Cover Up: What You Are Not Supposed to Know About Nuclear Power* (New York: Permanent Press, 1980) p. 13.

167. P.Z. Grossman and E.S. Cassedy, "Cost Benefit Analysis of Nuclear Waste Disposal," *Science, Technology and Human Values*, Vol. 10, No. 4, 1985.

168. As Dr. Helen Caldicott explains, "When exposed to air, plutonium ignites, forming very fine particles—like talcum powder—that are completely invisible. A single one of these particles could give you lung cancer. Hypothetically, if you could take one pound of plutonium and could put a speck of it in the lungs of every human being [she estimates a single microgram is sufficient], you would kill every man, woman, and child on earth—not immediately, but later, from lung cancer"; Freeman, *Nuclear Witnesses*, p. 294. Also see David Burnham, "Rise in Cancer Death Rate Tied in Study to Plutonium," *New York Times*, June 6, 1976.

169. Current planning now entails a "force reduction" in the number of such weapons to 3,500 by the year 2003; Charles Pope, "Nuclear Arms Cleanup Bill: A Tidy $230 Billion," *San Jose Mercury News*, Apr. 4, 1995.

170. Kuletz, *Tainted Desert*, p. 82; quoting William J. Broad, "The Plutonium Predicament," *New York Times*, May 2, 1995.

171. Pope, "Arms Cleanup."

172. U.S. Department of Energy, Office of Environmental Management, *Estimating the Cold War Mortgage: The 1995 Baseline Environmental Management Report* (Washington, D.C.: DOE/EM-0232, Mar. 1995); *Closing the Circle of the Closing of the Atom: The Environmental Legacy of Nuclear Weapons Production in the United States and What the Department of Energy is Doing About It* (Washington, D.C.: DOE/EM-0228, Jan. 1995).

173. U.S. Department of Energy, Office of Environmental Management, *Environmental Management 1995* (Washington, D.C.: DOE/EM-0228, Feb. 1995).

174. For analysis of the defects in this proposition, see Arjun Makhijana and Scott Saleska, *High-Level Dollars, Low-Level Sense: A Critique of Present Policy for the Management of Long-Lived Radioactive Wastes and Discussion of an Alternative Approach* (Takoma Park, MD: Institute for Energy and Environmental Research, 1992).

175. The Groundwork Collective, "The Illusion of Cleanup: A Case Study at Hanford," *Groundwork*, No. 4, Mar. 1994, p. 14. For the record, the classification scheme involved here, which is incorporated into the 1982 Nuclear Waste Policy Act (P.L. 97-425; 96 Stat. 2201), is problematic. The term "high-level wastes" pertains to spent fuel from nuclear power plants subject to reprocessing for extraction of plutonium and uranium-235. "Transuranic wastes" include substances like plutonium, neptunium and americium, "bred" from uranium-238. "Low-level wastes" include materials—e.g., worn out reactor parts—contaminated by exposure to high-level or transuranic substances. The classifications don't necessarily correspond to the degree of threat posed by a given material, only to the nature of the process by which it was produced; Concerned Citizens for Nuclear Safety, *The Nuclear Reactor*, Early Spring 1995.

176. Although tailings cleanup is mandated by the Uranium Mill Tailings Radiation Control Act of 1978, the program has been so chronically underfunded that it didn't really get started at all for eight years. When it did, its efforts consisted largely of moving tailings piles from particularly sensitive locations—such as downtown Edgemont, South Dakota, where the AEC had dumped about 3.5 million tons along the banks of the Cottonwood Creek, a quarter-mile upstream from the Cheyenne River—and relocating them to some "preferable" spot a few miles away, where they could be fenced-off for "safety" reasons; Ambler, *Iron Bonds*, pp. 178-90. Arguably, the dispersal involved in such procedures worsens rather than alleviates the problem. The plain fact is that nobody has a clue what to do with this body of carcinogenic material which, by the mid-'70s, was already large enough to "cover a four lane highway one foot deep from coast to coast"; Jeff Cox, "Nuclear Waste Recycling," *Environmental Action Bulletin*, No. 29, May 1976.

177. Nicholas Lenssen, *Nuclear Waste: The Problem that Won't Go Away* (Washington, D.C.: Worldwatch Institute, 1991) pp. 34-5.

178. Becky O'Guin, "DOE: Nation to burn and vitrify plutonium stores," *Colorado Daily*, Dec. 10, 1996.

179. The need for permanent repositories was formally enunciated for the first time in the Nuclear Waste Policy Act of 1982 (NWPA); the two-part scheme, authorizing establishment of MRS facilities as well as repositories, was included in the 1987 revision of NWPA; U.S. Department of Energy, Monitored Retrievable Storage Commission, "Nuclear Waste: Is There A Need For Federal Interim Storage?" in *Report of the Monitored Retrievable Storage Commission* (Washington, D.C.: U.S. Government Printing Office, 1989); Gerald Jacob, *Site Unseen: The Politics of Siting a Nuclear Repository* (Pittsburgh: University of Pittsburgh Press, 1990).

180. Valerie Taliman, "Nine tribes look at storage: Signs point to nuclear dump on Native land, *Smoke Signals*, Aug. 1993.

181. "Plutonium is so hazardous that if you . . . manage to contain the [amounts projected to exist by the turn of the century] 99.99 percent perfectly, it would still cause somewhere between 140,000 and 500,000 extra lung-cancer fatalities each year. . . The point is, if you lose a little bit of it—a terribly little bit—you're going to contaminate the earth, and people are going to suffer for thousands of generations"; quoted in Freeman, *Nuclear Witnesses*, pp. 108, 111.

182. In 1995, the few residents of Lincoln County, Nevada, attempted to negotiate a hefty fee for themselves in exchange for accepting an MRS. The state government quickly quashed the initiative; Kuletz, *Tainted Desert*, p. 106.

183. Grace Thorpe, "Radioactive Racism? Native Americans and the Nuclear Waste Legacy," *The Circle*, Apr. 1995.

184. Taliman, "Nine tribes."

185. On the NCAI grant, see Randel D. Hansen, "Mescalero Apache: Nuclear Waste and the Privatization of Genocide," *The Circle*, Aug. 1994. On the CERT funding, see Winona LaDuke, "Native

Environmentalism," *Earth Island Journal*, Summer 1993. CERT, created in the late 1970s by then Navajo Tribal Chairman Peter McDonald and federal lobbyist LaDonna Harris, has long been a major problem for those pursuing indigenous sovereignty; Philip S. Deloria, "CERT: It's Time for an Evaluation," *American Indian Law Newsletter*, Sept./Oct. 1982. Also see Geoffrey O'Gara, "Canny CERT Gets Money, Respect, Problems," *High Country News*, Dec. 14, 1979; Ken Peres and Fran Swan, "The New Indian Elite: Bureaucratic Entrepreneurs," *Akwesasne Notes*, Late spring 1980; Winona LaDuke, "CERT: An Outsider's View In," *Akwesasne Notes*, Summer 1980.

186. Ambler, *Iron Bonds*, pp. 115, 234.

187. The lease, which will soon expire, generates about 90 percent of the reservation's revenues. Without the MRS facility, the Goshutes would not only continue to suffer a high degree of contamination, but be totally without income as well; Kuletz, *Tainted Desert*, p. 110.

188. Quoted in Randel D. Hanson, "Nuclear Agreement Continues U.S. Policy of Dumping on Goshutes," *The Circle*, Oct. 1995.

189. Unidentified Mescalero, quoted in Winifred E. Frick, "Native Americans Approve Nuclear Waste Dump on Tribal Lands," *Santa Cruz on a Hill Press*, Mar. 16, 1995.

190. Quoted in ibid.

191. Rufina Laws, cited in Kuletz, *Tainted Desert*, p. 108. Chino died in November 1998.

192. Such a sense of emotional/spiritual malaise is hardly unique to Indians, albeit it may manifest itself especially strongly among groups like the Mescaleros, who are placed in extremis; see Joanna Rogers Macy, *Despair and Personal Power in the Nuclear Age* (Baltimore: New Society, 1983).

193. This, of course, leaves unaddressed the question of transuranic military waste—about 250,000 cubic meters of it—produced *before* 1970. Most of it is buried in shallow trenches at the Nevada Test Site and other locations, and is "difficult to retrieve" since the earth around it is now irradiated to an unknown depth. Present planning has gone no further than to leave it where it is, leaching into the environment at a steady rate; Rosenthal, *Heart of the Bomb*, p. 195.

194. Kuletz, *Tainted Desert*, p. 98; citing Concerned Citizens for Nuclear Safety, "What is WIPP?" *The Radioactive Rag*, Winter/Spring 1992.

195. National Academy of Sciences, Division of Earth Science, Committee on Waste Disposal, *The Disposal of Radioactive Waste on Land* (Washington, D.C.: NAS-NRC Pub. 519, 1957); Scientists' Review Panel on the WIPP, *Evaluation of the Waste Isolation Pilot Plant (WIPP) as a Water Saturated Nuclear Waste Repository* (Albuquerque, NM: Concerned Citizens for Nuclear Safety, Jan. 1988).

196. "Scientists Fear Atomic Explosion of Buried Waste," *New York Times*, Mar. 5, 1995.

197. About 10 percent of Yucca Mountain's capacity is earmarked for military wastes. As to civilian wastes, it will have been outstripped by the output of the country's 128 functioning commercial reactors before it is completed. Hence, a third repository is already necessary; Kuletz., *Tainted Desert*, p. 102.

198. Jacob, *Site Unseen*, p. 138.

199. The Low-Level Radioactive Waste Policy Act of 1980 makes the states responsible for the disposal of such materials, even if they've been federally/militarily produced (as they almost invariably are). California Governor Pete Wilson apparently opted to "assume the burden" of all 49 of his cohorts— on a fee-for-service basis—by dumping the aggregate contamination on a handful of Indians in a remote and unnoticed corner of his vast domain; Philip M. Klasky, "The Eagle's Eye View of Ward Valley: Environmentalists and Native American Tribes Fight Proposed Waste Dump in the Mojave Desert," *Wild Earth*, Spring 1994.

200. The plan is to "inter" the material—which contains plutonium, strontium and cesium among a wide range of hyperactive and longlived substances—in five unlined trenches, each about the size of a football field. The facility is to be run by U.S. Ecology, formerly Nuclear Engineering, a corporation whose track record includes oversight of a similar—now closed and badly leaking—facility at Barnwell, Utah, as well as the disastrous West Valley enterprise in upstate New York; Kuletz, *Tainted Desert*, pp. 156-7; Berger, *Nuclear Power*, p. 104.

201. The phrase does not accrue from "radical" rhetoric. See the unabashed advocacy of the trend, both technically and politically, advanced in Charles C. Reith and Bruce M. Thompson, eds., *Deserts as Dumps? The Disposal of Hazardous Materials in Arid Ecosystems* (Albuquerque: University of New Mexico Press, 1992).

202. For a more panoramic view of the phenomenon in its various dimensions, see Donald A. Grinde and Bruce E. Johansen, *Ecocide of Native America: Environmental Destruction of Indian Lands and Peoples* (Santa Fe, NM: Clear Light, 1995).

203. Felix S. Cohen, "The Erosion of Indian Rights, 1950-53: A Case-Study in Bureaucracy," *Yale Law Journal*, No. 62, 1953, p. 390.

204. Gyorgy, et al., *No Nukes*, p. 12; Sternglass, *Low Level Radiation*; Miller, *Under the Cloud*.

205. There is simply no substitute for natural uranium. Neither enriched uranium nor plutonium can be produced without it, and the thorium-derived U-233 does not fulfill the same requirements; David R. Inglis, *Nuclear Energy: Its Physics and Social Challenge* (Reading, MA: Addison-Wesley, 1973).

206. David Burnham, "8,000 pounds of Atom Materials Unaccounted for in U.S. Plants," *New York Times*, Aug. 5, 1977.

207. See, e.g., Gyorgy, et al., *No Nukes*; Falk, *Global Fission*.

208. Alex Haley, *The Autobiography of Malcolm X* (New York: Ballantine, 1965) p. 329.

209. For the most current overview, see Jay M. Gould, *The Enemy Within: The High Cost of Living with Nuclear Reactors* (New York: Four Walls Eight Windows, 1996). Also see Sternglass, *Low Level Radiation*; Gofman and Tamplin, *Poisoned Power*; Bertell, *No Immediate Danger ?*

210. A solid case can be made that the whole anti-tobacco craze of the 1990s has been—and continues to be—more than anything a well-calibrated diversion intended to draw public attention away from the mounting health effects of radioactive contamination (tobacco, unlike plutonium, having no strategic value). For a classic illustration, see Stanton A. Glantz, et al., *The Cigarette Papers* (Berkeley: University of California Press, 1996), introduced by former U.S. Surgeon General C. Everett Koop. The entire 497-page text is devoted to explaining how tobacco smoke is responsible for virtually every disease known to man, and how the cigarette-manufacturing industry knowingly suppressed such information for decades. Nuclear contamination is left altogether unmentioned—there are not even index references to substances like plutonium—as is the ongoing pattern of official suppression of relevant health data (overseen in part by Dr. Koop).

211. For elaboration, see Richard Leakey and Ronald Lewin, *The Sixth Extinction: Patterns of Life and the Future of Mankind* (New York: Doubleday, 1995).

212. This is essentially the strategy advocated by Jay M. Gould in his "The Future of Nuclear Power," *Monthly Review*, Vol. 35, No. 9, 1984. Also see the closing chapter of *The Enemy Within*.

213. See, e.g., Richard Drinnon, *Facing West: The Metaphysics of Indian-Hating and Empire Building* (Minneapolis: University of Minnesota Press, 1980).

214. For articulation of the legal arguments, see Lee C. Buckheit, *Succession: The Legitimacy of Self-Determination* (New Haven, CT: Yale University Press, 1978); Catherine Iorns, "Indigenous Peoples and Self-Determination: Challenging State Sovereignty," *Case Western Journal of International Law*, No. 24, 1992.

215. Robert Jay Lifton and Eric Markusen, *The Genocidal Mentality: Nazi Holocaust and Nuclear Threat* (New York: Basic Books, 1988).

216. For a good treatment of an analogous phenomenon, see Deborah Lipstadt, *Denying the Holocaust: The Growing Assault on Truth and Memory* (New York: Free Press, 1993).

217. Analysis on each of these points will be found in my *A Little Matter of Genocide: Holocaust and Denial in the Americas, 1492 to the Present* (San Francisco: City Lights, 1997).

218. This goes to the notion of "enlightened self-interest" as explicated by Ernst Cassirer in his *The Philosophy of Enlightenment* (Princeton, NJ: Princeton University Press, 1951).

219. See, e.g., Cynthia Peters, ed., *Collateral Damage: The "New World Order" at Home and Abroad* (Boston: South End Press, 1992).

220. A snapshot of such possibilities is contained in Samir Amin's *Delinking: Towards a Polycentric World* (London: Zed Books, 1985).

221. On Manson, see Ed Sanders' *The Family* (New York: Signet, [rev. ed.] 1990).

This essay was originally published in *American Indian Culture and Research Journal,"* Vol. 23, No. 4, Winter 1999.

# The Crucible of American Indian Identity
## Native Tradition versus Colonial Imposition in Postconquest North America

> Don't we have enough headaches trying to unite without. . .additional headaches? Why must people be categorized as full-bloods, mixed-bloods, etc.? Many years ago, the Bureau of Indian Affairs decided to establish blood quanta for the purpose of [tribal] enrollment. At the time, blood quantum was set at one-quarter degree, [a matter which] caused many people on the reservation to be categorized and labeled. The situation was caused solely by the BIA, with the able assistance of the Interior Department.
>
> —Tim Giago
> *Lakota Times*

Among the most vexing issues afflicting Native North America at the dawn of the twenty-first century are the questions of who does/does not hold a legitimate right to say he or she is American Indian, and by what criteria/whose definition this may or may not be true. Such queries, and the answers to them, hold an obvious and deeply important bearing, not only upon the personal sense of identity of millions of individuals scattered throughout the continent, but in terms of the degree to which some form of genuine self-determination can be exercised by indigenous nations in coming years. Conversely, they represent both an accurate gauge of the extent to which the sovereignty of North America's native peoples has been historically eroded or usurped by the continent's two preeminent settler-states, the U.S. and Canada, and a preview of how the remainder stands to be eradicated altogether in the not-so-distant future.[1]

Defining for itself the composition of its membership ("citizenry"), in whatever terms and in accordance with whatever standards it freely chooses, is, of course, the very bedrock expression of self-determination by any nation or people. The ability to maintain this prerogative is thus a vital measure of its sovereign standing.[2] By the same token, intervention in or preemption of this plainly internal function by an external entity may be taken as signifying the abridgment of a nation's right to self-determination and a corresponding diminishment of its sovereignty. For that very reason, under conditions of colonialism—where one nation is directly subordinated to the politicoeconomic or strategic interests of another, and most especially in the kind of "internal colonial" systems prevailing in North America, where the colonizing powers have quite literally subsumed the territoriality of the colonized within their own claimed geographies[3]—such domination assumes the weight of a structural imperative.[4]

Things cannot be put so straightforwardly in contemporary practice, however, since colonialism in all forms has been flatly prohibited by international law since at least as early as 1960.[5] In these circumstances, the kinds of subterfuge designed to create false appearances are an essential aspect of maintaining and perfecting the order of colonial rule. Hence, it is necessary for the colonizer not merely to preempt the sovereignty of the colonized, but to coopt it, inculcating a comprador consciousness among some segment of the subaltern population in which the forms of dominion imposed by colonization will be advocated as a self-determining expression of will emanating from the colonized themselves.[6]

At this point, with the codes of colonial domination embraced by many native people as comprising their own traditions, and articulation of the latter often perceived as a contravention of indigenous sovereignty, the colonized become for all practical intents and purposes self-colonizing.[7] In this most advanced and refined iteration of imperialism, confusion accomplishes much more cheaply, quietly and efficiently what raw force was once required to achieve.[8] Meaningful resistance, never mind decolonization, among those so thoroughly indoctrinated and deluded as to accept and enforce the terms of their own subjugation in the name liberation is, on its face, quite impossible. Yet both resistance and decolonization are not simply rights but obligations under international law and most other recent philosophical/moral schemas of justice.[9]

The situation presents a serious dilemma. Resolving it, and thereby actualizing the potential for a coherent and constructive indigenous response to the realties which now confront us, and which will confront our future generations, requires a systematic unraveling of the web of mystification through which North America's native peoples have been bound ever more tightly into the carefully crafted mechanisms of our oppression and eventual negation.[10] The purpose of the present essay is to make a contribution in this regard by sorting out that which has traditionally been part of the "Indian way" of identifying member/citizens from that which has not, and to sketch the mechanisms through which the latter has supplanted the former. From the resulting vantage point it should prove possible to ascertain with some clarity the methods which must be (re)asserted if we are ever to throw off the yoke of colonial bondage.

## The Traditional Way

There is not, and has never been, much of a genetic ("hereditary") distinction to be drawn between indigenous peoples in the Americas. In part, this devolves upon the probability that the great proliferation of culturally distinct groups evident in the hemisphere by the time the European invasions commenced around 1500 had all evolved from three, or perhaps four, discernible "gene stocks," figures correlating rather well to the evident number of root linguistic variants.[11] More to the point, native peoples have for the most part always maintained relatively high degrees of sociocultural inclusiveness and consequent reproductive interactivity ("inter-breeding") among one another.

Since time immemorial, Cheyennes (or their precursors) have intermarried with Arapahos, Ojibwes with Crees, Cayugas with Onondagas, Yaquis with Tarahumaras, Choctaws with Chickasaws, and so on, *ad infinitum*. In such instances, depending on whether the cultures in question were matrilinear or patrilinear, either the male or female spouse would become a part of the other's society, as would their offspring. Genealogy rather than genetics was the core component of societal composition, although procedures for incorporation of individuals and sometimes whole groups by adoption/naturalization and occasional merger were similarly well established and practiced with varying degrees of scale and frequency by most peoples, either periodically or continuously.[12]

Whatever else may be said of such processes, they served over time to erase any meaningful genetic distinctions between the groups involved. Indeed, there are recorded instances—as when the Mohawks absorbed significant portions of both the Hurons and the Susquehannocks during the seventeenth century—in which the number of outsiders incorporated into a given society noticeably exceeded that of the original members.[13] Given these historical circumstances, the contemporary notion of somehow being Mohawk "by blood" is self-evidently ludicrous, albeit no more so than similar claims advanced with respect to the Pawnee, Cherokee, Apache, Paiute or virtually any other native people.[14]

Once non-Indians began to appear in substantial numbers across the hemisphere, the same time-honored principles prevailed. Probably the earliest group of English to have simply melted into a native society were the inhabitants of Raleigh's "lost colony" of Roanoke in 1590.[15] A century later, there were literally thousands of "white Indians"—mostly English and French, but also Swedes, Scots, Irish, Dutch and others as well—who, diseased with aspects of their own cultures, had either married into, been adopted by, or petitioned for naturalization as member/citizens of indigenous nations.[16] By then, the phenomenon had become pronounced enough that it had long since precipitated a crisis among the Puritans of Plymouth Colony and figured in their waging of a war of extermination against the Pequots in 1637.[17]

The attraction of "going native" remained so strong, and the willingness of indigenous peoples to accept Europeans into their societies so apparent, that it prevailed even among those captured in Indian/white warfare.[18] During the 1770s, George Croghan and Guy Johnson, both acknowledged authorities on the native peoples of the mid-Atlantic region, estimated that the great bulk of the several hundred English prisoners of all ages and both genders taken by the Indians had been adopted by them rather than being put to death.[19] At about the same time, Benjamin Franklin lamented that:

> [W]hen white persons of either sex have been taken prisoners young by the Indians, and lived a while among them, tho' ransomed by their Friends, and treated with all imaginable tenderness to prevail with them to stay among the English, yet in a Short time they become disgusted with our manner of life, and the care and pains that are necessary to support it, and take the first good Opportunity of escaping again into the Woods, from thence there is no reclaiming them.[20]

The literature of the period is filled with similar observations. Virginia's Lieutenant Governor Francis Fauquier, for example, noted that whites "recovered" from Indians had to be "closely watched [lest] they will certainly return to the Barbarians."[21] Colonel Henry Bouquet, who headed a 1764 expedition to take charge of "captives" returned under terms of a treaty with England by the Shawnees, Miamis and other peoples of the Ohio River Valley, issued orders that "they are to be closely watched and well Secured [as] most of them, particularly those who have been a long time among the Indians, will take the first Opportunity to run away."[22] The Reverend

William Smith, chaplain and chronicler of Bouquet's foray, noted that most younger whites seemed to view their "liberators" as captors and "parted from the savages with tears."[23]

Some, like fourteen-year-old John McCullough, managed to escape Bouquet's column and quickly reunited himself with his native family.[24] Adults often expressed the same sentiments, as with the English wife of a native leader who shortly slipped away to rejoin her husband and their children.[25]

> Although most of the returned captives did not try to escape, the emotional torment caused by the separation from their adopted families deeply impressed the colonists. The Indians "delivered up their beloved captives with the utmost reluctance; shed torrents of tears over them, recommending them to the care and protection of the commanding officer." One young woman "cryed and roared when asked to come and begged to Stay a little longer." "Some, who could not make their escape, clung to their savage acquaintance at parting, and continued many days in bitter lamentations, even refusing sustenance." Children "cried as if they would die when they were presented to us." With only small exaggeration an observer . . . could report that "every captive left the Indians with regret."[26]

Many Indians reciprocated by refusing to surrender those they'd married, adopted, or otherwise accepted, especially children, under any but the most coercive circumstances.[27] In cases where there was no viable alternative, the record is replete with examples of adoptive native parents regularly visiting and otherwise maintaining familial relations with such children for the remainder of their own lives.[28] And, of course, children born of a union between Indian and non-Indian were almost invariably never relinquished at all (not least because whites, *not* Indians, tended to frown upon such "mixed-blood" offspring and thus made little or no effort to claim them).[29] One upshot is a marked proliferation of European surnames among indigenous peoples, not only in the East but the West as well; witness such sizable contemporary mixed-blood families as the Morriseaus, Robideaus, Peltiers and Bellecourts among the Chippewas, and the Pouriers, Garniers, Amiotts, Roubideauxs, Archambaults and Mousseaus among the Lakotas.[30]

With respect to blacks—mostly Africans brought to the southeastern quadrant of North America as chattel slaves, but the occasional "free man" as well—the situation was not dissimilar, albeit the imperative for them to reject a return to Euroamerican society was obviously greater than for whites, and a much larger proportion of adults was involved. Escaped slaves were typically accepted among the native peoples they encountered, married and produced children who were fully integrated into indigenous societies.[31]

So prominent was this process of intermingling that at some point around 1750 an entire people, the Seminole, was constituted as an amalgamation of the remnants of several thoroughly decimated indigenous nations and a very substantial element, about one-third of the whole, of blacks.[32]

Hence, by 1830 at the latest, the notion of defining "Indianness" in terms of "race" had been rendered patently absurd. It has been reliably estimated that something approaching half of all native people still residing east of the Mississippi River were at that point genetically intermixed not only with one another, but with "Negroid and Caucasoid racial stock," a demographic pattern which would spread rapidly westward over the next half-century.[33] There is little if any indication, moreover, that most indigenous societies viewed this increasing admixture as untoward or peculiar, much less threatening, in and of itself (this is as opposed to their often bitter resistance to the cultural, political and material encroachments of Euroamerican "civilization").

## On the Matter of Fidelity

It has become an article of faith among historical interpreters that mixed-bloods served as something of a Trojan Horse within indigenous societies during the era of Euroamerican conquest, undermining their cohesion and thereby eroding their ability to effectively resist the onslaught.[34] While it is true that the colonizing powers, especially the United States, often sought to use those of mixed ancestry in precisely this fashion, the realities of mixed blood performance were rather different. Indeed, their aggregate record in mounting a defense of native rights is not only equal in most respects to those who were of the "pure" variety, it was plainly stronger in certain instances. Examples abound, beginning with the above-mentioned Seminoles, who proved to be the U.S. Army's most successful adversaries east of the Mississippi.[35]

During the twenty-year period leading up to the Cherokee Removal of 1838, it was John Ross, a man "seven-eighths Scotch-Irish and one-eighth Cherokee by descent," who served as the primary leader of his people's effort to revitalize their traditional culture, prevent the loss of their homelands in the Georgia/Tennessee area and thereby avert mass relocation to Oklahoma Territory.[36] On the other hand, it was John Ridge—son of a full-blood leader called "Major" Ridge by whites, and himself only one-eighth white by pedigree—who headed the accommodationist ("sell-out") faction of Cherokee society. The dilution of unity that weakened Cherokee resistance, as well as the internal strife plaguing that nation for generations after its Trail of Tears, were thus demonstrably attributable to Ridge and his generally well-blooded followers rather than the "genetically marginal" Ross.[37]

Far to the west, a comparable example may be found in Quannah (Parker), "half-breed" son of Peta Nacona, principle leader of the Quahadi Comanches, and Cynthia Ann Parker, a white captive who was his wife.[38] Beginning in the late 1860s, after his father had been killed and his mother "recovered" by white raiders, Quannah emerged as a major galvanizer of military resistance to the United States, not just among Quahadis but with respect to all Comanches and allied Kiowas, Kiowa Apaches, Southern Cheyennes and Arapahos. After consummation of the U.S. conquest of the Southern Plains during the mid-1870s — the Quahadis were last to lay down their arms — Quannah shifted to a position of political leadership, a role which included introduction of the peyote religion, charting the Comanches' course through the perilous waters of the early reservation period and on into the twentieth century.[39]

Among the Cheyennes, there were the brothers George, Robert and Charlie Bent, sons of William Bent, a noted white trader, and his Cheyenne wife. While each struggled for their people's rights in his own way — George, for instance, fought briefly against the white invaders and testified on three separate occasions against perpetrators of the Colorado militia's infamous 1864 massacre of noncombatant Cheyennes and Arapahos at Sand Creek — Charlie is the better example (or at least the most reviled among mainstream commentators).[40] Accepted into the Cheyennes' élite Crazy Dog Society ("Dog Soldiers"), he acquired an almost legendary status because of his courage in physically defending his homeland. Ultimately, Charlie Bent gave his all, dying an agonizingly lingering death in 1868 of wounds suffered during a skirmish with Pawnees fighting for the United States.[41]

To the north, among the Oglala Lakotas, there was the all but mythic figure of Crazy Horse, the man who vanquished both Crook and Custer, establishing himself in the process as perhaps *the* preeminent symbol of native valor and integrity, both to his own people and to many others as well.[42] Slight, pale-complected, with fair, wavy hair — he was actually named "Curly" as a youth — the "strange man of the Oglalas" may well have been of mixed racial descent.[43] Regardless of Crazy Horse's ancestry, it is clear that men like Red Cloud, who figured most prominently in undercutting his ability to sustain the Lakota resistance, were themselves "full-bloods."[44] So too was Little Big Man, the former friend who pinned Crazy Horse's arms, allowing William Gentles, a U.S. Army private, to get close enough to bayonet him to death during the fall of 1877.[45]

The same could be said of Bull Head and the rest of the contingent of Indian police who murdered Sitting Bull in December 1890, the Arikara, Crow and Pawnee scouts who guided Custer and Colonel Ranald Mackenzie on their bloody paths across the plains, and the bulk of those who finally ran Geronimo to ground in the upper Sonora Desert.[46] Nor was it a question of genetics that prompted Crow Dog, a noted "recalcitrant," to kill the U.S.-sponsored Brûlé Lakota chief, Spotted Tail, whom the former viewed as having sacrificed his people's interest in favor of personal gain (both materially and in terms of imagined prestige).[47] The list goes on and on, with deadly repetition.

At the same time, it wasn't necessarily required that one be of any part "Indian blood" to assume a position of importance within an indigenous society. A salient example is that of Jim Beckwourth (or "Beckworth," or "Beckwith," there are various spellings), who was by all accounts of exclusively African descent. Having been adopted by the Crows during the mid-1820s and marrying a woman named Still Water shortly thereafter, he was elevated first to the station of counselor to the headmen and eventually to serving as a headman in his own right. Although he left the Crows for a time after the death of his second wife, he remained unstinting in his defense of Indian rights and returned in 1866 to die among the people who had accepted him as a naturalized leader.[48]

On balance, then, it is both fair and accurate to observe that questions concerning the likelihood an individual might display a strong loyalty to Indian interests never devolved upon his or her genetic makeup. Unquestionably, mixed-bloods and persons lacking even the pretense of a native gene stood among the foremost exemplars of patriotism in a number of indigenous nations during the nineteenth century (and earlier). By the same token, many native people "untainted" by any hint of admixture with whites or blacks conducted themselves with all the fidelity of Vidkun Quisling.[49] Such matters were well understood in traditional societies, which is precisely why they never considered blood quantum to be a useful factor in determining citizenship or cultural identity.

## The Racial Dimension of Divide and Rule

The intellectual establishment of the United States played a major role in pioneering such psuedoscientific "disciplines" as ethnology, craniometry, phrenology and eugenics from the early nineteenth century onwards.[50] In essence, although it has evidenced a variety of offshoots and subtexts over the years, the entire project—which has lasted into the present moment—has been devoted to devising "objective" criteria by which the human species may be subdivided into "races" according to certain "heritable" and "empirically demonstrable" characteristics. Values are then assigned to these genetically transmitted attributes in order to create the appearance that there is a "natural hierarchy of humanity" ranging upward from "Negroid" at the lowest level to "Caucasoid" at the highest.[51]

With publication of Samuel George Morton's *Crania Americana* in 1839, it is no overstatement to suggest that the Euroamerican intelligentsia stood at the cutting edge of "scholarly" efforts to lend both a patina of academic respectability and an aura of sheer inevitability to the white supremacist ideology attending European imperialism.[52] While it was put to various uses abroad, such material was utilized in the U.S. to justify both a domestic order of which black chattel slavery was an integral aspect and a continental trajectory of national expansion—America's "Manifest Destiny" to extend uninterruptedly "from sea to shining sea"—which could be consummated only at the direct expense of North America's indigenous population.[53]

It is instructive that while U.S. policymakers professed to embrace racism on both scientific and philosophical grounds, implying an at least minimal consistency in its application, their "pragmatic" implementation of its principles was at once transparently self-serving and utterly contradictory. Since blacks were considered to be property, yielding value not only in their labor but as commodities which could be bought and sold, it was profitable not only to employ but to breed them in ever larger numbers.[54] To this end, an elaborate system of quantifying their racial admixture was devised—classifications such as "maroon," "quadroon" and "octoroon"—by which to assess their relative worth.[55] The overriding premise, however, was the "one drop rule": a person with *any* amount of "Negroid blood" could be considered black for purposes of law, even if computation of their "quantum" revealed them to be 127/128 white.[56]

Native people, by contrast, were legally understood to *own* property— mainly land, and minerals within that land—coveted by whites.[57] It followed then, as it still does, that reductions in the number of Indians "at large" in North America corresponded directly to diminishment of the cloud surrounding the dominant society's claims of clear title to/jurisdictional rights over its purported landbase.[58] Hence, any racial admixture at all, especially with blacks, was often deemed sufficient to warrant individuals, and sometimes entire groups, being legally classified as a "non-Indians," regardless of their actual standing in indigenous society.[59] On this basis, most noticeably in the South but elsewhere as well, whole native peoples were declared "extinct" via the expedient of simply reclassifying them as "mulattos" or "coloreds."[60]

While the intermingling of natives with blacks was invariably cast in a negative light, the mixing of Indian with white "stock" came to be viewed more favorably. As no less than Thomas Jefferson observed in 1803, a calculated policy of subsuming native genetics within a much larger white gene pool might serve as an alternative to outright extermination in answering what he termed the "Indian Question."

> In truth, the ultimate point of rest and happiness for them is to let our settlements and theirs meet and blend together, to intermix, and become one people. Incorporating themselves with us as citizens of the United States, this is what the natural progress of things will, of course, bring on, and it will be better to promote than retard it.[61]

Completely oblivious to the reality of North America's abundant indigenous agriculture, and to the fact that whites had learned to cultivate corn and other crops from Indians rather than the other way round, America's "most admired . . . slaveholding philosopher of freedom" actually urged a delegation of Munsee, Lenni Lenâpé and Mohican leaders to adopt a "farming way of life" when they visited him in 1808.[62] "You will become one people with us," he went on to tell the astonished Indians, "Your blood will mix with ours, and will spread with ours across this great land."[63]

The sentiments underlying Jefferson's "humanitarian" strategy were framed less pleasantly, but with remarkable clarity, by J.C. Nott, a racial theorist whose views were endorsed by Morton and other prominent scientists of the day. With reference to the idea that at least five southern peoples— Cherokees, Choctaws, Chickasaws, Creeks and Seminoles—had become "civilized" in their own right before being forcibly evicted from their homelands during the 1830s,[64] he argued that:

> It has been falsely asserted that the *Choctaw* and *Cherokee* Indians have made great progress in civilization. I assert positively, after the most ample investigation of the facts, that the pure-blooded Indians are everywhere unchanged in their habits. Many white

persons, settling among the above tribes, have intermarried with them; and all such trumpeted progress exists among these whites and their mixed breeds alone. The pure-blooded savage still skulks untamed through the forest, or gallops athwart the prairie. Can any one call the name of a single pure Indian of the *Barbarous* tribes who—except in death, like a wild cat—has done anything worthy of remembrance (emphasis original)?[65]

It followed, according to the noted phrenologist Charles Caldwell, that the "only efficient scheme to civilize the Indians is to *cross the breed*. Attempt any other and you [will have no alternative] but to *extinguish the race* (emphasis original)."[66] Such views, posing the alternative of genetic/cultural absorption to literal "extirpation," were avidly embraced by none other than Lewis Henry Morgan, the "founding giant" of American anthropology. Indeed, Morgan was of the express opinion that the former option was preferable to the latter mainly because a blending of minute quantities of Indian "blood" into that of the white "mainstream" would serve to "toughen our race" even while it "painlessly" eradicated the indigenous population as such.[67]

All told, by 1860 or shortly thereafter, Euroamerican academicians had forged the full range of conceptual tools necessary for their government to use the traditionally inclusive structures of native societies in a manner which would facilitate their rapid division, fragmentation and, so it was thought at the time, ultimate dissipation.[68] Slowly but steadily, a national consensus was emerging to the effect that this represented the most appropriate (and final) solution to what was by then being called "The Indian Problem."[69] What remained necessary was for these tools to be applied systematically, through the design and implementation of a comprehensive set of policies. And, to this end, experimentation had long since begun.

### The Impositions of U.S. Policy

Probably the first concerted effort by U.S. officialdom to use the incorporation of whites and their mixed-blood offspring as a wedge with which to pry indigenous societies apart began in the late 1700s, when Moravian missionaries were asked to serve as de facto federal emissaries to the Cherokee Nation.[70] Imbued with the mystical notion that "Aryan" genetics correlated to such "innate" endowments as intellect and "moral capacity"—which in their minds corresponded with the potential to adopt "civilized" (Christian) outlooks and values—the Moravians and, after 1803, their Presbyterian colleagues "went out of their way to befriend" mixed-bloods rather than "pure" Indians while pursuing their goals of obtaining religious converts *cum* political allies.[71]

Predictably, this racial bias translated into a privileging of mixed-bloods in both political and material terms, regardless of their rank within the Cherokee polity and irrespective of whether they desired such "benefits," a situation which was quite reasonably resented by other Cherokees (most especially those whose authority was undermined or supplanted by such external manipulation). The result, obviously intended by the United States, was the opening of deep cleavages among Cherokees that greatly weakened them in military as well as political and cultural terms, circumstances which amplified considerably the decisive advantages the U.S. already enjoyed in its drive to dispossess them of their property.[72] Meanwhile, similar initiatives had been undertaken vis-à-vis the Creeks, Choctaws, Chickasaws and others.[73]

The U.S. largely refrained from attempting such maneuvers in a more formal sense during the first thirty years of its treatymaking with indigenous nations. This interval roughly corresponds to the period in which the young republic, a veritable revolutionary outlaw state, desperately required the legitimation which could be bestowed through native recognition of its sovereign status (indigenous sovereignty having already been recognized through treaties with the European powers).[74] Nonetheless, special provisions pertaining to mixed-bloods soon entered U.S. diplomacy with Indians, beginning with an 1817 Treaty with the Wyandots and several other peoples of the Ohio/Pennsylvania region.[75] Thereafter, the performance was repeated in compact after compact, at least 53 times by 1868.[76]

In only few instances, such as the 1847 Treaty with the Chippewa of the Mississippi and Lake Superior, in which it is recognized by the U.S. that "half or mixed bloods of the Chippewas residing with them [should simply] be considered Chippewas," is there acknowledgment of the right of indigenous nations to naturalize citizens as they saw fit.[77] In the great bulk of cases, such treaty provisions are plainly designed to accomplish the opposite effect, distinguishing those of mixed ancestry from the rest of their people, almost always by unilaterally privileging them in a material fashion. Usually, this followed upon the model established in the 1817 treaty, the eighth article of which provided that while the Indians themselves would hold certain lands in common, those "connected with said Indians, by blood or adoption" would receive individual tracts averaging 640 acres each.[78]

There were several variations on the theme. In one, exemplified by the

1818 Treaty with the Miami, chiefs as well as mixed-bloods and intermarried whites were assigned individual parcels, one-to-six sections each in this case, while the rest of the people were assigned a tract in common. Thus, not only were mixed-bloods figuratively elevated to the same standing as chiefs by external fiat, but the Miamis' actual leaders were implicitly linked to them rather than to their people as a whole.[79] On other occasions, as in the 1855 Treaty with the Winnebago, missionaries were substituted for chiefs.[80] On still others, as in the 1837 Treaty with the Sioux, money and/or other special provisions was substituted for land.[81] Even in cases like that of the 1861 Treaty with the Cheyenne and Arapaho, where full-bloods and mixed-bloods were nominally treated the same—i.e., everyone was allotted a parcel and/or monetary award—mixed-bloods were singled out to receive larger quantities.[82]

In a number of instances, as in the 1857 Treaty with the Pawnee, provisions were explicitly designed to induce an outright physical separation of mixed-bloods from their people, a particularly odious practice in cases such as that addressed by the 1865 Treaty with the Osage where "breeds" were the only group allowed (or coerced) to remain within a traditional homeland from which the rest of their nation was removed.[83] In the 1831 Treaty with the Shawnee, the notion of blood quantum was first applied in a formal way to determine who would—or, more importantly, who would *not*—be recognized by the U.S. as a "real" Indian.[84]

And, racism aside, the treaties often employed a virulent sexist bias, tracing descent, acknowledging authority and bestowing land titles along decidedly patriarchal lines even (or especially) in contexts where female property ownership, political leadership and matrilinearity were the indigenous norms. When combined with the usual racial manipulations, such gender criteria represented an extraordinarily potent means of subverting the integrity of native cultures, undermining their sociopolitical cohesion and confusing or nullifying their procedures for identifying member/citizens.[85]

In 1871, sensing that the capacity of most indigenous nations to offer effective military resistance was nearing an end, Congress suspended further treatymaking with Indians.[86] There then followed a decade of reorganization during which the government shifted from what had been primarily a policy of subjugating native peoples to an emphasis upon assimilating what remained of them, both geographically and demographically.[87] There were a number of aspects to this transition, notably the extension of U.S. criminal jurisdiction over reserved native territories via the Major Crimes Act of 1885.[88] Its hallmark, however, was passage of the 1887 General Allotment Act, a measure expressly intended to dissolve the collective relationship to land which was the fundament of traditional cultures by imposing the allegedly superior Anglo-Saxon system of individuated property ownership.[89]

The main ingredient of the Allotment Act was that each Indian recognized as such by the U.S. would be assigned an individually deeded parcel of land within existing reservation boundaries. These varied in size, depending on whether the Indian was a child (40 acres), unmarried adult (80 acres), or head of a family (160 acres). Once each Indian had received his/her personal allotment, becoming a U.S. citizen in the process, the law prescribed that the balance of reserved territory be declared "surplus" and opened up to homesteading by non-Indians, corporate usage, or placed in some form of perpetual federal trust status (i.e., designation as national parks and forests, military installations, etc.). In this manner, about two-thirds of the approximately 150 million acres of land still retained by indigenous nations at the outset "passed" to whites by 1934.[90]

The bedrock upon which the allotment process was built was the compilation of formal rolls listing those belonging to each reservation-based native people.[91] While the Act itself posited no specific criteria by which this would be accomplished, responsibility for completing the task was ultimately vested in the individual federal agents assigned to preside over the reservations. Endowed as they were with staunchly racialist perspectives, and fully aware that whatever definitional constraints might be applied in determining the overall number of Indians would translate directly into an increased availability of property to their own society, it was predictable that these men would rely heavily upon the sort of blood quantum "standards" already evident in treaty language.[92]

In practice, it was typically required that a potential enrollee/allottee be able to demonstrate that s/he possessed "not less than one-half degree of blood" in the particular group in which s/he wished to be enrolled ("intertribal" pedigrees were seldom accepted, even for ostensible full-bloods, and the overall standard was almost never allowed to slip below quarter-blood).[93] The upshot was that anywhere from a third to two-thirds of all those who might otherwise have been eligible to receive allotments were denied not only land but federal recognition as being member/citizens of their nations.[94] In sum, government functionaries admitted to the existence of only 237,196 native people within U.S. borders by the late 1890s, of whom only a small percentage were less than half-blood members of specific groups.[95]

To complete this racist reshaping of Indian identity, the Act provided that those enrolled as full-bloods would be placed under the legal presumption of being genetically incompetent to manage their own affairs. Hence, they were issued "trust patents" for their allotments, to be "administered in their behalf by the Secretary of the Interior or his delegate" (i.e., local Indian agents) for a quarter-century.[96] Mixed-bloods, by virtue of their white genetics, were deemed to be competent and issued patents in fee simple. This, along with other blatantly preferential treatment bestowed as a matter of policy upon those of mixed ancestry, drove the final wedges into many once harmonious indigenous societies.[97] In the more extreme instances, such as that of the Kaws in Kansas, the full-bloods' visceral response was to repudiate mixed-bloods altogether, demanding their elimination from the tribal roll and seeking to expel them as a body from their society.[98]

By the turn of the century, virtually every indigenous nation within the U.S. had, by way of an unrelenting substitution of federal definitions for their own, been stripped of the ability to determine for themselves in any meaningful way the internal composition of their polities. The manner in which this had been accomplished, moreover, ensured that rifts even among those still acknowledged as being Indians were of a nature which would all but guarantee eventual dissolution of native societies, at least in the sense they'd traditionally understood themselves. Allotment and the broader assimilation policy of which it was part had truly proven themselves to be, in the words of Indian Commissioner Francis E. Leupp, "a mighty pulverizing engine for breaking up the tribal mass."[99]

**Internalization**

The breakup and diminishment of the reservation landbase were not the only factors leading to confident predictions that there would be no Indians culturally recognizable as such in the United States by some point around 1935.[100] Beginning in the 1860s, there had been an increasing emphasis on "educating" native youth in the ways of the dominant society, a trend that was consolidated in the 1880s as a key aspect of assimilationist technique.[101] While there were several other options available, all of them less expensive and more humane, the mode selected for delivery of such instruction was primarily that of "off-reservation boarding schools" located in places as remote as possible from native communities.[102]

The model for what became an entire system was Pennsylvania's

Carlisle Indian School, established in 1875 by Captain Richard Henry Pratt, a man whose main qualification for the task seems to have been that he'd earlier served as warden of a military prison at Fort Marion, Florida.[103] Following Pratt's stated objective of "killing the Indian" in each student, Carlisle and other such facilities—Chilocco, Albuquerque, Phoenix, Haskell, Riverside; by 1902, there were two-dozen of them—systematically "deculturated" their pupils.[104] Children brought to the schools as young as age six were denied most or all direct contact with their families and societies for years on end. They were shorn of their hair and required to dress in the manner of Euroamerica, forbidden to speak their languages or practice their religions, prevented from learning their own histories or being in any other way socialized among their own people.[105]

Simultaneously, all students were subjected to a grueling regimen of indoctrination in Christian morality—mainly the "virtues" of private property, sexual repression and patriarchy—"proper" English and arithmetic, officially approved versions of history, civics and natural science, the latter devoted mostly to inculcating prevailing notions of racial heirarchy.[106] To instill the "work ethic"—that is, to prepare students for the lot assigned their racial group once it had been fully digested by Euroamerica—they were also required to spend half of each day during the school year engaged in "industrial vocational training" (i.e., uncompensated manual labor). During the summers, most of the older boys were "jobbed out" at very low wages to work on white-owned farms or local businesses; girls were assigned as domestics and the like.[107]

Individual native families and often whole societies resisted the process.[108] As a result, in 1891 and again in 1893 Congress authorized the use of police, troops and other forcible means to compel the transfer of children from reservations to boarding schools, and to keep them there once they'd arrived.[109] Hence, despite the best efforts of their elders, and not infrequently of the students themselves, a total of 21,568 indigenous children—about a third of the targeted age group—were confined in the schools in 1900.[110] As of the late 1920s, the system had been diversified and expanded to the point that upwards of half of each successive generation of native youth was being comprehensively "acculturated" in a more or less uniform fashion.[111]

By 1924, assimilation had progressed to the point that a "clean-up bill" was passed through which the responsibilities, though not necessarily the rights, of U.S. citizenship were imposed upon all Indians who had not already been naturalized under the Allotment Act or other federal initiatives.[112] Although it appeared that this might represent the culminating statutory ingredient necessary to bring about a final absorption of Native America, fate intervened in a most unexpected fashion to avert any such outcome (formally, if not in terms of more practical cultural, political and economic realities). This, rather ironically, took the form of resources: the mostly barren tracts of land left to Indians after allotment, thought to be worthless by nineteenth-century policymakers, had by the late 1920s been revealed as some of the more mineral-rich territory in the world.[113]

Loath to see these newfound assets thrown into the public domain (many had strategic value, real or potential), the more forward-looking federal economic planners quickly perceived the utility of retaining them in trust, where they might be exploited at controlled rates by preferred corporations for designated purposes and in the most profitable fashion imaginable. This resulted, in 1925, in the recommendation by a committee of one hundred officially selected academic experts and business leaders that allotment and the more draconian objectives of assimilation policy be abandoned in favor of preserving the reservations in some permanently subordinated capacity and inaugurating a policy of carefully calibrated "economic development" therein.[114]

This, in turn, led to passage of the 1934 Indian Reorganization Act (IRA), through which what remained of traditional native governments were for the most part supplanted by federally designed "tribal councils" meant to serve as the medium for longterm administration of the freshly conceived internal colonial domain.[115] Although the IRA was imposed behind the democratic facade of reservation-by-reservation referenda, the record reveals that BIA field representatives obtained favorable results by presenting skewed or patently false information to voters in a number of instances, flatly rigging the outcomes in others.[116] And, while democratic appearances were reinforced by the fact that the government of each reorganized reservation functioned on the basis of its own "tribal constitution," the reality is that these "founding" documents were essentially boilerplate contraptions resembling corporate charters hammered out on an assembly line basis by Bureau personnel.[117]

Nowhere is this last more obvious than in the language of the IRA constitutions pertaining to criteria of tribal membership. While there are certain variations between instruments, most simply aped the then-prevailing federal quantum standard of quarter-blood minimum, while all of them, regardless of the degree of blood required, advanced genetics as the linchpin of identity.[118] That there was no noteworthy resistance among native supporters of the IRA to this conspicuous usurpation of indigenous tradition is unsurprising, given that such persons were all but invariably drawn from the ranks of those indoctrinated in the boarding schools to see themselves in racial rather than national/political or cultural terms.[119]

With the embrace of the IRA constitutions by what were proclaimed as solid majorities on most reservations, Euroamerican definitions of and constraints upon Indian identity were formally as well as psychologically/intellectually internalized by Native America. From there on, the government could increasingly rely upon Indians themselves to enforce its race codes for it. Consequently, whenever racial formulations of native identity have been challenged, Washington has been able to lay the onus of responsibility directly at the feet of the IRA councils it not only invented and installed, but which remain utterly and perpetually dependent upon federal patronage for their base funding and whatever limited authority they might wield.[120] In turn, the councils defend Washington's negation of indigenous sovereignty in the name of maintaining it.[121] A more perfect shell game is impossible to imagine.

### Enter the "Purity Police"

The reconfiguration and structural assimilation of the mechanisms of indigenous governance— by the early 1990s, IRA-style councils were being openly referred to as a "third level" of the federal government itself—was facilitated and reinforced, not only through the increasingly pervasive indoctrination of native students via the educational system, but by lingering effects of allotment.[122] Foremost in this respect was the "heirship problem" created by the fact that the reserved native landbase had been reduced to a size corresponding to the number of Indians recognized as existing during the 1890s. No provision was made for a population rebound of any sort.[123] As the matter was politely explained in 1994:

> Upon the death of the original allottees the allotments, or portions of them, have descended to heirs or devisees. As these heirs in turn have died, their holdings have been subdivided among their heirs or devisees, and so on through the years. As a result, about half of the allotted Indian lands are in heirship status. The authors of the origi-

nal legislation failed to anticipate the problems that would be caused by the partition-ing of an individual's land following his death. Thousands of the allotments in an heir-ship status are subject to so many undivided interests that they can be utilized only with great difficulty by their Indian owners. . . Undivided interests in a single allotment can often be expressed by fractions with a common denominator of 1,000,000 or more [by this point].[124]

In other words, there was no reservation land available to accommo-date the 50 percent increase in the number of recognized Indians recorded by the U.S. Census between 1900 and 1950.[125] Rather than correcting the problem by transferring some portion of the territory unlawfully stripped away from native people back to its rightful owners,[126] the government launched a massive and sustained program to relocate the native "population surplus" from the land altogether, dispersing them for the most part into major urban areas. At the same time, as an incentive for them to leave, fund-ing for on-reservation programming of all sorts was sliced to the bone and sometimes deeper.[127] One result is that, while well over 90 percent of fed-erally recognized Indians lived on the reservations in 1900, fewer than 45 percent do so today.[128]

Another cost-cutting measure, inaugurated in the mid-1950s, was for the Congress to simply "terminate" its recognition of entire nations whose reservations were found to be devoid of minerals, or who were deemed to be too small and insignificant to warrant the expenditures necessary to administer them.[129] A total of 103 peoples, ranging from large groups like the Menominee in Wisconsin and Klamath in Oregon to the tiny "Mission Bands" of Southern California, were thereby dissolved, their remaining lands absorbed into the U.S. territorial corpus and their population effectively declared to be non-Indians before the process ran its course in the early '60s.[130] Only a handful, including the Menominee but not the Klamath, were ever reinstated.[131]

Predictably, far from seeking to combat such trends, federally installed-and-supported tribal councils amplified them. In the face of declining fed-eral appropriations to Indian Affairs, the councils by and large set out to reduce the number of Indians eligible to draw upon them. Arguing that the fewer people entitled to receive benefits such as healthcare and commodity foodstuffs, or to receive per capita payments against mineral extraction, water diversions and past land transfers, the larger the share for those who remained, the councils were able to peddle their bill of goods to many of their increasingly impoverished reservation constituents.[132] In short order, the IRA constitutions on many reservations were amended or rewritten to reflect higher blood quantum requirements for tribal enrollment.[133] In a number of instances, reservation residency was required as well, a stipulation which excluded the children of relocatees, regardless of their documentable degree of Indian blood.[134]

The council heads, through a federally funded lobbying organization dubbed the National Tribal Chairmen's Association (NTCA), then launched an aggressive campaign to once again recast the definition of "Indian" in the public consciousness—and, they made it clear, in law—this time as being *only* those "enrolled in a federally recognized tribe."[135] Consigned to the status of "non-Indians" in this perverse scenario were everyone from terminated peoples like the Klamaths to the unenrolled traditionals still living on and about many reservations, from nations like the Abenakis of Vermont who had never consented to a treaty with the U.S.—and who were thus officially "unrecognized"—to the NTCA members' own nieces and nephews residing in cities.[136] Also sacrificed in the proposed ethnic purge were thousands of hapless children, orphaned and otherwise, whom federal welfare agencies had caused to be adopted by non–Indian families.[137]

The government initially declined to accept the NTCA's simplistic nomenclature of Indianness. Instead, it conjured up a proliferation of what by now amount to at least eighty different and often conflicting definitions of its own, each of them conforming to some particular bureaucratic or policy agenda and sporting a larger or smaller clique of Indian subscribers queued up to defend it under the presumption they will somehow benefit by their endorsement.[138] Under such conditions, it is possible to challenge the legitimacy of virtually anyone identifying him/herself as Indian on one or several grounds (often having little or nothing to do with genuine concerns about identity, per se).[139] The result has been a steadily rising tide of infighting, occasioned in most instances by outright race-baiting, between and among native peoples over the past forty years.[140]

Things did not become truly pathological until 1990, however, when the NTCA's reactionary vision was at least partially realized at the federal level. With passage of the so-called Act for the Protection of American Indian Arts and Crafts in that year, it became a criminal offense punishable by fines of $250,000 to $1 million and imprisonment of up to fifteen years for anyone not enrolled in a federally recognized tribe to identify as an

Indian "for purposes of selling artwork."[141] Although Congress did not provide the statute an enabling clause to allow the Act's enforcement until 1996—not least because of concerns that to do so might technically require the arrest and prosecution of individuals deemed to be Indian under other elements of federal law—its very existence unleashed an utter frenzy of witch-hunting among Indians themselves.[142]

Within months, ad hoc patrols of "identity monitors" were prowling selected museums and galleries, demanding to see documentation of the pedigrees of the native artists exhibited therein, while freelance "Indian spokespersons" such as Suzan Shown Harjo advocated that comparable legislation pertaining to "ethnic fraud" should be enacted with respect to writers, educators, filmmakers and journalists, among many others.[143] The theme was quickly picked up, tabloid-style, by papers like *Indian Country Today* and *News From Indian Country*, while the Internet came figuratively alive with a swarm of essentially anonymous rumors that dozens of Native America's most distinguished artists, authors, thinkers and activists weren't "really" Indians after all.[144]

Perhaps most disgustingly, a literal flying squad of self-appointed "purity police" in the San Francisco Bay Area took it upon itself to systematically disrupt the functioning of all manner of community service organizations in 1992 and '93—their targets ranged from native programming on radio station KPFA, to an AIDS clinic administered by the Indian Health Service, to the local school district's Indian education project—to ensure that everyone involved fit their particular notion of what an Indian should be (children as young as eight years of age were button-holed and ordered to prove they were "genuine" Indians).[145] Meanwhile, back on the rez, at least some IRA leaders were arguing that the tribal constitutions should be amended yet again, this time to disenroll members who married non-Indians on the premise that such measures had become vital "to protect the purity of our Indian blood."[146]

**The Way Ahead**

The internalization of Euroamerica's conception of race by native peoples, the virulence with which it is now manifested in all too many sectors of the indigenous community, and the ubiquity of the confusion and divisiveness it has generated among Indians and their potential supporters, represents a culmination of federal policy initiatives originating nearly two hundred years ago. To all appearances, Native North America has been rendered effectively self-colonizing and, if present attitudes persist, it stands to become self-liquidating as well. The tale is told in the demographic data pertaining to those who are federally recognized.

> During the twentieth-century population recovery of American Indians there has been an increasing mixture between them and non-Indian peoples. Data concerning this may be obtained from the 1910 and 1930 U.S. censuses of American Indians. . . [In 1910] 56.5 percent of American Indians enumerated in the United States were full-blood—150,053 out of 265,682—with the blood quantum of 8.4 percent (22,207) not reported. . . In the U.S. census of 1930, however, 46.3 percent—153,933 out of 332,397—were enumerated as full-bloods and 42.4 percent (141,101) were enumerated as mixed-bloods, with the degree of Indian blood of 11.2 percent (37,363) not reported. Thus, whereas the American Indian population size increased by slightly over 66,000 from 1910 to 1930, the number of full-blood American Indians increased by only 4,000; most of the increase was among mixed-blood Indians.[147]

Such trends have not only continued but accelerated. By 1970, approximately two-thirds of the marriages of those on the tribal rolls were to people who were not, with the result that only 59 percent of births reflected a situation in which both parents registered themselves as possessing any Indian blood at all.[148] The number of supposed full-bloods has correspondingly dropped to almost nothing—among populous peoples like the Minnesota/ Wisconsin Chippewa they now represent only 5 percent of the whole—while the proportion and composition of mixed-bloods has climbed dramatically.[149] At present rates of intermarriage, the segment of the federally recognized native population evidencing less than one-quarter degree blood quantum, presently about 4 percent, will have climbed to 59 percent or more by 2080.[150] To tighten or even adhere to quantum requirements in the face of such realities is to engage in a sort of autogenocide by definitional/statistical extermination.[151] As historian Patricia Nelson Limerick has observed in this connection:

> Set the blood quantum at one-quarter, hold to it as a rigid definition of Indians, let intermarriage proceed as it [has] for centuries, and eventually Indians will be defined out of existence. When that happens, the federal government will be freed of its persistent "Indian problem."[152]

Cognizant of this, some smaller peoples like the Umatillas in Oregon have already undertaken to preserve racial cant while offsetting the consequent prospect of definitional self-extinguishment by proposing revision of their constitutions to require that future enrollees demonstrate some degree of Umatilla blood, no matter how minute, in addition to "at least one-quarter degree of blood . . . in another federally recognized tribe or tribes."[153] Left conspicuously unexplained in such convoluted formulations is exactly how being a quarter-blood Lakota or Mohawk supposedly makes a person one whit more Umatilla than does being a full-blood Irishman, Ibo or Han. Nor is it explained why a person genealogically connected to the group should be less Umatilla in orientation, absent some sort of generic "Indian" genetic structure, than a person who has it.

The implications of such nonsense become most striking when it is considered in juxtaposition to the actual—rather than federally recognized—size of the present indigenous population of the United States, and the potential power deriving from its scale. Jack Forbes, perhaps the closest examiner of the issue, has noted that since 1969, "the Bureau of the Census, conspiring with the Office of Management and Budget and political special interests, has [deliberately obfuscated] the 'racial' character of the U.S. population and, as part of the process, has 'lost' some six to eight million persons of Native American ancestry and appearance with a scientifically useless 'Hispanic/Spanish' category. In addition, [seven million or more] persons of mixed African and Native American ancestry remain uncounted as such because of the way census questions were asked and the answers tallied."[154]

Forbes estimates that, even using standard blood quantum criteria, the actual native population of the "lower 48" in 1980 was well over fifteen million rather than the 1.4 million officially admitted by the Census Bureau.[155] Employing traditional indigenous methods of identifying population rather than racial criteria would have resulted in an even higher number. And, as of 1990, when the official count reached nearly two million, inclusion of these most rapidly growing sectors of the native population results in an aggregate of as many as thirty million persons overall.[156] The ability to wield political and economic clout inherent to the latter tally, as opposed to the former—which comes to less than .5 percent of the overall U.S. population—is self-evident.

Fortunately, there is at least one concrete example of how things might be taken in the direction of realizing this potential. The Cherokee Nation of Oklahoma (CNO), in its 1975 constitution, took the unprecedented step, still unparalleled by other twentieth-century indigenous governments, of completely dispensing with blood quantum requirements in its enrollment procedures. Instead, the CNO placed its reliance upon the more traditional genealogical mode of determining citizenship.[157] This had the effect of increasing the number of persons formally identified as Cherokees from fewer than 10,000 during the late 1950s to slightly over 232,000 by 1980 (and about 300,000 today).[158]

On this basis, the Cherokees, whose reservation was dissolved pursuant to the 1898 Curtis Act, have been able to assert what amounts to a split jurisdiction over their former territory.[159] Moreover, while much has been made by assorted race mongers about how this course of action was "diluting" whatever was left of "real" Cherokee culture and society, the precise opposite result has obtained in practice.

> The Oklahoma Cherokee, without a reservation landbase, have been able to survive tribally by an inclusive definition of what it is to be Cherokee. Their definition allowed relatively large numbers of people with Cherokee lineage but relatively small amounts of Cherokee blood into the tribe. This allowed the tribe to reestablish itself after virtual "dissolution" and to achieve political power in Oklahoma. The tribe, in turn, has protected a smaller group of full-blood, more traditional Cherokee from American non-Indian ways of life.[160]

Plainly, in and of itself, the CNO initiative has neither ended the internecine bickering over identity which has precluded anything resembling unity among native people, much less established the basis upon which to free even the Cherokees from internal colonial domination by the U.S. It does, however, represent a substantial stride in the right direction. If the model it embodies is ultimately seized and acted upon by a broadening spectrum of indigenous nations in the years ahead, the tools required for liberating Native North America may at long last be forged. In the alternative, should the currently predominating racialist perspectives associated with the IRA régimes prevail, the road to extinction can be traversed rather quickly.[161]

# Notes

1. On the general concept of the settler state, see, e.g., J. Sakai, *Settlers: The Myth of the White Proletariat* (Chicago: Morning Star Press, 1983); Robert Harmon Atkinson, *God's Peoples: Covenant and Land in South Africa, Israel and Ulster* (Ithaca, NY: Cornell University Press, 1992). A little-known and incomplete, but especially useful analysis is provided in Frank Parella's *Lebensraum and Manifest Destiny: A Comparative Study in the Justification of National Expansion* (Washington, D.C.: M.A. Thesis, Georgetown University, 1950). An interesting correlation between settler-state colonialism and genocide is drawn by Robert Melson in his "Provocation or Nationalism: A Critical Inquiry into the Armenian Genocide of 1915," in Richard G. Hovannisian, ed., *The Armenian Genocide in Perspective* (New Brunswick, NJ: Transaction Books, 1986).

2. For discussion, see Andres Rigo Sureda, *The Evolution of the Right to Self-Determination* (Leyden: A.W. Sythoff, 1973); Aureliu Cristescu, *The Right to Self-Determination: Historical and Current Developments on the Basis of United Nations Instruments* (U.N. Doc. E/CN.4/Sub.2/404/Rev.1) (1981); Michla Pomerance, *Self-Determination in Law and Practice* (The Hague: Marinus Nijhoff, 1982).

3. For the most extensive explanation of the concept at issue, see Michael Hector, *Internal Colonialism: The Celtic Fringe in British National Development, 1536-1966* (Berkeley: University of California Press, 1975). A seminal application of the idea to the circumstance of American Indians will be found in Robert K. Thomas, "Colonialism: Classic and Internal," *New University Thought*, Winter 1966-67. Also see Menno Boldt, "Social Correlates of Nationalism: A Study of Native Indian Leaders in a Canadian Internal Colony," *Comparative Political Studies*, Vol. 14, No. 2, Summer 1981; Ward Churchill, "Indigenous Peoples of the U.S.: A Struggle Against Internal Colonialism," *Black Scholar*, Vol. 16, No. 1, Feb. 1985.

4. An excellent and succinct analysis is presented in Aimé Césaire's *Discourse on Colonialism* (New York: Monthly Review Press, 1972). More broadly, see Immanuel Wallerstein, *The Modern World System* (New York: Academic Press, 1974); Albert Szymanski, *The Logic of Imperialism* (New York: Praeger, 1981).

5. "[A]ll peoples have an inalienable right to complete freedom, the exercise of their sovereignty and the integrity of their national territory. . . The subjection of peoples to alien subjugation, domination and exploitation constitutes a denial of fundamental human rights, is contrary to the Charter of the United Nations and is an impediment to the promotion of world peace and cooperation. . . Any attempt aimed at the partial or total disruption of the national unity and the territorial integrity of a country is incompatible with the purposes and principles of the Charter of the United Nations. . . All States shall observe . . . noninterference in the internal affairs of all States, and respect for the sovereign rights of all peoples and their territorial integrity"; Declaration on the Granting of Independence to Colonial Countries and Peoples (U.N.G.A. Res. 1514(XV), 15 U.N. GOAR, Supp. (No. 16) 66, U.N. Doc. A/4684 (1961)), adopted by the United Nations General Assembly, Dec. 14, 1960). The right of all peoples to self-determination, as well the procedures and structures by which a rapid, orderly and universal process of decolonization was/is to occur, was enunciated as a matter of international law in the Charter of the United Nations (59 Stat. 1031, T.S. No. 993, 3 Bevans 1153, 1976 Y.B.U.N. 1043, Oct. 24, 1945). Both texts are included in Burns H. Weston, Richard A. Falk and Anthony D'Amato, eds., *Basic Documents in International Law and World Order* (St. Paul, MN: West Publishing, 1990) pp. 343-4, 16-32.

6. As Albert Memmi puts it, "In order for the colonizer to be a complete master, it is not enough for him to be so in actual fact, but he must also believe in [the colonial system's] legitimacy. In order for that legitimacy to be complete, it is not enough for the colonized to be a slave, he must also accept his role"; *The Colonizer and the Colonized* (Boston: Beacon Press, 1965) p. 89.

7. Probably the best examination of this phenomenon will be found in Frantz Fanon, *Black Skin, White Masks: The Experiences of a Black Man in a White World* (New York: Grove Press, 1967). Useful insights are also provided in Fanon's more famous work, *The Wretched of the Earth* (New York: Grove Press, 1965).

8. In external rather than internal contexts, the principle is manifested in the form of neocolonialism; see, e.g., Jack Woodis, *Introduction to Neocolonialism* (New York: International Publishers, 1967).

9. A good overview is provided in Richard Falk, *Human Rights and State Sovereignty* (New York: Holmes & Meier, 1981).

10. For useful theoretical discourses on the necessity of "demystification" as a predicate to concrete activity, see J.G. Merquior, *The Veil and the Mask: Essays on Culture and Ideology* (London: Routledge & Kegan Paul, 1979).

11. The three groupings are designated by linguists and geneticists alike as being "Amerind," "Na-Dene," and "Eskimo-Aleut"; Joseph H. Greenberg, *Language in the Americas* (Stanford, CA: Stanford University Press, 1988). Of the trio, Amerind is by far the oldest and most extensive, demonstrating a continuous presence in the hemisphere for at least 40,000 years—and perhaps 70,000 years or longer—and encompassing most of the area from central Canada to Tierra del Fuego; L.S. Cressman, *Prehistory of the Far West: Homes of Vanquished Peoples* (Salt Lake City: University of Utah Press, 1977); Richard Wolkomir, "New Find Could Rewrite the Start of American History," *Smithsonian*, No. 21, March 1991. The current argument that there may have been a fourth stock is well-made in Theodore Schurr, et al., "Amerindian Mitochondrial DNAs Have Rare Asian Mutations at High Frequencies, Suggesting They Derived from Four Primary Maternal Lineages," *American Journal of Human Genetics*, No. 46, 1990; also see Satoshi Harai, et al., "Peopling of the Americas: Founded by Four Major Lineages of Mitochondrial DNA," *Molecular Biology of Evolution*, Vol. 10, No. 1, 1993.

12. This is reflected even in the standard anthropological literature. See generally, Fred Egan, ed., *The Social Anthropology of American Indian Tribes* (Chicago: University of Chicago Press, 1955). Or, for a more recent but far less comprehensive overview, see Jay Miller, "A Kinship of Spirit" in Alvin M. Josephy, ed., *America in 1492: The World of the Indian Peoples Before the Arrival of Columbus* (New York: Alfred A. Knopf, 1992).

13. See generally, Francis Jennings, *The Ambiguous Iroquois Empire: The Covenant Chain Confederation of Indian Tribes with the New England Colonies* (New York: W.W. Norton, 1984).

14. Probably the most succinct observation on this matter I ever heard was made by the revered Oglala Lakota leader, Frank Fools Crow, then 90 years old, during the 1981 Wounded Knee Memorial conducted in the village of Manderson, on the Pine Ridge Reservation. He did not know who might be a "full-blood" Lakota, Fools Crow said, before observing that he doubted there were any. His reasoning? He himself admitted to having a Cheyenne grandmother, a matter which in his opinion made him a "mixed-blood" in terms of his biological "Lakotaness." It should be noted that the elder's statement was clearly intended to impress the younger members of his audience about the ridiculousness of their preoccupation with blood quantum.

15. The evidence is strong that the fate of the Roanoke colonists was to be accepted ("naturalized") as tribal members ("citizens") by the Croatoans: "Many years later, in 1650, the Croatoan Indians migrated from Hatteras to mainland North Carolina, where they were known as the Lumbees. Some of them were fair-haired and blue-eyed. Among their family names were the names of Roanoke settlers such as Dial, and there was a curious singsong in their speech, reminiscent, it was said, of Elizabethan English"; Ted Morgan, *Wilderness at Dawn: The Settling of the North American Continent* (New York: Simon and Schuster, 1993) p. 82.

16. See, e.g. James Axtell, "The White Indians of Colonial America," in his *The European and the Indian: Essays in the Ethnohistory of North America* (New York: Oxford University Press, 1981) pp. 168-206.

17. Richard Drinnon, *Facing West: The Metaphysics of Indian-Hating and Empire-Building* (New York: Schocken, [2nd. ed.] 1990), pp. 3-34.

18. See generally, J. Norman Heard, *White into Red: A Study of the Assimilation of White Persons Captured by the Indians* (Meyuchen, NY: Scarecrow Press, 1973). Also see Richard Drinnon, *White Savage: The Case of John Dunn Hunter* (New York: Schocken Books, 1972).

19. "The Opinions of George Croughan on the American Indian," *Pennsylvania Magazine of History and Biography*, No. 71, 1947, p. 157; "Guy Johnson's Opinions on the American Indians," *Pennsylvania Magazine of History and Biography*, No. 77, 1953, p. 322.

20. Benjamin Franklin, letter to Peter Collinson, May 9, 1753; in Leonard W. Larabee, et al., eds., *The Papers of Benjamin Franklin, Vol. 4* (New Haven, CT: Yale University Press, 1959) pp. 481-2. For analysis, see Edward H. Ackerknect, "White Indians: Psychological and Physiological Peculiarities of White Children Abducted and Reared by North American Indians," *Bulletin of the History of Medicine*, No. 15, 1944.

21. Sylvester K. Stevens and Donald H. Kent, eds., *The Papers of Col. Henry Bouquet*, 19 vols. (Harrisburg: Pennsylvania State Historical Society, 1940-43) Vol. 17, p. 51.

22. Ibid., p. 38.

23. William Smith, D.D., *Historical Account of Colonel Bouquet's Expedition Against the Ohio Indians,*

*1764* (Philadelphia: 1765) p. 80. Also see William S. Ewing, "Indian Captives Released by Colonel Bouquet," *Western Pennsylvania Historical Magazine*, No. 39, 1956.

24. Young McCullough, who had been tied to a horse with his natural father's garters in an effort to prevent just such an eventuality, was able to continue life as a Shawnee for another year before being captured by the English and taken to Fort Pitt "under strong guard"; *A Narrative of the Captivity of John McCullough, Esq.*, in Archibald Loudon, ed., *A Selection, of Some of the Most Interesting Narratives, of Outrages, Committed by the Indians, in Their Wars, with the White People*, 2 vols. (Carlisle, PA, 1808-11) Vol. 1, pp. 326-7.

25. Bouquet, to his credit, ordered that she not be pursued as it was clear "she would be happier with her Chief than she would if restored to her home"; James Sullivan, et al., eds., *The Papers of Sir William Johnson* 14 vols. (Albany: State Historical Society of New York, 1921-62)Vol. 11, p. 496-8. Such fidelity, and there are many other examples which might be cited, puts the lie to the standard Euroamerican myth that female prisoners were routinely raped by their native captors. Even so anti-Indian a source as William Smith was forced to admit that he knew of no instance in which a white woman taken by Indians had actually been violated; *Bouquet's Expedition*, p. 78. Nor were white women captives customarily forced to marry Indian men. As another observer on the Bouquet expedition put it, "there has not been a solitary instance among them of any woman having her delicacy injured by being compelled to marry. They have been left liberty of choice, and those who chose to remain single were not sufferers on that account"; "Provincial Correspondence: 1750 to 1765," *Register of Pennsylvania*, No. 4, 1839, pp. 390-1.

26. Axtell, "White Indians," p. 177. He is quoting from *Bouquet's Expedition*, pp. 390-1; "Provincial Correspondence," p. 500; "Relation of Frederick Post of Conversation with Indians, 1760," *Pennsylvania Archives*, No. 3, 1853.

27. Examples are numerous. Consider for instance the case of Elizabeth Gilbert, a twelve-year-old adopted by a native family after being taken in a raid during 1782. When the English tried to ransom her two years later, her adoptive father, called John Huston by the colonists, responded that neither he nor his wife was willing to sell their "own flesh and blood" for any amount of money; William Walton, *The Captivity and Sufferings of Benjamin Gilbert and His Family, 1780-83* (Philadelphia, 1784) pp. 103, 107.

28. For example, John Huston's lifelong relationship with Elizabeth Gilbert, even after she'd been returned to her biological parents; ibid., p. 181. Or, to offer another illustration, Sir William Johnson observed that "a Canadian Indian [came regularly] to Schenectady to visit one Newkirk of that place, who was some years a Prisoner in his House, and sent home about a year ago with this Indian's sister, who came with her Brother now purely to see Said Newkirk whom she calls her Son and is very fond of"; *Johnson Papers*, Vol. 10, p. 160; Vol. 11, p. 728. And again, the adoptive Shawnee parents of O.M. Spencer visited him annually, after he'd been "restored to civilization"; O.M. Spencer, *The Indian Captivity of O.M. Spencer* (New York: 1835). The same pertained to Thomas Ridout, another adopted Shawnee, for at least eleven years after his "release"; Thomas Ridout, "An Account of My Capture By the Shawanese Indians," *Blackburn's Magazine*, No. 223, 1928 reprint of 1788 original. The list goes on and on.

29. This tendency is remarked upon by Brewton Berry in the first chapter of his *Almost White: A Study of Certain Racial Hybrids in the Eastern United States* (New York: Macmillan, 1963).

30. Other factors entering into this circumstance have to do with missionaries assigning "Christian" names to Indians during baptismals and federal bureaucrats performing similar acts during the compilation of tribal rolls, mostly during the nineteenth century. See generally, Robert F. Berkhofer, Jr., *Salvation and the Savage: An Analysis of Protestant Missions and American Indian Response, 1787-1862* (New York: Atheneum, 1972; Clyde A. Milner II and Floyd A. O'Neil, eds., *Churchmen and the Western Indians, 1820-1920* (Norman: University of Oklahoma Press, 1985).

31. See Jack D. Forbes, *Black Africans and Native Americans: Race, Color and Caste in the Making of Red-Black Peoples* (London: Routledge, 1988). Also see William Katz, *Black Indians* (New York: Macmillan, 1986); bell hooks, "Revolutionary 'renegades': Native Americans, African Americans, and Black Indians," in her *Black Looks* (Boston: South End Press, 1992).

32. By 1800, the Seminoles consisted of about two-thirds Yamasee, Apalachee, Guale, Cofitachiqui and Timucuan Indians, the rest being of African descent. A few years later, in the aftermath of the Red Sticks War, a large group of Lower Creeks was also incorporated; Peter H. Wood, "The Changing Population of the Colonial South: An Overview by Race and Region, 1685-1790," in Peter H. Wood,

Gregory A. Waselkov and M. Thomas Hatley, eds., *Powhatan's Mantle: Indians in the Colonial Southeast* (Lincoln: University of Nebraska Press, 1989).

33. Jack D. Forbes, *Africans and Native Americans: The Language of Race and the Evolution of Red-Black Peoples* (Urbana: University of Illinois Press, [2nd. ed.] 1993) pp. 249-64. At least one credible analyst has gone further, asserting that the "available evidence indicates that the ethnic mixture between Indians and Negroes is of vastly greater proportions than has hitherto been realized. . . The American Negro population of today is a composite of African, White and Indian elements"; M.F. Ashley Montagu, "Origins of the American Negro," *Psychiatry*, Vol. 7, 1944.

34. This simplistically racist theme is pursued to a greater or lesser extent in much of the literature. For a recent example, see Edward Lazarus, *Black Hills, White Justice: The Sioux Nation versus the United States, 1775 to the Present* (New York: HarperCollins, 1991).

35. The U.S. waged three separate wars against the Seminoles during the first half of the nineteenth century. During the first pair, for "every two Seminoles who were sent West, one soldier died—1,500 in all. The war cost the federal government $20 million, and it ended in 1842 not through any victory on either side, but because the government simply stopped trying to flush out the remaining Seminoles who had hidden themselves deep in the Everglades"; John K. Mahon, *History of the Second Seminole War, 1835-1842* (Gainesville: University of Florida Press, 1967). The third campaign, which was pursued against these remnants from 1855 to 1858, was even less conclusive; Alan Axelrod, *Chronicle of the Indian Wars from Colonial Times to Wounded Knee* (New York: Prentice Hall, 1993) pp. 146-7.

36. Rachael E. Eaton, *John Ross and the Cherokee People* (Muskogee, OK: Cherokee National Museum, 1921); Walter H. Conser, Jr., "John Ross and the Cherokee Resistance Campaign, 1833-1838," *Journal of Southern History*, No. 44, 1978.

37. The elder Ridge's honorific was bestowed in recognition of his service to the U.S. in leading a force of Cherokee volunteers under overall command of Andrew Jackson against the Creek Redsticks in 1814. Son John led the small group which, secretly and in direct defiance of some 90 percent of all Cherokees, signed the treasonous Treaty of New Echota in December 1835, purportedly committing their nation to Removal. As a consequence, John Ridge and several of his associates were assassinated in Oklahoma in the years following the Trail of Tears. His son, John Rollin Ridge, was effectively exiled from the Cherokee Nation for most of his life; Thurman Wilkins, *Cherokee Tragedy: The Ridge Family and the Decimation of a People* (Norman: University of Oklahoma Press, [2nd ed.] 1986); James W. Parins, *John Rollin Ridge: His Life and Works* (Lincoln: University of Nebraska Press, 1991). The bitter factionalism among Cherokees resulting from Ridge's course of action lasted well into the twentieth century and is still somewhat in evidence to this day; see generally, Morris L. Wardell, *A Political History of the Cherokee Nation, 1838-1907* (Norman: University of Oklahoma Press, 1977 reprint of 1938 original); Duane H. King, *The Cherokee Nation: A Troubled History* (Knoxville: University of Tennessee Press, 1979). For the text of the Treaty of New Echota (7 Stat. 478; proclaimed May 23, 1836), see Charles Kappler, ed., *Indian Treaties, 1778-1885* (New York: Interland, 1973) pp. 439-49.

38. The case of Cynthia Ann Parker is one of the more celebrated of the so-called captive narratives, serving loosely as the basis for the 1956 John Ford/John Wayne film, *The Searchers*. Taken as a nine-year-old during one of the Comanches' almost continuous raids along the Texas frontier in May 1836, she was raised as a Quahadi and was plainly viewed as such (not least, by herself). After being forcibly "restored" to white society in 1860—her husband and several friends were killed in the process—she wasted steadily away and eventually died of what was described as a "broken heart"; Cynthia Schmidt Hacker, *Cynthia Ann Parker: The Life and the Legend* (El Paso: Texas Western Press, 1990).

39. Bill Neeley, *The Last Comanche Chief: The Life and Times of Quanah Parker* (New York: John Wiley, 1995).

40. Probably the best all-round study of the Bent family is David Lavender's *Bent's Fort* (Garden City, NY: Doubleday, 1954). Also see Samuel P. Arnold, "William Bent," in LeRoy R. Hafen, ed., *The Mountain Men and the Fur Trade in the Far West*, 8 vols. (Glendale, CA: Arthur H. Clark, 1965-71) Vol. 6, pp. 61-84.

41. It is instructive that while William Bent and his son George are frequently referenced in the literature, there is virtually no mention of Charlie. When his name comes up at all, it is almost invariably as a negative aside. On the Crazy Dogs, see, e.g., George Bird Grinnell, *The Fighting Cheyennes* (Norman: University of Oklahoma Press, 1956).

42. On Crazy Horse's rapid-fire defeats of a large column of troops under General George Crook at the Rosebud Creek on June 17, 1876, and decimation of Lt. Colonel George Armstrong Custer's 7th Cavalry at the Little Big Horn on June 25, see John E. Gray, *The Centennial Campaign: The Sioux War of 1876* (Norman: University of Oklahoma Press, 1988). Also see Stephen E. Ambrose, *Crazy Horse and Custer: The Parallel Lives of Two American Warriors* (Garden City, NY: Doubleday, 1975).

43. Mari Sandoz, *Crazy Horse: Strange Man of the Oglalas* (Lincoln: University of Nebraska Press, 1961).

44. See, e.g., James C. Olsen, *Red Cloud and the Sioux Problem* (Lincoln: University of Nebraska Press, 1965).

45. Robert A. Clark, ed., *The Killing of Chief Crazy Horse* (Lincoln: University of Nebraska Press, 1976).

46. John M. Carroll, ed., *The Arrest and Killing of Sitting Bull* (Glendale, CA: Arthur H. Clark, 1986); Thomas Dunlay, *Wolves for the Blue Soldiers: Indian Scouts and Auxiliaries with the U.S. Army, 1860-90* (Lincoln: University of Nebraska Press, 1982); Obie B. Faulk, *The Geronimo Campaign* (New York: Oxford University Press, 1969).

47. On Crow Dog's killing of Spotted Tail, see Leonard Crow Dog and Richard Erdoes, *Crow Dog: Four Generations of Sioux Medicine Men* (New York: HarperCollins, 1995) pp. 27-39.

48. Jim Beckwourth as told to Thomas D. Bonner, *The Life and Adventures of James P. Beckwourth* (Lincoln: University of Nebraska Press, 1971 reprint of 1866 original).

49. Quisling was a leading Norwegian collaborator with the German invaders of his country during the Second World War. Executed in October 1945, his name continues to be virtually synonymous with treason; Paul M. Hayes, *Quisling: The Career and Political Ideas of Vikdun Quisling, 1887-1945* (Bloomington: Indiana University Press, 1972).

50. There is a rather substantial literature on this point. One of the better overviews is presented in William Stanton's *The Leopard's Spots: Scientific Attitudes Towards Race in America, 1815-1859* (Chicago: University of Chicago Press, 1960). Concerning phrenology in particular, see John D. Davies, *Phrenology: Fad and Science; A Nineteenth Century American Crusade* (New Haven: Yale University Press, 1955). On the especially sinister role played by American intellectuals in developing the concept of eugenics ("racial hygiene"), see Stefan Kühl, *The Nazi Connection: Eugenics, American Racism, and German National Socialism* (New York: Oxford University Press, 1994).

51. A current example of this sort of tripe is the ponderous but highly touted tome coauthored by Richard J. Herrstein and Charles Murray entitled *The Bell Curve: Intelligence and Class Structure in American Life* (New York: Free Press, 1994), in which the authors purportedly prove that whites enjoy a congenital disposition of IQ rivaled only by Asians and, in varying degrees, vastly superior to that exhibited by blacks, hispanics and American Indians. Despite their proliferate deployment of graphs and charts, however, and their citation of myriad studies supposedly all leading up to their grand conclusion, Herrstein and Murray leave more than a few glaring gaps in their argument. They can't, for example, explain what "IQ" is (or even what it's supposed to be, with any degree of clarity), much less how it might be genetically transmitted. Nor, for that matter, do they even begin to define the presumed genetic composition of "hispanic"—a cultural/linguistic rather than biological designator—one of the groups to which they attribute "heritable" characteristics. For further analysis, see Russell Jacoby and Naomi Glauberman, eds., *The Bell Curve Debate: History, Documents, Opinions* (New York: Times Books, 1995). Broader perspectives on the implications of contemporary racial/biological scientism will be found in Troy Duster's *Backdoor to Eugenics* (London: Routledge, 1990) and R.C. Lwontin's *Biology as Ideology: The Doctrine of DNA* (New York: HarperPerennial, 1992).

52. Samuel George Morton, *Crania Americana, or, A Comparative View of the Skulls of Various Aboriginal Nations of North and South America to Which is Prefixed an Essay on the Varieties of the Human Species* (Philadelphia: John Pennington, 1839); also see his *Inquiry into the Distinctive Characteristics of the Aboriginal Race of America* (Philadelphia: John Pennington, 1844) and *Observations on the Ethnography and Archaeology of the American Aborigines* (New Haven, CT: Yale University Press, 1846). Morton's "craniometric method" was to fill specimen skulls with various materials—seeds were used at one point, buckshot at another—in order to measure cranial capacity, the premise being that this would correspond to brain size (true), and that this, in turn, would correspond to innate intelligence (false). By computing average cranial capacity

by race, he claimed to have thereby empirically demonstrated the inherent intellectual superiority of whites as compared to American Indians (and eventually all other non-whites as well). Although widely acclaimed at the time—by whites—the idea ultimately reduces to the absurdity that, even within the same race, a larger person "must" be smarter than a smaller one simply because his/her head is bigger. Whether or not Morton himself actually believed such patent nonsense is questionable insofar as he demonstrably rigged his measurements to obtain the desired results; Stephen Jay Gould, *The Mismeasure of Man* (New York: W.W. Norton, 1981) pp. 57-60. Be that as it may, the extent to which his and a raft of comparably psuedoscientific claptrap was popularized at the time is well examined in Madeleine Stern's *Heads and Headliners: The Phrenological Fowlers* (Norman: University of Oklahoma Press, 1971).

53. Overall, see Reginald Horsman, *Race and Manifest Destiny: The Origins of Racial Anglo-Saxonism* (Cambridge: Harvard University Press, 1981). On the justifications advanced for slavery in particular, see George M. Frederickson, *The Black Image in the White Mind: The Debate on Afro-American Character and Destiny, 1817-1914* (New York: Harper & Row, 1971).

54. Domestic breeding of blacks for the slave markets of America, always a lucrative enterprise, became an imperative during the early nineteenth century, once British efforts to end the transatlantic trade began to choke off the flow of chattel from Africa; Seymour Drescher, "The Ending of the Slave Trade and the Evolution of European Scientific Racism," in Joseph E. Inikori and Stanley L. Engerman, eds., *The Atlantic Slave Trade: Effects on Economies, Societies, and Peoples in Africa, the Americas, and Europe* (Durham, NC: Duke University Press, 1992).

55. The system appears to have been adapted from the far more comprehensive set of categories developed by the Spanish and Portuguese for use in Central and South America. The Latino schema, unlike its North American derivative, included classifications for black/Indian, Indian/white, and black/white/Indian admixtures; see, e.g., Magnus Mörner, *Race Mixture in the History of Latin America* (Boston: Little, Brown, 1967) p. 58; Nicolás Sánchez-Alboronoz, *The Population of Latin America: A History* (Berkeley: University of California Press, 1974) pp. 129-30.

56. For one of the better elaborations and analyses, see John Codman Hurd, *The Law of Freedom and Bondage in the United States* (New York: Negro Universities Press, 1968).

57. Perhaps the greatest conundrum confronting U.S. jurists during the early days of the republic was the fact that aboriginal peoples were clearly vested with property rights vis-à-vis their territories under the Doctrine of Discovery and other elements of international law; Robert A. Williams, Jr., *The American Indian in Western Legal Thought: The Discourses of Conquest* (New York: Oxford University Press, 1990). The nature of the logical/juridical subterfuges employed by Chief Justice John Marshall in his sustained effort to transcend this problem is analyzed in my "Perversions of Justice: Examining the Doctrine of U.S. Rights to Occupancy in North America," in this volume.

58. The premise was/is two-fold. First, under the principle that "vacant land" (*territorium res nullius*) could be claimed outright by whoever was willing to occupy and develop it, the U.S. incurred a clear official interest in pretending that, not only were there not large numbers of native peoples present in North America by the late eighteenth century, but there never had been (this is a theme still pursued with a vengeance by America's academic apologists and other professional liars). Second, by defining an ever-increasing proportion of even admitted indigenous populations out of existence on racial grounds, federal policymakers could conveniently negate much—sometimes all—of their residual property interests (this, too, is an ongoing theme). It should be noted that such factual/definitional manipulation was by no means the only manner in which native "disappearance" was achieved. Outright physical eradication of numerous native peoples, either partially or completely, was also an integral aspect of the process; for a more detailed and comprehensive examination of these issues, see my *A Little Matter of Genocide: Holocaust and Denial in the Americas* (San Francisco: City Lights, 1997). Also see the relevant sections of Russell Thornton's *American Indian Holocaust and Survival: A Population History Since 1492* (Norman: University of Oklahoma Press, 1987) and David E. Stannard's *American Holocaust: Columbus and the Conquest of the New World* (New York: Oxford University Press, 1992).

59. See, e.g., chapters 7 and 8 in Forbes, *Africans and Native Americans*. Also see Edward B. Reuter, *Race Mixture: Studies in Intermarriage and Miscegenation* (New York: McGraw-Hill, 1931).

60. This is essentially the same system of racial classification later adopted for somewhat different purposes by South Africa (albeit, the Afrikaners were concerned with East Indians rather than American

Indians intermixed with blacks). A detailed overview of how U.S. racial policies served as a model for South African practice will be found in George M. Frederickson's *White Supremacy: A Comparative Study in American and South African History* (New York: Oxford University Press, 1981). For examples in the U.S. outside the Deep South, see Joel Williamson, *The New People: Miscegenation and Mulattoes in the United States* (New York: Free Press, 1980).

61. Quoted in Julie Schimmel, "Inventing the Indian" in William H. Truettner, ed., *The West as America: Reinterpreting Images of the Frontier, 1820-1920* (Washington, D.C.: Smithsonian Institution Press, 1991) p. 174. On "unintendedly" genocidal implications of Jefferson's perspective, see Bernard W. Sheehan, *Seeds of Extinction: Jeffersonian Philanthropy and the American Indian* (Chapel Hill: University of North Carolina Press, 1973).

62. The characterization of Jefferson accrues from Stannard, *American Holocaust*, p. 120. On the nature, extent and quality of native agriculture (which greatly surpassed that of Europe on all counts), see Jack Weatherford, *Indian Givers: How the Indians of the Americas Transformed the World* (New York: Fawcett Columbine, 1988).

63. Quoted in Horsman, *Race and Manifest Destiny*, p. 108.

64. The notion that Indians might be "redeemed" through acculturation to "civilized" ways dates back at least as far as the arguments put forth in their regard by Bartolomé de Las Casas at Valladolid in 1550; see Lewis Hanke, *Aristotle and the Indians: A Study in Race Prejudice in the Modern World* (Chicago: Henry Regnery, 1959); *All Mankind Is One: A Study in the Disputation Between Bartolomé de Las Casas and Juan Ginés de Sepúlveda on the Intellectual and Religious Capacity of American Indians* (DeKalb: Northern Illinois University Press, 1974). In the U.S., a somewhat derivative argument—that apparent racial distinctions were "environmentally induced," and that Indians (and blacks) were thus as fully human as whites—was advanced by Samuel Stanhope Smith in his *Essay on the Causes of Variety of Complexion and Figure in the Human Species* (Cambridge: Harvard University Press, 1965 reprint of 1810 enlargement of 1787 original). The idea that the "Five Civilized Tribes" might be examples of this native potential was expounded by Secretary of War Henry Knox, among others, as early as 1792; Reginald Horsman, *Expansion and American Indian Policy, 1783-1812* (East Lansing: Michigan State University Press, 1967) pp. 54-65.

65. Quoted in Robert F. Berkhofer, Jr., *The White Man's Indian: Images of the American Indian from Columbus to the Present* (New York: Vintage, 1979) pp. 58-9. Unsurprisingly, Nott, along with his subsequent collaborator and coauthor, George R. Gliddon, ended up being a staunch advocate of racial wars of extermination in a manner which clearly prefigured Hitler: "Nations and races, like individuals, have an especial destiny: some to rule, and others to be ruled. . . No two distinctly marked races can dwell together on equal terms. Some races, moreover, seem destined to live and prosper for a time, until the destroying race comes, which is to exterminate and supplant them. . . [H]uman progress has arisen mainly from the war of the races. All the great impulses which have been given to it from time to time have been the results of conquests and colonizations"; J.C. Nott and George R. Gliddon, *Types of Mankind, or Ethical Researches, Based upon the Ancient Monuments, Paintings, Sculptures, and Crania of Races, and upon their Natural, Geographical, Philosophical, and Biblical History* (Philadelphia: Lippencott, Grambo, 1854) pp. 77, 79. For an example of Morton's encouragement of Nott's "research," see his letter in *Southern Quarterly Review*, No. 8, July 1845.

66. Quoted in R.W. Haskins, *History and Progress of Phrenology* (Buffalo, NY: n.p., 1839) pp. 110-11. Like Nott and Gliddon, Caldwell would become an open advocate of physical genocide. "Civilization," he opined, "is destined to exterminate [Indians], in common with wild animals"; Charles Caldwell, *Thoughts on the Original Unity of the Human Race* (New York: Harper Bros., 1830) p. 151. Varying analyses, all cogent, will be found in Roy Harvey Pearce, *The Savages of America: A Study of the Indian and the Idea of Civilization* (Baltimore: Johns Hopkins University Press, [2nd ed.] 1965); Richard Slotkin, *Regeneration Through Violence: The Mythology of the American Frontier, 1600-1860* (Middletown, CT: Wesleyan University Press, 1973); Brian Dippie, *The Vanishing American: White Attitudes and American Indian Policy* (Middletown, CT: Wesleyan University Press, 1982) esp. chap 2.

67. Quoted in Robert E. Beider, *Science Encounters the Indian, 1820-1880: The Early Years of American Ethnology* (Norman: University of Oklahoma Press, 1986) p. 220. Morgan has generally been cast as a "progressive," given that Karl Marx and Freidrich Engels were heavily influenced by his *League of the Ho-*

*de-no-sau-nee or Iroquois* (New York: Dodd, Meade, 1851) while preparing their book, *The Origins of the Family, Private Property and the State* (1884), included in *Marx and Engels: Selected Writings, Vol. 3* (Moscow: Foreign Language Publishers, 1973). *Origins*, in turn, has been highly touted by (white) socialist-feminists, then and now; see, e.g., Sheila Rowbotham, *Women, Resistance and Revolution: A History of Women and Revolution in the Modern World* (New York: Pantheon, 1972). In actuality, Morgan was not only a staunch eugenicist, as the statement quoted herein amply demonstrates, but a racist of what would now be called the "New Age" variety, belonging as he did to a peculiar precursor of Robert Bly's contemporary "Men's Movement" dubbed "The Grand Order of the Iroquois"; Michael Kammen, *Mystic Chords of Memory: The Transformation of Tradition in American Culture* (Ithaca, NY: Cornell University Press, 1991) p. 86. A sharing of some of these less remarked upon attributes may go some distance in explaining the virulent racism embodied in Marx's and Engels' endorsement of European colonialism in the Third World; see, e.g., Walker Connor, *The National Question in Marxist-Leninist Theory and Strategy* (Princeton, NJ: Princeton University Press, 1984) esp. chap 2. It may also offer insight into similar repugnant attitudes among feminists; for commentary and analysis, see bell hooks, *Ain't I A Woman: black women and feminism* (Boston: South End Press, 1981); *Feminist Theory: from margin to center* (Boston: South End Press, 1984). For broader overviews of Morgan and his work, see Bernard J. Stern, *Lewis Henry Morgan: Social Evolutionist* (New York: Russell and Russell, 1931); Carl Resek, *Lewis Henry Morgan: American Scholar* (Chicago: University of Chicago Press, 1960).

68. Again, the Deep South seems to have served as something of a model; see William S. Willis, "Divide and Rule: Red, White and Black in the Southeast," *Journal of Negro History*, Vol. 48, 1963.

69. For a good overview of this evolution, see Francis Paul Prucha, *Americanizing the American Indian: Writings of the "Friends of the Indian," 1800-1900* (Lincoln: University of Nebraska Press, 1973). Also see George D. Harmon, *Sixty Years of Indian Affairs: Political, Economic, and Diplomatic, 1789-1850* (Chapel Hill: University of North Carolina Press, 1941).

70. The Moravians, who were the first missionaries to be admitted by the Cherokees, had begun their efforts to establish a foothold in that people at least as early as 1735. They were unsuccessful until, having received federal backing four years earlier, they were able to arrange a formal meeting with the Cherokee National Council in 1799. The first mission in Cherokee country opened a year later; Edmund Schwarz, *History of the Moravian Missions among the Southern Indian Tribes of the United States* (Bethlehem, PA: Times Publishing, 1923). Also see Eugene C. Routh, "Early Missionaries to the Cherokees," *Chronicles of Oklahoma*, No. 15, 1937; Henry T. Malone, "The Early Nineteenth Century Missionaries in the Cherokee Country," *Tennessee Historical Quarterly*, No. 10, 1951. On broader federal policy during this seminal period, see Francis Paul Prucha, *American Indian Policy in the Formative Years: The Trade and Intercourse Acts, 1790-1834* (Cambridge: Harvard University Press, 1962).

71. William G. McLoughlin, *Cherokees and Missionaries, 1789-1839* (New Haven: Yale University Press, 1984) p. 26. It is reliably estimated that about a quarter of all Cherokees were mixed-bloods by 1825, although the missionary practice of seeking them out led to gross overestimations of their numbers, e.g., as early as 1805 federal agent Return J. Meigs reported that "the numbers of the real Indians and those of Mixed blood are nearly equal"; National Archives, Microfilm Record Group M-208. On the early Presbyterian missions in particular, see Harold S. Faust, "The Growth of Presbyterian Missions to the American Indians," *Journal of the Presbyterian Historical Society*, No. 22, 1944. "Aryanism," the belief that northern European "Germanic" peoples represent a sort of supreme gene pool, even among whites, was explained rather succinctly by J.C. Nott: "The ancient German may be regarded as the parent stock from which the highest modern civilization has sprung. The best blood of France and England is German; the ruling caste in Russia is German; and look at the United States, and contrast our people to the dark-skinned Spaniards. It is clear that the dark-skinned Celts are fading away before the superior race, and that they must eventually be absorbed"; J.C. Nott, *Two Lectures on the Connection between the Biblical and Physical History of Man* (New York: Negro Press, undated reprint of 1849 original) pp. 36-7. For later adaptations of such notions, see Robert Cecil, *The Myth of the Master Race: Alfred Rosenberg and Nazi Ideology* (New York: Dodd Meade, 1972). Overall, see Léon Poliakov, *The Aryan Myth: A History of Racist and Nationalistic Ideas in Europe* (New York: Barnes & Noble, 1971).

72. The clearest evidence of this was "White Path's Rebellion" in 1827-28, when traditionalists led by Nunnatsunega (White Path), one of the most respected elder chiefs, attempted to displace

missionary-aligned factions altogether. Although this has often been cast as a "full-blood/mixed-blood dispute" the reality, as is shown by notes 36 and 37 above, was hardly so simple. One of the better discussions will be found in W.G. McLoughlin and Walter H. Conser, Jr., "The Cherokees in Transition," *Journal of American History*, Vol. 64, No. 3, 1977. For overly sympathetic but nonetheless informative analyses of corresponding federal initiatives and responses, see Herman J. Viola, *Thomas L. McKinney: Architect of America's Early Indian Policy, 1816-1830* (Chicago: Sage Books, 1974); Ronald D. Satz, *American Indian Policy in the Jacksonian Era* (Lincoln: University of Nebraska Press, 1975).

73. See, e.g., Berkhofer, *Salvation and the Savage*; R. Pierce Beaver, *Church, State and the American Indian: Two and a Half Centuries of Partnership in Missions Between Protestant Churches and the Government* (St. Louis: Concordia, 1966), Henry W. Bowden, *American Indians and Christian Missions* (Chicago: University of Chicago Press, 1981). The Lower Creeks exhibited by far the sharpest response, their "recalcitrant" faction—called "Red Sticks" (*Baton Rouge*)—going to war in 1814 in an all-out attempt to drive the missionaries, white settlers and anyone aligned with them out of their territory; Joel W. Martin, *Sacred Revolt: The Muskogees' Struggle for a New World* (Boston: Beacon Press, 1991).

74. For explication of the point that early U.S. treatymaking with Indians was motivated by the need to obtain native recognition, see Vine Deloria, Jr., "Sovereignty," in Roxanne Dunbar Ortiz and Larry Emerson, eds., *Economic Development in American Indian Reservations* (Albuquerque: Native American Studies Center, University of New Mexico, 1979). On the background of European treatymaking with indigenous nations, see Dorothy V. Jones, *License for Empire: Colonialism by Treaty in Early Colonial America* (Chicago: University of Chicago Press, 1982).

75. 7 Stat. 160; proc. Jan. 4, 1819; text in Kappler, *Indian Treaties*, pp. 145-52. The other indigenous peoples were the Senecas, Lenni Lenapes (Delawares), Shawnees, Potawatomies, Ottawas and Chippewas.

76. There are 53 such instances in the incomplete compilation of 371 ratified treaty texts assembled by Kappler. There may, of course, be other examples among the dozen or so uncompiled instruments. More than 400 additional treaties went unratified for one reason or another. The pattern evident in the ratified instruments is doubtless reflected in these as well; conversation with Vine Deloria, Jr., April 1993.

77. 9 Stat. 904, proc. Apr. 3, 1848; Kappler, *Indian Treaties*, pp. 567-8. Other examples include 1866 treaties with the Seminoles (14 Stat. 755, proclaimed Aug. 16, 1866; ibid., pp. 910-15), Choctaw and Chickasaw (14 Stat. 769, proc. July 10, 1866; ibid., pp. 918-31); Creeks (14 Stat. 785, proc. Aug. 11, 1866; ibid., pp. 931-7) and Cherokee (14 Stat. 799, proc. Aug. 11, 1866; ibid. pp. 942-50). The second article of the Seminole, Creek and Cherokee treaties provide that blacks living among the Indians, whether full- or mixed-blood, "shall have and enjoy all the rights of native citizens." Articles 26 and 28 of the Choctaw/Chickasaw treaty acknowledged that "all persons who have become citizens by adoption or intermarriage of either of said nations, or who may hereinafter become such" would be accorded the right of any other Choctaw or Chickasaw, and that every "white person who, having married a Choctaw or Chickasaw, resides in the said Choctaw or Chickasaw Nation[s], or who has been adopted by the legislative authorities, shall be subject to the laws of the Choctaw and Chickasaw Nations according to his [or her] domicile, and to prosecution and trial before their tribunals, and to punishment according to their laws in all respects as though he was a native Choctaw or Chickasaw." A variation enunciated in the seventh article of the Cherokee treaty, repeated in various other instruments in which "consolidation of tribes" was effected, is that "other Indians" might be considered as naturalized Cherokees.

78. 7 Stat. 160. Related examples include the 1819 Treaty with the Chippewa (7 Stat. 203, proc. Mar. 25, 1820) in which three mixed-bloods named Riley are singled out to receive 640-acre tracts; the 1824 Treaty with the Quapaw (7 Stat. 232, proc. Feb. 19, 1825; ibid., pp. 210-11), Article 7 of which names mixed-bloods to receive their own parcels; the 1826 Treaty with the Chippewa (7 Stat. 290, proc. Feb. 7, 1827; ibid., pp. 268-73), Article 4 of which lists "half-breeds" assigned individual parcels; the 1829 Treaty with the Winnebago ( 7 Stat. 323, proc. Jan. 2, 1830; ibid., pp. 300-3), Article V of which lists mixed-bloods to receive individuals parcels; the 1830 Treaty with the Choctaw (7 Stat. 233, proc. Feb. 24, 1830; ibid., pp. 310-9), which, by an separate appended article (7 Stat. 340), sets out a long list of white men and mixed-bloods to receive personal tracts; the 1831 Treaty with the Ottawa (7 Stat. 359, proc. Apr. 6, 1832; ibid., pp. 335-9), Article XIV of which sets aside land specifically for "half-blood Ottoways" Hiram Theobault and William McNabb; the 1842 Treaty with the Wyandot (11 Stat. 581, proc. Oct. 5, 1842;

ibid. pp. 534-7), Article 4 of which allots parcels to specific individuals deemed "Wyandotts by blood or adoption"; the 1863 Treaty with the Red Lake and Pembina Bands of Chippewa (13 Stat. 667, proc. Mar. 1, 1864; ibid., pp. 853-5), Article 8 of which specifies that each "male half-breed or mixed blood who is related by blood to said Chippewas" will receive an individual 160-acre parcel; the 1865 Treaty with the Cheyenne and Arapaho (14 Stat. 704, proc. Feb. 2, 1867; ibid., pp. 887-91), Article 5 of which posits a whole list of mixed-bloods drawn from the Bent, Guerrier and other families to receive 640 acres each.

79. 7 Stat. 189, proc. Jan. 15, 1819; ibid., pp. 171-4. Another example is the 1826 Treaty with the Potawatomi (7 Stat. 295, proc. Feb. 7, 1827; ibid., pp. 273-7), Article 6 of which sets out a long list of mixed-bloods and intermarried whites to receive parcels along with designated chiefs.

80. 10 Stat. 1172, proc. Mar. 3, 1855; ibid., pp. 690-3. Another example is the 1855 Treaty with the Chippewa (10 Stat. 1165, proc. Mar. 3, 1855; ibid., pp. 685-9), Article 6 of which specifies that mixed-bloods and named missionaries will each receive 80-acre parcels.

81. Under Article 2d, $300,000 was placed in trust as compensation to the people as a whole for a land cession, while an additional $110,000 was allocated for payment to individual mixed-bloods of "one-quarter or more degree"; 7 Stat. 538, proc. June 15, 1838; ibid., pp. 493-4. Other examples include the 1833 Treaty with the Chippewa (7 Stat. 431, proc. Feb. 21, 1835; ibid., pp. 402-15), "Schedule A" of which sets out a long list of mixed-bloods meant to receive varying amounts of money "in lieu of land"; the 1837 Treaty with the Chippewa (7 Stat. 536, proc. June 15, 1838; ibid., pp. 491-3), Article 3 of which provides for special $100 payments to mixed-bloods; and the 1842 Treaty with the Chippewa (7 Stat. 591, proc. Mar. 23, 1843; ibid., pp. 542-5), Article IV of which allocates $15,000 for distribution among mixed-bloods. A novel variation here comes in the 1835 Treaty with the Cherokee (7 Stat. 478, proc. May 25, 1836; ibid., pp. 439-49), an addendum to which (7 Stat. 487) schedules payment to Osage "half-breeds" for land taken from their people by the U.S. to be reassigned to Cherokees removed to Oklahoma. Examples in which other special provisions are made for mixed-bloods include the 1836 Treaty with the Ottawa and Chippewa (7 Stat. 491, proc. May 27, 1836; ibid., pp. 450-6); the 1836 Treaty with the Menominee (7 Stat. 506, proc. Feb. 15, 1837; ibid., pp. 463-6); and both 1836 Treaties with the Sauk and Fox (7 Stat. 517, proc. Feb. 27, 1837; ibid., pp. 474-5; 7 Stat. 520, proc. Dec. 13, 1837; ibid., pp. 476-8).

82. Article 2 provides that each Indian will be assigned an individual 40-acre plot, while a "P.S.," added by the Senate post hoc, provides that two mixed-bloods, George Bent and Jack Smith, would be allotted 640 acres apiece; 12 Stat. 1163, proc. Dec. 5, 1861; ibid., pp. 807-11. A comparable example is found in the 1859 Treaty with the Sauk and Fox (15 Stat. 467, proc. July 9, 1860; ibid., pp. 796-9), Article 2 of which specifies that Indians would be assigned 80-acre plots while, under Article 10, mixed-bloods and women married to whites were allotted parcels of 320 acres each. In the 1848 Treaty with the Menominee (9 Stat. 952, proc. Jan. 23, 1849; ibid., pp. 572-4) Article 4 provides that $30,000 will be paid to chiefs, $40,000 to mixed-bloods.

83. Under Article 9, individually titled parcels are set aside for mixed-bloods wishing to live apart from their people; 11 Stat. 729, proc. Mar. 31, 1858; ibid., pp. 764-7. Other examples include the 1819 Treaty with the Cherokee (7 Stat. 195, proc. Mar. 10, 1819; ibid., pp. 177-81), Article 3 of which sets out a list of mixed-bloods to receive individually titled parcels separate from their nation; the 1830 Treaty with the Sauk and Fox (7 Stat. 328, proc. Feb. 24, 1831; ibid., pp. 305-10), Articles IX and X of which establish separate reservations for mixed-bloods; and the 1858 Treaty with the Ponca (12 Stat. 997, proc. Mar. 8, 1859; ibid., 772-5), Article 3 of which provides that individually titled parcels would be allotted to mixed-bloods wishing to live apart from their people. In the 1832 Treaty with the Sauk and Fox (7 Stat. 374, proc. Feb. 13, 1833; ibid., pp. 349-51), Article V reserves for Antoine LeClair, "interpreter and part-Indian," two sections of land in an area forcibly ceded by his people. Similarly, in the 1832 Treaty with the Potawatomi (7 Stat. 378, proc. Jan. 21, 1833; ibid., pp. 353-5), Article II sets aside tracts for persons "of Indian descent" within an area ceded by the Indians themselves. Other examples include the 1834 Treaty with the Miami (7 Stat. 458, proc. Dec. 22, 1837; ibid., pp. 425-8), Article 9 of which consists of a lengthy list of mixed-bloods and chiefs designated to retain parcels within an area ceded by the body of their people; and the 1865 Treaty with the Osage (14 Stat. 687, proc. June 26, 1866), Article 14 of which specifies that "half-breeds" shall retain 80-acre plots within a ceded area. Article 16 of the 1856 Treaty with the Stockbridge and Munsee (11 Stat. 663, proc. Sept. 8, 1856; ibid., pp. 742-55) assigns land patents to named mixed-bloods in exchange for their "separating from the Stockbridge tribe." Article 10 of the

234

1859 Treaty with the Sauk and Fox (15 Stat. 467, proc. July 9, 1860; *ibid.*, pp. 796-99) makes a similar provision for "mixed and half bloods of the tribe, and to such whole blood females as have intermarried with white men." Most harshly, there is the 1861 Treaty with the Sauk and Fox (12 Stat. 1171, proc. Feb. 6, 1861; ibid., pp. 811-3), Article 7 of which announces that "mixed bloods not resident" to the reservation would be simply "severed from the tribe."

84. Article XIII sets aside 640 acres for Joseph Parks, described as being of "one-quarter blood"; 7 Stat. 355, proc. Apr. 6, 1832; ibid., pp. 331-4. Also see the 1837 Treaty with the Sioux (note 81, above).

85. See, e.g., the 1863 Treaty with the Red Lake and Pembina Bands of Chippewa (note 78, above). The combination of racism and sexism on the part of U.S. treaty commissioners led to some rather bizarre outcomes, as when, under Article 5 of the 1818 Treaty with the Chickasaw (7 Stat. 192, proc. Jan. 7, 1819; ibid., pp. 174-5), a mixed-blood named John McCleish was awarded property "in consequence of his having married a white woman," thereby confounding the typically deep Euroamerican male aversion to native men mating with "their" females. In any event, the extraordinarily disruptive effects of the U.S. imposing patriarchal ("Christian") forms on traditionally matrilineal and gender-balanced native societies is well-documented; see, e.g., Rennard Strickland, *Fire and Spirits* (Norman: University of Oklahoma Press, 1975).

86. This was accomplished by attachment of a rider to the annual Appropriations Act (ch. 120, 16 Stat. 544, 566, now codified as 25 U.S.C. 71). It should be noted that, while canceling the government's prerogative to enter into new treaties, the rider provided that "nothing contained herein shall be construed to invalidate or impair the obligation of any treaty heretofore made with any such Indian tribe or nation."

87. The crux of this somewhat confused—and confusing—reordering of priorities can be located in the Grant administration; Elsie M. Rushmore, *The Indian Policy During Grant's Administration* (New York: Marion Press, 1914). More broadly, see Henry E. Fritz, *The Movement for Indian Assimilation, 1860-1890* (Philadelphia: University of Pennsylvania Press, 1963); Frederick A. Hoxie, *A Final Promise: The Campaign to Assimilate the Indians, 1880-1920* (Lincoln: University of Nebraska Press, 1984).

88. Ch. 341, 24 Stat. 362, 385, now codified at 18 U.S.C. 1153; also known as the Seven Major Crimes Act. The crimes at issue in this wholly unilateral U.S. assertion of jurisdiction over other nations were murder, manslaughter, rape, assault with intent to kill, larceny, burglary and arson. For background, see Sidney L. Harring, *Crow Dog's Case: American Indian Sovereignty, Tribal Law, and United States Law in the Nineteenth Century* (Cambridge: Cambridge University Press, 1994) pp. 100-41.

89. Ch. 119, 24 Stat. 388, now codified as amended at 25 U.S.C. 331 *et seq.*, also known as the "Dawes Act" or "Dawes Severalty Act," in honor of Massachusetts Senator Henry M. Dawes, its prime sponsor and supposed "Friend of the Indian"; D.S. Otis, *The Dawes Act and the Allotment of Indian Land* (Norman: University of Oklahoma Press, 1973); Wilcomb E. Washburn, *Assault on Tribalism: The General Allotment Law (Dawes Act) of 1887* (Philadelphia: J.B. Lippencott, 1975). On the "Friends," who were by this point organized as the "Indian Rights Association," see Prucha, *Americanizing the American Indian*; William T. Hagan, *The Indian Rights Association: The Herbert Welsh Years, 1882-1904* (Tucson: University of Arizona Press, 1985); Vine Deloria, Jr., "The Indian Rights Association: An Appraisal," in Sandra L. Cadwalader and Vine Deloria, Jr., eds., *The Aggressions of Civilization: Federal Indian Policy Since the 1880s* (Philadelphia: Temple University Press, 1984). Concerning the explicit intent of Dawes and others of his group to undermine and destroy any autochthonous sense of identity among native people, see Wilbert H. Ahern, "Assimilationist Racism: The Case of the 'Friends of the Indian'," *Journal of Ethnic Studies*, No. 4, 1976; Alexandra Harmon, "When Is an Indian Not an Indian? The 'Friends of the Indian' and the Problems of Indian Identity," *Journal of Ethnic Studies*, No. 18, 1990.

90. Orphaned children received the same 80-acre allotment as an unmarried adult; Kirk Kickingbird and Karen Ducheneaux, *One Hundred Million Acres* (New York: Macmillan, 1973); Janet A. McDonnell, *The Dispossession of the American Indian, 1887-1934* (Bloomington: Indian University Press, 1991).

91. There are numerous prototypes for what would become known as the "Dawes Rolls," dating back at least as far as the Cherokee "Immigrant Roll" in 1817. The common denominators are that they were invariably constructed in pursuance of some U.S., never indigenous, policy objective, and that their creation was always overseen by federal authorities; see, e.g., the relevant material in Charles C. Royce, *The Cherokee Nation of Indians, A Narrative of their Official Relations with the Colonial and U.S. Governments* (Washington, D.C.: Bureau of American Ethnology, Smithsonian Institution, 1887).

92. While blood quantum was seldom mentioned directly in treaty language—"half-breed" being a standard American colloquialism by which to describe persons of obvious Indian/white admixture, regardless of actual proportion—U.S. treaty commissioners and Indian agents habitually employed a quarter-blood minimum standard in compiling their lists of "mixed-bloods" scheduled to receive land titles, monetary awards, etc. Persons of less than one-quarter Indian blood were thus legally construed as being "non-Indian" by the U.S., even though they were often considered full members of native societies and discriminated against as "non-whites" by Euroamericans. For analogues, see Naomi Zack, *Race and Mixed Race* (Philadelphia: Temple University Press, 1993).

93. The problem was compounded by the fact that among some native peoples the strongest remaining elements of traditionalism declined to participate in the process at all. In the case of the Oklahoma Cherokees, for example, a sizable faction of full-bloods refused to enroll on the entirely appropriate bases that they neither desired to become citizens of the United States nor were willing to concede the prerogative of defining or recording who was/was not Cherokee to a foreign government. The result of this dynamic, in simplest terms, was that many of the most self-consciously *native* people left in the United States by 1890 were never officially recognized as such by the federal government, while the more acculturated were, almost by definition, enrolled. This clear bias in identification procedures has resulted in a marked and lingering accommodationist skew in "Indian" political perspectives. For a good emic examination of how these dynamics played out among the Cherokees, see Emmett Starr, *A History of the Cherokee Indians* (Oklahoma City: Warden, 1922).

94. Conversation with Jack D. Forbes, April 1993 (notes on file). Plainly, if the higher end of this estimated range is correct, there would have been precious little reservation land left for the U.S. to declare "surplus" after all Indians were allotted.

95. U.S. Bureau of the Census, "Table 2: Indian Population by Divisions and States, 1890-1930," *Fifteenth Census of the United States, 1930: The Indian Population of the United States and Alaska* (Washington, D.C.: U.S. Government Printing Office, 1937) p. 3. It should be noted that this is all that officially remained of an aggregate indigenous population that numbered perhaps fifteen million people in 1500, an approximate 97.5 percent reduction. Instructively, the latter figure corresponds perfectly with the 2.5 percent of its original landholdings this population was officially estimated to still retain by 1890; U.S. Bureau of the Census, *Report on Indians Taxed and Indians Not Taxed in the United States (except Alaska) at the Eleventh U.S. Census: 1890* (Washington, D.C.: U.S. Government Printing Office, 1894). On the size of the preinvasion native population, see Thornton, *American Indian Holocaust and Survival*. Also see Henry F. Dobyns, "Estimating Aboriginal American Population: An Appraisal of Techniques with a New Hemispheric Estimate," *Current Anthropology*, No. 7, 1966; *Their Numbers Become Thinned: Native American Population Dynamics in Eastern North America* (Knoxville: University of Tennessee Press, 1983). Even if, following the argument referenced in the preceding note, the actual size of the native population in 1890 was triple that admitted in official sources, it would not appreciably diminish the scale of attrition suffered by Native North America as a result of European invasion, conquest and colonization.

96. This enabled the agents to exercise "near dictatorial powers" over their hapless "wards," a matter which quickly resulted in the "checkerboarding"—that is, the longterm leasing of any usable land to non-Indian ranching and agricultural interests at discount rates, leaving only the least productive acreage under nominal native control—of many reservations; Vine Deloria, Jr., and Clifford M. Lytle, *American Indians, American Justice* (Austin: University of Texas Press, 1983) p. 10.

97. Mixed-bloods also tended to be allotted better properties—e.g., riverfront parcels—than were those enrolled as full-bloods.

98. For a close study of the process among the Kaws, see William E. Unrau, *Mixed Bloods and Tribal Dissolution: Charles Curtis and the Quest for Indian Identity* (Lawrence: University Press of Kansas, 1989).

99. Francis E. Leupp, *The Indian and His Problem* (New York: Scribner's, 1910) p. 93.

100. Turn of the century literature is replete with such references. See, e.g., "An Interesting Representative of a Vanishing Race," *Arena*, July 1896; Simon Pokagon, "The Future of the Red Man," *Forum*, Aug. 1897; William R. Draper, "The Last of the Red Race," *Cosmopolitan*, Jan. 1902; Charles M. Harvey, "The Last Race Rally of Indians," *World's Work*, May 1904; E. S. Curtis, "Vanishing Indian Types: The Tribes of the Northwest Plains," *Scribner's*, June 1906; James Mooney, "The Passing of the Indian," *Proceedings of the Second Pan American Scientific Congress, Sec. 1: Anthropology* (Washington, D.C.: Smithsonian

Institution, 1909-1910); Joseph K. Dixon, *The Vanishing Race: The Last Great Indian Council* (Garden City, NY: Doubleday, 1913); Stanton Elliot, "The End of the Trail," *Overland Monthly*, July 1915; Ella Higginson, "The Vanishing Race," *Red Man*, Feb. 1916; Ales Hrdlicka, "The Vanishing Indian," *Science*, No. 46, 1917; J.L. Hill, *The Passing of the Indian and the Buffalo* (Long Beach, CA: n.p., 1917); John Collier, "The Vanishing American," *Nation*, Jan. 11, 1928.

101. Actually, prototypes date back to 1617, when the Anglican Bishops allocated the sum of 500£ to establish the Henrico Academy in Virginia Colony for purposes of converting Indians to the "true faith"; Robert Land, "Henrico and Its College," *William and Mary Quarterly*, Vol. XXIV, 1938. Although the effort was initially unsuccessful, it was continued with the establishment of Harvard College in Massachusetts Colony in 1654; Andrew M. Davis, "The Indian College at Cambridge," *Magazine of American History*, Vol. XXIV, 1890. Then there were Moor's Charity School for Indians and Dartmouth College, both founded by the Reverend Eleazer Wheelock in the mid-1700s; Leon B. Richardson, *The History of Dartmouth College* (Hanover, NH: Dartmouth College Press, 1932). In 1693, another such institution, the College of William and Mary, was opened in Virginia; J.W. Randolph, *The History of William and Mary, 1660-1874* (Richmond, VA: Randolph and English, 1874). By the 1860s, largely as a result of missionary endeavors, primary and secondary school facilities had proliferated. Their potential to destroy native cultures was widely viewed as the "humanitarian alternative" to physical eradication in addressing the "Indian Question." See generally, Robert A. Trennert, Jr., *Alternative to Extinction: Federal Indian Policy and the Beginnings of the Reservation System, 1846-1851* (Philadelphia: Temple University Press, 1975); Loring Benson Priest, *Uncle Sam's Stepchildren: The Reformation of United States Indian Policy, 1865-1887* (Lincoln: University of Nebraska Press, 1975 reprint of 1942 original); Francis Paul Prucha, *American Indian Policy in Crisis: Christian Reformers and the Indian, 1865-1900* (Norman: University of Oklahoma Press, 1976).

102. Both reservation-based boarding schools and several varieties of missionary or BIA-run day schools offered lower attendant cost and avoided the isolation of students from familial and sociocultural input. Isolation must thus be considered a goal for which the government was willing to pay a certain premium; David Wallace Adams, *Education for Extinction: American Indians and the Boarding School Experience, 1875-1928* (Lawrence: University Press of Kansas, 1995) pp. 26-7. On the Christian day schools, see Francis Paul Prucha, *The Churches and the Indian Schools, 1888-1912* (Lincoln: University of Nebraska Press, 1979).

103. Fort Marion was the location to which many of the strongest native fighters of the Plains and Southwest Indian Wars—Cheyenne Dog Soldiers, Geronimo's Chiricahuas and others—were sent to be broken after laying down their arms; Frederick J. Stefon, "Richard Henry Pratt and His Indians," *Journal of Ethnic Studies*, No. 15, 1987. On the establishment of Carlisle, see Louis Morton, "How the Indians Came to Carlisle," *Pennsylvania History*, No. 29, 1962. For Pratt's own view of things, see his "American Indians, Chained and Unchained: Being an Account of How the Carlisle Indian School was Born and Grew in the First 25 Years," *Red Man*, June 1914.

104. Pratt's view that the role of education was to "kill the Indian . . . and save the man"—a play upon General Phil Sheridan's famous 1871 pronouncement that "the only good Indian is a dead one"—was first publicly articulated in a speech entitled "The Advantage of Mingling Indians with Whites," delivered in 1892 to the National Conference on Charities and Corrections. It is most famously repeated in his autobiographical *Battlefield and Classroom: Four Decades with the American Indian, 1867-1904* (New Haven, CT: Yale University Press, 1964 reprint of 1905 original). Studies of some of the other boarding schools mentioned include Lillie G. McKinney, "History of the Albuquerque Indian School," *New Mexico Historical Review*, No. 20, 1945; Robert A. Trennert, *The Phoenix Indian School: Forced Assimilation in Arizona, 1891-1935* (Norman: University of Oklahoma Press, 1988); K. Tsainina Lomawaima, *They Called It Prairie Light: The Story of the Chilocco Indian School* (Lincoln: University of Nebraska Press, 1994).

105. See generally, Adams, *Education for Extinction*; Sally J. McBride, *Ethnic Identity and the Boarding School Experience of West-Central Oklahoma American Indians* (Washington, D.C.: University Press of America, 1983); David Wallace Adams, "From Bullets to Boarding Schools: The Educational Assault on the American Indian Identity," in Philip Weeks, ed., *The American Indian Experience: A Profile* (Arlington Heights, IL: Forum Press, 1988); Michael C. Coleman, *American Indian Children at School, 1850-1930* (Jackson: University Press of Mississippi, 1993). Official confirmation of even the more extreme

characterizations of the process will be found in U.S. Bureau of Indian Affairs, *Rules for the Indian School Service* (Washington, D.C.: U.S. Government Printing Office, various editions, 1890-98, inclusive).

106. As Commissioner of Indian Affairs Thomas Jefferson Morgan put it in 1890, "The general purpose of the Government is preparation of Indian youth for assimilation into the national life by such a course of training as will prepare them for the duties and privileges of American citizenship"; *Annual Report of the Commissioner of Indian Affairs, 1890* (Washington, D.C.: U.S. Government Printing Office, 1890) p. cxlvi. To this end, the "Indian student would have to study American history and in the process come to internalize the national myths that were central to it, including the idea that the westward sweep of the American empire, that is to say the dispossession of Indian land, was clearly justifiable"; Adams, *Education for Extinction*, p. 24. Moreover, "Indians needed to be individualized. In many ways, the issue of individualization went to the very heart of the Indian question. In the [eurocentric] mind, Indians were savages mainly because tribal life placed a higher value on tribal community than on individual interests. Never was this more true than in the economic realm. Tribal society had somehow gotten matters all wrong: rather than operating on the progressive principle that the whole of society stood to benefit when the individual's acquisitive instincts were given their full play, tribal life was rooted in the idea that community welfare depended upon the individual curbing material desires. Whereas a Protestant American measured an individual's worth by his capacity to accumulate wealth, an Indian did so by what he [or she] gave away. . . It was not simply that [Christian whites] wished to snatch Indians' souls from a hellish fate; their commitment to Christianization was also rooted in the assumption that civilization, as the highest stage of social evolution, was erected upon a firm foundation of Christian morality"; ibid., pp. 22-3. Not only was all this incessantly drummed into students in the classroom setting, they were invariably required to join in extracurricular celebrations of salient events in the history of their own peoples' demise; Estelle Reel, *Course of Study for the Indian Schools of the United States: Industrial and Literary* (Washington, D.C.: Bureau of Indian Affairs, 1901).

107. In 1892, Indian Commissioner Morgan announced that "the whole underlying structure of the industrial school . . . is that intelligent, systematic labor by both men and women lies at the basis of civilization, and that if Indians are ever to be lifted to a higher plane it must be through the training of boys and girls alike to the performance of whatever manual labor may be essential for their welfare"; *Annual Report of the Indian Commissioner* (Washington, D.C.: U.S. Government Printing Office, 1892) p. 617. "In 1901, Commissioner William Jones announced that 'the ground work of all instruction in Indian Schools is the systematic inculcation of the principles of work.' That same year Superintendent of Indian Schools Estelle Reel unveiled a new course of study consistent with the new emphasis. Whereas before the curriculum had attempted to strike a balance between academic and industrial content, the new curriculum, although maintaining a half-day division between the two types of class work, made a concerted effort to infuse academic coursework with practical, job-related applications"; Adams, *Education for Extinction*, p. 315. The work experiences—performing stoop labor in Colorado's beet fields, for instance—were called "outings." For a good overview of the exploitation of males, see Robert A. Trennert, "From Carlisle to Phoenix: The Rise and Fall of the Indian Outing System, 1878-1930," *Pacific Historical Review*, No. 52, 1983. On more "feminine" applications, see Trennert's "Victorian Morality and the Supervision of Indian Women Working in Phoenix, 1906-1930," *Journal of Social History*, No. 22, 1988. For a good assessment of broader ramifications, see the collection of essays edited by Alice Littlefield and Martha C. Knack under the title *Native Americans and Wage Labor* (Norman: University of Oklahoma Press, 1996).

108. A contemporaneous survey of the extent of such resistance was offered by analyst Hamlin Garland in his article, "The Red Man's Present Needs," *North American Review*, No. 174, 1902. Its "major motivation," according to one current researcher, was that "a significant body of tribal opinion saw white education for what it was: an invitation to cultural suicide"; Adams, *Education for Extinction*, p. 212.

109. The first measure, effected on March 3, 1891, authorized the Commissioner of Indian Affairs to "make and enforce by proper means such rules and regulations as will secure the attendance of Indian children of suitable age . . . at schools established and maintained for their benefit"; *The Statutes at Large of the United States of America*, Vol. 26, p. 1014. The second specifically authorized the commissioner to "withhold rations, clothing and other annuities from Indian parents or guardians who refuse or neglect to send and keep their children . . . in school"; ibid., Vol. 27, p. 637. For implementation of both laws, see Office of Indian Affairs Circular No. 130, Jan. 15, 1906. It should be noted—and emphatically so—that

this forced transfer of children was nothing so innocuous as a "misguided policy." Such a course of governmental action is delineated as one of five categories of genocidal state conduct under Article II of the 1948 Convention on Prevention and Punishment of the Crime of Genocide; Ian Brownlie, ed., *Basic Documents on Human Rights* (Oxford: Clarendon Press, [3rd ed.] 1992) pp. 31-5. This may be one reason why the U.S., alone among major nation-states, declined to ratify the Genocide Convention for forty years after its promulgation as international law; Lawrence J. LeBlanc, *The United States and the Genocide Convention* (Durham, NC: Duke University Press, 1991).

110. Lawrence F. Schmeickebeir, *The Office of Indian Affairs* (Baltimore: Johns Hopkins University Press, 1927) p. 216. It was estimated in the April 6, 1912 issue of *Native American* that there were some 70,000 indigenous children in the overall "pool."

111. See Evelyn C. Adams, *American Indian Education: Government Schools and Economic Progress* (New York: King's Crown Press, 1946).

112. The Indian Citizenship Act of 1924 (ch. 233, 43 Stat. 25). Aside from the Allotment Act, other measures which had already conveyed citizenship upon selected groups of Indians was the Omnibus Bill of 1910 (which authorized the establishment of "competency commissions" to preside over the process) and a BIA policy announced by Indian Commissioner Cato Sells in 1917 pertaining to those who volunteered for military service; Michael T. Smith, "The History of Indian Citizenship," *Great Plains Journal*, No. 10, 1970; Gary C. Stein, "The Indian Citizenship Act of 1924," *New Mexico Historical Review*, No. 57, 1972.

113. Overall, the reservations contain about two-thirds of U.S. "domestic" uranium reserves, a quarter of the readily accessible low-sulfur coal, as much as a fifth of the oil and natural gas, as well as substantial deposits of copper, bauxite, molybdenum, zeolite, gold and much else; Ronald L. Trosper, "Appendix I: Indian Minerals," in American Indian Policy Review Commission, *Task Force 7 Final Report: Reservation Resource Development and Protection* (Washington, D.C.: U.S. Government Printing Office, 1977); Bureau of Indian Affairs, *Indian Lands Map: Oil, Gas and minerals on Indian Reservations* (Washington, D.C.: U.S. Government Printing Office, 1978).

114. Lewis Meriam, et al., *The Indian Problem: Resolution of the Committee of One Hundred by the Secretary of the Interior and Review of the Indian Problem* (Washington, D.C.: U.S. Government Printing Office, 1925); *The Problem of Indian Administration* (Baltimore: Johns Hopkins University Press, 1928).

115. Ch. 576, 48 Stat. 948, now codified at 25 U.S.C. 461-279; also known as the "Wheeler-Howard Act" after its main congressional sponsors, Senator Burton K. Wheeler and Representative Edgar Howard, although its major proponent was actually Indian Commissioner John Collier. There are a number of good studies of the IRA and its passage, among them Graham D. Taylor's *The New Deal and American Indian Tribalism: The Administration of the Indian Reorganization Act, 1934-1945* (Lincoln: University of Nebraska Press, 1980). Also see Kenneth R. Philp, *Assault on Assimilation: John Collier's Crusade for Indian Reform, 1920-1954* (Tucson: University of Arizona Press, 1977); Vine Deloria, Jr., and Clifford M. Lytle, *The Nations Within: The Past and Future of American Indian Sovereignty* (New York: Pantheon, 1984).

116. On disinformation and suppression of dissenting views, see Rupert Costo, "Federal Indian Policy, 1933-1945," in Kenneth R. Philp, ed., *Indian Self-Rule: First-Hand Accounts of Indian-White Relations from Roosevelt to Reagan* (Salt Lake City: Howe Bros., 1986). For what may be the most extreme example of rigging the outcome of a referendum, see Charles Lummis, *Bullying the Hopi* (Prescott, AZ: Prescott College Press, 1968). Another glaring illustration is described in Thomas Biolosi's *Organizing the Lakota: The Political Economy of the New Deal on the Pine Ridge and Rosebud Reservations* (Tucson: University of Arizona Press, 1992).

117. Of the 164 indigenous nations suffering reorganization, 92 were provided with such "constitutions"—effectively converting them into something more nearly approximating business entities than national polities—while 72 ended up with corporate charters, pure and simple; Kenneth R. Philp, "The Indian Reorganization Act Fifty Years Later," in his *Indian Self-Rule*.

118. For analysis of three such constitutions, see Thornton, *American Indian Holocaust and Survival*, pp. 190-200.

119. At Hopi, for example, only about 15 percent of the voting age population had been processed through the schools. It was precisely the same 15 percent who turned out to vote for reorganization while the remaining 85 percent, followers of the traditional Kikmongwe leadership, declined to participate in

any way at all; Oliver LaFarge, *Running Narrative of the Organization of the Hopi Tribe of Indians* (unpublished manuscript contained in the LaFarge Collection, University of Texas at Austin).

120. In what may be the best-known instance, the problem of blood quantum was raised by the 1972 Trail of Broken Treaties delegation to Washington in Point 11 of its 20-Point Program for reforming federal/Indian relations, demanding that the use of such criteria be abandoned. The Nixon administration responded that this would be "contrary to the position taken by the members of tribes in their referendums adopting constitutions setting forth their membership requirements" under the IRA. Taking up the issue with federal authorities is inappropriate and misguided, the administration concluded, since the "argument is really with the tribes who prescribe their membership pursuant to constitutions and by-laws that have been adopted"; Editors, *B.I.A., I'm Not Your Indian Any More: The Trail of Broken Treaties* (Mohawk Nation via Rooseveltown, NY: Akwesasne Notes, [3rd ed.] 1976) p. 76. For background, see Jack D. Forbes, *Native Americans and Nixon: Presidential Politics and Minority Self-Determination* (Los Angeles: UCLA American Indian Studies Center, 1981); Vine Deloria, Jr., *Behind the Trail of Broken Treaties: An Indian Declaration of Independence* (Austin: University of Texas Press, [2nd ed.] 1984).

121. Witness the performance of the National Tribal Chairmen's Association (NTCA), a federally subsidized association of presiding heads of IRA councils, whose officials defended the government by publicly attacking Trail of Broken Treaties participants as "irresponsible" and "unrepresentative of Indian interests," "renegades" who "possessed no constituency among Indians" and threatened "tribal sovereignty" by standing up for indigenous rights; *B.I.A., I'm Not Your Indian Any More*, pp. 31-2. It is worth noting that Webster Two Hawk, then President of the IRA council on the Rosebud Sioux Reservation, head of the NTCA, and the man who made these statements to the media—equivalent as they were to denunciations of the partisan resistance by Vichy French leader Pierre Laval during the occupation of France by Germany during World War II—was himself shortly voted out of office by his people. They replaced him with Robert Burnette, a major Trail organizer; Robert Burnette with John Koster, *The Road to Wounded Knee* (New York: Bantam, 1974). On the analogy to Laval and Vichy France, see Geoffrey Warner, *Pierre Laval and the Eclipse of France* (London: Macmillan, 1968); H.R. Kedward, *Resistance in Vichy France: A Study of Ideas and Motivations* (New York: Oxford University Press, 1978).

122. For articulation of the "third level" concept, see U.S. Senate, Select Committee on Indian Affairs, *Final Report and Legislative Recommendations: A Report of the Special Committee on Investigations* (Washington, D.C.: 101st Cong., 2d Sess., U.S. Government Printing Office, 1989). This is essentially the same subterfuge attempted by the French in placing administration of its Algerian colony under the Home Department rather than its Colonial Office during the 1950s; Joseph Kraft, *The Struggle for Algeria* (Garden City, NY: Doubleday, 1961).

123. For early analyses of the issue, see Ward Shepard, "Land Problems of an Expanding Population" and Allan G. Harper, "Salvaging the Wreckage of Indian Land Allotment," both in Oliver LaFarge, ed., *The Changing Indian* (Norman: University of Oklahoma Press, 1943).

124. Wilcomb Washburn, *Red Man's Land, White Man's Law* (Norman: University of Oklahoma Press, [2nd ed.] 1994) pp. 150-1. The analysis here is overly charitable, given that mere "oversights" in legislation are corrected by subsequent amendment. That the government was fully aware of the implications of the heirship problem by the late 1950s, and probably much earlier, is abundantly evidenced in its own documents; U.S. House of Representatives, Committee on Insular Affairs, *Indian Heirship Land Study* (Washington, D.C.: 86th Cong., 2d Sess., U.S. Government Printing Office, 1966). To date, nothing substantive has been done to alter the impacts.

125. There were 343,410 "official" Indians in the U.S. in 1950, up from less than a quarter-million fifty years earlier; U.S. Bureau of the Census, "Part 1: United States Summary," *Census of 1950, Vol. 2: Characteristics of the Population* (Washington, D.C.: U.S. Government Printing Office, 1953).

126. After 32 years of hearings and intensive investigative research, the Indian Claims Commission—the body officially ordained by Congress in 1946 to resolve indigenous grievances concerning territorial expropriations—admitted that it had been unable to find any sort of legal basis—no treaty, no agreement, not even a unilateral Act of Congress taking possession—of approximately 35 percent of the entire 48-states area; Indian Claims Commission, *Final Report* (Washington, D.C.: U.S. Government Printing Office, 1978); Russel L. Barsh, "Indian Land Claims Policy in the United States," *North Dakota Law Review*, No. 58, 1982. Nonetheless, despite the glaring inadequacy of the existing

reservation landbase, federal claims policy explicitly precluded land restoration. Instead, enabling legislation specifically provided that Indians found to have been illegally deprived of their property should be compensated for their loss at a rate commensurate with its value at the time it was taken. No interest accrual was awarded, and compensation amounts were offset against attorneys fees accumulated in obtaining a favorable judgment. Title to the land was then declared "quiet," whether the Indians agreed to the terms of the arrangement or not; John T. Vance, "The Congressional Mandate and the Indian Claims Commission," *North Dakota Law Review*, No. 45, 1969; Richard A. Nielson, "American Indian Land Claims: Land versus Money as a Remedy," *University Florida of Florida Law Review*, Vol. 19, No. 3, 1973.

127. See generally, Donald L. Fixico, *Termination and Relocation: Federal Indian Policy, 1945-1960* (Albuquerque: University of New Mexico Press, 1986).

128. Thornton, *American Indian Holocaust and Survival*, p. 227; U.S. Bureau of the Census, *1990 Census of the Population, Preliminary Report* (Washington, D.C.: U.S. Government Printing Office, 1991).

129. Termination occurred pursuant to House Concurrent Resolution 108, effected on August 1, 1953. The complete text appears in Part II of Edward H. Spicer's *A Short History of the Indians of the United States* (New York: Van Nostrand Rinehold, 1969). Dillon S. Myer, the man who had presided over the mass internment of Japanese Americans during World War II, was appointed Commissioner of Indian Affairs for the specific purpose of overseeing the process of tribal dissolution; Richard Drinnon, *Keeper of Concentration Camps: Dillon S. Myer and American Racism* (Berkeley: University of California Press, 1987).

130. Fixico, *Termination and Relocation*. Also see Larry W. Burt, *Tribalism in Crisis: Federal Indian Policy, 1953-1961* (Albuquerque: University of New Mexico Press, 1982).

131. On the struggle of the Menominee, see Nicholas Peroff, *Menominee DRUMS: Tribal Termination and Restoration, 1954-1974* (Norman: University of Oklahoma Press, 1982). Principal leader of this successful effort was a young woman named Ada Deer, a performance that established her political reputation and led, eventually, to her appointment as Commissioner of Indian Affairs under the Clinton administration. Perversely, she used this powerful position to champion the termination of other indigenous peoples.

132. The poverty is very real, albeit induced by intentional federal default on its treaty and other obligations to native people rather than by virtue of there being "too many Indian impersonators freeloading off the off the system," as one idiot recently put it. The poorest county in the United States throughout the 1950s and '60s was Shannon County, on the Pine Ridge Sioux Reservation, in South Dakota, where unemployment ran into the 90th percentile and per capita income averaged $1,200 per year into the early 1970s (things have not improved a lot since); Cheryl McCall, "Life at Pine Ridge Bleak," *Colorado Daily*, May 16, 1975. Overall, Indians remain by far the poorest population aggregate in North America, with all the dire effects this implies (average male life expectancy on the reservations is still well under fifty years); U.S. Department of Health and Human Services, Public Health Service, *Chart Series Book* (Washington, D.C.: U.S. Government Printing Office, 1988).

133. In the 1935 Constitution and Bylaws of the Confederated Salish and Kootenai Tribes of the Flathead Reservation, for example, enrollment criteria were delineated as consisting of all "persons of Indian blood whose names appear on the rolls of the Confederated Tribes [initially established at the time of the Dawes Commission] as of January 1, 1935." This was amended in 1960 to require that, to enroll, one must "possess one-quarter (1/4) degree or more blood of the Salish or Kootenai Tribes or both, of the Flathead Indian Reservation, Montana"; Thornton, *American Indian Holocaust and Survival*, pp. 197-8.

134. C. Matthew Snipp provides a convenient overview of enrollment requirements as Appendix 1 of his *American Indians: The First of This Land* (New York: Russell Sage Foundation, 1989).

135. The NTCA is now called the National Tribal Chairman's Fund. Its lobbying offensive during the mid-to-late '60s is covered by Robert Burnette in his book, *The Tortured Americans* (Engelwood Cliffs, NJ: Prentice-Hall, 1971). For more on the organization itself, see note 121, above.

136. At a meeting with members of the Abenaki National Council in 1991, it was explained to me that, in their view, the question of federal recognition put things exactly backwards. "The question is not whether we are recognized by the federal government," as one elder put it, "but whether we recognize *it*. After all, we Abenakis, not the United States or the State of Vermont, were the first people here. Unless they can show us a treaty in which our ancestors recognized their right to land which unquestionably

belonged to the Abenaki—which they can't—then it's still our land by law. Our law, their law, international law, it all comes out the same on this point."

137. Many of these children, almost none of whom were enrolled, were subjected to "blind adoptions." That is, they were denied by judicial decree, usually at the request of the adoptive family, all knowledge concerning the identity of their natural parents, much less the nature of their indigenous heritage; Tillie Blackbear Walker, "American Indian Children: Foster Care and Adoption," in U.S. Department of Education, Office of Educational Research and Development, National Institute of Education, *Conference on Educational and Occupational Needs of American Indian Women, October 1976* (Washington, D.C.: U.S. Government Printing Office, 1980).

138. In 1993, I had the misfortune to attend a so-called "Workshop on Identity" put on by an entity calling itself the "American Indian Advocacy Group" at my home institution, the University of Colorado at Boulder. Starting from the position that federal recognition is the essential ingredient of being Indian, the presenters—all native professionals, mostly counselors or administrators at the university—spent the balance of the afternoon belaboring the various financial, service and other benefits which might be expected by those "legitimately" entitled to identify as Indians, and the need to guard against "wannabees" seeking to "cash in." At no point was there discussion of such traditional concepts as lineage and genealogy, naturalization and loyalty to the people. At base, then, Indian identity was for this group little more than a commodity convertible to a cash value and/or some other set of preferences within the federal system.

139. My own experience in this regard may be instructive. In 1992, having attracted a certain notoriety as a codirector of the Colorado AIM chapter, I suddenly found my identity being challenged. A "real" Indian would make public the names of his/her indigenous relatives upon demand, it was asserted (although the question of why the right to privacy of my relatives—or of any native person—should be inherently less than other people's was never explained). After a time, I was convinced by an uncle to publish this information in a local newspaper. At that juncture, the "concern" of my critics instantly switched from genealogical issues to the question of whether I was recognized as native by the local Indian community (within which I'd lived and worked as an Indian for twenty years, and by a portion of which I'd been repeatedly elected to my AIM position). When this query provoked an outpouring of letters affirming such recognition, the criteria changed again, this time to demanding "proof" that I was "enrolled in a federally recognized tribe" (a position supposedly "affirming the sovereign right of tribes" to determine who is/isn't Indian). When it was established that I am in fact a duly enrolled member of the United Keetoowah Band of Cherokees, the Band itself was assailed as being "questionable," despite its having been federally recognized longer than any other Cherokee group. In the end, having met every one of the increasingly contrived "standards of Indianness" advanced by critics, I am *still* misrepresented as an "imposter" whenever they find it convenient. The only reasonable conclusion I can draw from the experience is that the "question" of my identity was never really at issue in the first place. Rather, it was raised quite cynically, for purposes of grinding other axes entirely. What these might be is readily discernable in the fact that two of the primary vehicles by which the campaign was conducted, *Indian Country Today* and *News From Indian Country*, are unabashed champions of IRA-style governance while I, obviously, rank among its harsher opponents. As to the matter of tribal sovereignty, the very idea that some self-appointed group of Lakotas, Chippewas and Cheyennes might exhibit such effrontery as to try and undermine the decision of a Cherokee government on a question of Cherokee identity tends to speak for itself.

140. For an altogether poignant and insightful examination of the impacts of this Fanonesque reality on all too many native people, see Patricia Penn Hilden, *When Nickels Were Indians: An Urban Mixed-Blood Story* (Washington, D.C.: Smithsonian Institution Press, 1995).

141. Public Law 101-644, enacted Nov. 29, 1990; gallery owners and others marketing such merchandise are subject to fines of up to $5 million. The background of the law is instructive. Its sponsor was Colorado Representative (now Senator) Ben Nighthorse Campbell, a millionaire and recently enrolled Northern Cheyenne. Campbell's wealth accrued in no small part from his manufacture and sale of silver jewelry—he identified himself as Indian all the while—during the period prior to his enrollment (an activity his bill defines as a Class-A Felony). His belated enrollment is itself a bit odd. The Northern Cheyenne constitution requires documentation of at least one-quarter degree blood, but Campbell has publicly admitted he's unsure what his quantum is. Others are regularly denied enrollment

on this basis, but Ben Campbell was accepted, a matter which may go far to explaining the end use of some of the $40,000 he estimates he spent getting "certified"; see generally, Herman J. Viola, *Ben Nighthorse Campbell: An American Warrior* (New York: Orion Books, 1993).

142. There is no indication that the impersonation of native fine artists by actual non-Indians is or ever was ever a significant problem in terms of displacing the former from opportunities to exhibit and sell (which is what the law supposedly covered). Targeted instead were Indian painters, sculptors and printmakers who were in various ways resistant to federal authority. There is no clearer example of this than the fact that both the Cherokee Cultural Heritage Center and the Five Civilized Tribes Museum were forced to close their doors during the week following the bill's passage because they featured work by the late Willard Stone, the wood carver who created the Great Seal of the Cherokee Nation but had always refused to enroll. It was necessary for the Cherokee National Council to posthumously certify Stone and several other obviously Cherokee artists in order to safely reopen the museums. Among the living artists targeted, meanwhile—others included Cherokees like Jimmie Durham and Burt Seabourn—was Stone's granddaughter, Jeanne Walker Rorex, who, although certainly eligible, has followed the traditionally honorable example of her grandfather and other Cherokee resisters in refusing enrollment; see generally, Gail K. Sheffield, *The Arbitrary Indian: The Indian Arts and Crafts Act of 1990* (Norman: University of Oklahoma Press, 1997).

143. Harjo, like Ben Campbell, was apparently enrolled as a Cheyenne under rather mysterious circumstances (she also identifies as Muskogee but is not enrolled as such, making her an "impostor" by her own articulated standards of "ethnic fraud"). She carried much of the weight in getting the 1990 Act passed, although the credit—or onus, depending on one's point of view—has mostly attached to the "Native American Artists Association" (NAAA), headed up by David Bradley, a failed painter and thoroughly deculturated White Earth Chippewa residing in Santa Fe, New Mexico. Some analysts have assessed the motives of NAAA as being more along the lines of restraint of trade—i.e., trying to secure the legalistic elimination of more talented competitors—than in protecting native identity; James J. Kilpatrick, "Government Playing the Indian Game," syndicated column © 1992, distributed by the Thomas Jefferson Center, Charlottesville, VA. On Harjo's role as a "prime mover" behind the Act, see Jonathan Tilove, "Who's an Indian Artist?" Newhouse News Service, Mar. 25, 1993. On Harjo's stated desire to expand the Act, see Sheffield, *Arbitrary Indian*, p. 52.

144. See, e.g., the 1993 series by Jerry Reynolds in *Indian Country Today* entitled "Indian Writers: The Good, the Bad, and the Could Be," in which the "pedigrees" of authors such as Michael Dorris, Roxanne Dunbar Ortiz and I are called into question on no apparent basis other than that we are mutually disliked by the paper's publisher, Tim Giago (such gratuitous smears likely contributed to the depression precipitating Dorris's recent suicide). With regard to *News From Indian Country*, see, e.g., the 1994-95 series by editor Paul DeMain titled "The AIM Paper Wars" in which a wide range of already-disproven rumors were reiterated as "fact," based upon a supposed "intensive investigation" of several individuals which turns out to have never occurred. Among those whose "Indian-ness" was called into question during the Internet barrage of 1993-95 were not only Dorris, Dunbar Ortiz and myself, but Vine Deloria, Jr., the late Robert K. Thomas, Glenn T. Morris, Linda Hogan, John Trudell, Donald A. Grinde, Jr., Chrystos, Leslie Marmon Silko, Wendy Rose, Paula Gunn Allen, Tim Coulter, Kay Miller, Robert Gish, Joseph Bruchac, Maurice Kenny, Kathy Chapman, Leonard Peltier, Louise Erdrich, Jimmie Durham and Bobby Castillo. One is tempted to say the definition employed by those using the Internet for such purposes was that anyone who'd ever accomplished anything must, for that reason alone, not be an Indian. A more objectively anti-Indian construct is hard to imagine.

145. The San Francisco group is headed by Carole Standing Elk, designated representative in Northern California of National AIM, Inc., a federally funded ($3.3 million in 1993 alone) Minnesota enterprise run by the brothers, Vernon and Clyde Bellecourt. The locus of operations in the Bay Area is the (also federally supported) Center for the SPIRIT, managed by John LaVelle, an unabashed apologist for federal identity policies running at least as far back as the Dawes Act; see his review of *Indians Are Us?* in the *American Indian Quarterly*, Vol. 20, No. 1, 1997. For details on National AIM, its funding and affiliations, and the activities mentioned here, see Faith Attaguile, *Why Do You Think We Call It Struggle? The Bellecourt Brothers and the Subversion of the American Indian Movement* (darknight e-postings, 2000).

146. Conversation with Twila Martin Catawba, at the time chair of the tribal council at the Turtle Mountain Chippewa Reservation in North Dakota, May 1992 (notes on file). For a good dose of analogous thinking, see Marc Hillel and Clarissa Henry, *Of Pure Blood: Hitler's Secret Program to Breed the "Master Race"* (New York: McGraw-Hill, 1976).

147. Thornton, *American Indian Holocaust and Survival*, pp. 174-5.

148. U.S. Department of Health, Education and Welfare, *A Study of Selected Socio-Economic Characteristics of Ethnic Minorities Based on the 1970 Census, Vol. 3: American Indians* (Washington, D.C.: U.S. Government Printing Office, 1974) pp. 74, 78.

149. Lenore Stiffarm and Phil Lane, Jr., "The Demography of Native North America: A Question of American Indian Survival," in M. Annette Jaimes, ed., *The State of Native America: Genocide, Colonization and Resistance* (Boston: South End Press, 1992) p. 45.

150. U.S. Congress, Office of Technology Assessment, *Indian Health Care* (Washington, D.C.: U.S. Government Printing Office, 1986) p. 78.

151. Some tribal councils have increased quantum requirements to one-half; Thornton, *American Indian Holocaust and Survival*, p. 190. On the concept of "autogenocide," coined to describe Khmer Rouge policies in Cambodia during the mid-to-late 1970s, see, e.g., Michael Vickery, *Cambodia, 1975-1982* (Boston: South End Press, 1984).

152. Patricia Nelson Limerick, *The Legacy of Conquest: The Unbroken Past of the American West* (New York: W.W. Norton, 1987) p. 338.

153. During the early '90s, the Umatilla tribal council commissioned University of Colorado anthropologist Deward E. Walker to conduct a study of what would happen if it simply adhered to its present quarter-blood Umatilla requirement for enrollment. The prognosis was that, given present rate of "outmarriage," there would be virtually no one enrollable as a Umatilla by some point around 2050. It was then that discussion of constitutional revisions began in earnest; conversation with Deward E. Walker, Apr. 1997 (notes on file).

154. Jack D. Forbes, "Undercounting Native Americans: The 1980 Census and Manipulation of Racial Identity in the United States," *Wicazo Sa Review*, Vol. VI, No. 1, 1990, p. 23. The Census Bureau itself inadvertently confirms the thrust of the argument, explaining that it construes the racial category "white" to include "all persons reporting Spanish origin. About 97 percent of persons of Spanish origin, about 99 percent of persons of Mexican origin, and 96 percent of persons of Puerto Rican origin were classified white" in the 1970 census; U.S. Bureau of the Census, *Selected Characteristics of Persons and Families of Mexican, Puerto Rican and Other Spanish Origin: March 1971* (Washington, D.C.: U.S. Government Printing Office, 1971) p. 15. That only 3,678 Mexican immigrants should have been classified as Indians in 1970—coming as they do from a population deriving overwhelmingly from indigenous "gene stocks" (Mörner, *Race Mixture*)—should speak for itself. Similarly, that only 1.9 percent (15,988 people) of the several million strong Mexican-American population should be so-categorized, is a travesty; U.S. Bureau of the Census, *Current Population Report: Characteristics of the Population by Ethnic Origin, November 1979* (Washington, D.C.: U.S. Government Printing Office, 1979).

155. Forbes, "Undercounting Native Americans".; U.S. Bureau of the Census, *Ancestry of the Population by State, 1980* (Washington, D.C.: U.S. Government Printing Office, 1983) p. 3.

156. For the official count, see U.S. Bureau of the Population, *General Characteristics of the Population, 1990* (Washington, D.C.: U.S. Government Printing Office, 1991) p. 9. A good in-depth discussion of such demographic trends will be found in Joane Nagel's *American Indian Ethnic Renewal: Red Power and the Resurgence of Identity and Culture* (New York: Oxford University Press, 1996).

157. Even this instrument fails to go the whole distance, making no provision for naturalization by marriage, adoption or petition. Moreover, since it takes as its point of departure the Dawes Rolls, it explicitly excludes the descendants of Cherokee resisters who refused to move to Oklahoma from Arkansas, Missouri, Kansas and Texas at the outset of the twentieth century. Still, the present CNO constitution accords much more closely with actual indigenous tradition than any other presently in existence. The constitution of my own Keetoowah Band follows not far behind, providing for enrollment based upon genealogy to anyone who can document it, but restricting voting, the holding of office and receipt of benefits to those of one-quarter or greater blood quantum. The Band also makes provision for "Honorary Members" who demonstrate no genealogical connection, but who provide service/display

loyalty to the group; Georgia Rae Leeds, *The United Keetoowah Band of Cherokee Indians in Oklahoma* (New York: Peter Lang, 1996) pp. 215-6.

158. U.S. Bureau of the Census, *1980 Census of the Population, Vol. II, Subject Reports: American Indians, Eskimos and Inuits on Identified Reservations and in Historic Use Areas of Oklahoma (excluding Urbanized Areas)* (Washington, D.C.: U.S. Government Printing Office, 1985) p. 99.

159. 30 Stat. 495; named in recognition of Charles Curtis, the mixed-blood Kaw who became Vice President of the United States; Unrau, *Mixed Bloods and Tribal Dissolution*.

160. Thornton, *American Indian Holocaust and Survival*, p. 200.

161. Indeed, there are already those such as New York attorney Allan van Gestel, who have begun to argue on this basis that American Indians are and have always been "legal fictions" created by the U.S. government for its own purposes. Having outlived its usefulness, he says, the "Indian myth" should now be abolished "in fairness to the country's non-Indian citizens"; see, e.g., his "When Fictions Take Hostages," in James A. Clifton, ed., *The Invented Indian: Cultural Fictions and Government Policies* (New Brunswick, NJ: Transaction, 1990). Van Gestel's cant, which has been widely applauded, finds echoes in many quarters; see, e.g., Fergus M. Bordewich, *Killing the White Man's Indian: Reinventing Native Americans at the End of the Twentieth Century* (New York: Doubleday, 1996).

This essay was originally published in *American Indian Culture and Research Journal*, Vol. 23, No. 1, Spring 1999. A somewhat condensed version also appears in Duane Champagne, ed., *Contemporary Native American Cultural Issues* (Walnut Creek, CA: AltaMira, 1999).

# Forbidding the "G-Word"
## Holocaust Denial as Judicial Doctrine in Canada

> Where scholars deny genocide, [they] contribute to the deadly psychohistorical dynamic in which unopposed genocide begets new genocides.
>
> —Roger W. Smith, Eric Markusen and Robert Jay Lifton
> "Professional Ethics and Denial of the Armenian Genocide" (1995)

Denial of genocide has become a matter of increasing concern in recent years, primarily as a result of efforts by a relative handful of neonazi "scholars" to rehabilitate their ideological heritage by advancing arguments and "evidence" that the Hitlerian Holocaust of the early 1940s never occurred.[1] So insidious has Holocaust denial been considered by many governments that they have criminalized it, and prosecutions of deniers have occurred in France, Canada and elsewhere.[2] The United States bars known deniers from entering the country, and has supported civil litigation against individuals and institutions engaging in such activities.[3]

A related but far less noticed phenomenon has been the efforts of a significant number of ostensibly more reputable scholars to indulge in a sort of reverse denial. According to this group, the Holocaust undoubtedly occurred, but it was something experienced exclusively by Jews.[4] Here, the fates of the Gypsies, Slavs, homosexuals and others at the hands of the nazis are routinely minimized and consigned to the ambiguous category of "nongenocidal suffering."[5]

In their more extreme formulations, proponents of Jewish exclusivism hold not only that the Holocaust was a uniquely Jewish experience, but that it is history's sole instance of "true" genocide. Exclusivists have gone on record, explicitly and repeatedly, denying that everything from the extermination of the Pequots in 1637, to the Turkish slaughter of more than a million Armenians between 1915 and 1918, to the more recent genocides in Cambodia, East Timor, Bosnia, Rwanda and Kosovo aren't really examples of genocide at all.[6] Hence, while neonazis deny a single genocide, exclusivists deny *many*.

There are of course other distinctions to be drawn between Holocaust deniers and those championing the exclusivity of suffering embodied in the nazi Judeocide. Although their influence often exceeds their actual numbers,[7] the propagandists of neonazism are by any definition a tiny fringe group. Those promoting ideas of Jewish exclusivism, on the other hand, comprise substantial majorities at the very hearts of the academic and media mainstreams. Moreover, their outlook has been adopted as official or quasi-official policy by numerous governments, including most prominently, those taking the strongest stands against neonazi deniers.[8] In sum, the Holocaust uniqueness postulations of Jewish exclusivism have assumed the status of an orthodoxy in historical/sociological interpretation, while those of neonazism have not (and hopefully never will).

The reasons for this are not especially mysterious. The magnitude of their people's catastrophe has generated among Jews an understandable need to find spiritual meaning in the experience, a matter which had led many to an unfortunate perversion of their own tradition in which they, a Chosen people, were uniquely selected by God to endure the Holocaust.[9] More pragmatically—or cynically—others have realized that such suffering can be translated into a kind of "moral capital" and used to political advantage, particularly in garnering support for the Israeli state.[10] There is thus a clear, and often quite overtly expressed, desire among many Jews to claim an absolute monopoly in terms of genocidal suffering.[11]

For the élites of gentile societies, meanwhile, affirming the pretensions of Jewish Holocaust exclusivism carries with it an automatic absolution: If only the nazi Judeocide can be qualified as genocide, it follows that only nazis have ever been perpetrators or beneficiaries of the crime. The point is not insignificant. Genocide has been all but universally decried as a not merely "incomparable," but an "unthinkable" offense,[12] one defying any possible redemption of those committing it (which is of course why neonazis seek to "prove" their ideological forebears did not engage in it). As the Germans have long since discovered, the citizenry of no nation can take pride in a history besmirched by genocidal comportment.[13] Nor can any citizenry be counted upon to conveniently acquiesce in contemporary policies of genocide carried out in their name.

Far more than mere conceptions of "national honor" are at stake.

Among those wishing to see themselves as "good people"—which is virtually everyone—the very term "genocide" provokes such deep and generalized revulsion that any official admission of its descriptive applicability to the national character, even historically, might threaten the hegemony upon which systemic stability largely depends.[14] Genocide must therefore be denied at all costs, most often by explaining it away as being or having been something else altogether. For this purpose, constraining perceptions of genocide to the terms set forth by Jewish exclusivism serves non-Jewish interests as readily as Jewish.

## Definitional Distortions

Genocide is not an old word, having "naturally" evolved over time to hold meanings contrary to its own. Nor was it meant to serve as a synonym for mass killing. When Raphaël Lemkin coined the term in 1944, he went to considerable lengths in explaining that it was intended to describe policies and processes designed to bring about the dissolution and disappearance of targeted human groups, as such. "Genocide has two phases," he wrote, "one, destruction of the national pattern of the oppressed group; the other, the imposition of the national pattern of the oppressor."[15] If these two conditions have been fulfilled, a genocide has occurred, even if every member of the targeted group has survived the process in a physical sense.

> Generally speaking, genocide does not necessarily mean the immediate destruction of a nation, *except* when accomplished by mass killings. . . It is intended rather to signify a coordinated plan of different actions aimed at the destruction of the essential foundations of the life of national groups, with the aim of annihilating the groups themselves. The objectives of such a plan would be a disintegration of political and social institutions, of culture, language, national feelings, religion, and the economic existence of national groups, and the destruction of personal security, liberty, health, dignity, and even the lives of the individuals belonging to such groups. Genocide is directed at the national group as an entity, and the actions involved are directed at individuals, not in their individual capacity, but as members of the national group (emphasis added).[16]

In 1946, Lemkin was retained by the United Nations Secretariat to draft an international convention codifying the crime. Therein, genocide—that is, "policies aimed at eradicating targeted ethnical, racial, national, religious or political groups"—was defined in a two-fold way: "(1) the destruction of a group," and "(2) preventing its preservation and development."[17] The offending policies were themselves grouped in three categories, all of equal gravity.

- *Physical Genocide*, meaning outright extermination as well as the imposition of "slow death measures" (i.e., subjection to conditions of life which, owing to lack of proper housing, clothing, food, hygiene and medical care or excessive work or physical exertion are likely to result in the debilitation and death of individuals; mutilations and biological experiments imposed for other than curative purposes; and deprivation of livelihood by means of looting or confiscation of property).

- *Biological Genocide*, meaning the prevention of births among the target group (i.e., involuntary sterilization or abortion, as well as compulsory segregation of the sexes).

- *Cultural Genocide*, meaning destruction of the specific characteristics of the group (i.e., forced dispersal of the population; forced transfer of children to another group; suppression of religious practices or the national language; forced exile of writers, artists, religious and political leaders or other individuals representing the culture of the group; destruction of cultural/religious shrines or monuments, or their diversion to alien uses; destruction or dispersion of documents and objects of historical, artistic or religious value, and objects used in religious worship).[18]

The draft was then turned over to a committee composed of nation-state delegates to be "revised and condensed" before its submission to the U.N. General Assembly. During this process, the United States and Canada, acting in concert, were able to arrange deletion of almost the entire provision on cultural genocide, as well as all explicit references to slow death measures.[19] As the matter was finally framed in international law on December 9, 1948, "genocide means any of the following acts committed with intent to destroy, in whole or in part, a national, ethnical, racial or religious group, as such:"

(a) Killing members of the group;

(b) Causing serious bodily or mental harm to members of the group;

(c) Deliberately inflicting on members of the group conditions of life calculated to bring about its physical destruction in whole or in part;

(d) Imposing measures intended to prevent births within the group;

(e) Forcibly transferring children of the group to another group.[20]

Strikingly, even in this greatly truncated delineation, only one in five criteria pertain to direct killing. Eighty percent of the legal definition of genocide thus devolves upon *nonlethal* policies and activities. The responses of the U.S. and Canada to this are instructive. The United States simply refused for forty years to accept the result. Finally, in 1988, embarrassed at being the only country so openly rejecting the rule of law, it attempted a ratification in which it claimed a "right" to exempt itself from compliance whenever convenient.[21]

Canada also submitted an invalid ratification, but much earlier, in 1952. The subterfuge in this case was to write domestic implementing legislation in such a way as to excise from the country's "legal understanding" those classifications of genocidal policy in which Canada was actually engaged,[22] retaining only those involving "physical destruction. . . killing, or its substantial equivalents" (that is, Article II(a), (c) and (d) of the 1948 Convention).

> For purposes of Canadian law, we believe that the definition of genocide should be drawn somewhat more narrowly than in the [already much narrowed] international Convention so as to include only killing and its substantial equivalents. . . The other components of the international definition, viz, causing serious bodily or mental harm to members of a group and forcibly transferring children of one group to another group with intent to destroy the group we deem inadvisable for Canada.[23]

In 1985, the parliament went further, removing the prohibition on involuntary sterilization (1948 Convention, Article II(d)) from Canada's genocide statute.[24] No country, of course, whether it be Canada or the U.S. or nazi Germany, holds a legitimate prerogative to pick and choose among elements of international law, electing to abide by some and others not. Less, does it possess a right to unilaterally "revise" the Laws of Nations in conformity with its own preferences. As the nazis were informed at Nuremberg, the requirements of customary law are binding, irrespective of whether individual sovereignties wish to accept them.[25]

Nonetheless, taking the cue from their governments, a range of "responsible" scholars shortly set themselves to the task of deforming Lemkin's concept even further. In 1959, Dutch law professor Pieter Drost published a massive two-volume study wherein he argued that usage of the term genocide should be restricted to its physical and biological dimensions, and that cultural genocide should be redesignated as "ethnocide," a term he erroneously attributed to "post-war French scholars."[26] Thereafter, biological genocide was also quietly dropped from discussion as writer after writer defined genocide exclusively in terms of killing.[27] Forty years of this continuous "genocide equals mass murder" distortion has yielded an altogether predictable effect, not only on the popular consciousness but on that of many otherwise critical activists and intellectuals. This last is readily evident in the recent release of a book by Native Hawaiian sovereigntist and professor Haunani-Kay Trask wherein genocide is defined as simply the "systematic killing of a people identified by ethnic/racial characteristics."[28]

## Friends of the Lubicon

Questions arise as to whether, after all this, Lemkinesque understandings of genocide still prevail at all, and, if so, whether they retain the capacity to galvanize public sentiment. The answers rest, to some extent, in a handful of examples. In 1968, as part of the Russell Tribunal's verdict condemning U.S. aggression in Vietnam, Jean-Paul Sartre concluded not only that the policy itself was genocidal, but that colonialism as a system inherently produces genocidal results.[29] Considerable support was lent to the latter of Sartre's findings in 1980, when the Tribunal published a report on conditions imposed upon the indigenous peoples of the Western Hemisphere.[30]

Still further expansions on the theme have accrued through publications like *Cultural Survival Quarterly*, and in the Native resistance movements which emerged during the 1980s in places like Wollaston Lake, James Bay and Big Mountain, Arizona.[31] Perhaps the most potent example, however, concerns the experience of a tiny Cree band at Lubicon Lake, in northern Alberta, who have been confronted with sociocultural eradication as the result of maneuverings on the parts of both the federal and provincial governments to allow the Daishowa Corporation, a transnational manufacturer of paper products, to "deforest" their traditional territory (within which government-sanctioned oil and gas exploration had already wrought a noticeable degree of havoc).[32]

After fruitlessly attempting to negotiate a resolution with both the corporation and participating governmental entities, the band, working through a non-Indian Toronto-based organization calling itself Friends of the Lubicon (FOL), announced a boycott of Daishowa products in 1991. The FOL made genocidal impacts of the corporation's planned clearcutting of Lubicon territory the centerpiece of its effort, developing a well-conceived media campaign to put its message across. As a Canadian court later put it, the "results of the Friends' campaign against Daishowa . . . were, in a word, stunning."[33] Not only did typical Canadians prove quite capable of understanding nonlethal modes of genocide, they displayed a pronounced willingness to decline to trade with businesses complicit in such processes. On this basis:

> Approximately fifty companies using paper products (mostly paper bags) from Daishowa were approached by the Friends. The list of these companies reads like a Who's Who of the retail and fast food industries in Ontario — Pizza Pizza, the Liquor Control Board of Ontario, Cultures, Country Style Donuts, Mr. Submarine, Bootlegger, A&W, Kentucky Fried Chicken, Woolworth's, Roots, Club Monaco,

Movenpeck Restaurants and Holt Renfrew, to name but a few. *Every one* of the companies approached by the Friends joined the boycott of Daishowa products. All but two did so . . . before their stores were picketed. . . Pizza Pizza was subjected to picketing outside its store on two occasions; Woolworth's had a single store picketed on two occasions. . . Both Pizza Pizza and Woolworth's joined the boycott.[34]

By 1994, the boycott was costing Daishowa millions of dollars annually in lost sales.[35] Under such circumstances, it stood to lose money rather than profiting by cutting timber on Lubicon land. One result was that, although Daishowa had indicated that it would commence logging operations "as soon as the ground freezes over" in the fall of 1991, not a tree was felled.[36] As FOL leader Kevin Thomas observed in 1997, the success of the boycott demonstrated clearly that there are viable alternatives for those genuinely opposed to genocide. Rather than simply bearing "moral witness" to what is happening half-a-world away in Tibet or Kosovo, it is entirely possible "to actually make a difference by focusing attention mainly on what our own government is doing right here at home and undertaking direct action to stop it."[37]

"This can have a precedential effect," Thomas suggests. "Halting genocide in one place helps lay the groundwork for halting it in all places. But, for this to happen, it's essential that people be made aware of what genocide actually is. We've all been pretty systematically misled on that score, but if we're confused, if we can't recognize genocide for what it is when it's happening right in front of us, there's no way in the world we can change anything for the better. That's why there's been so much effort expended on keeping everybody confused about it: business as usual pretty much depends on an ability to perpetrate genocide more-or-less continuously, without its being recognized as such and, as a result, without its encountering significant opposition from average citizens."[38]

### Judicial Repression in Canada

The lesson was lost on neither the corporate nor the governmental sectors of Canada's status quo. Consequently, naming Thomas and two other key organizers as principle defendants, Daishowa filed a SLAPP suit against the FOL on January 11, 1995. Citing millions in lost revenues and a steady erosion in its client base as damages, the corporation contended that the three men had conspired to employ tactics such as an illegal secondary boycott, and were guilty of defamation by using the word "genocide" in their public outreach efforts.[39]

Even before the defendants had an opportunity to file a response to the allegations against them, a temporary injunction was issued to prevent them from engaging in boycott activities of any sort for ninety days. By then, Daishowa's attorneys had requested an interlocutory injunction to extend the prohibition for the duration of the suit. This motion was "substantially dismissed," but the FOL was ordered not to describe Daishowa's planned activities as genocidal until a final ruling had been made.[40] The following trial ended with one of the more brilliantly obfuscatory rulings in Canadian history.

At one level, Judge J.C. MacPherson's lengthy verdict was a study in liberal legal scholarship, rejecting in an almost contemptuous tone each of Daishowa's claims that the FOL's boycott techniques had been in themselves unlawful. On the contrary, he concluded, "the manner in which the Friends have performed their picketing and boycott activities is a model of how such activities should be conducted in a democratic society."[41] All of this progressive cant, however, was simply a gloss meant to disguise the unmistakably reactionary core of what the judge had to say: that the FOL's characterization of Daishowa's corporate policy as genocidal constituted "an enormous injustice . . . bordering on the grotesque . . . cavalier and grossly unfair to Daishowa."[42] Having thus found that the FOL had indeed defamed the corporation, he forbade them—and everyone else in Canada—from ever again employing such accurate terminology to describe what the corporation was doing.[43]

It was not that MacPherson was unaware of the "plight" in which Daishowa's activities had placed the Lubicons. Indeed, he remarked upon it at some length.

> The essential subject matter of everything the Friends say and do is the plight of the Lubicon Cree. . . There can be little doubt that their plight, especially in recent years, is a tragic, indeed a desperate one. . . The loss of a traditional economy of hunting, trapping and gathering, the negative effect of industrial development on a people spiritually anchored in nature, the disintegration of a social structure grounded in families led by successful hunters and trappers, alcoholism, serious community health problems such as tuberculosis, and poor relations with governments and corporations engaged in oil and gas and forest operations on land the Lubicon regard as theirs—all of these have contributed to a current state of affairs for the Lubicon Cree which deserves the adjectives tragic, desperate and intolerable.[44]

Nor was he unaware that imposition of such conditions by "governments and corporations engaged in oil and gas and forest operations" conforms quite precisely with both the etymological and legal definitions of the crime of genocide, even under Canadian law. In his verdict, the judge quoted Raphaël Lemkin, the 1948 Convention and the relevant Canadian statute all three, only to disregard them, along with testimonies of a whole series of expert witnesses,[45] in favor of the "plain and ordinary meaning of the word 'genocide'" contained in *Webster's Dictionary*. This, he insisted—although the dictionary actually didn't—was "the intentional killing of a group of people."[46]

MacPherson never specified the point at which he believed the content of abridged dictionaries had come to outweigh black letter legal definition in Canadian jurisprudence.[47] Less did he explain how, using his "common sense" approach, anyone is supposed to distinguish between the nazi extermination of the Jews and such relatively trivial phenomena as the St. Valentine's Day Massacre (both involve the "intentional killing of a group of people," and would thus seem to be equally genocidal under the judge's "plain, ordinary" and utterly absurd interpretation).[48] Nevertheless, he went on to assert that characterizations of genocide deriving from other definitions—those found in international law, for example—do not constitute "fair comment" about perpetrators and their activities.[49]

It follows that organizations like the FOL, devoted not only to direct action but to what even the judge described as a broader "educational" purpose, are left with an ability to confront genocidal processes only by referring to them as something else (which is to say, in effect, by implicitly denying that they are genocide).[50] In the alternative, should such groups—or, presumably, the victims themselves—insist upon calling things by their right names, perpetrators have been perfectly positioned by MacPherson's judicial prevarications to claim "damages" and/or take other legal action against *them*.

### The Wages of Denial

As prominent exclusivist Deborah Lipstadt has noted, the "general public tends to accord victims of genocide a certain moral authority. If you devictimize a people, you strip them of their moral authority," and thus a substantial measure of their ability to attract public support.[51] Lipstadt was writing from an explicitly Jewish perspective, of course, and of her own people's natural desire to be compensated in various ways for the horrors of the nazi Judeocide. Her point, however, is equally valid with respect *any* genocidally victimized group. Moreover, where genocide is an ongoing process—as with the Lubicons—the need for public support goes not to securing compensation but survival itself.

This is by no means an academic consideration. Cumulatively, one result of a half-century of "scholarship" by people like Lipstadt has been the functional devictimization of literally hundreds of indigenous peoples, even as their very existence has been systematically extinguished. Refused moral authority by those better stationed to monopolize it for themselves, and thus unable to command public attention, much less support, a truly staggering number of Native societies have been pushed into oblivion since 1950.[52] It is in some ways a perverse testament to the effectiveness of exclusivist propaganda that most such passings—whether physical or "merely" cultural—have gone not only unprotested but unnoticed by the general populace.

In this, the convolutions of legalism have played their role. Arcane preoccupations with the standards of proof required in establishing perpetrator intent, and exactly what scale, mode, tempo or proportionality of killing should be necessary for instances of mass murder to be considered "genuinely" genocidal, have done far more to mask than to reveal the realities of genocide.[53] Small wonder that there has never been a concerted attempt by the international community to enforce the 1948 Convention. Comes now J.C. MacPherson to place his personal capstone on the whole sordid situation, entering a ruling which by implication transforms law from its potential as a weapon against genocide into one with which those engaged in it can shield themselves from any sort of effective exposure and intervention.

Denial of genocide, insofar as it plainly facilitates continuation of the crime, amounts to complicity in it. This is true whether the deniers are neonazis, Jewish exclusivists, renowned international jurists or provincial Canadian judges. Complicity in genocide is, under Article III of the 1948 Convention, tantamount to perpetration of genocide itself. It is formally designated a Crime Against Humanity, those who engage in it criminals of the worst sort. There is no difference in this sense between a J.C. MacPherson, a Deborah Lipstadt and an Adolf Eichmann.[54]

And what of the victims? Unquestionably, any group faced with the prospect of systemically imposed extinction holds not only the right but the obligation to defend and preserve itself by the best means available to it. Afforded the moral currency attending its circumstance, it may well be able to undertake this task both nonviolently and successfully. This, surely, is a primary lesson of the recent collaboration between the Lubicons and the FOL. Denied such currency, however, the victims can hardly be expected to simply "lie down in a ditch and die."[55] To paraphrase Martin Luther King, Jr., those who endeavor to make the success of peaceful resistance to genocide impossible only make violent resistance inevitable. They can have no complaint, morally, ethically or otherwise, when the chickens come home to roost.

# Notes

1. Pierre Vidal-Niquet, *Assassins of Memory: Essays on the Denial of the Holocaust* (New York: Columbia University Press, 1992); Deborah Lipstadt, *Denying the Holocaust: The Growing Assault on Truth and Memory* (New York: Free Press, 1993).

2. In France, there was the 1981 trial of Robert Faurisson, the country's leading denier, for defaming Holocaust witnesses and scholars. In Canada, the most notable cases have been the 1985 prosecutions of James Keegstra, an Alberta school teacher who'd spent fourteen years indoctrinating his students that the Holocaust was a "hoax," and Ernst Zündel, a Toronto-based publisher who is one of the world's leading purveyors of such tripe. See Nadine Fresco, "Denial of the Dead: On the Faurisson Affair," *Dissent*, Fall 1981; Alan T. Davies, "A Tale of Two Trials: Antisemitism in Canada," *Holocaust and Genocide Studies*, Vol. 4, 1989.

3. The primary case in the U.S. was *Mel Mermelstein v. Institute for Historical Review, et al.*, (Superior Court of California, Civ. No. 356542 (Feb. 1981)); British "historian" David Irving is among those barred from entering the United States because of his record as a denier.

4. See, e.g., Martin Gilbert, *The Holocaust: A History of the Jews of Europe During the Second World War* (New York: Henry Holt, 1985); Leni Yahil, *The Holocaust: The Fate of the European Jewry, 1932-1945* (New York: Oxford University Press, 1990).

5. This happens both directly and by way of omission. In Deborah Lipstadt's *Denying the Holocaust*, for example, there is not so much as an index entry for Gypsies, despite the fact that this smaller people was subject to exactly the same nazi racial decrees as Jews, were exterminated in precisely the same manner and in the same places as Jews, and, proportionately, suffered equivalent or greater population losses; Ian Hancock, "Responses to the Porrajmos: The Romani Holocaust," in Alan S. Rosenbaum, ed., *Is the Holocaust Unique? Perspectives in Comparative Genocide* (Boulder, CO: Westview Press, 1996). For direct assertions, see, e.g., Michael Berenbaum, ed., *A Mosaic of Victims: Non-Jews Persecuted and Murdered by the Nazis* (New York: New York University Press, 1990).

6. Although there are literally hundreds of iterations of the notion available from other authors, the most comprehensive assertion that the nazi Judeocide is "phenomenologically unique" has been that advanced by Steven T. Katz in his massive *The Holocaust in Historical Context, Vol. 1: The Holocaust and Mass Death Before the Modern Age* (New York: Oxford University Press, 1994).

7. A poll conducted in Italy during the fall of 1992, for example, revealed that nearly 10 percent of the country's adult population have been convinced that the Holocaust never happened; *Jewish Telegraph News Agency*, Nov. 11, 1992.

8. Examples of official policy include the quid pro quo entered into between the governments of Israel and Turkey by which the Israelis ban public characterizations of the Armenian genocide as genocide. In exchange, the Turks pronounce the nazi Judeocide as the only "real" genocide. Working together, the two governments were able to prevent the Armenians from being listed as victims of genocide in the U.S. Holocaust Memorial Museum in Washington, D.C.; Roger W. Smith, Eric Markusen and Robert Jay Lifton, "Professional Ethics and the Denial of the Armenian Genocide," *Holocaust and Genocide Studies*, No. 9, 1995. Insofar as it has received not inconsiderable governmental support and endorsement, the Holocaust Memorial Museum itself, though nominally private, may be viewed as an example of quasi-official policy.

9. See, e.g., Arthur A. Cohen, *The Tremendium: A Theological Interpretation of the Holocaust* (New York: Holmes & Meier, 1981); John Roth and Michael Berenbaum, *The Holocaust: Religious and Philosophical Implications* (New York: Paragon House, 1989). For critique, see John Murray Cuddahy, "The Holocaust: The Latent Issue in the Uniqueness Debate," in Philip F. Gallagher, ed., *Christians, Jews and Other Worlds: Patterns of Conflict and Accommodation* (Landham, MS: University Press of America, 1988); Arno J. Mayer, *Why Did the Heavens Not Darken? The Final Solution in History* (New York: Pantheon, [2nd ed.] 1990).

10. The term "moral capital" is taken from exclusivist writer Edward Alexander, *The Holocaust and the War of Ideas* (New Brunswick, NJ: Transaction, 1994) p. 195.

11. E.g., Yehuda Bauer, "Whose Holocaust?" and Edward Alexander, "Stealing the Holocaust," both in *Midstream*, Vol. 26, No. 9, 1980.

12. Roger Manvell and Heinrich Fraenkel,, *The Incomparable Crime; Mass Extermination in the 20th*

*Century: The Legacy of Guilt* (London: Hinemann, 1967); Israel W. Charny, *How Can We Commit the Unthinkable? Genocide, the Human Cancer* (Boulder, CO, Westview Press, 1982).

13. See generally, Richard Evans, *In Hitler's Shadow: West German Historians and the Attempt to Escape from the Nazi Past* (New York: Alfred A. Knopf, 1989).

14. As the Italian theorist Antonio Gramsci described it, hegemony functions by way of a master narrative designed to convince the great mass of people that the prevailing order is natural, right and thus inevitable. Any concession by ruling élites that there is anything fundamentally wrong with the order over which they preside would of course undermine the very belief system upon which their own ascendancy depends; Walter L. Adamson, *Hegemony and Revolution: A Study of Antonio Gramsci's Political and Cultural Theory* (Berkeley: University of California Press, 1980) esp. pp. 170-9.

15. Raphaël Lemkin, *Axis Rule in Occupied Europe: Laws of Occupation, Analysis of Government, Proposals for Redress* (Washington, D.C.: Carnegie Endowment for International Peace, 1944) p. 79.

16. Ibid.

17. U.N. Doc. A/362, June 14, 1947.

18. Ibid. For further discussion, see Robert Davis and Mark Zannis, *The Genocide Machine in Canada: The Pacification of the North* (Montréal: Black Rose Books, 1973) pp. 15-21.

19. On Canada's role, see *Canada and the United Nations* (Ottawa: Dept. of External Affairs, 1948) p. 191. Overall, see M. Lippman, "The Drafting of the 1948 Convention and Prevention and Punishment of the Crime of Genocide," *Boston University International Law Journal*, No. 3, 1984.

20. U.S.T. _____, T.I.A.S. _____, 78 U.N.T.S. 277 (1948), Article II. The Convention's third article makes it a crime not only to perpetrate genocide, but to conspire or attempt to commit it, to incite it, or to be otherwise complicit in its perpetration; for text, see Ian Brownlie, ed., *Basic Documents on Human Rights* (Oxford: Clarendon Press, [3rd ed.] 1992) pp. 31-4.

21. Lawrence LeBlanc, *The United States and the Genocide Convention* (Durham, NC: Duke University Press, 1991) pp. 7-12.

22. There can be no question whether parliament was aware its Indian residential school policy violated Article II(e) of the Genocide Convention, the prohibition on forced transfer of children. The issue was raised repeatedly during the debates on ratification; Canadian Civil Liberties Association, "Brief to the Senate Standing Committee on Legal and Constitutional Affairs, "April 26, 1969, p. 6. Yet this is one of the provisions deleted from the Canadian genocide statute, ostensibly because it had "no essential relevance to Canada where mass transfers of children to another group are unknown"; Special Committee on Hate Propaganda in Canada (1948); quoted in Davis and Zannis, *Genocide Machine*, p. 23. For background, see Roland Chrisjohn and Sherri Young with Michael Mauran, *The Circle Game: Shadows and Substance in the Residential School Experience in Canada* (Penticton, BC: Theytus Books, 1997); John S. Milloy, *A National Crime: The Canadian Government and the Residential School System, 1879-1986* (Winnipeg: University of Manitoba Press, 1999).

23. Special Committee on Hate Propaganda in Canada (1948); quoted in Davis and Zannis, *Genocide Machine*, p. 23.

24. Criminal Code, R.S.C. 1985, c. C-46.

25. As the matter was put by a principal advisor to the chief U.S. prosecutor at Nuremberg, many of the charges brought against the nazis were based in upon their violation of "customary international law—a system [evolving] under the impact of common consent and the demands of world security. Acquiescence of all members of the Family of Nations is not necessary for this purpose. All that is needed is reasonable proof of the existence of widespread custom"; Sheldon Glueck, "The Nuremberg Trial and Aggressive War," *Harvard Law Review*, No. 59, Feb. 1946, pp. 396-456. This rule was affirmed by the International Court of Justice with respect to the Genocide Convention in an Advisory Opinion issued on May 28, 1951: "The principles inherent in the Convention are acknowledged by civilized nations as binding on [any] country, even [those] without a conventional obligation." In effect, "reservations" to the Convention like that attempted by the U.S., or attempts to limit its scope by deleting portions of it in domestic implementing statutes, as Canada has, have no legal validity at all; see generally, Robert K. Woetzel, "The Eichmann Case in International Law," *Criminal Law Review*, Oct. 1962, pp. 671-82.

26. Pieter N. Drost, *Genocide* (Leyden: A.W. Sythoff, 1959); *The Crime of State* (Leyden: A.W. Sythoff, 1959). In actuality, Lemkin himself coined the term "ethnocide" in a footnote on page 79 of *Axis*

*Rule*—the same page on which the neologism "genocide" itself was invented—explaining therein that the two words are *synonyms*. Interestingly, subsequent researchers have simply repeated without further investigation Drost's false attribution of "ethnocide" to French scholarship, as well as his unfounded contention that it describes something other than genocide; see, e.g., Kurt Jonasohn and Frank Chalk, "A Typology of Genocide and Some Implications for the Human Rights Agenda," in Isador Walliman and Michael Dobkowski, eds., *Genocide and the Modern Age: Etiology and Case Studies of Mass Death* (Westport, CT: Greenwood Press, 1987) pp. 7, 37.

27. Frank Chalk, "Definitions of Genocide and Their Implications for Prediction and Prevention," in Yehuda Bauer, et al., eds., *Remembering for the Future: Working Papers and Addenda*, 2 vols. (Oxford: Pergammon Press, 1989) pp. 76-7.

28. Haunani-Kay Trask, *From a Native Daughter: Colonialism and Sovereignty in Hawai'i* (Honolulu: University of Hawai'i Press, [rev. ed.] 1999) p. 251.

29. Jean-Paul Sartre and Arlette El Kaim-Sartre, *On Genocide and a Summary of the Evidence and Judgments of the International War Crimes Tribunal* (Boston: Beacon Press, 1968). Although he was highly critical of Sartre's "overgeneralized" formulation, Leo Kuper, one of the more astute analysts of genocide, by and large incorporated it into his own books: Leo Kuper, *Genocide: Its Political Uses in the Twentieth Century* (New Haven, CT, Yale University Press, 1981); *International Action Against Genocide* (London: Minority Rights Group, [rev. ed.] 1984); *The Prevention of Genocide* (New Haven, CT: Yale University Press, 1985).

30. Russell Tribunal, *Report of the Fourth Russell Tribunal on the Rights of the Indians of the Americas* (Nottingham: Bertrand Russell Foundation, 1980).

31. *Cultural Survival Quarterly* is the journal of Cambridge, Massachusetts-based Cultural Survival, Inc. On the resistance movements, see Miles Goldstick, *Wollaston: People Resisting Genocide* (Montréal: Black Rose Books, 1987); Boyce Richardson, *Strangers Devour the Land: The Cree Hunters of the James Bay Area versus Premier Bourassa and the James Bay Development Corporation* (Post Mills, VT: Chelsea Green [rev. ed.] 1991); Ward Churchill, "Genocide in Arizona: The 'Navajo-Hopi Land Dispute' in Perspective," in my *Struggle for the Land: Native North American Resistance to Genocide, Ecocide and Colonization* (San Francisco: City Lights, [2nd ed.] 2002) pp. 135-74.

32. The story of the Lubicon is quite complex; see John Goddard, *Last Stand of the Lubicon Cree* (Vancouver/Toronto: Douglas & McIntire, 1991).

33. *Daishowa Inc. v. Friends of the Lubicon*, Ontario Court of Justice (Gen. Div.), File No. 95-CQ-59707, Verdict of Judge J. McPherson (Apr. 14, 1998) p. 21.

34. Ibid., pp. 21-2.

35. Thomas Claridge, "Judge to Rule May 19 on Lubicon boycott: Daishowa says $3-million annual sales lost," *Toronto Globe and Mail*, May 1, 1995.

36. FOL briefing paper distributed by the Sierra Legal Defense Fund, beginning in 1996 (copy on file).

37. Conversation with Kevin Thomas, June 14, 1997 (notes on file).

38. Ibid.

39. Christopher Genovali, "Multinational Pulp Company SLAPPs Suit Against Activist Group," *Alternatives Journal*, Vol. 22, No. 3, 1996.

40. *Daishowa Inc. v. Friends of the Lubicon* (1995), 30 C.R.R. (2d) 26 (Gen. Div.). The corporation immediately filed an appeal which resulted in reinstatement of the injunction against the FOL's boycott activities more generally. This higher court ruling was later expanded to prohibit the defendants, their attorneys, and even selected expert witnesses from publicly discussing the case; Christopher Genovali, "Daishowa Tries to Gag Critics," *Alternatives Journal*, Vol. 23, No. 2, 1997.

41. Verdict, p. 50.

42. Ibid., pp. 72, 68, 76.

43. Ibid., p. 76.

44. Ibid., pp. 42-3. MacPherson's description of the situation in which the Lubicon have been placed should be compared with the explanation offered by the Saudi delegate to the drafting committee of what was/is meant by the language contained in Article II(c) of the 1948. This includes not only the "planned disintegration of the political, social or economic structure of a group or nation," but the

"systematic debasement of a group, people or nation"; quoted in Davis and Zannis, *Genocide Machine*, p. 19.

45. Among the expert witness submissions MacPherson ignored were an article, "Modern Genocide," prepared by the McGill University law faculty and published in *Quid Novi* on November 30, 1987 (submitted in evidence as Defense Exhibit 30; Thomas Affidavit); a 1990 letter to Prime Minister Brian Mulroney prepared by the late James J.E. Smith, Curator of North American Ethnography for the Museum of the American Indian/Heye Foundation, in which it is concluded that "social and cultural genocide" is being perpetrated against the Lubicons (Defense Exhibit 4; Ominiyak Affidavit); a 1995 affidavit prepared by Dr. Joan Ryan, an anthropologist who combined 15 years experience documenting the destruction of Lubicon society with the very dictionary definitions the judge relied upon in arriving at a diametrically opposing conclusion. Both Dr. Ryan and I presented direct testimony during the trial. *None* of this is so much as mentioned in the Verdict.

46. Verdict, p. 71. MacPherson in fact quotes three different dictionaries, *none* of which posits "intentional killing" as synonymous with genocide. *Webster's* refers to "the deliberate and systematic *destruction* of a racial, political or cultural group (emphasis added)."

47. MacPherson claims to have followed the dictum that "defamatory meaning must be one which would be understood by an ordinary and reasonable person"; Verdict, pp. 70-1. He neglects to mention, however, that the rule pertains only to instances where the terms at issue are *not* defined in law; R.E. Brown, *The Law of Defamation in Canada* (2nd ed., Vol. 1, p. 52).

48. Even MacPherson seems a bit uncomfortable with his definition. He suggests at one point that "physical destruction" rather than direct killing alone might add up to genocide. But then, apparently realizing that the sorts of conditions he's already conceded the Lubicons are suffering would all too obviously fit this description, he simply drops the subject; Verdict, p. 71.

49. Ibid., p. 76.

50. Ibid., p. 39. This clearly goes to compelling the employment of euphemisms, the purpose of which is well-known. The nazis, after all, referred to their Judeocide as the "Final Solution," the transport of Jews to Auschwitz and other extermination centers as "Resettlement," the literal killing therein as "Special Handling." Such innocuous terminology was designed to obscure genocidal reality and thus constrain the probability of popular revulsion and unrest.

51. Lipstadt, *Denying the Holocaust*, pp. 7-8.

52. In the United States alone, nearly a hundred such peoples have been declared "culturally extinct" by the federal government during this period; Raymond V. Butler, "The Bureau of Indian Affairs: Activities Since 1945," *Annals of the American Academy of Political Science*, No. 435, 1978, pp. 50-60.

53. The implications were brought out clearly in March 1974, when, in one of the few instances where charges of genocide were filed with the U.N. Secretariat, the International League for the Rights of Man, the Inter-American Association for Democracy and Freedom and several other organizations accused the government of Paraguay of physically exterminating the Aché Indians. Paraguay's formal response to these allegations was that, "Although there are victims and victimizer, there is not the third element necessary to establish the crime of genocide—that is 'intent.' As there is no 'intent,' one cannot speak of 'genocide' "; Paraguayan Minister of Defense, quoted in Norman Lewis, "The Camp at Ceclio Baez," in Richard Arens, ed., *Genocide in Paraguay* (Philadelphia: Temple University Press, 1976) pp. 62-3.

54. Those who experience a visceral reaction to my "overstated" comparison should recall that Eichmann was not accused of actually killing anyone. Rather, he was convicted of having devoted his bureaucratic and technical expertise—that is, his intellect—to organizing the delivery of Jews and others to extermination centers; Hannah Arendt, *Eichmann in Jerusalem: A Report on the Banality of Evil* (New York: Penguin, 1964).

55. Unidentified Lubicon, quoted in Thomas Affidavit, p. 24.

This essay, originally published in the e-journal *Other Voices* during February 2000, is in part extracted from a longer essay entitled "Last Stand at Lubicon Lake: Genocide and Ecocide in the Canadian North," in my *Struggle for the Land: Native North American Resistance to Genocide, Ecocide and Colonization* (San Francisco: City Lights, [2nd ed.] 2002).

# The Bloody Wake of Alcatraz
## Repression of the American Indian Movement During the 1970s

> The only way to deal with the Indian problem in South Dakota is to put a gun to AIM leaders' heads and pull the trigger.
>
> —William Janklow
> South Dakota Attorney General
> 1975

In combination with the fishing rights struggles of the Puyallup, Nisqually, Muckleshoot and other nations in the Pacific Northwest from 1965 to 1970, the 1969-71 occupation of Alcatraz Island by the San Francisco Bay Area's Indians of All Tribes coalition ushered in a decade-long period of uncompromising and intensely confrontational American Indian political activism.[1] Unprecedented in modern U.S. history, the phenomenon represented by Alcatraz also marked the inception of a process of official repression of indigenous activists without contemporary North American parallel in its virulence and lethal effects.[2]

The nature of the post-Alcatraz federal response to organized agitation for native rights was such that by 1979 researchers were describing it as a manifestation of the U.S. government's "continuing Indian Wars."[3] For its part, in secret internal documents, the Federal Bureau of Investigation (FBI)—the primary instrument by which the government's policy of anti-Indian repression was implemented—concurred with such assessments, abandoning its customary counterintelligence vernacular in favor of the terminology of outright counterinsurgency warfare.[4] The result, as the U.S. Commission on Civil Rights officially conceded at the time, was the imposition of a virtual "reign of terror" upon certain of the less compliant sectors of indigenous society in the United States.[5]

In retrospect, it may be seen that the locus of both activism and repression in Indian Country throughout the 1970s centered squarely upon one group, the American Indian Movement (AIM). Moreover, the crux of AIM activism during the 1970s, and thus of the FBI's campaign to "neutralize" it,[6] can be found in a single locality: the Pine Ridge (Oglala Lakota) Reservation, in South Dakota. The purpose of the present essay, then, is to provide an overview of the federal counterinsurgency program against AIM on and around Pine Ridge, using it as a lens through which to explore the broader motives and outcomes attending it. Finally, conclusions will be drawn as to its implications, not only with respect to American Indians, but concerning non-indigenous Americans as well.

## Background

AIM was founded in 1968 in Minneapolis, by a group of urban Anishinabes (Chippewas) including Dennis Banks, Pat Ballanger, Clyde Bellecourt, Eddie Benton Benai and George Mitchell. Modeled loosely after the Black Panther Party for Self-Defense, established by Huey P. Newton and Bobby Seale in Oakland, California, two years previously, the group took as its first tasks the protection of the city's sizable native community from a pattern of rampant police abuse, and the creation of programs on jobs, housing and education.[7] Within three years, the organization had grown to include chapters in several other cities, and had begun to shift its focus from civil rights issues to an agenda more specifically attuned to the conditions afflicting Native North America.

What AIM discerned as the basis of the latter was not so much a matter of socioeconomic discrimination against Indians as it was their internal colonization by the United States.[8] This perception accrued from the fact that, by 1871, when federal treatymaking with native peoples was permanently suspended, the rights of indigenous nations to distinct, self-governing territories had been recognized by the U.S. more than 370 times through treaties duly ratified by its Senate.[9] Yet, during the intervening century, more than 90 percent of treaty-reserved native land had been expropriated by the federal government, in defiance of both its own constitution and international custom and convention.[10] One consequence of this was creation of the urban diaspora from which AIM itself had emerged; by 1970, about half of all Indians in the U.S. had been pushed off their land altogether.[11]

Within the residual archipelago of reservations, an aggregation of about 50 million acres, or roughly 2.5 percent of the forty-eight contiguous states, indigenous forms of governance had been thoroughly usurped through the imposition of U.S. jurisdiction under the federal government's self-assigned prerogative of exercising "plenary [full and absolute] power over Indian affairs."[12] Correspondingly, Indian control over what had turned out to be rather vast mineral resources within reservation boundaries—an estimated two-thirds of all U.S. "domestic" uranium deposits, a quarter of the low-sulfur coal, 20 percent of the oil and natural gas, and so on—was essentially nonexistent.[13]

It followed that royalty rates set by the U.S. Bureau of Indian Affairs (BIA), in its exercise of federal "trust" prerogatives vis-à-vis corporate extraction of Indian mineral assets, amounted to only a fraction of what the same corporations would have paid had they undertaken the same mining operations in nonreservation localities.[14] The same principle of underpayment to Indians, with resulting "super-profit" accrual to non-Indian business entities, prevailed with regard to other areas of economic activity handled by the Indian Bureau, from the leasing of reservation grazing land to various ranching interests to the harvesting of reservation timber by corporations such as Weyerhauser and Boise-Cascade.[15] Small wonder that, by the late 1960s, Indian radicals like Robert K. Thomas had begun to refer to the BIA as "the Colonial Office of the United States."[16]

In human terms, the consequence was that, as an aggregate, American Indians—who, on the basis of known resources, comprised what should have been the single wealthiest population group in North America—constituted by far the most impoverished sector of U.S. society. According to the federal government's own data, Indians suffered, by a decisive margin, the highest rate of unemployment in the country, a matter correlated to their receiving by far the lowest annual and lifetime incomes of any group in the country.[17] It also corresponded well with virtually every other statistical indicator of extreme poverty: a truly catastrophic rate of infant mortality and the highest rates of death from malnutrition, exposure, plague disease, teen suicide and accidents related to alcohol abuse. The average life-expectancy of a reservation-based Indian male was in 1970 less than 45 years; reservation-based Indian females could expect to live less than three years longer than their male counterparts; urban Indians of either gender were living only about five years longer on average than their relatives on the reservations.[18]

AIM's response to its growing apprehension of this squalid panorama was to initiate a campaign consciously intended to bring about the decolonization of Native North America: "Only by reestablishing our rights as sovereign nations, including our right to control our own territories and resources, and our right to genuine self-governance," as Dennis Banks put it in 1971, "can we hope to successfully address the conditions currently experienced by our people."[19]

Extrapolating largely from the example of Alcatraz, the Movement undertook a multifaceted political strategy combining a variety of tactics. On the one hand, it engaged in activities designed primarily to focus media attention, and thus the attention of the general public, on Indian rights issues, especially those pertaining to treaty rights. On the other hand, it pursued the sort of direct confrontation meant to affirm those rights in practice. It also began to systematically reassert native cultural/spiritual traditions.[20] Eventually, it added a component wherein the full range of indigenous rights to decolonization/self-determination were pursued through the United Nations venue of international law, custom and convention.[21]

In mounting this comprehensive effort, AIM made of itself a bona fide National Liberation Movement, at least for a while.[22] Its members consisted of "the shock troops of Indian sovereignty," to quote Oglala Lakota activist Birgil Kills Straight.[23] They essentially reframed the paradigm by which U.S.-Indian relations are understood in the late twentieth century.[24] They also suffered the worst physical repression at the hands of the United States of any "domestic" group since the 1890 massacre of Big Foot's Minneconjous by the 7th Cavalry at Wounded Knee.[25]

**Prelude**

AIM's seizure of the public consciousness may in many ways be said to have begun at the point in 1969 when Dennis Banks recruited a young Oglala named Russell Means to join the Movement. Instinctively imbued with what one critic described as a "bizarre knack for staging demonstrations that attracted the sort of press coverage Indians had been looking for,"[26] Means was instrumental in AIM's achieving several of its earliest and most important media coups: painting Plymouth Rock red before capturing the *Mayflower* replica on Thanksgiving Day 1971, for example, and staging a "4th of July Countercelebration" by occupying the Mt. Rushmore National Monument the same year.[27]

Perhaps more importantly, Means proved to be the bridge which allowed the Movement to establish its credibility on a reservation for the first time. In part, this was because when he joined AIM he brought along virtually an entire generation of his family—brothers Ted, Bill and Dale, cousin Madonna Gilbert, and others—each of whom possessed a web of friends and acquaintances on the Pine Ridge Reservation. It was therefore rather natural that AIM was called upon to "set things right" concerning the torture-murder of a middle-aged Oglala in the off-reservation town of Gordon, Nebraska, in late February 1972.[28] As Bill Means would later recall:

> When Raymond Yellow Thunder was killed, his relatives went first to the BIA, then to the FBI, and to the local police, but they got no response. Severt Young Bear [Yellow Thunder's nephew and a friend of Ted Means] then . . . asked AIM to come help clear up the case.[29]

Shortly, Russell Means led a caravan of some 1,300 Indians into the small town, announcing from the steps of the courthouse that, "We've come here today to put Gordon on the map . . . and if justice is not immediately forthcoming, we're going to take Gordon *off* the map." The killers, brothers named Melvin and Leslie Hare, were quickly arrested, and a police officer who had covered up for them suspended. The Hares soon became the first whites in Nebraska history sent to prison for killing an Indian and "AIM's reputation soared among reservation Indians. What tribal leaders had dared not do to protect their people, AIM had done."[30]

By fall, things had progressed to the point that AIM could collaborate with several other native rights organizations to stage the "Trail of Broken Treaties" caravan, bringing more than 2,000 Indians from reservations and urban areas across the country to Washington, D.C., on the eve of the 1972 presidential election. The idea was to present the incumbent chief executive, Richard M. Nixon, with a twenty-point program redefining the nature of U.S.-Indian relations. The publicity attending the critical timing and location of the action, as well as the large number of Indians involved, were calculated to force serious responses by the administration to each point.[31]

In the event, Interior Department officials who had earlier pledged logistical support to caravan participants once they arrived in the capitol reneged on their promises, apparently in the belief that this would cause the group to meekly disperse. Instead, angry Indians promptly took over the BIA headquarters building on November 2, evicted its staff, and held it for several days. Russell Means, in fine form, captured the front page of the nation's newspapers and the Six O'Clock News by conducting a press conference in front of the building while adorned with a makeshift "war club" and a "shield" fashioned from a portrait of Nixon himself.[32]

Desperate to end what had become a major media embarrassment, the administration publicly agreed to formally reply to the twenty-point program within a month, and to immediately provide $66,000 in transportation money, in exchange for a peaceful end to the occupation.[33] AIM honored its part of the bargain, leaving the BIA building on November 9. But, explaining that "Indians have every right to known the details of what's being done to us and to our property," it took with it a vast number of "confidential" files concerning BIA leasing practices, operation of the Indian Health Service (IHS), and so forth. The originals were returned as rapidly as they could be xeroxed, a process that required nearly two years to complete.[34]

Technically speaking, the government also honored its end of the deal, providing official—and exclusively negative—responses to the twenty points within the specified timeframe.[35] Concurrently, however, it initiated a campaign utilizing federally subsidized Indian "leaders" in an effort to discredit AIM members as "irresponsible . . . renegades, terrorists and self-styled revolutionaries."[36] There is also strong indication that it was at this point that the Federal Bureau of Investigation was instructed to launch a secret program of its own, one in which AIM's capacity to engage in further political activities of the kind and effectiveness displayed in Washington was to be, in the vernacular of FBI counterintelligence specialists, "neutralized."[37]

Even as this was going on, AIM's focus had shifted back to the Pine Ridge area. At issue was the January 23, 1973, murder of a young Oglala named Wesley Bad Heart Bull by a white man, Darld Schmitz, in the off-reservation village of Buffalo Gap, South Dakota. As in the Yellow Thunder case, local authorities had made no move to press appropriate charges against the killer.[38] At the request of the victim's mother, Sarah, Russell Means therefore called for a demonstration at the Custer County Courthouse, in which jurisdiction the scene of the crime fell. Terming western South Dakota "the Mississippi of the North,"[39] Dennis Banks simultaneously announced a longer-term effort to force abandonment "of the anti-Indian attitudes which result in Indian-killing being treated as a sort of local sport."[40]

When the Custer demonstration occurred on February 6, it followed a very different course than that of the protest in Gordon a year earlier. An anonymous call had been placed to the main regional newspaper, the *Rapid City Journal*, on the evening of February 5. The caller, saying he was "with AIM," asked that a notice canceling the action "because of bad weather" be prominently displayed in the paper the following morning. Consequently, relatively few Indians turned out for the protest.[41] Those who did were met by an amalgamated force of police, sheriff's deputies, state troopers and FBI personnel when they arrived in Custer.[42]

For a while, there was a tense standoff. Then, a sheriff's deputy manhandled Sarah Bad Heart Bull when she attempted to enter the courthouse. In the melée which followed, the courthouse was set ablaze—reportedly, by a police tear gas canister—and the local Chamber of Commerce building burned to the ground. Banks, Means and other AIM members, along with Mrs. Bad Heart Bull, were arrested and charged with riot. Banks was eventually convicted, sentenced to three years imprisonment, and became a fugitive; Sarah Bad Heart Bull herself served five months of a one-to-five-year sentence. Her son's killer never served a day in jail.[43]

### Wounded Knee

Meanwhile, on Pine Ridge, tensions were running extraordinarily high. The point of contention was an escalating conflict between the tribal administration headed by Richard "Dickie" Wilson, installed on the reservation with federal support in 1972, and a large body of reservation traditionals who objected to Wilson's nepotism and other abuses of his position.[44] Initially, Wilson's opponents had sought redress of their grievances through the BIA. The BIA responded by providing a $62,000 grant to Wilson for purposes of establishing a "Tribal Ranger Group"—a paramilitary entity reporting exclusively to Wilson which soon began calling itself "Guardians Of the Oglala Nation" (GOONs)—with which to physically intimidate the opposition.[45] The reason underlying this federal largesse appears to have been the government's desire that Wilson sign an instrument transferring title over a portion of the reservation known as the Sheep Mountain Gunnery Range—secretly known to be rich in uranium and molybdenum—to the National Park Service.[46]

In any event, forming what was called the Oglala Sioux Civil Rights Organization (OSCRO), the traditionals next attempted to obtain relief through the Justice Department and FBI. When this too failed to bring results, they set out to impeach Wilson, obtaining more signatures of more eligible voters on their petitions than had cast ballots for him in the first place. The BIA countered by naming Wilson himself to chair the impeachment proceedings, and the Justice Department dispatched a 65-member

"Special Operations Group" (SOG; a large SWAT unit) of U.S. Marshals to ensure that "order" was maintained during the travesty. Then, on the eve of the hearing, Wilson ordered the arrest and jailing of several members of the tribal council he felt might vote for his removal. Predictably, when the impeachment tally was taken on February 23, 1973, the tribal president was retained in office. Immediately thereafter, he announced a reservation-wide ban on political assemblies.[47]

Defying the ban, the traditionals convened a round-the-clock emergency meeting at the Calico Hall, near the village of Oglala, in an effort to determine their next move. On February 26, a messenger was sent to the newly established AIM headquarters in nearby Rapid City to request that Russell Means meet with the Oglala elders. As one of them, Ellen Moves Camp, later put it:

> We decided we needed the American Indian Movement in here. . . All of our older people from the reservation helped make that decision. . . This is what we needed, a little more push. Most of the reservation believes in AIM, and we're proud to have them with us.[48]

Means came on the morning of the 27th, then drove on to the village of Pine Ridge, seat of the reservation government, to try and negotiate some sort of resolution with Wilson. For his trouble, he was physically assaulted by GOONs in the parking lot of the tribal administration building.[49] By then, Dennis Banks and a number of other AIM members had arrived at the Calico Hall. During subsequent meetings, it was decided by the elders that what was necessary was to draw public attention to the situation on the reservation. For this purpose, a 200-person AIM contingent was sent to the symbolic site of Wounded Knee to prepare for an early morning press conference; a much smaller group was sent back to Rapid City to notify the media, and to guide reporters to Wounded Knee at the appropriate time.[50]

The intended press conference never occurred because, by dawn, Wilson's GOONs had established roadblocks on all four routes leading into (or out of) the tiny hamlet. During the morning, these positions were reinforced by uniformed BIA police, then by elements of the Marshals' SOG unit, and then by FBI "observers." As this was going on, the AIM members in Wounded Knee began the process of arming themselves from the stores of the local Gildersleeve Trading Post and building defensive positions.[51] By afternoon, General Alexander Haig, military liaison to the Nixon White House, had dispatched two special warfare experts—Colonel Volney Warner of the 82nd Airborne Division, and Colonel Jack Potter of the Sixth Army — to the scene.[52]

Documents later subpoenaed from the Pentagon revealed Colonel Potter directed the employment of 17 APCs [tanklike armored personnel carriers], 130,000 rounds of M-16 ammunition, 41,000 rounds of M-40 high explosive [for the M-79 grenade launchers he also provided], as well as helicopters, Phantom jets, and personnel. Military officers, supply sergeants, maintenance technicians, chemical officers, and medical teams [were provided on site]. Three hundred miles to the south, at Fort Carson, Colorado, the Army had billeted a fully uniformed assault unit on twenty-four hour alert.[53]

Over the next seventy-one days, the AIM perimeter at Wounded Knee was placed under siege. The ground cover was burned away for roughly a quarter-mile around the AIM position as part of the federal attempt to staunch the flow of supplies — food, medicine and ammunition — back-packed in to the Wounded Knee defenders at night; at one point such material had to be airdropped by a group of supporting pilots.[54] More than 500,000 rounds of military ammunition were fired into AIM's jerry-rigged "bunkers" by federal forces, killing two Indians — an Apache named Frank Clearwater and Buddy Lamont, an Oglala — and wounding several others.[55] As many as thirteen more people may have been killed by roving GOON patrols, their bodies secretly buried in remote locations around the reservation, while they were trying to carry supplies through federal lines.[56]

At first, the authorities sought to justify what was happening by claiming that AIM had "occupied" Wounded Knee, and that the Movement had taken several hostages in the process.[57] When the latter allegation was proven to be false, a press ban was imposed, and official spokespersons argued that the use of massive force was needed to "quell insurrection." Much was made of two federal casualties who were supposed to have been seriously injured by AIM gunfire.[58] In the end, it was Dickie Wilson who perhaps expressed matters most candidly when he informed reporters that the purpose of the entire exercise was to see to it that "AIM dies at Wounded Knee."[59]

Despite Wilson's sentiments — and those of FBI senior counterintelligence specialist Richard G. Held, expressed in a secret report prepared at the request of his superiors early in the siege[60] — an end to the standoff was finally negotiated for May 7, 1973. AIM's major condition, entered in behalf of the Pine Ridge traditionals and agreed to by government representatives, was that a federal commission would meet with the chiefs to review U.S. compliance with the terms of the 1868 Fort Laramie Treaty with the Lakota,

Cheyenne and Arapaho Nations.[61] The idea was to generate policy recommendations as to how the United States might bring itself into line with its treaty obligations. A White House delegation did in fact meet with the elders at the home of Chief Frank Fools Crow, near the reservation town of Manderson, on May 17. The delegates' mission, however, was to stonewall all efforts at meaningful discussion.[62] They promised a follow-up meeting on May 30, but never returned.[63]

On other fronts, the authorities were demonstrating no comparable lack of vigor. Before the first meeting at Fools Crow's, the FBI had made 562 arrests of those who had been involved in defending Wounded Knee.[64] Russell Means was in jail awaiting release on $150,000 bond; OSCRO leader Pedro Bissonette was held against $152,000; AIM leaders Stan Holder and Leonard Crow Dog against $32,000 and $35,000 respectively. Scores of others were being held pending the posting of lesser sums.[65] By the fall of 1973, agents had amassed some 316,000 separate investigative file classifications on those who had been inside Wounded Knee.[66]

This allowed federal prosecutors to obtain 185 indictments over the next several months (Means alone was charged with thirty-seven felonies and three misdemeanors).[67] Although in 1974 AIM and the traditionals used the 1868 Treaty as a basis upon which to challenge in federal court the U.S. government's jurisdiction over Pine Ridge, the trials of the "Wounded Knee Leadership" went forward.[68] Even after the FBI's and the prosecution's willingness to subvert the judicial process became so blatantly obvious that U.S. District Judge Fred Nichol was compelled to dismiss all charges against Banks and Means, cases were still pressed against Crow Dog, Holder, Carter Camp, Madonna Gilbert, Lorelei DeCora and Phyllis Young.[69]

The whole charade resulted in a meager fifteen convictions, all of them on such paltry offenses as trespass and "interference with postal inspectors in performance of their lawful duties."[70] Still, in the interim, the virtual entirety of AIM's leadership was tied up in a seemingly endless series of arrests, incarcerations, hearings and trials. Similarly, the great bulk of the Movement's fundraising and organizing capacity was diverted into posting bonds and mounting legal defenses for those indicted.[71]

On balance, the record suggests a distinct probability that the post-Wounded Knee prosecutions were never seriously intended to result in convictions at all. Instead, they were designed mainly to serve the time-honored—and utterly illegal—expedient of "disrupting, misdirecting, destabilizing or otherwise neutralizing" a politically objectionable group.[72] There is official concurrence with this view: As army counterinsurgency specialist Volney Warner framed matters at the time, "AIM's best leaders and most militant members are under indictment, in jail or warrants are out for their arrest. . . [Under these conditions] the government can win, even if nobody goes to [prison]."[73]

### The Reign of Terror

While AIM's "notables" were being forced to slog their way through the courts, a very different form of repression was being visited up the Movement's rank-and-file membership and grassroots traditionals of Pine Ridge. During the three-year period beginning with the Siege of Wounded Knee, at least sixty-nine members and supporters of AIM died violently on the reservation.[74] During the same period, nearly 350 others suffered serious physical assault. Overall, the situation on Pine Ridge was such that, by 1976, the U.S. Commission on Civil Rights was led to describe it as a "reign of terror."[75]

> Using only documented political deaths, the yearly murder rate on the Pine Ridge Reservation between March 1, 1973, and March 1, 1976, was 170 per 100,000. By comparison, Detroit, the reputed "murder capital of the United States," had a rate of 20.2 per 100,000 in 1974. The U.S. average was 9.7 per 100,000. . . In a nation of 200 million persons, the murder rate comparable with that on Pine Ridge between 1973 and 1976 would have left 340,000 persons dead for political reasons alone in one year; 1.32 million in three. . . The political murder rate at Pine Ridge was almost equivalent to that in Chile during the three years after a military coup supported by the United States killed President Salvador Allende.[76]

Despite the fact that eyewitnesses identified the assailants in twenty-one of these homicides, the FBI—which maintains preeminent jurisdiction over major crimes on all American Indian reservations—was responsible for not one of the killers ever being convicted.[77] In many cases, no active investigation of the murder of an AIM member or supporter was undertaken by the Bureau.[78] In others, those associated with the victims were falsely arrested as "perpetrators."[79]

When queried by reporters in 1975 as to the reason for his office's abysmal record in investigating murders on Pine Ridge, George O'Clock, agent in charge of the FBI's Rapid City Resident Agency—under which operational authority the reservation falls most immediately—replied that he "lacked the manpower" to assign agents such tasks.[80] O'Clock omitted to mention that, at the time, he had at his disposal the highest sustained ratio of agents to citizens enjoyed by any FBI office in the history of the Bureau.[81] He also neglected the fact that the same agents who were too busy to look into the murders of AIM people appear to have had unlimited time to undertake the investigative activities covered in the preceding section. Plainly, O'Clock's pat "explanation" was and remains implausible.

A far more likely scenario begins to take shape when it is considered that in each instance where there were eyewitness identifications of the individuals who had killed an AIM member or supporter, those identified were known GOONs.[82] The FBI's conspicuous inability to apprehend murderers on Pine Ridge may thus be located, not in the incompetence of its personnel, but in the nature of its relationship to the killers. In effect, the GOONs seem to have functioned under a more-or-less blanket immunity from prosecution provided by the FBI so long as they focused their lethal attentions upon targets selected by the Bureau. Put another way, the appearance is that the FBI used the GOONs as a surrogate force against AIM on Pine Ridge in precisely the same manner that Latin American death squads have been utilized by the CIA to destroy the opposition in countries like Guatemala, El Salvador and Chile.[83]

The roots of the FBI/GOON connection can be traced back at least as far as April 23, 1973, when U.S. Marshals Service Director Wayne Colburn, driving from Pine Ridge village to Wounded Knee, was stopped at what the Wilsonites referred to as "The Residents' Roadblock." One of the GOONs manning the position, vocally disgruntled with what he called the "soft line" taken by the Justice Department in dealing with AIM, leveled a shotgun at the head of Colburn's passenger, Solicitor General Kent Frizzell. Colburn was forced to draw his own weapon before the man would desist. Angered, Colburn drove back to Pine Ridge and dispatched a group of his men to arrest everyone at the roadblock. When the marshals arrived at the Pennington County Jail in Rapid City with those arrested, however, they found an FBI man waiting with instructions to release the GOONs immediately.[84]

By this point, Dickie Wilson himself had reestablished the roadblock, using a fresh crew of GOONs. Thoroughly enraged at this defiance, Colburn assembled another group of marshals and prepared to make arrests. Things had progressed to the point of a "High Noon" style showdown when a helicopter appeared, quickly landing on the blacktop road near the would-be combatants. In it was FBI counterintelligence ace Richard G. Held, who informed Colburn that he had received instructions "from the highest level" to ensure that no arrests would be made and that "the roadblock stays where it is."[85]

Humiliated, and increasingly concerned for the safety of his own personnel in a situation where the FBI was openly siding with a group hostile to them, Colburn ordered his men to disarm GOONs whenever possible.[86] Strikingly, as the marshals impounded the sort of weaponry the Wilsonites had up until then been using—conventional deer rifles, World War II surplus M-1s, shotguns, and other firearms normally found in a rural locality—the same GOONs Colburn's men had disarmed began to reappear, well-stocked with ammunition and sporting fully automatic military-issue M-16s.[87]

## The Brewer Revelations

It has always been the supposition of those aligned with AIM that the FBI provided such hardware to Wilson's GOONs. The Bureau and its apologists, meanwhile, pointing to the absence of concrete evidence with which to confirm the allegation, have consistently denied any such connection, charging those referring to its probability with journalistic or scholarly "irresponsibility."[88] It was not until the early 1990s, with publication of extracts from an interview with former GOON commander Duane Brewer, that AIM's premise was borne out.[89]

Not only does the one-time death squad leader make it clear that the FBI provided him and his men with weaponry, but with ample supplies of armor-piercing ammunition, hand grenades, "det cord" and other explosives, communications gear and additional paraphernalia.[90] Agents would drop by his house, Brewer maintains, to provide key bits of field intelligence which allowed the GOONs to function in a more efficient manner than might otherwise have been the case. And, perhaps most importantly, agents conveyed the plain message that members of the death squad would enjoy virtual immunity from federal prosecution for anything they did, so long as it fell within the realm of repressing dissidents on the reservation.[91]

Among other murders which Brewer clarifies in his interview is that of Jeanette Bissonette, a young woman shot to death in her car as she sat at a stop sign in Pine Ridge village at about one o'clock in the morning of March 27, 1975. The FBI has all along insisted, for reasons which remain mysterious, that it is "probable" Bissonette was assassinated by AIM members.[92] Brewer, on the other hand, explains on the basis of firsthand knowledge that the killing was "a mistake" on the part of his execution team, which mistook Bissonette's vehicle for that of local resistance leader Ellen Moves Camp.[93]

It is important to note, before moving ahead, that at the time he functioned as a GOON leader, Duane Brewer also served as second-in-command of the BIA police on Pine Ridge. His boss as a policeman, Delmar Eastman—primary liaison between the police and the FBI—was simultaneously in charge of all GOON operations on the reservation.[94] In total, it is reliably estimated that somewhere between one-third and one-half of all BIA police personnel on Pine Ridge between 1972 and 1976 moonlighted as GOONs. Those who didn't become directly involved, actively covered for their colleagues who did, or at least kept their mouths shut about the situation.[95]

Obviously, whatever meager hope for relief AIM and the Oglala traditionals might have extended to the workings of local law enforcement quickly disappeared under such circumstances.[96] In effect, the police were the killers, their crimes not only condoned, but for all practical intents and purposes commanded and controlled by the FBI. Other federal agencies did no more than issue largely uncirculated reports confirming that the bloodbath was in fact occurring.[97] "Due process" on Pine Ridge during the crucial period was effectively nonexistent.

### The Oglala Firefight

By the spring of 1975, with more than forty of their number already dead, it had become apparent to the Pine Ridge resisters that they had been handed a choice of either acquiescing to the federal agenda or being annihilated. All other alternatives, including a 1974 electoral effort to replace Dickie Wilson with AIM leader Russell Means, had been met by fraud, force and unremitting violence.[98] Those who wished to continue the struggle and survive were therefore compelled to adopt a posture of armed self-defense. Given that many of the traditionals were elderly, and thus could not reasonably hope to accomplish the latter on their own, AIM was asked to provide physical security for them. Defensive encampments were quickly established at several key locations around the reservation.[99]

For its part, the FBI seems to have become increasingly frustrated at the capacity of the dissidents to absorb punishment, and the consequent failure of the Bureau's counterinsurgency campaign to force submission. Internal

FBI documents suggest that the coordinators of the Pine Ridge operation had come to greatly desire some sensational event which might serve to justify in the public mind a sudden introduction to the reservation of the kind of overwhelming force which might break the back of the resistance once and for all.[100]

Apparently selected for this purpose was a security camp set up by the Northwest AIM Group at the request of traditional elders Harry and Cecelia Jumping Bull on their property, along Highway 18, a few miles south of the village of Oglala. During the early evening of June 25, 1975, two agents, Ron Williams and Jack Coler, escorted by a BIA policeman (and known GOON) named Bob Ecoffey, entered the Jumping Bull Compound. They claimed to be attempting to serve an arrest warrant on a seventeen-year-old Lakota and AIM supporter named Jimmy Eagle on spurious charges of kidnapping and aggravated assault.[101]

Told by residents that Eagle was not there and had not been seen for weeks, the agents and their escort left. On Highway 18, however, the agents accosted three young AIM members—Mike Anderson, Norman Charles and Wilfred "Wish" Draper—who were walking back to camp after taking showers in Oglala, drove them to the police headquarters in Pine Ridge village, and interrogated them for more than two hours. As the young men reported when they finally returned to the Jumping Bulls', no questions had been asked about Jimmy Eagle. Instead, the agents had wanted to know how many men of fighting age were in the camp, what sort of weapons they possessed, and so on. Thus alerted that something bad was about to happen, the Northwest AIM contingent put out an urgent call for support from the local AIM community.[102]

At about 11:00 a.m. the following morning, June 26, Williams and Coler returned to the Jumping Bull property. Driving past the compound of residences, they moved down into a shallow valley, stopped and exited their cars in an open area, and began to fire in the general direction of the AIM encampment in a treeline along White Clay Creek.[103] Shortly, they began to take a steadily growing return fire, not only from the treeline, but from the houses above. At about this point, agent J. Gary Adams and BIA police officer/GOON Glenn Two Birds attempted to come to Williams' and Coler's aid. Unexpectedly taking fire from the direction of the houses, they retreated to the ditch beside Highway 18.[104]

Some 150 SWAT-trained BIA police and FBI personnel were prepositioned in the immediate locale when the firefight began. This, especially when taken in combination with the fact that more than 200 additional FBI SWAT personnel were on alert awaiting word to proceed post haste to Pine Ridge from Minneapolis, Milwaukee and Quantico, Virginia, raises the probability that Williams and Coler were actually assigned to provoke an exchange of gunfire with the AIM members on the Jumping Bull land.[105] The plan seems to have been that they would then be immediately supported by the introduction of overwhelming force, the Northwest AIM Group destroyed, and the FBI afforded the pretext necessary to launch an outright invasion of the reservation.[106]

A number of local AIM members had rallied to the call to come to the Jumping Bulls'. Hence, instead of encountering the eight AIM "shooters" they'd anticipated, there were about thirty, and the two agents were cut off from their erstwhile supporters.[107] While the BIA police, reinforced by GOONs put up roadblocks to seal off the area, and the FBI agents on hand were deployed as snipers, no one made a serious effort to get to Williams and Coler until 5:50 p.m. By that point, they'd been dead for some time, along with a young Coeur D'Alene AIM member, Joe Stuntz Killsright, killed by FBI sniper Gerard Waring as he attempted to depart the compound.[108] Aside from Killsright, all AIM participants had escaped across country.

By nightfall, hundreds of agents equipped with everything from APCs to Vietnam-style Huey helicopters had begun arriving on the reservation.[109] The next morning, Tom Coll, an FBI "Public Information Specialist" imported for the purpose, convened a press conference in Oglala—the media was barred from the firefight site itself—in which he reported that the dead agents had been "lured into an ambush" by AIM, attacked with automatic weapons from a "sophisticated bunker complex," dragged wounded from their cars, stripped of their clothing, and then executed in cold blood while one of them pleaded with his killer(s) to spare him because he had a wife and children. Each agent, Coll asserted, had been "riddled with 15-20 bullets."[110]

Every word of this was false, as Coll well knew—the FBI had been in possession of both the agents' bodies and the ground on which they were killed for nearly eighteen hours before he made his statements—and the report was retracted in full by FBI Director Clarence Kelley at a press conference conducted in Los Angeles a week later.[111] By then, however, a barrage of sensational media coverage had "sensitized" the public to the need for a virtually unrestricted application of force against the "mad dogs of AIM." Correspondingly, the Bureau was free to run air assaults and massive sweeping operations on Pine Ridge—complete with the wholesale use of no-knock searches and John Doe warrants—for the next three months.[112] By the end of that period, its mission had largely been accomplished.[113] In the interim, on July 27, 1975, it was finally felt, given the preoccupation of all concerned parties with the FBI's offensive operations, that the time was right for Dickie Wilson to sign a memorandum transferring the Gunnery Range to the federal government; on January 2, 1976, a more formal instrument was signed and, in the spring, Congress passed a Public Law assuming U.S. title over this portion of Oglala territory.[114]

### The Case of Leonard Peltier

It is unlikely that the FBI intended its two agents be killed during the Oglala Firefight. Once Coler and Williams were dead, however, the Bureau capitalized upon their fate, not only as the medium through which to pursue its anti-AIM campaign with full ferocity, but as a mechanism with which to block an incipient congressional probe into what the FBI had been doing on Pine Ridge. This last took the form of a sympathy play: Bureau officials pleaded that the "natural" emotional volatility engendered among their agents by the deaths made it "inopportune" to proceed with the investigation "at the present time." Congress responded, on July 3, 1975, by postponing the scheduling of preliminary interviews, a delay which has become permanent.[115]

Still, with two dead agents, it was crucial for the Bureau's image that someone be brought directly to account. To fill this bill, four names were selected from this list of thirty "shooters" field investigators had concluded were participants in the exchange. Targeted were a pair of Anishinabe/Lakota cousins, Leonard Peltier and Bob Robideau, and Darrelle "Dino" Butler, a Tuni, the heads of Northwest AIM. Also included was Jimmy Eagle, whose name seems to have appeared out of expediency, since the Bureau claimed Williams and Coler were looking for him in the first place (all charges against him were later simply dropped, without investiture of discernible prosecutorial effort).[116]

Butler and Robideau, captured early on, were tried first, as codefendants, separate from Peltier.[117] The latter, having managed to avoid arrest in a trap set for him in Oregon, had found sanctuary in the remote encampment of Cree leader Robert Smallboy, in northern Alberta.[118] By the time he had been captured, extradited via a thoroughly fraudulent proceeding involving the presentation of an "eyewitness" affidavit from a psychotic Lakota woman named Myrtle Poor Bear to a Canadian court, and docketed in the U.S., the proceeding against Peltier's cohorts was ready to begin.[119] Peltier was thus scheduled to be tried later and alone.

During the Butler/Robideau trial, conducted in Cedar Rapids, Iowa, during the summer of 1976, the government's plan to turn the defendants—and AIM itself—into examples of the price of resistance began to unravel. Despite the calculated ostentation with which the FBI prepared to secure the judge and jurors from "AIM's potential for violence," and another media blitz designed to convince the public that Butler and Robideau were part of a vast "terrorist conspiracy," the carefully selected all-white Midwestern panel of jurors was unconvinced.[120] After William Muldrow of the U.S. Commission on Civil Rights was called by the defense to testify regarding the FBI-fostered reign of terror on Pine Ridge, and Director Kelley himself was forced to admit under oath that he knew of nothing which might support many of the Bureau's harsher characterizations of AIM, the jury voted to acquit on July 16, 1976.[121]

The "not guilty" verdict was based on the panel-members' assessment that—although both defendants acknowledged firing at the agents, Robideau that he had in fact hit them both[122]—they had acted in self-defense. Under the conditions described by credible witnesses, jury foreman Robert Bolin later recounted, "we felt that any reasonable person would have reacted the same way when the agents came in there shooting." Besides, Bolin continued, their personal observations of the behavior of governmental representatives during the trial had convinced most jury members that "it was the government, not the defendants or their movement, which was dangerous."[123]

Although the Cedar Rapids jury had essentially determined that Coler and Williams had not been murdered, the FBI and federal prosecutors opted to proceed against Peltier. In a pretrial conference they analyzed what had "gone wrong" in the Butler/Robideau case and, in a report dated July 20, 1976, concluded that among the problems encountered was the fact that the defendants had been allowed to present a self-defense argument, their lawyers allowed "to call and question witnesses" and subpoena government documents.[124] They then removed the Peltier trial from the docket of the judge at Cedar Rapids, Edward McManus, and reassigned it to another, Paul Benson, who they felt would be more amenable to their view.[125]

When Peltier was brought to trial in Fargo, North Dakota, on March 21, 1977, Benson ruled virtually everything presented by the defense at Cedar Rapids, including the Butler/Robideau trial transcript itself, inadmissible.[126] Prosecutors then presented a case against Peltier which was precisely the opposite of what they—and their FBI witnesses—professed to believe was true in the earlier trial.[127] A chain of circumstantial evidence was constructed, often through resort to fabricated physical evidence,[128] perjury[129] and the use of demonstrably coerced testimony,[130] to create a plausible impression among jurors—again all white Midwesterners—that the defendant was guilty.

Following a highly emotional closing presentation by Assistant Prosecutor Lynn Crooks, in which he waved color photos of the agents' bloody bodies under the jury's collective nose and graphically described the "cold-bloodedness" with which "Leonard Peltier executed these two wounded and helpless human beings," they voted on April 18, after only six hours of deliberation, to convict on both counts of first degree murder.[131] Benson then sentenced Peltier to serve two consecutive life terms in prison and he was transported straightaway to the federal "supermaximum" facility at Marion, Illinois.[132]

Almost immediately, an appeal was filed on the basis of FBI misconduct and multiple judicial errors on Benson's part. The matter was considered by a three-member panel of the Eighth Circuit Court—composed of judges William Webster, Donald Ross and Gerald Heaney—during the spring of 1978. Judge Webster wrote the opinion on behalf of his colleagues, finding that although the record revealed numerous reversible errors on the part of the trial judge, and many "unfortunate misjudgments" by the FBI, the conviction would be allowed to stand.[133] By the time the document was released, Webster was no longer there to answer for it. He had moved on to a new position as Director of the FBI. On February 12, 1979, the U.S. Supreme Court declined, without stating a reason, to review the lower court's decision.[134]

Undeterred, Peltier's attorneys had already filed a suit under the Freedom of Information Act (FOIA) to force disclosure of FBI documents withheld from the defense at trial. When the paperwork, more than 12,000 pages of investigative material, was finally produced in 1981, they began the tedious process of indexing and reviewing it.[135] Finding that the Bureau had suppressed ballistics reports which directly contradicted what had been presented at trial, they filed a second appeal in 1982.[136] This led to an evidentiary hearing and oral arguments in 1984 during which the FBI's chief ballistics expert, Evan Hodge, was caught in the act of perjuring himself,[137] and Lynn Crooks was forced to admit that the government "really has no idea who shot those agents."[138]

Crooks then attempted to argue that it didn't matter anyway, because Peltier had been convicted of "aiding and abetting in the murders rather than of the murders themselves."[139] This time, the circuit court panel—now composed of judges Heaney and Ross, as well as John Gibson—took nearly a year to deliberate. On October 11, 1986, they finally delivered an opinion holding that the content of Crooks' own closing argument to the jury, among many other factors precluded the notion that Peltier had been tried for aiding and abetting. They also concluded that the circumstantial ballistics case presented by the prosecution at trial was hopelessly undermined by evidence even then available to the FBI.[140]

Still, they refused to reverse Peltier's conviction because, "We recognize that there is evidence in this record of improper conduct on the part of some FBI agents, but we are reluctant to impute even further improprieties to them" by remanding the matter to trial.[141] On October 5, 1987, the Supreme Court once again refused to review the lower court's decision.[142] Most recently, a third appeal, argued on the basis of *habeas corpus*—if Peltier was never tried for aiding and abetting, and if the original case against him no longer really exists, why then is he in prison?—was filed. In November 1992, the Eighth Circuit, without ever really answering such questions, allowed his "conviction" to stand.[143] At this point, only a presidential pardon or commutation of sentence seems likely to bring about Peltier's release.

### Aftermath

The government repression of AIM during the mid-'70s had the intended effect of blunting the Movement's cutting edge. After 1977, things occurred in fits and starts rather than within a sustained drive. AIM's core membership, those who were not dead or in prison, scattered to the winds, many, like Wounded Knee security head Stan Holder, seeking other avenues into which to channel their activism.[144] Others, exhausted and intimidated by the massive violence directed against them, "retired" altogether from active politics.[145] Among the remainder, personal, political and intertribal antagonisms, often exacerbated by the rumors spread by federal provocateurs, instilled a deep and lasting factional fragmentation.[146]

In 1978, Dennis Banks, occupying the unique status in California of having been officially granted sanctuary by one state of the union against the extradition demands of another, sought to bring things back together by organizing what he called the "Longest Walk."[147] To some extent replicating on foot the Trail of Broken Treaties caravan of 1972, the Walk succeeded in its immediate objective; the walkers made it from Alcatraz Island—selected as a point of departure because of the importance of the 1969-71 occupation in forging AIM—to Washington, D.C., presenting a powerful manifesto to the Carter Administration in July.[148] But there was no follow-up, and the momentum was quickly lost.

Much hope was placed in the formation of the Leonard Peltier Defense Committee (LPDC) the same year, and, for a time it seemed as though it seemed as though it might serve as a kind of spark plug reenergizing the movement as a whole.[149] However, with the February 12, 1979, murder of AIM Chair John Trudell's entire family on the Duck Valley Reservation in Nevada, apparently as a deterrent to the effectiveness of Trudell's fiery oratory, things took an opposite tack.[150] The result was the abolition of all national officer positions in AIM; "These titles do nothing but provide a readymade list of priority targets for the feds," as Trudell put it at the time.[151] The gesture consummated a trend against centralization which began with the dissolution of AIM's national office at the time Banks had gone underground in 1975, a fugitive from sentencing after his conviction on charges stemming from the Custer Courthouse confrontation.[152]

In 1979 and '80, largescale "Survival Gatherings" were held outside Rapid City in an attempt to bring together Indian and non-Indian activists in collaborative opposition to uranium mining and other corporate "development" of the Black Hills.[153] An ensuing organization, the Black Hills Alliance (BHA), achieved momentary national prominence, but petered out after the demise of domestic uranium production in the early '80s dissolved several of the more pressing issues it confronted.[154]

Meanwhile, Russell Means, fresh out of prison, launched a related effort in 1981, occupying an 880-acre site in the Black Hills to establish a "sustainable, alternative, demonstration community" and "to initiate the physical reoccupation of Paha Sapa by the Lakota people and our allies." The occupation of what was dubbed Wincanyan Zi Tiospaye (Yellow Thunder Camp) in memory of Raymond Yellow Thunder lasted until 1985.[155] By that point, its organizers had obtained what on its face was a landmark judicial opinion from a federal district judge; not only did the Yellow Thunder occupiers have every right to do what they were doing, the judge decreed, but the Lakotas—and other Indians as well—are entitled to view entire geographic areas such as the Black Hills, rather than merely specific sites within them, to be of sacred significance.[156] The emergent victory was gutted, however, by the Supreme Court's controversial "G–O Road Decision" in 1988.[157]

Elsewhere, an AIM security camp was established on Navajo land near Big Mountain, Arizona, during the mid-'80s, to support the traditional Diné elders of that area in their resistance to forced relocation.[158] It is maintained through the present, and, somewhat comparably, AIM contingents began to become involved in the early '90s in providing physical security to Western Shoshone resisters to forced removal from their land in Nevada.[159] Similar scenarios have been played out in places as diverse as northern Minnesota and Wisconsin, Oregon, California, Oklahoma, Illinois, Florida, Georgia, Nebraska, Alaska and upstate New York. The issues confronted have been as wide-ranging as the localities in which they've been confronted.

Another potential bright spot which was ultimately eclipsed was the International Indian Treaty Council (IITC). Formed at the request of the Lakota elders in 1974 to "carry the message of indigenous people into the community of nations" and to serve more generally as "AIM's international diplomatic arm," it had by August 1977 gotten off to a brilliant start, playing a key role in bringing representatives of 98 native peoples throughout the Americas together in an unprecedented convocation before the United Nations Commission on Human Rights. This led directly to the establishment of a formal Working Group on Indigenous Populations—mandated to draft a Universal Declaration of the Rights of Indigenous Peoples for incorporation into international law—under the U.N. Economic and Social Council.[160]

Despite this remarkable early success, with the 1981 departure of its original director, Cherokee activist Jimmie Durham, IITC began to unravel.[161] By 1986, his successors were widely perceived as using the organization's reputation as a vehicle for personal profit and prestige, aligning themselves for a fee with various governments against indigenous interests. Allegations that they were also using their de facto diplomatic status as a medium through which to engage in drug trafficking also abounded. Whether or not such suspicions were accurate, IITC today has reduced itself to the stature of a small sectarian corporation, completely divorced from

AIM and the traditional milieu which legitimated it, subsisting mainly on donations from the very entities it was created to oppose.[162]

The early '90s, with the imminence of the Columbian Quincentennial Celebration, presented opportunities for the revitalization of AIM. Indeed, the period witnessed a more-or-less spontaneous regeneration of autonomous AIM chapters in at least sixteen localities around the country.[163] In Colorado, an escalating series of confrontations with Columbus Day celebrants organized by the local AIM chapter and beginning in 1989 led to the galvanizing of a coalition of some fifty progressive organizations, Indian and non-Indian alike, by 1992.[164] In Denver, the city where Columbus Day was first proclaimed an official holiday, Quincentennial activities were stopped in their tracks. Much the same process was evident in San Francisco and, to a lesser extent, other locations.

Perhaps ironically, the most vicious reaction to the prospect of a resurgent movement came, not from the government, but from a small group in Minneapolis professing itself to be AIM's "legitimate leadership." How exactly it imagined it had attained this exalted position was a bit murky, there not having been an AIM general membership conference to sanction the exercise of such authority since 1975. Nonetheless, in July 1993, the clique constituted itself under the laws of the State of Minnesota as "National-AIM, Inc.," announced formation of a "National Board" and "Central Committee," and provided the address to what it described as the "AIM National Office."[165] Among the very first acts of this interesting amalgam—which proudly reported it was receiving $4 million per year in federal funding, and more than $3 million annually from corporations like Honeywell—was the issuance of letters "expelling" most of the rest of the movement from itself.[166]

## A Legacy

It may be, as John Trudell has said, that "AIM died years ago. It's just that some people don't know it yet."[167] Certainly, as a viable organization, the evidence exhibits every indication of bearing him out. And yet there is another level to this reality, one which has more to do with the spirit of resistance than with tangible form. Whatever else may be said about what AIM was (or is), it must be acknowledged that, as Russell Means contends:

> Before AIM, Indians were dispirited, defeated and culturally dissolving. People were *ashamed* to be Indian. You didn't see the young people wearing braids or chokers or ribbon shirts in those days. Hell, *I* didn't wear 'em. People didn't Sun Dance, they didn't

Sweat, they were losing their languages. Then there was that spark at Alcatraz, and we took off. Man, we took a *ride* across this country. We put Indians and Indian rights smack dab in the middle of the public consciousness for the first time since the so-called Indian Wars. And, of course, we paid a heavy price for that. Some of us are still paying it. But now you see braids on our young people. There are dozens of Sun Dances every summer. You hear our languages spoken again in places they had almost died out. Most important, you find young Indians all over the place who understand that they don't have to accept whatever sort of bullshit the dominant society wants to hand them, that they have the right to fight, to struggle for their rights, that in fact they have an obligation to stand up on their hind legs and fight for their future generations, the way our ancestors did. Now, I don't know about you, but I call that pride in being Indian. And I think that's a very positive change. And I think—no, I *know*—AIM had a lot to do with bringing that change about. We laid the groundwork for the next stage in regaining our sovereignty and self-determination as nations, and I'm proud to have been a part of that.[168]

To the degree this is true, and much of it seems very accurate, AIM may be said to have succeeded in fulfilling its original agenda.[169] The impulse of Alcatraz was carried forward into dimensions its participants could not yet envision. And that legacy is even now being refashioned and extended by a new generation, as it will be by the next, and the next. The continuity of Native North America's traditional resistance to domination was reasserted by AIM in no uncertain terms.

There are other aspects of the AIM legacy, to be sure. Perhaps the most crucial should be placed under the heading of "Lessons Learned." These go to defining the nature of the society we now inhabit, the lengths to which its government will go to maintain the kinds of domination AIM fought to cast off, and the techniques it uses in doing so. The experience of the American Indian Movement, especially in the mid-1970s, provides what amounts to a textbook exposition of these things. It teaches what to expect, and, if properly understood, how to overcome many of these methodologies of repression. The lessons are applicable, not simply to American Indians, but to anyone whose lot in life is to be oppressed within the American conception of business as usual.[170]

Ultimately, the gift bestowed by AIM is in part an apprehension of the fact that the Third World is not something "out there." It is everywhere, behind the facade of liberal democracy masking the substance of the United States as much as anywhere else.[171] It is there on every reservation in the country, in the teeming ghettos of Brownsville, Detroit and Compton, in the barrios and migrant fields and sharecropping farms of the Deep South.[172] It is there in the desolation of the Appalachian coal regions. It is there in the burgeoning prison industry of America, warehousing by far the most incarcerated population on the planet.[173]

The Third World is there in the nation's ever more proliferate and militarized police apparatus. And it is there in the piles of corpses of those — not just AIM members, but Black Panthers, Brown Berets, Puerto Rican independentistas, labor organizers, civil rights workers and many others — who tried to say "no" and make it stick.[174] It is there in the fates of Malcolm X and Fred Hampton, Mark Clark and Ché Payne, Geronimo ji Jaga Pratt and Alejandrina Torres, Susan Rosenberg and Martin Luther King, George Jackson and Ray Luc Lavasseur, Reyes Tijerina, Mutulu Shakur, Marilyn Buck and so many others.[175]

To win, it is said, one must know one's enemy. Winning the sorts of struggles engaged in by the individuals and organizations just mentioned is unequivocally necessary if we are to effect a constructive change in the conditions they faced, and that we continue to face. In this, there are still many lessons to be drawn from the crucible of AIM experience. These must be learned by all of us. They must be learned well. And soon.

# Notes

1. American Friends Service Committee, *Uncommon Controversy: Fishing Rights of the Muckleshoot, Puyallup and Nisqually Indians* (Seattle: University of Washington Press, 1970); Peter Blue Cloud, ed., *Alcatraz Is Not An Island* (Berkeley: Wingbow Press, 1972).

2. This is not to say that others have not suffered severely and often fatally at the hands of official specialists in the techniques of domestic political repression in the United States. The distinction drawn with regard to American Indian activists in this respect is purely proportional. For background on the repression of non-Indians, see Robert Justin Goldstein, *Political Repression in Modern America, 1870 to the Present* (Cambridge/New York: Schenkman Publishing/Two Continents, 1978).

3. Bruce Johansen and Roberto Maestas, *Wasíchu: The Continuing Indian Wars* (New York: Monthly Review Press, 1979).

4. Counterinsurgency is *not* a part of law enforcement or intelligence-gathering missions. Rather, it is an integral subpart of low-intensity warfare doctrine and methodology, taught at the U.S. Army's Special Warfare School at Fort Bragg, North Carolina; see Maj. John S. Pustay, *Counterinsurgency Warfare* (New York: Free Press, 1965); Michael T. Klare and Peter Kornbluh, eds., *Low Intensity Warfare: Counterinsurgency, Proinsurgency, and Antiterrorism in the Eighties* (New York: Pantheon Book, 1988). For an illustration of the FBI's use of explicit counterinsurgency terminology to define its anti-Indian operations in 1976, see my and Jim Vander Wall's, *The COINTELPRO Papers: Documents from the FBI's Secret Wars Against Dissent in the United States* (Boston: South End Press, 1990) p. 26.

5. U.S. Department of Justice, Commission on Civil Rights, *Events Surrounding Recent Murders on the Pine Ridge Reservation in South Dakota* (Denver: Rocky Mountain Regional Office, Mar. 31, 1976).

6. In his at the time definitive study of the Bureau, Sanford J. Ungar quotes a senior counterintelligence specialist to the effect that "success in this area is not measured in terms of arrests and prosecutions, but in our ability to neutralize our targets' ability to do what they're doing"; Sanford J. Ungar, *FBI: An Uncensored Look Behind the Walls* (Boston: Little, Brown, 1975) p. 311.

7. On the early days of the Black Panther Party, see Gene Marine, *The Black Panthers* (New York: New American Library, 1969). On the beginnings of AIM, and its obvious reliance on the Panther model, see Peter Matthiessen, *In the Spirit of Crazy Horse* (New York: Viking, [2nd. ed.] 1991) pp. 34-7.

8. Although AIM was probably the first to begin attempting to put together a coherent program to challenge the internal colonization of American Indians, it was by no means the first to perceive the native situation in this light. That distinction probably belonged to the Cherokee anthropologist Robert K. Thomas, with his brief but influential essay "Colonialism: Internal and Classic," *New University Thought*, Vol. 4, No. 4, Winter 1966-67.

9. The U.S. is constitutionally prohibited, under Article 1, from entering into treaty relations with any entity other than another fully sovereign nation. Senate ratification of a treaty therefore confirms formal U.S. recognition of the sovereignty of the other party or parties to the instrument. The texts of 371 ratified treaties between the U.S. and various indigenous nations appear in Charles J. Kappler, *Indian Treaties, 1778-1883* (New York: Interland, 1972). The U.S. suspended such treatymaking by law in 1871 (ch. 120, 16 Stat. 544, 566, now codified at 25 U.S.C. 71) with the provision that "nothing herein contained shall be construed to invalidate or impair the obligation of any treaty heretofore lawfully made with any Indian nation or tribe."

10. Following the findings of the Indian Claims Commission in its 1979 *Final Report*, an independent researcher has summarized that, "about half the land area of the [U.S.] was purchased by treaty or agreement . . . another third of a [billion] acres, mainly in the West, were confiscated without compensation; another two-thirds of a [billion] acres were claimed by the United States without pretense of a unilateral action extinguishing native title"; see Russel L. Barsh, "Indian Land Claims Policy in the United States," *North Dakota Law Review*, No. 58, 1982, pp. 1-82. The last category mentioned, to which native title is still plainly applicable, amounts to about 35 percent of the 48 contiguous states; this should be contrasted to the approximately 2.5 percent of the "lower 48" currently retaining reservation trust status.

11. U.S. Department of Labor, Bureau of the Census, *1970 Census of the Population, Subject Report: American Indians* (Washington, D.C.: U.S. Government Printing Office, 1972).

12. U.S. Plenary Power Doctrine is perhaps best articulated in the Supreme Court's 1903 *Lone Wolf v. Hitchcock* opinion (187 U.S. 553). The most relevant statutes are the 1885 Major Crimes Act (ch

341, 24 Stat. 362, 385, now codified at U.S.C. 1153), 1887 General Allotment Act (ch. 119, 24 *Stat*. 388, now codified as amended at 25 U.S.C. 331 *et seq*.) and the Indian Reorganization Act (ch. 576, 48 Stat. 948, now codified at 25 U.S.C. 461-279).

13. On resource distribution, see generally Michael Garrity, "The U.S. Colonial Empire is as Close as the Nearest Indian Reservation," in Holly Sklar, ed., *Trilateralism: The Trilateral Commission and Elite Planning for World Government* (Boston: South End Press, 1980) pp. 238-68.

14. See generally, Joseph G. Jorgensen, ed., *Native Americans and Energy Development, II* (Cambridge, MA: Anthropology Resource Center/Seventh Generation Fund, 1984).

15. See generally, Roxanne Dunbar Ortiz, ed., *Economic Development in American Indian Reservations* (Albuquerque: Native American Studies Center, University of New Mexico, 1979).

16. Thomas, "Colonialism."

17. U.S. Department of Health, Education and Welfare (DHEW), *A Study of Selected Socio-Economic Characteristics of Ethnic Minorities Based on the 1970 Census, Vol. 3: American Indians* (Washington, D.C.: U.S. Government Printing Office, 1974). It should be noted that the economic and health data pertaining to certain sectors of other U.S. minority populations—inner city blacks, for example, or Latino migrant workers—are very similar to those bearing on American Indians. Unlike these other examples, however, the data on American Indians encompass the condition of the population as a whole.

18. U.S. Bureau of the Census, Population Division, Racial Statistics Branch, *A Statistical Profile of the American Indian Population* (Washington, D.C.: U.S. Government Printing Office, 1974).

19. Dennis J. Banks, speech before the United Lutheran Board, Minneapolis, Minnesota, Mar. 1971.

20. Notable in this respect was resuscitation of the Lakota Sun Dance, forbidden by the BIA since 1881, when in August 1972 AIM members showed up *en masse* to participate in the ceremony at Crow Dog's Paradise, on the Rosebud Reservation. As the revered Oglala spiritual leader Frank Fools Crow put it in 1980, "Before that, there were only one, two Sun Dances each year. Just a few came, the real traditionals. And we had to hold 'em in secret. After the AIM boys showed up, now there are [Sun Dances] everywhere, right out in the open, too. Nobody hides anymore. Now, they're all proud to be Indian." The same principle pertains to the resurgence of numerous other ceremonies among a variety of peoples.

21. The U.N. component was developed pursuant to the creation of the International Indian Treaty Council (IITC), "AIM's international diplomatic arm," in 1974. Under the directorship of Cherokee activist Jimmie Durham, IITC was responsible for convening the first Assembly of Indigenous Nations of the Western Hemisphere at the U.N. Palace of Nations in Geneva, Switzerland, during the summer of 1977. IITC then became the world's first Non-Governing Organization (NGO; Type-II, Consultative) to the U.N., and played a major role in bringing about the establishment of the Working Group on Indigenous Populations—charged with annual review of native grievances and the drafting a Universal Declaration on the Rights of Indigenous Peoples—under auspices of the U.N. Economic and Social Council (ECOSOC) in 1981. With Durham's departure from IITC the organization went into decline. The progressive dynamic it inaugurated, however, is ongoing. See generally, S. James Anaya, "The Rights of Indigenous Peoples and International Law in Historical and Contemporary Perspective," in Robert N. Clinton, Nell Jessup Newton and Monroe E. Price, eds., *American Indian Law: Cases and Materials* (Charlottesville, VA: Michie, 1991) pp. 1257-76.

22. The term "National Liberation Movement" is not rhetorical. Rather, it bears a precise meaning under Article I, Paragraph 4 of Additional Protocol I of the 1949 Geneva Convention. Also see United Nations Resolution 3103 (XXVIII), 12 Dec. 1973.

23. Birgil Kills Straight, mimeographed statement circulated by the Oglala Sioux Civil Rights Organization (Manderson, S.D.) during the 1973 Siege of Wounded Knee.

24. By the mid-'70s, even elements of the federal government had begun to adopt AIM's emphasis on colonialism to explain the relationship between the United States and American Indians. See, e.g., U.S. Commission on Civil Rights, *The Navajo Nation: An American Colony* (Washington, D.C.: U.S. Government Printing Office, Sept. 1975).

25. This remained true until the government's 1993 slaughter of 86 Branch Davidians in a single hour near Waco, Texas. The standard text on the 1890 massacre is, of course, Dee Brown's *Bury My Heart at Wounded Knee: An Indian History of the American West* (New York: Holt, Rinehart & Winston, 1970).

26. Robert Burnette with John Koster, *The Road to Wounded Knee* (New York: Bantam, 1974) p. 196.

27. Peter Matthiessen, *In the Spirit of Crazy Horse* (New York: Viking Press, [2nd ed.] 1991) pp. 38, 110.

28. Yellow Thunder, burned with cigarettes, was forced to dance nude from the waist down for the entertainment of a crowd assembled in the Gordon American Legion Hall. He was then severely beaten and stuffed, unconscious, into the trunk of a car where he froze to death; Rex Weyler, *Blood of the Land: The U.S. Government and Corporate War Against the American Indian Movement* (Philadelphia: New Society, [2nd ed.] 1992) p. 48; Matthiessen, *Spirit of Crazy Horse*, pp. 59-60.

29. Quoted in Weyler, *Blood of the Land*, p. 49.

30. Alvin M. Josephy, Jr., *Now That the Buffalo's Gone: A Study of Today's American Indian* (New York: Alfred A. Knopf, 1982) p. 237.

31. The best overall handling of these events, including the complete text of the 20-Point Program, is Vine Deloria, Jr.'s *Behind the Trail of Broken Treaties: An Indian Declaration of Independence* (Austin: University of Texas Press, [2nd ed.] 1974).

32. See Editors, *BIA, I'm Not Your Indian Anymore* (Rooseveltown, NY: Akwesasne Notes, 1973).

33. The money, comprised of unmarked twenty, fifty and hundred dollar bills, came from a slush fund administered by Nixon's notorious Committee to Re-Elect the President (CREEP), and was delivered in brown paper bags. The bagmen were administration aids Leonard Garment and Frank Carlucci (later National Security Council chief and CIA Director under Ronald Reagan); Paul Chaat Smith and Robert Allen Warrior, *Like a Hurricane: The American Indian Movement from Alcatraz to Wounded Knee* (New York: New Press, 1996) pp. 163-5.

34. It was from these files that, among other things, the existence of a secret IHS program to perform involuntary sterilizations on American Indian women was first revealed. See Brint Dillingham, "Indian Women and IHS Sterilization Practices," *American Indian Journal*, Vol. 3, No. 1, Jan. 1977.

35. The full text of administration response is included in *BIA, I'm Not Your Indian Anymore*.

36. The language is that of Webster Two Hawk, then President of the Rosebud Sioux Tribe and the federally funded National Tribal Chairmen's Association. Two Hawk was shortly voted out of both positions by his constituents, replaced as Rosebud President by Robert Burnette, an organizer of the Trail of Broken Treaties.

37. One firm indication of this was the arrest by the FBI of Assiniboin/Lakota activist Hank Adams and Les Whitten, an associate of columnist Jack Anderson, shortly after the occupation. They were briefly charged with illegally possessing government property. The men, neither of whom was an AIM member, were merely acting as go-betweens in returning BIA documents to the federal authorities. The point seems to have been to isolate AIM from its more "moderate" associations; Deloria, *Behind the Trail of Broken Treaties*, p. 59.

38. Although he had stabbed Bad Heart Bull repeatedly in the chest with a hunting knife, Schmitz was charged only with second-degree manslaughter and released on a mere $5,000 bond; Weyler, *Blood of the Land*, p. 68.

39. Don and Jan Stevens, *South Dakota: The Mississippi of the North, or Stories Jack Anderson Never Told You* (Custer, SD: self-published pamphlet, 1977).

40. More broadly, AIM's posture was a response to what it perceived as a nationwide wave of murders of Indians by whites. These included not only those of Yellow Thunder and Bad Heart Bull, but of a nineteen-year-old Papago named Phillip Celay by a sheriff's deputy in Arizona, an Onondaga Special Forces veteran (and member of the honor guard during the funeral of John F. Kennedy) named Leroy Shenandoah in Philadelphia, and, on September 20, 1972, of Alcatraz leader Richard Oaks near San Francisco; see my and Jim Vander Wall's, *Agents of Repression: The FBI's Secret Wars Against the Black Panther Party and the American Indian Movement* (Boston: South End Press, 1988) p. 123.

41. The individual receiving the call was reporter Lynn Gladstone. Such calls are a standard FBI counterintelligence tactic used to disrupt the political organizing of targeted groups; Brian Glick, *War at Home: Covert Action Against U.S. Activists and What We Can Do About It* (Boston: South End Press, 1989).

42. A Jan. 31, 1973, teletype delineates the fact that the FBI was already involved in planning the police response to the Custer demonstration; reproduced in *COINTELPRO Papers*, p. 241.

43. Weyler, *Blood of the Land*, pp. 68-9.

44. The average annual income on Pine Ridge at this time was about $1,000; Cheryl McCall,"Life on Pine Ridge Bleak," *Colorado Daily*, May 16, 1975. Wilson hired his brother, Jim, to head the tribal planning office at an annual salary of $25,000 plus $15,000 in "consulting fees"; *New York Times*, April 22, 1975. Another brother, George, was hired at a salary of $20,000 to help the Oglalas "manage their affairs"; Wilson's wife was named director of the Reservation Head Start program at a salary of $18,000; his son, "Manny" (Richard, Jr.) was placed on the GOON payroll, along with several cousins and nephews; Wilson also upped his own salary from $5,500 per year to $15,500 per year, plus lucrative consulting fees, within his first six months in office; Matthiessen, *Spirit of Crazy Horse*, p. 62. When queried about the propriety of all this, Wilson replied,"There's no law against nepotism"; Robert Anderson, et al., eds., *Voices From Wounded Knee, 1973* (Rooseveltown, NY: Akwesasne Notes, 1974) p. 34.

45. In addition to this BIA "seed money," Wilson is suspected of having misappropriated some $347,000 in federal highway improvement funds to meet GOON payrolls between 1972 and 1975. A 1975 General Accounting Office report indicates that the funds had been expended without any appreciable road repair having been done, and that the Wilsonites had kept no books with which to account for this mysterious situation. Nonetheless, the FBI declined to undertake a further investigation of the matter.

46. The Gunnery Range, comprising the northwestern eighth of Pine Ridge, was an area "borrowed" from the Oglalas by the War Department in 1942 as a place to train aerial gunners. It was to be returned at the end of World War II, but never was. By the early '70s, the Oglala traditionals had begun to agitate heavily for its recovery. The deposits had been secretly discovered in 1971, however, through a technologically elaborate survey and mapping project undertaken jointly by the National Aeronautics and Space Administration (NASA) and a little-known entity called the National Uranium Resource Evaluation Institute (NURE). At that point, the government set out to obtain permanent title over the property. Its quid pro quo with Wilson seems to have been his willingness to provide it. See J.P. Gries, *Status of Mineral Resource Information on the Pine Ridge Indian Reservation, S.D.* (Washington, D.C.: BIA Bulletin No. 12, U.S. Department of Interior, 1976). Also see Jacqueline Huber, et al., *The Gunnery Range Report* (Pine Ridge, SD: Office of the Oglala Sioux Tribal President, 1981).

47. Anderson, et al., *Voices From Wounded Knee*, pp. 17-26.

48. Quoted in Matthiessen, *Spirit of Crazy Horse*, p. 66.

49. Burnette and Koster, *Road to Wounded Knee*, p. 74.

50. The action was proposed by OSCRO leader Pedro Bissonette and endorsed by traditional Oglala chiefs Frank Fools Crow, Pete Catches, Ellis Chips, Edgar Red Cloud, Jake Kills Enemy, Morris Wounded, Severt Young Bear and Everette Catches; Anderson, et al., *Voices From Wounded Knee,*, p. 36.

51. Weyler, *Blood of the Land*, pp. 76-8.

52. One of their first actions was to meet with Colonel Vic Jackson, a subordinate of future FEMA head Louis Giuffrida, brought in from California to "consult." Through an entity called the California Civil Disorder Management School, Jackson and Giuffrida had devised a pair of "multi-agency domestic counterinsurgency scenarios" code named "Garden Plot" and "Cable Splicer" in which the government was interested. There is thus more than passing indication that what followed at Wounded Knee was, at least in part, a field test of these plans; Weyler, *Blood of the Land*, pp. 80-81. Also see Ken Lawrence, *The New State Repression* (Chicago: International Network Against the New State Repression, 1985).

53. Weyler, *Blood of the Land*, p. 83. The quantity of M-16 ammunition should actually read 1.3 million rounds. The military also provided state-of-the art communications gear, M-14 sniper rifles and ammunition, "Starlight" night vision scopes and other optical technology, teargas rounds and flares for M-79 grenade launchers, and field provisions to feed the assembled federal forces. All of this was in violation of the *Posse Comitatus* Act (18 USCS § 1385), which makes it illegal for the government to deploy its military against "civil disturbances." For this reason, Colonels Warner and Potter, and the other military personnel they brought in, wore civilian clothes at Wounded Knee in an effort to hide their involvement.

54. Bill Zimmerman, *Airlift to Wounded Knee* (Chicago: Swallow Press, 1976).

55. Clearwater was mortally wounded on Apr. 17, 1973, and died on Apr. 25. Lamont was hit on April 27, after being driven from his bunker by teargas. Federal gunfire then prevented help from reaching him until he died from loss of blood; Anderson, et al., *Voices From Wounded Knee*, pp. 179, 220.

56. Robert Burnette later recounted how, once the siege had ended, Justice Department Solicitor General Kent Frizzell asked his assistance in search for such graves; Burnette and Koster, *Road to Wounded Knee.*, p. 248; Anderson, et al., *Voices From Wounded Knee,* p. 193.

57. The "hostages" were mostly elderly residents of Wounded Knee: Wilbert A. Reigert (aged 86), Girlie Clark (75), Clive Gildersleeve (73), Agnes Gildersleeve (68), Bill Cole (82), Mary Pike (72) and Annie Hunts Horse (78). Others included Guy Fritz (aged 49), Jeanne Fritz (47), Adrienne Fritz (12) and Father Paul Manhart (46). When South Dakota Senators George McGovern and James Abourezk went to Wounded Knee on Mar. 2 to "bring the hostages out," the supposed captives announced they had no intention of leaving. Instead they stated they wished to stay to "protect [their] property from federal forces" and that they considered the AIM people to be the "real hostages in this situation"; Burnette and Koster, *Road to Wounded Knee,* pp. 227-8.

58. The first federal casualty was an FBI agent named Curtis Fitzpatrick, hit in the wrist by a spent round on Mar. 11, 1973. Interestingly, with his head swathed in bandages, he was evacuated by helicopter before a crowd of reporters assembled to witness the event; Burnette and Koster, *Road to Wounded Knee,* pp. 237-8. The second, U.S. Marshal Lloyd Grimm, was struck in the back and permanently paralyzed on Mar. 23. Grimm was, however, *facing* the AIM perimeter when he was hit. The probability is therefore that he was shot—perhaps unintentionally—by one of Wilson's GOONs, who were at the time firing from positions behind the those of the marshals; Anderson, et al., *Voices From Wounded Knee,* p. 128.

59. Quoted in ibid., p. 47.

60. Held was simultaneously serving as head of the FBI's Internal Security Section and as Special Agent in Charge (SAC) of the Bureau's Chicago Office. He had been assigned the latter position, in addition to his other duties, in order that he might orchestrate a cover-up of the FBI's involvement in the 1969 murders of Illinois Black Panther leaders Fred Hampton and Mark Clark. At the outset of the Wounded Knee Siege, he was detached from his SAC position, a very unusual circumstance, and sent to Pine Ridge in order to prepare a study of how the Bureau should deal with AIM "insurgents." The result, entitled "FBI Paramilitary Operations in Indian Country"—in which he argued, among other things, that "shoot to kill" orders should be made standard—is extremely significant in light of subsequent FBI activities on the reservation and Held's own role in them.

61. The terms of the stand down agreement are covered in Anderson, et al., *Voices From Wounded Knee,* p. 231. The full text of the treaty will be found in Charles J. Kappler, *Indian Treaties and Agreements, 1778-1883* (New York: Interland, 1972) pp. 594-6.

62. Federal representatives plainly obfuscated, arguing that they were precluded from responding to questions of treaty compliance because of Congress's 1871 suspension of treatymaking with Indians (Title 25 USC § 71). As Lakota elder Matthew King rejoined, however, the Indians were not asking that a new treaty be negotiated. Rather, they were demanding that U.S. commitments under an *existing* treaty be honored, a matter which was not only possible under the 1871 Act, but *required* by it; Anderson, et al., *Voices From Wounded Knee,* p. 252-4.

63. Instead, a single Marshal was dispatched to Fools Crow's home on the appointed date to deliver to those assembled there a note signed by White House Counsel Leonard Garment. The missive stated that "the days of treaty-making with Indians ended in 1871, 102 years ago"; quoted in ibid., pp. 257-8.

64. U.S. House of Representatives, Committee on the Judiciary, Subcommittee on Civil and Constitutional Rights, *1st Session on FBI Authorization, March 19, 24, 25; April 2 and 8, 1981* (Washington, D.C.: 97th Cong., 2nd Sess., 1981).

65. Weyler, *Blood of the Land,* p. 95; Burnette and Koster, *Road to Wounded Knee,* p. 253.

66. Subcommittee on Civil and Constitutional Rights, *1st Session on FBI Authorization* (1981).

67. Ibid. Means was convicted on *none* of the forty federal charges. Instead, he was finally found guilty in 1977 under South Dakota State Law of "Criminal Syndicalism" and served a year in the maximum security prison at Sioux Falls. He was, and will remain, the only individual ever convicted under this statute; the South Dakota legislature repealed the law while he was imprisoned. Amnesty International was preparing to adopt him as a Prisoner of Conscience when he was released in 1979; Amnesty International, *Proposal for a commission of inquiry into the effect of domestic intelligence activities on criminal trials in the United States of America* (New York: Amnesty International, 1980).

68. Roxanne Dunbar Ortiz, ed., *The Great Sioux Nation: Sitting in Judgment on America* (New York/San Francisco: International Indian Treaty Council/Moon Books, 1977).

69. Tried together in the second "Leadership Trial," Crow Dog, Holder and Camp were convicted of minor offenses during the spring of 1975. Holder and Camp went underground to avoid sentencing. Crow Dog was granted probation (as were his codefendants when they surfaced), and then tried on charges unrelated to Wounded Knee the following November. Convicted, and sentenced to five years, he was imprisoned first in the federal maximum security facility at Lewisburg, Pennsylvania, and then at Leavenworth, Kansas. The National Council of Churches and Amnesty International were preparing to adopt him as a Prisoner of Conscience when he was released on parole in 1977; Weyler, *Blood of the Land*, p. 189.

70. As a congressional study concluded, this was "a very low rate considering the usual rate of conviction in Federal Courts and a great input of resources in these cases"; Subcommittee on Civil and Constitutional Rights, *1st Session on FBI Authorization* (1981).

71. This is a classic among the counterintelligence methods utilized by the FBI. For example, according to a Bureau report declassified by a Senate Select Committee in 1975, agents in Philadelphia offered as an "example of a successful counterintelligence technique" their use of "any excuse for arrest" as a means of "neutralizing" members of a targeted organization, the Revolutionary Action Movement (RAM) during the summer of 1967. "RAM people," the document went on, "were arrested and released on bail, but they were re-arrested several times until they could no longer make bail." The tactic was recommended for use by other FBI offices to "curtail the activities" of objectionable political groups in their areas. Complete text of this document will be found in *Agents of Repression*, pp. 45-47.

72. This is the standard delineation of objectives attending the FBI's domestic counterintelligence programs (COINTELPROs); see the document reproduced in *COINTELPRO Papers*, pp. 92-3.

73. Quoted in Martin Garbus, "General Haig of Wounded Knee," *The Nation*, Nov. 9, 1974.

74. A complete list of those killed and dates of death is contained in *COINTELPRO Papers*, pp. 393-4.

75. Commission on Civil Rights, *Events Surrounding Recent Murders*.

76. Johansen and Maestas, *Wasíchu*, pp. 83-4.

77. FBI jurisdiction on reservations accrues under the 1885 Major Crimes Act (ch. 341, 24 Stat. 362, 385, now codified at 18 USC 1153).

78. As examples: Delphine Crow Dog, sister of AIM's spiritual leader, beaten unconscious and left to freeze to death in a field on Nov. 9, 1974; AIM member Joseph Stuntz Killsright, killed by a bullet to the head and apparently shot repeatedly in the torso after death on June 26, 1975.

79. Consider the case of the brothers Vernal and Clarence Cross, both AIM members, who were stopped along the road with car trouble outside Pine Ridge village on June 19, 1973. Individuals firing from a nearby field hit both men, killing Clarence and severely wounding Vernal. Another bullet struck 9-year-old Mary Ann Little Bear, who was riding in a car driven by her father and coming in the opposite direction, in the face, blinding her in one eye. Mr. Little Bear identified three individuals to police and FBI agents as being the shooters. None of the three were interrogated. Instead, authorities arrested Vernal Cross in the hospital, charging him with murdering Clarence (the charges were later dropped). No charges were ever filed in the shooting of Mary Ann Little Bear; Weyler, *Blood of the Land*, p. 106.

80. Quoted in Johansen and Maestas, *Wasíchu*, p. 88. Actually, O'Clock's position fits into a broader Bureau policy. "When Indians complain about the lack of investigation and prosecution on reservation crime, they are usually told the Federal government does not have the resources to handle the work"; U.S. Department of Justice, *Report of the Task Force on Indian Matters* (Washington, D.C.: U.S. Government Printing Office, 1975) pp. 42-3.

81. In 1972, the Rapid City Resident Agency was staffed by three agents. This was expanded to 11 in March 1973, and augmented by a 10-member SWAT team shortly thereafter. By the spring of 1975, more than thirty agents were assigned to Rapid City on a longterm basis, and as many as two dozen others were steadily coming and going while performing "special tasks"; Johansen and Maestas, *Wasíchu*, p. 93; Department of Justice, *Report of the Task Force on Indian Matters*, pp. 42-3.

82. In the Clarence Cross murder, for example, the killers were identified as John Hussman, Woody Richards and Francis Randall, all prominent members of the GOONs. Or again, in the Jan. 30,

1976, murder of Byron DeSersa near the reservation hamlet of Wanbli, at least a dozen people identified GOONs Billy Wilson (Dickie Wilson's younger son), Charles David Winters, Dale Janis and Chuck Richards as being among the killers. Indeed, the guilty parties were still on the scene when two FBI agents arrived. Yet the only person arrested was a witness, an elderly Cheyenne named Guy Dull Knife, because of the vociferousness with which he complained about the agents' inaction. The BIA police, for their part, simply ordered the GOONs to leave town; U.S. Commission on Civil Rights, *American Indian Issues in South Dakota: Hearing Held in Rapid City, South Dakota, July 27-28, 1978* (Washington, D.C.: U.S. Government Printing Office, 1978) p. 33.

83. On the CIA's relationship to Latin American death squads, see Penny Lernoux, *Cry of the People: United States Involvement in the Rise of Fascism, Torture, and Murder, and the Persecution of the Catholic Church in Latin America* (New York: Doubleday, 1980).

84. Anderson, et al., *Voices From Wounded Knee*, p. 189. Frizzell himself has confirmed the account.

85. Ibid., p. 190.

86. The directive was issued on Apr. 24, 1973.

87. Anderson, et al., *Voices From Wounded Knee*, p. 213; Weyler, *Blood of the Land*, pp. 92-3.

88. See, e.g., Athan Theoharis, "Building a Case Against the FBI," *Washington Post*, Oct. 30, 1988.

89. See my "Death Squads in the United States: Confessions of a Government Terrorist," in my *From a Native Son: Selected Essays in Indigenism, 1985-1995* (Boston: South End Press, 1996) pp. 231-70.

90. "Det cord" is detonation cord, a rope-like explosive often used by the U.S. military to fashion booby traps. Brewer also makes mention of Bureau personnel introducing himself and other GOONs to civilian right-wingers who provided additional ordnance.

91. Another example of this sort of thing came in the wake of the Feb. 27, 1975, beating and slashing of AIM defense attorney Roger Finzel, his client, Bernard Escamilla, and several associates at the Pine Ridge Airport by a group of GOONs headed by Duane Brewer and Dickie Wilson himself. The event being too visible to be simply ignored, Wilson was allowed to plead guilty to a petty offense carrying a $10 penalty in his own tribal court. Federal charges were then dropped on advice from the FBI—which had spent its investigative time polygraphing the victims rather than their assailants—because pressing them might constitute "double jeopardy"; Weyler, *Blood of the Land*, pp. 172-3; Matthiessen, *Spirit of Crazy Horse*, pp. 130-1.

92. At one point, the Bureau attempted to implicate Northwest AIM leader Leonard Peltier in the killing. This ploy was abandoned only when it was conclusively demonstrated that Peltier was in another state when the murder occurred; Matthiessen, *Spirit of Crazy Horse*, p. 133.

93. Both Moves Camp and Bissonette drove white over dark blue Chevrolet sedans. Goon leader Duane Brewer subsequently confirmed that his men had killed Bissonette by "mistake"; "Death Squads," pp. 247-8. The victim, who was not herself active in supporting AIM, was the sister of OSCRO leader Pedro Bissonette, shot to death under highly suspicious circumstances by BIA police officer *cum* GOON Joe Clifford on the night of Oct. 17, 1973; *Agents of Repression*, pp. 200-3; Weyler, *Blood of the Land*, pp. 107-10.

94. Eastman, although a Crow, is directly related to the Dakota family of the same name, made famous by the writer Charles Eastman earlier in the century. Ironically, two of his relatives, the sisters Carole Standing Elk and Fern Matthias, purport to be AIM members in California.

95. "Death Squads," p. 237.

96. Structurally, the appropriation of the formal apparatus of deploying force possessed by client states for purposes of composing death squads, long a hallmark of CIA covert operations in the Third World, corresponds quite well with the FBI's use of the BIA police on Pine Ridge; A.J. Languuth, *Hidden Terrors: The Truth About U.S. Police Operations in Latin America* (New York: Pantheon Press, 1978); Edward S. Herman, *The Real Terror Network: Terrorism in Fact and Propaganda* (Boston: South End Press, 1982).

97. Commission on Civil Rights, *Events Surrounding Recent Murders*.

98. In late 1973, Means took a majority of all votes cast in the tribal primaries. In the 1974 run-off, however, Wilson retained his presidency by a 200-vote margin. A subsequent investigation by the U.S. Commission on Civil Rights revealed that 154 cases of voter fraud—non-Oglalas being allowed to vote—had occurred. A further undetermined number of invalid votes had been cast by Oglalas who did not meet tribal residency requirements. No record had been kept of the number of ballots printed or how

and in what numbers they had been distributed. No poll watchers were present in many locations, and those who were present at the others had been appointed by Wilson rather than an impartial third party. There was also significant evidence that pro-Means voters had been systematically intimidated, and in some cases roughed up, by Wilsonites stationed at each polling place; U.S. Commission on Civil Rights, *Report of Investigation: Oglala Sioux Tribe, General Election, 1974* (Denver: Rocky Mountain Regional Office, October 1974). Despite these official findings, the FBI performed no substantive investigation, and the BIA allowed the results of the election to stand.

99. As the Jumping Bulls' daughter, Roselyn, later put it, "We asked those AIM boys to come help us [defend ourselves against] Dickie Wilson and his goons."; quoted in an unpublished manuscript by researcher Candy Hamilton, p. 3 (copy on file).

100. See, e.g., a memorandum from SAC Minneapolis (Joseph Trimbach) to the FBI Director, dated June 3, 1975, and captioned "Law Enforcement on the Pine Ridge Indian Reservation," in which it is recommended that armored personnel carriers be used to assault AIM defensive positions.

101. No such warrant existed. When an arrest order was finally issued for Eagle on July 9, 1975, it was for the petty theft of a pair of used cowboy boots from a white ranchhand. Eagle was acquitted even of this when the case was taken to trial in 1976. Meanwhile, George O'Clock's assignment of two agents to pursue an Indian teenager over so trivial an offense at a time when he professed to be too shorthanded to investigate the murders of AIM members speaks for itself; Matthiessen, *Spirit of Crazy Horse*, p. 173.

102. Ibid., p. 156.

103. The agents followed a red pickup truck which, unbeknownst to them, was full of dynamite onto the property. In the valley, the truck stopped and its occupants got out. Williams and Coler also stopped and got out of their cars. They then began firing toward the pickup, a direction which carried their rounds into the AIM camp, where a number of noncombatant women and children were situated. AIM security then began to fire back. It is a certainty that AIM did not initiate the firefight because, as Bob Robideau later explained, "Nobody in their right mind would start a gunfight, using a truckload of dynamite for cover." Once the agents were preoccupied, the pickup made its escape. Northwest AIM was toying with the idea of using the explosives to remove George Washington's face from the nearby Mount Rushmore National Monument; interview with Bob Robideau, May 1990 (notes on file).

104. Matthiessen, *Spirit of Crazy Horse*, p. 158.

105. An additional indicator is that William Janklow also seems to have been on alert, awaiting a call telling him things were underway. In any event, when called, Janklow was able to assemble a white vigilante force in Hot Springs, S.D., and drive about fifty miles to the Jumping Bull property, arriving there at about 1:30 p.m., an elapsed time of approximately two hours.

106. A further indication of preplanning by the Bureau is found in a June 27, 1975, memorandum from R.E. Gebhart to Mr. O'Donnell at FBIHQ. It states that Chicago SAC/Internal Security Chief Richard G. Held was contacted by headquarters about the firefight *at the Minneapolis field office* at 12:30 p.m. on June 26. It turns out that Held had already been detached from his position in Chicago and was in Minneapolis—under which authority the Rapid City resident agency, and hence Pine Ridge, falls—awaiting word to temporarily take over from Minneapolis SAC Joseph Trimbach. The only ready explanation for this highly unorthodox circumstance, unprecedented in Bureau history, is that it was expected that Held's peculiar expertise in political repression would be needed for a major operation on Pine Ridge in the immediate future; Johansen and Maestas, *Wasíchu*, p. 95.

107. Matthiessen, *Spirit of Crazy Horse*, pp. 483-5.

108. The FBI sought to "credit" BIA police officer Gerald Hill with the lethal long range shot to the head, fired at Killsright at about 3 p.m., despite the fact that he was plainly running away and therefore presented no threat to law enforcement personnel (it was also not yet known that Coler and Williams were dead). However, Waring, who was with Hill at the time, was the trained sniper of the pair, and equipped accordingly. In any event, several witnesses who viewed Killsright's corpse *in situ* —including Assistant South Dakota Attorney General William Delaney and reporter Kevin Barry McKiernan— subsequently stated that it appeared to them that someone had fired a burst from an automatic into the torso from close range and then tried to hide the fact by putting an FBI jacket over the *postmortem* wounds; Matthiessen, *Spirit of Crazy Horse*, p. 183.

109. The agents' standard attire was Vietnam-issue "boonie hats, jungle fatigues and boots. Their weapons were standard army M-16s. The whole affair was deliberately staged to resemble a military operation in Southeast Asia; see the selection of photographs in *Agents of Repression*.

110. Williams and Coler were each shot three times. The FBI knew, from the sound of the rifles during the firefight if nothing else, that AIM had used no automatic weapons. Neither agent was stripped. There were no bunkers, but rather only a couple of old root cellars and tumbledown corrals, common enough in rural areas and not used as firing positions in any event (the Bureau would have known this because of the absence of spent cartridge casings in such locations). Far from being "lured" to the Jumping Bull property, they had returned after being expressly told to leave (moreover, they were supposed to be serving a warrant). Instructively, nobody in the nation's press corps thought to ask how, exactly, Coll might happen to know either agent's last words, since nobody from the FBI was present when they were killed; Joel D. Weisman, "About that 'Ambush' at Wounded Knee," *Columbia Journalism Review*, Sept.–Oct. 1975.

111. The director's admission, during a press conference conducted at the Century Plaza Hotel on July 1, 1975, in conjunction with Coler's and Williams' funerals. It was accorded inside coverage by the press, unlike the page-one treatment given Coll's original disinformation; Tom Bates, "The Government's Secret War on the Indian," *Oregon Times*, Feb.–Mar. 1976.

112. Examples of the air assault technique include a 35-man raid on the property of AIM spiritual leader Selo Black Crow, near the village of Wanbli, on July 8, 1975. Crow Dog's Paradise, on the Rosebud Reservation, just across the line from Pine Ridge, was hit by a hundred heliborne agents on Sept. 5. Meanwhile, an elderly Oglala named James Brings Yellow had suffered a heart attack and died when agent J. Gary Adams suddenly kicked in his door during a no-knock search on July 12. By August, such abuse by the FBI was so pervasive that even some of Wilson's GOONs were demanding that the agents withdraw from the reservation; *COINTELPRO Papers*, pp. 268-70.

113. By September, it had become obvious to everyone that AIM lacked the military capacity to protect the traditionals from the level of violence being imposed by the FBI by that point. Hence, it began a pointed disengagement in order to alleviate pressure on the traditionals. On Oct. 16, 1975, Richard G. Held sent a memo to FBIHQ advising that his work in South Dakota was complete and that he anticipated returning to his position in Chicago by Oct. 18; a portion of this document is reproduced in *COINTELPRO Papers*, p. 273.

114. "Memorandum of Agreement Between the Oglala Sioux Tribe of South Dakota and the National Park Service of the Department of Interior to Facilitate Establishment, Development, Administration and Public Use of the Oglala Sioux Tribal Lands, Badlands National Monument" (Washington, D.C.: U.S. Department of Interior, January 2, 1976). The Act assuming title is P.L. 90-468 (1976). If there is any doubt as to whether the transfer was about uranium, consider that the law as amended in 1978—in the face of considerable protest by the traditionals—to allow the Oglalas to recover *surface* use rights any time they decided by referendum to do so. Subsurface (mineral) rights, however, were permanently retained by the government. Actually, the whole charade was illegal insofar as the still-binding 1868 Fort Laramie Treaty requires three-fourths express consent of all adult male Lakotas to validate land transfers, not land recoveries. Such consent, obviously, was never obtained with respect to the Gunnery Range transfer; Huber, et al., *Gunnery Range Report*.

115. The congressional missive read: "Attached is a letter from the Senate Select Committee (SSC), dated 6-23-75, addressed to [U.S. Attorney General] Edward S. Levi. This letter announces the SSC's intent to conduct interviews relating . . . to our investigation at 'Wounded Knee' and our investigation of the American Indian Movement . . . On 6-27-75, Patrick Shae, staff member of the SSC, requested we hold in abeyance any action . . . in view of the killing of the Agents at Pine Ridge, South Dakota."

116. The selection of those charged seems to have served a dual purpose: 1) to "decapitate" one of AIM's best and most cohesive security groups, and 2) in not charging participants from Pine Ridge, to divide the locals from their sources of outside support. The window dressing charges against Jimmy Eagle were explicitly dropped in order to "place the full prosecutorial weight of the government on Leonard Peltier"; quoted in Jim Messerschmidt, *The Trial of Leonard Peltier* (Boston: South End Press, 1984) p. 47.

117. Butler was apprehended at Crow Dog's Paradise during the FBI's massive air assault there on Sept. 5, 1975. Robideau was arrested in a hospital where he was being treated for injuries sustained when his car exploded on the Kansas Turnpike on Sept. 10; *Agents of Repression*, pp. 448-9.

118. Acting on an informant's tip, the Oregon State Police stopped a car and a motor home belonging to the actor Marlon Brando near the town of Ontario on the night of Nov. 14, 1975. Arrested in the motor home were Kamook Banks and Anna Mae Pictou Aquash, a fugitive on minor charges in South Dakota; arrested in the automobile were AIM members Russell Redner and Kenneth Loudhawk. Two men—Dennis Banks, a fugitive from sentencing after being convicted of inciting the 1972 Custer Courthouse "riot" in South Dakota, and Leonard Peltier, a fugitive on several warrants, including one for murder in the deaths of Williams and Coler—escaped from the motor home. Peltier was wounded in the process. On Feb. 6, 1976, acting on another informant's tip, the Royal Canadian Mounted Police arrested Peltier, Frank Black Horse (Frank DeLuca) and Ronald Blackman (Ron Janvier) at Smallboy's Camp, about 160 miles east of Edmonton, Alberta; Matthiessen, *Spirit of Crazy Horse*, pp. 249-51, 272-8. On the outcome for Dennis Banks and the others, see my, "Due Process Be Damned: The Case of the Portland Four," *Z Magazine*, Jan. 1988.

119. Poor Bear, a clinically unbalanced Oglala, was picked up for "routine questioning" by agents David Price and Ron Wood in February 1976 and held incommunicado for nearly two months in the Hacienda Motel, in Gordon, Nebraska. During this time she was continuously threatened with dire consequences by the agents unless she "cooperated" with their "investigation" into the deaths of Coler and Williams. At some point, Price began to prepare for her signature affidavits incriminating Leonard Peltier. Ultimately, she signed three mutually exclusive "accounts"; one of them—in which Peltier is said to have been her boyfriend, and to have confessed to her one night in a Nebraska bar that he'd killed the agents—was submitted in Canadian court to obtain Peltier's extradition on June 18, 1976. Meanwhile, on Mar. 29, Price caused Poor Bear to take the stand against Richard Marshall in Rapid City, during the AIM member's trial for killing Martin Montileaux. She testified that she was Marshall's girl friend and that he had confessed the murder to her one night in a Nebraska bar. Marshall was then convicted. Federal prosecutors declined to introduce Poor Bear as a witness at either the Butler/Robideau or Peltier trials, observing that her testimony was "worthless" due to her mental condition. She has publicly and repeatedly recanted her testimony against both Peltier and Marshall, saying she never met either of them. For years, members of the Canadian parliament have been demanding Peltier's return to their jurisdiction due to the fraud perpetrated by U.S. authorities during his extradition proceeding. The Poor Bear affidavits are reproduced in *COINTELPRO Papers*, pp. 288-91. On her testimony against Marshall and recantations, see *Agents of Repression*, pp. 339-42. On the position of the Canadian Parliament, see, e.g., "External Affairs: Canada-U.S. Extradition Treaty—Case of Leonard Peltier, Statement of Mr. James Fulton," in *House of Commons Debate, Canada* , Vol. 128, No. 129 (Ottawa: 1st Sess., 33rd Par. Official Report, Thurs., Apr. 17, 1986).

120. The disinformation campaign centered in Bureau's "leaks" of the so-called "Dog Soldier Teletypes" on June 21 and 22, 1976—in the midst of the Butler/Robideau trial—to "friendly media representatives." The documents, which were never in any way substantiated but were nonetheless sensationally reported across the country, asserted that 2,000 AIM "Dog Soldiers," acting in concert with SDS (a long-defunct white radical group) and the Crusade for Justice (a militant Chicano organization), had equipped themselves with illegal weapons and explosives and were preparing to embark on a campaign of terrorism which included "killing a cop a day . . . sniping at tourists . . . burning out farmers . . . assassinating the Governor of South Dakota . . . blowing up the Fort Randall Dam" and breaking people out of the maximum security prison at Sioux Falls. The second teletype is reproduced in *COINTELPRO Papers*, pp. 277-82.

121. Defense attorney William Kunstler queried Kelley as to whether there was "one shred, one scintilla of evidence" to support the allegations made by the FBI in the Dog Soldier Teletypes. Kelley replied, "I know of none." Nonetheless the FBI continued to feature AIM prominently in its *Domestic Terrorist Digest*, distributed free of charge to state and local police departments nationally; Churchill and Vander Wall, *COINTELPRO Papers*, p. 276.

122. The initial round striking both Coler and Williams was a .44 magnum. Bob Robideau testified that he was the only AIM member using a .44 magnum during the firefight; Robideau interview, Nov. 1993 (tape on file).

123. Videotaped NBC interview with Robert Bolin, 1990 (raw tape on file).

124. FBI personnel in attendance at this confab were Director Kelley and Richard G. Held, by

then promoted to the rank of Assistant Director, James B. Adams, Richard J. Gallagher, John C. Gordon and Herbert H. Hawkins, Jr. Representing the Justice Department were prosecutor Evan Hultman and his boss, William B. Grey; memo from B.H. Cooke to Richard J. Gallagher, August 10, 1976.

125. McManus professes to have been "astonished" when he was removed from the Peltier case; Matthiessen, *Spirit of Crazy Horse.*, p. 566.

126. *United States v. Leonard Peltier*, (CR-75-5106-1, U.S. District Court for the District of North Dakota, 1977; hereinafter referred to as *Peltier Trial Transcript*).

127. Butler and Robideau were tried on the premise that they were part of conspiracy which led to a group slaying of Williams and Coler. Peltier was tried as the "lone gunman" who had caused their deaths. Similarly, at Cedar Rapids, agent J. Gary Adams had testified the dead agents followed a red pickup onto the Jumping Bull property; during the Fargo trial, he testified they'd followed a "red and white van" belonging to Peltier. The defense was prevented by the judge's evidentiary ruling at the outset from impeaching such testimony on the basis of its contradiction of sworn testimony already entered against Butler and Robideau; see *Peltier Trial Transcript* and *United States v. Darrelle E. Butler and Robert E. Robideau* (CR76-11, U.S. District Court for the District of Iowa, 1976). For purposes of comparison; the matter is well analyzed in Messerschmidt, *Trial of Leonard Peltier.*

128. No slugs were recovered from Williams' and Coler's bodies, and two separate autopsies were inconclusive in determining the exact type of weapon from which the fatal shots were fired. The key piece of evidence in this respect was a .223 caliber shell casing which the FBI said was ejected from the killer's AR-15 rifle into the open trunk of Coler's car at the moment he fired one of the lethal rounds. The Bureau also claimed its ballistics investigation proved only one such weapon was used by AIM during the firefight. *Ipso facto*, whichever AIM member could be shown to have used an AR-15 on June 26, 1975, would be the guilty party. The problem is that the cartridge casing was not found in Coler's trunk when agents initially went over the car with fine tooth combs. Instead, it was supposedly found later, on one of two different days, by one of two different agents, and turned over to someone whose identity neither could quite recall, somewhere on the reservation. How the casing got from whoever and wherever that was to the FBI crime lab in Washington, D.C., is, of course, equally mysterious. This is what was used to establish the "murder weapon"; *Peltier Trial Transcript*, pp. 2114, 3012-13, 3137-38, 3235, 3342, 3388.

129. Agent Frank Coward, who did not testify to this effect against Butler and Robideau, claimed at the Fargo trial that shortly after the estimated time of Coler's and Williams' deaths, he observed Leonard Peltier, who he conceded he'd never seen before, running away from their cars and carrying an AR-15 rifle. This sighting was supposedly made through a 7x rifle scope at a distance of 800 meters (a half mile) through severe atmospheric heat shimmers while Peltier was moving at an oblique angle to the observer. Defense tests demonstrated that any such identification was impossible, even among friends standing full-face and under perfect weather conditions. In any event, this is what was used to tie Peltier to the "murder weapon"; *Peltier Trial Transcript*, p. 1305.

130. Seventeen-year-old Wish Draper, for instance, was strapped to a chair at the police station at Window Rock, Arizona, while being "interrogated" by FBI agents Charles Stapleton and James Doyle; he thereupon agreed to "cooperate" by testifying against Peltier; *Peltier Trial Transcript*, pp. 1087-98. Seventeen-year-old Norman Brown was told by agents J. Gary Adams and O. Victor Harvey during their interrogation of him that he'd "never walk this earth again" unless he testified in the manner they desired; *Peltier Trial Transcript*, pp. 4799-4804, 4842-43. Fifteen-year-old Mike Anderson was also interrogated by Adams and Harvey. In this case, they offered both the carrot and the stick: to get pending charges dismissed against him if he testified as instructed, and to "beat the living shit" out of him if he didn't; *Peltier Trial Transcript*, pp. 840-42. All three young men acknowledged under defense cross examination that they'd lied under oath at the request of the FBI and federal prosecutors.

131. Crooks' speech is worth quoting in part: "Apparently Special Agent Williams was killed first. He was shot in the face and hand by a bullet . . . probably begging for his life, and he was shot. The back of his head was blown off by a high powered rifle. . . Leonard Peltier then turned, as the evidence indicates, to Jack Coler lying on the ground helpless. He shoots him in the top of the head. Apparently feeling he hadn't done a good enough job, he shoots him again through the jaw, and his face explodes. No shell comes out, just explodes. The whole bottom of his chin is blown out by the force of the concussion. Blood splattered against the side of the car"; *Peltier Trial Transcript*, p. 5011.

132. Peltier's being sent directly to Marion contravenes federal Bureau of Prisons regulations restricting placement in that facility to "incorrigibles" who have "a record of unmanageability in more normal penal settings." Leonard Peltier had no prior convictions and therefore no record, unmanageable or otherwise, of behavior in penal settings.

133. *United States v. Peltier* (858 F.2d 314, 335 (8th Cir. 1978)).

134. *United States v. Peltier* (440 U.S. 945, *cert. denied* (1979)).

135. Another 6,000-odd pages of FBI file material on Peltier are still being withheld on the basis of "National Security."

136. At trial FBI ballistics expert Evan Hodge testified that the actual AR-15 had been recovered from Bob Robideau's burned-out car along the Wichita Turnpike in September 1975. The weapon was so badly damaged by the fire, Hodge said, that it had been impossible to perform a match-comparison of firing-pin tool marks by which to link it to the cartridge casing supposedly found in the trunk of Coler's car. However, by removing the bolt mechanism from the damaged weapon and putting it in an undamaged rifle, he claimed, it had been possible to perform a rather less conclusive match-comparison of extractor tool marks, with which to tie the Wichita AR-15 to the Coler Car Casing. Among the documents released under provision of the FOIA in 1981 was an Oct. 2, 1975, teletype written by Hodge stating that he *had* in fact performed a firing pin test using the Wichita AR-15, and that it failed to produce a match to the crucial casing; *United States v. Peltier*, Motion to Vacate Judgment and for a New Trial (Crim. No. CR-3003, U.S. District Court for the District of North Dakota, (filed Dec. 15, 1982)). The Eighth Circuit Court's decision to allow the appeal to proceed, despite Judge Benson's rejection of the preceding motion, is listed as *United States v. Peltier* (731 F.2d 550, 555 (8th Cir. 1984)).

137. During the evidentiary hearing on Peltier's second appeal, conducted in Bismarck, North Dakota, during late October 1984, it began to emerge that AIM members had used — and the FBI had *known* they had used — not one but several AR-15s during the Oglala Firefight. This stood to destroy the "single AR-15" theory used to convict Peltier at trial. Moreover, the evidentiary chain concerning the Coler Car Casing was brought into question. In an effort to salvage the situation, Bureau ballistics chief Evan Hodge took the stand to testify that he, and he *alone*, had handled ballistics materials related to the Peltier case. Appeal attorney William Kunstler then queried him concerning margin notes on the ballistics reports which were not his own. At that point, he retracted, admitting that a lab assistant, Joseph Twardowski had also handled the evidence and worked on the reports. Kunstler asked whether Hodge was sure that only Twardowski and himself had had access to the materials and conclusions adduced from them. Hodge responded emphatically in the affirmative. Kunstler then pointed to yet another handwriting in the report margins and demanded a formal inquiry by the court. Two hours later, a deflated Hodge was allowed by Judge Benson to return to the stand and admit he'd "mispoken" once again; he really had no idea who had handled the evidence, adding or subtracting pieces at will.

138. *United States v. Peltier* (CR-3003, Transcript of Oral Arguments Before the U.S. Eighth Circuit Court of Appeals, St. Louis, MO, Oct. 15, 1985) p. 19.

139. Ibid., p.18.

140. U.S. Eighth Circuit Court of Appeals, Appeal from the United States District of North Dakota in the Matter of *United States v. Leonard Peltier* (Crim. No. 85-5192, St. Louis, MO, Oct. 11, 1986).

141. Ibid., p. 16.

142. The high court declined review despite the fact that the Eighth Circuit decision had created a question — deriving from a Supreme Court opinion rendered in *U.S. v. Bagley* (U.S. 105 S. Ct. 3375 (1985)) — of what standard of doubt must be met before an appeals court is bound to remand a case to trial. The Eighth Circuit had formally concluded that while the Peltier jury might "possibly" have reached a different verdict had the appeals evidence been presented to it, it was necessary under *Bagley* guidelines that the jury would "probably" have rendered a different verdict for remand to be appropriate. Even this ludicrously labored reasoning collapses upon itself when it is considered that, in a slightly earlier case, the Ninth Circuit had remanded on the basis that the verdict might *possibly* have been different. It is in large part to resolve just such questions of equal treatment before the law that the Supreme Court theoretically exists. Yet it flatly refused to do its job when it came to being involved in the Peltier case; see my "Leonard Peltier: The Ordeal Continues," *Z Magazine*, Mar. 1988.

143. Once again, the Supreme Court has declined to review the matter.

144. Holder moved into secondary education, and works for Indian control of their schools in Kansas and Oklahoma. Others, such as Wilma Mankiller, Ted Means and Twila Martin, have moved into more mainstream venues of tribal politics. Still others, like Phyllis Young and Madonna (Gilbert) Thunderhawk have gone in the direction of environmentalism.

145. Examples include Jimmie Durham and John Arbuckle, both of whom now pursue—in dramatically different ways—careers in the arts.

146. Actually, this began very early on, as when AIM National President Carter Camp shot founder Clyde Bellecourt in the stomach in 1974 over a factional dispute instigated by Bellecourt's brother, Vernon. In the ensuing turmoil, Russell Means openly resigned from AIM, but was quickly reinstated; see Matthiessen, *Spirit of Crazy Horse*, pp. 85-6.

147. Banks was granted sanctuary by California Governor Jerry Brown in 1977, because of such campaign statements by South Dakota Attorney General William Janklow as "the way to deal with AIM leaders is a bullet in the head" and that, if elected, he would "put AIM leaders either in our jails or under them." An enraged Janklow responded by threatening to arrange early parole for a number of South Dakota's worst felons on condition they accept immediate deportation to California. During his time of "refugee status" Banks served as chancellor of the AIM-initiated D-Q University, near Sacramento; *Rapid City Journal*, Apr. 7, 1981.

148. Rebecca L. Robbins, "American Indian Self-Determination: Comparative Analysis and Rhetorical Criticism," *Issues in Radical Therapy/New Studies on the Left*, Vol. XIII, Nos. 3-4, Summer-Fall 1988.

149. An intended offshoot of the Peltier Defense Committee, designed to expose the identity of whoever had murdered AIM activist Anna Mae Pictou Aquash in execution style on Pine Ridge sometime in February 1976 (at the onset, it was expected this would be members of Wilson's GOONs), quickly collapsed when it became apparent that AIM itself might be involved. It turned out that self-proclaimed AIM National Officer Vernon Bellecourt had directed security personnel during the 1975 AIM General Membership Meeting to interrogate Aquash as a possible FBI informant. They were, he said, to "bury her where she stands" if unsatisfied with her answers. The security team, composed of Northwest AIM members, did not act upon this instruction, instead incorporating Aquash into their own group. The Northwest AIM Group was rapidly decimated after the Oglala Firefight, however, and Aquash was left unprotected. It is instructive that, once her body turned up near Wanbli, Bellecourt was the prime mover in quashing an internal investigation of her death. For general background, see Johanna Brand, *The Life and Death of Anna Mae Aquash* (Toronto: James Lorimer Publishers, 1978).

150. Killed were Trudell's wife, Tina Manning, their three children—Ricarda Star (age five), Sunshine Karma (age three) and Eli Changing Sun (age one)—and Tina's mother, Leah Hicks Manning. They were burned to death as they slept in the Trudells' trailer home; the blaze occurred less than twelve hours after Trudell delivered a speech in front of FBI headquarters during which he burned an American flag; although there was ample reason to suspect arson, no police or FBI investigation ensued; *Agents of Repression*, pp. 361-4.

151. Personal conversation with the author, 1979.

152. None of this is to say that LPDC did not continue. It did, even while failing to fulfill many of the wider objectives set forth by its founders. In terms of service to Peltier himself, aside from maintaining an ongoing legal appeals effort, the LPDC is largely responsible for the generation of more than 14 million petition signatures worldwide, all of them calling for his retrial. It has also been instrumental in bringing about several television documentaries, official inquiries into his situation by several foreign governments, an investigation by Amnesty International, and Peltier's receipt of a 1986 human rights award from the government of Spain.

153. *Keystone to Survival* (Rapid City, SD: Black Hills Alliance, 1981).

154. See "Breach of Trust," in this volume.

155. Weyler, *Blood of the Land*, pp. 251-64.

156. *United States v. Means, et al.* (Civ. No. 81-5131, U.S. District Court for the District of South Dakota (Dec. 9, 1985)).

157. *Lyng v. Northwest Indian Cemetery Protection Association* (485 U.S. 439 (1988)).

158. Anita Parlow, *Cry, Sacred Ground: Big Mountain, USA* (Washington, D.C.: Christic Institute, 1988).

159. See my, "The Struggle for Newe Segobia: The Western Shoshone Battle for Their Homeland," in *Struggle for the Land*, pp. 173–89.

160. Weyler, *Blood of the Land.*, pp. 212–50.

161. On Durham's recent activities, see his *A Certain Lack of Coherence: Writings on Art and Cultural Politics* (London: Kala Press, 1993).

162. Glenn T. Morris' and my "Between a Rock and a Hard Place: Left-Wing Revolution, Right-Wing Reaction, and the Destruction of Indigenous Peoples," *Cultural Survival Quarterly*, Vol. 11, No. 3, Fall 1988.

163. Colorado, Dakota, Eastern Oklahoma, Florida, Illinois, Maryland, Mid-Atlantic (LISN), Northern California, New Mexico (Albuquerque), Northwest, Ohio, Southeast (Atlanta), Southern California, Texas, Western Oklahoma, Wraps His Tail (Crow). These organized themselves as the Confederation of Autonomous AIM Chapters at a national conference in Edgewood, New Mexico, on Dec. 17, 1993.

164. M.A. Jaimes, "Racism and Sexism in the Media: The Trial of the Columbus Day Four," *Lies Of Our Times*, Sept. 1992.

165. Incorporation documents and attachments on file. The documents of incorporation are signed by Vernon Bellecourt, who is listed as a Central Committee member; the address listed for annual membership meetings is Bellecourt's residence. Other officers listed in the documents are Clyde Bellecourt, Dennis Banks, Herb Powless, John Trudell, Bill Means, Carole Standing Elk and Sam Dry Water. Trudell and Banks maintain that they were neither informed of the incorporation nor agreed to be officers.

166. Expulsion letter and associated documents on file. Bill Means states that he was asked, but refused to sign the letter.

167. Statement during a talk at the annual Medicine Ways Conference, University of California at Riverside, May 1991.

168. Statement during a talk at the University of Colorado at Denver, Feb. 1988 (tape on file).

169. This assessment, of course, runs entirely counter to those of pro-Wilson publicists such as syndicated columnist Tim Giago—supported as he is by a variety of powerful non-Indian interests—who has made it a mission in life to discredit and degrade the legacy of AIM through continuous doses of disinformation. Consider, as one example, his eulogy to Dickie Wilson—in which he denounced careful chroniclers of the Pine Ridge terror such as Onondaga faithkeeper Oren Lyons and Peter Matthiessen, described the victims of Wilson's GOONs as "violent" and "criminal," and embraced Wilson himself as a "friend"—in the Feb. 13, 1990, edition of *Lakota Times*. In a more recent editorial, Giago announced that his research indicates that "only 10" people were actually killed by Wilson's gun thugs on Pine Ridge during the mid-'70s although the FBI itself has conceded more than forty such fatalities. Then, rather than professing horror that his "friend" might have been responsible for even his revised number of murders, Giago uses this faulty revelation to suggest that the Wilson régime really wasn't so bad after all, especially when compared to AIM's "violence" and irreverence for "law and order."

170. A good effort to render several of these lessons will be found in Glick, *War at Home*.

171. For superb analysis of this point, see Isaac Balbus, *The Dialectic of Legal Repression* (New York: Russell Sage Foundation, 1973).

172. A fine survey of the conditions prevailing in each of these sectors will be found in Teresa L. Amott and Julie A. Matthaei, *Race, Gender and Work: A Multicultural Economic History of the United States* (Boston: South End Press, 1991).

173. For details and analysis, see my and J.J. Vander Wall's coedited, *Cages of Steel: The Politics of Imprisonment in the United States* (Washington, D.C.: Maisonneuve Press, 1992).

174. For a survey of the repression visited upon most of these groups, see *COINTELPRO Papers*.

175. For biographical information concerning those mentioned who are currently imprisoned by the United States, see *Can't Jail the Spirit: Political Prisoners in the United States* (Chicago: Committee to End the Marion Lockdown, 2002).

This essay was originally published in *American Indian Culture and Research Journal*, Vol. 18, No. 4, Fall 1995. It was subsequently published in Troy Johnson, Joane Nagel and Duane Champagne, eds., *American Indian Activism: Alcatraz to the Longest Walk* (Urbana: University of Illinois Press, 1997).

## "To Judge Them by the Standards of Their Time"

### America's Indian Fighters, the Laws of War and the Question of International Order

> I want no prisoners. I wish you to kill and burn. The more you kill and burn, the better you will please me.
>
> — General Jacob H. Smith
> Philippines (1901)

The expansion of the United States from a strip of territory situated east of the Appalachian Mountains on North America's Atlantic coast, first to continental scale, then to a position of global ascendancy, is a history replete with the use of military force.[1] Quite apart from the armed struggle by which it freed itself from English colonization, the new country's sheer bellicosity was evidenced as early as May 31, 1779, when future president George Washington issued written orders to Major General John Sullivan, instructing him to undertake a "preemptory" campaign against the Senecas and other members of the Haudenosaunee (Six Nation Iroquois Confederation) in upstate New York.[2]

Sullivan's mission was not so much to overrun Seneca territory as to destroy it, Washington wrote, and he was forbidden to "listen to any overture of peace before the total ruin of their settlements is effected."[3] The general thereupon did as he was directed. In 1838, historian William L. Stone "described in detail Sullivan's scouring the countryside, the 'war of extermination [he] waged against the very orchards.' At the town of Genesee alone Sullivan's army destroyed over a hundred houses, 'mostly large and very elegant,' laid waste extensive fields of ripening corn and beans, and 'with axe and torch soon transformed the whole of that beautiful region from the character of a garden to a scene of drear and sickening desolation.' "[4]

Among the trophies with which Sullivan's men returned from their victorious expedition were the scalps and tanned skins of their vanquished foes, the latter neatly fashioned into leggings.[5] Small wonder, all-in-all, that

Washington became known as "Town Destroyer" to the Haudenosaunee, and, as the Seneca leader Cornplanter remarked to America's "Founding Father" in 1792, "our women turn pale and look behind them, and our children cling close to the necks of their mothers" whenever his name was mentioned.[6]

A year after Sullivan wrought havoc upon the Six Nations, General George Rogers Clark—whose rangers still serve as the prototype after which the Army's élite units are modeled[7]—was engaged in a similar offensive against the Shawnees and other peoples in what are now the states of Ohio, Indiana and Illinois. Clark's men, who are known to have scalped their captives alive,[8] destroyed an estimated "five hundred acres of corn . . . as well as every species of edible vegetable" at the towns of Chillicothe and Piqua alone.[9]

Clark's effort was followed by that of General Anthony Wayne, still operating under the direction of Washington, in 1794. "Mad" Anthony's troops laid waste a huge swath through the Shawnee heartland, "remaining three days on the banks of the Maumee [River] during which time all the houses and . . . immense fields of corn . . . were consumed and destroyed" for a distance of fifty miles.[10] In the aftermath, leggings crafted from tanned human skin again made their appearance, this time along the Ohio frontier.[11]

Ultimately, the Shawnees were not defeated until the Battle of Tippecanoe on November 6, 1811. There, soldiers serving under future president William Henry Harrison indulged themselves in atrocities identical in their grotesquerie to those marking the Sullivan, Clark and Wayne campaigns a generation earlier. Emblematic of the whole was the troops' mutilation of the fallen Shawnee leader Tecumseh.

> The souvenir hunters got to work, and when the warrior had been stripped of his clothing . . . Kentuckians tore the skin from his back at thigh. . . The rapacious soldiery so thoroughly scalped the corpse that some of them came away with fragments the size of a cent piece and endowed with a tuft of hair. When one of them was interviewed in 1868 he was still able to display a piece of Tecumseh's skin.[12]

On March 27, 1814, following his massacre of the Muscogee Red Sticks at Horseshoe Bend, in Alabama, General Andrew Jackson "supervised the mutilation of 800 or more Indian corpses—cutting off their noses to count and preserve a record of the dead, slicing long strips of flesh from their bodies to tan and turn into bridle reins."[13] Thereafter, especially during his successful bid for the presidency in 1828, Jackson, who'd meanwhile gone on record urging that the Cherokees be similarly "scurged," would frequently boast that he'd "on all occasions preserved the scalps of my killed."[14]

In 1833, general and future president Zachary Taylor—in whose militia still another president-to-be, Abraham Lincoln, was serving at the time—unleashed the massacre of about 300 Sacs and Foxes led by Black Hawk on the Bad Axe River, in present-day Wisconsin.[16] Taylor's men ran wild, engaging in "an eight-hour frenzy of clubbing, stabbing, shooting [and] scalping."[15] The bones of Black Hawk himself were later disinterred and put on display in a local museum in Iowaville, Iowa, for well over a century.[16]

A recounting of this sort could be extended to great length, and expanded to include related matters—the proclamation of bounties on the scalps of Indians in every one of the "Lower 48,"[17] for instance, or the annihilation of entire native peoples by well-armed and -organized groups of "private citizens" in California[18]—but the illustrations provided above should prove sufficient to mark a conspicuous pattern of atrocity committed by the U.S. Army against American Indians during the entire period leading up to the Civil War.

They should also serve to demonstrate quite clearly that, far from being officially repudiated or socially condemned, such actions were undertaken as a matter of policy and with support of a majority of citizens enthusiastic enough to propel one perpetrator after another into the White House. Reward, not punishment or stigma, was the rule for even the worst of America's Indian-killers, any number of whom have come to be immortalized as national heroes.[19]

### "To Judge Them by the Standards of Their Time"

These realities are entirely disconsonant with the carefully cultivated air of "American Innocence" adopted by the United States, both as a self-concept and as an image projected internationally.[20] Correspondingly, such "unpleasantness" has been downplayed to the point of invisibility by generations of "responsible" historians, especially those authoring popular narratives and texts intended for absorption by schoolchildren,[21] and/or inverted in literature, cinema and the mass media.[22] Hence, the "tendency of [most] Americans is to deny such abuses and even to assert that they could never exist in their country."[23]

"Patriots" of this variety can of course be pinned down from time to time, usually after an infinity of hairsplitting over whether things "really" happened in the manner described, on the fact that one or even several of these "unfortunate occurrences" actually took place. The implications are seldom acknowledged, however. All but invariably, when uncomfortable facts are conceded a second level of sophistry ensues: that which threatens the sanctity of American purity of purpose is quickly consigned to the realm of aberration or anomaly.[24]

Alternately—or concomitantly—it is argued that things are being "interpreted out of context" by a process in which critics project contemporary values backwards into history, imposing them upon events, persons and entire settings where, having yet to be conceived, they bear no possible relevance. Neither actions nor implications, it is concluded, can be properly judged other than "by the standards of their time." In effect, no genuine onus can be assigned to massacres like Bad Axe and Horseshoe Bend because "everybody else was doing the same thing," or, in any event, "there was no law against it" when they happened.[25]

Strictly speaking, such arguments to technical innocence have never held water. Since its inception, the conduct of the United States, no less than that of any other country, has always been subject to the Law of Nations.[26] More specifically, the conduct of the U.S. military has been subject to the Laws of War. No recent moral innovation is involved, since "the regulation of armed conflict has occupied the attention of scholars, statesmen, and soldiers for thousands of years [and the] idea that the conduct of armed conflicts is governed by rules appears to have been found in almost all societies, without geographical limitation."[27]

> The foundation of the current legal regime is very old. . . The Greeks and Romans customarily observed certain humanitarian principles which have become fundamental rules of the contemporary laws of war. . . As the body of international law began to develop in Europe, early writers (such as Legnano, Victoria, Belli, Ayala, Gentili, and Grotius) gave priority to consideration of hostility in international relations. The work of Grotius, published during the Thirty Years War (1618-48) . . . has since come to be regarded as the first systematic treatment of international law, and one in which the laws of war played a principle part. Over this period, the practice of states led to the gradual emergence of customary principles regarding the conduct of armed hostilities.[28]

The relevant body of international customary law would certainly seem to suggest a reasonable standard of contemporaneous values and legitimacy to which the actions of men like George Washington, William Henry Harrison, Andrew Jackson and Zachary Taylor might be assessed for purposes of historical understanding.[29] Americans, Angloamericans in particular, have always had extraordinary difficulty grasping the concept that their behavior might ultimately be subject to some set of rules other than their own.

Thus, when the argument is advanced that there was "no law against" George Rogers Clark's scalping of living human beings, or John Sullivan's making breeches from the skins of his victims, it should be understood as meaning only that the United States itself had effected no statute prohibiting such practices. The polemic is at root identical to that offered by the nazi defendants at Nuremberg in arguing that their conduct was legitimate in that it had conformed to the requirements of Germany's domestic legal code (which they themselves had written).[30] To their eternal credit, the panel of jurists presiding over the nazis' prosecution dismissed such claims to "national sovereignty" as preposterous.[31]

Instead, the Nuremberg Tribunal asserted that "international law has imposed obligations upon states to punish certain acts committed in their territory," or under their authority.[32] These obligations encompass all international customs and conventions, including the Laws of War. No country possesses a right—as distinct from the power—to exempt itself from meeting this responsibility. Still less does it hold a right to "legitimate" violations of international legality by advancing formulations within its own statutes. Abridgement of these principles renders the offending state subject to international sanction and, depending on the magnitude of the issues involved, the jurisdiction of an international court.[33]

### The Lieber Code

Unlike Germany, moreover, the United States has always promoted itself as being the very avatar of enlightened legality, "a nation of laws, not men."[34] Within this self-congratulatory discourse, the Laws of War have featured quite prominently and the American prototype has been not infrequently offered as a model for worldwide emulation.

> The most famous early example of a national manual outlining the laws of war for the use of armed forces, and one of the first attempts to codify the laws of land warfare, was the 1863 'Instructions for the Government of Armies of the United States in the Field' prepared by Dr Francis Lieber of Columbia University. This manual, which became known as the 'Lieber Code,' was issued to the Union Army on 24 April 1863, and was applied to the forces of the United States during the American Civil War. It became the model for many other national manuals (for example, those of the Netherlands in 1871, France in 1877, Serbia in 1879, Spain in 1882, Portugal in 1890, and Italy in 1896).[35]

The Lieber Code is highly illuminating in that it conclusively demonstrates the extent to which America's legal community was familiar with the customary laws applicable to their country's warfare. Article 22, for example, holds that "as civilization has advanced during the last centuries, so has likewise steadily advanced, especially in war on land, the distinction between the private individual belonging to a hostile country and the hostile country, with its men at arms. The principle has been more and more acknowledged that the unarmed citizen is to be spared in person, property, and honor." In Article 23, it is stated that "Private citizens are no longer murdered . . . and the inoffensive individual is as little disturbed in his private relations as the commander of the hostile troops can afford to grant."

> 37. The United States acknowledge and protect, in hostile countries occupied by them . . . the persons of the inhabitants, especially women. . . Offenses to the contrary shall be rigorously punished.

> 44. All wanton violence committed against persons in the invaded country . . . all rape, wounding, maiming or killing of such inhabitants, are prohibited under penalty of death, or other such severe penalty as may seem adequate for the gravity of the offense.

These passages represent little more than amplifications of Emmerich de Vattel's famous observation, made a century earlier, that by the then–prevailing Laws of War "the people, the peasantry, the townspeople have nothing to fear from the sword of their enemies."[37] Lieber, however, with a smugness largely absent in Vattel, then proceeded to expend two articles explaining that the extension of such protections to noncombatants proved the superiority of European and euroderivate cultures to their "savage" or "barbarous" nonwestern counterparts.

> 24. The almost universal rule in remote times was, and continues to be with barbarous armies, that the private individual of the hostile country is destined to suffer every privation of liberty and protection, and every disruption of family ties. Protection was, and still is with uncivilized peoples, the exception.

> 25. In modern regular wars of Europeans, and their descendants in other parts of the globe, protection of the inoffensive citizen of the hostile country is the rule. . .

While many of the Code's remaining articles concern matters marginal to how wars against "savages" were to be waged, there are several that bore directly on the methods traditionally employed by the Army's Indian fighters. Article 68, borrows from Clausewitz's famous dicta, first published in 1827,[38] in stating that "modern wars are not internecine wars, in which killing the enemy is the object. The destruction of the enemy in modern war, and, indeed, modern war itself, are means to obtain that objective of the belligerent which lies beyond the war."

> 60. It is [therefore] against the usage of modern war to resolve, in hatred and revenge, to give no quarter. . . [A] commander is permitted to direct his troops to give no quarter [only] in great straits, when his own salvation makes it *impossible* to cumber himself with prisoners [emphasis in original].

Prefiguring the 1864 Geneva Convention on Wounded and Sick by nearly a year[39]—it was under discussion while the Code was being written—Lieber included two articles of obvious relevance in *any* sort of armed conflict.

> 61. [Even troops compelled by circumstance to] give no quarter have no right to kill enemies already disabled on the ground. . .

> 71. Whoever intentionally inflicts additional wounds on an enemy already wholly disabled, or kills such an enemy, or who orders or encourages soldiers to do so, shall suffer death, if duly convicted. . .

He followed Montesquieu and Rousseau in Article 56,[40] stipulating that prisoners of war, whether enemy civilians or captured combatants, were "subject to no punishment for being [enemies], nor is any revenge wreaked upon [them] by the intentional infliction of suffering, or disgrace, by cruel imprisonment, want of food, by mutilation, death, or any other barbarity." Article 75 reaffirmed this point, stating that "prisoners of war are subject to confinement or imprisonment . . . but are to be subjected to no other intentional suffering or indignity." Additionally,

> 67. The law of nations . . . admits of no rules or laws different from those of regular warfare regarding the treatment of prisoners of war, although they may belong to the army of a government which the captor may consider as a wanton and unjust assailant.

> 76. Prisoners of war shall be fed upon plain and wholesome food, whenever practicable, and treated with humanity.

> 79. Every captured enemy shall be medically treated, according to the ability of the medical staff.

Concerning armistices, Lieber also followed long-established legal custom, noting in Article 135 that an "armistice is the cessation of hostilities for a period agreed upon between the belligerents. It must be agreed upon in writing, and duly ratified by the highest authorities of the contending parties," and, in Article 138, that it "may be general, and valid for all points and lines of the belligerents; or special, that is, referring to certain troops or certain locales only." In Article 142, he goes on to clarify that, whether general or special, "an armistice is not a partial or a temporary peace; it is only the suspension of military operations to the extent agreed upon by the parties."

There can be no claim that the Code was meant to be situational, applicable in some instances and not in others. It was clearly designed to have a universally binding effect upon the conduct of U.S. troops in the field, irrespective of who they were fighting. Article 57, for example, stipulates that "no belligerent has the right to declare that enemies of a certain class, color, or condition . . . will not be treated by him [like other enemies]." Article 58 reinforces this point, emphasizing that the "law of nations knows of no distinction on the basis of color."

Thus did the government of the United States establish, concisely and in black letter form, the set of standards by which its wartime comportment may be evaluated. Whatever legal ambiguities may have attended earlier atrocities—and, as should be apparent, things were never so murky in this respect as apologists would now have it—they were dispelled on April 24, 1863. Thereafter, intellectual honesty and the law itself require that the conduct of America's Indian fighters be judged through the lens of the Lieber Code. Hence, standards in hand, we may resume our examination of their activities.

### The View From Sand Creek

On the morning of November 29, 1864, a reinforced regiment of U.S. volunteer cavalry, about 900 men in all, attacked a Cheyenne encampment along the Sand Creek, in southeastern Colorado. Of the 700-odd Indians residing therein, a lopsided majority were women, children and elderly men, all of them assembled on the order of territorial governor John Evans, disarmed and mostly dismounted, their safety "guaranteed" by the Army.[41] Their leader, Black Kettle, was a prominent member of the Cheyenne "peace faction" who displayed an American flag presented him by President Lincoln over his tipi.[42] In addition to the stars and stripes, a white ensign of surrender flew above the village when the soldiers came storming in.[43]

Flags aside, there can be no question that the cavalrymen mistook the village for one occupied by "hostiles." Colonel John M. Chivington, in charge of all Colorado volunteer units, had assumed personal command of the assault force. He'd been present when, as the condition of a special armistice, Evans had instructed Black Kettle to place his noncombatants under the protection of military authorities at Fort Lyon. [44] They were camped close to the post, at a spot approved by the post commander. Chivington, moreover, took extraordinary precautions to prevent the defenseless Cheyennes being warned of the fate about to befall them. [45]

Nor can there be the least confusion as to whether what happened at Sand Creek was simply a "tragedy" of the sort sometimes resulting when officers "lose control" over their troops in the heat of combat. Chivington addressed his men immediately prior to the attack, directing them to "kill and scalp all, big and little" [46] under his oft-stated premise that "nits make lice." [47] The soldiers, most of whom had overstayed their enlistments to participate in the bloodletting—promised weeks beforehand [48]—can thus be said to have conducted themselves in rather strict conformity to their orders.

The exact toll taken in the orgiastic slaughter thus unleashed remains unclear. In his after-action reports, Chivington himself put the bodycount at "400-500." He and other officers later pushed it even higher. [49] Most estimates today place the number killed at around 150. [50] Be that as it may, there is nothing mysterious about the manner in which the killing was done.

> The Indians fled in all directions, but the main body of them moved up the creek bed, which alone offered some protection from the soldiers' bullets. They fled headlong until they came to a place above the camp where the banks of the [stream] were cut back by breaks. Here, the Indians frantically began digging in the loose sand with their hands to make holes in which to hide. The larger percentage of these were women and children. [51]

As the scene was later described by Robert Bent, a mixed-blood Cheyenne who had accompanied the attackers:

> There were some thirty or forty [women] collected in a hole for protection; they sent out a little girl about six years old with a white flag on a stick; she had not proceeded but a few steps when she was shot and killed. All the [women] in the hole were afterwards killed. . . [They'd] offered no resistance. Every one I saw dead was scalped. I saw one [woman] cut open with an unborn child, as I thought, lying by her side. . . I saw quite a number of infants in arms killed with their mothers. [52]

John Smith, a veteran scout, recounted much the same.

> [The soldiers] used their knives, ripped open women, clubbed little children, knocked them in the head with their guns, beat their brains out, mutilated their bodies in every

sense of the word . . . worse mutilated than any I saw before. . . [C]hildren two or three months old; all lying there; from sucking infants up to [the elderly].[53]

Even Army officers concurred.

I did not see a body of man, woman or child but was scalped, and . . . mutilated in the most horrible manner—men, women and children's privates cut out, &c; I heard one man say that he had cut out a woman's private parts and had them for exhibition on a stick. . . [There were] numerous instances in which men had cut out the private parts of females and stretched them over saddle bows and wore them over their hats while riding in ranks.[54]

The day after the massacre, the few prisoners taken, including several women and an infant, were summarily executed.[55] The butchers then set out for Denver, the territorial capitol, where they proudly paraded down Larimer Street, a main thoroughfare, displaying bloody body parts of their victims to more than a thousand wildly cheering people who'd turned out to greet them.[56] Meanwhile, the slaughter was celebrated in the *Rocky Mountain News*—which had for more than a year been championing a "war of extermination" against the Cheyennes—as "an unparalleled feat of arms [which would] live forever in the annals of martial glory."[57]

These local sentiments notwithstanding, what had occurred was a war crime—or, rather, a cluster of war crimes—of the very grossest sort. Chivington's actions, and those of most of the other officers and men at Sand Creek,[58] violated every article of the Lieber Code cited in the preceding section. Such was the finding of not one but *three* federal investigations—one each by the Senate, the House, and the War Department—in the months following the massacre.[59] Yet, although there was thus ample predication for the filing of capital charges against those responsible, no prosecutions ensued.

The rationalization adorning this outcome contained all the ingredients of a farce. Since their crimes had been committed while the perpetrators were serving in the Army, civilian authorities purported no standing upon which to try them; because they'd since returned to civilian life, the War Department disavowed jurisdiction as well.[60] It is obvious, however, that the travesty did not result from jurisdictional loopholes. Military officers, then as now, served at the discretion of the president. Their commissions, once bestowed, were permanent. Chivington and his cohorts could thus have been recalled to active duty and court-martialed at any time.[61] The case against them was both unassailable and potentially precedential. All that was required was a genuine desire to hold them accountable for what they'd done.

312

Given that the merit of any legal codification resides not so much in its comprehensiveness or the elegance of its phraseology as in its enforcement,[62] the fact that no such desire was evidenced highlights the gulf separating the glowing rhetoric attending U.S. policy pronouncements from the grimy reality of how those policies were actually implemented. To all appearances, neither the Army nor civilian authorities wished to see a judicial precedent which might serve to deter the perpetration of further Sand Creeks. This, of course, says quite a lot about the true nature of America's "national character."

The more so, in view of treatment subsequently accorded Colorado's war criminals. To this day, a town near the massacre site is named in honor of John Chivington.[63] Streets in Denver similarly memorialize his principle subordinates. Until 1988, a building on University of Colorado's Boulder campus bore the name of David M. Nichols, a captain whose company was singled out for its "exceptional" performance at Sand Creek.[64] A monument stationed just outside the state capitol building still commemorates Chivington, his officers, and his troops as "gallant men."

## An "Anomaly Theory" of History?

While the example of Sand Creek can in many respects be left to speak for itself, to do so would be to beg the question of whether the massacre might be considered in some way "historically anomalous."[65] That it was not, can be readily appreciated in the nature of the "Kit Carson Campaign" conducted against the Navajos the same year. Although not so well-documented as the actions of Chivington and his troops, the record of Carson's command is replete with atrocity (e.g., soldiers playing catch with breasts hacked off living women).[66] Nor is there a shortage of comparably grisly examples.

Take, for instance, the "Battle of the Washita" on November 28, 1868, in which Lt. Colonel George Armstrong Custer's vaunted Seventh Cavalry Regiment slammed into Black Kettle's noncombatant Cheyennes for a second time. Replicating Chivington's feat almost exactly, and a day short of four years later, Custer's men left their Oklahoma killing ground strewn with 103 corpses.[67] Of these, "93 were women, old men, and children — as well as Black Kettle himself, who had been cut down with his wife as they were riding double on a pony in a desperate attempt to forestall the attack."[68] Needless to say, Custer — one of the more "glamorous" figures in U.S. military history — was not prosecuted.[69]

Then there was the Marias Massacre, in Montana, on January 23, 1870.

In this "incident," two companies of the Second Cavalry under Major Eugene M. Baker slaughtered 173 Piegans, only fifteen of whom were fighting-age males.[70] Although it turned out that Baker had hit the wrong village, and that most of his victims had been incapacitated by a recent smallpox epidemic, he went unprosecuted. On the contrary, like Custer's at the Washita, Baker's actions were vigorously applauded by General Phil Sheridan, in whose military district the massacres took place and who would later serve as Army Chief of Staff.[71]

On January 9, 1879, the much-suffering Cheyennes were made to bleed again, this time when a group of about 150 noncombatants led by Dull Knife attempted to escape from confinement at Camp Robinson, Nebraska. Sick, malnourished, afoot and almost entirely unarmed, they were quickly chased down. At least 85 were killed—the last 32 by massed soldiers firing point-blank volleys into a buffalo wallow where the Indians had sought refuge—and another 23 wounded. As usual, the victims were mostly old men, women and children. With equal predictability, no one was prosecuted for murdering them.[72]

Probably the best known of all such massacres occurred at Wounded Knee, South Dakota, on December 28, 1890. There, having disarmed and immobilized a group of about 500 Minneconjou Lakotas, the Seventh Cavalry, commanded at the time by Colonel George A. Forsyth, set about annihilating their captives in a manner entirely reminiscent of Sand Creek.

> [All] witnesses agree that from the moment it opened fire, [the Seventh] became a mass of infuriated men intent upon butchery. Women and children attempted to escape by running up a dry ravine, but were pursued and slaughtered—there is no other word—by hundreds of maddened soldiers, while shells from Hotchkiss guns, which had been moved up to sweep the ravine, continued to burst among them. The line of bodies was found to extend more than two miles from the camp—and they were all women and children. A few survivors eventually found shelter in brushy gullies here and there, and their pursuers had scouts call out that women and children could come out of hiding because they had nothing to fear. . . Some small boys crept out and were surrounded by soldiers who then butchered them. Nothing Indian that lived was safe.[73]

At about the same time, several lesser massacres were perpetrated in nearby locations.[74] Afterwards, as many as 350 corpses were unceremoniously dumped in a mass grave atop a hill overlooking the primary killing field.[75] Not only was no one prosecuted for this spectacular slaughter, twenty-three soldiers were awarded medals of honor for participating in it.[76] The most prominent public criticism, moreover, appears to have been that the Army failed to "finish the job" by completing "the total annihilation of the few remaining Indians" (this from newspaper editor Frank L. Baum, gentle author of *The Wizard of Oz*).[77]

After adding in the myriad smaller, mostly forgotten, and always unprosecuted massacres of American Indians—that of 27 Cheyennes on the Sappa Creek on April 20, 1875, to offer but one example[78]—one cannot help wondering just how many "anomalies" it takes to make a norm. The significance of such queries is accentuated when backdropped by Army Chief of Staff William Tecumseh Sherman's view, expressed in 1866, that his troops should "act with vindictive earnestness against the [Indians], even to their extermination, men, women, and children."[79] Still more, the notorious observation made three years later by Sherman's subordinate, Phil Sheridan, that "the only good Indian is a dead Indian."[80]

These flat contradictions of the Lieber Code's noble-sounding principles represented a consensus outlook among ranking generals, field officers and troops, not to mention apparent majorities of their civilian overseers and the public.[81] Viewed in this light, can it *really* have been a matter of mere "happenstance" or "coincidence" that the Cheyennes, Arapahos, Comanches, Kiowas and several other native peoples upon whom the Army warred during the period had all suffered population reductions in the 90th percentile by 1891, when the fighting for the most part ended, or that each experienced a dramatic numerical "rebound" thereafter?[82]

### The "Indians of the Philippines"

With the notion of anomaly thus thoroughly debunked, it will be useful to address the fallback position most often assumed by apologists for the Army's consistently criminal conduct during the "Indian Wars."[83] This concerns the claim that "special" or "unique" circumstances, usually having to do with the "savage nature" of the Indians themselves,[84] necessitated resort to tactics and behaviors outlawed not only in the Lieber Code but, increasingly, by the formalism of international convention as well.[85]

Leaving aside the fact that Al Capone might well have entered a similar argument—and with tangibly more justification—concerning the rival gangsters he ordered machine-gunned on St. Valentine's Day 1929,[86] a much larger factual problem presents itself. To put it simply, were there the least substance to such victim-blaming contentions, the illegalities at issue would have been limited to North America and ceased at some point before the beginning of the twentieth-century. And, of course, neither of these things is true.

Nowhere was this more obvious than in the Philippines during the years 1899–1902. There, having "liberated" the islands from Spanish colonization in 1898, the U.S. set about converting them into a colony of its own.[87] When the Filipinos resisted, they were described as "savages no better than our Indians" by American officials, and treated accordingly.[88] "The reasoning which justifies our making war against Sitting Bull also justifies our checking the outbreaks" of Filipinos, announced incipient president Theodore Roosevelt in 1900.[89] An Army officer framed the matter more frankly still:

> There is no use mincing words. . . If we decide to stay, we must bury all qualms and scruples about Weylerian cruelty, the consent of the governed, etc., and stay. We exterminated the American Indians, and I guess most of us are proud of it, or at least, believe the end justified the means; and we must have no scruples about exterminating this other race standing in the way of progress and enlightenment.[90]

With that end very much in mind, the War Department dispatched Major General Adna R. Chaffee, a veteran of campaigns against the Comanches, Cheyennes, Kiowas, and Apaches, to take charge.[91] As primary field commanders, Chaffee selected brigadier generals J. Franklin Bell, who'd fought the Cheyennes and Lakotas, and Jacob H. ("Hell-Roaring Jake") Smith, whose experience accrued from the Geronimo Campaign and the massacre at Wounded Knee.[92] They, in turn, brought in numerous subordinates with similar backgrounds. Small wonder that the Philippine endeavor was soon described as "just another Injun War," albeit, one waged overseas and against a vastly larger population.[93]

Bell was assigned to the Batangas region of Luzon, where he conducted "a particularly murderous campaign that depopulated large sections of the province."[94] By his own estimate, his tactics left one-sixth of the populace—some 616,000 people—dead within three years.[95] His officers were recorded as boasting that their general "had found the secret of pacification of the archipelago. . . They never rebel in [southern] Luzon because there isn't anybody there to rebel."[96] Although one of his subordinates, General R. P. Hughs, admitted during congressional testimony that none of this comported "with the ordinary rules of civilized warfare,"[97] Bell was never prosecuted for his crimes. Instead, the "Butcher of Batangas" received a presidential commendation for his ghastly record, and was later promoted to Army Chief of Staff.[98]

In the Samar district of northern Leyte, Jake Smith went even further, ordering the deaths of "all persons . . . *capable* of bearing arms in . . . hostilities against the United States [emphasis added]."[99] In response to a query from a subordinate about age limits, these instructions were refined to encompass every male "over ten years of age, as the Samar boys of that age were equally as dangerous as their elders."[100] The results were shortly reported in the press.

> Our men have been relentless; have killed to exterminate men, women, children, prisoners and captives, active insurgents and suspected people, from lads of ten and up, an idea prevailing that a Filipino, as such, was little better than a dog, a noisome reptile in some instances, whose best disposition was the rubbish heap.[101]

By 1902, such exposure had begun to tarnish the U.S. image internationally, rendering the Roosevelt administration vulnerable to criticism by its liberal opponents. A Senate investigation was duly convened.[102] Hence, the War Department went through the motions of charging a total of ten junior officers with "cruelties," including murder.[103] The outcomes obtaining from the resultant courts martial speak for themselves.

> One was convicted of "firing into a town," and "looting" and sentenced to a "reprimand." Lieutenant Bissell Thomas was found guilty of "assaulting prisoners and cruelty"; the court remarked that his cruelty had been "very severe and amounted almost to acute torture"; his sentence was a fine of $300 and "a reprimand." More appropriate was the disposition of the case of First Lieutenant Preston Brown, who was found guilty of "killing a prisoner of war" and sentenced to dismissal from the service and confinement "at hard labor for five years." . . .Brown's sentence [was, however,] commuted [on January 27, 1902] to a loss of thirty-five places in the army list and forfeiture of half his pay for nine months.[104]

Things did go a bit awry for the War Department during the trial of Littleton L.T. Waller, a Marine Corps major charged with one of the smaller slaughters he'd perpetrated while serving as Hell-Roaring Jake's right-hand man in Samar.[105] The prospects of Waller's paying much of a price were of course all but nil, the Army having appointed yet another of its "bald old Indian fighters," to hear the case. Unsurprisingly, although the accused candidly acknowledged presiding over not one but numerous massacres, he was promptly exonerated.[106]

Unfortunately for Smith, however, the judge bumbled the verdict, acquitting Waller not on the basis of his acts themselves being somehow legitimate, but because they'd been undertaken in obedience to superior orders.[107] This lapse made it necessary that the Hell-Roarer himself be charged with precipitating Waller's criminal activities. Nonetheless, "Smith was tried not for war crimes, or even for murder, but . . . for *conduct to the prejudice of good order and military discipline* [emphasis in the original]."[108] Found guilty of that remarkably trivial offense, he was sentenced to be "admonished by the President," allowing Roosevelt to "punish" the 62-year-old mass murderer with a grant of early retirement on full pension.[109]

This wrist slap, if it can be called even that, represented the total penalty paid by senior officers against the staggering welter of atrocities perpetrated under their authority. Against Chaffee, who was shown to have instructed Smith—and Bell, for that matter—to use "any means" in accomplishing their objectives, there were no charges whatever.[110] Rather, in August 1903, Roosevelt rewarded his orchestration of holocaustal initiatives consuming the lives of as many as a million Filipinos by appointing him Army Chief of Staff.[111] As was mentioned above, his successor in this exalted position, appointed in 1906, was "the *real* terror of the islands," J. Franklin Bell.[112]

Concerning America's pitiless war against the "Indians of the Philippines," Roosevelt—whose stern visage would soon affront the face of Mount Rushmore, enshrining him for all time as one of the four "greatest" U.S. presidents—had by then declared it "the most glorious in the country's history" and "a triumph of civilization over the black chaos of savagery and barbarism."[113] General Arthur MacArthur may have come closer to the mark when he explained to the Senate that, in his opinion, the whole affair signified nothing so much as a "fulfillment of the destiny of our Aryan ancestors."[114]

### The Exception as Rule

MacArthur's comment was revealing, suggesting as it did that the "special circumstances" precipitating extermination of peoples indigenous to U.S. "home" territory had little to do with anything "unique" to the victims themselves. Rather, that American Indians, like Filipinos, were *not white* was the issue. The Army, as saturated with the "scientific" racist perspectives pervading nineteenth-century American society as any other institution, simply followed the country's intellectual élite in viewing peoples of color as "species" biologically inferior to—i.e., less human than—whites.[115] Hence, nonwhites were seen as being "naturally" subordinate to their European/euroderivative "betters" (of whom MacArthur's "Aryans"—Anglo-Saxons—were deemed best of the best).[116]

It follows that the measure of inhumanity believed to be incarnated in particular groups of nonwhites was adduced not from their modes of fighting, but simply from the degree and tenacity of resistance they offered to assuming their "rightful" place under white domination; the greater the resistance, the less the humanity, to the point that—as with both Native Americans and Filipinos—they were construed as something altogether *other* than human beings (i.e., "nits," "lice," "dogs," "noisome reptiles," "squaws," "savages"). In turn, this reduction of "recalcitrant" nonwhites to a repugnant, dehumanized status licensed the Army to employ "exceptional" means in waging war against them.[117]

In effect, the situation could be—and was—considered exceptional whenever the Army took the field against anyone aside from "Europeans and their descendants in other portions of the globe."[118] Thus, as a practical matter, the prohibition against treating enemies differently on the basis of color enshrined in Articles 57 and 58 of the Lieber Code were nullified at the level of military doctrine in the very moment of its promulgation. From there, the rest of the Code's lofty principles fell like dominoes every time a conflict with nonwhites occurred.

And, since the great bulk of the fighting in which U.S. troops have engaged since 1863 has been against peoples of color[119]—that is, in settings where the military has indulged in self-exemption from its own professed standards of legality—it can be seen that "exceptions" once again constitute the rule. The illegalities inherent to Indian-fighting thereby emerge as both the model and the norm of behavior for the United States Army during armed conflicts. This remains true, whether the opponent is composed or regular or irregular forces, so long as the opponent is nonwhite.[120]

The institutionalization of this implicitly racist distinction was as apparent during operations against the Japanese in World War II as it had been forty years earlier, against the Filipinos, or forty years before that, against the Cheyennes, or forty years earlier still, against the Shawnees. Although U.S. troops adhered, more-or-less, to the laws of war in the course of fighting Germans and Italians in North Africa and Europe,[121] the Pacific War against Japan was waged on very different terms. As a veteran war correspondent recounted in *Atlantic Monthly*:

> We shot prisoners in cold blood, wiped out hospitals, strafed lifeboats, killed or mistreated enemy civilians, finished off the enemy wounded, tossed the dying into a hole with the dead, and in the Pacific boiled the flesh off enemy skulls to make table ornaments for sweethearts, or carved their bones into letter openers.[122]

Commanded by General Douglas MacArthur, Arthur's son, American soldiers "torture[d] and mutilate[d] with impunity,"[123] making a "fetish [of] collecting grisly battlefield trophies from the Japanese dead and near dead, in the form of gold teeth, ears, bones, scalps, and skulls."[124] None of this can be said to have happened secretly, without the knowledge of responsible officers, civilian authorities, or the general public. Rather, it was widely and often pridefully publicized, as when *Life* magazine accompanied a 1944 "human interest story" with "a full-page photograph of an attractive blonde posing with a Japanese skull she'd been sent by her fiancé [serving] in the Pacific."[125] Plainly, not much had changed since 1814, when, as a celebratory gesture, Andrew Jackson encouraged his men to distribute body parts cut from the corpses of Red Sticks slain at Horseshoe Bend among "the ladies of Tennessee."[126]

Nor was this the worst of it. Following in the tradition of George Washington's order that General Sullivan "not . . . listen to any overture of peace before the total ruin of [Seneca] settlements is effected,"[127] U.S. officials steadfastly refused Japan's attempts to surrender until after a series of massive "fire raids"—culminating in the nuclear bombings of Hiroshima and Nagasaki in August—were conducted against the country's cities during the spring and summer of 1945.[128] Although not prompted by any discernable military necessity,[129] this final air offensive cost the lives of well over a half-million Japanese civilians.[130]

In 1794, Washington had referred to the infliction of such needless suffering upon those he saw as biologically lesser beings as "chastizement."[131] In 1902, General Bell described it as a "thrashing" of "unruly" natives.[132] In 1945, America's leaders framed it in terms of a mysterious requirement that Japan's surrender be "unconditional."[133] Regardless of the phrasing, however, the meaning was always the same. As President George Herbert Walker Bush would put it in 1991, such policies of systematic atrocity were and remain necessary to "send a message" to brown-skinned people—in this case, the Iraqis—that "what we say, goes."[134]

### "Indian Country" (Again)

Once Japan's capitulation had converted the entire Pacific Basin into an "American lake," the U.S. turned to defending its "new frontier" on the periphery.[135] Wars fought along the Pacific Rim during the 1950s and 60s, often through surrogates, were especially brutal affairs,[136] conducted against "yellow dwarfs"[137] without regard to—and often in outright defiance of—the rule of law.[138] Although the U.S. "police action" fought in Korea from 1950-53 was in many respects a worthy contender,[139] this tendency was most pronounced during America's "ten thousand day war" in Indochina, centering on Vietnam and designed to prevent the peoples of the entire region from exercising their legal rights to self-determination.[140]

After 1965, the ferocity of the assault became almost unimaginable, involving the wholesale relocation and internment of an estimated two-thirds of the entire population of South Vietnam,[141] and the massive use of white phosphorus, napalm, and other incendiary ordnance against civilian targets.[142] One small area, the Panhandle of North Vietnam, became the most heavily bombed locale in history.[143] The Plain of Jars, in Laos, and portions of Cambodia were hit almost as hard.[144] Whole new technologies of inflicting pain—cluster bombs containing fiberglass shrapnel which would not show up on x-rays, for example—were developed to achieve the goal of "pacifying" the population.[145] Eventually, the ecosystem itself was targeted for eradication.[146]

Strategically, General William Westmoreland, overall commander of U.S. forces in Southeast Asia, articulated no concept other than to cause such "attrition" among "enemy personnel"—that is, the populace—that resistance would be unsustainable.[147] General Maxwell D. Taylor, who served as personal military advisor to President John F. Kennedy and as U.S. ambassador to Vietnam under Kennedy's successor, Lyndon Johnson, drew the obvious parallel to an "Indian War."[148] "Westy" himself was more blunt, likening his mission to that of an "exterminator" killing "termites."[149] Other ranking officers concurred, describing the Vietnamese as "ants" and "flies," Vietnam itself as a "manure pile."[150]

The sentiments bound up in these restatements of Bell's attitudes and policies in Batangas—and those of Sherman, Sheridan and Chivington on the Great Plains of North America—were lost on neither the field commanders nor their troops. From the outset, all territory other than that directly occupied by Americans was referred to by officers and men alike as "Indian Country."[151] Officers compared the tactical difficulties they faced to the "Indian Problem [in the] Old West" and announced they would "solve the . . . problem like we solved the Indian problem."[152] The indigenous population itself was habitually disparaged as being comprised of "gooks," "dinks," "slopes," even "zipperheads."[153]

Unsurprisingly, a "Mere Gook Rule," otherwise known as the "MGR,"[154] was adopted by the troops, translated by one soldier as "the Indian idea . . . the only good gook is a dead gook," by another as "the only good dink is a dead dink."[155] The killing was utterly indiscriminate because, as a Marine Corps officer explained, "the troops think [the Vietnamese] are all fucking savages" anyway.[156] The techniques routinely employed in dispatching the "savages" were described rather graphically by combat veterans Vernado Simpson, Jr., Gary Garfolo and James Bergthold in 1971 (there are hundreds of such accounts, many of them officially recorded).[157]

> *Simpson*: [We'd] mutilate the bodies and everything. [We'd] hang 'em up . . . or scalp 'em.
>
> *Garfolo*: Like scalps, you know, like from Indians. Some people were on an Indian trip over there.
>
> *Bergthold*: [We] cut ears off a guy and stuff like this here, without knowing if they were [enemy combatants] or not. If you got an ear, you got an [enemy].[159]

"Anybody we saw that was over twelve years old and that we thought was a male, was to be considered an enemy and engaged as such," recounted infantryman Robert A. Kruch.[159] Thus, "anything that's dead and isn't white" was tallied as "an enemy."[160] Perhaps the best summation of the prevailing attitude was offered by Lieutenant William L. Calley, who, accused of responsibility for the massacre of "at least 102 Oriental human beings" at a hamlet known as My Lai 4 on March 16, 1968, responded that he'd not set out "to kill human beings, really. . . We were there to kill . . . I don't know. . . Blobs. Pieces of flesh."[161]

In actuality, Calley and his men slaughtered 347 "old men, women, children, and babies," all of them unarmed, before "systematically burn[ing] their homes and huts" and reporting that they'd killed "128 enemy soldiers during an intense firefight."[162] Although the truth was known by Calley's superiors—his battalion executive officer observed the action from a helicopter and reported it to Colonel Oran Henderson, the battalion commander, who then relayed the information to the brigade commander, Major General Samuel W. Koster[163]—his unit was shortly congratulated by Westmoreland himself for its "outstanding action."[164] From there, "efforts were made at every level of command from company to division to withhold and suppress information concerning the incident."[165]

Only the unusual conscience and initiative displayed by a young ex-soldier named Ron Ridenhour forced the story into the open, nearly a year after the fact, and mainly because a growing segment of the body politic had become disenchanted with the war's spiraling costs (the administration of Richard Nixon, who replaced Johnson in 1969, was by then under a degree pressure, both domestically and internationally, making that faced by Theodore Roosevelt in 1902 seem paltry by comparison).[166] Nonetheless, after Ridenhour sent a letter detailing what had happened at My Lai to the president and twenty members of Congress on March 29, 1969,[167] the military continued to stonewall for several months.

It was not until information began to appear in the press that the Army finally charged Calley,[168] and even then it attempted to conduct his court-martial in secret.[169] By that point the story was uncontainable, however—an article by journalist Seymour Hersh appeared in thirty newspapers on November 11[170]—and the government's propaganda specialists thereupon recommended an exercise in "damage control." The resulting public relations extravaganza, beginning with a pair of "high-level reviews" of the massacre—one by the House,[171] the other by the Army[172]—was plainly intended to impress upon the world both how seriously the United States took its obligations under the Laws of War, and how "aberrant" or "anomalous" the massacre had been. As the House (Hébert Committee) report concluded:

> What happened at My Lai was wrong. It was contrary to the Geneva Conventions, the Rules of Engagement, and the MACV [Westmoreland's Military Assistance Command, Vietnam] Directives. In fact it was so wrong and so foreign to the normal character and actions of our military forces as to raise a question as to the legal sanity at the time of those men involved.[173]

Soon, thirty officers, including General Koster—but not, to be sure, William Westmoreland or any of his MACV staff[174]—were charged with offenses ranging from murder to obstruction of justice. Even without resort to the insanity defense, however, the accused fared about the same as their predecessors during the Philippines Trials of 1902.

> Calley was the only person among the 30 held to account through the system of military justice. Three others were brought to trial but acquitted. Charges brought against 12 of the 30 were dismissed before trial. Administrative action . . . demotion, or reprimand, or the like . . . was taken against seven of the twelve and one of the three acquitted after trial.[175]

Like Hell-Roaring Jake Smith before him, Koster—who, because of his "exemplary service" in Vietnam had been appointed superintendent of the U.S. Military Academy at West Point—was reprimanded and placed on early retirement.[176] Also like Smith, Colonel Henderson was tried only on only relatively petty charges (dereliction of duty, failure to obey regulations); unlike Smith, he was acquitted even of those.[177] Calley's company commander, Captain Ernest Medina—who, like Chivington at Sand Creek, had given his subordinate specific instructions to do what he did at My Lai—was charged with complicity in the massacre.[178] He, too, was exonerated.[179] The rest walked away with little more than tepid letters of censure or reprimands, remaining for the most part on active duty.[180]

As to Calley himself, barred by the Nuremberg precedent from using the "superior orders" defense employed so successfully by Littleton Waller in 1902, he was a natural scapegoat. His penalty was by no means great, however. Convicted on March 29, 1971, he was initially sentenced with much fanfare to serve "life at hard labor." Spared the labor while he appealed to the commander of the Third Army, his sentence was reduced, five months after his conviction, to twenty years imprisonment. In April 1974, Secretary of the Army Howard H. Callaway cut it to ten years, and the conviction itself was reversed on September 24. Having served three-and-a-half years on house arrest—about three days per victim, about eight hours if the nearly 250 unacknowledged murders at My Lai are added in—"Rusty" Calley was a free man.[181] Preston Brown would have felt right at home.

### (. . .and Again)

My Lai was extraordinary only in the sense that it was publicized and therefore resulted in the token punishment of a perpetrator. As Oran Henderson put it, "every unit of brigade size had its My Lai hidden some place" although "every unit [didn't] have a Ridenhour" to make an issue of it.[182] Proof of this came, ironically enough, during the Army's field investigation of My Lai itself, when evidence was turned up that a second massacre had occurred at more-or-less the same time at the hamlet of My Khe 4 (or Co Luy, as it was also known), about two miles southeast of Calley's killing ground.[183]

> In this "other massacre," members of a separate company piled up a body count of perhaps a hundred peasants—My Khe was smaller than My Lai—"just flattened the village" by dynamite and fire, then threw a few handfuls of straw on the corpses. The next morning, the company moved on down the Batangan peninsula by the South China Sea, burning every hamlet they came to, killing water buffalo, pigs, chickens, and ducks,

324

and destroying crops. And, as one of the My Khe veterans said later, "what we were doing was being done all over." Said another: "We were having a good time. It was sort of like being in a shooting gallery."[184]

General William Peers, heading up the Army's "review" of the slaughter at My Lai, "falsely stated to newsmen that no evidence had been presented of another massacre,"[185] then set about suppressing it. Hence, although the unit commander at My Khe, Captain Thomas K. Willingham, was charged with the "unpremeditated murder [of] at least twenty Vietnamese civilians" in February 1970,[186] the case against him was dismissed in June for "lack of [the very] evidence" Peers had buried.[187] To this day, the general's findings on My Khe remain highly classified.[188] So, too, are the files on Truong Khanh 2, another place "pacified" in 1968:

> "[The] troops stormed the hamlet, which was occupied mostly by old people, women, and children," going from house to house, killing everyone they found, in the end, 62 villagers. The people of the village were broom makers. When they were dead. . . "the troops put the bodies on a pile, covered them with straw, and set them on fire."[189]

Despite the best efforts of men like Peers to keep the lid on information about Truong Khanh, the massacre was described by former infantryman Daniel Notley in testimony before a congressional committee in March 1970.

> [As] we moved into the [village] nobody said anything but all of a sudden these guys start shooting. They were shooting women and kids . . . there weren't any men there. . . It was just like cut and dried like it was understood this was going to happen. . . [They] did this so systematically like it was something they'd done many times before, it was easy. . . [T]here weren't any men in [the village] at all. There were some male children, but there were women and children only.[190]

"How many other incidents of this kind took place the West will never know, and in fact does not much care,"[191] although many have been recounted by American soldiers who witnessed or participated in them.[192] Even less attention is paid to the atrocities committed by the approximately 7,000 South Korean mercenaries employed from 1965 to 1973 to augment U.S. ground forces in Vietnam.[193] The standard operating procedure of these surrogates, as was certainly known to Westmoreland and other officers at MACV, included shooting one of ten civilians in villages they occupied.[194] Their record, moreover, includes at least forty-three major massacres, a dozen claiming upwards of a hundred victims.[195] Australian "contributions to the war effort," actively solicited by the U.S., took much the same form.[196]

More insidious still were the sorts of ongoing massacre that never crystallized in a largescale "event" like My Lai, My Khe or Truong Khanh. These took the form of a steady, grinding propensity of U.S. troops to carry out "innumerable, isolated killings . . . rapes and tortures,"[197] machine-gunning random peasants from passing helicopters,[198] obliterating entire villages — and their inhabitants — with artillery barrages and airstrikes (sometimes called in for no other reason than "to have something to do").[199]

> One brigade commander ran a contest, celebrating his unit's 10,000[th] enemy kill by giving the GI who shot him [or her, or "it"] a week's pass. . . Many battalions staged contests among their rifle companies for the highest score in enemy kills, with the winning unit getting additional time for passes.[200]

The earlier-quoted definition of an "enemy" being "anything dead that isn't white" tells the tale, however. As *Newsweek* reporter Kevin Buckley observed with respect to an operation conducted in the single province of Kien Hoa during a six-month period of 1968:

> All the evidence I gathered pointed to a clear conclusion: a staggering number of noncombatant civilians . . . were killed by U.S. firepower to "pacify" Kien Hoa. . . There is overwhelming evidence that virtually all [enemy combatants] were armed. Simple civilians were, of course, not armed. And the enormous discrepancy between the body count [11,000] and the number of captured weapons [748] is hard to explain — except by the conclusion that many victims were unarmed innocent civilians. . . The death toll there made My Lai look trifling by comparison.[201]

An experienced U.S. official concurred with Buckley's assessment, stating that the "actions of the 9th Division [which conducted the Kien Hoa offensive] in inflicting civilian casualties were far worse" than those of Calley's men.[202]

> The sum total of what the 9th did was overwhelming. In sum, the horror was worse than My Lai. But with the 9th, the civilian casualties came in dribbles and were pieced together over a long period.[203]

Colonel George S. Patton III, grandson of the legendary World War II general, also agreed with Buckley, but from a radically different perspective. Describing his troops as "a bloody good bunch of killers,"[204] Patton went on to reflect upon how he considered their "present ratio of 90 percent killing and 10 percent pacification just about right."[205] Celebrating Christmas 1968 with a card displaying the photo of a dismembered Vietnamese over the legend "Peace on Earth," Patton returned to the U.S. carrying a polished human skull, complete with a bullet hole over the left eye, presented at his farewell party by adoring subordinates.[206] Soon to be promoted brigadier general, he'd already been awarded the Legion of Merit and characterized by Westmoreland's successor, General Creighton Abrams, as "one of our finest young officers."[207]

Fittingly, under the circumstances, U.S. troops all over Vietnam painted slogans like "Kill 'em All. . . Let God Sort 'em Out" on their helicopters and armored vehicles, along with SS death's head insignia (which also figured prominently in the impromptu patches and "beer can insignia" adopted by élite units like the Special Forces).[208] Many wore necklaces of human ears, while others posed for photos, proudly positioned beside the severed heads of those they'd killed.[209] To paraphrase another slogan popular with GIs, "killing was their business and business was good."[210]

All told, an estimated 3.2 million Indochinese perished as the result of U.S. actions in Southeast Asia.[211] Against that, for all practical intents and purposes, can be balanced Lieutenant William Calley's travesty of a punishment and that of First Lieutenant James Duffy, found guilty in 1970 of the premeditated murder of a prisoner. Almost immediately afterwards, however, Duffy's offense was "revised" to read "involuntary manslaughter" and his sentence reduced to six months incarceration—already served—plus a $150 fine.[212] Once again, Preston Brown might have felt right at home, a circumstance underscoring how little had changed since 1902 (or 1864, for that matter).

### Standards (Again)

By the time it went to war in Indochina, the U.S. military had considerably refined its Rules of Engagement. Those set forth in the Lieber Code had been updated over the intervening century to incorporate a steadily growing body of international law. The directives in effect when the massacres at My Lai and My Khe occurred indicated that "the United States recognizes the conflict in Vietnam as an international conflict to which both customary and written or conventional law apply, and . . . has declared its intent to observe this law."[213] Several elements of written law were noted as being of cardinal importance.

1. Hague Convention No. IV Respecting the Laws and Customs of War on Land and the Annex thereto which embodies the Regulations Respecting the Laws and Customs of War on Land.[214]

2. The four 1949 Geneva Conventions for the protection of the wounded and sick of armed forces in the field; wounded, sick, and shipwrecked members of the armed forces at sea; prisoners of war; and civilian persons in times of war.[215]

3. The 1929 Geneva Conventions relative to treatment of prisoners of war and the amelioration of the conditions of the wounded and sick of armies in the field.[216]

Article 6(b) of the Charter of the International Military Tribunal at Nuremberg (1945), defining "war crimes" as "violation of the laws or customs of war [including,] but not limited to, murder, ill treatment or deportation to slave labor or for any other purpose of civilian population of or in occupied territory, murder or ill treatment of prisoners of war or persons on the high seas, killing of hostages, plunder of public or private property, wanton destruction of cities, towns or villages, or devastation not justified by military necessity" was also of obvious relevance.[217]

Acknowledging that the primary purposes of these conventions devolve upon "protecting both noncombatants and combatants from unnecessary suffering" and "safeguarding certain fundamental human rights of persons who fall into the hands of the enemy, particularly prisoners of war, the wounded and sick, and civilians," the directives pledge the United States to investigate, prosecute and punish "grave breaches" of them through its own Uniform Code of Military Justice.[218] Something of the magnitude to which the Army defaulted in this regard should have been obvious in the preceding two sections.

This was but the tip of the proverbial iceberg, however. The entire strategic context in which massacres of both abrupt and protracted varieties occurred—that of using "awesome firepower" to achieve "a demographic reconfiguration" of Indochina which would deny "population resources to the "enemy" (however defined)[219]—was illegal on its face. This would have been true, even if, to advance a patently absurd hypothesis often employed by U.S. apologists,[220] not a single civilian were killed in the process.

Article 25 of the 1907 Hague Convention, for example, states that the "attack or bombardment, by whatever means, of towns, dwellings or buildings which are undefended is prohibited."[221] Article 22 of the 1923 Hague Rules of Aerial Warfare states that "aerial bombardment for purposes of terrorizing the civilian population, or of destroying or damaging private property not of a military character, or of injuring noncombatants is prohibited."[222] Article 3 of the 1949 Geneva Convention IV Relative to the Protection of Civilian Persons in Times of War affords similar protections.[223]

During the earlier-discussed 1968 Ninth Infantry offensive, codenamed "Operation Speedy Express," there were 3,183 tactical airstrikes by fighter-bomber aircraft.[224] This is aside from continuous ground support missions flown by fifty helicopter gunships equipped with rockets and miniguns (a sort of Gatling gun capable of firing 6,000 rounds per minute).[225] It is also aside from round-the-clock fire missions carried out by the fifty heavy and dozens of smaller artillery pieces committed to the operation,[226] and scores of "Arclight strikes"—the radio-directed saturation bombing of often unseen targets—by B-52 strategic bombers flying eight miles above the earth.[227]

The great bulk of this ordnance—something on the order of 80 percent—was expended against rural villages possessed of neither air defenses nor military installations, the residents of which were comprised, even in the estimation of military intelligence analysts, all but exclusively of noncombatant peasants. As was mentioned, more than 10,000 Vietnamese civilians appear to have been killed during Speedy Express, as opposed to less than a thousand enemy combatants. More importantly, from the perspective of U.S. strategists, some 120,000 others were driven from their homes, away from the "free fire zone," and thus "denied" as a "resource" to the enemy.[228]

Speedy Express involved a single infantry division during six months of the seven-year period, 1965-72, in which substantial American ground forces were deployed. At its peak, MACV had nine Army and two Marine divisions "on the ground" in Vietnam, as well as five independent infantry brigades, an independent armored regiment, and substantial elements of another airborne division.[229] There were more than two-dozen offensives on the scale of Speedy Express during the war, and even this does not begin to tell the whole story, since the bombardment continued unabated during the intervals in between. All told, the quantity of aerial ordnance expended in the area of U.S. ground operations by the end of 1972 was "over 3.9 million tons . . . about double the total bomb tonnage used by the United States in all theaters during World War II."[230] The result was well over a million dead noncombatants and upwards of ten million permanently "displaced" from their homes.[231]

So it was in Laos, a country against which U.S. officials insisted "no military operations [were] being conducted."[232] Although only a small number of American ground troops were committed to the "secret war" in Laos, most of them Special Forces and CIA clandestine operations personnel, the Plain of Jars and the more southerly Laotian panhandle comprised one of "the most heavily-bombed regions in the history of warfare."[233] By 1969, fighter bombers were flying "an average of 200–300 sorties a day over northern Laos, and 1,200 daily over the southeast . . . bombing both day and night, dropping 500 pound bombs, delayed-action bombs, napalm, phosphorous bombs and, most of all, CBU [cluster bomb unit] antipersonnel bombs."[234] Arclight strikes by B-52s were also frequent.[235]

Although the air offensive was ostensibly designed to support the war effort in Vietnam by targeting enemy troop sanctuaries and interdicting supply routes, "everything [in Laos] was attacked—buffaloes, cows, rice fields, schools, temples . . . both the villages and their outskirts . . . and [even] tiny shelters erected outside the villages."[236] As a survivor recounted, "During the bombing, if the planes couldn't select a place to bomb, but they saw some animals or people, they would simply drop the bombs on them."[237] An American airman concurred:

> The only place people could exist up there on the Plain of Jars was in caves. And we were bombing caves. A single human path was enough for us to bomb. All human activity was considered enemy activity.[238]

The goal of the saturation bombing in Laos was identical to that enunciated for Vietnam. To quote U.S. Congressman Pete McClosky, the "uncontestable conclusion is that at least 76 percent of [the] small villages in northern Laos were destroyed by bombing in 1969" alone.[239] "Cluster bombs and white phosphorous were used against the civilian population of a country with which the United States [was] not at war."[240] This served to "cause a population flow away from" the targeted areas, into locales preferred by U.S. strategic planners.[241] By 1970, an estimated "350,000 men, women and children [had] been killed . . . and a tenth of the population of three million uprooted" in the process of "destroying the social and economic infrastructure" upon which U.S. strategists believed their "enemies" depended.[242]

Yet another "secret" bombing campaign was conducted in Cambodia. Although the U.S. was "not at war" with that country either, and, according to the Pentagon itself, the targets selected usually posed at most "a *potential* threat to friendly forces [emphasis added],"[243] the air offensive reached a crescendo in 1973.

> In all of 1972 the B-52s dropped just under 37,000 tons of bombs into Cambodia. In March 1973 they dropped over 24,000, in April bout 35,000 and in May almost 36,000 tons. So with the fighter bombers. In 1972 they had loosed 16,513 tons of bombs at

their targets. In April 1973 alone, they dropped almost 15,000 tons, and the figure rose monthly to over 19,000 tons in July.[244]

As in Vietnam and Laos, "the bombs were falling upon the most heavily populated areas of Cambodia,"[245] generating heavy casualties among the peasantry and destroying the basis of their economy for no purpose remotely fitting accepted definitions of "military necessity." Before the bombing ended in April 1975, an estimated 4,500 undefended villages and hamlets had been destroyed, along with half the livestock and a quarter of the farmland (cratered beyond use).[246] A minimum of 445,000 noncombatants were killed or wounded—estimates run as high as a million—and some four million of Cambodia's 7.7 million people driven from their homes.[247]

A quarter-century later, none of the three largest societies impacted by the onslaught—Vietnamese, Lao and Khmer—have come close to recovering. Once comprising the "rice bowl of Asia," they remain destitute,[248] struggling with the combination of environmental devastation and intractable social trauma resulting from the sustained savagery of U.S. "pacification."[249] For the smaller "tribal" societies of the area—the upland Hmong of Laos, for example, and the so-called Montagnards of Vietnam—conditions are by all indications even worse.[250] To paraphrase the (in)famous observation of an American major after he'd leveled the town of Ben Tre in 1968, "it was necessary to destroy an entire way of life in order to save it" from existing in a manner free of American domination.[251] No American Indian familiar with his/her own history would be surprised by the expression of such sentiments.

### Do As We Say (Never As We Do)

As early as 1966, England's Lord Bertrand Russell had outlined the basis upon which the overall U.S. Indochina strategy should be considered criminal.[252] A year later, he sponsored an International War Crimes Tribunal, usually referred to as the "Russell Tribunal," to hear testimony and otherwise examine matters in greater detail. Composed of noted jurists, scholars and intellectuals and first convened in November 1967, the panel considered evidence over a period of several months, eventually concluding that the United States was guilty, as a matter of policy, not only of major war crimes, but others, including genocide.[253]

Although there was considerable "controversy" over the Russell Tribunal's findings,[254] the situation was clear enough by 1970 that even General Telford Taylor, who had served as chief counsel for the prosecution at Nuremberg, acknowledged that what was being done in Vietnam, Laos and Cambodia was "what we hanged and imprisoned Japanese and German generals for doing."[255] Were the same standards applied to Americans as were applied against the nazis, he observed, there was "a very strong possibility" that both the military and the civilian leadership of the United States "would come to the same end [they] did."[256]

That Taylor relied upon the standards set at Nuremberg when assessing U.S. conduct was especially appropriate not only because of his experience in prosecuting violators, but because the United States had all but single-handedly established such standards in the first place.[257] It was, after all, Supreme Court Justice Robert H. Jackson, while serving as chief U.S. prosecutor at Nuremberg, who'd articulated the principle that the laws under which the nazis were tried were as applicable to "all men [and] any other nations, including those which now sit here in judgement" as they were to Germany and the men then in the defendants' dock.[258]

> If certain acts and violations of treaties are crimes, they are crimes whether the United States does them or Germany does them. We are not prepared to lay down a rule of criminal conduct against others which we are not willing to have invoked against us.[259]

This, to be sure, proved demonstrably false. Not one U.S. airman, much less a general or high civilian official, faced charges accruing from their roles in the systematic destruction of whole Indochinese societies. On the contrary, throughout its war(s) in Indochina, representatives of the American government openly described the idea it might be bound in *any* palpable way by the Nuremberg precedent as "absurd."[260] In the astonishingly revealing estimation of one senior diplomat, "war crimes tribunals would be the worst thing that could happen, [because] they would amount to . . . a system of legal guilt for top [U.S.] officials" who violated international law.[261] Thus did the United States categorically exempt itself from the rules imposed upon those it presumed to judge.

The glaring double-standard belying Jackson's rhetoric had been there all along. Germany's Grand Admiral Karl Dönitz, for instance, was convicted of war crimes at Nuremberg for having conducted a campaign of "unrestricted U-boat warfare" against Allied shipping in the North Atlantic despite an affidavit from U.S. Admiral Chester A. Nimitz admitting he'd employed the same methods against the Japanese in the Pacific.[262] Reichsmarschall Hermann Göring was also prosecuted in part for ordering the "terror bombings" of Warsaw, Rotterdam and Coventry, although these charges were quietly abandoned after the defense pointed out that the British/American strategic bombing of Germany—most especially the incendiary attacks on Hamburg and Dresden—far surpassed anything Göring's Luftwaffe had done.[263] Plainly, a crime was a crime at Nuremberg only insofar as the U.S. and its allies had not also perpetrated it (and, in the *Dönitz* case, even when they had).

The same was true of the "Other Nuremberg" convened in Tokyo to try Japanese war criminals.[264] Although Japan was not a signatory, several members of the Japanese general staff were executed under provision of Article 26 of the 1929 Geneva Convention Relative to the Treatment of Prisoners of War, through which they were held responsible for murders and other atrocities committed against POWs by their subordinates.[265] The best-known example is that of General Tomoyuki Yamashita, the "Tiger of the Philippines" (who was actually tried in Manila).[266] Quite apart from the fact that the record of Yamashita's men pales in comparison to that of Chaffee's only forty years earlier,[267] it was common knowledge that U.S. soldiers and Marines had routinely dispatched Japanese prisoners all over the Pacific.[268]

Nor was a different attitude adopted with regard to enemies of lesser rank. While American field officers and troops were nowhere charged for torturing and murdering their captured opponents—shooting hundreds of wounded Japanese on Bougainville, to provide one illustration,[269] machine-gunning "a line of unarmed Japanese soldiers who had just surrendered" on Okinawa, to offer another[270]—scores of vanquished foes were prosecuted for comparable offenses during the numerous "Little Nurembergs" that followed the main events of 1945-46.[271] SS Obersturmbannführer (Lt. Colonel) Jochen Peiper, to take the most memorable example, was sentenced to death—later commuted to 35 years imprisonment—for having ordered the 1944 massacre of 84 U.S. POWs at Malmédy, Belgium.[272]

Unquestionably, the atrocities perpetrated by the SS and their Japanese counterparts against prisoners in their charge merited the punishments meted out. No more so, however, than those committed by U.S. troops against Japanese and, to a much lesser degree, German soldiers.[273] Nor more so than either the "water cure" and similar tortures performed by American soldiers upon thousands of Filipino prisoners decades before World War II.[274] Nor the ubiquitous "Bell telephone hour"—torture by electric shock—and other such brutalities routinely committed against the

Indochinese twenty years later,[275] all of which went not just unpunished but in many cases was actively rewarded.

The same pattern can be traced much deeper in time, as when, following "Little Crow's War" in 1863, the Army conducted drumhead courts-martial of 400 defeated Santee Dakotas and sentenced 303 of them to death for alleged crimes against white "settlers" who'd flooded into their treaty-guaranteed Minnesota homeland.[276] Only the "humanitarian intervention" of President Lincoln reduced the number to 37, all hanged together in the largest mass execution in American history.[277] The Army itself, which had slaughtered native noncombatants with its usual abandon during the war, had by then confined the bulk of the starving survivors in a concentration camp, and proclaimed a $200 bounty on the scalps of the rest.[278]

Similarly, although the Army had engaged in avowedly exterminatory campaigns against their peoples, several thousand native men of fighting age—the majority of them Cheyennes, Kiowas, Comanches and Apaches—were accused of crimes against whites invading their territories during the 1860s, '70s, and '80s.[279] Sometimes tried, sometimes not, the warriors were consigned for long periods and with deadening regularity to the Fort Marion Military Prison in Florida. Probably the ugliest example is that of Geronimo's Chiricahua Apaches, 400 of whom were sent first to the Florida facility, then to Fort Sill, Oklahoma, and never allowed to return to their homes.[280]

Then there was the case of Captain Henry Wirtz, a Confederate officer prosecuted for war crimes under the terms of the Lieber Code and hanged on November 10, 1865. The allegation was that while serving as its commandant, Wirtz been responsible for the hideous conditions prevailing in the Andersonville POW camp and that some 13,000 Union prisoners had died as a result. While the charges against the captain were accurate enough, they plainly blinked the fact that conditions in U.S. prison camps had been just as bad, the death rates therein comparable, and that "the Union had been much more capable of feeding its POWs but had deliberately reduced the amount of rations many times."[281]

Even more to the point is the reality that at the time Wirtz was tried, the Army was holding virtually the entire Navajo Nation as POWs at a concentration camp in Bosque Redondo, outside Fort Sumner, New Mexico, and would continue to do so for another three years.[282] Conditions there were such that, before the survivors were finally released in 1868, more than half the prisoners had died of exposure, malnutrition and disease.[283] The death rate at Bosque Redondo was much higher than those prevailing in such infamous nazi camps as Dachau and Buchenwald eighty years later.[284] Unlike the nazis, however—or Henry Wirtz, for that matter—no U.S. officer was prosecuted for the crimes that consumed the Navajos.

On balance, it is accurate to conclude that U.S. practice concerning war crimes and related offenses has been to insist that others "do as we say, not as we do." Not only does this make a mockery of America's hallowed pretense of dispensing "equal justice before the law," it places the country in the position of conducting its affairs as a veritable outlaw state.[285] *Whatever* standards have been in effect at any given moment, the U.S. high command and its civilian counterparts have run very far afoul of them. This accounts in no small degree for what the Hébert Committee called "the normal character and actions of [American] military forces,"[286] albeit in a manner diametrically opposed to how the committee meant it.

### Under Penalty of Law

Actually, where rank-and-file U.S. troops were concerned, "doing as we say" may never have entered in. No one seems to have bothered to say anything to them about the legal issues involved in combat, one way or the other. Despite the detailed references in the showpiece 1956 edition of its Rules of Engagement,[287] America's military establishment provided not even a modicum of training in such matters to junior officers or enlisted personnel. As a former artillery sergeant explained in testimony before Congress, "I was never taught anything about the Geneva Convention as far the use of artillery goes."[288]

Graduates of the U.S. military academies were no better off, as is reflected in the recollection of an Army captain during the same hearings that, "I received no meaningful instruction whatever on the law of land warfare while I was at West Point. I did not know what the law of land warfare was until I returned from Vietnam in 1969."[289] The captain's observation was affirmed by that of a classmate:

> Never in my time in the military, [and] at one time I was going to West Point, [was] I ever given training on rules of warfare, Nuremberg trials, handling of prisoners of war, or anything like that.[290]

The same was true of Marine officers:

> Never during the course of my enlisted service in boot camp and in infantry training nor during my cadet days in flight school nor as an officer did I receive any instruction

regarding the Hague or Geneva Conventions, the Nuremberg Principles, or the treatment of POWs.[291]

Many veterans recalled having been issued small cards upon their arrival in Vietnam inscribed with eleven general rules of behavior they were to observe while "in-country."[292] Some, however, recounted receiving manuals, classified "Top Secret," outlining the obviously illegal operational techniques they were expected to employ during prisoner interrogations.[293] In what might be described as the "best-case scenario," a two-hour briefing on the rules of engagement—heavily intermixed with information on the behavior expected of U.S. troops were they themselves to be taken prisoner—was extended to new recruits during their sixteen weeks of basic and advanced individual training.[294]

Still, in at least some cases soldiers were sufficiently conversant with the requirements of international law, and took seriously enough their obligations under the Nuremberg Principles, to refuse obedience to what they considered unlawful orders. The official response in such instances is instructive. While doing everything in its power to avoid prosecuting—or even charging—the My Lai defendants and others accused of specific war crimes, the military frequently visited what it called "the full penalty of law" upon those who resisted participation in such atrocities.[295]

A prime example is that of Captain Charles Levy, a medical officer who in 1966 refused either to serve in Vietnam or to train Special Forces personnel because he believed that doing so would make him complicit in the crimes their units were committing throughout Indochina. Levy was quickly court-martialed for, among other things, "disobedience to orders" and "conduct unbecoming an officer," then sentenced to three years at hard labor in the military prison at Fort Leavenworth, Kansas.[296] He was not alone:

> Air Force Capt. Dale Noyd [was] sentenced to a year in prison at Clovis Air Force Base, New Mexico, for refusing to train airmen for Vietnam. A private at Fort Dix, New Jersey, applied for conscientious objector status and when it was denied refused to wear his uniform. He [was] sentenced to a year at Leavenworth. A lieutenant at Shaw Air Force Base refused to assist in training for the war and [was] also convicted and sentenced.[297]

A "dozen other cases of overt resistance" involving "about forty" defendants and all resulting in convictions had been tried by April 1968.[298] Among them were the "Fort Hood Three"—Army privates Dennis Mora, David Samas and James Johnson—who refused orders to go to Vietnam because they viewed what was happening in Indochina to be "unjust, immoral, and illegal . . . a war of extermination."[299] Like Levy, they were sentenced to hard labor at Leavenworth.[300] In several instances, the punishments were still more severe.[301]

Even the military élite was subject to sanctions. The best, or at least best-known, example is that of Lt. Colonel Anthony B. Herbert, the most decorated combat veteran of Korea and a soldier of such overall prowess that his photo appeared on the cover of the Army's Ranger Training Manual. When Herbert, assigned to the 173rd Airborne Brigade in Vietnam, objected to his superiors' condoning of conspicuous war crimes, he was strongly advised to "cease and desist" in his complaints. When he nonetheless pushed the issue "upstairs," first to MACV and then the Pentagon, he was relieved of his command and forced into early retirement.[302]

While he was still on active duty, Herbert was forbidden by Secretary of the Army Stanley Resor from testifying before a congressional committee conducting war crimes hearings.[303] Other veterans who attempted to draw public attention to what they'd seen or done in Indochina were taken under investigation by the Army's Criminal Intelligence Division (CID), although many had already been discharged from military service.[304] The FBI also became heavily involved in such cases, most notably in an illegal counterintelligence program designed to "neutralize" Vietnam Veterans Against the War (VVAW), a group of whistle-blowing protestors organized in 1970.[305] Army intelligence personnel were assigned to collaborate with the FBI in such constitutionally prohibited operations.[306]

Yet another measure of how "The Law" was used to prevent individuals from fulfilling their obligations under the Nuremberg Principles concerns the extent to which the FBI was harnessed to enforcing the Selective Service Act (i.e., the "Draft"). By 1971, the Bureau's own records reveal that 14 percent of its time and energy was devoted to the "investigation leading where possible to successful prosecution" of young men whose only "offense" was refusing conscription by a military establishment they believed to be conducting itself in a criminal fashion.[307] A second, closely related preoccupation of both the FBI and military authorities was apprehension of active-duty soldiers who deserted rather than accept assignment to Vietnam (or rejected their orders once they got there).[308]

The virulence of this enforcement bias served for a considerable period to convince most of those who might otherwise have resisted that there was no realistic alternative to going along, obeying orders, no matter how illegitimate. When a group of thirty-five GIs at Fort Jackson, South Carolina, attempted to raise questions about the legality of the war among their peers in 1968, for instance, they were warned by their commander that if they didn't stop they'd "end up in prison like Dr. Levy."[309] The result was what might be properly described as an American correlate to the oft-remarked "Good German Syndrome," even among soldiers who, despite the best efforts of the Pentagon to keep them in the dark, had become reasonably conversant with the Nuremberg Principles.

> If you are smart you will go along with it because it's the only way out, so you go along with it. You go through the basic training and [advanced individual training] and you are then in a dream world. You don't believe this is going on, but there it is. And there's no way out. . . You have to go along with it. . . Any moral questions in your mind about the whole thing, you just have to put those out of your mind.[310]

Major Gordon Livingston, an Army psychologist, further illuminated the process, explaining that not only did the "system [actively] discourage the assumption of individual responsibility for preventing" atrocities, it consciously fostered a "pathological association environment" making it almost impossible for lower-ranking soldiers to meet such obligations.[311]

> The system is so large and so well organized that even an individual who finds what is happening to be morally [or legally] repugnant in some way is led to question his own values. . . The question always arises, am I crazy or is what is going on here crazy? When it is so large and so well organized as Vietnam, it is hard for an individual to assert himself [especially when s/he is subject to harsh punishment for doing so].[312]

There was thus "a fabric, a method, a climate, call it what you will," designed to prevent soldiers "from speaking out or acting against the incredible, incredible brutality" occurring daily in Indochina,[313] even if they were not personally afflicted with the attitudes infecting the bulk of their peers. For the United States, things had progressed little since 1865, when Silas Soule, a captain in the Colorado Volunteers who had refused to allow his men to participate in the massacre at Sand Creek, was gunned down in the streets of Denver to prevent his testifying against those who had.[314] Only the mechanisms by which conformity to the country's unstated standards of inhumanity was enforced, not the underlying values themselves, had been refined in the interim.

## A Certain Unmistakable Consistency

In the aftermath of the carnage in Indochina, a battery of new conventions were put in place by the international community to prevent a recurrence of what the U.S. had done there. These included the 1977 United Nations Convention on the Prohibition of Military or Any Other Hostile Use of Environmental Modification Techniques,[315] a reference to the massive use of "Agent Orange" and other chemical defoliants to denude vast portions of the South Vietnamese landscape.[316] In 1977, two Additional Protocols to the 1949 Geneva Conventions were also effected, prohibiting, among other things, such standard American practices as saturation ("carpet") bombing and bombardments "expected to cause incidental loss of civilian life [or] injury to civilians [i.e., 'collateral damage']."[317] Indeed, the entire U.S. Indochina strategy was declared illegal.

> It is prohibited to attack, destroy, remove or render useless objects indispensable to the survival of the civilian population, such as foodstuffs, agricultural areas for the production of foodstuffs, crops, livestock, drinking water installations and supplies and irrigation works, for the specific purpose of denying their sustenance value to the civilian population or to the adverse Party, whatever the motive, whether in order to starve out the civilians, to cause them to move away, or for any other motive.[318]

This was followed, in 1978, by the Red Cross Fundamental Rules of Humanitarian Law Applicable to Armed Conflicts,[319] and, in 1981, by the United Nations Convention on Prohibition of Certain Conventional Weapons.[320] In the latter, the use of "any weapon the primary effect of which is to injure by fragments which in the human body escape detection by X-rays"—which, as was mentioned earlier, the U.S. developed specifically for employment in Indochina—was banned altogether.[321] The use of incendiary weapons, which were employed by the U.S. more extensively in Indochina than by any other country in any other war,[322] was very sharply circumscribed, especially, under Article 2, concerning the potential impact on noncombatants.

1. It is prohibited in all circumstances to make the civilian population as such, individual civilians or civilian objects the object of attack by incendiary weapons.

2. It is prohibited in all circumstances to make any military objective located within a concentration of civilians the object of an attack by air-delivered incendiary weapons.

3. It is further prohibited to make any military objective located within a concentration of civilians the object of attack by means of incendiary weapons other than air-

delivered incendiary weapons [i.e., by artillery or landmines], except when such military objective is clearly separated from the concentration of civilians and all feasible precautions are taken to limiting the incendiary effects to the military objective. . .[323]

Although the United States expressed "reservations" on each of these additions to legal convention, it duly signed off and added the appropriate references when its Rules of Engagement were updated in 1984.[324] None of this mattered, however, when in August 1990 U.S. troops were deployed in the Persian Gulf against Iraq. Although President George Bush invoked the Augustinian principle of "Just War" as a basis for using overwhelming force to "roll back" what he called the "naked aggression" entailed in Iraq's attempted recovery of Kuwait[325]—an Iraqi province until the British partition of 1916[326]—he ordered a campaign as fundamentally criminal as any in history.

This began with the opening round of "Operation Desert Storm," as the war was called, an intensive air offensive designed in part to eliminate the capacity of Iraq's military to offer meaningful resistance before U.S. ground forces began their invasion of what was once again referred to as "Indian Country."[327] This objective was easily achieved, with Iraq's air defense system "utterly obliterated" in the first days.[328] Well over 100,000 essentially defenseless Iraqi soldiers—"Sand Niggers," in the parlance of American troops—were then butchered in place, their corpses eventually bulldozed into mass graves.[329] Once the ground assault began, those who'd survived the bombing were often pinned down by machine-gun fire and, thus denied the option of surrender, buried alive by tanks mounted with specially modified bulldozer blades.[330]

Given that the U.S. suffered a total of 148 killed—at least twenty of them by "friendly fire"—in the course of the "fighting," the entire campaign has been rightly described as a "massacre . . . reminiscent of the Gatling gun vs. the bow and arrow."[331] Such characterizations seem all the more apt in that, as with the Senecas in 1794, and Japan in 1945, the U.S. refused as a matter of policy to entertain any overture for peace until a certain exemplary quota of killing was completed.[332] In fact, the slaughter not only continued but escalated after Iraq had submitted, beginning the complete withdrawal of its troops from Kuwait in compliance with stated U.S. demands.[333]

The Iraqi capitulation, previously communicated to U.S. officials by Soviet intermediaries on February 21, was publicly announced by Iraqi President Saddam Hussein on February 26, 1991.[334] By then, his troops had begun a rather chaotic retreat—a "panicked flight," according to some observers—flying white flags over many of their vehicles.[335] They were plainly "out of combat" and therefore legally exempt from attack under provision of the Geneva Convention, Common Article III.[336] Nonetheless, Bush announced that the U.S. would "continue to prosecute the war" and ordered them targeted for annihilation.[337] His specific instruction was that "no quarter be given,"[338] a gross violation of the 1907 Hague Convention, the 1864 Geneva Convention on Wounded and Sick, and even the Lieber Code.[339]

Provided such license to "find anything moving and take it out,"[340] American fliers responded with an enthusiasm that might have made Hermann Göring blush.

> The fleeing Iraqis took two roads that meet near the Kuwaiti town of al-Mutlaa and their exodus quickly became a traffic jam of immense proportions. U.S. Marines allowed the convoy of cars, trucks, and every sort of vehicle to get out of Kuwait City before bombing the front and [rear] of the convoy. Kill zones were then assigned along the seventy miles of highway so that planes would not crash into each other [as they destroyed their defenseless and immobilized prey].[341]

Thus began an "orgy of slaughter" along what is known as the "Highway of Death."[342] The pilots, in a frenzy to make second and third attacks on what they laughingly described as "fish in a barrel," didn't even bother to take time reloading with the proper ordnance;"from cluster bombs to 500 pound bombs, [they] took whatever happened to be close" at hand.[343] Anything lethal would do. Ultimately, they "continued to drop bombs on the convoy until all humans were killed."[344] Their tally was estimated at more than 25,000 people, including not only Iraqi soldiers, but thousands of Palestinians, Jordanians and East Indian contract-workers and their families attempting to escape the war zone.[345]

On March 2, a second "outright massacre"—albeit much smaller, and not involving civilians—occurred near Basra.

> On May 8, 1991, an article appeared in *New York Newsday* [describing what it called] "the largest battle of the war." The catch was that the "battle" occurred two days after Bush had ordered the final cease-fire, and eight days after Iraq had announced its full withdrawal, and fighting had ceased. It was a violation even of the cease-fire guidelines. A division of the Republican Guard withdrawing on a long, unprotected causeway, high above a swamp . . . was attacked. [U.S. Commanding] General ["Stormin' Norman"] Schwartzkopf . . . ordered the attack, claiming that a single Iraqi infantry-man had fired a round at a U.S. patrol. . . The U.S. [24th Infantry Division then

deployed] attack helicopters, tanks, [and] artillery, and opened fire with laser-guided weapons.[346]

As the division's commander later recounted gleefully, "We went right up the column like a turkey shoot. We *really* waxed 'em!"[347] In fact, while some 2,000 Iraqi guardsmen were slaughtered, the U.S. suffered no casualties at all.[348] The Wounded Knee–like quality of the "Battle of Basra," especially when considered in combination with the scale of other military fatalities inflicted upon Iraq for no discernable military purpose, lends considerable credence to contentions that the overall U.S. objective was not simply to win the war, but "to so decimate the military-age male population that Iraq could not raise a substantial force for half a generation."[349]

Both the goal and the methods used in attaining it were obviously a far cry from then–Defense Secretary, now Vice President Dick Cheney's 1991 claim that the American campaign would be "remembered for its effort, within the bounds of war, to be humane," and very much within the bounds of legality. There was instead, as historian Howard Zinn observed at about the same time, "a certain unmistakable consistency" uniting Desert Storm with the illegitimate modes of exterminatory warfare the U.S. had waged against American Indians and other peoples of color since its inception.[350]

### "Collateral Damage"

The validity of Zinn's view, and the sheer depravity of Cheney's, is most readily confirmed by the fate imposed upon Iraqi noncombatants from the air. More than 109,000 sorties were flown by U.S. attack planes, during which 136,755 "conventional" bombs (including thousands of incendiaries), 44,922 cluster bombs and rockets, and 4,077 precision-guided ("smart") bombs—over 88,000 tons in all—were "delivered." This is aside from the launching of 217 Walleye and 2,095 HARM missiles.[352] Much of this ordnance was expended against Baghdad, Iraq's capitol and largest city, as well as the cities of Basra, Urbil, Sulamaneiya and other such obvious "concentrations of civilians."[353]

Despite the Geneva Conventions and the 1981 prohibitions on employing incendiaries in such fashion, the U.S. "used napalm against civilians. It used napalm and other heat-intensive explosives to start fires in anything that was highly [flammable]. . . . It used fuel-air explosives which can incinerate hundreds, even thousands of people at once."[354] Since fuel-air bombs are aerosol devices consuming all the oxygen in a two–square–kilometer area upon detonation, they cause death by asphyxiation as well as burning.[355] They are therefore arguably illegal under the 1925 Geneva Protocol for the Prohibition of the Use in War of Asphyxiating, Poisonous or Other Gases.[356]

In any event, much was made during the war about the precision displayed by so-called "smart bombs," which apparently hit their targets about 80 percent of the time.[357] These accounted for less than 3 percent of the bombs dropped, however. The remaining 97 percent consisted of "dumb" bombs, with a "miss rate" of approximately 75 percent.[358] This was especially true of those dropped by B-52s engaged in the legally prohibited practice of carpet bombing from their customary altitude of 40,000 feet, as was done to Basra, Iraq's second-largest city.[359] All told, U.S. "planes came in with bombs and destroyed residential neighborhoods in every city, every major town, and most villages," killing about 113,000 civilians, two-thirds of them children.[360] Some 300,000 others were wounded.[361]

Actually, the worst civilian suffering did not result from the rain of dumb bombs. It accrued instead, according to senior U.S. officials, "from precision-guided weapons that hit exactly where they were aimed—at electrical plants, oil refineries, and transportation networks."[362] To this might be added hospitals, schools, mosques, transportation centers, sanitation and water purification facilities, pharmaceutical production facilities, as well as food production and storage capacities.[363]

> When hostilities . . . finally ceased, the city of Urbil had only five of its forty-two community health centers functioning; Basra had five of nineteen; Sulamaneiya had six out of twenty. Likewise, in Baghdad four hospitals were destroyed. Iraq lost its only laboratory for producing vaccines as well as its available stores in the bombardment. . .[364]

The effects of obliterating the Iraqi power grid were even more egregious.

> Without electricity, water cannot be purified, sewage cannot be treated, water-borne diseases flourish, and hospitals cannot treat curable illnesses. This absence of electricity, coupled with direct damage to the sewage treatment facilities, has rendered the sewage treatment system as a whole inoperable. . . The pollution of the water supply has led to epidemics of typhoid, cholera, and gastroenteritis which threaten the entire population, and children in particular.[365]

None of these "infrastructural targets" were selected to "influence the course of the conflict itself," thus meeting the minimum standard of military necessity necessary to legitimate them.[366] Nor was such damage in any way "collateral to the bombing of legitimate military targets," as U.S. officials claimed; Air Force Chief of Staff Michael J. Duggan was on record as early as September 1990 outlining plans to do exactly what was done.[367] The idea was simply to bomb the entire country "back to the Stone Age" so that the United States could "gain a post-war leverage over Iraq," especially when such calculated damage was combined with a longterm economic embargo and other such sanctions.[368] Quite predictably—indeed it *was* predicted[369]—the consequences of this "systematic destruction of the civilian infrastructure" have proven catestrophic for Iraqi noncombatants.[370]

In addition to spiraling rates of disease and thousands of deaths from otherwise treatable wounds accruing from the pinpoint bombing of Iraq's medical, electrical and sanitation facilities, "famine [had] already begun to aggravate an already dire situation" even before the war ended.[371] According to a March 1991 United Nations report, Iraq's food supplies were by that point "critically low," in part because its food storage/production capacity had been systematically destroyed, but also because its ability to acquire foodstuffs abroad had been eliminated by the U.S.-orchestrated embargo.[372] Certain items—infant formula, for example, after a baby food factory was hit by a smart bomb[373]—had all but disappeared from Iraqi inventories, and the daily calorie intake for the population had "been cut by half and the entire [population] was beginning to suffer acute malnutrition."[374]

> Iraq now [evidences] a couple of manifestations of hunger never seen before in [the] region, [including] marasmus, the condition that makes kids under two suddenly look like wizened old men, the bony face, the skull; and kwashiokor, the malnutrition that turns a child's hair a rusty red and gives him a pot belly. . . [Y]ou see it all over the place now, even in Baghdad.[375]

By May, a study conducted by the Harvard School of Public Health concluded that approximately 3,000 Iraqi infants had died of malnutrition during the six months of hostilities, and that the mortality rate among children under five had subsequently doubled. The researchers projected the "deaths of an additional 170,000 children beyond normal rates of mortality among the younger age group" over the next year, unless the embargo was lifted and "humanitarian intervention" to repair the Iraqi agricultural and sanitation systems undertaken on "an emergency basis."[376] In response, the U.S. not only maintained but tightened the sanctions, with the result that by 1996 an estimated *half-million* children had perished in a country whose total population was barely 18 million.[377]

As lately as 1999, there were over 10,000 sorties by U.S. fighter-bombers over Iraq delivering more than a thousand bombs and missiles against 400 of the usual targets, "killing and wounding many hundreds of people," while keeping the quality of life suffered by the population at the U.S.-prescribed level of misery.[378] The United States, moreover, insists that it holds "the right" to do this with what amounts to impunity. As the matter was put by Air Force Brigadier William Looney, the aptly named chief of air operations in the Gulf Region:

> If they turn on their radars we're going to blow up their goddamn [air defenses]. They know we own their country. We own their airspace... We dictate the way they live and talk. And that's what's great about America right now. [379]

In 1998, U.N. Assistant Secretary General Denis J. Halliday resigned his position in protest of this ongoing U.S. inversion of Clausewitz—i.e., making "policy an extension of war"—describing it as not only criminal but genocidal.[380] That this is so has been openly confirmed by U.S. officials at the highest levels. In 1996, U.S. Ambassador to the United Nations Madeleine Albright, opined on the television program *60 Minutes* that it is "worth the price" of starving an entire generation of Iraqi children to death, so long as U.S. policy objectives are met.[381] Undoubtedly because of the enlightened humanitarianism and close attention to legality embodied in her views, Albright was shortly promoted by President Bill Clinton to serve as his Secretary of State.

She is but one example. Her successor at the helm of the State Department is General Colin Powell, whose major job qualification appears to have been that, as Chairman of the Joint Chiefs of Staff, he supervised the military's entire Gulf War strategy.[382] Asked in 1991 about Iraqi casualties, most especially among children and other civilians, he replied that it was "not a number I'm terribly interested in."[383] This response was undoubtedly honest enough, coming as it did from a man whose earlier military credentials included an active role in covering up the massacres at My Lai, My Khe and elsewhere in Vietnam.[384]

### The Penalties of Law (Again)

Even as it was running roughshod over the Laws of War and every conceivable standard of international humanitarian legality in Iraq, the U.S. was once again wielding "The Rule of Law" to punish anyone attempting to obey it. Seven members of a Marine reserve unit at Camp LeJeune, North

Carolina, who refused orders to participate in what they publicly denounced as a "racist war" were quickly court-martialed and "sentenced to 'bad [conduct]' discharges and prison terms ranging from one to 30 months."[385] An Air Force reservist in California was sentenced to a year's imprisonment under similar circumstances, while three noncommissioned officers in an Army reserve unit at Fort Hood received sentences of up to six years for "attempting to lead 100 fellow troopers in a work stoppage."[386]

Active-duty personnel typically fared worse than reservists, as is witnessed by two GIs at Fort Bliss, Texas, and a sergeant at Fort Riley, Kansas, sentenced to six years each.[387] This was true even of Captain Yolanda Huet-Vaughn, a medical officer who was able to muster witnesses as credible as former U.S. Attorney General Ramsey Clark to testify that since "America's civil and military leaders are guilty of war crimes under the Nuremberg" Standards, she had no legal alternative but to refuse to accept her orders.[388]

> At a pre-trial hearing at Fort Leonard Wood, Missouri . . . Huet-Vaughn became the first resister to base her defense on international law. Her attorney, Louis Font of Boston, called [not only Clark, but] Francis Boyle, a renowned international law expert, to buttress Clark's testimony. The University of Illinois professor outlined the international laws and treaties that are binding on the U.S. government and that were violated by U.S. forces during Desert Storm—including the Hague and Geneva Conventions. Boyle testified that to convict Huet-Vaughn of desertion, the army had to prove that she absented herself "without authority." In his opinion, she had the necessary authority under international law.[389]

Having listened politely to this learned recitation of the Army's own Rules of Engagement and Code of Conduct, the military court promptly ruled such issues "irrelevant to the charges before us," then convicted Huet-Vaughn of "desertion with intent to avoid hazardous duty" and sentenced her to thirty months imprisonment and a dishonorable discharge.[390] By then, more than forty other soldiers, airmen and marines had shared her fate, while an undetermined number of others were summarily handcuffed and shipped off to the war zone despite their announced intent to refuse service therein.[391]

As all this was going on, George Bush was busily pontificating on the importance of bringing Saddam Hussein, falsely accused by U.S. propagandists of ordering the removal of 300 Kuwaiti babies from incubators, "before an international tribunal to account for this atrocity and many other crimes against humanity."[392] This was, of course, the very same George Bush who bore ultimate responsibility for the murders of so many thousands of Iraqi youngsters, openly rejecting the idea that the International Court of Justice (ICJ or "World Court") might hold any authority at all with regard to U.S. conduct abroad.[393] Indeed, he was already on record responding to queries about his own country's crimes with the bald assertion that he would "never apologize for the United States of America. I don't care *what* the facts are."[394]

In 1993, a year after Bush left office, a tribunal was indeed brought into being in the Hague, fathered and for the most part funded by the U.S.[395] Although Hussein was never hauled before it—it had been decided that leaving him in power would best serve U.S. interests in the Mideast, so long as his military capacity could be maintained at a properly "degraded" level through perpetual bombing and embargo[396]—it functioned mainly as an accoutrement to U.S. policy pronouncements for several years.[397] The extent to which the U.S. intended things to remain so became clear when the United Nations set out to convert the American-owned travesty into an actual court of international criminal law (à la Nuremberg).[398]

> Finally, in 1998 in Rome, the nations of the world drafted the charter of The International Criminal Court [ICC]. American negotiators, however, insisted on provisions in the charter that would, in essence, give the United States veto power over any prosecution through its seat on the [UN] Security Council. The American request was rejected, and primarily for this reason the U.S. refused to join 120 other nations who supported the charter.[399]

Senior officials have stated repeatedly and quite categorically that they will continue to reject any jurisdictional arrangement allowing international prosecution of its own civilian authorities or military personnel for war crimes as an "infringement upon U.S. national sovereignty" (thereby recapitulating the previously noted premise of the Third Reich).[400] Objections have also been raised with regard to any curtailment of self-assigned U.S. prerogatives to shield its clients—usually referred to as "friends"—from prosecution for crimes committed under its sponsorship (e.g., Suharto and other Indonesian officials responsible for the slaughter of approximately one-third of the East Timorese population from 1975 through 1995, and Turkish officials presiding over the ongoing "pacification" of Kurdistan).[401]

Concomitantly, the U.S. has become increasingly open in thumbing its nose at elements of international law it finds inconvenient, often refusing even to go through the motions of signing off. One of the more noteworthy recent examples has been the International Treaty Banning the Use,

Production, Stockpiling and Transfer of Anti-Personnel Mines, which entered into force on March 1, 1999, without the United States as a signatory.[402] Here, it was argued that while every other country should be strictly bound by the treaty, the U.S. has "unique needs" entitling it—and it alone—to be formally exempted from compliance. When the signatory nations rejected this absurd proposition, U.S. representatives effectively withdrew from further discussions.[403]

The same has been true with regard to a number of other important treaties, declarations and conventions over the past two decades. On December 31, 1979, for example, the U.S. was one of only three member-states voting against a U.N. General Assembly Resolution to implement the 1960 Declaration Granting Independence to Colonial Peoples and Countries.[404] In 1981, 1982 and 1983, it was the only member-state voting against a declaration that "education, work, health care, proper nourishment and self-determination" are basic human rights.[405] In 1984, it alone voted against implementing the 1966 International Convention on Elimination of All Forms of Racial Discrimination, which it did not ratify until 1994, and then with numerous reservations.[406] Since 1994, it has been one of only two countries—the other is Somalia—refusing to ratify the International Convention on the Rights of the Child.[407]

There are scores of comparable examples.[408] Even the 1948 Convention on Prevention and Punishment of the Crime of Genocide went unsigned by the United States for forty years, and was ratified in 1988 only after the Senate attached a "Sovereignty Package" by which the U.S. claimed a "right" to exempt itself from compliance at its own discretion.[409] Meanwhile, American diplomats have become ever more sanctimonious in advancing "international human rights enforcement" as a pretext for U.S. military interventions, both overt and covert, on a continuous and quite literally planetary basis.[410]

By far the most blatant illustration occurred in 1999, when the U.S., with an eye towards dictating the structure of Europe's internal relations, departed from its usual practice of reserving such treatment for the world's darker peoples long enough to launch "Operation Allied Force," a fullscale air offensive against Serbia.[411] Ostensibly undertaken to halt atrocities against resident Albanians in Kosovo,[412] the attack was accompanied by the filing of formal charges with the emergent ICC—at that point called the International Criminal Tribunal (ICT)—against Serbia's president, Slobodan Milosevic, and other members of his régime.[413]

The worm turned a bit, however, when independent groups of international legal experts from several countries began filing criminal complaints against Bill Clinton, Madeline Albright, Defense Secretary William Cohen, and numerous other high-ranking officials for targeting Serbia's civilian infrastructure in much the same way Bush and his cohorts had targeted Iraq's.[414]

> Amongst the charges filed were: "grave violations of international humanitarian law," including "willful killing [. . .] employment of poisonous weapons and other weapons to cause unnecessary suffering, wanton destruction of cities, towns and villages, unlawful attacks on civilian objects, [and] attacks on undefended buildings and dwellings," [all] in "open violation" of the United Nations Charter . . . the Geneva Conventions and the Principles of International Law Recognized by the International Military Tribunal at Nuremberg.[415]

The official U.S. response was "disbelief, shock, anger, and denial" at these "unjustified and appalling allegations."[416] All civilian casualties and/or damage to nonmilitary targets was purely "accidental and unintended," U.S. spokespersons maintained, until Canadian researchers produced a Pentagon document showing that there was actually a formal classification called "unintended civ casualties" used in strategic planning.[417] "It's a little difficult to see how civilian casualties can be both planned for *and* 'unintended'," as one attorney put it.[418]

With that, Secretary Albright brought a bit of not-so-subtle pressure to bear on Swiss jurist Carla Del Ponte, retained by the ICT to review all charges related to the "Balkan Crisis." Still denying that the tribunal held the least jurisdiction over the United States, Albright explained to Del Ponte that unless her investigation of U.S. war crimes was immediately terminated, the U.S. would withdraw its financial support of the ITC, thereby making it impossible for the prosecutor to proceed against anyone at all. Thus confronted with the American version of how "impartial justice" is best administered, Del Ponte caved in and did as her potential defendant instructed.[419]

Much the same set of power relations have become evident in the conduct of a second tribunal, established in 1995 to try the perpetrators of the genocide carried out under French authority against the Tutsis in Rwanda a year earlier.[420] Here, as with the ICT devoted to the "Balkan Crisis," the U.S. and allied "Western governments made their support for the tribunal incumbent on the assurance that their own military and civilian representatives would escape the magistrates' scrutiny. In order to avoid any embarrassment, they even [prevented] their agents from collaborating with the court . . .

refusing to cooperate with an institution they were allegedly supporting."[421] To date, although hundreds of well-publicized indictments were returned as early as 1996, there has yet to be a single prosecution.

### "Indian Country" Forever?

In 1999, French Prime Minister Lionel Jospin stated publicly that the increasingly overbearing nature of U.S. behavior in its foreign relations represented "a new problem on the international scene."[422] Jospin's foreign minister, Hubert Vedrine, concurred, noting with palpable irritation that "the predominant weight of the United States and the absence for the moment of a counterweight . . . leads it to hegemony,"[423] and thus an ever more imperious belief in its prerogative to dictate the terms by which the rest of the world will live or die. "Never before in modern history has a country dominated the earth so totally as the United States does today," observed the editors of the German newsmagazine *Der Spiegel*.[424]

The commentators were referring in part to the position of near-total economic primacy enjoyed by the U.S. at the dawn of the twenty-first century.[425] Their main point, however, concerned the dramatic imbalance of military technology/power which followed the collapse during the late 1980s of America's greatest rival in this sphere, the Soviet Union.[426] The contest of "Gatling guns vs. bows and arrows" once defining the U.S. relationship to America's native peoples, and mentioned above with reference to Iraq, has been extrapolated to truly global proportions. At this juncture, the entire planet can be viewed as "Indian Country" by U.S. élites, its inhabitants as "Indians" subject to extermination whenever, wherever and to whatever end their overweening sense of self-interest and entitlement may prescribe.[427]

The U.S. of course continues to seek—and to find—collaborators in pursuing even its most blatantly domineering aspirations. As Madeline Albright bluntly informed the international community fifteen years ago, however, "we will behave multilaterally when we can, unilaterally when we must."[428] Working in concert with other nations is thus seen as a matter of mere expedience or efficiency by U.S. policymakers, and often as a purely cosmetic gesture, never as a posture devolving upon any sense of genuine reciprocity, moral commitment or the meeting of legal obligations. Should its "allies" decline to play their assigned roles at any given moment, the U.S. has made it clear that it will override any and all objections to its course of action, "going it alone," and "making it stick."[429] In other words, to repeat the earlier-quoted phrase of George Bush, "What we say, goes."[430] This, as Bush announced in 1991, parroting Adolf Hitler's pronouncement of a half-century before, is the "New World Order."[431]

That things have reached such a pass is due not only to the consistency with which the U.S. has since its first moments refused the most rudimentary adherence to law, but the manner in which it has substituted legalistic pretension for actual legality, brandishing the resultant deformity as a club with which to bludgeon those struggling to curb its criminal propensities.[432] Unchecked in such endeavors, it has by now positioned itself to consummate a final subversion of international jurisprudence, transforming it into just another weapon with which to work its will upon the world. To paraphrase Antonio de Nebrija, law, or at least the illusion of legality, has for the United States become "a perfect companion to empire."[433]

A much more fundamental layer of consideration underlies this elaborate subterfuge. It pertains to the near-universal degree of consent, only partially "manufactured" through the mechanisms of propaganda,[434] that grassroots Americans have habitually extended to the unending torrent of crimes against peace and humanity perpetrated by their country. Such resonance derives from the smug "air of innocence" so eagerly personalized by average citizens—quite irrespective of factual circumstance—a ubiquitous, comfortable and entirely self-serving affectation which readily lends itself to acceptance of even the most transparently inane official mythologies concerning the "altruism" supposedly guiding U.S. actions, ambitions and attendant policy formation.[435]

To describe the mindset at issue as "delusional" is to be clinically precise in terms of mass psychology.[436] The more so, given the virulently pathological racialism—deepset, intractable, and for the most part vociferously denied—which, now more than ever, comprises the institutional reality of mainstream U.S. society.[437] Add in the compulsive braggadocio and violent aggressiveness with which Euroamericans in particular have sought historically to compensate for their abiding sense of cultural inferiority,[438] and the outcome is an aggregate condition which has been aptly described as a "genocidal mentality."[439] This, of course, goes a very long way towards explaining how and why the "ordinary men" of the U.S. military have so regularly and enthusiastically acquitted themselves as they have.[440]

That an objectively psychopathic collectivity such as the United States should have come to hold the physical capacity to indulge its lethal fantasies worldwide, and to do so with the knowledge that it can act without fear of retribution or accountability, bespeaks a reality far more awful in its portents than anything discussed thus far. Pretending things are otherwise will not help. Quite the opposite. Denial is the crux of the pathology itself.[441] The urgency of the need for a radical change in the existing relations of power, both globally and domestically, is not a matter subject to debate or equivocation by anyone imbued with the least sanity.[442] The only question is how best—that is, most expeditiously and completely—to achieve it.

The options on this score are limited: those in opposition may endeavor to kill the beast, to cage it, to cure it, or to undertake some combination. Actually, since attempting any of the first three inevitably involves aspects of the others, it would perhaps be best to view them as forming an interactive continuum rather than as discrete and mutually exclusive components.[443] Put another way, the last option is the only viable alternative; opposition to the status quo must proceed at all times, at every possible level, and by all conceivable means, towards the common destination of abolishing it. To frame the matter in still another fashion, the goal must be to at last force judgement upon the United States in accordance with articulated standards, and to hold it accountable to the verdict.

## The Ingredients of Radical Change

Although it will undoubtedly be disparaged in some quarters as a "liberal" position, there is considerable merit to the proposition that recourse to law represents the best available avenue along which to pursue a transformative agenda. While it can be conceded that explicitly revolutionary theoretical constructions hold a greater emotional appeal, it must also be acknowledged that the point of departure in any liberatory process must be where things stand, not where they "should be" or where oppositionists wish they were.[444] It is also true that the body of extant law, especially the Nuremberg Principles, can—and arguably should—be interpreted in a manner accommodating a very broad range of oppositionist objectives (including even those typically ascribed to anarchism).[445]

The point to be taken in this connection is that there is no entity "out there" to which an appeal can be made for the enforcement of international law. Tribunals of the sort convened at Nuremberg function on the basis of the military defeat of those on trial, or, as is envisioned with the ICC, their submitting more-or-less voluntarily to prosecution.[446] Absent such submission, and given that the aversion of armed conflict is the paramount objective of international legality,[447] the principle extended at Nuremberg is that enforcement responsibility inheres first and foremost in the citizenry of each country.[448] Oppositionists are thereby vested with not only the right, but a legal obligation to employ any means necessary to compel compliance with international law (particularly in the realm of humanitarian law).[449]

Most problematic in this respect is the question of how to motivate a sufficient number of U.S. citizens to act that the government will be forced to move in the desired direction. Even at the height of the popular mobilization against the U.S. assault on Indochina—over a million people participated in demonstrations attending the November 1969 Moratorium to End the War in Vietnam[450]—the "critical mass" was not achieved. At this point, the prospects of generating a popular response of the requisite scale seem dimmer than ever; not only is the mental imbalance of the middle-American main-stream more pronounced than ever, but increasingly larger segments of tradi-tionally oppressed populations—African Americans, for example, and American Indians—have become locked into the military apparatus itself.[451]

Fortunately, the unprecedented degree of dominance America's élites have attained has rendered them arrogant to the point of sowing the seeds of their own potential destruction in a number of important ways. Overall, the short-run success of their economic globalization schemes has emboldened them to discount the importance of maintaining the standard of living enjoyed by 75 percent of all Americans—dismantling social services, "ratio-nalizing" health care, and so on—as a means of "freeing up capital" (i.e., increasing corporate profitability and the affluence of the stockholding quar-ter of the population).[452]

To the same end, firms operating within the U.S. have steadily "down-sized," relocating their production facilities to draw upon cheap labor pools situated in neocolonial settings abroad, marginalizing the American work-force itself.[453] The specter of "runaway shops" and attendant disemployment has served as a vehicle upon which to roll back the wage gains achieved by the American labor movement over the past seventy years, as well as to cut such overhead costs as worker safety measures, pension packages, and envi-ronmental protection measures, thereby amplifying corporate profitability/ élite affluence at still another level.[454]

Not even the troops upon which the élites depend have been safe from such ravages. The negative health effects of U.S. weapons technologies on successive generations of American soldiers—nuclear testing during the

1950s, for example, as well as the use of chemical defoliants like Agent Orange in Vietnam, and depleted uranium ammunition during Desert Storm—have been consistently denied and left untreated as a Pentagon "cost-cutting measure."[455] Meanwhile, despite the fact that the United States is confronted by no credible opponents, "investment" of tax dollars in the development/deployment of the technologies themselves has skyrocketed.[456] Most recently, in the face of overwhelming opposition by the international community, the U.S. announced it would "go forward" with developing a sophisticated and lavishly-expensive laser "defense" system in outer space.[457]

Manifestations of social discontent accruing from these trends have been met not by the traditional methods of concession and cooptation, but by ever-harsher modes of state repression. This has been most visible in a vast proliferation of paramilitary police units since 1970,[458] and an expansion of the U.S. penal system by more than 100 percent during the same period.[459] By the late 1990s, the United States had incarcerated a greater proportion of its population than any country in the world,[460] and prison construction/administration had become the most rapidly expanding sectors of America's domestic economy.[461] Concomitantly, with one-in-four young men of color imprisoned, a literal—and very profitable—system of slave labor has reemerged in North America.[462]

"The chickens," in the words of Malcolm X , are truly "coming home to roost."[463] The U.S. domestic populace is being not-so-gradually reduced to a dehumanized status of expendability resembling that typically assigned the Third World populations to which they have so long accustomed themselves to feeling superior.[464] The potentially positive implications of this dynamic should be neither ignored nor underestimated. It was, after all, the revelation of rather analogous attitudes within the régime that finally precipitated what may otherwise have remained impossible: a generalized disenchantment of the German public with the "ideals" and policies of nazism.[465] And, notwithstanding the dissident upsurge of the 1960s, the last time a genuinely revolutionary potential was evident in the U.S. was amidst the deteriorated socioeconomic environment of the Great Depression.[466]

**The Ingredients of Radical Change**

To the extent that the American body politic may now be more open to hearing that what has been happening is wrong than at any point in the past several generations, the question becomes how best to interpret this perceived truth so as to give it form, substance and strike the most responsive chord amongst the greatest number of people. An array of moral, economic and libertarian arguments have been employed in the past, and, while each has merit, none have worked to any appreciable degree.[467] What has not been evident, at least not in any unified and coherent form, has been an attempt to couch things in the terms the general public has been most thoroughly conditioned to believe it accepts: the Rule of Law.

As the work of Noam Chomsky in particular has long since demonstrated, depictions of circumstances as being not simply wrong, but criminally so, especially when accompanied by straightforward representations of the black letter law(s) at issue, carry with them a credibility and psychological weight with average citizens which, rightly or wrongly, is missing from other modes of articulation.[468] Bringing such analyses to bear allows oppositionists not only to connect with a wide range of people "where they are"—or where they think they are—but to preempt the rhetoric of "law enforcement" which forms a cornerstone of élite discourse, turning it against itself in an immediate sense.

More broadly, the deployment of codified law as an essential standard by which the propriety of each phase in the U.S. historical trajectory is assessed stands to challenge the "master narrative" by which America's élites purport to explain and justify themselves, introducing a serious dimension of cognitive dissonance into popular understandings of the status quo.[469] Reformulated, this goes to the notion that most approaches to remedying psychological maladies are predicated in recognition on the part of sufferers that they are not "well," much less representative of an acceptable norm, and thus in need of modifying the manner in which they perceive, understand and act within the world.[470]

At its most basic level, the therapeutic dynamic at play embodies a conscious withdrawal of consent from the functioning of power—that is, a decay in the hegemonic structure of thought control by which élites hold sway—which leads all but inevitably to a widespread desire for some tangible rearrangement of power relations.[471] For what should be obvious reasons, these can be capitalized upon most effectively when linked over the short term to concrete goals which can at once be seen as eminently "reasonable" from the standpoint so recently occupied by those in psychointellectual transition *and* readily conceded by élite defenders in their efforts to contain and ultimately coopt expressions of discontent.[472]

Within the analytical framework of this essay, an excellent place to begin would be with resuscitating recommendations advanced at the time of the My Lai/My Khe travesty to remove jurisdiction over war crimes from the "military justice system" and lodge it under civilian courts.[473] Mostly ignored at the time as an "insufficiently radical" idea, and now all but forgotten, the proposal was/remains important in that it would for the first time make the U.S. military even symbolically accountable to *some* entity other than itself. This, in turn, stands to significantly undermine the confidence with which real or potential war crimes perpetrators receive assurances of near-blanket immunity from punishment heretofore provided by the Pentagon (in military terms, this presents a "command, control and morale problem" of considerable magnitude).[474]

The logic guiding this simple alteration of its domestic judicial structure, of course, points unerringly towards the far more significant adjustment embodied in U.S. acceptance of ICC jurisdiction. And that, in turn, expands the realm of legal consideration from the Laws of War, per se, to that of international humanitarian law en toto, making U.S. officials subject to scrutiny and potential adjudication for noncompliance with accepted standards pertaining to child welfare,[475] penal conditions,[476] methods of policing[477] and the like. The "trickle down effects" from this development are obvious, bound up as they must be in the imposition of external control over the federal Bureau of Prisons and its state-level counterparts,[478] civilian rather than internal review boards to oversee the police,[479] and so on.

Each step along these lines, no matter how partial, entails a diminishment in the centralized authority/autonomy of the State and a corresponding curtailment of its capacity to exert physical force. Conversely, each represents a relative empowerment of oppositionists, as well as an incremental reorientation of the popular consciousness to embrace the constructive potentialities of legalism rather than rhetorical and repressive (mis)appropriations of it. As the latter evolves, the door is opened to a general (re)appraisal of various other matters — the lawfulness of U.S. pretensions to jurisdictional rights over indigenous national territories with its claimed boundaries, for example[480] — each of which stands to impair the ideological structure of U.S. self-legitimation and, ultimately, its geographical integrity.[481]

Tracing this devolution to its logical terminus, the United States, at least in the sense that it has been previously constructed, could no longer exist. In its stead, one would encounter a proliferation of interactive "autonomous zones," of the permanent rather than transient variety, functioning on the basis of group affinity and human scale.[482] Self-evidently the sort of military practice which has defined the flow of U.S. history and which now threatens the world with endless replications—indeed, the military itself—would be impossible in such an environment. Less still, the configuration of corporate domination which has sprouted and matured on the back of American militarism over the past century-and-a-half.[483]

In effect, inculcating a *genuine* desire for law enforcement among the American public—that is, a demand for adherence by the State and its appendages to the baseline of international legality—could represent "the end of world order" in the sense that George Bush, Madeline Albright and Adolf Hitler have each used the term.[484] Ultimately, the antidote or antithesis to such cancerous behavioral/attitudinal phenomena as have been described herein may be discerned within the planetary rearrangement of relations between peoples such a prescription entails. On this basis, and probably on this basis alone, we, all of us, collectively, will be able to achieve a new set of standards, standards with which all might willingly abide. In effect, the result will at last be standards of *our* times, not "theirs," which is to say that they will be standards worthy of our children, our children's children, and theirs as well.

## Postscript

This essay was completed during the fall of 2000. Approximately one year later, on September 11, 2001—a date now and forever enshrined in the American memory as corresponding to the emergency telephone sequence "9-1-1"—someone finally grew tired of waiting for U.S. "progressives" to stop pretending that the abolition of ashtrays in airports was a "gain" transcending the importance of doing anything tangible to halt their country's ongoing genocide in Iraq.[485] In the five years following Madeleine Albright's open admission that the United States was consciously exterminating the youngsters of that much-battered populace had been marked by no detectable outcry from the purportedly more enlightened sectors of the perpetrator society—nothing on the scale of, say, the campaign for designer speedbumps and better bike paths in Boulder, Colorado[486]—it was deemed necessary that an emphatic sort of "wake up call" be delivered.

Commandeering four civilian airliners, the messengers conducted a carefully coordinated and surgically precise operation in which one of the

"300,000 pound cruise missiles" was flown directly into the U.S. military's central command and control complex at the Pentagon, while another pair eliminated the twin towers of New York's World Trade Center (WTC), both symbolically and in some ways more tangibly the hub of America's global economic dominance.[487] The fourth plane, reputedly targeting either the U.S. capitol building or the White House and quite possibly shot down by Air Force interceptors, crashed in Pennsylvania.[488] All told, some 3,275 people were killed,[489] while the technical infrastructure of U.S. finance suffered immense damage — a "hit" from which it has yet to fully recover[490] — and the economy was "degraded" by perhaps $100 billion.[491]

Even before the WTC had come crashing to the ground, all three major cable "news" networks had launched a concerted propaganda offensive, pronouncing the attacks to be "senseless," the dead both "innocent" and "Americans" (several hundred turned out to be foreign nationals).[492] By nightfall, completely ignoring the fact the U.S. had been flying daily "peacetime" combat missions over Iraq for a full decade — and that it had routinely dispensed less sustained but nonetheless comparable aggression to several other countries during the same period — officials announced that a "new and unprovoked" war had been declared against the United States.[493] A day later, President George W. Bush, unelected son of George "What We Say Goes" Bush, came out of hiding long enough to explain the motives of the "cowards" who'd willingly sacrificed their lives to give Americans a small taste of what they'd for so long — and so blithely — dished out to others. The attackers were "evil," he confided, people who "hate freedom" and whose sole objective was to destroy it.[494]

Bush the Younger's characterization seemed a bit peculiar, even for him, given that the 9-1-1 attackers had at that point been identified as members of a radical Islamicist entity known as al-Qaida. The organization figured prominently among the CIA-trained and -equipped "freedom fighters" — to borrow a description from George the Elder, during his days as Ronald Reagan's vice president — who'd waged a protracted U.S. proxy war against the Soviets in Afghanistan, after the USSR invaded the country in 1979.[495] "Freedom," as employed in the vernacular of U.S. diplomacy, is a very slippery concept, however. When, in the aftermath of the 1989 Soviet defeat in Afghanistan, it turned out that al-Qaida was *genuinely* committed to Islamic self-determination — that is, as ready to fight capitalists as communists in its dedication to preventing or repealing western dominion over

Islam—the group was quietly excommunicated from America's roster of "freedom-loving friends" abroad and assigned to the State Department's list of international terrorist organizations.[496]

Al-Qaida's nominal head, a wealthy Saudi named Usama bin-Laden, was quite prepared to accept responsibility for the 9-1-1 operation, as he was for earlier attacks on U.S. embassies in Nairobi and Dar es Salaam, and upon the *U.S.S. Cole* in Yemen.[497] His explanation of why the assaults been carried out, released by videotape to the Arab al-Jazeera television network in early October 2001, nonetheless stood in stark contrast to Bush's.[498] In his electronic missive, bin-Laden made it clear that the assault had been undertaken not only as a concrete response to the ongoing holocaust of Iraqi children,[499] but to the collective fate suffered by Palestinians as a result of the U.S. support of patently illegal "settlement" policies pursued by Israel for a full generation,[500] and other such "aggression against Islam." Among the latter, he specified the continuing presence of substantial U.S. forces in Saudi Arabia, location of Mecca and others of Islam's most sacred sites.[501]

Bin-Laden might as easily have mentioned, but didn't, the shoot-down of an unoffending Iranian airliner by the *U.S.S. Vincennes* on July 3, 1988, killing 290 civilians (an "accident" for which no indemnity was paid nor even a formal apology issued, and despite which both the ship's captain and the air defense officer who fired the lethal missile were awarded the Legion of Merit in 1990).[502] Or he might have remarked upon a series of U.S. provocations in the Gulf of Sidra in 1981, including the sinking of several boats and a toll of 50 dead, which provided the pretext for the subsequent downing of two Libyan fighter planes.[503] As well, there were the U.S. bombing raids on Tripoli and Benghazi on April 14, 1986, undertaken for the most spurious of reasons and resulting in massive damage and another 100 deaths (including the adopted infant daughter of Libyan president Muamar al-Qadaffi).[504] Still again, he might have noted the thousands dead in the Sudan as a result of the August 1998 U.S. bombing of that country's only pharmaceutical plant, al-Shifa, near Khartoum, "justifying" its action with the falsehood that the factory was manufacturing chemical weapons (the vacuousness of this allegation stood revealed in the subsequent U.S. refusal to allow a UN inspection of the ruins, intended to ascertain whether such activity had in fact occurred).[505] A number of other obvious possibilities offered themselves, but on these, too, bin-Laden remained mute.[506]

Despite such deficiencies in bin-Laden's formulation, the official response to the prospect that Americans might be in any way apprised of the 9-1-1 attackers' actual motives—and thus perhaps confront the possibility that they were quite "rational" in their own way, their crimes against "innocent Americans" entirely consistent with those routinely perpetrated by the U.S. and its surrogates in *their* homelands—was to block any but the most carefully edited excerpts of bin-Laden's statements from being broadcast in the United States (this, under the preposterous pretext that airing unedited material might enable him to pass "coded instructions to his followers").[507] Considerable pressure was also brought to bear on the Emir of Qatar, where al-Jazeera is based, to "rein in" that network's coverage of al-Qaida communiqués.[508]

Meanwhile, having disgraced the dead by holding a veritable pep rally atop their corpses in the smoldering ruins of the WTC,[509] Bush declared what he called a "war on terrorism" and demanded that the Taliban government of Afghanistan, where bin-Laden then resided, hand him over.[510] The régime, which had come into being in the first place partly as a result of the CIA's manipulation of the Afghani polity during the 1980s,[511] replied that it might comply with the "request for extradition"—albeit, the U.S. had never deigned to enter into an extradition treaty with Afghanistan—but only at such time as the United States submitted a standard offer of proof (i.e., tangible evidence of bin-Laden's guilt).[512] The U.S. reply was that in its newest global war there was/is no room for observance of such "legal niceties" and that there were/are only two real options open to *any* government: immediately and unconditionally "cooperate" with U.S. demands or face destruction ("What we say, goes," in clear refrain).[513]

When the U.S. assault on the Taliban was launched, early in October 2001, the first gambit was to employ air strikes to seal off Afghanistan's border with Pakistan, over which virtually all medical and food supplies to the destitute country were transported and across which an estimated 1.5 million refugees were frantically attempting to flee.[514] In short order, some 7.5 million Afghanis were placed in imminent danger of starvation, according to the UN World Food Program.[515] Under intense international criticism for its near-instantaneous creation of a "humanitarian crisis of epic proportions," the U.S. inaugurated a program of air drops so inadequate as to be dismissed even in establishmentarian publications like the *Financial Times* as "a propaganda ploy rather than a way to get aid to Afghans who really need help."[516] No solid estimate is available concerning the number of people who ultimately died as a result of this cynical maneuver, but by even the most conservative guess it would have to have been several times the number who perished on 9-1-1.

Aside from "contributing" massive airpower to its own campaign, the U.S. followed up mostly by deploying a range of special operations units[517]—Army Special Forces, Delta Force, Navy SEALs and so on—to coordinate operations undertaken by an odd assortment of anti-Taliban Afghani groups somewhat cryptically referred to as the "Northern Alliance." In truth, the Alliance was the same amalgam of war lords and opium-smugglers who'd held power before the Taliban deposed them in 1995, largely because their three-year tenure had been "the worst in Afghanistan's history," marked as it was by "mass rapes. . .the killing of tens of thousands of civilians. . .and other atrocities."[518] Afterwards, they'd mounted an unrelenting effort to undermine the new government, butchering some 3,000 prisoners in a single 1997 massacre, and more generally carrying out "massive ethnic cleansing in areas suspected of Taliban sympathies."[519]

True to form, the Alliance troops, now armed, equipped and otherwise supported by the United States—and with U.S. "advisers" overseeing their activities—proceeded to commit every conceivable variety of war crime, including the castration and summary execution of a captured Taliban fighter chronicled in full color by photojournalist Tyler Hicks.[520] Altogether, an estimated 4,770 people were killed in the direct fighting, perhaps 10 percent of them during massacres of Taliban captives at the Shiberghan prison and a school, both in or near the town of Mazar-i-Sharif.[521] The Boston-based Physicians for Human Rights has also estimated that another 3,000 or so were suffocated while being transported in sealed shipping containers to the prison.[522] The Pentagon has of course denied that U.S. personnel were involved in—or even aware of—such crimes, but witnesses interviewed in a British documentary film entitled *Massacre at Mazar* have uniformly indicated their willingness to testify to the contrary before a bona fide war crimes tribunal.[523]

As the fighting wound down towards the end of the year, it became obvious that Usama bin-Laden had quietly slipped away. Indeed, there was little indication that appreciable damage had been done to al-Qaida in any way at all. U.S. officials put a certain gloss on this potentially embarrassing situation by conflating captured Taliban fighters with al-Qaida members, declaring both to be "illegal combatants" and flying about 350 of them—

allegedly the "most knowledgeable and dangerous"—halfway around the world, to the U.S. naval installation at Guantánamo Bay, Cuba.[524] There, they've been held under conditions openly defiant of the Geneva Convention's minimum standards for the treatment, not just of POWs but "of *all* persons captured during armed conflict,"[525] while they are subjected to a sustained interrogation under the guise that they possess "crucial intelligence information" about the workings of "international terrorism."

A hint as to the methods used on at least some of these unfortunates can be discerned in the fact that Brigadier General Rick Baccus, in charge of the "Camp X-Ray" facility where the prisoners are held, was recently relieved of command because of "philosophical differences" with interrogators operating therein.[526] In October 2002, moreover, the first real glimpse of the quality of the "threat" posed by those caged at Guantánamo Bay became possible when the first four were finally released. One them, Faiz Muhammad, turned out to be a 78-year-old—he believes he is 105—suffering from Alzheimer's, while a second, Muhammad Siddiq, is at least 90 years of age.[527] According to Pakistani intelligence officers collaborating with their U.S. counterparts in the camp, *all* of their 53 countrymen presently held there are mere "Taliban foot soldiers," *none* of them privy to anything resembling an al-Qaida secret.[528] The same can likely be said of the remaining prisoners as well, but their very existence has served the dual purpose of convincing a significant segment of the U.S. populace that something "meaningful" in terms of "combating terrorism" was accomplished in Afghanistan and, by holding the threat of trial by military tribunal over the heads of the captives, consolidating a rather confused base of public support for the presidential exercise of plainly extralegal powers.[529]

Even before the first prisoner arrived at Camp X-Ray, the latter impulse had spilled over into the domestic arena, with the Senate's passage, on October 25, 2001, of the USA PATRIOT Act. The huge tract had obviously been in preparation long before 9-1-1—and therefore cannot be accurately described as a "response to the attack"—but, "under the circumstances," it was overwhelmingly endorsed without substantive review by both U.S. legislative bodies.[530] Signed into law on October 26, the PATRIOT Act embodied a "wish list" on the part of America's apparatus of internal repression, the capstone to a list of earlier statutes—the 1984 Bail Reform Act, for example, and the Antiterrorism and Effective Death Penalty Act of 1996—which already criminalized dissident politics and empowered the agencies involved to employ ever more draconian techniques in eradicating them.[531] Among other things, PATRIOT eliminates previously existing barriers between police and intelligence agencies, vastly expands the latitude of politically motivated surveillance—including unwarranted bugs, phone taps, e-mail monitors and physical searches—enjoyed by police/intelligence agencies, formalizes guilt by association as a "legal" concept, sanctions ethnic, gender and ideological profiling as investigative techniques, greatly expands the ability of authorities to indulge in the arbitrary detention of "suspects" and to impound their assets, and, by implication, authorizes the "neutralization" rather than prosecution of those who, for whatever reason, are secretly designated as "domestic terrorists."[532]

This last appears particularly ominous, given the marked erosion over the past twenty years of the 1877 *Posse Comitatus* Act's prohibition against the use of military personnel for domestic policing purposes[533]—a constraint already considerably offset by the rampant militarization of police departments around the country[534]—all the more so given the recent revelation of a so-called Praetor Guideline (or "Praetor Protocol") by which the past several presidents have secretly assigned themselves an extraconstitutional "discretionary authority" to employ élite military units like Delta Force in "quelling civil disturbances."[535] Such developments are certainly in keeping with the joint military/police/intelligence "domestic counterinsurgency exercises" conducted under authority of the then-newly-established Federal Emergency Management Agency (FEMA) during the mid-1980s.[536]

In any event, by the time the PATRIOT Act was effected, several of its key ingredients were undergoing a fullfledged field test, using immigrants from Islamic countries as subjects. In short order, some 5,000 students and other legal Muslim aliens were grilled by the FBI, and 6,000 others were marked for expedited deportation (all because of minor status infractions). A further 2,000 or more were simply "disappeared"—that is, indefinitely detained without charge and denied contact with either their attorneys or, in many cases, their families—in a manner so secretive that it is still impossible to ascertain with any degree of certainty who was scooped up or where they're being held.[537] Attorney General John Ashcroft has recently made it clear that, in principle, his office considers such techniques as applicable to "domestic extremists" as to foreign nationals, a matter clearly raising the specter of a proliferation of Camp X-Rays housing American citizens "guilty" of expressing—or perhaps simply holding—"objectionable" political views.[538]

Such "internal security" mechanisms well in hand, the Bush administration rapidly blurred its initial pretense that the invasion of Afghanistan had anything to do with "fighting terrorism." In this connection, bin-Laden and al-Qaida were mentioned less and less—at this point almost never—as the U.S. installed a handpicked "democratic" régime headed by Hamid Karzai, a maneuver guaranteed to result in approval of rights of way for American oil companies to build a cost-efficient pipeline from the lush but landlocked oil fields of Turkmenistan, Uzbekistan and Kazakhstan to the Pakistani port of Gwaddar (the Taliban had been adamantly blocking the plan).[539] The new client government is equally sure to make no objection to Afghani territory being used as a U.S. forward staging area, should military "stabilization operations" in any of the three Central Asia republics—or an invasion of neighboring Iran—become "necessary."[540] The quid pro quo, at least in part, is that those who served as U.S. proxies in 2001 have been allowed to resume opium production, which the Taliban had all but eradicated, with the result that Afghanistan has already (re)emerged as the world's leading exporter of the drug (most of it destined for North America's inner cities).[541]

Even as it disappeared as a topic in official discourse on Afghanistan, al-Qaida has continued to serve a useful propaganda purpose in other respects. Well before the end of 2001, much was being made of the "more than sixty countries" in which the "bin-Laden network" was supposedly active.[542] While these included Canada, Germany, France, England, Pakistan, Morocco, Egypt and Saudi Arabia—as well as the U.S. itself—the "need for a military option" was expressed only with regard to countries on the official U.S. enemies list, primarily Somalia, the Sudan and, with a transparent flourish, Libya (a decisively *anti*-Islamicist state).[543] By January 2002, Special Forces units had in fact been dispatched to the southern Philippines to combat the "al-Qaida-connected" Abu Sayyaf guerrillas—generally believed by other oppositionists in those islands to be a CIA front—as well as the former Soviet republic of Georgia, to disperse "al-Qaida-linked" Chechen rebels based therein, and Yemen, where "important al-Qaida cells" were said to thrive.[544]

On January 31, 2002, Bush finally laid bare the cynicism with which U.S. policymakers were using the "war on terror" as a cover for other designs. In his State of the Union Address, the president defined an "Axis of Evil" against which he was imminently prepared to order the use of significant military force.[545] Tellingly, although Bush larded his rhetoric with references to "the continuing terrorist threat," alleged al–Qaida "hosts" were not among his three-country "Axis." Instead, the first two, Iraq and Iran, are not only mutually hostile, but emphatically so with respect to al–Qaida's brand of Islamicism (and vice versa).[546] The third, North Korea, is neither Islamic nor known to support international terrorism.[547] To all appearances, the only real commonality uniting the "Axis" countries resides in the consistency with which each has rejected U S. dictates. Ultimately, the picture painted by the president was so implausible that even Madeleine Albright publicly scolded him for it.[548]

Seemingly surprised by such criticism, and anxious to retain his base of domestic support, Bush quickly refocused his pitch (the "Axis of Evil" line hasn't been used in months). His demotion of al–Qaida from its position of preeminence nevertheless continued, with ever-increasing emphasis placed upon "Saddam Hussein's violation of sixteen United Nations resolutions" and the "certainty" that Iraq has thereby (re)acquired "weapons of mass destruction."[549] These supposedly consist at present of both chemical and biological agents—the basis for which were secretly provided by the U.S. during the 1980s, when Hussein's brutal Ba'athist régime was considered a useful club for purposes of bludgeoning Iran[550]—although Scott Ritter, a Gulf War veteran and one of the chief UN weapons inspectors working in Iraq until 1998, has vociferously contested such contentions.

> Contrary to popular mythology, there's no evidence Iraq [ever] worked on smallpox, Ebola, or any other horrific nightmare weapons the media likes to talk about today. . . They actually made. . .anthrax in liquid bulk agent form [and] produced a significant quantity of liquid botulinum toxin. . . Liquid anthrax, even under ideal storage conditions, germinates in three years, becoming useless. . . Iraq has no biological weapons today, because both the anthrax and botulinum toxin [they produced have expired, and] they'd have to reconstitute a biological manufacturing base.[551]

As to chemical weapons:

> Iraq manufactured three kinds of nerve agents: Sarin, Tabun, and VX. Some people who want war with Iraq describe 20,000 munitions filled with Sarin and Tabun nerve agents that could be used against Americans. The facts, however, don't support this. Sarin and Tabun have a shelf-life of five years. Even if Iraq had somehow managed to hide this vast number of weapons from inspectors, what they're now storing is nothing more than useless, harmless goo. . . VX is different, for a couple of reasons [but the] real question is: Is there a VX nerve agent factory in Iraq today? Not on your life. . . Real questions exist as to whether Iraq perfected the stabilization process [and even] if Iraq had held on to stabilized VX agent, it's likely it would have degraded by today.[552]

365

Hussein is also alleged to be on the verge of developing nuclear weapons, although, as Ritter again points out, absolutely no evidence has been presented to substantiate the claim.[553] At any rate, conspicuously missing from the framing of charges against Iraq is the fact that neighboring Israel, with full and ongoing U.S. support, has over the past forty years thumbed its nose at a far greater number of UN resolutions than the Iraqis have lately disregarded,[554] and that the Israelis actually—not to mention quite unlawfully—possess a substantial stockpile of nuclear weapons.[555] So does Pakistan, another country recently added to the U.S. "friends" list, and India.[556] Israel, moreover—again, compliments of the United States—possesses a delivery capacity vis-à-vis such weapons vastly superior to Iraq's.[557] All these illegalities notwithstanding, nobody in U.S. policy circles is attempting to build a case for war against Israel.

Bush has sought to finesse this blatant contradiction by claiming that in April 2001 Mohammed Atta, the man ostensibly in charge of the 9-1-1 attack teams, had met with an Iraqi intelligence officer in Prague. This "clear link" between Iraq and al-Qaida—used both to discount the sharp ideological differences separating the two, and to imply Iraqi sponsorship of the 9-1-1 attack itself—dissolved when Czech intelligence publicly announced that the meeting was a fiction (Atta was in Florida when the fabled liaison supposedly occurred).[558] The same sort of fate has befallen several other U.S. efforts to come with something which might be plausibly advanced as the "smoking gun" tying Iraq into 9-1-1.[559] Still, by October 2002, a Pew Research poll revealed that fully two-thirds of all Americans were finding it convenient to "believe Saddam Hussein helped terrorists carry out the Sept. 11 attacks."[560]

A decisive majority of his constituents thus prepped, the president set about finalizing the U.S. subversion of international law, delivering an ultimatum to the UN closely resembling his "you're either with us or against us and therefore subject to immediate destruction" speeches of late 2001. On September 12, 2002, Bush appeared before the General Assembly to demand that the Security Council pass a resolution authorizing the U.S. to use whatever force it deems necessary not only to "disarm" Iraq, but to precipitate a "regime change" in the country.[561] In the alternative, he made it clear, the U.S. would no longer view the UN as a "credible" legislative and enforcement body, and he would be "compelled" to appoint his own administration its replacement. In substance, the message once again was "do as you're told, what *we* say, goes."[562]

Actually, this "UN initiative" would probably have been launched earlier, had the U.S. not had to contend with fallout resulting from Israel's having seized upon the rhetoric of "global antiterrorism" as a pretext upon which to launch yet another of its endless offensives against the Palestinian West Bank (this one lasted three months, April through June 2002, despite Bush's having openly demanded early on that Israeli premier Ariel Sharon "immediately" withdraw his forces).[563] During the invasion, which was as always carried out in defiance of urgent UN resolutions, many Israeli troops indulged in their usual behavior, committing hundreds of "unlawful killings, torture and ill-treatment of prisoners, [as well as the] wanton destruction of homes [while others regularly] blocked access to ambulances and denied humanitarian assistance, leaving the wounded and dead lying in the streets for days, and used Palestinians as 'human shields' while searching for suspected militants."[564] The pattern of atrocity appears to have been especially pronounced in the West Bank towns of Nablus and Jenin.[565]

His own ineffectuality in bringing America's primary Mideastern ally quickly to heel—a matter which, rather accurately, was widely interpreted as indicating a continuing U.S. support of Israel's systematically criminal comportment—to some extent slowed the Bushian rush to wax bellicose in condemning Iraq's illegalities.[566] It also served to seriously undermine the degree of cooperation and support the U.S. could expect from members of the Arab League during a war with Iraq. The Saudis, for example, withdrew their permission for airstrikes to be launched from bases in their territory, and several months were required to negotiate an adequate alternative with Oman.[567] By late October 2002, however, these difficulties had been for the most part resolved and Bush "turned up the heat" on the UN.[568]

The result, coming in the wake of American voters' endorsement of Bush's "don't confuse me with the facts" approach to world policy during the midterm election held on November 5, 2002, was a "compromise" resolution unanimously approved by the Security Council on November 8.[569] Predicated upon Iraq's granting "unconditional and immediate" access to any and all sites by UN weapons inspectors, the resolution contains only a pro forma requirement that the U.S. obtain Security Council approval before launching a fullscale military invasion in response to Iraqi "obstruction" (as defined, to all appearances, by the United States). The very same afternoon, an exultant Bush displayed himself on TV, crowing that Saddam now had "no choice but to submit."[570] As he spoke, additional major U.S. forces were deploying in the Persian Gulf.

Plainly, the wake-up call delivered so forcefully on 9-1-1 has not been heeded. Rather, Americans for the most part continue to wallow in the self-serving and misbegotten notion of their own radical innocence, the same mindless outlook that has all along deformed their collective self-concept into a pathological condition.[571] Quite predictably under these circumstances, the "Prussians" among the country's élites have moved quickly in an effort to realize the ancient and infantile fantasy of outright world domination.[572] The grim scenario described in the section of this essay entitled " 'Indian Country' Forever?" is coming together at breakneck speed, while the positive alternatives hinted at in the conclusion recede with equal rapidity.

True, a certain alternative potential purports to present itself in an incipient (re)emergence of a mass antiwar movement for the first time since Vietnam.[573] In the main, however, its participants have, as they did during the Vietnam era, seemed far more concerned with establishing an appearance of personal purity than with attempting anything materially disruptive to the U.S. war-making capacity.[574] Acting upon their own vibrant sense of American exceptionalism, most have forsworn on "philosophical" grounds the range of oppositional tactics that have proven necessary—and most effective—elsewhere, arguing with all due sanctimony that circumstances unique to the United States render such methods "inappropriate" to the task of compelling transformative change on the "home front."[575] Their stance thus mirroring that of their ostensible opponents, they place themselves a priori in a self-neutralizing posture, leaving themselves utterly incapable of retarding—much less averting—the horrors they insist it is their purpose to halt.[576]

On the face of it, then, the normative ambit of dissent in the U.S. is being drawn, as it always has, to displace the burden of blood onto Others, "out there" somewhere (*anywhere* but here). It is to be for "Them," as ever, to do the fighting and the dying, to bear the maiming and the burns, the starvation and endemic disease, suffering all the vast and ghastly toll of American military aggression while a self-styled "resistance" within the perpetrator country performs sanitary genuflections of symbolic protest, bearing "moral witness" to Their agony. To all appearances, it is presumed that this should remain the lot of these faceless, nameless multitudes of Others to endure *whatever* may be imposed upon them for *however* long it might take for America's enlightened oppositionists, through some alchemy never quite explained, to abolish the structural basis of U.S. aggression and genocide "nonviolently" (i.e., in a manner painless to themselves).[577]

From the perspective of those on the receiving end of what the U.S. so habitually dispenses to Others, there can thus be little by which to distinguish the glaring sense of self-entitlement exhibited by America's "peace movement" from that manifested by the state/corporate edifice whose policies and comportment it ostensibly opposes.[578] The extent to which there is truth to this perception is precisely the extent to which all but the most committed and self-sacrificing sectors of the U.S. opposition have historically defaulted—and are defaulting even now—upon the most fundamental responsibilities enshrined both in the customary standards of elemental human decency and in law. Here, the premise enunciated in Nuremberg Doctrine is as irreducibly simple as it is disquieting to those who would claim virtue in their pursuit of a comfort zone politics: When *any* government defies the basic tenets of international legality—as the nazis did, and as the U.S. government always has—the citizenry is bound by the legal obligation to utilize any and all means necessary to enforce compliance.[579]

There are no lines, legal or moral, constraining citizen action in such endeavors.[580] The only illegality is entailed in shirking one's obligation to cross whatever lines have been established to ensure the stability of criminal governments.[581] Those guilty of this offense are—as more than a few Good Germans were informed in the aftermath of World War II—in certain respects no less accountable to those who've suffered their country's aggression than are the officials they wildly applauded, or quietly embraced, or in any event failed to unseat. There are no bystanders to war crimes, genocide and other crimes against humanity. There are only victims, perpetrators and those complicit in the perpetration by way of either their endorsement or their acquiescence. Among the last three groups, children and mental incompetents aside, *no one* is "innocent." *All* are to one or another extent responsible.[582]

Such was the message—a warning, really—sent on 9-1-1. The days of smugness in which Americans might anoint themselves with a "god-given right" to exemption from the pain they as a country impose on Others are over. Insofar as U.S. citizens are accepting of the proposition that the economy of another people represents a legitimate military target—as they have since John Sullivan's troops laid waste the Seneca orchards and cornfields in 1779[583]—then "infrastructural" entities like the WTC are unquestionably fair game. To the degree that Americans are comfortable with the idea that the employment of tactics and technologies resulting inevitably in the slaughter of "enemy" civilians is acceptable under the rubric of "collateral damage"—as they've been since at least as early as Anthony Wayne's 1794 campaign against the Shawnees[584]—they've no logically or morally defensible basis to complain when the same devaluation is applied to them. In the sense that Americans have been perfectly willing to condone policies targeting entire populations of Others for eradication—as they have since Indian scalp bounties were promulgated during the first moments of their republic[585]—they can have no complaint when they themselves are explicitly taken as a target and subjected to the same treatment. What goes around does in fact ultimately come around, and only the most shortsighted—and arrogant—of peoples might ever have believed they could permanently forestall actualization of that simple truth.

The lapse in comparable operations inside the United States with which "the terrorists" have followed up their carefully focused attacks of 9-1-1 seems to have been intended more than anything to afford the American public a breathing space, time to draw appropriate lessons from the bitterness of its rather minor loss. Put another way, U.S. citizens were offered one last chance to finally grasp the fact—*really* grasp it rather than paying occasional and perfunctory lip service to it—that Americans are *not* a "special" or "chosen" people, either individually or collectively, that the lowliest "sand nigger" is worth just as much as the most self-absorbed yuppie braying business transactions into his cell phone while golfing at Myrtle Beach, that every wide-eyed little waif starving to death in Iraq and the reservations of Native North America is of a value identical to that with which a Jonbenet Ramsey or Danielle van Dam is currently imbued.[586] From this realization, had it occurred, one could hope that certain conclusions might accrue, conclusions resulting not just in an American "regime change," but in an alteration of public sensibility that left the likes of Henry Kissinger and Madeleine Albright sitting where by rights they belong: in a defendants' dock overshadowed by the gallows.[587]

At the very least, it was reasonable to expect that it might at last dawn on average folk that, to quote Georgia State University law professor Natsu Saito, "if Americans want their own kids to be safe again, the way to make it happen is really not very complicated—stop killing other people's babies."[588] Even this cognitive threshold has been beyond reach, however. The public, refusing the obviousness of such formulations, has gathered itself in its usual collectivity of denial, queuing up to place its faith in the "security" offered by such absurdities as the impoundment of tweezers contained in the carry-on luggage of airline passengers, and demanded a restoration of its accustomed "right" to kill with impunity.[589] The message of 9-1-1, to all appearances, has thus been lost (another disgrace to the memory of those who died). It will therefore have to be repeated (in pedagogical theory, the technique involved is referred to as being "recursive," highly effective with slow learners).

For this reason, on November 12, 2002, Usama bin-Laden, whose long silence had lulled many into the hope that he might be dead, made a taped appearance on al-Jazeera to explain the situation in no uncertain terms. "As you kill, you will be killed," he informed those applauding the prospect of another major war in the Persian Gulf, "As you bomb, you will bombed."[590] To make it clear that al-Qaida retains the capability to deliver on its words, bin-Laden took implicit credit for a whole series of actions over the year of his invisibility, including the recent bombing of a nightclub in Bali claiming a heavy toll of Australians[591] and the even more recent Chechen takeover of a theater in Moscow which resulted in well over a hundred fatalities.[592] As a subtext, he observed that every U.S. action since September 2001 had served to solidify al-Qaida's worldwide base of grassroots support, and that any major military action against Iraq would expand its recruitment base immensely.

It is no doubt true, as U.S. officials keep reminding us, that neither al-Qaida nor any other such organization holds — or is likely ever to hold — the capacity to defeat the United States in purely military terms. Nor do they possess the means to truly destroy America's economic system. What they do have, nonetheless, is the means and the will — both of them in increasing rather than diminishing proportions — to make U.S. citizens pay in the dearest possible terms, and in numbers making 9-1-1 look like the sneak preview it actually was, for the lethal effrontery embodied in their effort to resume business as usual. As the Israelis can all-too-readily attest, there really is no effective defense against people driven to the depths of such despair that they will gladly sacrifice themselves, if only it means taking a few of their tormentors with them.[593] In this regard, justice sometimes assumes the most awful sort of symmetry, but it will always, and irrespective of the power relations involved, prevail.

There is no Eighth Air Force available to hammer America into the kind of humility and self-recognition that lends itself to legal compliance. Nevertheless, Americans, like the Germans before them, are now confronted with a plain and unavoidable choice concerning the measure of suffering they are willing to endure in order to maintain the delusional pretensions marking their objectively criminal way of life. One can hope they will choose correctly, and soon. The scourges of smallpox, VX and dirty bombs would be a hideous price to pay for recalcitrance,[594] but American recalcitrance equates, as it's always equated, to mounds of rotting corpses in whatever chunk of territory the U.S. chooses to view as "Indian Country" at any given moment. Come what may, there is solace to be had in the knowledge that Americans no longer enjoy the option of pretending they can avoid the choice itself.

# Notes

1. See, e.g., Edwin P. Hoyt, *America's Wars and Military Excursions* (New York: McGraw-Hill, 1987).

2. The complete text of the order will be found in John C. Fitzgerald, ed., *Writings of George Washington* (Washington, D.C.: U.S. Government Printing Office, 1936) pp. 189-93.

3. Ibid., p. 93.

4. Quoted in Richard Drinnon, *Facing West: The Metaphysics of Indian-Hating and Empire-Building* (Minneapolis: University of Minnesota Press, 1980) p. 332.

5. Anthony Wallace, *The Death and Rebirth of the Seneca* (New York: Alfred A. Knopf, 1970) pp. 141-4.

6. Quoted in Drinnon, Facing West, p. 332.

7. Shelby L. Stanton, *Rangers at War: Combat Recon in Vietnam* (New York: Orion Books, 1992) pp. 1-6.

8. Col. Henry Hamilton, "The Hamilton Papers," *Michigan Pioneer and Historical Collections*, No. 9, 1886, pp. 501-2.

9. Henry Howe, quoted in Richard Drinnon, *Keeper of Concentration Camps: Dillon S. Myer and American Racism* (Berkeley: University of California Press, 1987) p. 23.

10. Ibid. Also see Gerard Fowke, *Archaeological History of Ohio: The Mound Builders and Later Indians* (Columbus: Ohio State Archaeological and Historical Society, 1902) pp. 478-80.

11. For the best overall account of combat in the Ohio River Valley during this period, see Allan W. Eckert, *That Dark and Bloody River: Chronicles of the Ohio River Valley* (New York: Bantam, 1995).

12. John Sugden, *Tecumseh's Last Stand* (Norman: University of Oklahoma Press, 1985) p. 180.

13. David E. Stannard, *American Holocaust: Columbus and the Conquest of the New World* (New York: Oxford University Press, 1992) p. 121. Also see H.S. Halbert and T.H. Hall, *The Creek War of 1813 and 1814* (Tuscaloosa: University of Alabama Press, 1969) pp. 276-7.

14. Quoted in Stannard, *American Holocaust*, p. 121.

15. See generally, Edward J. Nichols, *Zach Taylor's Little Army* (Garden City, NY: Doubleday, 1963).

16. Alan Axelrod, *Chronicle of the Indian Wars from Colonial Times to Wounded Knee* (New York: Prentice Hall, 1993) p. 151.

17. On scalp bounties, see my *A Little Matter of Genocide: Holocaust and Denial in the Americas, 1492 to the Present* (San Francisco: City Lights, 1997) pp. 178-88.

18. Robert F. Heizer, ed., *The Destruction of California Indians* (Lincoln: University of Nebraska Press, [2nd ed.] 1993).

19. I am referring here not to the men whose faces appear on U.S. currency—although several would plainly qualify—but to less overtly political figures like Daniel Boone, Davy Crockett, Kit Carson and George Armstrong Custer. Perhaps the best analysis of how this came about will be found in Richard Slotkin's *Fatal Environment: The Myth of the Frontier in the Age of Industrialization, 1800-1890* (Norman: University of Oklahoma Press, [2nd ed.] 1998): on Boone, see pp. 65-8; on Crockett, see 162-72, 269-70; on Carson, see pp. 200-207; on Custer, see pp. 369-74, 500-1, 528-30.

20. Stuart Creighton Miller, *"Benevolent Assimilation": The American Conquest of the Philippines, 1899-1903* (New Haven, CT: Yale University Press, 1982) pp. 1-2, 253-67.

21. Patricia Nelson Limerick, to name a prominent example, offers a "revised" interpretation of "how the West was won" that manages to omit all mention of such "unpleasantness"—the term is hers—as massacres; see her much-touted *The Legacy of Conquest: The Unbroken Past of the West* (New York: W.W. Norton, 1987).

22. See Richard Slotkin, *Gunfighter Nation: The Myth of the Frontier in Twentieth-Century America* (Norman: University of Oklahoma Press, [2nd ed.] 1998).

23. Miller, *"Benevolent Assimilation"*, pp. 1-2.

24. Notably, Samuel Flagg Bemis, in his supposedly magisterial study, *A Diplomatic History of the United States* (New York: Henry Holt, 1936), opined that imperialism was "a great aberration in American history."

25. Examples of such formulations are legion. A classic illustration will be found in J.H. Elliot's review of Stannard's *American Holocaust* published in the *New York Review of Books* on June 24, 1993. More broadly, see the polemics offered by James Axtell in his *The European and the Indian: Essays in the Ethnohistory of Colonial North America* (New York: Oxford University Press, 1981); *After Columbus: Essays*

*in the Ethnohistory of Colonial North America* (New York: Oxford University Press, 1988); *Beyond 1492: Encounters in Colonial North America* (New York: Oxford University Press, 1992).

26. "The concept of offenses against the law of nations *(delicti juris gentium)* was recognized by classical text-writers on international law and . . . was regarded as sufficiently tangible in the eighteenth century that United States courts sustained indictments charging acts as an offense against the law of nations, even if there were no statutes defining the offense"; Quincy Wright, "The Law of the Nuremberg Trial, Part II," in Jay Baird, ed., *From Nuremberg to My Lai* (Lexington, MA: D.C. Heath, 1972) p. 37.

27. Adam Roberts and Richard Guelff, eds., *Documents on the Laws of War* (Oxford, U.K.: Clarendon Press, 1982) p. 2.

28. Ibid., pp. 2-3.

29. See, e.g., Hedley Bull, Benedict Kingsbury and Adam Roberts, eds., *Hugo Grotius and International Relations* (Oxford, UK: Clarendon Press, 1992).

30. See the opening statement of Hermann Jahrreiss, lead counsel for the defense, in *Trial of the Major Nazi War Criminals before the International Military Tribunal*, 42 vols. (Nuremberg: International Military Tribunal, 1949) Blue Series, Vol. 17, pp. 458-94.

31. See, e.g., Henry L. Stimson, "The Nuremberg Trial: Landmark in Law," *Foreign Affairs*, No. XXV, 1947.

32. Wright, "The Law of the Nuremberg Trial," p. 38.

33. Affirmation of the Principles of International Law Recognized by the Charter of the Nuremberg Tribunal, U.N.G.A. Res. 95(I), U.N. Doc. A/236 (1946), at 1144.

34. For an especially nauseating articulation of this thesis, see Wilcomb E. Washburn, *Red Man's Land, White Man's Law* (New York: Scribner's, 1971).

35. Roberts and Guelff, *Documents on the Laws of War*, p. 7; United States Army, *General Orders No. 100: Instructions for the Government of United States Armies in the Field* (Washington, D.C.: U.S. Dept. of War, Apr. 24, 1863; hereinafter referred as "Lieber Code").

37. Quoted in Joseph B. Kelley, "A Legal Analysis of the Changes in War," *Military Law Review*, July 1961.

38. "War is merely the continuation of policy by other means. . . War is thus an act of force to compel our enemy to do our will. . . The political object is the goal, war is the means of reaching it, and means can never be considered in isolation from their purpose"; Carl von Clausewitz, *On War* (Princeton, NJ: Princeton University Press, 1976) pp. 75, 87.

39. Roberts and Guelff, *Documents on the Laws of War*, p. 3.

40. "Murders in cold blood after the heat of battle were condemned by all nations of the world. . . [O]ne had the right to kill the defenders of the state as long as they bore arms, but when they surrendered they ceased to be enemies or instruments of the enemy and became men. Their killing was unnecessary to achieve the purpose of the war, namely the destruction of the enemy state. . . The philosophical premises of the law were formulated by such philosophers of the Enlightenment as Montesquieu and Rousseau"; Allan Rosas, *The Legal Status of Prisoners of War: A Study in International Humanitarian Law Applicable in Armed Conflicts* (Helsinki: Suomalainen Tiedeakatemia, 1976) p. 57.

41. On the numbers involved, and the meeting at which the protected status of the village was guaranteed, see Stan Hoig, *The Sand Creek Massacre* (Norman: University of Oklahoma Press, 1961) pp. 12, 116-7, 120.

42. Simon J. Ortiz, *From Sand Creek* (Oak Park, NY: Thunder's Mouth Press, 1981) p. 8. Also see Stan Hoig, *Peace Chiefs of the Cheyenne* (Norman: University of Oklahoma Press, 1980).

43. Hoig, *Sand Creek Massacre*, p. 150.

44. The armistice was negotiated in mid-September during a meeting conducted at Camp Weld, outside Denver, at Black Kettle's behest; ibid., pp. 110-28.

45. Ibid., p. 140.

46. Quoted in ibid., p. 147.

47. Chivington was paraphrasing the observation of H.L. Hall, an Indian-killer prominent in California at about the same time, that American Indian infants should be butchered whenever possible because "a nit would make a louse"; see generally, Lynwood Carranco and Estle Beard, *Genocide and*

*Vendetta: The Round Valley Wars of Northern California* (Norman: University of Oklahoma Press, 1981) esp. Chap. 4. Hall himself may well have been borrowing from a Puritan rhyme likening Indians to "rats and mice or swarms of lice," written in the aftermath of their 1637 extermination of the Pequots; Drinnon, *Facing West*, p. 55.

48. The Third Colorado Volunteer Cavalry Regiment, comprising the bulk of Chivington's assault force, was formed during the first weeks of August 1864 for the express purpose of "exterminating" hostile Cheyennes and allied Arapahos. The term of enlistment was 100 days. Hence, the soldiers' obligations were met by mid-November, although they'd by then come upon only a handful of Indians to exterminate, and were therefore embarrassed to be known as the "Bloodless Third." At the last moment, they were inspired to stay on—for purposes of attacking Black Kettle's noncombatants—during a visit by Gen. Patrick E. Connor, who had, on Jan. 27, 1863, led a force of California volunteers in slaughtering several hundred Shoshones at Bear River, in southern Idaho; *Rocky Mountain News*, Nov. 14, 16, 1864. On Connor's "accomplishment," see Brigham M. Madsen, *The Shoshoni Frontier and the Bear River Massacre* (Salt Lake City: University of Utah Press, 1985) esp. pp. 189-92.

49. Hoig, *Sand Creek Massacre*, pp. 172-99.

50. Ortiz places the number at "105 women and children and 28 men"; *From Sand Creek*, p. 8.

51. Hoig, *Sand Creek Massacre*, p. 151.

52. U.S. Senate, *Reports of the Committees: The Chivington Massacre* (Washington, D.C.: 39th Cong., 2d Sess., 1867) pp. 95-6.

53. Ibid., p. 42.

54. Ibid. p. 53. Corroborating testimony is too voluminous to cite adequately herein. For additional extracts, see Hoig, *Sand Creek Massacre*, pp. 177-92.

55. The infant was considered a "nuisance." Her throat was therefore slit. Jack Smith, a mixed-blood Cheyenne, was also shot; U.S. Senate, *Chivington Massacre*, p. 155.

56. *Rocky Mountain News*, Dec. 22, 1864.

57. Gov. Evans also advocated extermination; U.S. Dept. of War, Commissioner of Indian Affairs, *Annual Report* (Washington, D.C.: 38th Cong., 1st Sess., 1864) pp. 239-46. Overall, see David Svaldi, *Sand Creek and the Rhetoric of Extermination: A Case-Study in Indian-White Relations* (Landham, MD: University Press of America, 1989).

58. It should be noted that Capt. Silas S. Soule refused to allow his company to participate in the massacre; Hoig, *Sand Creek Massacre*, p. 151.

59. U.S. Senate, *Chivington Massacre*; U.S. House of Representatives, *Report on the Conduct of the War: Massacre of Cheyenne Indians* (Washington, D.C.: 38th Cong., 2d Sess., 1865); U.S. Department of War, *Report of the Secretary of War: The Sand Creek Massacre* (Washington, D.C.: Sen. Exec. Doc. 26, 39th Cong., 2d Sess., 1867).

60. Hoig, *Sand Creek Massacre*, p. 169.

61. Serious consideration was in fact given to recalling several officers to stand trial. They were, however, to be charged only with misappropriating horses and other booty taken at Sand Creek, a violation of Article 31 of the Lieber Code. The proposal foundered when it was realized that there was no way of bringing them under military jurisdiction for this purpose without opening them up to prosecution on the far more serious charges pending against them; ibid.

62. "The state of the law cannot be properly judged by referencing the written law alone"; Roberts and Guelff, *Documents on the Laws of War*, p. 16.

63. There are also several thoroughly squalid books eulogizing the colonel's supposed virtues. See, as examples, Reginald S. Craig, *The Fighting Parson: A Biography of Col. John M. Chivington* (Tucson, AZ: Westernlore, 1959); Lt. Col. William R. Dunn, *"I Stand by Sand Creek": A Defense of Colonel John M. Chivington and the Third Colorado Cavalry* (Ft. Collins, CO: Old Army Press, 1985).

64. Patricia Nelson Limerick, "What's in a Name? Nichols Hall: A Report" (Boulder: unpublished study commissioned by the Regents of the University of Colorado, 1987).

65. M.A. Sievers, "The Shifting Sands of Sand Creek Historiography," *Colorado Magazine*, No. 49, 1972.

66. See generally, Clifford E. Trafzer, *The Kit Carson Campaign: The Last Great Navajo War* (Norman: University of Oklahoma Press, 1982).

67. Stan Hoig, *The Battle of the Washita* (Garden City, NY: Doubleday, 1976) p. 74. Also see Don Turner, *Custer's First Massacre: The Battle of the Washita* (Amarillo, TX: Gulch Press, 1968).

68. Axelrod, *Chronicle of the Indian Wars*, p. 209.

69. W.A. Graham, *The Custer Myth: A Sourcebook on Custeriana* (Lincoln: University of Nebraska Press, [2nd ed.] 1981).

70. Robert G. Athearn, *William Tecumseh Sherman and the Settlement of the West* (Norman: University of Oklahoma Press, 1956) pp. 278-9. The best overall handling of the Marias Massacre and its backdrop will be found in James Welch, *Killing Custer: The Battle of the Little Big Horn and the Fate of the Plains Indians* (New York: W.W, Norton, 1994).

71. Paul Andrew Hutton, *Phil Sheridan and His Army* (Lincoln: University of Nebraska Press, 1985) pp. 192-4.

72. Dee Brown, *Bury My Heart at Wounded Knee: An Indian History of the American West* (New York: Holt, Rinehart and Winston, 1970) pp. 346-7.

73. Ralph K. Andrist, *The Long Death: The Last Days of the Plains Indian* (New York: Macmillan, 1964) pp. 351-2.

74. Mario Gonzalez and Elizabeth Cook-Lynn, *The Politics of Hallowed Ground: Wounded Knee and the Struggle for Indian Sovereignty* (Urbana: University of Illinois Press, 1999) pp. 177, 253.

75. As at Sand Creek, the exact number of dead is "controversial," since no accurate count was made at the time; Andrist, *Long Death*, p. 352.

76. Gonzalez and Cook-Lynn, *Hallowed Ground*, p. 107.

77. Quoted in Elliot J. Gorn, Randy Roberts and Terry D. Bilhartz, *Constructing the American Past: A Sourcebook of a People's History* (New York: HarperCollins, 1972) p. 74.

78. William D. Street, "Cheyenne Indian Massacre on the Middle Fork of the Sappa ," *Transactions of the Kansas State Historical Society*, Vol. X, 1907-1908.

79. Quoted in Axelrod, *Chronicle of the Indian Wars*, p. 203.

80. Sheridan's actual phrase was, "The only good Indians I ever saw were dead"; Hutton, *Phil Sheridan*, p. 180.

81. Svaldi, *Sand Creek and the Rhetoric of Extermination.*

82. For demographic data, see Donald J. Berthrong, *The Cheyenne and Arapaho Ordeal: Reservation and Agency Life, 1875-1907* (Norman: University of Oklahoma Press, 1976); William T. Hagan, *United States-Comanche Relations: The Reservation Years* (Norman: University of Oklahoma Press, [2nd ed.] 1990); Mildred P. Mayhall, *The Kiowas* (Norman: University of Oklahoma Press, 1962). More broadly, see Russell Thornton, *American Indian Holocaust and Survival: A Population History Since 1492* (Norman: University of Oklahoma Press, 1987).

83. The term "Indian Wars" is itself a misnomer. In all cases, the conflicts resulted from the invasion of native nations by the United States. A more accurate descriptor would therefore be "Wars of U.S. Aggression."

84. As an example: "[B]efore there were whites to rob and plunder and steal from, the [Indians] robbed and stole from each other. Before there were white men in the country to kill, they killed each other. Before there were white women and children to scalp and mutilate and torture, the Indians scalped and mutilated and tortured the women and children of enemies of their own race"; Duane Schultz, *Month of the Freezing Moon: The Sand Creek Massacre, November 1864* (New York: St. Martin's Press, 1990) p. 16.

85. Although the 1868 Additional Articles to the 1864 Geneva Convention on the Wounded and Sick are certainly germane, the 1874 Brussels Declaration incorporating the "fundamental customary principle . . . that the right of belligerents to adopt means of injuring the enemy is not unlimited" goes more to the point. As formulated in the 1899 Hague Convention, this meant that "the principle of humanity prohibits any kind or degree of force not actually necessary for military purposes"; Roberts and Guelff, *Documents on the Laws of War*, pp. 3, 5.

86. For background on the St. Valentine's Day Massacre, see Robert J. Schoenberg, *Mr. Capone* (New York: William Morrow, 1992) pp. 207-29.

87. See generally, Miller, *"Benevolent Assimilation"*; Robert E. Welch, Jr., *Response to Imperialism: The United States and the Philippine-American War, 1899-1902* (Chapel Hill: University of North Carolina Press, 1979).

88. Unidentified General Officer (probably Wesley Merritt), quoted by Senator George Frisbee Hoar, *Congressional Record*, Vol. XXXIII, Jan. 9, 1901, p. 714.

89. Theodore Roosevelt, *The Winning of the West*, 7 vols. (New York: Putnam's, 1907) Vol. III, p. 145.

90. Anonymous Army officer, quoted in Moorfield Storey and Julian Codman, *"Marked Severities" in Philippine Warfare* (Boston: George H. Ellis, 1902) p. 99. The "Weylerian" reference is to the Spanish general, Valeriano Weyler, known as the "Butcher of Cuba"; Miller, *"Benevolent Assimilation"*, p. 9.

91. Drinnon, *Facing West*, p. 315.

92. Ibid., pp. 324-5. Miller, *"Benevolent Assimilation"*, p. 219.

93. Ibid., pp. 196-218.

94. Slotkin, *Gunfighter Nation*, p. 119.

95. In a manner which would later become fashionable in Vietnam, Bell may have exaggerated his bodycount. Closer study reveals that his policies may have accounted for "only" 220,000 people (estimated as being composed of 20,000 combatants and 200,000 civilians); Glenn May, "Filipino Resistance to American Occupation: Batangas, 1899-1902," *Pacific Historical Review*, No. 48, 1979, pp. 555-6.

96. Storey and Codman, *"Marked Severities"*, pp. 26-7.

97. Miller, *"Benevolent Assimilation"*, p. 218.

98. Ibid., pp. 237, 260.

99. Slotkin, *Gunfighter Nation*, p. 119.

100. Drinnon, *Facing West*, p. 328.

101. *Philadelphia Ledger*, Nov. 19, 1901.

102. U.S. Senate, Committee on the Philippine Islands, *Hearings Before the Senate Committee on the Philippine Islands* (Washington, D.C.: S. Doc. 331, 57th Cong., 1st Sess., 1902).

103. U.S. Department of War, *Letter From the Secretary of War Relative to the Reports and Charges in the Public Press of Cruelty and Oppression Exercised by Our Soldiers Towards Natives of the Philippines* (Washington, D.C.: S. Doc. 205., 57th Cong., 1st Sess., 1902).

104. Drinnon, *Facing West*, p. 522; Storey and Codman, *"Marked Severities"*, pp. 136-7.

105. At issue were the deaths of only eleven people; Drinnon, *Facing West*, p. 327.

106. Ibid.

107. Miller, *"Benevolent Assimilation"*, p. 232.

108. Drinnon, *Facing West*, p. 328.

109. Slotkin, *Gunfighter Nation*, p. 121.

110. Senate, *Hearings on the Philippines*, p. 1591.

111. For the best concise summary of the evidence on Filipino fatalities during Chaffee's tenure, see Luzviminda Francisco, "The Philippine-American War," in Daniel B. Schirmer and Stephen Rosskamm Shalom, eds., *The Philippines Reader: A History of Colonialism, Neocolonialism, Dictatorship, and Resistance* (Boston: South End Press, 1987) p. 19.

112. On the appointments of both Chaffee and Bell, see Miller, *"Benevolent Assimilation"*, p. 260.

113. Quoted in ibid., pp. 250-1.

114. Senate, *Hearings on the Philippines*, pp. 867-8.

115. See William Stanton, *The Leopard's Spots: Scientific Attitudes Towards Race in America, 1815-1859* (Chicago: University of Chicago Press, 1960); Stephen Jay Gould, *The Mismeasure of Man* (New York: W.W. Norton, 1981).

116. An excellent overview of such thinking, and its effects on U.S. policy formation, will be found in Reginald Horsman, *Race and Manifest Destiny: The Origins of American Racial Anglo-Saxonism* (Cambridge, MA: Harvard University Press, 1981).

117. This is not to argue that such dynamics and sensibilities are in any way unique to the United States. For examination of analogous contexts, see, e.g., Sven Lindquist, *"Exterminate All the Brutes": One Man's Odyssey into the Heart of Darkness and the Origins of European Genocide* (New York: New Press, 1996).

118. Lieber Code, Article 25.

119. Hoyt, *America's Wars*.

120. For an excellent handing of the mythic aspects attending this continuity, see Slotkin, *Gunfighter Nation*, pp. 313-43, 441-86.

121. There were, of course, exceptions to this, mainly associated with the strategic bombing campaign against Germany. Probably the most notorious illustration was the incendiary attack on Dresden on the night of Feb. 13, 1945, inflicting an estimated 150,000 civilian casualties; G.E. Hopkins, "Bombing and the American Conscience in World War II," *Historian*, No. XXVIII, 1966.

122. Quoted in John W. Dower, *War Without Mercy: Race and Power in the Pacific War* (New York: Pantheon, 1986) p. 64.

123. Stannard, *American Holocaust*, p. 252.

124. Dower, *War Without Mercy*, pp. 64–5.

125. Ronald Takaki, *Iron Cages: Race and Culture in 19th-Century America* (New York: Alfred A. Knopf, 1979) p. 96. Other examples are offered in Dower, *War Without Mercy*.

126. Stannard, *American Holocaust*, p. 252.

127. See note 3.

128. "It was known that the Japanese had instructed their ambassador in Moscow to work on peace negotiations with the Allies. Japanese leaders had begun talking of surrender a year before this"; Howard Zinn, *A People's History of the United States* (New York: Harper & Row, 1980) pp. 413–5.

129. "The [official] justification for these atrocities was that this would end the war quickly, making unnecessary an invasion of Japan. Such an invasion would cost a huge number of lives, the government said—a million, according to Secretary of State [James F.] Byrnes; a half-million, Truman claimed was the figure given him by General George Marshall. . . These estimates of losses . . . seemed to be pulled out of the air to justify bombings"; ibid., p. 413. Also see Ronald Takaki, *Hiroshima: Why America Dropped the Atomic Bomb* (Boston: Little, Brown, 1995); Gar Alperovitz. *The Decision to Drop the Bomb* (New York: Alfred A. Knopf, 1995).

130. As many as 130,000 people died in the Tokyo incendiary bombing alone. The longterm toll of the Hiroshima and Nagasaki bombings are estimated as being 200,000 and 240,000, respectively; Lifton and Markusen, *The Genocidal Mentality*, pp. 21, 24.

131. Quoted in Drinnon, *Facing West*, p. 331.

132. Ibid.

133. "On July 13, [1945,] Foreign Minister Shigenori Togo had wired his ambassador in Moscow: 'Unconditional surrender is the only obstacle to peace. . .' If only the Americans had not insisted on unconditional surrender—that is, if they were willing to accept one condition to surrender, that the Emperor, a holy figure to the Japanese, remain in place [a stipulation the U.S. later decided was in its own interests in any event]—the Japanese would have agreed to stop the war"; Zinn, *People's History*, p. 415.

134. Quoted in Noam Chomsky, " 'What We Say Goes': The Middle East in the New World Order," in Cynthia Peters, ed., *Collateral Damage: The "New World Order" at Home and Abroad* (Boston: South End Press, 1992) p. 52.

135. "Modernizing Turner: The Ideology of the New Frontier," in Slotkin, *Gunfighter Nation*, pp. 491–7.

136. Consider, for example, the performance of the U.S.-backed military junta headed by General Suharto in Indonesia, which, after overthrowing the populist President Sukarno in 1965, exterminated at least 500,000 peasant "communists" while establishing a "business-friendly climate" in the region; Noam Chomsky and Edward S. Herman, *The Political Economy of Human Rights, Vol. 1: The Washington Connection and Third World Fascism* (Boston: South End Press, 1979) pp. 205–17.

137. The characterization is of the Vietnamese, by President Lyndon B. Johnson, also known to refer to their homeland as a "damn little pissant country"; quoted in Stanley Karnow, *Vietnam: A History* (New York: Viking Press, 1983) p. 395.

138. This is true in respects well beyond the use of tactics violating the Laws of War. A classic example is that of the U.S. sabotage of the 1954 Geneva Peace Accords calling for the reunification of Vietnam two years later. In the process, it violated not only the accords, but the United Nations Charter and several other elements of international legality; Ralph Stavins, Richard J. Barnet and Marcus G. Raskin, *Washington Plans an Aggressive War* (New York: Random House, 1971) pp. 3–18. Also see Quincy Wright, "Legal Aspects of the Vietnam Situation," in Richard Falk, ed., *The Vietnam War and International Law* (Princeton, NJ: Princeton University Press, 1968) pp. 271–91.

139. I.F. Stone, *The Hidden History of the Korean War, 1950-1951* (Boston: Little, Brown, [2nd ed.] 1988).

140. Michael MacClear, *The Ten Thousand Day War: Vietnam, 1945-1975* (New York: St. Martin's Press, 1981); Noam Chomsky, *At War with Asia* (New York: Pantheon, 1970).

141. The point of this "Civic Action Program" was to "deprive the enemy of the his strategic base" by forcibly driving the entire rural population into "protected hamlets," most often by employing "air and artillery to terrorize the peasantry and raze the countryside"; Neil Sheehan, "Should We Have War Crimes Trials?" *New York Times*, Mar, 28, 1971.

142. Stockholm International Peace Research Institute (Malvern Lumsden), *Incendiary Weapons* (Stockholm/Cambridge, MA: Almquist & Wiksell International/MIT Press, 1975) pp. 49-63.

143. In the area around the Marine base at Khe Sanh alone, "we delivered more than 110,000 tons of bombs [in] eleven weeks . . . the greatest volume of explosives in the history of warfare"; Michael Herr, *Dispatches* (New York: Alfred A, Knopf, 1978) p. 153.

144. Noam Chomsky, *For Reasons of State* (New York: Vintage, 1973) pp. 172-6, 180-4, 187-90, 227-8.

145. Like the M-16 rifle, this type of ordnance was designed to effect technical compliance with, while achieving practical circumvention of, an unbroken line of black letter international law dating from the 1899 Hague Declaration 3 Concerning Expanding Bullets, all of it intended to prohibit the use of weapons inflicting wounds of "exceptional cruelty"; Roberts and Guelff, *Documents on the Laws of War*, pp. 39-42.

146. Barry Weisberg, *Ecocide in Indochina: The Ecology of War* (San Francisco: Canfield Press, 1970).

147. Karnow, *Vietnam*, pp. 17, 18, 480, 512.

148. Quoted in Drinnon, *Facing West*, p. 369.

149. Quoted in Francis Fitzgerald, *Fire in the Lake: The Vietnamese and the Americans in Vietnam* (New York: Vintage, 1973) p. 460.

150. Quotes in Drinnon, *Facing West*, p. 451; Karnow, *Vietnam*, p. 325.

151. Ibid.; Chomsky, *Reasons of State*, p. 120. Also see Citizen's Commission of Inquiry, *The Dellums Committee Hearings on War Crimes in Vietnam* (New York: Vintage, 1972) p. 52.

152. Testimony of International Voluntary Service Director Hugh Manke before Congress, 1971; quoted in Drinnon, *Facing West*, p. 449.

153. The term "gook" has been wrongly classified as an American corruption of a Korean word originating during the early 1950s. In actuality, it is a racial epithet invented much earlier to describe Haitians. According to the July 10, 1920, issue of the *Nation*, "officers wearing the United States uniform in the interior of Haiti talk of 'bumping off' (i.e., killing) 'Gooks' as if it were a variety of sport like duck hunting"; see the chapter entitled "Of Gooks and Men" in Robert Jay Lifton's *Home From the War* (New York: Simon and Schuster, 1973) pp. 189-216.

154. Unidentified junior officer from the Americal Division, quoted in the *New York Times*, Mar. 10, 1970. Also see Sheehan, "War Crimes"; Lifton, *Home From the War*, pp. 189-216; Drinnon, *Facing West*, p. 455; Chomsky, *Reasons of State*, p. 224; R.W. Apple, "The Real Guilt," *New Statesman*, Apr. 2, 1971, p. 34.

155. Both quotes come from Joseph Strick's 1971 documentary, *Interviews with My Lai Veterans*. Also see Lifton, *Home From the War*, p. 47; Charles Levy, *Spoils of War* (Boston: Houghton-Mifflin, 1974) p. 26.

156. Quoted in Drinnon, *Facing West*, p. 457.

157. One hundred similar testimonies were read into the *Congressional Record* by Senator Mark O. Hatfield on April 6 and 7, 1971 (Vol. CXVII, pp. 2825-900, 2903-36). The same material was subsequently published as a book; Vietnam Veterans Against the War, *The Winter Soldier Investigation: An Inquiry into American War Crimes* (Boston: Beacon Press, 1972). Also see Citizen's Commission of Inquiry, *Dellums Hearings*.

158. Strick, *Interviews with My Lai Veterans*.

159. Hatfield, *Congressional Record*, p. 2928.

160. Drinnon, *Facing West*, p. 451.

161. Quoted in the *New York Times*, Mar, 31, 1971. Also see John Sack, *Lieutenant Calley: His Own Story* (New York: Viking, 1971) pp. 31, 104-5. The term "Oriental human beings" was used by the Army

in Calley's charge sheet; Seymour M. Hersh, *My Lai 4: A Report on the Massacre and Its Aftermath* (New York: Random House, 1970) p. 125.

162. Drinnon, *Facing West*, p. 451; also see Chomsky, *At War with Asia*, pp. 81-2.

163. Joseph Goldstein, Burke Marshall and Jack Schwartz, *The My Lai Massacre and Its Cover-Up: Beyond the Reach of the Law?* (New York: Free Press, 1976) p. 47. This book contains the text of the Army's official report on My Lai, otherwise known as the "Peers Report" (see note 172, below). Citations of/quotations from that report will therefore be made from the volume cited here.

164. Quoted in Drinnon, *Facing West*, p. 451.

165. Goldstein, Marshall and Schwartz, *My Lai Massacre*, p. 56.

166. One concern was with the mounting toll of American casualties (though never much with the millions of slaughtered Asians). Another was with the sheer fiscal cost of waging a protracted, high-tech war; see Paul Joseph, *Cracks in the Empire: State Politics in the Vietnam War* (Boston: South End Press, 1981).

167. Reproduced in Goldstein, Marshall and Schwartz, *My Lai Massacre*, pp. 34-7.

168. Ridenhour began to put out feelers through an agent in June 1969. *Life*, *Look*, *Harper's* and *Newsweek* magazines all expressed no interest in the story. Only the left-leaning *Ramparts* responded favorably; Hersh, *My Lai 4*, p. 115.

169. Ibid. p. 133.

170. Ibid., pp. 134-5. *Life* and *Look* were still not interested.

171. U.S. House of Representatives, Committee on the Armed Services, *Report on the My Lai Incident* (Washington, D.C.: 91st Cong., 2nd Sess., July 15, 1970); usually referred to as the "Hébert Committee Report," after Representative F. Edward Hébert, who chaired the subcommittee that prepared it. For analysis, see Seymour M. Hersh, *Cover-Up* (New York: Random House, 1972).

172. Lt. Gen. William Peers, et al., *Report of the Department of the Army Review of Preliminary Investigations into the My Lai Incident*, 3 vols. (Washington, D.C.: U.S. Dept. of the Army, No. 13, 1974).

173. House of Representatives, *Report on My Lai*, quoted in Drinnon, *Facing West*, p. 452.

174. Years later, "Westy" would still claim, all evidence to the contrary notwithstanding, that everything that had happened "on his watch" in Vietnam would measure up "before the bar of justice and the court of history"; William Westmoreland, *A Soldier Reports* (Garden City, NY: Doubleday, 1976) p. 379.

175. Goldstein, Marshall and Schwartz, *My Lai Massacre*, pp. 3-4.

176. Koster was also demoted to brigadier general (for purposes of computing his retirement pay), and stripped of his Distinguished Service Medal (he kept the rest, including, presumably, his Good Conduct Medal); ibid., pp. ix-x.

177. Ibid.

178. Hersh, *My Lai 4*, pp. 40-3.

179. Goldstein, Marshall and Schwartz, *My Lai Massacre*, pp. x, 465-7.

180. Three members of Koster's staff—Brig. Gen. Young, Col. Johnson, and Maj. Johnson—were each stripped of a medal and reprimanded, but all remained on active duty; ibid., pp. ix-x.

181. See generally, Sack, *Lieutenant Calley*.

182. Quoted in Chomsky, *Reasons of State*, p. 222.

183. Hersh, *My Lai 4*, p. 177.

184. Drinnon, *Facing West*, pp. 452-3. Also see Seymour M. Hersh, "The Army's Secret Inquiry Describes a 2nd Massacre, Involving 90 Civilians," *New York Times*, June 5, 1972.

185. Chomsky, *For Reasons of State*, p. xx.

187. Willingham had been a lieutenant when the massacre occurred; Hersh, *My Lai 4*, pp. 177-8.

188. Goldstein, Marshall and Schwartz, *My Lai Massacre*, p. ix.

188. For background, see Hersh, *Cover-Up*.

189. Chomsky and Herman, *Washington Connection*, p. 318; quoting from Earl S. Martin, *Reaching the Other Side* (New York: Crown, 1978) p. 133.

190. Citizens Commission of Inquiry, *Dellums Hearings*, pp. 188-9.

191. Chomsky and Herman, *Washington Connection*, p. 318.

192. See note 157.

193. Chomsky, *For Reasons of State*, p. 122. The troops were paid for with supplements to the annual aid package the U.S. awarded its South Korean client régime ($134 million in 1973, for example); Chomsky and Herman, *Washington Connection*, p. 322.

194. Robert M. Smith, "Vietnam Killings Laid to Koreans," *New York Times*, Jan. 10, 1970.

195. Chomsky and Herman, *Washington Connection*, pp. 321-2.

196. See, e.g., Alex Carey, *Australian Atrocities in Vietnam* (Sydney: self-published, 1968).

197. Chomsky and Herman, *Washington Connection*, p. 321. To illustrate, consider that Vernado Simpson, one of the soldiers quoted earlier (see note 158), admitted he'd personally "killed eight or ten Vietnamese civilians on March 16, 1968"; Hersh, *My Lai 4*, pp. 179-80.

198. "Many officers stalked Vietnamese in the free fire zones from the air, shooting at anyone who moved below"; ibid., p. 9. Also see the testimony of former helicopter gunship pilot David Bessum in Citizens Commission of Inquiry, *Dellums Hearings*, pp. 282-94.

199. Ibid., pp. 60-1, 96-7, 190, 205, 213, 266-9.

200. Hersh, *My Lai 4*, p. 9.

201. Kevin Buckley, "Pacification's Deadly Price," *Newsweek*, June 19, 1972; quoted in Chomsky and Herman, *Washington Connection*, pp. 314-5.

202. Ibid., p. 316.

203. Ibid., p. 317.

204. "The Colonel Speaking of His Men," excerpts from an interview on WABC-TV (New York), in Mitchell Goodman, ed., *Movement Towards a New America* (Philadelphia/New York: Pilgrim Press/Alfred A. Knopf, 1970) p. 625.

205. Quoted in Hersh, *My Lai 4*, p. 9. On the operations of Patton's 11th Armored Cavalry Regiment, see Citizens Commission of Inquiry, *Dellums Hearings*, pp. 143-56.

206. Hersh, *My Lai 4*, pp. 9-10.

207. Chomsky and Herman, *Washington Connection*, p. 319.

208. Leroy Thompson, *Elite Unit Insignia of the Vietnam War* (London: Arms and Armour Press, 1986).

209. Herr, *Dispatches*, pp. 34-5, 198-9; also see the photo in Goodman, *Movement*, p. 315.

210. Buckley, quoted in Chomsky and Herman, *Washington Connection*, p. 314.

211. The estimate was offered during a 1996 interview of former Defense Secretary Robert S. McNamara by Charlie Rose; also see McNamara's *In Retrospect: The Tragedy and Lessons of Vietnam* (New York: Vintage, 1996).

212. Drinnon, *Facing West*, pp. 454-5. On Apr. 7, 1971, the *New York Times* reported that the Army claimed there had been a total of 81 soldiers prosecuted for murder as a result of their actions in Vietnam. Of these, 38 were said to have been convicted of the main charge(s), 20 of lesser charges, and 23 acquitted. Of those convicted of murder, however, it turned out that 27 had been charged with killing other Americans. Of the 11 convicted of murdering Vietnamese, none was charged with participation in a My Lai-type incident, and, as with Duffy, all were bestowed with a postconviction "revision" of the offense/reduced sentence.

213. Peers Report, in Goldstein, Marshall and Burke, *My Lai Massacre*, p. 207. The formulation referenced is *Field Manual 27-10: The Law of Land Warfare* (Washington, D.C.: U.S. Dept. of the Army, 1956).

214. Ibid. The full text of the 1907 Hague Convention IV will be found in Roberts and Guelff, *Documents on the Laws of War*, pp. 43-59.

215. Peers Report, in Goldstein, Marshall and Burke, *My Lai Massacre*, p. 207. The texts of four 1949 Geneva Conventions will be found in Roberts and Guelff, *Documents on the Laws of War*, pp. 169-337. Of particular relevance are the 1949 Geneva Convention III Relative to Treatment of Prisoners of War (pp. 215-270) and the 1949 Geneva Convention IV Relative to the Protection of Civilian Persons in Times of War (pp. 271-37).

216. Peers Report, in Goldstein, Marshall and Burke, *My Lai Massacre*, pp. 207-8.

217. Agreement for the Prosecution and Punishment of the Major War Criminals of the European Axis Powers and Charter of the International Military Tribunal (Aug. 8, 1945); text in Burns H. Weston, Richard A. Falk and Anthony D'Amato, eds., *Basic Documents in International Law and World Order* (St. Paul, MN: West, 1990) pp. 138-9, quote at 138.

218. Peers Report, in Goldstein, Marshall and Burke, *My Lai Massacre*, pp. 208-9.

219. See note 141. For further background, see Robert L. Gallucci, *Neither Peace nor Honor: The Politics of American Military Policy in Vietnam* (Baltimore: Johns Hopkins University Press, 1975); Neil Sheehan, *A Bright Shining Lie: John Paul Vann and America in Vietnam* (New York: Random House, 1988).

220. This goes to the oft-stated contention that where infliction of civilian casualties is not a specifically articulated policy objective—or the express goal of particular applications of tactics—they must be considered "inadvertent" and therefore not a matter of criminal culpability. Such reasoning has no basis in law (or common sense). The policies and/or tactical expedients at issue are prohibited because it is understood a priori that, if they are pursued, civilian casualties will *inevitably* result. There can thus be nothing inadvertent in their infliction. Hence, the Laws of War offer no legitimate exception(s) to compliance; see generally, Sydney Bailey, *Prohibitions and Restraints in War* (New York: Oxford University Press, 1972).

221. Roberts and Guelff, *Documents on the Laws of War*, p. 53.

222. Text, ibid., pp. 123-35; article cited at p. 126.

223. Ibid., p. 273.

224. Buckley, quoted in Chomsky and Herman, *Washington Connection*, p. 314.

225. Ibid. On miniguns, see Herr, *Dispatches*, pp. 132-3.

226. Buckley, quoted in Chomsky and Herman, *Washington Connection*, p. 314.

227. Arclight missions "usually involved a three-ship 'cell,' bombing in close trail to saturate a target 'box' roughly one kilometer wide and three kilometers long [with overlapping craters made by 500 pound bombs]. Bombing from above 30,000 feet, the B-52s could be neither seen nor heard by" anyone below; Drew Middleton, *Air War—Vietnam* (New York: Arno Press, 1978) p. 201. Also see the photos of B-52s dropping their "payload and of bombs detonating in an Arclight box pattern at pp. 180-81.

228. Buckley, quoted in Chomsky and Herman, *Washington Connection*, p. 314.

229. Along with support units, this added up to over 525,000 men in 1968. See generally, Karnow, *Vietnam*; Shelby L. Stanton, *Vietnam Order of Battle* (Washington, D.C.: U.S. News Books, MCMLXXXI).

230. Chomsky and Herman, *Washington Connection*, pp. 311-2.

231. Noam Chomsky and Edward S. Herman, *The Political Economy of Human Rights, Vol. II: Postwar Indochina and the Reconstruction of Imperial Ideology* (Boston: South End Press, 1979) pp. 66-7.

232. Hugh Toye, *Laos: Buffer State or Battleground?* (London: Oxford University Press, 1968).

233. "It is a region that has had, by conservative estimate, more than two million tons of bombs dropped on it"; Citizens Commission of Inquiry, *Dellums Hearings*, p. 311.

234. Fred Branfman, "Presidential War in Laos, 1964-1970," in Nina S. Adams and Alfred W. McCoy, eds., *Laos: War and Revolution* (New York: Harper & Row, 1970) pp. 233-4.

235. Most of the B-52 strikes were conducted along the Truong Son supply route—known by Americans as the "Ho Chi Minh Trail"—in the Laotian panhandle; see the photographs in John L. Plaster, *SOG: A Photo History of the Secret Wars* (Boulder, CO: Paladin Press, 2000) pp. 53, 58, 67.

236. Branfman, "Presidential War," p. 233.

237. Quoted in Chomsky, *For Reasons of State*, p. 176.

238. Quoted in ibid., p. 175.

239. Quoted in Citizens Commission of Inquiry, *Dellums Hearings*, p. 314.

240. Ibid. Also see U.S. Senate, Committee on Foreign Relations, *United States Security Agreements and Commitments Abroad: The Kingdom of Laos* (Washington, D.C.: 91$^{st}$ Cong., 2d Sess., Oct. 20-22, 1969).

241. Citizens Commission of Inquiry, *Dellums Hearings*, p. 313.

242. On civilian casualties; *New York Times*, Aug. 24, 1975. On destruction of "infrastructure"; Citizens Commission of Inquiry, *Dellums Hearings*, p. 313 (quoting Robert Shaplen, *Foreign Affairs*, Apr. 1970).

243. U.S. Joint Chiefs of Staff, quoted in William Shawcross, *Sideshow: Kissinger, Nixon and the Bombing of Cambodia* (New York: Simon and Schuster, 1979) pp. 272-3.

244. Ibid., 272.

245. This is according to maps prepared for a classified history of the B-52 campaign by the U.S. Air Force; ibid., p. 272.

246. Thus deprived of their livestock, the peasants were reduced to working as "human buffaloes" in a desperate effort to plow what fields they had left; *New York Times*, June 14, 1976.

247. Chomsky and Herman, *Postwar Indochina*, p. 165. The higher estimate was confirmed as "close" by U.S. State Department official Timothy Carney in 1976; ibid., p. 173.

248. Ibid., pp. 73-7, 128-34, 160-3; David Dellinger, *Vietnam Revisited: Covert Action to Invasion to Reconstruction* (Boston: South End Press, 1986) pp. 166-90.

249. Westmoreland has gone on record saying that the United States "won the war" because the whole Indochina remains a "basketcase"; *Boston Globe*, Mar. 14, 1991. Overall, see Chomsky and Herman, *Postwar Indochina*.

250. Robert L. Mole, *The Montagnards of South Vietnam: A Study of Nine Tribes* (Rutland, VT: Charles E. Tuttle, 1970). On the fate of the Hmong, see Chomsky and Herman, *Postwar Indochina*, pp. 119-26.

251. The original quote was "we had to destroy the town in order to save it"; Herr, *Dispatches*, p. 71. Also see Clark Dougan and David Fulghum, eds., *The Vietnam Experience: Nineteen Sixty-Eight* (Boston: Boston Publishing Co., 1983) p. 21.

252. Bertrand Russell, *War Crimes in Vietnam* (New York: Monthly Review Press, 1967).

253. John Duffett, ed., *Against the Crime of Silence: Proceedings of the International War Crimes Tribunal* (New York: Clarion, 1970).

254. See, e.g., Judith Coburn and Geoffrey Cowan, "The War Criminals Hedge Their Bets," *Village Voice*, Dec. 4, 1969.

255. Telford Taylor, *Nuremberg and Vietnam: An American Tragedy* (Chicago: Quadrangle, 1970) p. 169.

256. Statement made on television talk show; quoted in Drinnon, *Facing West*, p. 550.

257. The other participating powers—Great Britain, France and the USSR—actually opposed the Nuremberg procedure. Winston Churchill and John A. Simon, respectively the English prime minister and lord chancellor, argued strongly for summary execution of the nazi leaders rather than risking the establishment of legal precedents at trial; Bradley F. Smith, *The Road to Nuremberg* (New York: Basic Books, 1981) pp. 45-7.

258. Robert H. Jackson, "Opening Statement for the United States before the International Military Tribunal, November 21, 1945," in Jay W. Baird, ed., *From Nuremberg to My Lai* (Lexington, MA: D.C. Heath, 1972) p. 28.

259. Justice Jackson, quoted in Russell, *War Crimes*, p. 125.

260. See, e.g., Townsend Hoopes, "The Nuremberg Suggestion," *Washington Monthly*, Jan. 1970.

261. Hoopes, quoted in Coburn and Cowan, "War Criminals."

262. Nimitz's order in fact "went far beyond the German one"; Davidson, *Trial of the Germans*, p. 421. Nonetheless, it was the U.S. alternate on the tribunal, John J. Parker, who proved most insistent that Dönitz be convicted; Bradley F. Smith, *Reaching Judgement at Nuremberg* (New York: Basic Books, 1977) pp. 260-1.

263. Robert E. Conot, *Justice at Nuremberg* (New York: Harper & Row, 1983) pp. 493-4. On Dresden, see note 121. On Hamburg, see Robert Sherry, *The Rise of American Air Power: The Creation of Armageddon* (New Haven, CT: Yale University Press, 1986) pp. 152-5.

264. Arnold C. Brackman, *The Other Nuremberg: The Untold Story of the Tokyo War Crimes Trials* (New York: Quill, 1987).

265. Ibid., pp. 409-12.

266. Ibid., p 51. Also see A. Frank Reel, *The Case of General Yamashita* (Chicago: University of Chicago Press, 1949).

267. Yamashita was accused of responsibility in the murders of 131,028 POWs and noncombatant Filipinos; Brackman, *Other Nuremberg*, p. 244. Without diminishing the significance of these deaths in any way, they should be compared to the 616,000 tallied by J. Franklin Bell in 1902 (see note 95).

268. See, e.g., George S. Andrew. Jr., "The 41st Didn't Take Prisoners," *Saturday Evening Post*, July 27, 1946. Also see Dower, *War Without Mercy*, pp. 60-71.

269. Denis Warner and Peggy Warner, *The Sacred Warriors: Japan's Suicide Legions* (New York: Avon, 1982) pp. xi, 36.

270. William Manchester, *Goodbye, Darkness: A Memoir of the Pacific War* (New York, Dell, 1980) p. 439.

271. John Alan Appleman, *Military Tribunals and International Crimes* (Westport, CT: Greenwood Press, 1954) pp. 267-89.

272. Michael Reynolds, *The Devil's Adjutant: Jochen Peiper, Panzer Leader* (New York: Sarpedon, 1995) pp. 92, 252-9.

273. Slicing open the cheeks of wounded Japanese and prying out their gold teeth with K-bar knives, for example; E.B. Sledge, *With the Old Breed at Peleliu and Okinawa* (San Francisco: Presidio Press, 1981) p. 120.

274. Drinnon, *Facing West*, pp. 316, 320; Miller, *"Benevolent Assimilation"*, pp. 225-6, 250-1.

275. Citizens Commission of Inquiry, *Dellums Hearings*, pp. 83-156.

276. On the war and its causes, see Dee Brown, *Bury My Heart at Wounded Knee: An Indian History of the American West* (New York: Macmillan, 1970) pp. 37-65.

277. The Indians whose death sentences were overturned were not freed. Lincoln merely commuted there punishments to varying terms of imprisonment; Sidney L. Harring, *Crow Dog's Case: American Indian Sovereignty, Tribal Law, and United States Law in the Nineteenth Century* (Cambridge, UK: Cambridge University Press, 1994) p. 262.

278. Brown, *Wounded Knee*, pp. 60, 63-4.

279. Harring, *Crow Dog's Case*, p. 262.

280. Michael Lieder and Jake Page, *Wild Justice: The People of Geronimo vs. the United States* (New York: Random House, 1997).

281. Lonnie R. Speer, *Portals to Hell: Military Prisons in the Civil War* (Mechanicsburg, PA: Stackpole Books, 1997) pp. 291-2.

282. See generally, Trafzer, *Kit Carson Campaign*; Lynn R. Baily, *The Long Walk* (Los Angeles: Westernlore, 1964); Lawrence C. Kelly, *Navajo Roundup* (Boulder, CO: Pruett, 1970).

283. Roberto Mario Salmon, "The Disease Complaint at Bosque Redondo (1864-1868)," *Indian Historian*, No. 9, 1976; Gerald Thompson, *The Army and the Navajo: The Bosque Redondo Reservation Experiment, 1863-1868* (Tucson: University of Arizona Press, 1982).

284. The death rate at Dachau was 36 percent, at Buchenwald, 19 percent; Michael Burleigh, *Ethics and Extermination: Reflections on the Nazi Genocide* (Cambridge, UK: Cambridge University Press, 1997) pp. 210-1.

285. See Noam Chomsky, *Rogue States: The Rule of Force in World Affairs* (Cambridge, MA: South End Press, 2000).

286. See note 173.

287. U.S. Army, *Laws of Land Warfare* (see note 213).

288. Citizens Commission of Inquiry, *Dellums Hearings*, p. 267.

289. Ibid., p. 41.

290. Ibid., p. 329.

291. Ibid., p. 295.

292. Ibid., pp. 60, 62.

293. Ibid., p. 107.

294. Ibid., pp. 295, 304 .

295. See generally, Robert Sherrill, *Military Justice is to Justice as Military Music is to Music* (New York: Harper & Row, 1970).

296. Andrew Kopkind, "Doctor's Plot" and "The Trial of Captain Levy II," both in his *The Thirty Years' Wars: Dispatches and Diversions of a Radical Journalist, 1965-1994* (London: Verso, 1995) pp. 72-82, 104-11.

297. Kopkind, "Levy Trial II," p. 110.

298. Ibid., pp. 109-10.

299. Dennis Mora, David Samas and James Johnson, "The Fort Hood Three: The Case of Three GIs Who Said "No" to the War in Vietnam," in Judith Claire Albert and Stewart Edward Albert, eds., *The Sixties Papers: Documents of a Rebellious Decade* (New York: Praeger, 1984) p. 303.

300. Kopkind, "Levy Trial II," p. 109.

301. See Sherrill, *Military Justice*.

302. Anthony B. Herbert with James T. Wooten, *Soldier* (New York: Holt, Rinehart and Winston, 1973).

303. Citizens Commission of Inquiry, *Dellums Hearings*, pp. 83-4.

304. Ibid., pp. 154-5.

305. Fred J. Cook, "Justice in Gainesville," *The Nation*, Oct. 1, 1973; Sanford J. Ungar, *FBI* (Boston: Little, Brown, 1976) pp. 483-4, 504.

306. Athan Theoharis, *Spying on Americans: Political Surveillance from Hoover to the Huston Plan* (Philadelphia: Temple University Press, 1978) pp. 120-1, 124-5, 178-9.

307. Editors, "From the Citizens Commission to Investigate the FBI," *Win*, Vol. VIII, Nos. 4-5, Mar. 1/15, 1972, p. 9. Also see my and Jim Vander Wall's *Agents of Repression: The FBI's Secret Wars Against the Black Panther Party and the American Indian Movement* (Boston: South End Press, 1988) pp. 395-6.

308. Officially, there were 65,643 desertions from the Army alone in 1970, a half-million from all services during the years 1967-72. Army intelligence estimated that some sixty per week were actually "crossing over to the other side" in Vietnam by early 1971; George Katsiaficas, *The Imagination of the New Left: A Global Analysis of 1968* (Boston: South End Press, 1987) p. 141; H. Bruce Franklin, *M.I.A., or, Mythmaking in America* (Chicago: Lawrence Hill, 1992) pp. 23-4.

309. Kopkind, "Levy Trial II," p. 109.

310. Citizens Commission of Inquiry, *Dellums Hearings*, pp. 245-6.

311. Ibid., p. 37.

312. Ibid.

313. Representative Parren J. Mitchell; ibid., pp. 118-9.

314. On Soule's performance at Sand Creek, see note 58. On his murder, see Hoig, *Sand Creek Massacre*, p. 172.

315. Full text will be found in Roberts and Guelff, *Laws of War*, pp. 377-85.

316. The issues also included cloud seeding, the saturation or "carpet" bombing of rural areas, and other such techniques employed by the U.S.; see Weisberg, *Ecocide in Indochina*, esp. pp. 17-32, 49-63. Also see Thomas Whiteside, *The Withering Rain: America's Herbicidal Folly* (New York: Dutton, 1971); John Dux and P.J. Young, *Agent Orange: The Bitter Harvest* (Sydney: Hodder and Stoughton, 1980).

317. Full text of Additional Protocol I will be found in Roberts and Guelff, *Laws of War*, pp. 387-446; Additional Protocol II at pp. 447-64. The language quoted accrues from Additional Protocol I, Article 51, Section 5, Clauses a and b; it will be found at p. 416.

318. Ibid., Additional Protocol I, Article 54, Section 2, at p. 417.

319. Full text will be found in ibid., pp. 465-6.

320. Full text will be found in ibid., pp. 467-82.

321. Ibid., p. 475. On the weaponry, see note 145.

322. "This was particularly so during the periods of active engagement of U.S. ground, sea and air forces from 1961-1973," with an emphasis on napalm and white phosphorous munitions; SIPRI, *Incendiary Weapons*, pp. 49-50.

323. Roberts and Guelff, *Laws of War*, p. 481.

324. *Field Manual 31-12: The Law of Land Warfare* (Washington, D.C.: U.S. Dept. of the Army, 1984).

325. Quoted in George Cheney, " 'Talking War': Symbols, Strategies and Images," *New Studies on the Left*, Vol. XIV, No. 3, Winter 1990-91. On the concept involved, see Michael Walzer, *Just and Unjust Wars: A Moral Argument with Illustrations* (London: Allen Lane, 1978).

326. Kuwait was first demarcated for administrative separation from Iraq, then called Mesopotamia and under Ottoman rule, by the British, in its 1916 Sykes-Picot Treaty with France. Following the defeat of the Ottomans in World War I, the partition was "finalized" by the League of Nations, with boundaries being "set" in 1922. Iraq, however, never agreed to the arrangement and began pressing claims for a formal restoration of its territory, beginning with its independence from British "protectorate" status in 1932; Joe Stork and Ann M. Lesch, "Why War?", in Peters, *Collateral Damage*, pp. 161-2.

327. Holly Sklar, "Brave New World Order," in Peters, *Collateral Damage*, p. 8.

328. Erika Munck, "The New Face of Techno-War," *The Nation*, May 6, 1991.

329. There were 49 such graves filled with what may in fact have been "hundreds of thousands" of Iraqi casualties. The Pentagon has refused to meet its legal obligation to inform the Red Cross as to their location; Ramsey Clark, et al., *War Crimes: A Report on United States War Crimes Against Iraq* (Washington, D.C.: Maisonneuve Press, 1992) pp. 3, 17, 89. On use of the term "Sand Niggers," see Sklar, "New World Order," p. 8.

330. "U.S. soldiers practiced for months techniques for burying alive Iraqi soldiers"; Clark, *War Crimes*, p. 35. Patrick J. Sloyan, "U.S. Officers Say Iraqis Were Buried Alive," *San Francisco Chronicle*, Sept. 12, 1991.

331. Sklar, "New World Order," p. 15.

332. The first Iraqi attempt was made on Aug. 12, 1990, and such efforts continued into mid-Feb. 1991; Clark, *War Crimes*, p. 13. Also see Michael Emry, "How the U.S. Avoided the Peace," *Village Voice*, Mar. 5, 1991.

333. These were articulated in United Nations Security Council Resolution 660, which Iraq formally accepted on Feb. 21, 1991; Clark, *War Crimes*, p. 91.

334. Ibid., p. 91.

335. Rowan Scarborough, "Pool Report Aboard the USS Blue Ridge," *Washington Times*, Feb. 27, 1991; William M. Arkin, Damian Durrant and Marianne Cherni, *On Impact: Modern Warfare and the Environment—A Case Study of the Gulf War* (Washington, D.C.: Greenpeace, May 1991) pp. 105-15.

336. "Persons taking no active part in the hostilities, including soldiers who have laid down their arms, and those placed *hors de combat* [by] any cause, shall in all circumstances be treated humanely"; Roberts and Guelff, *Laws of War*, pp. 195, 217, 273.

337. Quoted in Clark, *War Crimes*, p. 91.

338. Actually, the posture had been assumed rather earlier; Edward Cody, "U.S. Briefers Concede No Quarter," *Washington Post*, Feb. 14, 1991.

339. Article 23 (d) of the 1907 Hague Convention states that "it is especially forbidden. . . To declare that no quarter will be given"; Roberts and Guelff, *Laws of War*, p. 52. On the 1864 Geneva Convention, see note 39.

340. Quoted in Arkin, Durrant and Cherni, *On Impact*, p. 109.

341. Clark, *War Crimes*, pp. 50-1.

342. Ibid., pp. 51, 90-3.

343. Randall Richard of the *Providence Journal*, quoted in ibid., p. 91.

344. Clark, *War Crimes*, p. 92. Also see "Trapped in the Killing Ground at Mutlaa," *Manchester Guardian Weekly*, Mar. 17, 1991; Michael Kelly, "Highway to Hell," *New Republic*, Apr. 1991.

345. Clark, *War Crimes*, pp. 17.

346. Ibid., p. 30, citing Patrick J. Sloyan, "Massive Battle After Cease Fire," *New York Newsday*, May 8, 1991. Also see Sloyan's "War's Fiercest Ground Battle Was After Cease Fire," *Oakland Tribune*, May 8, 1991.

347. Quoted in Patrick J. Sloyan, "Pullback a Bloody Mismatch: Route of Iraqis Became Savage 'Turkey Shoot'," *New York Newsday*, Mar. 31, 1991.

348. Arkin, Durrant and Cherni, *On Impact*, p. 112.

349. Clark, *War Crimes*, p. 17.

350. Quoted in Sklar, "New World Order," pp. 11-2.

351. Interview, radio station WBAI, New York, May 1991.

352. Clark, *War Crimes*, pp. 14, 17-8, 20, 85; Arkin, Durrant and Cherni, *On Impact*, p. 160n377.

353. Upwards of 3,000 bombs, including several GBU-28 devices weighing 2.5 tons each, were dropped on Baghdad alone; Clark, *War Crimes*, p. 17-8, 85; John D. Morrocco and David Fulghum, "USAF Developed a 4,700-lb. Bomb in Crash Program to Attack Iraqi Leaders in Hardened Bunkers," *Aviation Week & Space Technology*, May 6, 1991.

354. Clark, *War Crimes*, p. 18.

355. Ibid., pp. 45, 86. Also see Barbara Starr, "FAEs Used to Clear Mines," *Jane's Defense Weekly*, Feb. 23, 1991.

356. Full text will be found in Roberts and Guelff, *Laws of War*, pp. 137-45.

357. Clark, *War Crimes*, pp. 47-8.

358. Ibid., pp. 48

359. Mark Fineman, "Smoke Blots Out Sun in Bomb-Blasted Basra," *Los Angeles Times*, Feb. 5, 1991; Clark, *War Crimes*, pp. 16, 35, 87-8.

360. Clark, *War Crimes*, pp. 35, 15.

361. Eric Hooglund, "The Other Face of War," in Peters, *Collateral Damage*, p. 183. For an early but exhaustively detailed itemization of the impact of the air war upon Iraqi noncombatants, see Middle

East Watch, *Needless Deaths in the Gulf War: Civilian Casualties During the Air Campaign and Violations of the Laws of War* (New York: Human Rights Watch, 1991).

362. Barton Gellman, "Storm Damage in the Persian Gulf: U.S. strategy against Iraq went beyond strictly military targets," *Washington Post Weekly*, July 8-14, 1991.

363. Clark, *War Crimes*, pp. 22, 35.

364. Ibid., 53-4.

365. Ibid., p. 54, citing Bill Moyers, *PBS Special Report: After the War*, Spring 1991.

366. Br. Gen. Jack Neil, quoted in the *Washington Post*, Feb. 2, 1991.

367. Quoted in Mark Fineman, "Eyewitnesses Describe Allied Raids' Devastation," *San Francisco Chronicle*, Feb. 5, 1991. Also see Barbara Nimri Aziz, "Targets—Not Victims," in Anthony Arnove, ed., *Iraq Under Siege: The Deadly Impact of Sanctions and War* (Cambridge, MA: South End Press, 2000) pp. 127-36.

368. Gellman, "Storm Damage"; Jack Calhoun, "UN: Iraq Bombed Back to Stone Age," *Manchester Guardian*, Apr. 3, 1991; Patrick E. Tyler, "Disease Spirals in Iraq as Embargo Takes Its Toll," *New York Times*, June 24, 1991.

369. E.g.: a secret 1990 Air Force study, predicting that damage to Iraq's sanitation and fresh water processing facilities would generate epidemics among the civilian population, was revealed in a CNN special report entitled *The Unfinished War* on Jan. 21, 2001.

370. Clark, *War Crimes*, p. 88.

371. Ibid, p. 56.

372. U.N. Resolutions 661, 666, cited in "Hunger, Disease Stalk a Ravaged Iraq," *Manchester Guardian*, Mar. 13, 1991. Also see George Cappaccio, "Sanctions: Killing a Country and a People," in Arnove, *Iraq Under Siege*, pp. 137-48.

373. Gen. Colin Powell, Chairman of the Joint Chiefs of Staff, claimed the factory was a "biological weapons production facility," an idea refuted even by such U.S. allies as New Zealand; *Washington Post*, Feb. 1, 1991.

374. Joyce Price, "Embargo and Air War Diminish Iraq's Food Supply to a Record Low," *Washington Times*, Feb. 28, 1991; Clark, *War Crimes*, p. 56, 164-9; Phyllis Bennis and Dennis J. Halliday (interviewed by David Barsamian), "Iraq: The Impact of Sanctions and U.S. Policy," in Arnove, *Iraq Under Siege*, pp. 35-46.

375. Quoted in Moyers, *After the War*; Clark, *War Crimes*, pp. 56-7.

376. *Harvard Study Team Report: Public Health in Iraq After the Gulf War*, cited in Sklar, "New World Order," p. 14; Clark, *War Crimes*, p. 56, 99-101. For more current information, see Dr. Peter L. Pellett, "Sanctions, Food, Nutrition, and Health in Iraq," in Arnove, *Iraq Under Siege*, pp. 151-68.

377. William Blum, *Rogue State: A Guide to the World's Only Superpower* (Monroe, ME: Common Courage Press, 2000) p. 5. Also see Steven Lee Myers, "In Intense But Little-Noticed Fight, Allies Have Bombed Iraq All Year," *New York Times*, Aug. 13, 1999.

378. *Washington Post*, Aug. 30, 1999.

379. Quoted in the *Washington Post*, June 24, 1996.

380. Denis J. Halliday, "Introduction," in Phyllis Bennis, *Calling the Shots: How the U.S. Dominates Today's UN* (New York: Olive Branch Press, 2000) p. xiv. Halliday also appeared in CNN's *Unfinished War*. On the Clausewitz dictum, see note 38.

381. May 12, 1996; quoted in Blum, *Rogue State*, pp. 5-6.

382. An excellent overview of Powell's pedigree as a war criminal will be found in ibid., p. 69.

383. Quoted in *New York Times*, Mar. 23, 1991.

384. "In the headquarters staff of the Americal Division in Chu Lai . . . a reassuring memorandum was prepared for the Adjutant General [investigating the massacres] by Major Colin Luther Powell, the assistant chief of staff (operations). . . Showing all the signs of a soldier who had triumphed in the battle of military paperwork, Powell wrote what his superiors clearly wanted to hear. He described the Vietnamese people as being truly appreciative [of] the direct interest the division's soldiers took in their welfare and improvement of . . . standard of living. Maj. Powell . . . concluded even more complacently: 'Although there may be isolated cases of mistreatment of civilians and POWs this by no means reflects the general attitude throughout the division. In direct refutation of [allegations of the division's war crimes at My Lai and elsewhere] is the fact that relations between Americal soldiers

and the Vietnamese people are excellent' "; Michael Bilton and Kevin Sim, *Four Hours at My Lai* (New York: Viking, 1992) p. 213.

385. The shorter sentences resulted from negotiated settlements in which defendants pleaded guilty to the charge of "missing a troop movement"; Tod Ensign, "Military Resisters during Operation Desert Shield/Storm," in Peters, *Collateral Damage*, p. 290. Also see William Kunstler, "Harsh Government Prosecution of War Resisters," in Clark, *War Crimes*, pp. 201-3.

386. Ensign, "Military Resisters," pp. 294, 291.

387. Ibid., pp. 293-4.

388. Quoted in ibid., p. 292.

389. Ibid.

390. Ibid., p. 293.

391. Ibid., pp. 291-4.

392. Quoted in Cheney, " 'Talkin' War'," p. 19. On the incubator fable, see Dana Priest, "Kuwait Baby-Killing Report Disputed," *Washington Post*, Feb. 7, 1992.

393. Bush of course served as vice president in the Reagan administration, which, when the ICJ ruled in 1985 that the U.S. had no legal right to mine Nicaraguan harbors as a "peacetime" policy expedient, replied that ICJ held no authority to decide the matter; Abraham Sofaer, "The United States and the World Court," *Current Affairs*, No. 769, Dec. 1985; "U.S. Terminates Acceptance of ICJ Compulsory Jurisdiction," *Department of State Bulletin*, No. 86, Jan. 1986.

394. Quoted in *Newsweek*, Aug. 15, 1988.

395. In May 1999, Secretary of State Madeleine Albright announced that the U.S. was "the major provider of funds for the Tribunal and [had] pledged even more money to it." The balance, according to NATO spokesperson Jamie Shae, was contributed by U.S. partners in the North Atlantic Treaty Alliance; Blum, *Rogue State*, pp. 74-5.

396. Noam Chomsky, "U.S. Iraq Policy: Motives and Consequences," in Arnove, *Iraq Under Siege*, pp. 47-56; *Rogue States*, pp. 37-8.

397. See, e.g., . Francis A. Boyle, *The Bosnian People Charge Genocide: Proceedings of the International Court of Justice Concerning Bosnia* vs. Serbia *on the Prevention and Punishment of the Crime of Genocide* (Amherst, MA: Aletheia Press, 1996).

398. In effect, creation of the judicial venue implied in the Affirmation of Nuremberg Principles signed by the U.S. in 1946; see note 33.

399. Blum, *Rogue State*, p. 77. Six other countries—Libya, Iraq, Sudan, China, Qatar and Israel—also refused to sign on; Bennis, *Calling the Shots*, p. 277.

400. Blum, *Rogue State*, p. 77; Bennis, *Calling the Shots*, p. 276; statements of Albright and others in the *New York Times*, Dec. 2, 1998; Jan. 3, 2000. On the dismissal of such arguments at Nuremberg, see note 31.

401. Chomsky, "East Timor Retrospective," in *Rogue States*, pp. 51-61. On Kurdistan, see, e.g., A.R. Ghassemlou, et al., *People Without a Country: The Kurds and Kurdistan* (London: Zed Press, 1980); Chomsky, *Rogue States*, pp. 41-2, 63-4.

402. Blum, *Rogue State*, p. 101; Bennis, *Calling the Shots*, p. 280.

403. Bennis, *Calling the Shots*, pp. 279-80.

404. Blum, *Rogue State*, p. 187. The text of the Declaration will be found in Ian Brownlie, ed., *Basic Documents on Human Rights* (Oxford, UK: Clarendon Press, [3$^{rd}$ ed.] 1992) pp. 28-30.

405. Blum, *Rogue State*, pp. 189, 192-3.

406. Ibid., p. 194. For text, see Brownlie, *Basic Documents*, pp. 148-61; on U.S. ratification, see Frank Newman and David Weissbrodt, *International Human Rights: Law, Policy, and Process* (Cincinnati, OH: Anderson, [2nd ed.] 1996) pp. 42-43.

407. Bennis, *Calling the Shots*, pp. 280-1.

408. A detailed itemization for the years 1978-86 will be found in Blum, *Rogue State*, pp. 185-97.

409. Lawrence J. LeBlanc, *The United States and the Genocide Convention* (Durham, NC: Duke University Press, 1991); the text of the U.S. "Sovereignty Package" appears as Appendix C, pp. 253-4.

410. A subplot has been to use Western notions of individual rights as a lever to pry apart the group cohesion evident in nonwestern, collectivist cultural settings, especially those of indigenous

peoples; Gustavo Esteva and Madhu Suri Prakash, *Grassroots Postmodernism: Remaking the Soil of Cultures* (London: Zed Books, 1998) pp. 110-46.

411. James Hooper, "Kosovo: America's Balkan Problem," *Current History*, Apr. 1999; Chomsky, "Crisis in the Balkans," in *Rogue States*, pp. 34-50.

412. For analysis of this packaging and its implications, see Noam Chomsky, *The New Military Humanism: Lessons from Kosovo* (Monroe, ME: Common Courage Press, 1999).

413. Serbia's conduct in Kosovo was indeed criminal, but by no means as extreme as the "ethnic cleansing" operations it carried out in Bosnia during the early '90s. The U.S. stood aside while the latter occurred; Marshall Harris, "Introduction," in Boyle, *Bosnian Genocide*, pp. xi-xix; David Rieff, *Slaughterhouse: Bosnia and the Failure of the West* (New York: Simon and Schuster, 1995); Michel Feher, *Powerless by Design: The Age of the International Community* (Durham, NC: Duke University Press, 2000) esp. pp. 2-4, 70-2, 78-82, 84-92.

414. Separate actions were filed by groups of Canadian, British and Greek international legal experts, as well as the American Association of Jurists; Blum, *Rogue State*, p. 73.

415. Ibid.

416. Quoted in ibid., pp. 75-6.

417. *Washington Post*, Sept. 20,1999.

418. Prof. Michael Mandel, University of Toronto Law School, Sept. 21, 1999.

419. *The Observer*, Dec. 26, 1999; *New York Times*, Dec. 30, 1999; *Washington Times*, Dec. 31, 1999.

420. Feher, *Powerless by Design*, pp. 66-7, 71-4. Also see Alaine Destexhe, *Rwanda and Genocide in the Twentieth Century* (New York: New York University Press, 1995); Gérard Prunier, *The Rwanda Crisis: History of a Genocide* (New York: Columbia University Press, 1995).

421. Feher, *Powerless by Design*, p. 86.

422. John Vincour, "Going It Alone: U.S. Upsets France So Paris Begins a Campaign to Strengthen Multilateral Institutions," *International Herald Tribune*, Feb. 3, 1999.

423. Ibid.

424. Sept. 1, 1997. Also see William Drozdiak, "Even Allies Resent U.S. Dominance: America Accused of Bullying World," *Washington Post*, Nov. 4, 1997.

425. Joyce Kolko, *Restructuring the World Economy* (New York: Pantheon, 1988); Richard Barnet and John Cavanaugh, *Global Dreams: Imperial Corporations and the New World Order* (New York: Simon and Schuster, 1994); Noam Chomsky, *World Orders, Old and New* (New York: Columbia University Press, 1996).

426. Richard M. Nixon, *Seize the Moment: America's Challenge in a One-Superpower World* (New York: Simon and Schuster, 1992); Jack Nelson-Pallmeyer, *Brave New World Order* (Maryknoll, NY: Orbis Books, 1992); Michael Parenti, *Blackshirts and Reds: Rational Fascism and the Overthrow of Communism* (San Francisco: City Lights Books, 1997).

427. Valdas Anelauskas, *Discovering America As It Is* (Atlanta: Clarity Press, 1999) pp. 409-66.

428. Quoted in Chomsky, "U.S. Iraq Policy," p. 54. Albright repeated precisely the same formulation as recently as Jan. 2, 2000, on NBC's *Meet the Press*.

429. George Bush, quoted in Cheney, " 'Talkin' War'," p. 19.

430. See note 134.

431. Bush first employed the term on Jan. 29, 1991; quoted in Chomsky, *World Orders*, p. 7.

432. An excellent overview—far beyond what can be offered herein—will be found in Isaac Balbus, *The Dialectic of Legal Repression* (New York: Russell Sage Foundation, 1973).

433. Nebrija's 1492 observation concerned the utility of language in consolidating colonial enterprises; quoted in Patricia Seed, *Ceremonies of Possession in Europe's Conquest of the New World, 1492-1640* (Cambridge, UK: Cambridge University Press, 1995) p. 8.

434. This is not to deny the importance of propaganda in shaping either the form or extent of apparent consensus. For analysis, see Jacques Ellul, *Propaganda: The Formation of Men's Attitudes* (New York: Vintage, 1973); Edward S. Herman and Noam Chomsky, *Manufacturing Consent: The Political Economy of the News Media* (New York: Pantheon, 1988); Noam Chomsky, *Necessary Illusions: Thought Control in Democratic Societies* (Boston: South End Press, 1989); Michael Parenti, *Inventing Reality: The Politics of the News Media* (New York: St. Martin's Press, 1993).

435. "The idea of 'altruism' has been a recurrent feature of America's love affair with itself'"; Blum, *Rogue State*, p. 12.

436. See, e.g., Wilhelm Reich, *The Mass Psychology of Fascism* (New York: Farrar, Straus & Giroux, 1970); R.D. Laing, *The Politics of Experience* (New York: Ballantine, 1967) esp. pp. 28-30.

437. Joel Kovel, *White Racism: A Psychohistory* (New York: Columbia University Press, [2nd ed.] 1984); Michael Omi and Howard Winant, *Racial Formation in the United States From the 1960s to the 1990s* (New York: Routledge, 1994).

438. Slotkin, *Gunfighter Nation*; also see his *Regeneration Through Violence: The Mythology of the American Frontier, 1600-1860* (Norman: University of Oklahoma Press, [2nd ed.] 2000).

439. Martin Jay Lifton and Eric Markusen, *The Genocidal Mentality: Nazi Holocaust and Nuclear Threat* (New York: Basic Books, 1988).

440. For analogues, see Christopher R. Browning, *Ordinary Men: Police Battalion 101 and the Final Solution in Poland* (New York: HarperCollins, 1992); Daniel Jonah Goldhagen, *Hitler's Willing Executioners: Ordinary Germans and the Final Solution* (New York: Alfred A. Knopf, 1996). A range of useful insights will also be found in Hannah Arendt's *Eichmann in Jerusalem: A Report on the Banality of Evil* (New York: Penguin, 1964).

441. An excellent overview is presented in Stanley Cohen's *States of Denial: Knowing About Atrocities and Suffering* (Cambridge, UK: Polity Press, 2001). For more clinical appreciations of the phenomenon, see Donald A. Nathanson, "Denial, Projection, and the Empathic Wall," and Léon Wurmser, "Cultural Paradigms of Denial," both in E.L. Edelstein, Donald L. Nathanson and Andrew M. Stone, eds., *Denial: A Clarification of Concepts and Research* (New York: Plenum, 1989) pp. 37-60, 277-86.

442. The word "radical" is used here, not in the colloquial sense of meaning "extreme"—although extreme measures may well under the circumstances be both warranted and necessary—but in accordance with its actual definition: "at the root or most elemental level."

443. For the theoretically inclined, this is a specifically dialectical reading of the possibilities; see, e.g., Michael Albert and Robin Hahnel, *Unorthodox Marxism: An Essay on Capitalism, Socialism and Revolution* (Boston: South End Press, 1978) pp. 14-6, 90-4.

444. A good forum on this point will be found in Michael Albert, et al., *Liberating Theory* (Boston: South End Press, 1986) esp. pp. 127-45.

445. See generally, David S. Caudill and Steven Jay Gold, eds., *Radical Philosophy of Law: Contemporary Challenges to Mainstream Legal Theory and Practice* (Atlantic Highlands, NJ: Humanities Press, 1995).

446. Bennis, *Calling the Shots*, pp. 274-9.

447. Francis Anthony Boyle, *Foundations of World Order: The Legalist Approach to International Relations, 1898-1922* (Durham, NC: Duke University Press, 1999) pp. 22-3.

448. Karl Jaspers, "The Significance of the Nuremberg Trials for Germany and the World," *Notre Dame Law Review*, Vol. XXII, Jan. 1947.

449. Jean-Paul Sartre, "Inaugural Statement," in Duffett, *Crimes of Silence*, esp. pp. 41-4; Richard Falk, *Human Rights and State Sovereignty* (New York: Holmes and Meier, 1981) esp. the chapter entitled "Keeping Nuremberg Alive," pp. 195-201.

450. See generally, Francis M. Wilhoit, *The Politics of Massive Resistance* (New York: Braziller, 1973).

451. Rachel L. Jones, "Minorities in the Military," in Peters, *Collateral Damage*, pp. 237-53.

452. Francis Fox-Piven and Richard Cloward, *The New Class War: Reagan's Attack on the Welfare State and Its Consequences* (New York: Pantheon, 1988); Martin Carnoy, *Faded Dreams: The Politics and Economics of Race in America* (Cambridge, UK: Cambridge University Press, 1994); Ruth Sidel, *Keeping Women and Children Last: America's War on the Poor* (New York: Penguin, 1996); Irene Gugenmoos-Holzman, Uwe Flick and M. Harvey Brenner, *Quality of Life and Health* (Iowa City: Iowa State University Press, 1997); Noam Chomsky, *Profit Over People: Neoliberalism and Global Order* (New York: Seven Stories Press, 1999).

453. Barry Bluestone and Bennett Harrison, *The Deindustrialization of America: Plant Closings, Community Abandonment, and the Dismantling of Basic Industry* (New York: Basic Books, 1982); Bennett Harrison and Barry Bluestone, *The Great U-Turn: Corporate Restructuring and the Polarization of America* (New York: Basic Books, 1988); Sakia Sassen, *Mobility of Labor and Capital* (Cambridge, UK: Cambridge University Press, 1997).

454. Lawrence Mishel, Jared Bernstein and John Schmitt, *The State of Working America, 1998-1999* (Ithaca, NY: Cornell University Press, 1999); Richard W. Judy and Carol D'Amico, *Workforce 2020: Work and Workers in the Twenty-First Century* (Indianapolis: Hudson Institute, 1997); William Julius Wilson, *When Work Disappears: The World of the New Urban Poor* (New York: Vintage, 1997).

455. As examples: Howard I. Rosenberg, *Atomic Soldiers: American Victims of Nuclear Experiments* (Boston: Beacon, 1980); Fred Wilcox, *Waiting for an Army to Die: The Tragedy of Agent Orange* (New York: Vintage, 1983); Depleted Uranium Citizens' Network, *Radioactive Battlefields of the 1990s: The United States Army's Use of Depleted Uranium and Its Consequences for Human Health and the Environment* (Lewiston, ME: Military Toxics Project, 1996).

456. Chris Hellman, "Pentagon May seek Substantial Increase in Fiscal Year 2000 Top-line," *Weekly Defense Monitor*, Dec. 10, 1998; "Last of the Big Spenders: U.S. Military Budget Still the World's Largest, and Growing," *Center for Defense Information Fact Sheet*, Feb. 1, 1999; "Administration Seeks More Money for the Pentagon," *Weekly Defense Monitor*, Feb. 4, 1999.

457. Pacifica Network News, Feb. 3, 2001. For background, see Anelauskas, *America As It Is*, pp. 418-20.

458. Peter B. Kraska and Victor E. Kappler, "Militarizing American Police: The Rise and Normalization of Paramilitary Units," *Social Problems*, Vol. 44, No. 1, Feb. 1997; Christian Parenti, *Lockdown America: Police and Prisons in the Age of Crisis* (London: Verso, 1999) pp. 139-60.

459. See, e.g., Sabina Virgo, "The Criminalization of Poverty," in Elihu Rosenblatt, *Criminal Injustice: Confronting the Prison Crisis* (Boston: South End Press, 1996) pp. 47-60.

460. Marc Mauer, "Americans Behind Bars: A Comparison of International Rates of Incarceration," in my and J.J. Vander Wall's coedited, *Cages of Steel: The Politics of Imprisonment in the United States* (Washington, D.C.: Maisonneuve Press, 1992) pp. 22-37.

461. Katherine Beckett, *Making Crime Pay: Law and Order in Contemporary American Politics* (New York: Oxford University Press, 1997); Parenti, *Lockdown*, pp. 211-42.

462. See, e.g., the section entitled "Workin' for the Man: Prison Labor in the U.S.A.," in Daniel Burton-Rose, Dan Pens and Paul Wright, eds., *The Celling of America: An Inside Look at the U.S. Prison Industry* (Monroe, ME: Common Courage Press, 1998) pp. 102-31.

463. Malcolm X as told to Alex Haley, *The Autobiography of Malcolm X* (New York: Ballantine Books, [2nd ed.] 1973) p. 329.

464. Donald L. Barlett and James B. Steel, *America: What Went Wrong?* (New York: Simon and Schuster, 1992); Michael Perelman, *The Pathology of the U.S. Economy: The Costs of a Low-Wage System* (New York: Macmillan, 1993).

465. Erosion of public support for nazism did not set in until German troop losses in the USSR rose to catastrophic levels during the winter of 1941-42. This decline in the régime's popularity became more and more pronounced over the next year, as defeats piled up, the Allied air war commenced in earnest, and the German people began to suffer the fate they'd celebrated when their military had visited it upon others; Michael Burleigh, *The Third Reich: A New History* (New York: Hill and Wang, 2000) pp. 758-60.

466. Zinn, *People's History*, 368-97.

467. See, e.g., Ken Hurwitz, *Marching Nowhere* (New York: W.W. Norton, 1971); David Zane Mairowitz, *The Radical Soap Opera: Roots of Failure in the American Left* (New York: Discus, 1974).

468. For explication, see Robert F. Barsky, *Noam Chomsky: A Life of Dissent* (Cambridge, MA: MIT Press, 1998). Also see Chomsky's own *Radical Priorities*, edited by C.P. Otero (Montréal: Black Rose Books, 1981) esp. pp. 137-66; *Powers and Prospects: Reflections on Human Nature and the Social Order* (Boston: South End Press, 1996); as well as titles already cited.

469. On the concept of a "master" or "grand" narrative, see Jean François Lyotard, *The Postmodern Condition: A Report on Knowledge* (Minneapolis: University of Minnesota Press, 1984) pp. xxi-xix, 31-40. As nearly as I can tell, the idea of "cognitive dissonance" was introduced to critical theory by C. Wright Mills, in his *The Sociological Imagination* (London: Oxford University Press, 1959).

470. This is as true of radical alternatives to traditional psychotherapy, as it is for orthodoxy itself. The one exception may be found in B.F. Skinner's behavior modification techniques. See generally, Jerome Angel and the Radical Therapist Collective, *The Radical Therapist: Therapy Means Change, Not*

*Adjustment* (New York: Ballantine, 1971). For a devastating critique of Skinner, see Noam Chomsky, "Psychology and Ideology," in *For Reasons of State*, pp. 318-65.

471. See Walter L. Adamson, *Hegemony and Revolution: A Study of Antonio Gramsci's Political and Cultural Theory* (Berkeley: University of California Press, 1980) pp. 170-9, 241-5.

472. On statist strategies of cooptation, see Katsiaficas, *New Left*, pp. 156-7, 161-4, 186-8, 195-7, 209-11.

473. Goldstein, Marshall and Schwartz, *My Lai Massacre*, pp. 11-4.

474. Although different in configuration, the dimension of the problem is potentially analogous to that unsuccessfully confronted by the military hierarchy towards the end of the war in Indochina, when enlisted personnel began to ignore orders en masse; Cincinnatus, *Self-Destruction: The Disintegration and Decay of the United States Army During the Vietnam Era* (New York: W.W. Norton, 1981).

475. As of January 2001, the United States was one of only two countries—the other was Somalia—which had refused to ratify the 1994 International Convention on the Rights of the Child. One of the main sticking points was an optional protocol prohibiting military service by youngsters under the age of 18; Bennis, *Calling the Shots*, pp. 280-1.

476. More than a decade ago, the United Nations nongovernmental consultative organization Human Rights Watch conducted a survey of 27 representative U.S. prisons and documented "numerous human rights abuses and frequent violations of the [1977] U.N. Standard Minimum Rules for the Treatment of Prisoners"; *Prison Conditions in the United States* (New York: Human Rights Watch, 1991) p. 4. The Rules are an offshoot of the International Convention Against Torture and Other Forms of Cruel, Inhuman or Degrading Treatment or Punishment (1984); for text, see Weston, Falk and D'Amato, *Basic Documents*, pp. 463-71.

477. The United Nations nongovernmental consultative organization Amnesty International recently released a report documenting chronic violation of international human rights protections by U.S. police departments; Kwame Dixon and Patricia E. Allard, *Police Brutality and International Human Rights in the United States: The Report on Hearings Held in Los Angeles, California, Chicago, Illinois, and Pittsburgh, Pennsylvania, Fall 1999* (New York: Amnesty International USA, Feb. 2000) pp. 39-42. More broadly, see Paul Chevigny, *The Edge of the Knife: Police Violence in the Americas* (New York: W.W. Norton, 1995) pp. 31-144; Parenti, *Lockdown*, pp. 69-139.

478. Like the military's, BoP regulations and violations thereof are not typically subject to normal judicial oversight; see, e.g., Mary K. O'Melveny, "Lexington Prison High Security Unit: U.S. Political Prison," in Rosenblatt, *Criminal Injustice*, pp. 322-33.

479. Efforts to create oversight boards to extend direct community control over the police have a long standing in the U.S., and were included as a recommendation by Amnesty International in its 2000 report; Dixon and Allard, *Police Brutality*, p. 44. For background, see Tony Platt, et al., *The Iron Fist and the Velvet Glove: An Analysis of the U.S. Police* (San Francisco: Synthesis, 1982) pp. 189-90, 220-1.

480. Serious challenges have been mounted in this connection, most notably during the "Sioux Sovereignty Hearing" of 1974; John William Sayer, *Ghost Dancing the Law: The Wounded Knee Trials* (Cambridge, MA: Harvard University Press, 1997) pp. 204-5. For detail, see Roxanne Dunbar Ortiz, *The Great Sioux Nation: Sitting in Judgement on America* (New York/San Francisco: International Indian Treaty Council/Moon Books, 1977). For a broader overview, see "Perversions of Justice," in this volume.

481. See the essay entitled "I Am Indigenist: Notes on the Ideology of the Fourth World," in my *Struggle for the Land: Native North American Resistance to Genocide, Ecocide and Colonization* (San Francisco: City Lights, [2nd ed.] 2002) pp. 367-402.

482. Reference is made here to the concepts articulated by Hakim Bey in his *T.A.Z.: The Temporary Autonomous Zone* (Brooklyn, NY: Autonomedia, 1991), and Kirkpatrick Sale, in *Human Scale* (New York: Coward, McCann & Geoghegan, 1980).

483. Those who would receive this formulation as evidence of a "knee-jerk radical" outlook would do well to recall that by 1961 no less conservative a figure than outgoing President—and former General of the Army—Dwight David Eisenhower was warning of the implications embodied in the "military-industrial complex" that had long since become a central feature of U.S. political and economic life; see Eisenhower's "Farewell Address," *Annals of America*, Vol. 18, No. 3, 1976. For contemporaneous background, see C. Wright Mills, *The Causes of World War III* (New York: Simon & Schuster, 1958). For a more recent analysis, see Leah Renae Kelly, "The More Things Change, the More They Stay the Same:

NSC 68, Reaganomics, and the End of the Cold War," in her *In My Own Voice: Essays on the Sociopolitical Context of Art and Cinema* (Winnipeg: Arbeiter Ring, 2001) pp. 104-7.

484. For elaboration, see Richard Falk's "Anarchism and World Order," in his *The End of World Order: Essays on Normative International Relations* (New York: Holmes & Meier, 1983) pp. 277-98. Also see the section entitled "The 'Rule of Law' Versus 'Rule by Law' " in Terrance Edward Paupp, *Achieving Inclusionary Governance: Advancing Peace and Development in First and Third World Nations* (Ardsley, NY: Transnational, 2000) pp. 232-40.

485. There is absolutely no scientific basis upon which to conclude that "second-hand tobacco smoke" is a "public health hazard." For data and policy analysis, see Jacob Sullum, *For Your Own Good: The Anti-Smoking Crusade and the Tyranny of Public Health* (New York: Free Press, 1998). The most current technical summaries concerning the "problem" will be found in Ronald R. Watson and Mark Witten, eds., *Environmental Tobacco Smoke* (Boca Raton, FL: CRC Press, 2001). This is a classic instance of the personal preferences of a self-indulgently privileged-sector segment being imposed under glaringly false premises upon the public as a whole, the poor and otherwise marginalized in particular.

486. Much as the drive to create "smoke-free environments" was pursued under the prevarication of "public health," the campaign to proliferate speedbumps in places like Boulder has been waged under the spurious premise that "public safety" would be increased thereby. In actuality, all that has been accomplished—aside from enhancing the already extravagant "quality of life" enjoyed by those demanding that the public wealth be expended in this fashion—is that the transit of ambulances and fire trucks has been noticeably slowed, a result which demonstrably *diminishes* public safety.

487. The "cruise missile" phrase description was used by Defense Secretary Donald Rumsfeld during a press conference carried by CNN, Sept. 13, 2001.

488. The story of the fourth airliner's demise is quite murky. It began with word that one passenger had managed to secretly make telephone contact with her husband from a lavatory, and that this communication was abruptly terminated by a "loud noise." Shortly thereafter, there were reports the plane had crashed. A while after *that*, it emerged that numerous others had supposedly contacted their loved ones by cell phone while seated in the cabin, in full view of the hijackers. With that, all mention of the loud noise which marked the end of the first caller's conversation disappeared from the airwaves, as did reference to the caller herself. She was replaced by a young man who was said to have given his family the details of how he and several others were planning to assault their captors, recovering control of the aircraft. From there, it was an easy step to the final version, in which it is claimed that the passengers themselves dived the plane into an open field, preventing its use as a weapon and instantly converting themselves from victims into "heroes." Rousing as the latter portrayal of events may be, it cannot be accepted until the loud noise—an auditory signature consistent with the impact of an air-to-air missile—reported in the first version is explained rather than simply expunged from the narrative.

489. There were 2,824 fatalities at the WTC, 184 at the Pentagon and 266 in the four airliners. All told, this comes to less than half the tally of "7,000 innocent Americans" announced by Sen. Orin Hatch on Dec. 11, 2001, during an appearance of CNN's *Larry King Live*.

490. Those killed on the upper floors of the WTC included hundreds of the most highly skilled technicians of international finance available in the U.S. (Cantor Fitzgerald alone lost roughly 700 of 1,000 employees); Eric Roston, "A CEO's Story: All His Office Mates Gone," *Time* (Special Issue: "America digs out—and digs in"), Sept. 24, 2001. The reacquisition of such expertise takes a considerable period of time. A clandestine intelligence-gathering facility in the WTC was also obliterated; James Risen, "Secret C.I.A. Site in New York Was Destroyed on Sept. 11: Attack Seriously Disrupted Spying Operations," *New York Times*, Nov. 4, 2001.

491. The estimate is conservative. In addition to the billions in material damage resulting from the attacks, and the further billions required to clear the rubble, the already ailing air transport and related industries took a serious nosedive in the aftermath, and the stock market has yet to rebound from a period of decline first strongly manifested in the wake of 9-1-1. For a ridiculously optimistic—or, more accurately, propagandistic—"forecast" of a rapid recovery, see Bernard Baumohl, Maggie Sieger and Adam Zagorin, "The Economy: Up From the Ashes," *Time* (Special Issue: "America digs out—and digs in"), Sept. 24, 2001.

492. People from 86 different countries, including 78 British nationals, are reported to have been killed; U.S. Attorney General John Ashcroft, press briefing carried on CNBC, Nov. 29, 2001.

493. "American warplanes have methodically and with virtually no public discussion been attacking Iraq. . . In the last eight months, American and British pilots have fired more than 1,100 missiles against 359 targets in Iraq. . . This is triple the number of targets attacked in four furious days of strikes in December [1998]"; Myers, "In Intense But Little-Noticed Fight." "After eight years of enforcing a 'no-fly zone' in northern [and southern] Iraq, few targets remain. . . 'We're down to the last outhouse,'" one Pentagon spokesperson announced; Ronald G. Shafer, "Washington Wire," *Wall Street Journal*, Oct. 22, 1999. A list of operations is provided in Gore Vidal's *Perpetual War for Perpetual Peace: How We Got to be So Hated* (New York: Thunder's Mouth Press/Nation Books, 2002) pp. 24-5. Overall, see Naseer Aruri, "America's War Against Iraq: 1990-1999," in Arnove, *Iraq Under Siege*, pp. 23-33.

494. Such Bushian rhetoric was quickly adopted and refined by pundits like Ronald Steel, who opined in the *New York Times* on Sept. 14, 2001, that, "They hate us because we champion a 'new world order' of capitalism, secularism and democracy that should be the norm everywhere." Meanwhile, those, like aesthetician Susan Sontag and ABC talk show host Bill Maher, who took even mild exception to the prevailing presidential idiocies were publicly savaged on "moral" grounds in the *Washington Post* and elsewhere. White House press secretary Ari Fleischer thereupon explained that those raising their voices in the "land of the free" would henceforth do well to "watch what they say"; Celestine Bohlen, "In New War on Terrorism, Words Are Weapons, Too," *New York Times*, Sept. 29, 2001.

495. For background, see John K. Cooley, *Unholy Wars: Afghanistan, America and International Terrorism* (London: Pluto Press, [2nd ed.] 2000).

496. A broad sample of the State Department material appears in Yonah Alexander and Michael S. Swetnam, *Osama bin-Laden's al-Qaida: Profile of a Terrorist Network* (Ardsley, NY: Transnational, 2001).

497. The "real assault on America would begin in earnest only in the summer of 1998, in East Africa. On the morning of August 7, 1998, truck bombs devastated the areas around the American embassies in Nairobi, Kenya, and Dar es Salaam, Tanzania. The Nairobi bomb killed 247 people, including 12 Americans in a portion of the embassy which collapsed, and wounded thousands"; Cooley, *Unholy Wars*, p. 220. "Al-Qaida is also suspected of mounting the October 12, 2000, suicide bombing of the *USS Cole*, killing 17 and wounding 39 American sailors in Aden harbor, Yemen"; Alexander and Swetman, *al-Qalda*, p. vvii.

498. *Wall Street Journal*, Oct. 5, 2001.

499. By Aug. 1999, UNICEF had completed an exhaustive study in which the child death toll attributable to sanctions was once again confirmed; Milan Rai, *War Plan Iraq: Ten Reasons Against War on Iraq* (London: Verso, 2002) p. 176. Also see Capaccio, "Sanctions," pp. 137-48.

500. The "U.S. is a prime supporter of the Israeli occupation of Palestinian territory, now in its thirty-fifth year. It's been harsh and brutal from the beginning, extremely repressive. Most of this hasn't been discussed here, and the U.S. role has been virtually suppressed. . . Even simple facts are not reported. For example, as soon as the current fighting began last September 30, Israel immediately, the next day, began using U.S. helicopters (they can't produce helicopters) to attack civilian targets. In the next couple of days they killed several dozen people in apartment complexes and elsewhere. The fighting was all in Palestinian territories and there was no Palestinian fire. . . Meanwhile the settlement policies, which have taken over substantial parts of the territories and are designed to make it virtually impossible for an independent [Palestinian] state to develop, are supported by the U.S. The U.S. provides the funding, the diplomatic support. It's the only country that's blocked the overwhelming international consensus on condemning all this under the Geneva Convention"; Noam Chomsky, interviewed by David Barsamian, "The United States is a Leading Terrorist State," *Monthly Review*, Vol. 53, No. 6, Nov. 2001, p. 13. For in-depth background, see Noam Chomsky, *The Fateful Triangle: The United States, Israel and the Palestinians* (Boston: South End Press, 1983); Avi Shlaim, *The Iron Wall: Israel and the Arab World* (New York: W.W. Norton, 2000); Nur Masalha, *Imperial Israel and the Palestinians* (London: Pluto Press, 2000); Naseer Aruri, ed., *Palestinian Refugees: The Right of Return* (London: Pluto Press, 2001).

501. For a full rendering of bin-Laden's/al-Qaida's position in this regard, see Appendices 1A and 1B— "Declaration of War against the Americans Occupying the Land of the Two Holy Places: A Message from Osama bin Muhammad bin Laden unto his Muslim Brethren all over the world generally, and in the Arab Peninsula specifically" (Sept. 4, 1996) and "Jihad Against Jews and Crusaders: World Islamic Front Statement" ( Feb. 23,1998)—in Alexander and Swetnam, *al-Qaida*.

502. The Iranian airliner had only just taken off and was well within a commercial air lane. According to U.S. Navy Commander David Carlson, it was shot down out of "a need to prove the viability of Aigis," the ship's state-of-the-art air defense system; quoted in Noam Chomsky, *Deterring Democracy* (New York: Hill and Wang, 1992) p. 379. In 1989, and again in 1990, the Iranians attempted to bring an action before the International Court of Justice; "Iran submits complaint over U.S. downing of airliner in '88," *Chicago Tribune*, July 25, 1990. Such recourse to legality was useless, however, since the U.S. had repudiated ICJ jurisdiction over its actions four years earlier (see note 393). Even among "progressives," there has been almost no serious expression of outrage over this blatant U.S. atrocity, a circumstance usefully compared to the outpouring of horror concerning the 1983 Soviet shootdown of Korean Airlines Flight 007—on which there were relatively few Americans aboard, and only after the plane had deeply penetrated Soviet air space—or the Libyans' alleged 1988 bombing of Pan Am Flight 103 over Lockerbie, Scotland. On KAL Flight 007, see Edward S. Herman and Gerry O'Sullivan, *The Terrorism Industry: The Experts and the Institutions that Shape Our View of Terror* (New York: Pantheon, 1989) pp. 197-8. On the destruction of Pan Am Flight 103, for which Abdel Basset Ali al-Megrahi, a Libyan intelligence officer, was sentenced to life imprisonment in January 2001—and because of which Libya recently effected a settlement with the families of the victims—see "Lockerbie lawyers said to reach 2.7-billion-dollar deal with Libya," Agence France-Presse, Oct. 30, 2002.

503. The U.S. claims an "inherent right" to shoot down any "hostile" aircraft approaching within 200 miles of its coastline. By its own account, the Pentagon sent fighter-bombers within 40 miles of the Libyan coast during the 1981 Gulf of Sidra "exercise." In actuality, according to a British engineer who was monitoring a radar screen during the entire confrontation, U.S. aircraft penetrated 8 miles into airspace over the Libyan landmass itself. "I don't think the Libyans had any choice but to hit back," he said. "In my opinion they were reluctant to do so." This reluctance prevailed despite the fact that the U.S. had already implemented a policy of firing on "any Libyan boat that enters international waters in the Gulf of Sidra for as long as the U.S. naval exercise in that region continues—no matter how far away the boat might be from U.S. ships"; all quotes in Noam Chomsky, *Pirates and Emperors: International Terrorism and the Real World* (New York: Claremont, 1986) pp. 144-5.

504. The U.S. claimed the strikes were in retaliation for Libya's sponsorship of bombings at the Rome and Vienna airports on Dec. 27, 1985, in which a single American child, 11-year-old Natasha Simpson, was killed. Instructively, both the Italian and Austrian intelligence agencies stated unequivocally that Libya had nothing to do with the attacks. A second pretext was that Libya was behind the Apr. 5, 1986 bombing of the La Belle discothèque in Berlin, in which a U.S. serviceman was killed, although German intelligence was equally adamant that there was no "Libyan connection" at issue (instructively, U.S. military intelligence shared this view); Chomsky, *Pirates and Emperors*, pp. 135, 148. In the aftermath of the U.S. raids, which clearly targeted Qadaffi himself—his home was bombed—in violation of both U.S. domestic and international law, and in which a number of children besides Qadaffi's were killed, "65 claims were filed with the White House and the Department of Defense under the Federal Tort Claims Act and the Foreign Claims Act on behalf of those killed or injured. The claimants, who were asking for up to $5 million for each wrongful death, included Libyans, Greeks, Egyptians, Yugoslavs and Lebanese. . . [N]one of the claims got anywhere in the American judicial system, with the Supreme Court declining to hear the case"; Blum, *Rogue State*, p. 230. Arguably, it was this "due process" outcome that prompted the bombing of Pan Am Flight 103, and it should be compared to Libya's recent award of $10 million per victim who perished in that incident (see note 502).

505. All told, al-Shifa manufactured "90 percent of Sudan's pharmaceutical products." Among other things, it "provided 50 percent of the Sudan's medicines, and its destruction has left the country with no supplies of chloroquine, the standard treatment for malaria" and it was the only factory "producing TB drugs—for more than 100,000 patients [as well as] veterinary drugs. . .to kill the parasites which pass from herds to herders, one of Sudan's principle causes of infant mortality." As a result of the plant's destruction, "Sudan's death toll. . .has continued, quietly, to rise. . .tens of thousands of people—many of them children—have suffered and died from malaria, tuberculosis, and other treatable diseases." According to Germany's ambassador to the Sudan, "It is difficult to assess how many people died in this poor African country died as a consequence of the al-Shifa factory bombing, but several tens of thousands seems a reasonable guess"; Noam Chomsky, *9-11* (New York: Seven Stories Press, 2001) pp.

48-9; quoting Patrick Wintour, *Observer*, Dec. 20, 1998; James Astill, *The Guardian*, Oct. 2, 2001; Jonathan Belke, *Boston Globe*, Aug. 22, 1999; Werner Daum, "Universalism and the West," *Harvard International Review*, Summer 2001.

506. A salient example would be the staunchness with which the U.S. supported Israel after the Israeli Air Force knowingly shot down a Libyan airliner in Feb. 1973, killing all 109 aboard. In that instance, the *New York Times*, reflecting the official U.S. stance, editorialized that, "No useful purpose is served by an acrimonious debate over the assignment of blame for the downing of a Libyan airliner over the Sinai Peninsula." The *Times*' position in the 1973 case is usefully compared to that taken on Sept. 2, 1983 by America's "newspaper of record" concerning the Soviets' shootdown of KAL Flight 007: "There can be no conceivable excuse for any nation shooting down a harmless airliner." This neatly reversed "standard" was, of course, reversed again with respect to the U.S. Navy's obliteration of an Iranian airliner in 1988 (see note 501). Actually, U.S. forgiveness of its "friends'" terrorist attacks on civilian airliners is standard, having applied not only to the 1973 Israeli atrocity against Libya, but to the 1976 bombing of a Cuban airliner, killing 73, by the Cuban expatriate Orlando Bosch (a longtime CIA client), the highly lethal shootdown of an Angola Airlines plane by Joseph Savimbi's UNITA forces on Nov. 3, 1983 (Savimbi and his organization were from the outset CIA-supported), and the planting of a bomb aboard an Air India jumbo jet in 1985, killing 329, by Sikh extremists (one of whom had received explosives instruction at a "private" military training camp in Alabama); Herman and O'Sullivan, *Terrorism Industry*, pp. 197-8; Chomsky, *Pirates and Emperors*, p. 136; Edward S. Herman, *The Real Terror Network: Terrorism in Fact and Propaganda* (Boston: South End Press, 1982) p. 63.

507. See, e.g., Dean E. Murphy, "With Anger and Disgust, Region Views Tape of bin Laden's Boasts," *New York Times*, Dec. 14, 2001.

508. Chomsky, *9-11*, p. 114.

509. See, e.g., the cover of *Time* (Special Issue: "America digs out—and digs in"), as well as the photo spread at pp. 24-5. It should be noted that these stills do not convey the impact of the massed firemen and other emergency workers responding to the president's squalid rhetoric with chants worthy of a football locker room—a truly disgusting spectacle.

510. It should be noted that by "the summer of 1998, the leader of the Taliban, Mullah Omar [had] struck a secret deal with the Saudis to expel [bin-Laden]. But just before Mullah Omar's order. . .was carried out, President Clinton ordered an illegal missile strike on Afghanistan. . .in retaliation for the bombing of U.S. embassies in Africa. Prince Turki al-Faisal, the head of Saudi intelligence who had brokered the deal, said 'The Taliban attitude changed 180 degrees' "; Rai, *War Plan Iraq*, p. 202. For further framing, see As'ad AbuKhalil, *Bin Laden, Islam and America's New "War on Terrorism"* (New York: Seven Stories Press, 2002).

511. The best overview is provided in Ahmed Rashid's *Taliban: Militant Islam, Oil and Fundamentalism in Central Asia* (New Haven, CT: Yale University Press, 2001).

512. As Arundhati Roy put it, "The Taliban's response to U.S. demands for the extradition of bin Laden has been uncharacteristically reasonable: produce the evidence, then we'll hand him over. President Bush's response is that the demand is non-negotiable"; quoted in Chomsky, *9-11*, p. 103. Roy also points out that the U.S. has been steadfast in its refusal to honor India's extradition request, complete with a solid evidentiary offer concerning his criminal culpability, for Union Carbide CEO Warren Anderson, an untended gas leak at whose Bhopal plant killed more than 16,000 people in 1984. Similarly, the U.S. has consistently refused Haiti's request for the extradition of Emmanuel Constant, a paramilitary leader believed to be responsible for the murders of at least 5,000 people in that tiny country (i.e., close to twice the number of U.S. citizens killed on 9-1-1, and proportionately the equivalent of several hundred thousand Americans). The pattern is not new, as is witnessed in the U.S. refusal to turn over its deposed ally, Mohammed Reza Shah Pahlavi, for trial in Iran, a matter figuring prominently in the 1980 "hostage crisis" at the U.S. embassy in Teheran; Nikki R. Keddie, *Roots of Revolution: An Interpretive History of Modern Iran* (New Haven, CT: Yale University Press, 1981) p. 270.

513. The formulation of this "stark choice" derives from that articulated by Bush himself, as quoted by R. W. Apple in the *New York Times*, Sept. 14, 2001.

514. "UN concern as air strikes bring relief efforts to a halt," *Financial Times*, Oct. 9, 2001.

515. "Relief workers hit at linking of food drops with air raids," *Financial Times*, Oct. 9, 2001.

516. Among the complainants were Oxfam International, Doctors Without Borders, Christian Aid, Save the Children and an array of UN officials; "Scepticism grows over US food drops," *Financial Times*, Oct. 10, 2001.

517. Altogether, a carrier fleet, plus some "fifty thousand American military personnel and four hundred aircraft were moved from the Red Sea to the Indian Ocean, about mid-November" to participate in the Afghanistan operation. These substantial ground forces were used mainly for "mop-up" and occupation purposes, however; Kolko, *Another Century*, p. 3.

518. Joost Hilterman, a Middle East specialist for Human Rights Watch; quoted in Chomsky, *9-11*, p. 96. Also see Ross Benson, "Chilling truth about the butchers who routed the Taliban," *Daily Mail*, Nov. 14, 2001.

519. Ibid. Also see the chapter entitled "Mazar-E-Sharif 1997: Massacre in the North," in Rashid, *Taliban*, pp. 53-66.

520. Wayne Veysey, "I saw the killing of a Taliban Soldier," *Scottish Daily Record*, Nov. 16, 2001.

521. Yvonne Abraham, "UN Backs Reports of Mass Execution: Says Opposition Killed Recruits Hiding at School," *Boston Globe*, Nov. 14, 2001; Chris Brummet, "U.N. Probes Alleged Afghan Killings," *New York Times*, Oct. 18, 2002.

522. "Afghan massacre puts Pentagon on the spot," *The Guardian*, Sept. 14, 2001.

523. Kate Connolly and Rory McCarthy, "New film Accuses US of war crimes," *The Guardian*, June 13, 2002.

524. As of Oct. 29, 2002, there were reportedly 625 prisoners at "Gitmo."

525. Barbara Olshansky, *Secret Trials and Executions: Military Tribunals and the Threat to Democracy* (New York: Seven Stories Press, 2002) p. 47. In general, Taliban soldiers are entitled to status as POWs, and are thus subject to the protections of the Third Geneva Convention, while al-Qaida personnel fall under the heading of "unprivileged combatants," and are thus subject to the protections of Geneva IV. "Illegal combatant" is not a valid classification. In any case, the conditions prevailing at Guantánamo Bay—holding prisoners in open air cages, for example—are legally impermissible. In no instance, moreover, is the U.S. empowered under either international or its own domestic law to try prisoners before military tribunals, as, on Nov. 13, 2001, George Bush announced it would do (the groundwork was laid in Defense Secretary Rumsfeld's Military Commission Order No. 1, Mar. 21, 2002). The texts of Geneva III and IV will be found in Roberts and Guelff, *Laws of War*, pp. 215-70. 271-38. For relevant domestic law, see *Ex Parte Milligan* (71 U.S. (4 Wall) 2 (1866)); *Zadvydas v. Davis* (121 S. Ct. 2491, 2500 (2001)). Overall, see Natsu Taylor Saito, "Will Force Trump Legality After September 11? American Jurisprudence Confronts the Rule of Law," *Georgetown Immigration Law Journal* (forthcoming).

526. "Detention Camp Commander Is Removed," *New York Times*, Oct. 15, 2002.

527. "Babbling at times like a child, the partially deaf, shriveled old man was unable to answer simple questions. He struggled to complete sentences and strained to hear words that were shouted at him. His faded mind kept failing him"; David Rohde, "Afghans Freed from Guantánamo Speak of Heat and Isolation," *New York Times*, Oct. 29, 2002.

528. Ibid.

529. On the authorization of tribunals, see note 524, esp. Olshansky, *Secret Trials and Executions*.

530. "The bill was never the subject of Committee debate or mark-up in the Senate. There was a truncated process in the House, which heard no official testimony from opponents of the bill but at least held a full Committee mark-up. But the result of that process was put aside by the Administration and the House leadership and never brought to a vote in the full House. . . It is virtually certain that not a single member of the House read the bill for which he or she voted"; David Cole and James X. Dempsey, *Terrorism and the Constitution* (New York: New Press, 2002) p. 151.

531. Uniting and Strengthening America by Providing Appropriate Tools Required to Intercept and Obstruct Terrorism (USA PATRIOT) Act of 2001 (115 Stat. 272). The Bail Reform Act of 1984 (18 U.S.C. § 3142) empowers authorities to nullify the right of accused individuals to bail upon argument by a prosecutor that s/he represents a "danger to the community." Since the Act's passage, such arguments have been made in more than 40 percent of all cases brought before federal courts (and every single "political" case; see my introductory essay, "The Third World at Home: Political Prisons and Prisoners in the United States," in *Cages of Steel*, p. 9-10. The Antiterrorism and Effective Death Penalty Act of 1996 (110 Stat. 214)

allows the secretary of state to define terrorism in entirely arbitrary ways, criminalizes even the most indirect support to organizations and/or individuals thus defined, and authorizes police and intelligence agencies to engage in previously illegal "counterintelligence" operations against those thus criminalized; see Cole and Dempsey, *Terrorism and the Constitution*, pp. 117-46. On counterintelligence techniques, see my and Jim Vander Wall's, *The COINTELPRO Papers: Documents from the FBI's Secret Wars Against Dissent in the United States* (Cambridge, MA: South End Press, [Classics Ed.] 2002).

532. Cole and Dempsey, *Terrorism and the Constitution*, pp. 147-75; Nancy Chang, *Silencing Political Dissent: How Post-September 11 Anti-Terrorism Measures Threaten Our Civil Liberties* (New York: Seven Stories Press, 2002). On "neutralization" as a counterintelligence objective, see my and Jim Vander Wall's *Agents of Repression: The FBI's Secret Wars Against the Black Panther Party and the American Indian Movement* (Cambridge, MA: South End Press, [Classics Ed.] 2002).

533. *Posse Comitatus* Act (18 U.S.C.S. § 1385). The Act is amended at 10 U.S.C. § 332, to allow the president to use the military to restore order, should enforcement of the law by civil authorities become literally "impracticable" (a very high threshold). Also at issue is an amendment accruing under Ronald Reagan's Economy Act (105 Stat. 1494), allowing the *noncombat* employment of military personnel in waging the so-called War on Drugs.

534. On police militarization, see the chapter entitled "Carrying the Big Stick: SWAT Teams and Paramilitary Policing," in Parenti, *Lockdown America*, pp. 111-38; Pat Cascio and John McSweeney, *SWAT Battle Tactics* (Boulder, CO: Paladin Press, 1996). On the HRT, which has never rescued a hostage, but which has repeatedly brought military Special Forces tactics to bear in the U.S. domestic context, see David T. Hardy and Rex Kimball, *This is Not an Assault: Penetrating the Web of Official Lies Regarding the Waco Incident* (San Antonio, TX: Xlibris, 2001) pp. 240-1.

535. On the Praetor Protocol, see my prefatory essay, "*The COINTELPRO Papers*: More Relevant Than Ever," in *COINTELPRO Papers*, at pp. xlvi-xlviii. For the record here, Delta Force personnel, wearing FBI field jackets, were deployed by Ronald Reagan during the 1987 Atlanta prison riot, by George Bush (the 41st) during the 1992 insurrection in Los Angeles, and Bill Clinton during both the 1993 siege of Branch Davidians near Waco, Texas, and during the 1998 WTO demonstrations in Seattle. The quasiofficial version of how all this came about is that, in 1987, Reagan secretly signed a "waiver" of the *Posse Comitatus* Act. According to then White House cybersecurity czar Richard Clark, "The president can waive this law at a moment's notice"; quoted in Robert Dreyfuss, "Spying on Ourselves," *Rolling Stone*, Mar. 28, 2002. The chief executive, of course, holds *no* lawful authority to "waive" *any* statute.

536. The exercises were conducted under headings such as "Rex-84." They conformed quite closely to "integrated force counterinsurgency scenarios" developed a decade earlier under the code names "Garden Plot" and "Cable Splicer" by founding FEMA director Louis O. Giuffrida at the behest of then-California governor Ronald Reagan; see *Agents of Repression*, pp. 194-5, 447.

537. David Cole, "Enemy Aliens," *Stanford Law Review*, Vol. 54, No. 5, 2002, p. 985.

538. The idea of using "internment centers"—concentration camps, by any other name—to neutralize the activities of political dissident Americans is not new. It was authorized under the Internal Security Act of 1950 (66 Stat. 163), a law that was not repealed until the early 1970s; see Thomas I. Emerson, *The System of Free Expression* (New York: Vintage, 1970) esp. p. 145; Kirkpatrick Sale, *SDS* (New York: Random House, 1973) p. 443. That preparations for such a move have been underway for some time are to some extent evidenced by the recent revelation that the Denver Police Department's intelligence unit has been compiling files on local activists under the caption "Criminal Extremist-G" for such nefarious activities as signing petitions and attending rallies; *American Friends Service Committee, et al., v. City and County of Denver* (Civ. No. 02-N-0740 (D. Colo.) (2002)). Also see Sarah Huntley, "Cops have 'spy files,' groups say," *Rocky Mountain News*, Mar. 12, 2002; "Denver Police Files Raise Rights Concerns," *New York Times*, Mar. 14, John C. Ensslin, "Spy files have storied past," *Rocky Mountain News*, Mar. 14, 2002; 2002; Judy Cart, "Denver Police Spied on Activists, ACLU Says," *Los Angeles Times*, Mar. 22, 2002. Relatedly, see Katharine Q. Seelye, "Appeals Court Again Hears Case of American Held Without Charges or Counsel," *New York Times*, Oct. 29, 2002.

539. See the chapter entitled "Dictators and Oil Barons: The Taliban and Central Asia, Russia, Turkey and Israel," in Rashid, *Taliban*, pp. 143-56. Also see the map at p. xii.

540. For strategic context, see Ahmed Rashid, *The Resurgence of Central Asia: Islam or Nationalism?* (London: Zed Books, 1994).

541. David Rohde, "Afghans Lead World Again in Poppy Crop," *New York Times*, Oct. 28, 2002; Chris Brummet, "Concerns Over Afghan Drug War," AP On-Line, Oct. 30, 2002. For background on the historical role of Afghanistan in the international drug trade, see the chapter entitled "Poppy Fields, Killing Fields and Druglords," in Cooley, *Unholy War*, pp. 127-61. For a broader view of how drug trafficking has figured in U.S. foreign policy, see Alfred W. McCoy, *The Politics of Heroin: CIA Complicity in the Global Drug Trade* (Brooklyn, NY: Lawrence Hill, 1991).

542. Sec. of Defense Rumsfeld, quoted in Gabriel Kolko, *Another Century of War?* (New York: New Press, 2002) p. 2. "55" is the more usual number, cited in Alexander and Swetnam, *al-Qaida*, p. viii. Either way, the implication is that the "war," as V.P. Dick Cheney put it on Oct. 18, 2001, "may never end. At least, not in our lifetime"; Kolko, *Another Century*, p. 2. For further analysis, see AbuKhalil, *"War on Terrorism"*.

543. "Colonel Muamar al-Qadaffi had combated the Islamists in his country from the time he seized power in Libya in a coup in 1969... Whenever disorders or violent opposition to his rule erupted in Libya, as it did in the eastern parts of his country during the later 1990s, travelers reaching Egypt would insist that Islamist groups had identified themselves as the authors"; Cooley, *Unholy War*, p. 214. More broadly, see Jonathan Bearman, *Qadhafi's Libya* (London: Zed Books, 1986). The idea of a "Qadaffi/al-Qaida connection" can thus be viewed as a pretext for settling longstanding and completely unrelated scores. For background, see the essay entitled "Libya in U.S. Demonology," in Chomsky, *Pirates and Emperors*, pp. 129-74.

544. On Abu Sayyaf, see the chapter entitled "More Contagion: The Philippines," in Cooley, *Unholy Wars*, pp. 248-58; on Islamicist activities in Chechnya and elsewhere in the Caucasus region, see the chapter entitled "Russia: Bitter Aftertaste and Reluctant Return," esp. pp. 174-84. On the Yemen "cells," see "Bin Laden Groomed Yemen Ties for Two Years," *Gulf News*, Oct. 21, 2000.

545. William Safire, "U.S. prepares to battle 'axis of evil,'" *San Francisco Chronicle*, Feb. 1, 2002.

546. "Misrepresentations of bin Laden abound. For example, he is sometimes portrayed as an ally of Saddam Hussein, although he clearly despises Hussein's secular leadership and brutal persecution of fundamentalists in Iraq." By the same token, Iran is an all but exclusively Shi'ite country. Al-Qaida "considers Shi'ites to be infidels, and [its] unofficial spokesman, Abu Qatada, calls them *rawafid*—literally, rejectionists...a pejorative term applied by some Sunnis to Shi'ites"; AbuKhalil, *"War on Terrorism"*, p. 76. On the mutual hostility of Iran and Iraq, see Dilip Hiro, *Neighbors, Not Friends: Iraq and Iran After the Gulf Wars* (New York: Routledge, 2001).

547. Far from being a sponsor of international terrorism, the communist state of North Korea is usually described as "reclusive" or "isolationist." Like its Caribbean counterpart, Cuba—which *is* routinely listed as a terrorist sponsor by the State Department—North Korea's involvement in such things seems mainly to have consisted of being on the receiving end of the terrorism practiced by CIA client organizations; see Herman, *The Real Terror Network*.

548. Matthew Lee, "Former secretary of state Albright blasts Bush for 'axis of evil' tag," Agence France-Presse, Feb. 1, 2002.

549. For a survey of official pronouncements, see Jonathan Wright, "U.S. Rhetoric on Iraq Puts Credibility On Line," *New York Times*, Aug. 20, 2002.

550. One of the conduits through which the materials necessary to Iraq's illegal armaments programs passed during the '80s was the Halliburton Corp., a board member of which was the current U.S. Vice President, Dick Cheney; William Rivers Pitt, "An Interview with Scott Ritter," in William Rivers Pitts with Scott Ritter, *War on Iraq: What Team Bush Doesn't Want You to Know* (New York: Context Books, 2002) pp. 38-9. Also see Patrick E. Tyler, "Reagan Aided Iraq Despite Use of Gas," *New York Times*, Aug. 18, 2002. A still broader view is provided in Alan Friedman's *Spider's Web: The secret history of how the White House illegally armed Iraq* (New York: Bantam Books, 1993).

551. Pitt, "Interview with Scott Ritter," pp. 41, 42.

552. Ibid., pp. 33, 34, 36-7.

553. "The Vice President has been saying that Iraq might be two years away from building a nuclear bomb. Unless he knows something we don't, that's nonsense. And it doesn't appear he does,

because whenever you press the Vice President or other Bush administration officials on these claims, they fall back on testimony by Richard Butler, my former boss, an Australian diplomat, and Khidre Hamza, an Iraqi defector who claims to be Saddam's bomb-maker. Neither of these people provide anything more than speculation to back up their assertions. The Vice President's continued claims about Iraq's nuclear weapons capability are unsubstantiated speculation. And of course that's not good enough, especially when we have the United Nations record of Iraqi disarmament from 1991 to 1998. That record is without dispute. . . We eliminated the nuclear program, and for Iraq to have reconstituted it would require undertaking activities eminently detectable by intelligence services"; ibid. p. 32.

554. These include the Security Council's 1967 Resolution 242, calling upon Israel to withdraw from territory beyond its borders; Security Council Resolution 338 (1973), essentially reiterating Resolution 242; Security Council Resolution 425 (1978), calling upon Israel to withdraw its forces from Lebanon; Security Council Resolution 465 (1980), calling upon Israel halt its pattern of violation the Geneva IV Convention; and Security Council Resolution 1322 (2000), reiterating Resolution 465 in even more emphatic terms. Also at issue are General Assembly Resolution 181 (1947), establishing Israel's original borders; a 1967 General Assembly Resolution affirming the right of Palestinians to national self-determination; and a 1997 General Assembly Resolution calling for an end to all settlement activities in the Occupied Territories. During the 1988 General Assembly session alone, nearly a score of resolutions were passed—and mostly vetoed by the U.S.—condemning Israel for violations of the Geneva (IV) Convention during its bloody repression of the Palestinian Intifada. Israel has also been repeatedly condemned by the Security Council for specific acts of aggression beginning with the Oct. 1953 massacre at Qibya perpetrated by Ariel Sharon's notorious Unit 101; Shlaim, *Iron Wall*, pp. 261, 291, 303, 310, 321, 322, 338, 356, 456, 322, 338, 356, 495, 592, 25, 333, 454-5, 92; Noam Chomsky, "Terror and Just Response," in Rai, *War Plan Iraq*, p. 30.

555. Precisely when and how Israel acquired nuclear arms capability remains unclear, but it had 10 operational devices by 1968; David Burnham, "U.S. Agencies Suspected Missing Uranium Went to Israel for Arms," *New York Times*, Nov. 6, 1977. Irrespective of the details, the Israeli acquisition is contrary to the International Treaty on Non-Proliferation of Nuclear Weapons (1970). Overall, see Seymore M. Hersh, *The Sampson Option: Israel, America and the Bomb* (London: Faber and Faber, 1991).

556. India tested its first device in 1974, Pakistan a decade later; Anna Gyorgy and Friends, *No Nukes: Everyone's Guide to Nuclear Power* (Boston: South End Press, 1979) p. 304.

557. "Prior to the Gulf War, Iraq acquired a lot of technology, as well as parts, from Germany, which has a record of precision machinery. After the war, the Iraqis tried to replicate that, but with very little success. . . I hear people talking about Iraq having multi-staging rockets, but Iraq doesn't have multi-staging capability. They tried that once, back in 1989 when the country had full access to technology, and the rocket blew up in midair. I hear people talk about clustering, but Iraq tried that, too, and it didn't work. The bottom line is that Iraq doesn't have the capability to do long-range ballistic missiles. They don't even have the capability to do short-range ballistic missiles"; Pitt, "Interview with Scott Ritter," p. 47.

558. David Rennie, "Czechs deny meeting of 9/11 leader and Iraqi official: False report was 'smoking gun' linking Saddam to terrorist attack," *National Post*, Oct. 22, 2002.

559. David S. Cloud, "Missing Links: Bush Efforts to Tie Hussein to al Qaeda Lack Clear Evidence," *Wall Street Journal*, Oct. 23, 2002.

560. Rennie, "Czechs deny."

561. Bill Kemper with Jill Zuckman, "Bush to UN: Act on Iraq," *Chicago Tribune*, Sept. 13, 2002.

562. Chris McCann, "U.S. is at a 'Defining Moment' in Its History: Rule of Law or Renegade?" *Seattle Post-Intelligencer*, Oct. 5, 2002.

563. In fairness, Sharon had probably been led to believe that his actions would receive the usual unqualified U.S. support. On Dec. 14, 2001, for example, the U.S. vetoed a Security Council resolution calling for the introduction of UN peacekeepers to the West Bank in hopes of averting an escalation of hostilities there. Ten days earlier, it had boycotted—and thus effectively scuttled—an international conference called in Geneva to reaffirm Israel's obligation to comply with the Geneva IV Convention's requirements for protecting "enemy" civilians in times of armed conflict; Chomsky, "Terror and Just Response," pp. 29-30.

564. "Group accuses Israel of War Crimes," *Chicago Tribune*, Nov. 5, 2002.

565. John Ward Anderson, "Report ties Israel with war crimes: Human rights group says West Bank raids used excessive force against Palestinians," *Washington Post*, Nov. 4, 2002.

566. Israel's pretense that it was merely "responding" to a "wave of terrorism" embodied in Palestinian suicide bombings may have played well in Peoria—and on Fox News—but virtually nowhere outside the U.S. and Israel itself. Most of the rest of the world remains rational enough to realize that suicide bombing is a tactic employed only by disempowered and utterly desperate people in a forlorn hope of gaining some sort of military parity with their oppressors. In other words, it is generally understood that it is the *Palestinians* who are "responding" to perpetual Israeli terrorism, a matter readily borne out in the lopsided fatality rates they've suffered all along; for background, see Zachary Lockman and Joel Beinin, *Intifada: The Palestinian Uprising Against Israeli Occupation* (Boston: South End Press, 1989); Roane Carey, ed., *The New Intifada: Resisting Israel's Apartheid* (London: Verso, 2001).

567. MSNBC and CNN broadcasts, Nov. 8, 2002.

568. Robert Holloway, "Bush turns up heat on UN Security Council to act against Iraq," Agence France-Presse, Oct. 29, 2002.

569. Patrick E. Tyler, "Bush Signal: Time Is Now," *New York Times*, Nov. 8, 2002.

570. George W. Bush, press statement broadcast of CNN, Nov. 8, 2002. Also see David E. Sanger and Julia Preston, "President Warns Hussein to Heed a Call to Disarm: U.N. Vote Set for Today," *New York Times*, Nov. 8, 2002.

571. See note 435.

572. McCann, "Defining Moment."

573. Monte Reel and Manny Fernandez, "100,000 Rally, March Against War in Iraq," *Washington Post*, Oct. 27, 2002.

574. Narrower forms of crass self-interest underlay the rhetorical purity of principle marking the Vietnam-era antiwar movement. Witness, for example, the rapidity with which the mass movement withered after the draft was reformed (1969) and U.S. ground forces withdrawn (1972). The war itself was continued on the basis of U.S. support for another three years—and Vietnamese died at rates as great as ever—but without substantial protest from the American "antiwar" activists. In effect, once they themselves were no longer faced with the prospect of having to fight it, average protestors' "concerns of conscience" about the war abated both quickly and dramatically; Terry H. Anderson, *The Movement and the Sixties: Protest in America from Greensboro to Wounded Knee* (New York: Oxford University Press, 1995) pp. 379–80.

575. Deborah L. Madsen, *American Exceptionalism* (Jackson: University of Mississippi Press, 1998). For framing in the dimension at issue here, see my and Mike Ryan's *Pacifism as Pathology: Reflections on the Role of Armed Struggle in North America* (Winnipeg: Arbeiter Ring, 1998).

576. For an especially biting analysis, see Mairowitz, *The Radical Soap Opera*.

577. The "master work" in this connection is Gene Sharp's *The Politics of Nonviolent Action*, 3 vols. (Boston: Porter Sargent, 1973). Also see Staughton Lynd and Alice Lynd, eds., *Nonviolence in America: A Documentary History* (Maryknoll, NY: Orbis Books, 1995).

578. This critique is not new, having been advanced by the Revolutionary Youth Movement faction of Students for a Democratic Society (SDS) from 1967 onward; see, e.g., Ron Jacobs, *The Way the Wind Blew: A History of the Weather Underground* (London: Verso, 1997) pp. 1–23. Also see Karin Ashley, et al., "You Don't Need a Weatherman to Know Which Way the Wind Blows," in Harold Jacobs, ed., *Weatherman* (San Francisco: Ramparts Press, 1970) pp. 51–90.

579. "In post-Nuremberg settings, a government that flagrantly violates international law is engaged in criminal behavior even on the domestic plane, and as far as internal law is concerned, its policies are not entitled to respect. To disobey is no longer, as with Thoreau, to engage in 'civil disobedience,' an initiative designed to point up the discrepancy between 'law' and 'morality,' and the priority of the latter for the person of conscience. Such a tension no longer exists. To resist reasonably a violation of international law is a matter of legal right, possibly even of legal duty if knowledge and a capacity for action exists. [R]esisters who properly invoke the authority of Nuremberg stand on firm legal ground, and should not be sent off to jail, but should be exonerated. Or better, the courts should lend the weight of their authority to the claim that a given direction of foreign policy or national security doctrine [is] incompatible with international law, and its principle executors are subject to prosecution"; Richard

Falk, "Introduction" to Francis Anthony Boyle, *Defending Civil Resistance Under International Law* (Dobbs Ferry, NY: Transnational, 1988) p. xxi.

580. The principle is closely related to that expressed in UN Res. 42/159 (1987), asserting that what would otherwise be classified as "terrorism"—that is, "the calculated and illegal use of violence or threat of violence to attain goals that are political, religious, or ideological in nature"—is permissible when its purpose is to obtain "the right to self-determination, freedom, and independence, as derived from the Charter of the United Nations, of people forcibly deprived of that right. . .particularly peoples under colonial and racist regimes and foreign occupation; Chomsky, "Terror and Just Response," p. 23.

581. This principle is generally accepted, even in the U.S., so long as the "right" government is at issue. Witness all the recent chatter emanating from the departments of state and defense about the desirability of the Iraqis themselves "removing" Saddam Hussein (through means always left to the imagination). More classic is America's postwar valorization of the group of army officers who attempted to assassinate Adolf Hitler and seize control of Germany in 1944; see Peter Hoffmann, *The History of the German Resistance, 1933-1945* (Montréal: McGill-Queens University Press, [3rd ed.] 1996) esp. "Part VI: Assassination Attempts, 1933-1942" (pp. 251-62) and "Part VIII: Stauffenberg and the Replacement Army" (pp. 315-503). U.S. adherence to legal norms in advocating/orchestrating citizen violence against selected governments is, however, entirely situational. Consider, for instance, the immediate and massive support accruing to the openly fascist Pinochet régime in Chile, following the CIA-backed 1973 coup in which, among other things, Pinochet's insurgents assassinated Chile's duly-elected president, Salvador Allende, and committed the mass murder of some 4,000 Chilean progressives; see Mary Helen Spooner, *Soldiers in a Narrow Land: The Pinochet Regime in Chile* (Berkeley: University of California Press, [2nd ed.] 1999) pp. 17-82; Hugh O'Shaughnessy, *Pinochet: The Politics of Torture* (New York: New York University Press, 2000) pp. 49-63. Given their own record and posture, for U.S. officials to contend that it would be "wrong"—much less "illegal"—for American citizens to use force as a means of compelling governmental adherence to international human rights law and/or the laws of war is utterly ludicrous.

582. For further explication of this principle, see Karl Jaspers, E.B. Ashton and Joseph W. Koterski, *The Question of German Guilt* (New York: Fordham University Press, 2002).

583. See notes 4, 5, and accompanying text.

584. See note 11 and accompanying text.

585. See note 17 and accompanying text.

586. There are currently no fewer than 24 books in print concerning the Jonbenet Ramsey case; see, as examples, Carlton Smith, *Death of a Little Princess: The Tragic Story of the Murder of Jonbenet Ramsey* (New York: St. Martin's Press, 1997); Cyril H. Wecht and Charles Bosworth, Jr., *Who Killed Jonbenet Ramsey? A Leading Forensic Expert Uncovers the Shocking Facts* (New York: Signet, 1998); Lawrence Schiller, *Perfect Murder, Perfect Town: The Uncensored Story of the Jonbenet Murder and the Grand Jury's Search for the Final Truth* (New York: Harper, 1999). On the far more recent, but equally sensationalized case of Danielle van Dam, see Tony Perry, "Van Dams Agree With Jury Penalty Decision: Death for her daughter's killer is 'right,' but life in prison without parole would be acceptable," *Los Angeles Times*, Sept. 18, 2002. It should be noted that the now 7-year-old Ramsey case was still being treated as an appropriate subject of "in-depth" media analysis as recently as Nov. 14, 2002, when MSNBC aired a lengthy segment featuring clips taken from the Boulder (Colorado) Police Department's interrogations of her parents.

587. Christopher Hitchens presents one case rather well in his *The Trial of Henry Kissinger* (London: Verso, 2001). The specification of charges against Albright would be similar. These two are merely representative. A long list of still-living U.S. officials are of course guilty of comparable criminality.

588. Prof. Natsu Taylor Saito, interview on the National Public Radio *Powerpoint* program, broadcast on Atlanta radio station WCLK, Nov. 4, 2001.

589. For an itemization of the "stupid rule list," see Keith L. Alexander, "Some Rules Deserve to Go, TSA Agrees," *Washington Post*, Oct. 16, 2002.

590. James Risen with Neil MacFarquhar, "New Recording May Be Threat from bin Laden," *New York Times*, Nov. 13, 2002.

591. 180 people were killed in the Bali blasts, most of them Australian tourists, targeted because of their government's endorsement of the U.S. "war on terrorism"; see Ellen Nakashima and Alan Sipress, "Bombing Kills at Least 180 in Indonesian Club; Site Popular with Foreigners; 2nd Blast Hits Near U.S.

Office," *Washington Post*, Oct. 13, 2002; Mike Corder, "Al-Qaida involved in Bali bombings and more attacks to come, says Australia's spy chief," Associated Press, Oct. 31, 2002. Bin-Laden also mentioned that a French oil tanker off Yemen was heavily damaged in another recent al-Qaida operation; Sebastian Rotella and Esther Schrader, "Tanker Blast Likely a Terror Attack; Debris indicates small boat was apparently used to attack the ship of Yemen; U.S. sees incident as part of new campaign," *Los Angeles Times*, Oct. 11, 2002; Ahmed al-Haj, "Attack on French tanker similar to *USS Cole* bombing," Associated Press, Oct. 24, 2002.

592. The Chechens had managed to move large quantities of explosives into Moscow, despite Russia's supposedly "airtight" security, then seized a theater in which some 800 members of the Russian élite were viewing a performance, threatening to blow it up unless the government altered its policy of denying self-determination to Chechnya. Ultimately, the Spetznatz (Russian Special Forces) "rescued" the hostages by using a gas which killed 118 of them; Sarah Karush, "Russian lawmaker: Putin pledges to appoint official to answer lingering questions about hostage crisis," Associated Press, Nov. 15, 2002. For insight into the "terrorists'" motives, see "Human rights groups say Russian troops have killed 20,000 Chechens in 3 years," Associated Press, Nov. 15, 2002.

593. "Palestinian militants have carried out about 80 suicide bombings, killing almost 300 people, since the [second intifada] began just over two years ago"; Laurence Copans, "Palestinian suicide bomber strikes at Jewish settlement, four killed," Associated Press, Oct., 27, 2002. Also see "Chronology of major anti-Israeli attacks in Palestinian uprising," Agence France-Presse, Sept. 18, 2002. It should be noted that several of the more significant Arab terrorist organizations were spawned in response to specific Israeli acts of aggression. The Palestine Liberation Organization (PLO) was established in 1964 with the support of Egyptian president Abdul Gamal Nasser, mainly in reaction to Israel's ongoing refusal to resolve territorial issues arising from its drive to the Suez a decade earlier. The Iranian/Syrian-backed Hizbullah (Party of God) was created in the wake of Israel's 1982 invasion of Lebanon. Hamas (Zeal) was born in 1988, as a reaction to Israel's draconian repression of the decidedly nonviolent intifada. Both Hamas and the Islamic Jihad were in decline until Prime Minister Benyamin Netanyahu's 1997 escalation of Israeli "settlement" efforts in the West Bank—a direct violation of the 1995 Oslo II Peace Accords—prompted an upsurge in suicide bombings by both groups; Shlaim, *Iron Wall*, pp. 187, 427, 459, 584. For further background, see Kameel B. Nasr, *Arab and Israeli Terrorism* (Jefferson, NC: McFarland, 1997).

594. This is not to say that it would be Iraq providing such weapons. There are several U.S. "allies"—Pakistan, for instance—possessed of them. Indeed, Scott Ritter has laid out a scenario in which he believes U.S. or Israeli actions against Iraq could lead Pakistan and/or Iran to "turn over nuclear capability to terrorists [and] within ten years the United States would be struck by a terrorist nuclear bomb"; Pitt, *War on Iraq*, p. 65.

# Appendix A

# Declaration on the Granting of Independence to Colonial Countries and Peoples

## United Nations General Assembly Resolution 1514 (XV)

## December 14, 1960

THE GENERAL ASSEMBLY.

*Mindful* of the determination proclaimed by the peoples of the world in the Charter of the United Nations to reaffirm faith in fundamental human rights, in the dignity and worth of the human person, in the equal rights of men and women and of nations large and small and to provide social progress and better standards of life in larger freedom,

*Conscious* of the need for creation of conditions of stability and well-being and peaceful and friendly relations based on respect for the principles of equal rights and self-determination for all peoples, and of universal respect for, and observance of, human rights and fundamental freedoms for all without distinction as to race, sex, language or religion,

*Recognizing* the passionate yearning for freedom in all dependent peoples and the decisive role of the freedom of such peoples, which constitute a serious threat to world peace,

*Aware of* the increasing conflicts resulting from the denial of or impediments in the way of the freedom of such peoples, which constitute a serious threat to world peace,

*Considering* the important role of the United Nations in assisting the movement for independence in Trust or Non-Self-Governing Territories,

*Recognizing* that the peoples of the world ardently desire the end of colonialism in all its manifestations,

*Convinced* that the continued existence of colonialism prevents the development of international economic co-operation, impedes the social, cultural and economic development of dependent peoples and militates against the United Nations ideal of universal peace,

*Affirming* that peoples may, for their own ends, freely dispose of their natural wealth and resources without prejudice to any obligations arising out of international economic co-operation, based upon the principle of mutual benefit, and international law,

*Believing* that the process of liberation is irresistible and irreversible and that, in order to avoid serious crises, an end must be put to colonialism and all practices of discrimination and segregation associated therewith,

*Welcoming* the emergence in recent years of a large number of dependent territories into freedom and independence, and recognizing the increasingly powerful trends towards freedom in such territories which have not yet attained independence,

*Convinced* that all peoples have the inalienable right to complete freedom, the exercise of their sovereignty and the integrity of their national territory,

*Solemnly proclaims* the necessity of bringing to a speedy and unconditional end colonialism in all its forms and manifestations;

And to this end

*Declares* that:

1. The subjection of peoples to alien subjugation, domination and exploitation constitutes a denial of fundamental human rights, is contrary to the Charter of the United Nations and is an impediment to the promotion of world peace and co-operation.

2. All peoples have the right to self-determination; by virtue of that right they freely determine their political status and freely pursue their economic, social and cultural development.

3. Inadequacy of political, economic, social or educational preparedness should never serve as a pretext for delaying independence.

4. All armed actions or repressive measures of all kinds directed against

dependent peoples shall cease in order to enable them to exercise peacefully and freely their right to complete independence, and the integrity of their national territory shall be respected.

5. Immediate steps shall be taken, in Trust and Non-Self-Governing Territories and all other territories which have not yet attained independence, to transfer all powers to the peoples of those territories, without any conditions or reservations, in accordance with their freely expressed will and desire, without any distinction as to race, creed or colour, in order to enable them to enjoy complete independence and freedom.

6. Any attempt aimed at the partial or total disruption of the national unity and the territorial integrity of a country is incompatible with the purpose and principles of the Charter of the United Nations.

7. All States shall observe faithfully and strictly the provisions of the Charter of the United Nations, the Universal Declaration of Human Rights and the present Declaration on the basis of equality, noninterference in the internal affairs of all States, and respect for the sovereign rights of all peoples and their territorial integrity.

# Appendix B

# Congressional Apology to Native Hawaiians

## Public Law 103-150

### 1993

To acknowledge the 100th anniversary of the January 17, 1893 overthrow of the Kingdom of Hawaii, and to offer an apology the Native Hawaiians on behalf of the United States for the overthrow of the Kingdom of Hawaii.

Whereas, prior to the arrival of the first Europeans in 1778, the Native Hawaiian people lived in a highly organized, self-sufficient, subsistent social system based on communal land tenure with a sophisticated language, culture, and religion;

Whereas, a unified monarchical government of the Hawaiian Islands was established in 1810 under Kamehameha I, the first king of Hawaii;

Whereas, from 1826 until 1893, the United States recognized the independence of the Kingdom of Hawaii, extended full and complete diplomatic recognition to the Hawaiian Government, and entered into treaties and conventions with the Hawaiian monarchs to govern commerce and navigation in 1826, 1842, 1849, 1875, and 1887;

Whereas the Congregational Church (now known as the United Church of Christ), through its American Board of Commissioners for Foreign Missions, sponsored and sent more than 100 missionaries to the Kingdom of Hawaii between 1820 and 1850;

Whereas, on January 14, 1893, John L. Stevens (hereafter referred to in this Resolution as the "United States Minister"), the United States Minister assigned to the sovereign and independent Kingdom of Hawaii conspired with a small group of non-Hawaiian residents of the Kingdom of Hawaii, including citizens of the United States, to overthrow the indigenous and lawful Government of Hawaii;

Whereas, in pursuance of the conspiracy to overthrow the Government of Hawaii, the United States Minister and the naval representatives of the United States caused armed naval forces of the United States to invade the sovereign Hawaiian nation on January 16, 1893, and to position themselves near the Hawaiian Government buildings and the Iolani Palace to intimidate Queen Liliuokalani and her Government;

Whereas, on the afternoon of January 17, 1893, a Committee of Safety that represented the American and European sugar planters, descendents of missionaries, and financiers deposed the Hawaiian monarchy and proclaimed the establishment of a Provisional Government;

Whereas the United States Minister thereupon extended diplomatic recognition to the Provisional Government that was formed by the conspirators without the consent of the Native Hawaiian people or the lawful Government of Hawaii and in violation of treaties between the two nations and of international law;

Whereas, soon thereafter, when informed of the risk of bloodshed with resistance, Queen Liliuokalani issued the following statement yielding her authority to the United States Government rather than to the Provisional Government:

I Liliuokalani, by the Grace of God and under the Constitution of the Hawaiian Kingdom, Queen, do hereby solemnly protest against any and all acts done against myself and the Constitutional Government of the Hawaiian Kingdom by certain persons claiming to have established a Provisional Government of and for this Kingdom... That I yield to the superior force of the United States of America whose Minister Plenipotentiary, His Excellency John L. Stevens, has caused United States troops to be landed at Honolulu and declared that he would support the Provisional Government... Now to avoid any collision of armed forces, and perhaps the loss of life, I do this under protest and impelled by said force yield my authority until such time as the Government of the United States shall, upon facts being presented to it, undo the action of its representatives and reinstate me in the authority which I claim as the Constitutional Sovereign of the Hawaiian Islands.

Done at Honolulu this 17th day of January, A.D. 1893

Whereas, without the active support and intervention by the United States diplomatic and military representatives, the insurrection against the Government of the Queen Liliuokalani would have failed for lack of popular support and insufficient arms;

Whereas, on February 1, 1893, the United States Minister raised the American flag and proclaimed Hawaii to be a protectorate of the United States;

Whereas the report of a Presidentially established investigation conducted by former Congressman James Blount into the events surrounding the insurrection and overthrow of January 17, 1893, concluded that the United States diplomatic and military representatives had abused their authority and were responsible for the change in government;

Whereas, as a result of this investigation, the United States Minister to Hawaii was recalled from his diplomatic post and the military commander of the United States armed forces stationed in Hawaii was disciplined and forced to resign his commission;

Whereas, in a message to Congress on December 18, 1893, President Grover Cleveland reported fully and accurately on the illegal acts of the conspirators, described such acts as an "act of war, committed with the participation of a diplomatic representative of the United States and without authority of Congress," and acknowledged that by such acts the government of a peaceful and friendly people was overthrown;

Whereas President Cleveland further concluded that a "substantial wrong has thus been done which a due regard for our national character as well as the rights of the injured people requires we should endeavor to repair" and called for the restoration of the Hawaiian monarchy;

Whereas the Provisional Government protested President Cleveland's call for the restoration of the monarchy and continued to hold state power and pursue annexation to the United States;

Whereas the Provisional Government successfully lobbied the Committee on Foreign Relations of the Senate (hereafter referred to in this Resolution as the "Committee") to conduct a new investigation into the events surrounding the overthrow of the monarchy;

Whereas the Committee and its chairman, Senator John Morgan, conducted hearings in Washington, D.C., from December 27, 1893, through February 26, 1894, in which members of the Provisional

410

Government justified and condoned the actions of the United States Minister and recommended annexation of Hawaii;

Whereas, although the Provisional Government was able to obscure the role of the United States in the illegal overthrow of the Hawaiian monarchy, it was unable to rally the support from two-thirds of the Senate needed to ratify a treaty of annexation;

Whereas, on July 4, 1894, the Provisional Government declared itself to be the Republic of Hawaii;

Whereas, on January 24, 1895, while imprisoned in Iolani Palace, Queen Liliuokalani was forced by representatives of the Republic of Hawaii to officially abdicate her throne;

Whereas, in the 1896 United States Presidential election, William McKinley replaced Grover Cleveland;

Whereas, on July 7, 1898, as a consequence of the Spanish-American War, President McKinley signed the Newlands Joint Resolution that provided for the annexation of Hawaii;

Whereas, through the Newlands Resolution, the self-declared Republic of Hawaii ceded sovereignty over the Hawaiian Islands to the United States;

Whereas the Republic of Hawaii also ceded 1,800,000 acres of crown, government and public lands of the Kingdom of Hawaii, without the consent of or compensation to the Native Hawaiian people of Hawaii or their sovereign government;

Whereas the Congress, through the Newlands Resolution, ratified the cession, annexed Hawaii as part of the United States, and vested title to the lands in Hawaii in the United States;

Whereas the Newlands Resolution also specified that treaties existing between Hawaii and foreign nations were to immediately cease and be replaced by United States treaties with such nations;

Whereas the Newlands Resolution effected the transaction between the Republic of Hawaii and the United States Government;

Whereas the indigenous Hawaiian people never directly relinquished their claims to their inherent sovereignty as a people or over their national lands to the United States, either through their monarchy or through a plebiscite or referendum;

Whereas, on April 30, 1900, President McKinley signed the Organic Act that provided a government for the territory of Hawaii and defined the political structure and powers of the newly established Territorial Government and its relationship to the United States;

Whereas, on August 21, 1959, Hawaii became the 50th State of the United States;

Whereas the health and well-being of the Native Hawaiian people is intrinsically tied to their deep feelings and attachment to the land;

Whereas the long-range economic and social changes in Hawaii over the nineteenth and early twentieth centuries have been devastating to the population and to the health and well-being of the Hawaiian people;

Whereas, the Native Hawaiian people are determined to preserve, develop and transmit to future generations their ancestral territory, and their cultural identity in accordance with their own spiritual and traditional beliefs, customs, practices, language, and social institutions;

Whereas, in order to promote racial harmony and cultural understanding, the Legislature of the State of Hawaii has determined that the year 1993 should serve Hawaii as a year of special reflection on the rights and dignities of the Native Hawaiians in the Hawaiian and American societies;

Whereas the Eighteenth General Synod of the United Church of Christ in recognition of the denomination's historical complicity in the illegal overthrow of the Kingdom of Hawaii in 1893 directed the Office of the President of the United Church of Christ to offer a public apology to the Native Hawaiian people and to initiate the process of reconciliation between the United Church of Christ and the Native Hawaiians; and

Whereas it is proper and timely for the Congress on the occasion of the impending one hundredth anniversary of the event, to acknowledge the historic significance of the illegal overthrow of the Kingdom of Hawaii, to express its deep regret to the Native Hawaiian people, and to support the reconciliation efforts of the State of Hawaii and the United Church of Christ with Native Hawaiians: Now therefore be it

*Resolved by the Senate and House of Representatives of the United States of America in Congress assembled,*

## Section 1: Acknowledgement and Apology

The Congress—

(1) on the occasion of the 100th anniversary of the illegal overthrow of the Kingdom of Hawaii on January 17, 1893, acknowledges the historical significance of this event which resulted in the suppression of the inherent sovereignty of the Native Hawaiian people;

(2) recognizes and commends efforts of reconciliation initiated by the State of Hawaii and the United Church of Christ with Native Hawaiians;

(3) apologizes to Native Hawaiians on behalf of the people of the United States for the overthrow of the Kingdom of Hawaii on January 17, 1893 with the participation of agents and citizens of the United States, and the deprivation of the rights of Native Hawaiians to self-determination;

(4) expresses its commitment to acknowledge the ramifications of the overthrow of the Kingdom of Hawaii, in order to provide a proper foundation for reconciliation between the United States and the Native Hawaiian people; and

(5) urges the President of the United States to also acknowledge the ramifications of the overthrow of the Kingdom of Hawaii and to support reconciliation efforts between the United States and the Native Hawaiian people.

## Section 2: Definitions

As used in this Joint Resolution, the terms "Native Hawaiian" means any individual who is a descendent of the aboriginal people who, prior to 1778, occupied and exercised sovereignty in the area that now constitutes the State of Hawaii.

## Section 3: Disclaimer

Nothing in this Joint Resolution is intended to serve as a settlement of any claims against the United States.

## Appendix C

# Draft United Nations Declaration on the Rights of Indigenous Peoples

## A Report of the Sub-Commission on Prevention of Discrimination and Protection of Minorities

### 46th Session, August 1994

*Affirming* that indigenous peoples are equal in dignity and rights to all other peoples, while recognizing the right of all peoples to be different, to consider themselves different, and to be respected as such,

*Affirming also* that all peoples contribute to the diversity and richness of civilizations and cultures, which constitute the common heritage of mankind,

*Affirming further* that all doctrines, policies and practices based on or advocating superiority of peoples or individuals on the basis of national origin, racial, religious, ethnic or cultural differences are racist, scientifically false, legally invalid, morally condemnable and socially unjust,

*Reaffirming also* that indigenous peoples, in the exercise of their rights, should be free of discrimination of any kind,

*Concerned* that indigenous peoples have been deprived of their human rights and fundamental freedoms, resulting, *inter alia*, in their colonization and dispossession of their lands, territories and resources, thus preventing them from exercising, in particular, their right to development in accordance with their own needs and interests,

*Recognizing* the urgent need to respect and promote the inherent rights and characteristics of indigenous peoples, especially their rights to their lands, territories and resources, which derive from their political, economic and social structures and from their cultures, spiritual traditions, histories and philosophies,

*Welcoming* the fact that indigenous peoples are organizing themselves for political, economic, social and cultural enhancement and in order to bring an end to all forms of discrimination and oppression wherever they occur,

*Convinced* that control by indigenous peoples over developments affecting them and their lands, territories and resources will enable them to maintain and strengthen their institutions, cultures and traditions, and to promote their development in accordance with their aspirations and needs,

*Recognizing also* that respect for indigenous knowledge, cultures and traditional practices contributes to sustainable and equitable development and proper management of the environment,

*Emphasizing* the need for demilitarization of the lands and territories of indigenous peoples, which will contribute to peace, economic and social progress and development, understanding and friendly relations among nations and peoples of the world,

*Recognizing* in particular the right of indigenous families and communities to retain shared responsibility for the upbringing, training, education and well-being of their children,

*Recognizing also* that indigenous peoples have the right freely to determine their relationships with States in a spirit of coexistence, mutual benefit and full respect,

*Considering* that treaties, agreements and other arrangements between States and indigenous peoples are properly matters of international concern and responsibility,

*Acknowledging* that the Charter of the United Nations, the International Covenant on Economic, Social and Cultural Rights and the International Covenant on Civil and Political Rights affirm the fundamental importance of the right of self-determination of all peoples, by virtue of which they freely determine their political status and freely pursue their economic, social and cultural development,

*Bearing in mind* that nothing in this Declaration may be used to deny any peoples their right of self-determination,

*Encouraging* States to comply with and effectively implement all international instruments, in particular those related to human rights, as they apply to indigenous peoples, in consultation and cooperation with the peoples concerned,

*Emphasizing* that the United Nations has an important and continuing role to play in promoting and protecting the rights of indigenous peoples,

*Believing* that this Declaration is a further important step forward for the recognition, promotion and protection of the rights and freedoms of indigenous peoples and in the development of relevant activities of the United Nations system in this field,

*Solemnly proclaims* the following United Nations Declaration on the Rights of Indigenous Peoples:

## PART I

### Article 1

Indigenous peoples have the right to the full and effective enjoyment of all human rights and fundamental freedoms recognized in the Charter of the United Nations, the Universal Declaration of Human Rights and international human rights law.

### Article 2

Indigenous individuals and peoples are free and equal to all other individuals and peoples in dignity and rights, and have the right to be free from any kind of adverse discrimination, in particular that based on their indigenous origin or identity.

### Article 3

Indigenous peoples have the right of self-determination. By virtue of that right they freely determine their political status and freely pursue their economic, social and cultural development.

## Article 4

Indigenous peoples have the right to maintain and strengthen their distinct political, economic, social and cultural characteristics, as well as their legal systems, while retaining their rights to participate fully, if they so choose, in the political economic, social and cultural life of the State.

## Article 5

Every indigenous individual has the right to a nationality.

## PART II

## Article 6

Indigenous peoples have the collective right to live in freedom, peace and security as distinct peoples and to full guarantees against genocide or any other act of violence, including the removal of indigenous children from their families and communities under any pretext.

In addition, they have the individual rights to life, physical and mental integrity, liberty and security of persons.

## Article 7

Indigenous peoples have the collective and individual right not to be subjected to ethnocide and cultural genocide, including prevention of and redress for:

(a) Any action which has the aim or effect of depriving them of their integrity as distinct peoples, or of their cultural values or ethnic identities;

(b) Any action which has the aim or effect of dispossessing them of their lands, territories or resources;

(c) Any form of population transfer which has the aim or effect of violating or undermining any of their rights;

(d) Any form of assimilation or integration by other cultures or ways of life imposed on them by legislative, administrative or other measures;

(e) Any form of propaganda directed against them.

## Article 8

Indigenous peoples have the collective and individual right to maintain and develop their distinct identities and characteristics, including the right to identify themselves as indigenous and to be recognized as such.

## Article 9

Indigenous peoples and individuals have the right to belong to an indigenous community or nation, in accordance with the traditions and customs of the community or nation concerned. No disadvantage of any kind may arise from the exercise of such a right.

## Article 10

Indigenous peoples shall not be forcibly removed from their lands or territories. No relocation shall take place without the free and informed consent of the indigenous peoples concerned and after agreement on just and fair compensation and, where possible, with the option of return.

## Article 11

Indigenous peoples have the right to special protection and security in periods of armed conflict.

States shall observe international standards, in particular the Fourth Geneva Convention of 1949, for the protection of civilian populations in circumstances of emergency and armed conflict, and shall not:

(a) Recruit indigenous individuals against their will into the armed forces and, in particular, for use against other indigenous peoples;

(b) Recruit indigenous children into the armed forces under any circumstances;

(c) Force indigenous individuals to abandon their lands, territories or means of subsistence, or relocate them in special centres for military purposes;

(d) Force indigenous individuals to work for military purposes under any discriminatory conditions.

## PART III

### Article 12

Indigenous peoples have the right to practise and revitalize their cultural traditions and customs. This includes the right to maintain, protect and develop the past, present and future manifestations of their cultures, such as archaeological and historical sites, artifacts, designs, ceremonies, technologies and visual and performing arts and literature, as well as the right to the restitution of cultural, intellectual, religious and spiritual property taken without their free and informed consent or in violation of their laws, traditions and customs.

### Article 13

Indigenous peoples have the right to manifest, practise, develop and teach their spiritual and religious traditions, customs and ceremonies; the right to maintain, protect, and have access in privacy to their religious and cultural sites; the right to the use and control of ceremonial objects; and the right to the repatriation of human remains.

States shall take effective measures, in conjunction with the indigenous peoples concerned, to ensure that indigenous sacred places, including burial sites, be preserved, respected and protected.

### Article 14

Indigenous peoples have the right to revitalize, use, develop and transmit to future generations their histories, languages, oral traditions, philosophies, writing systems and literatures, and to designate and retain their own names for communities, places and persons.

States shall take effective measures, whenever any right of indigenous peoples may be threatened, to ensure this right is protected and also to ensure that they can understand and be understood in political, legal and administrative proceedings, where necessary through the provision of interpretation or by other appropriate means.

# PART IV

## Article 15

Indigenous children have the right to all levels and forms of education of the State. All indigenous peoples also have this right and the right to establish and control their educational systems and institutions providing education in their own languages, in a manner appropriate to their cultural methods of teaching and learning.

Indigenous children living outside their communities have the right to be provided access to education in their own culture and language.

States shall take effective measures to provide appropriate resources for these purposes.

## Article 16

Indigenous peoples have the right to have the dignity and diversity of their cultures, traditions, histories and aspirations appropriately reflected in all forms of education and public information.

States shall take effective measures, in consultation with the indigenous peoples concerned, to eliminate prejudice and discrimination and to promote tolerance, understanding and good relations among indigenous peoples and all segments of society.

## Article 17

Indigenous peoples have the right to establish their own media in their own languages. They also have the right to equal access to all forms of non-indigenous media.

States shall take effective measures to ensure that State-owned media duly reflect indigenous cultural diversity.

## Article 18

Indigenous peoples have the right to enjoy fully all rights established under international labour law and national labour legislation.

Indigenous individuals have the right not to be subjected to any discriminatory conditions of labour, employment or salary.

## PART V

### *Article 19*

Indigenous peoples have the right to participate fully, if they so choose, at all levels of decision-making in matters which may affect their rights, lives and destinies through representatives chosen by themselves in accordance with their own procedures, as well as to maintain and develop their own indigenous decision-making institutions.

### *Article 20*

Indigenous peoples have the right to participate fully, if they so choose, through procedures determined by them, in devising legislative or administrative measures that may affect them.

States shall obtain the free and informed consent of the peoples concerned before adopting and implementing such measures.

### *Article 21*

Indigenous peoples have the right to maintain and develop their political, economic and social systems, to be secure in the enjoyment of their own means of subsistence and development, and to engage freely in all their traditional and other economic activities. Indigenous peoples who have been deprived of their means of subsistence and development are entitled to just and fair compensation.

### *Article 22*

Indigenous peoples have the right to special measures for the immediate, effective and continuing improvement of their economic and social conditions, including in the areas of employment, vocational training and retraining, housing, sanitation, health and social security.

Particular attention shall be paid to the rights and special needs of indigenous elders, women, youth, children and disabled persons.

### *Article 23*

Indigenous peoples have the right to determine and develop priorities and strategies for exercising their right to development. In particular, indigenous peoples have the right to determine and develop all health, housing and other economic and social programmes affecting them and, as far as possible, to administer such programmes through their own institutions.

## Article 24

Indigenous peoples have the right to their traditional medicines and health practices, including the right to the protection of vital medicinal plants, animals and minerals.

They also have the right to access, without any discrimination, to all medical institutions, health services and medical care.

## PART VI

### Article 25

Indigenous peoples have the right to maintain and strengthen their distinctive spiritual and material relationship with the lands, territories, waters and coastal seas and other resources which they have traditionally owned or otherwise occupied or used, and to uphold their responsibilities to future generations in this regard.

### Article 26

Indigenous peoples have the right to own, develop, control and use their lands and territories, including the total environment of the lands, air, waters, coastal seas, sea-ice, flora and fauna and other resources which they have traditionally owned or otherwise occupied or used. This includes the right to the full recognition of their laws, traditions and customs, land-tenure systems and institutions for the development and management of resources, and the right to effective measures by States to prevent any interference with, alienation of, or encroachment upon these rights.

### Article 27

Indigenous peoples have the right to the restitution of the lands, territories and resources which they have traditionally owned or otherwise occupied or used, and which have been confiscated, occupied, used or damaged without their free and informed consent. Where this is not possible, they have the right to just and fair compensation. Unless otherwise freely agreed upon by the peoples concerned, compensation shall take the form of lands, territories and resources equal in quality, size and legal status.

## Article 28

Indigenous peoples have the right to the conservation, restoration and protection of the total environment and the productive capacity of their lands, territories and resources, as well as to assistance for this purpose from States and through international cooperation. Military activities shall not take place in the lands and territories of indigenous peoples, unless otherwise freely agreed upon by the peoples concerned.

States shall take effective measures to ensure that no storage or disposal of hazardous materials shall take place in the lands and territories of indigenous peoples.

States shall also take effective measures to ensure, as needed, that programmes for monitoring, maintaining and restoring the health of indigenous peoples, as developed and implemented by the peoples affected by such materials, are duly implemented.

## Article 29

Indigenous peoples are entitled to the recognition of the full ownership, control and protection of their cultural and intellectual property.

They have the right to special measures to control, develop and protect their sciences, technologies and cultural manifestations, including human and other genetic resources, seeds, medicines, knowledge of the properties of fauna and flora, oral traditions, literatures, designs and visual and performing arts.

## Article 30

Indigenous peoples have the right to determine and develop priorities and strategies for the development or use of their lands, territories and other resources, including the right to require that States obtain their free and informed consent prior to the approval of any project affecting their lands, territories and other resources, particularly in connection with the development, utilization or exploitation of mineral, water or other resources. Pursuant to agreement with the indigenous peoples concerned, fair and just compensation shall be provided for any such activities and measures taken to mitigate adverse environmental, economic, social, cultural or spiritual impact.

# PART VII

## Article 31

Indigenous peoples, as a specific form of exercising their right to self-determination, have the right to autonomy or self-government in matters relating to their internal and local affairs, including culture, religion, education, information, media, health, housing, employment, social welfare, economic activities, land and resources management, environment and entry by non-members, as well as ways and means for financing these autonomous functions.

## Article 32

Indigenous peoples have the collective right to determine their own citizenship in accordance with their customs and traditions. Indigenous citizenship does not impair the right of indigenous individuals to obtain citizenship of the States in which they live.

Indigenous peoples have the right to determine the structure and to select the membership of their institutions in accordance with their own procedures.

## Article 33

Indigenous peoples have the right to promote, develop and maintain their institutional structures and their distinctive juridical customs, traditions, procedures and practices, in accordance with internationally recognized human rights standards.

## Article 34

Indigenous peoples have the collective right to determine the responsibilities of individuals to their communities.

## Article 35

Indigenous peoples, in particular those divided by international borders, have the right to maintain and develop contacts, relations and cooperation, including activities for spiritual, cultural, political, economic and social purposes, with other peoples across borders.

States shall take effective measures to ensure the exercise and implementation of this right.

## Article 36

Indigenous peoples have the right to the recognition, observance and enforcement of treaties, agreements and other constructive arrangements concluded with States or their successors, according to their original spirit and intent, and to have States honour and respect such treaties, agreements and other constructive arrangements. Conflicts and disputes which cannot otherwise be settled should be submitted to competent international bodies agreed to by all parties concerned.

## PART VIII

## Article 37

States shall take effective and appropriate measures, in consultation with the indigenous peoples concerned, to give full effect to the provisions of this Declaration. The rights recognized herein shall be adopted and included in national legislation in such a manner that indigenous peoples can avail themselves of such rights in practice.

## Article 38

Indigenous peoples have the right to have access to adequate financial and technical assistance, from States and through international cooperation, to pursue freely their political, economic, social, cultural and spiritual development and for the enjoyment of the rights and freedoms recognized in this Declaration.

## Article 39

Indigenous peoples have the right to have access to and prompt decision through mutually acceptable and fair procedures for the resolution of conflicts and disputes with States, as well as to effective remedies for all infringements of their individual and collective rights. Such a decision shall take into consideration the customs, traditions, rules and legal systems of the indigenous peoples concerned.

### Article 40

The organs and specialized agencies of the United Nations system and other intergovernmental organizations shall contribute to the full realization of the provisions of this Declaration through the mobilization, *inter alia*, of financial cooperation and technical assistance. Ways and means of ensuring participation of indigenous peoples on issues affecting them shall be established.

### Article 41

The United Nations shall take the necessary steps to ensure the implementation of this Declaration including the creation of a body at the highest level with special competence in this field and with the direct participation of indigenous peoples. All United Nations bodies shall promote respect for and full application of the provisions of this Declaration.

## PART IX

### Article 42

The rights recognized herein constitute the minimum standards for the survival, dignity and well-being of the indigenous peoples of the world.

### Article 43

All the rights and freedoms recognized herein are equally guaranteed to male and female indigenous individuals.

### Article 44

Nothing in this Declaration may be construed as diminishing or extinguishing any existing or future rights indigenous peoples may have or acquire.

### Article 45

Nothing in this Declaration may be interpreted as implying for any State group or person any right to engage in any activity or to perform any act contrary to the Charter of the United Nations.

# Appendix D

## National Security Council
### Washington, D.C. 20204

### January 18, 2001

Ms. Kristie A. Kenny
Executive Secretary
Department of State

Ms. Julie Faulkner
Director of Executive Secretariat
Department of Interior

Mr. Francis P. Townsend
Council for Intelligence Policy
Representative Department of Justice

Mr. Chris Klein
Staff Assistant of the
Of the U.S. to the U.N.

Subject:  Indigenous Peoples

The President has determined that the United States will announce its support for U.S. positions described in the attached cable.

The State Department will ensure delivery of the attached message this evening, so as to ensure that the U.S. delegation to the OAS can implement its instruction to inform appropriate foreign government counterparts of these U.S. positions on January 19.

(signed)
Robert A. Bradtke
Executive Secretary

# Attached Cable

1. This message provides guidance for the U.S. delegates to the UN Commission on Human Rights, the Commission's Working Group on the UN Draft Declaration on Indigenous Rights and to the OAS Working Group on the similar OAS Draft Declaration, and to the preparatory meetings to the World Conference Against Racism. It relates to text we can accept in the Draft Declarations being considered in these forums.

2. The U.S. delegation to the OAS is instructed to inform appropriate foreign government counterparts, and the OAS Secretariat, of the following U.S. positions on January 19. The U.S. observer delegation to the Africa Region Preparatory Conference for the World Conference Against Racism is instructed to inform appropriate foreign government counterparts of the following U.S. positions on January 22. Other U.S. delegations to negotiations considering these matters should also be guided by these instructions.

3. The USDEL should support use of the term "internal self-determination" in both the UN and OAS Declarations on Indigenous Rights, defined as follows:

"Indigenous Peoples have the right to internal self-determination. By virtue of that right, they may negotiate their political status within the framework of the existing nation-state and are free to pursue their economic, social, and cultural development. Indigenous Peoples, in exercising their right of internal self-determination, have the internal right to autonomy or self-government in matters relating to their local affairs, including determination of membership, culture, language, religion, education, information, media, health, housing, employment, social welfare, maintenance of community safety, family relations, economic activities, lands and resource development, environment and entry by non-members, as well as ways and means for financing these autonomous activities."

This language combines aspects of Articles 3 and 31 of the current draft of the UN Declaration.

4. Because the term "internal self-determination" is carefully defined in the text, it is not necessary to include language in the text stating what the term does not mean. Instead, the U.S. Delegation to both the UN and OAS Working Groups on the Indigenous Declaration will read a prepared statement that expresses the U.S. understanding of the term "internal self-determination" and indicates that it does not include a right of independence or permanent sovereignty over natural resources. This statement allows the U.S. to state its understanding of the Article of Internal Self-Determination. The statement is intended to be read by the Delegation, and is not intended for inclusion in the Declaration or any related document. The text of the statement is as follows:

"Under United States domestic law, the U.S. recognizes Indian tribes as political entities with inherent powers of self-government. In this domestic context, self-determination means promoting tribal self-government and autonomy over a broad range of internal and local affairs similar to those rights articulated in Article 31 of the current draft of the United Nations (Article 15 of the Organization of American States) Draft Declaration of Indigenous Rights. While the U.S. domestic concept of self-determination is similar to the rights articulated in the Draft Declaration, it is not necessarily synonymous with more general understandings of self-determination under international law.

Generally, under international law, self-determination means the full enjoyment and exercise of civil and political rights in a representative, democratic government. More specifically, however, the United States has historically understood this term, as enunciated in the United Nations Charter and Common Articles 1(1) of the Covenants, to mean the right of all 'Peoples' to choose their political status, including the right to choose independence, among other possibilities, and to exercise permanent sovereignty over natural resources.

In an effort to harmonize U.S. domestic and foreign policy on the right of self-determination for indigenous groups, we have considered the views of indigenous representatives, other governments, and scholars, including the views that 1) Self-determination is an evolving concept; 2) Self-determination includes both external and internal aspects and that the latter would apply to groups within existing States; 3) Self-determination is limited by the principle of territorial integrity and, therefore, must be exercised within the existing States; 4) Self-determination as articulated in the Draft Declaration is specifically limited by Article 48 [Article 26] protecting the territorial integrity of existing nation-states.

Although self-determination may be an evolving concept under international law and although the Draft Declaration may contain limitations on the exercise of self-determination, to protect the territorial integrity of the existing State[s], it is the position of the United States that the Draft Declaration should be more explicit with regard to the civil and political rights enjoyed by indigenous peoples. Thus, the United States would be able to endorse the concept of self-determination in the Declaration if the Declaration itself specifically characterized the right as one of 'internal self-determination.' The term 'internal self-determination' would include those rights articulated in Article 31 [Article 15] and thus be consistent with U.S. domestic law, but would not include the right of independence or permanent sovereignty over natural resources. With the understanding that this Declaration sets forth the civil and political rights enjoyed by indigenous groups, the U.S. can also support the use of the term 'Indigenous Peoples' in this Declaration."

5. Caveat on "Peoples" in other international documents.

The UN and OAS Declarations set forth the rights enjoyed by Indigenous Peoples. In particular, the United States supports final Declarations stating that Indigenous Peoples have a right to internal self-determination, and defining that right as one exercised within the framework of the State and involving internal control over local affairs (see para 3, above, for exact language). Moreover, a separate statement to be read by the Delegation will express our understanding that the right of internal self-determination as defined in the Declaration does not include independence or permanent sovereignty over natural resources (see para 4, above). Accordingly, it is not necessary to qualify the term "Peoples" in these Declarations with an express caveat in the text stating that it does not imply a right to independence or permanent sovereignty over natural resources as set forth in Article 1(1) of the Covenants.

However, although the purpose of the UN and OAS Declarations is to set forth the rights enjoyed by Indigenous Peoples, other international declarations, action plans, etc., that do not define the rights of Indigenous Peoples with respect to self-determination and sovereignty over natural resources may nonetheless make reference to indigenous groups. In such instances, the United States would be able to support the use of the term Indigenous "Peoples," but only with a footnote that states as follows:

"The use of the term 'Peoples' in this document shall not be construed as having any implications as regards the rights that may attach to the term under international law."

6. Collective rights.

International human rights instruments generally recognize the rights of individuals. We accept, however, that some collective rights are appropriate for indigenous communities.

We believe that collective and individual rights can coexist in the indigenous context without undermining the individual rights that are firmly rooted in international human rights law. In general, when considering how best to express our position in human rights instruments, the U.S. has used the phrase "individuals in community with others." This formula clearly recognizes the collective aspect of some human rights while at the same time protects the rights of the individual. U.S. domestic law recognizes collective rights for Native Americans, Alaskan Natives, and Native Hawaiians, and, in the domestic indigenous context, collective rights are viewed as furthering the rights of individuals.

7. Scope of the definition of Indigenous Peoples.

In the context of the UN Declaration, no definition of Indigenous Peoples has been offered, nor is it expected that one will be offered. The U.S. has determined it does not need to define who is indigenous in order to accept a final draft. We can apply the term domestically consistent with our domestic policy on federally recognized tribes while supporting any approach to this issue that takes account of differing historical experiences in other countries and regions.

If it should become necessary to provide some benchmarks in defining who is indigenous, it will be the position of the United States that the scope of "Indigenous Peoples" should be determined with reference to fundamental criteria, including but not limited to self-identification, Aboriginal Status, and distinct culture and customs. The application and relative weight of these criteria should account for differing historical circumstances around the world. For example, in the United States, Aboriginal Status is a necessary criterion in identifying Indigenous Peoples. In other countries or regions, it could be appropriate to apply the criteria differently in light of different historical experiences, including histories of colonization, migration patterns (including forced migrations), the formation of existing or prior States in those areas, and efforts to assimilate Indigenous Peoples into surrounding cultures or societies.

In the context of the OAS Declaration, a definition of Indigenous Peoples is under discussion. The U.S. should therefore support the approach described above, but recognize the shared experience of aboriginal, precolonial peoples in the Americas region.

# Index

## A

A&W restaurants: 252

Abourezk, Sen. James: 292n57

Abrams, Gen. Creighton: 327

Abyssinia, *see* Ethiopia/Ethiopians

Act for the Protection of American Indian Arts and Crafts (1990): xvi; criminal penalties under: 220-1, 242n141; divisive effects of: 221

Adams, Hank: 290n37

Adams, SA J. Gary: 277, 296n112; interrogation techniques of: 298n130; perjury of: 298n127

Adams, SA James B.: 298n124

Adams, John: 5

Afghanis/Afghanistan: 360-1; bin-Laden evades U.S. forces in: 361; border with Pakistan of: 360; CIA operations in: 358, 360; Karzai régime installed in: 364; Mazar-i-Sharif massacre in: 361; "Northern Alliance" in: 361; opium production in: 364; Shiberghan prison in: 361; Soviet invasion of: 358; Taliban régime in: 360, 361, 364, 396n510, 396n512; relations with Saudis of: 396n510; U.S. conflation of Taliban and al-Qaida prisoners in: 361-2, 397n525; U.S. invasion of: 360-1; U.S.-instigated humanitarian crisis in: 360; U.S. oil interests in: 364; U.S. strategic interests in: 364; war crimes in: 361; 1998 U.S. missile strike on: 396n510

Africa: European colonization of: 39, 43, 50; decolonization of: 90; 1884-85 Berlin Conf. concerning: 50

Agricolia, Georgius: 160

al-Faisal, Prince Turki: 396n510

al-Jazeera television network: 359, 360, 371

al-Megrahi, Abdel Basset Ali: 395n502

al-Qaida: 358-61, 362, 364, 371; attack on *U.S.S. Cole* by: 359, 394n497,; attacks on U.S. embassies by: 359, 394n497; attitude towards Shi'ites of: 399n546; "Axis of Evil" speech and: 365; CIA training of: 358; connection to Abu-Sayyef of: 364; positions of: 394n501; proclaimed "illegal combatants" by U.S.: 361, 397n525; proclaimed "terrorist organization" by U.S.: 359; radical Islamicism of: 358, 365;

recruitment base of: 371; 9-1-1 attack by: 357-8; 2002 Bali bombing and: 371, 402n591; 2002 Moscow theater debàcle and: 371; 2002 oil tanker bombing and: 403n591; *also see* bin-Laden, Usama

Alaska: U.S. colonization of: 49, 153

Alaska Native Claims Settlement Act (1971): 18

Albright, Sec. of State Madeline: 34, 106, 349, 357, 365, 370, 388n395, 402n587; as UN ambassador: 345; as proponent of U.S. unilateralism: 350; criminal charges filed against: 349; on *60 Minutes*: 345

Albuquerque Indian School: 216

Alcatraz Island: 283; 1969-71 Indians of All Tribes occupation of: 263, 266, 283, 286, 290n40

Alexander, Samuel: 111n43

Aleutian Islands: 114n115; Amchitka Island nuclear weapons tests in: 176, 197n160

Alfonso Martinez, Miguel: 30n110

Algeria/Algerians: as French colony: 49, 66n137, 91, 101, 242n122; 1830 French conquest of: 50

Allen, Elisha: 78, 80

Allen, Paula Gunn: 243n144

Allende, Salvador: 273, 402n581

Aloha Assoc.: 97

Alsace- Lorraine:0 Prussian annexation of: 61-1n40

Aluli, Noa Emmett: 100, 118n197; *Aluli v. Rumsfeld* case of: 119n215

American Assoc. of Jurists: 389n414

American Cancer Inst.: Environmental Cancer Section of: 161

American Indian Movement (AIM): 31n118, 141, 171, 264-87; and Alcatraz occupation: 263, 266, 283, 286; and Big Mt. resistance: 284; and Black Panther Party: 264; and UN: 266; and revitalization of Lakota Sun dance: 289n20; and Western Shoshone land struggle: 284; armed self-defense posture of: 276; autonomous chapters of: 285, 301n163; Calico Hall meeting and: 270; Colorado chapter of: 242n139, 285; decolonization agenda of: 266; "Dog Soldier Teletypes" and: 297n120; early reputation among Indians of: 267; FBI disinformation about: 278-9, 280,

433

296n110, 296n111; FBI repression of: xvii, 19, 264-87; federal "reign of terror" against: 263, 273-9; founding of: 264; fragmentation of: 282; general membership meetings of: 300n149; Gildersleeve Trading Post sacked by: 270; International Indian Treaty Council of: 284; legacy of: 285-7; national office dissolved: 283; Northwest AIM Group of: 277, 278, 294n92, 300n149; occupies BIA headquarters: 33, 267; 1971 *Mayflower* protest of: 266; 1971 Mt. Rushmore protest of: 266; 1972 Gordon protest of: 267; 1972 Custer County Courthouse protest of: 268-9; 1972 Trail of Broken Treaties and: 240n120, 267, 283; 1973 Wounded Knee siege and: 270-71; 1974-75 leadership trials of: 272; 1975 Oglala Firefight and: 277-9, 296n110, 300n149; 1978 "Longest Walk" of: 283; 1979-80 Black Hills Survival Gatherings and: 283; 1981-85 Yellow Thunder Camp occupation by: 283; 1989-92 Columbus Day protests of: 285; 1993 Edgewood Conf. of: 301n163; *also see* Banks, Dennis; Means, Russell; "National AIM, Inc."

"American Innocence": after 9-1-1: 358; as "altruism": 389n435; as "purity of purpose": 306; traditional assertions of: 305, 351

American Institute on International Law: "Draft on the Problem of Conquest" of (1925): 65n105

American Labor Relations Board: 85

"American" Samoa: as U.S. colony: 19, 153

Americans for Indian Opportunity: 33

American Indian Chicago Conf. (1961): Declaration of Purpose of: 142

AMEX Corp.: 165

Amfac, *see* "Big Five" corporations

Amiott family: 205

Amnesty International: 293n69, 300n152, 392n477

Anaconda Copper Corp.: 192n98; as ARCO subsidiary: 166; Jackpile-Paguate uranium mining complex of: 166-7, 191n85; Laguna "improvement" programs of: 169-70

*Anarchy* (magazine): 126

Anderson, Judge Aldon: 163

Anderson, Jack: 290n37

Anderson, Mike: 277, 298n130

Anderson, Warren: 396n512

Andersonville POW camp: 334

Angola: as Portuguese colony: 91, 101; airliner bombing in: 396n506; independence struggle in: 67n139; UNITA org. in: 396n506

anti-imperialists/anti-imperialism: 50; American variant of: 113n90

Antiterrorism and Effective Death Penalty Act (1996): 362, 397n531

Aquash, Anna Mae Pictou: 297n118; badjacketing of: 300n149; murder of: 300n149

Aquinas, Thomas: 23n9; as author of *Summa Theologica Secunda Secundae*: 61n49

Arab League: 367

Arbuckle, John: 300n145

Archambault family: 205

Archer, Victor E.: 163, 164

Argentina/Argentines: 44

Ariyoshi, Gov. George: 94

Armenia/Armenians: and U.S. Holocaust Memorial Museum: 258n8; genocide of: 247; Turkish/Israeli denial of genocide suffered by: 258n8

Armstrong, Richard: 78

Asahi Development Corp.: 95, 96

Ashcroft, Att'ny Gen. John: 363

Ashford, Volney: 109n16

Asia: European colonization of: 39

*Atlantic Monthly* (magazine): 319

Atlantic-Richfield (ARCO) Corp.: 165, 166; Hanford "tank farm" of: 173; *also see* Anaconda Copper Corp.

Atomic Energy Act (1946): 161, 189n63

Atomic Energy Commission (AEC), *see* U.S. Dept. of Energy

Atta, Mohammed: 366

Australia/Australians: 54, 114n115; as British colony: 77; as settler state: 51; contributions to Vietnam War effort of: 325; internal colonialism in: 51; losses in 2002 Bali bombing of: 371, 402n591; uranium mining in: 167

Austria/Austrians: 40, 64n86, 395n504; Carpathian silver miners in: 160; 1938 German seizure of: 46

Austrohungarian Empire: 40, 64n86

Axis Powers: 1

Azore Islands: 67n139

## B

Baccus, Gen. Rick: 362

Bad Heart Bull, Sarah: 269

Bad Heart Bull, Wesley: 268, 290n38, 290n40

Bail Reform Act (1984): 362, 397n531
Baker, Maj. Eugene: 314
Balance of Power politics: 38–41; *also see* geopolitics
Baldwin, Henry: 111n43
Ball, Milner S.: 119n209
Ballanger, Pat: 264
Bangladesh: separation of, from Pakistan: 158
Bank of America: 88, 92
Bank of Hawaii: 88
Bank of the Pacific: 88
Banks, Dennis: 266, 268, 270; as AIM founder: 264; as chancellor of D-Q University: 300n147; as fugitive: 297n118, 300n147; rejects assoc. with "National AIM, Inc.": 301n165; riot conviction of: 269, 297n118; Wounded Knee charges dismissed against: 272
Banks, Kamook: 297n118
Baum, Frank L.: as author of *The Wizard of Oz*: 315; calls for "complete annihilation" of Lakotas: 315
Bear, Leon: 179
Bechtel Corp.: 176
Beckwourth, Jim (Jim Beckworth; Jim Beckwith): 208
Begay, Kee: 194n126
Belgians/Belgium: "Belgian Thesis" on decolonization of: 50; classical empire of: 48; colonization of the Congo by: 50, 89; Malmédy Massacre perpetrated in: 333
Bell, Gen. J. Franklin: 320, 321, 377n95, 383n267; as army chief of staff: 316, 318; as "Butcher of Batangas": 316
Bellecourt family: 205
Bellecourt, Clyde: 243n145, 300n146, 301n165; as AIM founder: 264
Bellecourt, Vernon: 243n145; AIM turmoil instigated by: 300n146; and Aquash badjacketing: 300n149; and "internal investigation" of Aquash murder: 300n149; as head of "National AIM, Inc.": 301n165
Belli, Pierino: 306
Bellinger, John: 94, 96
Benson, Judge Paul: 280, 299n136, 299n137; reversible errors of: 281
Bent family: 234n78
Bent, Charlie: 228n41; as Cheyenne Dog Soldier: 207; mixed-bloodedness of: 207
Bent, George: 207, 228n41, 234n82
Bent, Robert: 207, 311
Bent, William: 228n41

Benton Benai, Eddie: 264
Bergthold, James: 322
Bermuda: as British colony: 101
Bernays, Col. Murray C.: 148n81
Bertell, Rosalie: 162
Beverly, Bob: 188n44
Biddle, Att'ny Gen. Francis: 133, 150n122; as Nuremberg Tribunal member: 136
Big Bear (Cree leader): xix, xx
"Big Five" corporations: Alexander and Baldwin: 79, 88; C. Brewer: 79; Castle and Cooke: 79, 83, 84, 85, 86, 88, 93, 111n50; Theo Davies: 79, 88; Hackfield (Amfac): 79, 88, 117n162
Big Foot (Minneconjou Lakota leader): 266
bin-Laden, Usama: 359–60, 364, 371, 396n512; as head of al-Qaida: 359; attack on *U.S.S. Cole* and: 359, 394n497; attacks on U.S. embassies and: 359, 394n497; audiotapes of: 371; evades U.S. forces in Afghanistan: 361; misrepresentations of: 399n546; positions of: 394n501; relationship to Taliban of: 396n510; videotapes of: 359, 360; 2002 Bali bombing and: 371, 402n591; 2002 Moscow theater debàcle and: 371; 2002 oil tanker bombing and: 403n591; *also see* al-Qaida
Bishop, Charles Reed: 80
Bison, American (buffalo): extermination of: 12
Bissonette, Jeanette: 275-6, 294n93
Bissonette, Pedro: 272, 291n50, 294n93
Black, Bob: 126
Black Crow, Selo: 296n112
Black Hawk (Sac leader): 305
Black Hills Alliance: 283
Black Horse, Frank (Frank DeLuca): 297n118
Black Kettle (Cheyenne leader): 310, 311, 313, 375n48
"Black Indians": phenomenon of: 205-6, 228n33; policies towards: 209; Seminoles as: 206, 227n32, 233n77; treaty provisions regarding: 233n77
Black Panther Party (for Self-Defense): 264, 287
Blackman, Ronald (Ron Janvier): 297n118
Blaine, Sec. of State James: 81
Blaisdell, Kekuni: 99, 119n214
Blanco, Hugo: 53
"blood quantum standards": 13, 98, 203-24, 236n92; and General Allotment Act: 214; and Indian Reorganization Act: 218, 220; applied to Cherokees: 212; applied to Chippewas: 212; applied to Creeks, Choctaws and Chickasaws: 212; applied

to Miamis: 213; applied to Osages: 213; applied to Pawnees: 213; as "definitional genocide": 230n58; as opposed to traditional modes of identity: 203-6, 208, 213; contemporary Cherokee rejection of: 223-4; contemporary federal manipulations of: 222-3; contemporary "tribal" manipulations of: 220, 222-3; imposed upon Shawnees: 213; "purity police" and: 221; "one drop rule" of: 209; South African utilization of: 230-1n60; 1990 Arts and Crafts Act and: 221; *also see* racism/racial theory

Blount, Rep. James: 82, 112n71, 112n78

"Blue Water Thesis," *see* colonialism/colonization; Org. of African Unity

Bly, Robert: : 232n67

Boise-Cascade Corp.: 117n161, 265

Bokum Minerals Corp.: Laguna uranium mill of: 169

Bolin, Robert: 280

Bolsheviks/Bolshevism: 41

Bolton Finch, Capt. William: 78

Bonfils, Henry: 38

Boone, Daniel: 373n19

Bootlegger restaurants: 252

Bosch, Orlando: 396n506

Bougainville: 333

Boulder, CO: 357, 393n486; Jonbenet Ramsey case in: 402n586

Bouquet, Col. Henry: 204-5, 227n25

Boyd, Robert: 80, 81

Boyle, Francis Anthony: 346

Bradley, Sen. Bill: 151n133

Bradley, David: 243n143

Branch Davidians: 398n535; 1993 slaughter of: 289n25

Brando, Marlon: 297n118

Brazil/Brazilians: 44, 54, 88; as internal colonial state: 51

Brewer, Duane: 275-6, 294n90, 294n91; as BIA policeman: 276; as Pine Ridge GOON leader: 275; on GOON/FBI collaboration: 275-6; on Jeanette Bissonette murder: 294n93

Brings Yellow, James: 296n112

Brown Berets: 287

Brown, Gov. Jerry: 300n147

Brown, Norman: 298n130

Brown, Lt. Preston: 317, 324, 327

Bruchac, Joseph: 243n144

Brussels Declaration (1874): 376n85

Buck, Marilyn: 287

Buckley, Kevin: 326

Bull Head (Hunkpapa Lakota): 208

*Bulletin of New York Academy of Medicine*: 161

Bureau of Indian Affairs (BIA): 154, 201, 239n112; AIM occupies headquarters building of: 33, 267; as "Colonial Office of the United States": 265; as part of Interior Dept.: 12, 33, 154; as part of War Dept.: 12; collaboration with AEC: 164-6; finds Pine Ridge GOON squads: 269; leasing practices of: 16, 128, 155-6, 165, 236n96; mineral royalty rates set by: 167, 265; police units of: 270, 276, 277-8; SWAT teams of: 277; "trust authority" of: 154, 167, 265

Bureau of the Census, *see* U.S. Dept. of Commerce

Burgess, Hayden (Poka Laenu): 119n203

Burke, Indian Comm. Charles: 15

Burma (Myanmar): Karen independence struggle in: 52

Burnette, Robert: 240n121, 290n36, 292n56

Burns, C.E.: 117n162

Burns, Gov. John: 91, 92, 93, 117n168

Bush, Pres. George Herbert Walker: 320, 346-7, 349, 358, 398n535; as Vice President under Reagan: 358, 388n393; illegal orders of: 341; "Just War" concept of: 21, 340; rhetoric compared to Hitler's: 351, 357

Bush, Pres. George W.: 358, 359, 367, 394n494, 396n512, 397n525; "Axis of Evil" speech of: 364-5; disgraces WTC dead: 360, 396n509; on Israel: 367; ultimatum to UN General Assembly of: 366

Butler, Darrelle ("Dino"): 279, 296n117, 298n127; 298n129; acquitted of murdering FBI agents: 280; and Oglala Firefight: 279

Butler, Richard: 399n553

Byrnes, Sec. of State James F.: 378n129

## C

C-Span 2 (tv channel): 33

Caldicott, Helen: 197n168

Caldwell, Charles: 211

California Civil Disorder Management School: "Cable Splicer" counterinsurgency scenario of: 291n52, 398n536; "Garden Plot" counterinsurgency scenario of: 291n52, 398n536; also see Federal Emergency Management Agency

(FEMA); Giuffrida, Louis O.
Callaway, Sec. of the Army Howard H.: 324
Calley, Lt. William L. ("Rusty"): 322, 324, 326,
    327; and My Lai Massacre: 322; court-
    martial of: 323, 324; sentence reductions
    of: 324
Cambodia/Cambodians: 321; civilian fatalities
    among: 331; Khmer people of: 331; U.S.
    aerial ordnance expended against: 330-1;
    villages destroyed in: 331; wartime civilian
    displacement among: 331
Camp, Carter: 272, 293n69, 300n146
Campbell, Sen. Ben "Nighthorse": 242-3n141,
    243n143
Canada/Canadians: xv, 54, 55, 201, 364; and
    League of Nations: 42; and Vienna
    Convention on the Law of Treaties:
    71n213, 71n221; as British colony: 77; as
    settler state: 56; courts of: xv, xvi, xviii, 5,
    253-5; criminalization of Holocaust
    denial in: 247; demands return of Peltier:
    297n119; domestic genocide statute of:
    251; *Friends of the Lubicon* trial in: xvi,
    252-5; Indian reservation system in:
    24n19; Indian residential schools in:
    xxin13; invalid ratification of Genocide
    Convention by: 251; James Bay: 252;
    *Keegstra* trial in: 258n2; Liquor Control
    Board of Ontario: 253; Lubicon Lake:
    252; native resistance movements in: 252;
    treaty obligations of: 57; Peltier's
    extradition from: 280, 297n119; Royal
    Canadian Mounted Police (RCMP) of:
    297n118; UN performance of: 19-20;
    uranium mining in: 167; U.S. economic
    domination of: 53; U.S. judicial precedent
    and: xv, 19, 61-2n54; Wollaston Lake: 252;
    *Zündel* trial in: 258n2
Cantor Fitzgerald Corp.: 393n490
Capone, Al: 315
Caracas Protocol (1883): 65n105
Caribbean Basin: U.S. investment in: 95
Carlisle Indian School: 216
Carlsbad Caverns: as WIPP site: 180
Carlson, Cmdr. David: 394n502
Carlucci, CIA Dir. Frank: as National Security
    Council head under Reagan: 290n33; as
    Nixon bag man: 33, 290n33
Caroline Islands: 76; U.S. occupation of: 49
Carson, Kit: 373n19
Carter, Henry: 80
Carter, Pres. Jimmy: 283
Case, St. Rep. Ed: 119-20n216

Castle, Samuel: 111n50
Castle, William R.: 83, 84
Castillo, Bobby: 243n144
Catawba, Twila Martin: 244n146, 300n144
Catches, Everette: 291n50
Catches, Pete: 291n50
Catholics/Catholicism: 2-5; Vatican of: 61n49
Catlin, George: 125
Celay, Phillip: 290n40
Center for the SPIRIT: 243n145
Central Intelligence Agency (CIA): 399n547; and
    Abu Sayyef guerrillas: 364; and Allende
    assassination: 402n581; and bombing of
    Angolan airliner: 396n506; and bombing
    of Air India jumbo jet: 396n506; and
    bombing of Cuban airliner: 396n506; and
    Jonas Savimbi: 396n506; and Orlando
    Bosch: 396n506; coordination of death
    squads by: 274, 294n96; operations in
    Laos of: 329; training of al-Qaida by: 358;
    WTC facility of: 393n490
Ceylon, *see* Sri Lanka
Chaco Declaration (1932): 45
Chaffey, Gen. Adna R.: 316, 377n111;
    responsibility for Philippines atrocities:
    318; promotion as Army Chief of Staff:
    318
Chapman, Kathy: 243n144
Charles, Norman: 277
Chase-Manhattan Bank: 92
Cheney, Vice Pres. Dick: 342, 399n542, 399n553;
    and Halliburton: 399n550; as Sec. of
    Defense: 342
Cherokees/Cherokee Nation: 9, 204, 228n37,
    242n139, 284; blood quantum criteria
    and: 223-4, 232n71; contemporary CNO
    enrollment policies of: 223-4, 244n157;
    contemporary population of: 224;
    Cultural Heritage Ctr. of: 243n142;
    "Dawes Roll" of: 235n91, 244n157; Great
    Seal of: 243n142; Moravians and: 211,
    232n70; National Council of: 232n70,
    243n142; preremoval resistance of: 206;
    resistance to enrollment among "full-
    bloods" of: 236n93, 243n142, 244n157;
    "sell-out" faction of: 206, 228n37; Trail of
    Tears of: 11-2, 206-7, 228n37; United
    Keetoowah Band of: 242n139, 244n157;
    "White Path's Rebellion" of: 232-3n71;
    1817 "Immigrant Roll" of: 235n91; 1975
    constitutions of: 223, 244n157
Cheyennes: 171, 242n139, 315, 316, 319, 334;
    Bent family and: 207; Crazy Dog Society

("Dog Soldiers") of: 207, 237n103; enrollment criteria of: 242-3n141; 1864 Sand Creek massacre of: 207, 310-2, 324, 338, 375n48; 1868 Washita massacre of: 11, 313, 314; 1875 Sappa Creek massacre of: 11, 315; 1879 Camp Robinson Massacre of: 11, 314

Chile/Chileans: Pinochet régime in: 402n581; 1973 coup in: 273, 402n581; 1973-76 violent death rate in: 273

Chilocco Indian School: 216

China/Chinese: 54; and Angola: 67n139; Han hegemony in: 51; internal colonialism in: 51; 1949 maoist revolution in: 49

Chino, Wendell: 180

Chips, Ellis: 291n50

Chivington, Col. John M.: 310-3, 321; as commander at Sand Creek: 310-1, 324, 375n48; "nits make lice" statement of: 311, 374n47; violations of Lieber Code by: 312; nonprosecution of: 312; town named after: 313

Chomsky, Noam: xiii, 355

Chrystos: 243n144

Chung, Hyun-Kyung: 119n209

Churchill, Ward (Kizhiinaabe): xi, xiv-xx; as activist: xx; as author of *A Little Matter of Genocide*: xiv; as author of *Perversions of Justice*: xiv; as author of *Struggle for the Land*: xiv; as Colorado AIM codirector: 242n139; as rapporteur of 1993 International Peoples Tribunal: 119n209; as speaker of truth, xx; attacks upon identity of: 242n139, 243n144; testifies at FOL trial: 261n45; tribal affiliation of: xiv, 242n139

Churchill, Winston S.: 383n257

cigarettes, *see* tobacco/smoking

Citizens' Party: 33

Clark, Gen. George Rogers: 304; atrocities committed by: 307

Clark, Girlie: 292n57

Clark, Mark: 287, 292n60

Clark, Att'ny Gen. Ramsey: 346

Clark, Richard: 398n535

Clausewitz, Carl von: 308, 345

Clean Water Act(1972): 190n79

Clearwater, Frank: 271, 291n55

Cleaver, Eldridge: 106, 123n274

Cleaver, Kathleen: 123n274

Cleveland, Pres. Grover: commissions "Blount Report": 82, 112n71; denounces U.S. aggression in Hawai'i as "unprovoked act of war": 76; recognizes "Republic of Hawaii": 76, 82

Clifford, Joe: 294n93

Climax Uranium Corp.: 165

Clinch River: nuclear contamination of: 177

Clinton, Pres. Bill: 241n131, 345, 398n535; criminal charges filed against: 349; signs P.L. 103-150: 73; orders 1998 missile attack on Afghanistan: 396n510; 1998 WTO protests and: 398n535

Club Monaco restaurants: 252

Cochrane, Rep. John J.: 133

Cohen, Felix S.: 123n264, 182, 185

Cohen, Sec. of Defense William: 349

Colburn, Wayne: 274

Cole, Bill: 292n57

Coler, SA Jack: 277, 295n103, 297n122, 299n136; death of: 278, 295n108, 296n110, 298n127, 298n128, 298n129, 298-9n131; funeral of: 296n111

Coll, SA Tom: 278, 296n110

Collier, Indian Comm. John: 29n86

Colmer, Rep. William M.: 134

colonialism/colonization: 34, 38-40, 89-90, 184, 225n6; "Belgian Thesis" on: 50; "Blue Water Thesis" ("Salt Water Thesis") concerning: 20, 51, 53, 158; classical form of: 1-2, 64n90; European rationalization of: 39; internal form of: 20-1, 34-5, 64n90, 128, 158, 201, 288n8; John Marshall's rationalization of: 9, 40; legal disparities of: 39-40; neocolonialism: 64n90, 90, 353; "radioactive" form of: xvi; Sartre's equation to genocide: 52, 128, 158-9; settler state form: xiii, 1-2, 64n90, 158; *also see* imperialism

Colorado River Indian Tribes Reservation: 181

Colorado Plateau: "uranium frenzy" on: 165

Colorado State Medical Society: 161-2

Columbia River: nuclear contamination of: 173, 177, 195n140

Columbus, Christopher (Christobal Colón): annual celebrations of: 285; 141; voyages of: 2; 1992 Quincentennial celebration of: 285

Commoner, Barry: 33

Congo: and the "Belgian Thesis": 50; as Belgian colony: 50; as internal colonial state: 50; Katanga independence struggle in: 52

Connor, Gen. Patrick E.: 375n48

Conoco Corp.: 165

Continental Congress, *see* United States

Cook, Capt. James: 77

Constant, Emmanuel: 396n512
Cornplanter (Seneca leader): 304
Coulter, Tim: 243n144
Council of Energy Resource Tribes (CERT): 179, 199n185
Country Style Donuts: 252
Coward, SA Fred: 298n129
Crazy Horse (Oglala Lakota leader): xix, xx; assassination of: 208; complexion of: 207; defeats Crook: 207, 229n42; defeats Custer: 207, 229n42
Creeks (Muscogees): 7, 149n97, 210, 227n32; atrocities committed against: 304; massacred at Horseshoe Bend: 304, 320; Red Sticks (Baton Rouge) faction of: 7, 227n32, 228n37, 320
Crimes Against Humanity, concept of: 21, 254
Crimes Against Peace, concept of: 21
Crockett, Davy: 373n19
Croghan, George: 204
Crook, Gen. George: xix; defeat at Rosebud Creek of: 207, 229n42
Crooks, AUSA Lynne: closing argument against Peltier of: 281, 282; concedes falsity of argument: 282
Cross, Clarence: 293n79, 293n82
Cross, Vernal: 293n79
Crow Dog (Brûlé Lakota): 208
Crow Dog, Delphine: 293n78
Crow Dog, Leonard: 272, 293n69
Crow Dog's Paradise: 296n112, 296n117
Crow Reservation: 171
Crusade for Justice: 297n120
Crusades: 2; Third Crusade: 61n49
Cuba/Cubans: 399n542; and Angola: 67n139
*Cultural Survival Quarterly* (journal): 252
Cultures restaurants: 252
Curtis, Vice Pres. Charles: 245n159
Curtis Act (1898): 224
Custer, Lt. Col. George Armstrong: xix, 208, 373n19; as commander at Washita Massacre: 313, 314; defeat at Little Big Horn of: 207, 229n42
Czechs/Czechoslovakia: 64n86; city of Prague in: 366; slave labor employed in: 190n66; supposed al-Qaida/Iraqi mtg. in: 366; 1938 German seizure of: 46

**D**

Daishowa Corp.: 252-5, 260n40; "deforesting" operations of: 252, 253; effects on the Lubicon Cree of: 254; SLAPP suit against FOL by: 253-5; 1991-94 FOL boycott of:

252, 260n40
Dartmouth College: 237n101
Dawes, Sen. Henry M.: 235n89
Dawes Act, *see* General Allotment Act
Dawn Mining Corp.: Blue Creek uranium mine/mill of: 194n127
death squads: CIA coordination of: 274, 294n96; in Chile: 274; in El Salvador: 274; in Guatemala: 274; on Pine Ridge: 274, 275-6
Death Valley National Monument: 176
DeCora, Lorelei: 272
Deer, Ada: 241n131
Del Ponte, Carla: 349
Delaney, SD Ass't Att'ny Gen. William: 295n108
Deloria, Vine Jr.: 128, 140, 243n144
DeMain, Paul: 243n144
Denmark/Danes/Danish: 31n118
Denver (CO) Police Dept.: "Criminal Extremist" files of: 398n538
*Der Spiegel* (German newspaper): 350
Deskaheh (Cayuga statesman): 42
Despagnet, Frantz: 38
Dial family: 226n15
Diamond, Henry: 111n43
Dickenson, Emily: xi
Dilco: 88, 115n121
Dillingham, Walter: 115n121
Dinstein, Yoram: 36
Divine Right of Kings, concept of: 36
Doctrine of Discovery: xiv, 2-5, 39, 61n49, 230n57; acquisition of land title under: 3-5, 25-5n27; criteria of: 3; framing of "Just Wars" in: 3; John Marshall's interpretation of: 8-9; Norman Yoke concept applied to: 4-5, 8, 24n19; origins of: 2-3; origins of Indian treaties in: 4; role of missionaries under: 3; *terra nullius* doctrine of: 3, 230n58; *also see* Right of Conquest
Dole, Sanford: 80, 83, 84
Dole Fruit Co.: 80
Dörnitz, Gr. Adm. Karl: 332, 333
Dorris, Michael: 243n144
Doyle, SA James: 298n130
Draper, Wilfred ("Wish"): 277, 298n130
Driver, Harold: 26n56
Drost, Pieter: 251
Dry Water, Sam: 301n165
Duffy, Lt. James: 327, 381n212
Duggan, Gen. Michael J.: 344
Dull Knife (Cheyenne leader): 314
Dull Knife, Guy: 294n82
Dunbar Ortiz, Roxanne: 243n144
DuPont, Admiral A,E.: 79, 111n52

439

Durham, Jimmie: 243n142, 243n144, 300n145; and 1977 "Indian Summer in Geneva": 289n21; as founding IITC director: 284, 289n21; resignation from IITC: 289n21

Dutch, *see* Netherlands/Dutch

# E

Eagle, Jimmy: 277, 279, 295n101, 296n116

Eastman, Charles: 294n94

Eastman, Delmar: 276, 294n94

Ecoffey, Bob: 277

*Economic World* (magazine): 96

Ecuador: as internal colonial state: 51

Edgemont, SD: nuclear contamination of: 198n176

Egypt/Egyptians: 364, 399n543, 403n593

Eichmann, Adolf: 256, 261n54

Eighth Pan-American Conf. (1938): Declaration on the Non-Recognition of Territory Acquired by Force of: 45

Eisenbud, Merril: 161

Eisenhower, Pres. Dwight D.: 392n483

Engels, Freidrich: 231-2n67

England/English: 204, 364; alterations of Discovery Doctrine by: 4-5; colonization of Ireland by: 39; French and Indian Wars of: 4-5; German bombing of Coventry in: 333; internal colonization of the Scots by: 39, 187n27; internal colonization of the Welsh by: 39, 187n27; North American colonies of: 5, 204; War with the Shawnees of: 204; *also see* Great Britain/British

Environmental Protection Agency (EPA): 193n117, 194n127; report on Río Molino contamination of: 166; report on Río Paguate contamination of: 166

Erdrich, Louise: 243n144

Escamilla, Bernard: 294n91

Ethiopia/Ethiopians: Italian invasion of: 46

Evans, Gov. John: 310, 311, 375n57

Equitable Insurance Group, Inc.: 92

Exxon Corp.: 165

# F

Falk, Richard: 119n209

Fanon, Frantz: as author of *Black Skins, White Masks*: xvii; as author of *Wretched of the Earth*: 73

Farrington, Joseph: 85

Faurisson, Robert: 258n2

Fauquier, Francis: 204

Federal Bureau of Investigation (FBI): 293n80, 295n108, 300n150; Chicago Field Office of: 292n60, 295n106, 296n113; collaboration with Army Intelligence of: 337; crime lab of: 298n128; disinformation employed by: 278-9, 280, 296n110, 296n111, 297n120, 297n121; *Domestic Terrorist Digest* of: 297n121; fabrication of evidence by: 281; Hostage Rescue Team (HRT) of: 398n534; illegal detentions and: 363; illegal operations against VVAW by: 337; Internal Security Section of: 292n60; Milwaukee Field Office of: 278; Minneapolis Field Office of: 278, 295n100, 295n106; "no-knock" raids by: 279; perjured testimony of agents: 282; pursuit of Vietnam era draft resisters by: 337; pursuit of Vietnam era military deserters by: 337; Rapid City Resident Agency of: 273-4, 293n81, 295n106; relationship to Pine Ridge GOONs of: 274-6, 294n82, 294n91, 294n96; repression of AIM by: xvii, 19, 263-83; repression of RAM by: 293n71; reservation "reign of terror" perpetrated by: 271-9; suppression of evidence by: 281; SWAT teams of: 277, 278, 293n81; Quantico training facility of: 278; *also see* Coler, SA Jack; Held, SAC Richard G.; Kelley, FBI Dir. Clarence; Williams, SA Ron

Federal Emergency Management Agency (FEMA): 291n52, 363; and "Cable Splicer" counterinsurgency scenario: 398n536; and "Garden Plot" counterinsurgency scenario: 398n536; "Rex-84" counterinsurgency scenario of: 398n536; *also see* California Civil Disorder Management School; Giuffrida, Louis O.

Federal Tort Claims Act: 395n504

Ferdinand, Austrian Archduke Franz: assassination of: 40

Fifth International American Conf. (1923): 44

Fiji: U.S. investment in: 95

*Financial Times* (newspaper): 360

Finzel, Roger: 294n91

Fiore, Pasquale: 38

First Hawaiian Bank: 88, 94, 96

First Inter-American Conf. (1826): 65n105

First International American Conf. (1899): 44

First World War, *see* World War I

Fitzpatrick, SA Curtis: 292n58

Five Civilized Tribes Museum: 243n142

Flathead Indian Reservation: 241n133
Fleischer, Ari: 394n494
Florida: as Spanish colony: 5
Font, Louis: 346
Fools Crow, Frank (Oglala Lakota leader):
    226n14, 272, 291n50, 292n63; and
    revitalization of the Sun Dance: 289n20
Foote Mineral Corp.: 165
Forbes, Jack D.: 223
Foreign Claims Act: 395n504
*Foreign Relations* (journal): 109n17
Ford, John: 228n38
Forsyth, Col. George A.: 314
"Fort Hood 3": 336-7
Fort Mojave Indian Reservation: 181
Foster, Sec. of State John: 81, 83, 112n74, 113n81
Fourth World ("host world"): 105; concept of:
    51-5; self-determining rights of: 56-8
Fox News Channel: 401n566
France/French: 40, 364; and Nuremberg Trials:
    383n257; classical empire of: 1, 48, 89;
    colonization of Algeria by: 49, 66n137, 91,
    101, 240n122; colonization of New
    Caledonia (Kanaky) by: 49, 101;
    colonization of Somaliland by: 122n259;
    condemns U.S. unilateralism: 350;
    criminalization of Holocaust denial in:
    247; *Faurisson* trial in: 258n2; "French and
    Indian Wars" of: 4-5; in Vietnam: 67n140;
    Louisiana Purchase and: 6; World War II
    partisan movement in: 240n121; 1877
    codification of the Laws of War by: 307;
    *also see* Vichy France
Franklin, Benjamin: 204
Frazier, Sen. Linn: 131
Freedom of Information Act (FOIA; 1975): 281,
    299n136
Friends of the Indian: 235n89
Friends of the Lubicon (FOL): 252-5; Daishowa
    SLAPP suit against: 253-5; 1991-94
    Daishowa boycott of: 252
Fritz, Adrienne: 292n57
Fritz, Guy: 292n57
Fritz, Jeanne: 292n57
Frizzell, Sol. Gen. Kent: 274, 292n56

## G

Galeano, Eduardo: 156, 157
Gallagher, SA Richard J.: 298n124
Garafolo, Gary: 322
Garment, Leonard: 33-5, 55, 56, 58, 292n63; as
    Nixon bag man: 33, 290n33
Garnier family: 205

Gatesby Jones, Capt. Thomas ap: 77, 79
General Allotment Act ("Dawes Act"; 1887): 13,
    14, 78, 217, 235n89; as cornerstone of
    U.S. assimilation policy: 215; compilation
    of tribal rolls and: 214; property
    implications of: 214, 218-9; racial criteria
    of: 214-5
Geneva Convention on Wounded and Sick
    (1864): 309, 336, 341, 345, 349; 1868
    Additional Articles to: 376n85
Geneva Protocol for the Prohibition of the Use
    in War of Asphyxiating, Poisonous or
    Other Gases (1925): 336, 343, 346, 349
Genera Conventions (1926): 328, 336, 346, 349
Geneva Convention Relative to Treatment of
    Prisoners of War (1929): 333, 336, 346,
    349, 362
Geneva Conventions (1949): 323, 328, 336, 342,
    346, 349, 362, 394n500; Additional
    Protocol I to (1977): 118n200, 289n22,
    339, 362; Additional Protocol II to
    (1977): 339; Common Article III of: 341;
    Convention III Relative to Treatment of
    Prisoners of War: 381n215, 397n525;
    Convention IV Relative to Protection of
    Civilian Persons in Times of War: 328,
    381n215, 397n525, 400n554, 400n563
Geneva Peace Accords (1954): 378n138
Gentles, Pvt. William: 208
genocide: 155, 184, 368; as primarily nonlethal
    phenomenon: 250; "autogenocidal" form
    of: 185; "biological" form of: 250, 251;
    Canadian restrictions in describing: xvi,
    253-5; in Bosnia: 247; "cultural" form of:
    250, 251; Drost distorts meaning of: 251;
    euphemistic language and: 261n50;
    Hitlerian form of: 247; in Cambodia: 247;
    in Kosovo: 247, 253; in Rwanda: 247, 349;
    in Tibet: 253; Jewish exclusivist
    interpretations of: 247-9, 258n6, 258n8;
    Judeocide as form of: 248, 258n6, 258n8,
    261n50; legal criteria of: 186-7n15, 250;
    Lemkin's coinage of term: 149n94, 249;
    Lemkin's description of: 249-50;
    McPherson distorts meaning of: 255; of
    Achés: 261n53; of the Armenians: 247; of
    East Timorese: 247; of Gypsies: 247; of
    homosexuals: 247; of Jews: 247-8; of
    Pequots: 247; of Slavs: 247; "physical"
    form of: 250, 251; Sartre's equation to
    colonialism of: 52, 128, 158;
    "statistical/definitional variety" of: xvi;
    Trask's definition of: 251; *Webster's*

*Dictionary* definition of: 255
Genocide Convention (Convention on
    Prevention and Punishment of the Crime
    of Genocide (1948)): 20; Article II
    criteria of: 186-7n15, 250, 251, 259n22,
    260-1n44; Article III criteria of: 256,
    259n20; as customary law: 31n116, 251,
    259n25; Canadian ratification of: 251;
    subversions of, in Canadian law: 251-5;
    U.S. nonratification of: 31n116, 145n22,
    250, 348; U.S. "sovereignty package" and:
    31n116, 145n22, 250, 259n25, 348
Georgia State University: 370
Gentili, Alberico: 306
geopolitics, concepts of: 39; *also see* Balance of
    Power politics
Germans/Germany: 57, 364, 369, 371, 395n505;
    behavior of U.S. troops towards: 319;
    Buchenwald concentration camp in: 335,
    384n284; "Good Germans," concept of:
    58, 338, 369; Dachau concentration camp
    in: 335, 384n284; post-World War I loss
    of colonies: 43; pre-World War II
    expansionism of: 42; Schneeberg mining
    reason of: 161; Soviets and: 41; support for
    nazism of: 391n465; supposed "racial
    superiority" of: 232n71; unrestricted
    submarine warfare during World War II
    by: 332, 383n262; uranium production in:
    190n66; World War I and: 40; World War
    II casualties of: 65n110, 391n465; World
    War II firebombing of Dresden in: 333,
    378n121; World War I firebombing of
    Hamburg in: 333;1938 seizure of Austria
    by: 46; 1939 seizure of Czechoslovakia by:
    46; 1944 coup attempt in: 402n581
Geronimo (Chiricahua Apache leader): 208;
    exiled to Oklahoma: 334; imprisoned at
    Fort Marion: 237n103, 334
Getty Oil Corp.: 165
Ghana: as British colony: 50; as internal colonial
    state: 50
Giago, Tim: 201, 243n144; eulogy to Dickie
    Wilson by: 301n169
Gibson, Judge John: 282
Gilbert, Elizabeth: 227n27, 227n28
Gilbert (Thunderhawk), Madonna: 267, 272,
    300n144
Gildersleeve, Agnes: 292n57
Gildersleeve, Clive: 292n57
Gish, Robert: 243n144
Giuffrida, Louis O.: 291n52, 398n536
Gladstone, Lynn: 290n41

"globalization": 53, 106, 353
Goa: Portuguese occupation of: 103
Gofman, John W.: 162, 178, 189n58
Goodwin, Francis A.: 146n50
Gordon, SA John C.: 298n124
Göring, Hermann: 332-3, 341
Gramsci, Antonio: xiv; and concept of
    hegemony: 259n14
Grants Uranium Belt: milling along: 168-71;
    mining along: 164-8
Great Britain/British: 40; and Australian colony:
    77; and "Blue Water Thesis": 51; and
    Canadian colony: 77; and Nuremberg
    Trials: 383n257; classical empire of: 1, 4-5,
    31n118, 48, 136; colonization of Bermuda
    by: 101; colonization of Ceylon (Sri
    Lanka) by: 101; colonization of India by:
    50; colonization of Malaya by: 51;
    colonization of Malta by: 101-2;
    colonization of Nigeria by: 50;
    colonization of Oman by: 116n152;
    colonization of Rhodesia by: 101;
    interests in Hawai'i: 77; nationals killed in
    9-1-1 attacks: 393n492; War of 1812 and:
    7; 1916 partition of Iraq by: 21, 340,
    385n326; *also see* England/English
Great Russian Empire, *see* Romanov Empire
Grey, AUSA William B.: 298n124
Griffin, Susan: as author of *A Chorus of Stones*:
    153
Griffith, D.W.: *Birth of a Nation* (film) made by:
    63n81
Grinde, Donald A. Jr.: 243n144
Grimm, U.S. Marshal Lloyd: 292n58
Grotius, Hugo: 36-8, 47, 55; Pufendorf's critique
    of: 37; on Laws of War: 306; writes *De
    Jure Belli ac Pacis*: 36
Guam: 54, 76, 105; as U.S. colony: 19, 40, 49, 83,
    153; U.S. investment in: 95; 1905 Organic
    Act concerning: 66n136
Guerrier family: 234n78
"Guardians of the Oglala Nation" (GOONs):
    295n99, 301n169; and shooting of U.S.
    Marshal Grimm: 292n58; and Wounded
    Knee siege: 270-1; as Pine Ridge death
    squad: 274, 275-6; as "Tribal Ranger
    Group": 269; BIA funding of: 269; federal
    highway funds used to underwrite:
    291n45; confrontations with U.S.
    Marshals of: 274-5; formation of: 269;
    relationship to FBI of: 274-6, 291n45
Guatemala/Guatemalans: slaughter of Mayas by: 52
guerrillas/guerrilla movements: Hukbalahap:

66n132; Sendero Luminoso: 69n181
Gulf Oil Corp.: 165; San Mateo uranium mine
of: 190n78

# H

Hague Convention (1899): 328, 346, 376n85;
  Declaration 3 Concerning Expanding
  Bullets of: 379n145
Hague Convention IV Respecting the Laws and
  Customs of War (1907): 327, 328, 336,
  341, 346; Article 23 of: 386n339
Hague Rules of Aerial Warfare (1923): 328, 336,
  346
Haig, Gen. Alexander: 270
Haiti/Haitians: 379n153, 396n512
Hall, H.H.: 374-5n47
Halliburton Corp.: 399n547
Halliday, UN Ass't. Sec. Gen. Denis J.: 345
Hamas: 403n593
Hampton, Fred: 287, 292n60
Hamza, Khidre: 399n553
Hanford Nuclear Weapons Research and
  Production Facility: 174; as possible
  nuclear waste repository: 179; cancer rates
  among workers at: 162; DoD/DoE cover-
  up at: 173-4; establishment of: 159;
  experimental isotope releases from: 173;
  nuclear contamination from: 173,
  195n140; nuclear wastes at: 173-4, 178;
  "tank farm" at: 173
Hapsburg Empire, see Austrohungarian Empire
Hare, Leslie: 267
Hare, Melvin: 267
Harjo, Suzan Shown: 221, 243n143
Harper's (magazine): 380n168
Harris, Sen. Fred: 33
Harris, Charles: 80
Harris, LaDonna: 33, 199n185
Harrison, Pres. William Henry: 306; as army
  general: 304
Härting, E.H.: 160
Harvard University: School of Public Health of:
  344
Harvey, SA O. Victor: 298n130
Haskell Indian School: 216
Hatch, Sen. Orin: 393n489
Haudenosaunee (Iroquois Six Nations
  Confederacy): 42; atrocities committed
  against: 303; Cayugas: 42, 203; Hurons
  absorbed by: 203; Mohawks: 203, 223;
  Oneidas: 141, 203; Onondagas: 203,
  290n40; Senecas: 303-4, 340; Sullivan's
  campaign against: 303-4, 340, 369;

Susquehannocks absorbed by: 203; town
  of Genesee of: 303; traditional mode of
  membership identification among: 203-4
Hawai'i/Native Hawaiians (Kanaka Maoli): xviii,
  18, 21, 54, 73-107, 153, 251; and U.S.
  Pacific Rim Strategy: 87-8; "Big Five"
  corporations in: 79, 84; British interests
  in: 77, 111n49; Chinese laborers imported
  to: 79, 112n68; "Committee of Public
  Safety" activities in: 75-6, 109n16;
  constitutional monarchy overthrown:
  62n63, 73-4; constitutions of: 78, 81,
  111n66; contemporary population of: 98;
  contemporary sovereignty movement in:
  97-100; Cook's "discovery" of: 77; cost of
  living in: 93; development of tourism
  industry in: 92-6, 116-7n160, 117n121;
  dispossession of: 78-9, 86, 92; effect of
  Old World diseases upon: 77; exports
  from: 84; Filipino laborers imported to:
  79, 85; French interest in: 111n49; Great
  Mahele in: 78-9, 80; Greens Party in: 98;
  Hawaiian Crown Lands ("ceded lands")
  in: 78, 83, 92, 99; Hawaiian Homes Land
  in: 86, 99; "Hawaiian League" activities in:
  80, 109n16; health data on: 95; Hilo
  Airport development in: 95; Honolulu
  International Airport development in: 95;
  "Honolulu Rifles'" activities in: 76,
  109n16; imports to: 84-5; impoverishment
  of: 93-4, 117n170; inherent rights of: 74-
  5; Japanese investment in: 95-6; Japanese
  laborers imported to: 79; Ka Lahui
  "sovereignty march" in: 98-9; Kaho'olawe
  protests in: 97, 100; Kona Airport
  development in: 92; missionaries arrive in:
  77; missionary activity in: 77-9; National
  Guard in: 85; national lottery in: 112n68;
  Office of Hawaiian Affairs in: 100; opium
  tax in: 112n68; police in: 85; population
  decline among: 77, 86, 111n46; price
  disparities in: 84-5; repressive legislation
  in: 85; "Republic" of: 62n63, 76;
  sandalwood trade in: 77, 110n32; Sandy
  Beach protests in: 97; school system in:
  78; "Second Mahele" in: 92;
  strikes/strikebreaking in: 85; sugar
  production in: 84; tax structure in: 92-3,
  94-5; TH-3 highway development in: 95;
  Third World character of: 97; treaty with
  Denmark of: 111n49; treaty with
  Hamburg (Germany) of: 111n49; "Tyler
  Doctrine" concerning: 79; UN

obligations to: 100-7; U.S. acquisition/use of Pearl Harbor in: 76, 77, 80, 81, 82, 83, 86; U.S. annexation of: 40, 62n63, 76; U.S. colonization of: 49; U.S. economic penetration of: 78-9, 87-8, 92; U.S. gunboat diplomacy and: 77-82; U.S. military aggression against: 73-4, 80, 81, 82, 109n17; U.S. militarization of: 86; U.S. statehood imposed upon: 73, 90, 101; U.S. treaties with: 62n63, 79, 80, 111n57; 1993 U.S. apology to: 73-5; 1873 revolt in: 80; 1903 Organic Act concerning: 83; *al-4so see* "Big Five" corporations

Hawaiian Agricultural Co.: 84

Hawaiian Autonomy Act ("Case Act"; 1998): 100, 119-20n216

Hawaiian Homes Commission Act (1920): 86

Hawaiian Sugar and Commercial Co.: 84

Hawkins, SA Herbert H. Jr.: 298n124

Heaney, Judge Gerald: 281, 282

Held, SAC Richard G.: 271, 274-5, 295n106, 296n113; as FBI asst. dir.: 298n124; as head of FBI Internal Security Section: 292n60; as author of "Paramilitary Operations in Indian Country": 292n60; orchestrates cover-up of Hampton/Clark assassinations: 292n60

Helm, George: 97, 118n197

Helms, Sen. Jesse: 106

Henderson, Col. Oran: 322, 324

Herbert, Col. Anthony: 337

Herman, Edward S.: xiv

Hersh, Seymore: 323

Hesse, W.: 160

Hicks, Tyler: 361

Hill, Gerald: 295n108

Hinds, Lennox: 119n209

Hiroshima: U.S. nuclear bombing of: 174, 197n160, 320, 378n130

Hitler, Adolf: xiii, 148n85, 351, 357; and genocide: 247; as author of *Mein Kampf*: xiii, 27n58, 135; attempted assassination of: 57, 402n581; "Big Lie" concept of: xiii-xiv: Hössbach Memorandum and: 148n82; *Lebensraumpolitik* of: 12, 26-7n58, 135-6; Münich diplomacy of: 144n1

Hizbullah: 403n593

Hodge, SA Evan: 282; perjury of: 299n136, 299n137

Hogan, Linda: 243n144

Holder, Stan: 272, 282, 293n69, 300n144

Holiday Inns Corp.: 92

Holocaust denial: criminalization of, in Canada: 247; criminalization of, in France: 247; Jewish exclusivism as form of: 247-9; neonazi form of: 248-9

Holt Renfrew restaurants: 253

Honeywell Corp.: 285

Hong Kong: U.S. investments in: 88

Honolulu-Hilo Inland Boatman's Union: 85

Honolulu International Country Club: 96

Hössbach, Col. Freidrich: 148n82

Howard, Rep. Edgar: 239n115

Huepner, William C.: AEC constrains public presentations of: 161-2; as author of *Occupational Tumors and Allied Diseases*: 161

Huet-Vaughn, Capt. Yolanda: 346

Hultman, AUSA Evan: 298n124

Human Rights Watch: 392n476

Hungary/Hungarians: 64n86

Hunts Horse, Annie: 292n57

Hussein, Saddam: 340, 346, 347, 365, 367, 399n553, 402n581; anti-Islamicism of: 399n546; supposed link to 9-1-1 of: 366

Hussman, John: 293n82

Huston, John: 227n27, 227n28

**I**

India: 396n512; as British colony: 50; Air India jumbo jet bombing: 396n506; as internal colonial state: 51; Naga independence struggle in: 52; nuclear weapons pgm. in: 366; Sikh independence struggle in: 396n506; U.S. refuses extradition to: 396n512; 1984 Bhopal disaster in: 396n512

Indian boarding/residential school system: 215-6, 237n102, 238n106, 238n107, 238n108; as cornerstone of U.S./Canadian assimilation policies: 215; as cultural genocide: 238n108, 239n109, 259n22; as industrial schools: 238n107; establishment of: 216; in Canada: xxin13; methods used in: 216, 238-9n109; stated objectives of: 216; *also see* Albuquerque Indian School; Carlisle Indian School; Chilocco Indian School; Haskell Indian School; Phoenix Indian School; Pratt, Capt. Richard Henry; Riverside Indian School

Indian Citizenship Act (1924): 14-5; as assimilationist "clean-up" measure: 216-7

Indian Civil Rights Act (1968): 31n118

Indian Claims Commission (ICC): xv, 19, 50, 129-43, 240n126; as PR gesture: 136-7; extensions of: 139; final report of: 153-4, 187n30, 288n10; funding of: 150n121;

Justice Dept. obstructions of: 139, 150n122; *Loyal Creeks v. U.S.* docket of: 149n97; number of dockets filed with: 139-40, 150n114; "Pit River Land Claims Settlement" effected by: 149-50n106; procedures of: 18, 139-41; *Pueblo de Taos* docket of: 149n96; unresolved dockets of: 140; Western Shoshone Land Claim and: 151n125

Indian Claims Commission Act (1946): 18, 137, 151n131; Justice Dept. recommends changes to: 148n87; legislative background of: 147-8n75; relationship to Nuremberg prosecutions: 135-7; relationship to termination legislation: 138

*Indian Country Today* (newspaper): 221, 242n139, 243n144

Indian Reorganization Act (IRA; "Wheeler-Howard Act"; 1934): xvii, 16, 217-8; corporate charters written under: 239n117; NTCA and: 240n121; "tribal councils" created by: 16, 19, 34, 217; tribal constitutions written under: 217, 218, 220, 239n117; tribal membership criteria posited under: 218, 220

Indian Rights Assoc.: 235n89

Indian Self-Determination and Educational Assistance Act (1975): 31n118, 34

"Indian Wars": 35, 127, 148n85, 304-5, 376n83; absence of in Canada: 55; as "settlers' wars": 25n42; "Black Hawk's War": 305; continuing forms of: 263; Euroamerican atrocities committed during: 303-7, 310-5; "Little Crow's War": 334; Seminole Wars: 228n35; "special circumstances" pertaining to: 315, 319; 1899-1902 Philippines campaign as: 315-8; *also see* massacres; U.S. Army

Indians of All Tribes: 263

indigenous peoples: Abenakis: 220, 241-2n136; Achés: 52, 261n53; Acoma Pueblo: 167, 169, 171; alcoholism among: 127, 155, 254; Aleuts: 18, 176; Apaches: 204, 316, 334; Apalachees: 227n32; Arapahos: 194n127, 203, 207, 315, 375n48; Arikaras: 208; as "subhumans": 319; assimilation policies aimed against: 132-3, 213-8; Basques: 39, 187n27; Berbers: 52; Catalans: 39; Celts: 39; Chamorros: 105; Chechens: 52, 364; Chemehuavis: 181; Chickasaws: 203, 210; Chippewas: 205, 222, 242n139, 264; Choctaws: 203, 210;

Cochiti Pueblo: 172; Cocopahs: 181; Coeur d'Alenes: 278; Cofitichiquis: 227n32; Comanches: 207, 228n38, 315, 334; contemporary demographic data on: 17, 28n82, 186n7, 222, 223, 236n95, 240-1n126; Cree: xiii, xix, 203, 252, 253, 254, 256, 279; Croatans: 226n15; Crows: 171, 208; death rates among: 52, 127, 155; diaspora of: 15, 52, 219, 264; Goshutes: 175, 177, 199n187; Guales: 227n32; Havasupi: 177; health data on: 17, 52, 127, 154-5, 254, 265, 289n17; Hopis: 52, 141, 171, 239-40n119; Hmongs: 52, 331; Hualapis: 177; Hurons: 203; Hutus: 52; Ibos: 52, 223; impoverishment of: 17, 52, 126-7, 154, 241n132, 254, 265, 289n17; independence struggles of: 52, 347; involuntary sterilization of: 290n34; Inuits: 18; Isleta Pueblo: 171; Jemez Pueblo: 172; Kaibabs: 177; Kanakys: 49; Kaws: 215, 245n159; Kiowa Apaches: 207; Kiowas: 207, 315, 316, 334; Klamaths: 131, 138, 219, 220; Kootenai: 241n133; Kurds: 52, 187n27, 347; land rights/holdings of: 142, 154, 186n5, 240n126, 264, 288n10; language groups of: 226n11; Lenni Lenâpé (Delawares): 210; Lumbees: 226n16; Mayas: 52; Menominees: 138, 150n108, 219, 241n131; Mesquakis ("Foxes"): 305; Miamis: 204; mineral resources of: 15-6, 154, 156, 217, 239n113, 265; Miskitos: 52; "Mission Bands": 138, 219; Moapas: 175; Mohicans: 210; Montagnards: 52, 331; Munsees: 210; Muckleshoots: 263; Nagas: 52; Nez Perce: 146n50, 179; Nisquallys: 263; Ojibwes: 203; Osage: 131; "outmarriage" rates of: 222; Paiutes: 175, 176, 181, 204; Papagos: 290n40; Pawnees: 204, 207, 208; Pequots: 204, 247; Piegans: 314; Poncas: 150n108; population reductions of: 11, 12, 26n56; Puyallups: 141, 263; Qechuas: 53; Quechanis: 181; Ramas: 52; reductions in landholdings of: 12, 13, 40, 52, 129-46, 214, 219, 264; relocation pgms. and: 219; Sacs (Sauks): 305; Salish: 241n133; San Ildefonso Pueblo: 159, 172; San Juan Pueblo: 172; Santa Clara Pueblo: 172; Santees: 334; Scots: 39, 187n27; self-determining rights of: 20, 57; Seminoles: 206, 210, 227n32; Shoshones: 131, 182, 194n127, 373n48; Siletz: 150n108; Spokanes: 173, 194n127; Stillaquamish:

445

141; suicide rates among: 155; Sumus: 52; Suquamish: 141; Susquehannocks: 203; Tamils: 101; Tarahumaras: 203; Timacuans: 227n32; Timorese: 52, 347; traditional modes of identification among: 203-6, 208, 213; Tutsis: 52, 349; Umatillas: 179, 222-3, 244n153; U.S. statutes effecting: 13; Utes: 171; Welsh: 39, 187n27; Western Shoshones: 141; Wichitas: 131; Yakimas: 159, 173, 179, 182; Yamasees: 227n32; Yaquis: 203; Zia Pueblo: 172; Zuni Pueblo: 171; *also see* Cherokees/Cherokee Nation; Cheyennes; Creeks (Muscogees); Haudenosaunee; Hawai'i/Native Hawaiians; Laguna Pueblo; Lakotas; Mescalero Apache Reservation; Navajo Nation; Philippine/Filipinos; Shawnees; Skull Valley Reservation

Indonesia/Indonesians: as internal colonial state: 51; slaughter of Timorese by: 52, 347; 2002 Bali bombing in: 371, 402n591; 1965 Suharto coup in: 378n136; *also see* Java

Inouye, Sen. Daniel: 21, 31n118

Inter-American Assoc. for Democracy and Freedom: 261n53

Inter-American Conf. for the Promotion of Peace (1938): 45, 47

International Court of Justice (ICJ; "World Court"): 20, 31n115; creation of: 46; *Nicaragua v. U.S.* opinion of (1985): 21n115, 388n393; Iranian attempts to bring action before: 394-5n502; League of Nations precursor to: 42, 55; U.S. repudiates jurisdiction of: 20, 31n115, 347, 388n393, 394-5n502

International Criminal Court (ICC): 347, 352-3, 356; as International Criminal Tribunal (ICT): 348-9, 388n395; U.S. refuses jurisdiction of: 347

International Indian Treaty Council (IITC): 289n21; as "AIM's international diplomatic arm": 284; as UN Type-II NGO: 289n21; current irrelevance of: 284-5; drug trafficking allegations against: 284; founding of: 284; Jimmie Durham as founding director of: 284, 289n21

International League for the Rights of Man: 261n53

International Monetary Fund (IMF): 92

International Peoples Tribunal on the Rights of Indigenous Hawaiians (1993): 99, 119n209

International Symposium on the Peaceful Uses of Atomic Energy (1955): 161

international tort law: 74, 121n243

Iran/Iranians: as Shi'ite country: 399n546; attempts to bring ICJ action by: 394-5n502; "Axis of Evil" speech and: 365; hostility of al-Qaida to: 399n546; hostility to al-Qaida of: 365; U.S. shoots down civilian airliner of: 359, 394-5n502; 1979-80 "hostage crisis" in: 396n512

Iraq/Iraqis: 340-5, 350, 359, 367, 370, 399n547, 400n557, 402n581; alleged biological weapons in: 365; alleged chemical weapons in: 365; alleged nuclear weapons in: 366, 399n553; alleged links to al-Qaida of: 366; as "Indian Country": 340; as "Mesopotamia": 385n326; "Axis of Evil" speech and: 365; Basra massacre in: 341-2; Ba'athist régime in: 365; city of Baghdad in: 343; city of Basra in: 341, 342, 343; city of Sulamaneiya in" 342, 343; city of Urbil in: 342; civilian casualties in: 343, 344-5, 386n361; current U.S. plans to invade: 367-8; disarmament of: 399-400n553; depleted uranium munitions used against: 354; epidemics in: 343, 387n369; "Highway of Death" massacre in: 341; hostility to al-Qaida of: 365; "infrastructural" targets in: 343-4; invasion of Kuwait by: 21, 340; Kurdish independence struggle in: 52; postwar bombing of: 344-5; postwar embargo of: 344; relations with Iran of: 365; relationship of to Kuwait: 21, 340, 385n326; Republican Guard of: 341; supposed link to 9-1-1 of: 366; U.S. aerial ordnance expended against: 342-3, 386n353, 393n493; U.S. propaganda concerning: 346; U.S. war crimes against:340-5, 385n329; 1990-91 U.S. war against: 21, 340-4; 1991 capitulation of: 340; 1991 UN report on: 344

Irish/Ireland: 204, 223; English colonization of: 39

Iroquois, *see* Haudenosaunee

Islamic Jihad: 403n593

Israel/Israelis: and shootdown Libyan airliner: 395-6n506, 403n594; as settler state: 2; atrocities against Palestinians by: 367, 394n500; defiance of UN resolutions by: 367, 400n554; failure of security in: 371; holocaust denial policies of: 258n8;

occupation policies of: 394n500; political support of: 248; repression of the Intifada by: 400n554; secret nuclear weapons program of: 192n93, 366, 400n555; Oslo II Peace Accord and: 403n593; "settlement" policies of: 359, 394n500, 400n554, 403n593; terrorism and: 401n566; terrorism of: 401n566; quid pro quo with Turkey of: 258n8; U.S. military/political support to: 367, 394n500, 395-6n506, 400n563; violation of Non-Proliferation Treaty by: 400n555

Italy/Italians: 395n504; behavior of U.S. troops towards: 319; invasion of Ethiopia by: 46; League of Nations sanctions against: 46; post-World War II leadership trials of: 47; pre-World War II expansionism of: 42, 46; 1896 codification of the Laws of War by: 307

# J

Jackson, George: 287

Jackson, Pres. Andrew: 306; as army general: 304; atrocities committed by: 304, 320

Jackson, Sen. Henry M. ("Scoop"): 137, 151n131

Jackson, Justice Robert H.: 134; as U.S. prosecutor at Nuremberg: 57, 71n221, 136, 332; "Menagerie Theory" of: 134, 136; *Northwest Bands of Shoshone* opinion of (1945): 134, 136, 147n71

Jackson, Te Moana Nui A Kiwa: 119n209

Jackson, Col. Vic: 291n52

Janis, Dale: 294n82

Janklow, Gov. William: 295n103; as South Dakota att'ny gen.: 263, 300n147

Japan/Japanese: 49, 67n140, 114n115, 332, 340; Pacific mandates of: 49; Manila war crimes trials of: 333; post-World War II leadership trials of: 47; pre-World War II expansionism of: 42, 44; significance of the Emperor to: 378n133; Tokyo war crimes trials of: 333; "unconditional surrender" demanded from: 320, 378n133; U.S. war crimes against: 319-20, 333, 384n273; World War II defeat of: 174, 320; World War II fire raids against: 320, 378n130; World War II surrender attempts of: 378n128, 378n133; 1941 U.S. embargo of: 46; *also see* Hiroshima; Nagasaki

Japan Airlines: 95

Jarach, Lawrence: 126

Jarvis, James Jackson: 80

Java: 1609 Dutch conquest of: 50

Javits, Sen. Jacob: 66n136

Jefferson, Pres. Thomas: 5; racial views of: 210

Johnson, Guy: 204

Johnson, Pvt. James: 336-7

Johnson, Pres. Lyndon B.: 321, 323, 378n137

Johnson, Sir William: 227n28

Jones, Indian Comm. William: 238n107

Jospin, Lionel: 350

*Journal of the National Cancer Institute*: 161

Judd, Gerrit: 78, 111n43

Jumping Bull, Cecilia: 277, 278

Jumping Bull, Harry: 277, 278

Jumping Bull, Roselyn: 295n99

Jumping Bull Compound: 277

"Just War," concepts of: 3, 8, 11, 21

# K

Ka Lahui Hawai'i: 98-100, 119n214; founding of: 98; "Four Arenas of Sovereignty" program of: 100; Master Plan of: 99, 102; participation in International People's Tribunal by: 99; 1993 "sovereignty march" of: 98-9

Ka Pakaukau: 99, 119n214

Kaibab Reservation: 177

Kaiser, Henry J.: 88, 115n120

Kaiser Permanente Corp.: 88

Kanaka Maoli, *see* Hawai'i/Native Hawaiians

Karzai, Hamid: 364

Kazaks/Kazakistan: 364

Keegstra, James: 258n2

Kelley, FBI Dir. Clarence: 278, 280, 297n121, 298n124

Kellogg-Briand Pact (Pact of Paris; 1928): 44, 47; influence on UN Charter of: 45

Kennedy, Pres. John F.: 290n40, 321

Kenny, Maurice: 243n144

Kent, Noel: 77

Kentucky Fried Chicken Corp.: 252

Kenya/Kenyans: Nairobi embassy bombing in: 359, 394n497

Kerr-McGee Nuclear Corp.: 164, 191n79; Grants uranium mill of: 169; Laguna uranium mill of: 168, 169; Church Rock job training pgm. run by: 167, 191n91; Church Rock No. 1 uranium mine: 165, 166; Red Rock uranium mine of: 164, 166; sued for damages by Red Rock uranium miners: 193n106; Shiprock uranium mill of: 169, 193n105; Shiprock uranium mine of: 164, 165, 166; worker safety violations of: 164

Khader, Asma: 119n209
Kills Enemy, Jake: 291n50
Kills Straight, Birgil: 266
Killsright, Joe Stuntz: 278, 293n78, 295n108
King George III: Treaty of Paris and: 6; 1763
    Royal Proclamation of: 5, 6, 24–5n27
King Kalakua (David Kalakua): "Bayonet
    Constitution" imposed upon: 81; seated as
    Hawaiian King: 80; death of: 81
King Kamehameha I: 77
King Lunalilo: 80
King, Matthew ("Noble Red Man"): 292n62
King, Martin Luther Jr.: 256, 287
Kintetsu International Corp.: 96
Kipling, Rudyard: "Gunga Din" poem of: xvii
Kissinger, Sec. of State Henry: 34, 370
Knox, Sec. of War John: 231n64
Koop, Surgeon Gen. C. Everett: 200n210
Korea/Koreans: 114n115, 399n547; "Axis of Evil"
    speech and: 365; "contributions" to
    Vietnam War effort of: 325, 380–1n193;
    KAL Fl. 007 shootdown: 395n502,
    396n506; U.S. "police action" in: 321
Korman, Sharon: 38, 43; as author of The Right of
    Conquest: 33
Koster, Gen. Samuel W.: 380n176; and My Lai
    Massacre: 322; appointed superintendent
    of West Point: 323–4; nonprosecution of:
    323
KPFA (radio station): 221
Kroeber, Alfred L.: 26n56
Kruch, Robert A.: 322
Kuleana Act (1850): 78
Kunstler, William: 297n121, 299n137
Kuper, Leo: critique of Sartre by: 260n29
Kuwait: 340–1, 346, 385n326; as 19th Iraqi
    province: 21, 340, 385n326; Kuwait City
    in:341; town of al-Mutlaa in: 341; 1990
    Iraqi invasion of: 21, 340
Kuykendall, Indian Claims Comm. Jerome: 139

## L

Laguna Pueblo: 183; Anaconda "improvement"
    pgms. and: 169–70; and Four Corners
    National Sacrifice Area: 171;
    environmental contamination at: 166–7,
    169–70, 168, 192n98; health data on: 167,
    170; Jackpile-Paguate uranium mining
    complex at: 166–7; Kerr-McGee uranium
    mill at: 168; unemployment at: 167,
    191n89
Lakota Times (newspaper): 201, 301n169
Lakotas/Lakota Nation ("Sioux"): xix, 223,
242n139, 280, 316; and Black Hills
    National Sacrifice Area: 171; and World
    War I: 28n78; Brûlé (Sicangu) band of:
    208; Cheyenne River Reservation of:
    171; Crow Creek Reservation of: 171;
    IRA imposed upon: 29n86; Minneconjou
    Band of: 314; Oglala band of: 19, 141,
    207, 264, 266, 267, 268, 271, 279, 291n46,
    294–5n98, 296n114; Standing Rock
    Reservation of: 171; Sun dance revitalized
    among: 289n20; Sun Dance suppressed
    among: 28n76, 289n20; traditional mode
    of member identification among: 205;
    1890 Wounded Knee Massacre of: 11,
    28n78, 266, 314; 1974 "Sioux Sovereignty
    Hearing" concerning: 392n480; also see
    Pine Ridge Reservation; Rosebud Sioux
    Reservation
Lamont, Buddy: 271, 291n55
Lanaians for Sensible Growth: 98
Land Mines Treaty (International Treaty Banning
    the Use, Production, Stockpiling and
    Transfer of Anti-Personnel Mines (1999):
    347–8; U.S. refusal of: 348
Laos/Laotians: 329–31; as U.S. "secret war" zone:
    329; civilian fatalities among: 330; Hmong
    people in: 52, 331; panhandle region of:
    329, 382n235; Plain of Jars region of: 321,
    329–30; Truong Son supply route ("Ho
    Chi Minh Trail") in: 382n235; U.S. aerial
    ordnance expended against: 330,
    382n233; wartime population
    displacement among: 330
Larry King Live (tv show): 393n489
Las Casas, Bartolomé de: 231n64
Las Vegas Paiute Colony: 175
Laval, Pierre: 240n121
Lavasseur, Ray Luc: 287
LaVelle, John (the "Italian Stallion"): 243n145
Law of Nations: 35, 37, 306, 374n26
Laws, Rufina: 180
Laws of War: xv, 56, 356, 378n138, 382n220; as
    customary law: 307; history of: 306; Red
    Cross Fundamental Rules of
    Humanitarian Law Applicable to Armed
    Conflicts (1978): 339; also see Geneva
    Conventions; Hague Conventions; Land
    Mines Treaty; Lieber Code; United
    Nations
League of Nations: 42–6, 47, 385n326; Covenant
    of: 63–4n85, 64n92; creation of: 42;
    ineffectuality of: 46; sanctions against Italy
    of: 46; U.S. refuses to join: 42; "World

Court" of: 42, 46
LeClair, Antoine: 234n83
Lemkin, Raphaël: 251, 252, 255; as author of *Axis Rule in Occupied Europe*: 259–60n26; coins term "ethnocide" as synonym for "genocide": 259–60n26; coins term "genocide": 149n94, 249; describes genocidal processes: 249–50; 1946 draft Genocide Convention prepared by: 249–50
Lenin, Vladimir Illich: 49; 1917 "Decree of Peace" by: 42
leninists/leninism: 43
Leonard Peltier Defense Committee (LPDC): 283, 300n149, 300n152
Leupp, Indian Comm. Francis: 13, 132, 133, 215
Levi, Att'ny Gen. Edward S.: 296n115
Levy, Capt. Howard: 336, 337, 338
Libya/Libyans: 364; alleged bombing of La Belle discotèque by: 395n504; alleged bombing of Pan Am Fl. 103 by: 395n502; alleged bombing of Rome Airport by: alleged bombing of Pan Am Fl. 103 by: 395n504; alleged bombing of Vienna Airport by: alleged bombing of Pan Am Fl. 103 by: 395n504; city of Benghazi in: 359; city of Tripoli in: 359; civilian airliner of, shot down by Israel: 395–6n506; compensation to families of Pan Am victims: 395n504; 1981 "Gulf of Sidra Incident" and: 359, 395n503; 1986 U.S. bombing of: 359
Lieber, Francis: 307, 308
Lieber Code ("Instructions for the Government of Armies of the United States in the Field"; 1863): 307–10, 327, 334, 341, 375n61; and 1864 Geneva Convention: 309; contents of: 308–10; doctrinal nullification of: 319; influence of: 307; influence of Clausewitz upon: 308; influence of Montesquieu upon: 309; influence of Rousseau upon: 309; influence of Vattel upon: 308; promulgation of: 307; U.S. Army violations of: 310–5; *also see* Laws of War
Liechtenstein: sovereignty of: 144n3
*Life* (magazine): 320, 380n168
Lifton, Robert Jay: 247
Limerick, Patricia Nelson: 222, 373n21
Lincoln, Pres. Abraham: 310, 334, 384n277; in "Black Hawk's War": 305
Lind, Ian: 118n197
Lipstadt, Deborah: as author of *Denying the Holocaust*: 258n5; as holocaust denier: 256; as Jewish exclusivist: 255–6; neglect of

Gypsies by
Little Bear, Mary Ann: 293n79
Little Big Man (Oglala Lakota): 208
Livingstone, Maj. Gordon: 338
*Look* (magazine): 380n168
Looking Elk, Stanley: 193n117
Looney, Gen. William: 345
Lorenser, S.: 161
Lorenz, Egon: 161
Los Alamos National Scientific Laboratory: 174; Area G of: 172; Bayo Canyon area of: 172; establishment of: 159; recommends creation of National Sacrifice Areas: 170; nuclear contamination from: 172; nuclear wastes at: 172, 195n131
Loud Hawk, Kenneth: 297n118
Louisiana Land Corp.: 117n161
Louisiana Purchase (1803): 6
Low Level Nuclear Waste Policy Act (1980): 199n199
Ludwig, P.: 161

## M

MacArthur, Gen. Arthur: 318
MacArthur, Gen. Douglas: 320
Mackenzie, Col. Ranald: 208
Madagascar: as French colony: 50; as internal colonial state: 50
Madison, Pres. James: 5
Maher, Bill: 394n494
Major Crimes Act (1885): 12, 14, 213, 235n88
Makoto, Oda: 119n209
Malaya (Malaysia): as British colony: 50–1; as internal colonial state: 50, 51; U.S. investments in: 88
Malcolm X: 57, 183, 287, 354
Malta: as British colony: 101; decolonization of: 102
Mancuso, Thomas F.: 162
Manhart, Fr. Paul: 292n57
Manifest Destiny: concept of: 209; as "imperial destiny": 109n24; compared to nazi *Lebensraumpolitik*: 12, 25n40
Mankiller, Wilma: 300n144
Manning, Leah Hicks: 300n150
Manson, Charlie: 185
Mao Zedong: "Third World" concept of: 39
maoists/maoism: 49
Maori Legal Service: 119n209
Marcuse, Herbert: 106
Margold, Nathan R.: 133
Marianas Islands, U.S. occupation of: 49
Markusen, Eric: 247

Marshall, Gen. George C.: 378n129

Marshall, Chief Justice John: xiv, 8, 17, 43;
*Cherokee* opinions of: 9-10, 25n36, 25n37,
64n92; colonialist theories of: 9, 40;
Discovery Doctrine interpreted by: 8-9;
*Fletcher v. Peck* opinion of: 8, 10; *Johnson v.
McIntosh* opinion of: 8, 10; *Marbury v.
Madison* opinion of: 122n258; "Just War"
principle interpreted by: 10, 11;
landholdings of: 8; law of nations
subverted by: 10; legal doctrine of: 10-4,
16, 19, 20, 21; Norman Yoke principle
applied by: 8

Marshall, Richard ("Dickie"): 297n119

Marshall Islands: as U.S. colony: 19; U.S. nuclear
weapons testing in: 174, 195n144; Bikini
Atoll in: 195n144, 197n160; Enewetak
Atoll in: 195n144

Marx, Groucho: 1

Marx, Karl: 39; endorses European colonialism: :
232n67; influence of Morgan upon:
231n67

marxists/marxism: 50

Massachusetts Colony: Harvard College in:
237n101

*Massacre at Mazar* (film): 361

massacres: 317, 325, 340; Bad Axe River (1833):
305, 306; Basra (1991): 341; Bear River
(1863): 11, 375n48; Blue River (1854): 11;
Camp Robinson (1878): 11, 314;
"Highway of Death" (1991): 341;
Horseshoe Bend (1814): 304, 306, 320;
Malmédy (1944): 333; Marias River:
(1870): 11, 314; Mazar-i-Sharif (2001):
361; My Khe 4 (Co Luy; 1968): 324-5,
326, 327, 345; My Lai 4 (Son My; 1968):
322-4, 326, 327, 345; Qibya (1953):
400n554; Sand Creek (1864): 11, 207,
310-3, 324, 338, 375n48, 375n61; Sappa
Creek (1875): 11, 315; Truong Khanh 2
(1968): 325, 326; Washita River (1868):
11, 313, 314; Wounded Knee (1890): 11,
148n85, 266, 314, 342

master narratives: 391n469; U.S. triumphalist
variety of: 35; *also see* metanarrative

Mathis, Fern: 294n94

Matías de Paz, Juan: 3, 61n49

Maxwell, Charles: 97

McDonald, Peter: 199n185

McClosky, Rep. Pete: 330

McCullough. John: 205, 227n24

McGill University: law faculty of: 261n45

McGovern, Sen. George: 292n57

McKiernan, Kevin Barry: 295n108

McKinley, Pres. William: 83; as "eager
imperialist": 109n23

McLeish, John: 235n85

McManus, Judge Edward: 280, 298n125

McNabb, William: 233n78

McNamara, Sec. of Defense Robert S,: 381n211

McPherson, Judge J.C.: 256, 260n44, 261n47,
261n48; as holocaust denier: 256; hears
*Friends of the Lubicon* case: 254-5; ignores
expert witness testimony: 261n45;
privileges dictionary over legal definitions
at trial: 255, 261n46; ruling of: 254;
subversion of international law by: 255

Means, Bill: 267, 301n165

Means, Russell: 31n118, 141, 143, 171, 285; and
BIA headquarters occupation: 267;
"criminal syndicalism" conviction of:
292n67; joins AIM: 266; leads 1971
*Mayflower* protest: 266; leads 1971 Mt.
Rushmore protest: 266; leads 1972
Gordon protest: 267; media skills of: 266;
resigns from AIM: 300n146; riot charges
against: 269; Wounded Knee charges
dismissed against: 272; 1974 electoral
campaign of: 276, 294-5n98

Means, Ted: 267, 300n144

Medina, Capt. Ernest: 324

Melville, Commodore George: 76

Memmi, Albert: 225n6

"Men's Movement," *see* "New Age"

Meriam Commission: 133

Merritt, Assist. Indian Comm. Edgar B.: 132

Mescalero Apache Reservation: as possible MRS
site: 179, 180; proximity to White Sands
Test Range: 159, 180; "Trinity" nuclear
test near: 159

metanarrative (grand narrative): 391n469; concept
of: xiv

Mexico/Mexicans: 54; Mayan independence
struggle in Chiapas: 52

Micronesia: U.S. investments in: 88

Miles, Ellen: 118n197

Miller, Kay: 243n144

Miller, Justice Samuel F.: 12

Mills, C. Wright: 128, 391n469

Milosevic, Slobodan: 348

missions/missionaries: 3, 211, 227n30, 232n70;
American Missionary Board of: 111n43;
subvert Hawaiian monarchy: 77-82

Mitchell, George: 264

Mitchell, James Kimo: 97, 118n197

Mitterand, François: 66n137

Moehler, William: 170
Mojave Desert: nuclear contamination of: 176; Ward Valley nuclear waste facility in: 181
Monaco: sovereignty of: 144n3
Monroe, Pres. James: "Monroe Doctrine" of: 79
Montesquieu: 309, 374n40
Montevideo Convention on the Rights and Duties of States (1933): 45, 47
Montileaux, Martin: 297n119
Montluc: 38
Mooney, James: 26n56
Moor's Charity School for Indians: 237n101
Mora, Pvt. Dennis: 336-7
Moratorium to End the War in Vietnam: 353
Morgan, Sen. John T.: 112n78
Morgan, Lewis Henry: 211
Morgan, Indian Comm. Thomas Jefferson: 238n106, 238n107
Moroccans/Morocco: 364
Morris, Glenn T.: 119n209, 243n144
Morris, Steve: 118n197
Morriseau family: 205
Morton, Samuel George: 210; as author of *Crania Americana*: 209; fraudulent methods of: 229-10n52
Mousseau family: 205
Movenpeck Restaurants: 253
Moves Camp, Ellen: 270, 276, 294n93
Mozambique: as Portuguese colony: 91, 101
MSNBC: 402n587
Muldrow, William: 280
Muhammad, Faiz: 362
Mullah Omar: 396n510
Muller, H.J.: 162
Mulroney, Pr. Min. Brian: 261n45
Mundt, Rep. Karl: 137
MX missile system: 176, 197n163
Myer, Indian Comm. Dillon S.: presides over World War II internment of Japanese Americans: 241n129; presides of Indian termination policy: 241n129
Myanmar, *see* Burma

# N

Nagasaki: U.S. nuclear bombing of: 320, 378n130
Namibia: uranium mining in: 167
Napier, Alex: 93, 117n162
Napoleonic Wars: 38
Nasser, Abdul Gamal: 403n593
National Academy of Sciences: 171, 180
National Aeronautics and Space Admin. (NASA): 291n46
"National AIM, Inc.": 243n145; corporate charter of: 285, 301n165; corporate funding of: 285; federal funding of: 243n145, 285; those associated with: 301n165; Vernon Bellecourt and: 301n165
National Conf. On Charities and Corrections (1892): 237n104
National Congress of American Indians (NCAI): 179
National Council of Churches: 293n69
National Sacrifice Areas: and Nixon admin.: 194n123; Black Hills National Sacrifice Area: 171; concept of: xvi, 17; Four Corners National Sacrifice Area: 171; Los Alamos recommendation and: 170-1; National Academy of Sciences recommendation and: 171
National Tribal Chairmen's Assoc. (NTCA): 220; and Trail of Broken Treaties: 240n121, 290n36; becomes National Tribal Chairmen's Fund: 241n135
National Uranium Resource Evaluation Institute (NURE): 291n46
Native American Artists Assoc.: 243n143
NATO (North Atlantic Treaty Org.): 67n139, 388n395
Navajos/Navajo Nation: and federal livestock impoundment pgm.: 192n96; and Four Corners National Sacrifice Area: 171; Big Mountain resistance movement among: 252; Black Mesa coal deposit and: 156, 171; Bosque Redondo internment of: 12, 334; Cañoncito Reservation of: 171; environmental contamination at: 165, 168, 171, 194n126; forced relocation of: 156; Four Corners Power Plant and: 156; health data on: 160,161, 163, 164-5, 166; Navajo Health Authority of: 165; poverty of: 156-7, 160; Ramah Reservation of: 171; Red Rock District of: 164, 166; Shiprock District of: 164-6, 169, 183; town of Window Rock in: 298n130; uranium milling and: 168-71; uranium mining and: 159,160-8; 1979 Church Rock spill and: 170, 183, 193n114, 194n118
nazis/nazism: xvii, 18, 21, 143, 369; antigypsy decrees of: 258n5; antijewish decrees of: 258n5; Buchenwald concentration camp of: 335; Dachau concentration camp of: 335; euphemistic language used by: 261n50; genocide and: 247-9, 261n50; German disenchantment with: 354; Holocaust denial and: 247-9; "Master Plan" of: 148n81; "Nuremberg Defense"

of: 307; Nuremberg Trials and: 21, 47, 57, 135-6, 148n81, 383n257; racial theories of: 26-7n58, 135; SS org. of: 327

Nebrija, Antonio de: 106, 351, 389n433

neocolonialism, *see* colonialism/colonization

Netherlands/Dutch: 31n118, 204; classical empire of: 1, 48; colonization of Surinam by: 122n256; 1871 codification of the Laws of War by: 307; German bombing of Rotterdam in: 333

"New Age": "Men's Movement" variant of: : 232n67

New Caledonia: 102, 103; as French colony: 49, 101

"New World Order": 106; concept of: 2, 21, 185, 351

New York Life Insurance Group, Inc.: 92

*New York Newsday*: 341

*New York Review of Books*: 373n25

*New York Times*: 109n23, 381n212, 394n494, 396n506

*News from Indian Country* (newspaper): 221, 242n139, 243n144

*Newsweek*: 326, 380n168

Newlands Resolution (1898): 76, 77

Newton, Huey P.: 264

Nicaragua/Nicaraguans: and U.S. mining of harbors: 388n393; Miskito/Sumu/Rama autonomy struggle in: 52; 1985 *Nicaragua v. U.S.* ICJ opinion and: 21n115, 388n393

Nichol, Judge Fred: 272

Nichols, Capt. David M.: 313

Nielson, Richard A.: 142

Nietschmann, Bernard: 52; "Third World War" postulation of: 53

Nigeria: as British colony: 50; as internal colonial state: 50; Ibo (Biafra) independence struggle in: 52

Nimitz, Adm. Chester A.: 332, 383n262

Nishimura, Shiro: 117n162

Nixon, Pres. Richard M.: 33, 323; and National Sacrifice Area concept: 194n123; Committee to Re-Elect the President (CREEP) of: 290n33; response to Trail of Broken Treaties of: 240n120, 267

Nkrumah, Kwame: 51

Norris, Kathleen: xi

Northern Cheyenne Reservation: 171

Northern Ireland: as settler state: 2

Northwest Ordinance (1787): 6, 125

Notley, Daniel: 325

Nott, J.C.: 210, 231n65, 232n71

Noyd, Capt. David: 336

Nuclear Engineering Corp. (now U.S. Ecology Corp.): 199n200

nuclear materials: antimony-125: 175; barium-140: 175; berylium-7: 175; cadmium-109: 175; carcinogenic properties of: 160, 177, 178, 197n168, 198n181; cesium-137: 173, 175; cobalt-60: 175; europium-155: 175; health effects of: 160-4, 166, 178; iodine-131: 175; iridium-192: 175; krypton: 175; lantaum-140: 175; lead-210: 170; mutagenic effects of: 165-6; plutonium: 159, 162, 172, 173, 177, 178, 182, 200n210; plutonium-238: 175; plutonium-239: 173, 175; plutonium-240: 175; polonium-210: 170; polonium-218: 160; radioactive iodides: 182; radium: 160; radium-236: 166, 170; radon: 161, 163, 165, 168; radon-222: 160; radon daughters: 160; rhodium-106: 175; ruthenium: 173; ruthenium-103: 175; ruthenium-106: 173; sodium-22: 175; strontium: 182; strontium-90: 172, 173, 175; thorium-230: 170; thoron: 165, 168; tritium: 172, 173, 175; uranium: 159-71, 172; uranium-233: 162; "yellowcake": 168, 169; *also see* tobacco/smoking

nuclear waste: anticipated clean-up costs of: 177; fallout: 174-6, 182; "monitored retrievable storage" (MRS) sites for: 178; plutonium: 177, 178, 195n131; uranium mill tailings: 168-71, 182, 192n101, 193n105, 193n109, 198n176; volume of: 177-8, 182, 199n193; "waste isolation pilot plant" (WIPP) for: 180-1; Yucca Mt. repository for: 181, 199n197

Nuclear Waste Policy Act (1982): 198n175, 198n179

Nunnatsunega ("White Path"; Cherokee leader): 232-3n72

Nuremberg Trials: 21, 47, 57, 148n81, 148n85, 332-3, 335; application of customary law in: 259n25, 307; *Dörnitz* case: 331; *Göring* case: 331-2; *Streicher* case: 136; U.S. instigation of: 383n257; 1945 London Charter for: 135-6, 328

Nuremberg Tribunal: 347, 352-3; application of customary law by: 259n25, 307; refutation of nazi "Nuremberg Defense" by: 307; U.S. representation on: 136; 1945 London Charter of: 135-6, 328

Nuremberg Doctrine/Principles/Standards: 35, 47, 53, 57, 324, 328, 336, 337, 338, 346, 349, 352, 369, 401n579

# O

Oaks, Richard: 290n40
Occidental Life Insurance Group, Inc.: 92
Oceania, *see* Pacific Basin
O'Clock, ASAC George: 273-4, 293n80,
    295n101
Oglala Sioux Civil Rights Org. (OSCRO): 269
Ohbayashi Construction Co.: 96
Okinawa: 333
O'Malley, Rep. Thomas: 134
Oman: 367; as British colony: 116n152
Omnibus Bill of 1910: 239n112
Oppenheim, Lassa: 24, 35, 38
Org. of African Unity (OAU): 51
Org. of American States (OAS): Charter of: 46-7,
    70n212; U.S. delegation to: 54
Ortiz, Simon J.: 168
Osana, Kenji: 96
Osana, Kokusai: 95
Oslo II Peace Accord (1995): 403n593
OSS, *see* U.S. Office of Strategic Services
Ottoman Empire: 42, 385n326

# P

Pacific Basin (Oceania): 87; European
    colonization of: 39, 43; as "American
    Lake": 87, 320; U.S. investments in: 88;
    war against Japan fought in: 319
Pacific Rim Strategy: 90; military dimensions of:
    87, 114-5n115, 320-1; politicoeconomic
    dimensions of: 87-8
Pact of Paris, *see* Kellogg-Briand Pact
Pahrump Paiute Reservation: 175
Pahvlavi, Shah Mohammed Reza (Shah of Iran):
    396n512
Pakistan/Pakistanis: 362, 364, 403n594; border
    with Afghanistan of: 360; port of
    Gwaddar in: 364; nuclear weapons pgm.
    of: 366; separation from India of: 158;
    separation of Bangladesh from: 158
Palestine/Palestinians/"Palestine Question": 158;
    city of Jenin in: 367; city of Nablus in:
    367; fatality rates among: 401n566;
    Intifadas of: 400n554, 403n593; Israeli
    atrocities against: 367, 394n500; Israeli
    occupation of: 394n500; Israeli
    "settlement" policy and: 359, 394n500,
    400n554; suicide bombings by: 401n566,
    403n593; UN Res. guaranteeing right of
    self-determination to: 400n554
Palestine Liberation Org. (PLO): 403n593
Palestinian Rights Society: 119n209

Pan-Africanists/Pan-Africanism: 51
Pan-American Conf. (1890): 65n105
Paraguay/Paraguayans: extermination of the Aché
    by: 52; 261n53
Parenti, Michael: xiv
Parker, Cynthia Ann: 207, 228n38
Parker, John J.: 383n262
Parker, Quannah: as Quahadi Comanche patriot:
    207; mixed-bloodedness of: 207
Patton, Gen. George S.: 326
Patton, Col. George S. III: 326-7
Payne, Ché: 287
Peabody Coal Co.: 171
Peers, Gen. William: 325
Peiper, Lt. Col. Jochen: 333
Peltier family: 205
Peltier, Leonard: 243n144, 279, 294n92, 298n127,
    298n129, 298n130, 298n131; and Oglala
    Firefight: 279; appeals of: 281-2, 299n137,
    299n142; as federal fugitive: 297n118;
    convicted of murdering FBI agents: 281,
    299n137; FOIA documents and: 281;
    evidence fabricated against: 281;
    fraudulent extradition from Canada of:
    280; human rights award received by:
    300n152; incarceration of: 281-82,
    299n132; "national security" documents
    and: 299n135; perjurious testimony
    against: 281; prosecutor's closing argument
    against: 281; seeks sanctuary at Smallboy's
    Camp: 279, 297n118; Poor Bear affidavits
    against: 280, 297n119; *also see* Butler,
    Darrelle; Coler, SA Jack; Leonard Peltier
    Defense Committee; Robideau, Bob;
    Williams, SA Ron
Pentagon, *see* U.S. Dept. of Defense
Permanent Peoples Tribunal (Rome): 119n209
Persian Gulf: 21
Peta Nacona (Quahadi Comanche leader): 207
Peru: Sendero Luminoso movement in: 69n181
Peterson, Randolph: 88
Pew Research Polls: 366
Philippines/Filipinos: 76, 113n80; Abu Sayyef
    guerrillas in: 364; as "Indians of the
    Philippines": 318; as "subhumans": 319;
    Batangas region in: 316, 321; city of
    Manila in: 333; general pattern of U.S.
    atrocities in: 316-7, 333; independence of:
    48-9, 66n132, 114n114; island of Leyte
    in: 317; island of Luzon in: 316; Huk
    guerrillas in: 66n132; U.S. colonization of:
    40; Samar district of: 317; U.S. military
    bases in: 87, 114n114; 1899-1802 U.S.

military campaign in: 316-8; U.S. war crimes in: 316-8; Yamashita trial conducted in: 333

Phoenix Indian School: 216

Physicians for Human Rights: 361

Pike, Mary: 292n57

Pine Ridge Sioux Reservation: xvii, 19, 267, 268; airport on: 294n91; and Black Hills National Sacrifice Area: 171; FBI repression of AIM on: 264; GOON squads on: 269-79; Head Start Pgm. on: 291n44; Highway 18 on: 277; housing quality on: 127, 154; minerals on: 269, 291n46; nuclear contamination of: 193n117; poverty on: 126, 154, 241n132; proximity of Igloo uranium mine/mill to: 193n117; Red Shirt Table area of: 193n117; "reign of terror" on: 273-9; Shannon County portion of: 126, 154, 241n132; Sheep Mt. Gunnery Range on: 269, 279, 291n46; village of Manderson on: 226n14, 272; village of Oglala on: 277; village on Pine Ridge on: 270, 277, 293n79; village of Wanbli on: 294n82, 296n112, 300n149; White Clay Creek on: 277; Wilson régime on: 269-79; 1973 Wounded Knee siege on: 270-3; 1973-76 homicide rate on: 273; 1981 Wounded Knee Memorial on: 226n14

Pinochet, Col. Augusto: 402n581

Pizza Pizza restaurants: 252, 253

plenary power: 84; concept of: xv-xvi, 12, 153, 265, 288n12; and federal "trust" prerogatives: 14, 15, 20, 62n58, 127, 184

Plymouth Colony: 204

Poles/Poland: 64n86; German bombing of Warsaw in: 333; partitions of: 39; 1939 German invasion of: 141, 148n82;

Poor Bear, Myrtle: 280; and Marshall trial: 297n119; and Peltier affidavits: 280, 297n119; recantations of: 297n119

Popes/Papacy: Alexander VI: 23n8; and Discovery Doctrine: 3; Bulls of: 2, 23n8, 23n13, 61n49; Innocent IV: 2, 23n9, 61n49

Portugal/Portuguese: as NATO member: 67n139; classical empire of: 1, 48; colonization of Angola by: 67n139, 91, 101; colonization of the Azores by: 67n139; colonization of Mozambique by: 91, 101; colonization of Timor by: 50; occupation of Goa by: 103; system of racial classification employed by: 230n55; 1890 codification of the Laws of War by: 307

Posse Comitatus Act (1877): 291n53, 363, 398n533: Economy Act and: 398n533

postcolonialism, concept of: xiii, 50, 52

postmodernism, concept of: xiv, 52

Potlatch ceremony, suppression of: 28n76

Potter, Col. Jack: 271, 291n53

Pourier family: 205

Powell, Sec. of State: as chairman of the joint chiefs of staff: 345, 387n373; My Lai Massacre cover-up and: 345, 387n384

Powless, Herb: 301n165

Pradier-Fodére, Pierre: 38

Pratt, Geronimo ji Jaga: 287

Pratt, Capt. Richard Henry: 237n104; as superintendent of Indian schools: 216; as warden on Ft. Marion military prison: 216, 237n103

Prejean, Kawaipuna: 118n197

Price, SA David: 297n119

Price, Morton E.: 151n137

Protestants/Protestantism: 4-5, 238n106; Anglicans: 237n101; Congregationalists: 77, 111n43; Moravians: 211, 232n70; Presbyterians: 211; Puritans: 204, 375n47

Prudential Insurance Group, Inc.: 92

Public Law 280 (1956): 15

Pueblo Lands Board: 194n96

Puerto Rico: 105; as U.S. colony: 19, 49, 83, 158; independence movement in: 287; made U.S. "commonwealth" (1950): 66n136; 1917 Organic Act concerning: 66n136; 1993 plebiscite in: 122n259

Pufendorf, Samuel: 38, 47; critique of Grotius: 37; influence of: 38; Vitoria's influence on: 37, 38

## Q

Qadaffi, Muamar al: 359, 395n504; anti-Islamicism of: 399n543

Qatada, Abu: 399n546

Qatar: Emir of: 360; al-Jazeera located in: 360

Queen Emma: 80

Queen Lili'uokalani: 76, 112n66; betrayed by Cleveland: 76, 82-3; coronation of: 81; overthrow of: 76, 82, 98; Wilcox's attempt to reinstate: 83

Quinn, Gov. William: 92, 96

Quisling, Vikdun: xvii, 208, 229n49

## R

racism/racial theory: as U.S. policy: 209-10, 212-24; Herrstein/Murray version of: 229n51;

Jefferson's views on: 210; Morgan's
version of: 211; Morton's version of: 209-
10, 229-30n52; nazi variants of: 26-7n58,
135; Nott's version of: 210, 231n65,
232n71; property implications of: 209-10,
214, 236n94; "scientific" form of: 209,
210, 211, 229n51; Spanish/Portuguese
classifications of: 230n55; U.S.
classifications of: 209; also see "blood
quantum standards"
radioactive substances, see nuclear materials
Ramada Inns Corp.: 92
Ramsey, Jonbenet: 370
Ramparts (magazine): 380n168
Randall, Francis: 294n82
Rapid City Journal (newspaper): 268
Reagan, Pres. Ronald: 31n115, 176, 290n33, 358,
388n393, 398n535; as California
governor: 398n536; Economy Act of:
398n533; "War on Drugs" of: 398n533
Red Cloud (Oglala Lakota leader): 207
Red Cloud, Edgar: 291n50
Red Cross: 385n329
Redner, Russell: 297n118
Reel, Estelle: 238n107
Reigert, Wilbert A.: 292n57
Republic of Georgia: Chechen guerrillas in: 364
restitution, principles of: 103, 152n142
Revolutionary Action Movement (RAM):
293n71
Reynolds, Jerry: 243n144
Rhodesia (now Zimbabwe): as British colony:
101; as independent settler state: 101
Rice, Walter: 111n43
Rich, Norman: 136
Richards, Chuck: 294n82
Richards, Woody: 294n82
Ricord, John: 78
Ridenhour, Ron: 322-3, 324, 380n168
Ridge, John: 228n37
Ridge, John Rollin: 228n37
Ridge, Major: as Cherokee sell-out: 206-7,
228n37; "blood" pedigree of: 206
Ridout, Thomas: 227n28
Right of Conquest: 37-58; Dinstein on: 36;
Grotius on: 36-7; Leonard Garment's
version of: 34-5, 55-6; international
repudiation of: 43-51; Oppenheim on:
35-6, 38; Pufendorf on: 37; Vattel on: 36,
38; Vitoria on: 37
Right of Self-Determination: xi, 20, 43, 99-100,
158, 184, 201-2; and right of secession:
57; as law: 34-5, 40, 48, 50, 53, 89-91,

100-5, 108n8, 122n256, 122n259, 157,
225n5, 321, 348, 402n580; U.S. concept of
"internal" self-determination and: 54; also
see plenary power
Río Molino: nuclear contamination of: 166
Río Paguate: nuclear contamination of: 166
Río Puerco: nuclear contamination of: 170,
193n114, 194n118
Rio Tinto Zinc Corp.: 191n93
Ritt, Walter Jr.: 118n197
Ritter, Scott: 365, 366, 403n594
Riverside Indian School: 216
Roanoke Colony: 204, 226n15
Robideau family: 205
Robideau, Bob: 279, 295n103, 297n117,
298n127, 298n129; acquitted of
murdering FBI agents: 280; and Oglala
Firefight: 279, 297n122
Rockwell International Corp.: 165
Rocky Mountain News (newspaper): celebration of
Sand Creek Massacre by: 312
Romanov Empire (Great Russian Empire): 40;
Bolshevik Revolution in: 40
Roosevelt, Pres. Franklin D.: 134
Roosevelt. Pres. Theodore: 316, 317, 318, 323
Roots restaurants: 252
Rorex, Jeanne Walker: 243n142
Rosco, Robert J.: 160
Rose, Charlie: 381n211
Rose, Wendy: 243n144
Rosebud Sioux Reservation: 154, 290n36; and
Black Hills National Sacrifice Area: 171;
Crow Dog's Paradise on: 296n112,
296n117
Rosenberg, Susan: 287
Rosenthal, Harvey D.: 126, 129, 130, 143
Ross, Judge Donald: 281, 282
Ross, John: as Cherokee patriot: 206-7; "blood"
pedigree of: 206
Roubideaux family: 205
Rousseau, Jean-Jacques: 38, 47, 374n40; influence
on Lieber Code of: 309
Roy, Arundhati: 396n512
Rumania/Rumanians: 64n86
Rumsfeld, Sec. of Defense Donald: 493n487;
Military Commission Order No. 1 of:
397n525
Russell, Bertrand: 331
Russell Tribunals: on the rights of indigenous
peoples: 252; on U.S. crimes in Vietnam:
252, 331
Russia/Russians: Chechen rebels in: 52, 364, 371,
403n592; 2002 Moscow theater debàcle

in: 371, 403n592; Spetznatz troops of: 403n592; *also see* Soviets/Soviet Union
Rwanda: Hutu/Tutsi conflict in: 52, 349
Ryan, Joan: 261n45

# S

Saavedra Lamas Pact (1933): 45
Safe Drinking Water Act (1974): 190n79
Sainte-Marie, Buffy: xiii
Saito, Natsu: 370
"Salt Water Thesis," *see* colonialism/colonization
Samas, Pvt. David: 336-7
San Marino: sovereignty of: 144n3
Sandwich Islands, *see* Hawai'i/Native Hawaiians
Sartre, Jean-Paul: 35, 39; equates colonialism to genocide: 52, 128, 158-9, 252; Kuper's critique of: 260n29
Saudis/Saudi Arabia: 364, 367; city of Mecca in: 359; intelligence service of: 396n510; relations with Taliban of: 396n510; U.S. forces in: 359; Usama bin-Laden as: 359
Savannah River: nuclear contamination of: 177
Savimbi, Jonas: 396n506
Schmitz, Darld: 268, 290n38
Schwartzkopf, Gen. Norman ("Stormin' Norman"): 341
Scots/Scotland: 204; English conquest/colonization of: 39
Seabourn, Burt: 243n142
Seale, Bobby: 264
*Searchers, The* (film): 228n38
Second World War, *see* World War II
Sells, Indian Comm. Cato: 239n112
Seibu Corp.: 96
September 11, 2001 ("9-1-1"): 366, 370; as "wake-up" call: 357, 368; as warning: 369, 371; fatalities caused by: 358, 393n489, 393n492, 396n512; illegal detention of Muslims following: 363; monetary damage caused by: 358, 393n491; motivations underlying: 358-60; occupations of those killed during: 393n490; Pennsylvania airliner crash during: 358, 393n488; symbolism of targets selected: 358; U.S. propaganda concerning: 358; USA PATRIOT Act and: 362
Serbs/Serbia: 1-2, 348; atrocities against Kosovo Albanians by: 348, 389n413; "ethnic cleansing" in Bosnia by: 389n413; "infrastructural" targets in: 349; U.S. war crimes in: 349; 1879 codification of the Laws of War by: 307; 1914 "Sarajevo

Incident" in: 39-40; 1999 U.S. war against: 348
Seventh Pan-American Conf. (1933): 45
Seward, Sec. of State William: 79
Shae, Jamie: 388n395
Shae, Patrick: 296n115
Shakur, Mutulu: 287
Sharon, Ariel: 367, 400n563; Unit 101 of: 400n554; Qibya Massacre and: 400n554
Shawnees: 204, 227n28, 319; atrocities committed against: 304; Battle of Tippecanoe and: 304; Clark's campaign against: 304; town of Chillocothe of: 304; town of Piqua of: 304; Wayne's campaign against: 304, 370; *also see* Tecumseh
Shenandoah, Leroy: 290n40
Sheraton Hotels, Inc.: 95
Sheridan, Gen. Phil: 314, 321; "only good Indian is a dead Indian" statement of: 237n104, 315, 322, 376n80
Sherman, Gen. William Tecumseh: 315, 321
Siddiq, Muhammad: 362
Signal Oil Corp.: 117n160
Silko, Leslie Marmon: 243n144
Simon, John A.: 383n257
Simpson, Natasha: 395n504
Simpson, Vernado: 322, 381n197
Singapore: U.S. investments in: 88
Sioux Nation, *see* Lakotas
Sitting Bull (Hunkpapa Lakota leader): 208, 316
Skerritt, Admiral Joseph: 82, 109n17
Skinner, B.F.: 391n470
Skull Valley Reservation: nuclear contamination of: 177, 179; as MRS site: 179-80
Smallboy, Chief Robert: 279
Smith, Gen. Jacob ("Hell Roaring Jake"): 113n80, 303, 323, 324; as brigadier in Philippines campaign: 316; as participant in Wounded Knee Massacre: 316; early retirement of: 318; illegal orders of: 317
Smith, Jack: 234n82
Smith, James J.E.: 261n45
Smith, John: 311
Smith, John Stanhope: 231n64
Smith, Roger W.: 247
Smith, William: 205, 227n25
Smithsonian Institution: 125
Smuts, Gen. J.C.: 43
Somaliland (Somalia): as French colony: 122m259, 364
Sontag, Susan: 394n494
Soule, Capt. Silas: 338, 375n58
South Africa: 43; as settler state: 2; secret nuclear

456

weapons program of: 192n93
Southern Ute reservation: 171
Southwest Research and Information Ctr.: 170
Soviets/Soviet Union (USSR): 43, 46, 50, 177,
    350, 391n465; and Angola: 67n139; and
    Nuremberg Trials: 383n257; as
    continuation of Great Russian Empire: 1–
    2; as intermediaries in U.S./Iraqi war:
    340; as internal colonial state: 51;
    Bolshevik creation of: 41; collapse of: 21,
    106; Chernobyl nuclear disaster in: 173,
    195n137; establishment of "Soviet Bloc"
    by: 49; invasion of Afghanistan by: 358;
    KAL Fl. 007 by: 395n502, 396n506; slave
    labor employed in: 163-4, 190n66; World
    War II casualties of: 65n110; *also see*
    Russia/Russians
Spain/Spanish: classical empire of: 48, 136; gives
    human rights award to Peltier: 300n152;
    internal colonization of the Basques by:
    39, 187n27; internal colonization of the
    Catalans by: 39; supposed "racial
    inferiority" of: 232n71; system of racial
    classification employed by: 230n55; 1550
    Valladolid debates in: 231n64; 1882
    codification of Laws of War by: 307
Spotted Tail (Brûlé Lakota leader): 208
Sri Lanka (Ceylon): as British colony: 101; Tamil
    settlements in: 101
St. Valentine's Day Massacre: 255, 315
Standard Oil Corp. of Ohio (Sohio): 165;
    Cebolleta uranium mill of: 193n109;
    Laguna uranium mill of: 169
Standing Ilk, Carole: 243n145, 294n94; assoc.
    with "National AIM, Inc.": 301n165
Stannard, David E.: as author of *American
    Holocaust*: 373n25
Stapleton, SA Charles: 298n130
Steel, Ronald: 394n494
Sternglass, Ernest J.: 162
Stevens, U.S. Min. to Hawai'i J.L.: 76, 81, 82,
    112n74, 112n75, 112-3n79, 113n81
Stewart, Fred W.: 161
Still Water (Crow): 208
Stimson, Sec. of State Henry: 44; "Stimson
    Doctrine" of: 44-5, 47
Stone, Willard: 243n142
Streicher, Julius: 136
Students for a Democratic Society (SDS):
    297n120; *New Left Notes* newspaper of:
    123n274
Sudan/Sudanese: 364; al-Shifa pharmaceutical
    plant in: 359, 387n373, 395n505; city of

Khartoum in: 359; 1998 U.S. bombing of:
    359
Suharto: 347, 378n136
Sukarno: 378n136
Sullivan, Gen. John: 303-4, 320, 369; atrocities
    committed by: 307
Sun Oil Corp.: 165
Surinam: as Dutch colony: 122n256;
    independence of: 122n256
Susquehannah-Western Corp.: Riverton uranium
    mill of: 194n127
Sutton, Imre: 128
Swedes/Sweden: 204
Syracuse University: 123n274

**T**

Taiwan: 114n115; U.S. investments in: 88
Tahiti: U.S. investment in: 95
Tanzania/Tanzanians: Dar es Salaam embassy
    bombing in: 359, 394n497
Taylor, Gen. Maxwell D.: 321
Taylor, Gen. Telford: 331
Taylor, Pres. Zachary: 306; as army general: 305
Tecumseh (Shawnee leader): 7; defeated at
    Tippecanoe: 304; mutilation of: 304
*territorium res nullius (terra nullius)*, *see* Doctrine of
    Discovery
Thailand: U.S. investments in: 88
Thatcher, Margaret: xiv
Theobault, Hiram: 233n78
Third Reich: xiv, 347
Third World: xvii, 43, 49, 51, 97, 286, 287; anti-
    imperialist movement in: 50, 51;
    contrasted to First and Second Worlds: 41,
    51, 53; decolonization in: 90; Fourth
    World and: 51; IMF/World Bank policies
    towards: 94; Mao's conception of: 39;
    poverty in: 127, 354; superprofits extracted
    from: 156
Thirty Years War: 306
Thomas, Lt. Bissell: 317
Thomas, Sen. Elmer: 138
Thomas, Kevin: 253
Thomas, Robert K.: 243n144, 265, 288n8
Thompson, Frank: 85
Thoreau, Henry David: 401n579
Thorpe, Grace: 178
Three Mile Island nuclear disaster: 173, 193n113
Thurston, Lorrin: 77, 83
Tibet/Tibetans: 253
Tijerina, Reyes: 287
Timor: 1636 Portuguese conquest of: 50
tobacco/smoking: 357; as diversion from health

effects of nuclear materials: 160, 183, 191n91, 200n210; "secondhand" smoke: 191n91, 393n485

Togo, Shigenori: 378n133

Tonga: U.S. investments in: 88

Torres, Alejandrina: 287

Tracy, Sec. of the Navy B.G.: 82, 113n81

Trail of Broken Treaties (1972): 240n120, 240n121, 267; 20-Point Program of: 240n120, 267

Trask, Haunani-Kay: 97, 98, 251

Trask, Mililani: 98, 100

treaties: German/Hawaiian Treaty (1848): 111n49; Danish/Hawaiian Treaty (1847): 111n49; International Treaty on Non-Proliferation of Nuclear Weapons (1970): 400n555; Sykes-Picot Treaty (1916): 385n326; Treaty of Paris (1783): 6; Treaty of Sainte-Germain (1919): 120n239; Treaty of Westphalia (1648): 55; U.S. Treaty with the Sandwich Islands (1826): 79; U.S. Treaty with Hawaiian Kingdom (1849): 80; U.S./Hawaiian Treaty of Commercial Reciprocity with Hawaiian Kingdom (1875): 62n63; *also see* U.S. treaties with Indians

treatymaking: 71n213; mutually binding effects of: 56; origins of Indian treaties: 4; principle of *pacta sunt servanda* ("treaties are to be observed"): 74; U.S. defaults upon: 11; U.S. subversion of: 26n44; *also see* Vienna Convention on the Law of Treaties

Trimbach, SAC Joseph: 295n100, 295n106

Troy, New York: nuclear contamination of: 182

Trudell, Eli Changing Sun: 300n150

Trudell, John: xiii, 243n144, 285, 300n150; family murdered: 283, 300n150; rejects assoc. with "National AIM, Inc.": 301n165

Trudell, Ricarda Star: 300n150

Trudell, Sunshine Karma: 300n150

Trudell, Tina Manning: 300n150

Truman, Pres. Harry S.: 125, 129; orders nuclear bombing of Hiroshima: 378n129; signs Claims Commission Act: 137

Turkmen/Turkmenistan: 364

Turks/Turkey: genocide of Armenians by: 247; holocaust denial policies of: 258n8; internal colonization of Kurds by: 187n27, 347; Kurdish independence struggle in: 52; quid pro quo with Israel of: 258n8

Turtle Mt. Chippewa Reservation: 244n146

Twardowski, SA Joseph: 299n137

Two Birds, Glenn: 277

Two Hawks, Webster: 240n121, 290n36

Tyler, Pres. John: doctrine on Hawai'i of: 79, 111n49

## U

Umetco Minerals Corp.: 165

Ungar, Sanford J.: 288n6

Union Carbide Corp. (formerly Vanadium Corp. of America, now Umetco Minerals Corp.): 165, 188n36, 188n44; 1984 Bhopal disaster and: 396n512

United Nations (UN): 90, 105, 106, 126, 365, 400n553; Charter of: 34, 46, 48, 50, 51, 59n12, 70n212, 75, 89, 90, 91, 102, 103, 105, 108n8, 128, 150n123, 157, 158, 187n30, 349, 378n138, 402n580; Commission on Human Rights of: 97-8, 284; Committee of 24 of: 104, 121n250; Convention Against Torture and Other Forms of Cruel, Inhuman or Degrading Torture or Punishment of: 392n476; Convention on Elimination of All Forms of Racial Discrimination of: 20, 348; Convention on the Rights of Children of: 348, 392n475; Covenant on Civil and Political Rights of: 20; Covenant on Economic, Social and Cultural Rights of: 20; Declaration of the Granting of Independence to Colonial Countries and Peoples (Resolution 1514 (XV)) by: 48, 51, 102, 104, 157-8, 348; decolonization procedures of: 89-91; Draft Declaration of the Rights of Indigenous Peoples by: 20, 30n110, 98, 126, 289n21; Economic and Social Council (ECOSOC) of: 19, 98, 284, 289n21; founding of: 89; GA Res. 181 of: 400n554; GA Res. 742 (VIII) of: 91, 122n256; GA Res. 946 of: 122n256; GA Res. 1469 of: 122n256; GA Res. 1503 (XLVIII): 99; GA Res. 1541 (XV) of: 20, 67-8n157, 158; GA Res. 1654 (XVI): 104; GA Res. 2625 (VIII) of: 105, 122n253; GA Res. 3103 (XXVIII) of: 289n22; General Assembly (GA) of: 47, 91, 102, 122n256, 250, 348, 366, 400n554; "Indian Summer in Geneva" of (1977): 97, 284, 289n21; inspection teams of: 359, 365, 367; International Law Commission of: 53; obligations of, to Native Hawaiians: 100-7; peacekeepers of: 400n563; SC Res. 242 of: 400n554; SC Res. 338 of; 400n554; SC Res. 425 of:

400n554; SC Res. 465 of: 400n554; SC Res. 660 of: 386n333; SC Res. 1322 of: 400n554; Secretariat of: xviii, 89, 90, 103, 249, 261n53; Security Council (SC) of: 108n8, 347, 366, 367, 400n563; Special Committee on Decolonization of: 101, 122n259; Standard Minimum Rules for the Treatment of Prisoners established by: 392n476; UNICEF reports of: 394n499; Universal Declaration of Human Rights by: 20; U.S. delegation to: 54; U.S. unilateralism and: 350-1; Working Group on Indigenous Populations of: 19, 30n110, 98, 99, 284, 289n21; World Food Pgm. of: 360; 1946 Affirmation of the Principles of International Law Recognized by the Charter of the Nuremberg Tribunal by: 47; 1970 Declaration on Principles of International Law by: 47; 1977 Convention on the Prohibition of Military or Other Environmental Modification Techniques of: 339; 1981 Convention on Prohibition of Certain Conventional Weapons of: 339-40, 342; 1991 report on Iraq of: 344; *also see* Genocide Convention; International Court of Justice; Vienna Convention on the Law of Treaties

United Nuclear Corp.: 165, 193n114; Church Rock uranium mill of: 170, 193n113

United States (U.S.): 40, 54, 201; and "Blue Water Thesis": 51; and League of Nations: 42; Articles of Confederation of: 6, 24n24; as settler state: 56; assertion of plenary power over Indians by: 12, 14, 62n58, 127, 153, 265, 288n12; Civil War of: 305, 307, 334; Continental Congress of: 5, 144n1; domestic economy of: 354, 371; Indian assimilation policy of: 132-3, 215; Indian reservation system of: 24n19; Indian termination policy of: 138, 150n108, 241n129; internal colonial policies of: 20-1, 34-5; OAS delegation of: 54; General Accounting Office (GAO) of: 131, 140, 146n45, 150n122, 166-7, 291n45; incarceration rates in: 354; Institute for Government Research of: 133; nuclear weapons inventory of: 177, 197n169; Pacific Rim Strategy of: 87-8; refuses ICC jurisdiction: 347; rejects ICJ jurisdiction: 20, 31n115, 347, 388n393; Security Council vetoes by: 400n563; termination policy of: 15-6; territorial acquisitions of:

6, 56, 129-30, 139-41; UN delegation of: 54; War of Independence of: 5, 303; War of 1812 and: 7; War with Spain (1898-99): 83; World War II casualties of: 65n110; 1993 apology to Native Hawaiians by: 73-5

Uniting and Strengthening America by Providing Appropriate Tools Required to Intercept and Obstruct Terrorism Act (USA PATRIOT Act; 2001): 362-3, 397n531

University of Colorado/Boulder: American Indian Advocacy Group at: 242n138; Nichols Hall at: 312

University of Hawaii: annual budget of: 117n178; East-West Ctr. of: 87

uranium: *see* nuclear materials

uranium mines/miners: 283; AEC Igloo mine: 193n117, 194n122; and world uranium market: 167, 191-2n93; Blue Creek mine (Spokane): 194n127; death rates among: 160, 164; "dewatering" procedures at: 165, 166; in Australia: 167; in Canada: 167; in Namibia: 167; Jackpile-Paguate mining complex (Laguna): 166-7, 191n93; Lagunas as: 167; lung cancer rates among: 160-1, 163, 164, 167, 194n126; Navajos as: 160, 161, 163-6; Red Rock mine (Navajo): 164; Rossing mine (Namibia): 191n93; Shiprock mine (Navajo): 164, 165, 166; suits brought by: 163, 193n106; ventilation of: 165; working conditions in: 160-4

uranium mills/mill-workers: 168-71; AEC Igloo mill (Edgemont, SD): 193n117, 194n122; AEC secret mill (Fernald, OH): 192n102; and world uranium market: 167, 191-2n93; Blue Creek mill (Spokane): 194n127; Bokum Minerals mill (Laguna): 169; groundwater contamination from: 193n117; Kerr-McGee mill (Grants, NM): 169; Kerr-McGee mill (Laguna): 168, 169; Kerr-McGee mill (Shiprock): 169; Riverton mill (Wind River): 194n127; Sherwood mill (Spokane): 194n127; Sohio-Reserve mill (Cebolleta, NM): 193n109; Sohio-Reserve mill (Laguna): 169; working conditions in: 169

Uranium Mill Tailings Control Act (1978): 198n176

U.S. Air Force: 344, 345, 346, 358; and Laws of War: 328-9, 339-40, 343; "Arclight" bombing technique of: 382n227; bombing in Cambodia by: 321, 330-31,

382n227; bombing in Laos by: 321, 329-30, 382n227, 382n235; bombing in Vietnam by: 321, 329, 379n143, 382n227; Uniform Code of Military Justice and: 328; 1986 bombing of Libya by: 359, 395n504; 1990-2002 bombing of Iraq by: 342-4, 386n353, 387n369, 393n493; 1998 bombing of al-Shifa pharmaceutical plant by: 359, 387n373, 395n505; 2001-2 bombing of Afghanistan by: 360-1

U.S. Army: 86; xv, 6; and the Laws of War: xv, 323, 327-8, 345; Americal Div. of: 387n384; Bosque Redondo concentration camp of: 12, 334-5; Code of Conduct of: 346; contemporary rules of engagement of: 323, 327-8, 335, 340, 346; Criminal Intelligence Div. (CID) of: 337; Delta Force of: 361, 363, 398n535; Intelligence Div. of: 337, 385n308; investigation of My Lai Massacre (Peers Commission investigation) by: 323, 325; medals of honor awarded after Wound Knee Massacre by: 324; Military Assistance Command, Vietnam (MACV) of: 323, 325, 329, 337; *Posse Comitatus* Act and: 291n53, 363; Praetor Guideline/Protocol of: 363; ranger units of: 304, 337; Special Forces units of: 290n40, 327, 329, 336, 361, 364, 398n534; Special Warfare School of: 288n4; Uniform Code of Military Justice of: 328; Vietnam deployment of: 329; Vietnam era desertions from: 385n308; violations of Lieber Code by: 310-5; West Point Military Academy of: 324, 335; 2nd Cav. Rgt. of: 314; 3rd Army of: 324; 3rd Colorado Vol. Cav. Rgt. of: 375n48; 6th Army of: 271; 7th Cav. Rgt. of: 313; 8th Air Force of: 371; 9th Inf. Div. of: 326, 329; 11th Armored Cav. Rgt.: 381n205; 24th Inf. Div. of: 341-2; 82nd Airborne Div. of: 271; 173rd Airborne Brig'd of: 337; 1779 campaign against the Iroquois of: 303-4, 320, 369; 1780 campaign against the Shawnees of: 304; 1794 campaign against the Shawnees of: 304, 370; 1811 campaign against the Shawnees of: 304; 1814 campaign against the Creeks of: 304, 320; 1833 campaign against the Sac and Fox of: 305; 1863 campaign against the Santees of: 334; 1864 campaign against the Cheyennes and Arapahos of: 310-3; 1864 campaign against the Navajos ("Kit Carson Campaign") of: 313; 1868 campaign against the Cheyennes of: 313; 1883 Geronimo Campaign of: 316; 1899-1902 Philippines Campaign of: 215-8; 1941-45 campaign against Japan pursued by: 319-20; 1950-53 Korean "police action" of: 321; 1961-75 Indochina campaign of: 320-31, 353; 1990-91 Persian Gulf campaign of ("Desert Shield"/"Desert Storm"): 340-4, 346, 354; 1999 Serbian campaign of ("Operation Allied Force"): 348; 2001-02 Afghanistan campaign (operations "Infinite Justice" and "Enduring Freedom"): 396-7n517; *also see* Lieber Code; massacres

U.S. Constitution: 6; Article I of: 24n24, 25n37, 121n238, 288n9; Article V of: 151n133; Article VI of: 24n24, 74; Commerce Clause of: 24n24

U.S. Court of Claims: 132, 135, 138, 141, 148n87, 150n122; Indians denied access to: 129-30; Indians permitted access to: 130; native claims filed before: 130, 146n49; receives unresolved ICC claims: 140

U.S. Dept. of Commerce: Bureau of the Census of: 11, 28n82, 98, 219, 223; Small Business Admin. (SBA) of: 160, 188n42

U.S. Dept. of Defense (DoD; "Pentagon"; formerly Dept. of War): 173, 291n46, 316, 317, 330, 337, 338, 354, 361, 385n329, 395n503; BIA as part of: 12; investigation of Sand Creek Massacre by: 312; "Manhattan Project" of: 159; "Nutmeg Project" of: 174; sued by Libya: 395n504; 9-1-1 attack upon: 358, 393n489; *also see* Hanford Nuclear Weapons Research and Production Facility; Los Alamos National Scientific Laboratory; U.S. Army; U.S. Marine Corps; U.S. military installations; U.S. Navy

U.S. Dept. of Energy (DoE; formerly Atomic Energy Commission): 150-76, 177, 198n176; collaboration with BIA: 164-5; collaboration with SBA: 160, 188n42; domestic uranium ore-buying program of: 163; establishment of: 160; Igloo uranium mine/mill of: 193n117; Lawrence Livermore Laboratories of: 162; Navajo uranium mining program of: 160, 161, 163-4; uranium stockpiling quotas of: 167; secret Fernald (Ohio) uranium mill of: 192n102; sued for damages by Red

Rock uranium miners: 163, 193n106; suppression of health data by: 160-4, 196n154; *also see* Hanford Nuclear Weapons Research and Production Facility; Los Alamos National Scientific Laboratory

U.S. Dept. of Health and Human Services (formerly Dept. of Health, Education and Welfare (DHEW)): 166; Indian Health Service of: 166, 170, 221, 290n34; National Cancer Institute of: 162, 189n58; National Institutes of Health of: 97, 161; National Institute for Occupational Safety and Health of: 160, 163, 168; Public Health Service of: 162, 163

U.S. Dept. of Interior: 140, 201; and Trail of Broken Treaties: 267; National Park Service of: 269; *also see* Bureau of Indian Affairs

U.S. Dept. of Justice: 131, 133, 138, 140; and Pine Ridge conflict: 269-70, 274; Bureau of Prisons of: 356, 392n478; Commission on Civil Rights of: 263, 273, 280, 294n98; Marshals Service of: 19, 270; .obstructions of ICC process by: 139, 150n122; recommends changes to ICC: 148n87; *also see* Federal Bureau of Investigation

U.S. Dept. of Labor: Church Rock job training pgm. funded by: 167, 191n91

U.S. Dept. of State: attacks on embassies of: 359, 394n497; list of "international terrorist organizations" maintained by: 359; list of "international terrorist sponsors" maintained by: 399n547

U.S. Holocaust Memorial Museum: 258n8

U.S. House of Representatives: 132, 135, 146-7n75; and USA PATRIOT ACT: 397n525; approves creation of ICC: 135; Concurrent Resolution 108 of: 15, 28n80, 241n129; investigation of My Lai Massacre by (Hébert Committee investigation): 323, 335; investigation of Sand Creek Massacre by: 312

U.S. Marine Corps: 62n63, 86, 322, 345; and the Laws of War: xv, 323, 327-8, 345; Uniform Code of Military Justice and: 328; invasions of Hawai'i by: 76, 80, 81, 82, 109n17; Laws of War and: 335-6; Vietnam deployment of: 329; war crimes in the Philippines by: 317-8; 1941-45 campaign against Japan pursued by: 319-20; 1968 Khe Sanh siege and: 379n143

U.S. military installations: Alamogordo Bomb Range (NM): 159; Barber's Point Naval Air Station (HI): 86; Bellows Air Field (HI): 86; Camp LeJeunne (NC): 345-6; Camp McKinley (HI): 86; Camp Robinson (NB): 11, 314; Camp X-Ray (Cuba): 362, 363; China Lake Naval Weapons Ctr. (CA): 176, 195n156; Clark Naval Air Station (Philippines): 87, 114n114; Clovis Air Force Base (NM): 336; Dugway Proving Grounds (UT): 180, 197n165; Edwards Air Force Base (CA): 176; Deseret Test Ctr. (UT): 197n165; Fallon Navy Training Range (NV): 175; Fish Springs Nuclear Weapons Range (NV): 197n165; Ft. Armstrong (HI): 86; Ft. Bliss (TX): 346; Ft. Bragg (NC): 288n4; Ft. Cason (CO): 271; Ft. DeRussy (HI): 86; Ft. Dix (NJ): 336; Ft. Hood (TX): 336, 346; Ft. Irwin (CA): 176; Ft. Jackson (SC): 338; Ft. Leonard Wood (KS): 346; Ft. Kamehameha (HI): 86; Ft. Leavenworth (KS): 336, 337; Ft. Lyon (CO): 311; Ft. Marion (FL): 216, 237n103, 334; Ft. Riley (KS): 346; Ft. Ruger (HI): 86; Ft. Shafter (HI): 86; Ft. Sill (OK): 334; Ft. Sumner (NM): 334; Guantánamo Bay (Cuba): 362; Hart Military Operations Area (NV): 175; Hawthorne Army Ammunition Depot (NV): 175; Hickham Field (HI): 86; Hill Air Force Training Range (Nevada): 197n165; Kaho'olawe Gunnery Range (HI): 86; Los Vegas/Tonopah Bomb Range (NV): 174; Luke Air Force Base (AZ): 197n164; Nellis Test Range (NV): 174, 175; Nevada Test Site: 174, 175, 177, 179, 197n164, 199n193; Paradise Military Operations Area (NV): 175; Pearl Harbor Naval Base (HI): 80, 81, 82, 83, 86; Reno Military Operations Area (NV): 175; Schofield Barracks (HI): 86; Utah Training Range: 175; Shaw Air Force Base (CA): 336; Subic Bay Naval Base (Philippines): 87, 114n114; Tooele Army Weapons Depot (UT): 179, 197n165; Twentynine Palms Marine Corps Base (CA): 176; Wendover Test Range (NV): 197n165; Wheeler Air Field (HI): 86; White Sands Test Range (NM): 159, 196n157; Yuma Proving Grounds (AZ): 197n164

U.S. Navy: and the Laws of War: xv, 323, 327-8, 341, 345; Uniform Code of Military

Justice and: 328; 1981 "Gulf of Sidra Incident" and: 359, 395n503; 1988 shootdown of Iranian airliner by: 359; 1991 "Highway of Death" slaughter by: 341; unrestricted submarine warfare during World War II by: 332, 383n262; 2001 Red Sea buildup of: 396-7n517

U.S. Office of Strategic Services (OSS): in Vietnam: 67n140

U.S. Senate: 135, 146-7n75, 318; approves creation of ICC: 135; blocks U.S. entry into League of Nations: 42; Indian treaties ratified by: 56-7; investigation of Philippines atrocities by: 317; investigation of Sand Creek Massacre by: 312; "Morgan Report" of: 82, 112n78;

Select Committee on Indian Affairs of: 21, 31n118, 131; Select Committee on Intelligence Activities and the Rights of Americans ("Church Committee") of: 293n71, 296n115; treaties with Hawai'i ratified by: 62n63; USA PATRIOT Act passed by: 362, 397n525; votes to annex Hawai'i: 109n23

U.S. Supreme Court: xiv, 134, 136, 150n122, 153, 395n504; Black Hills Land Claim and: 19; *Cherokee v. Georgia* opinion of (1832): 64n92; *Lone Wolf v. Hitchcock* opinion of (1903): 14, 27n70, 62n58, 127, 144n17, 288n12; *Lyng v. Northwest Cemetery Protective Association* opinion of ("G-O Road" opinion; 1988): 284; repeatedly denies *cert.* in Peltier: 282, 299-300n142; *Rice v. Cayetano* opinion of (2000): 103; *Sioux Nation v. U.S.* opinion of (1980): 151n133; *Standing Bear v. Crook* opinion of (1879): 130; *U.S. v. Bagley* opinion of (1985): 299n142; Western Shoshone Land Claim and: 19; *also see* Jackson, Justice Robert H.; Marshall, Chief Justice John

U.S. treaties with Indians: 33, 130, 145n30, 233n76, 264, 288n9; racial criteria of: 212-3, 233n78; Treaty of Fort Laramie (Treaty with the Sioux, Cheyenne and Arapaho; 1868): 19, 151n168, 271, 296n114; Treaty of Ruby Valley (1863): 196n146; Treaty with the Cherokee (1819): 234n83; Treaty with the Cherokee (Treaty of New Echota; 1835): 228n37, 234n81; Treaty with the Cherokee (1866): 233n77; Treaty with the Cheyenne and Arapaho (Treaty of Ft. Wise; 1861): 26n44, 213; Treaty with the

Cheyenne and Arapaho (1865): 234n78; Treaty with the Chippewa (1819): 233n78; Treaty with the Chippewa (1826): 233n78; Treaty with the Chippewa (1833): 234n81; Treaty with the Chippewa (1837): 234n81; Treaty with the Chippewa (1842): 234n81; Treaty with the Chippewa (1855): 234n80; Treaty with the Chippewa of the Mississippi and Lake Superior (1847): 212; Treaty with the Choctaw (1830): 233n78; Treaty with the Choctaw and Chickasaw (1866): 233n77; Treaty with the Creeks (1866): 233n77; Treaty with the Menominee (1836): 234n81; Treaty with the Menominee (1848): 234n82; Treaty with the Miami (1818): 213; Treaty with the Miami (1834): 234n83; Treaty with the Osage (1865): 213, 234n83; Treaty with the Ottawa (1832): 233n78; Treaty with the Ottawa and Chippewa (1836): 234n81; Treaty with the Pawnee (1857): 213; Treaty with the Ponca (1858): 234n83; Treaty with the Potawatomi (1833): 234n83; Treaty with the Potawatomi (1836): 234n79; Treaty with the Quapaw (1825): 233n78; Treaty with the Red Lake and Pembina Bands of Chippewa (1863): 234n78, 235n85; Treaty with the Sauk and Fox (1830): 234n83; Treaty with the Sauk and Fox (1832): 234n83; Treaty with the Sauk and Fox (1836): 234n81; Treaty with the Sauk and Fox (1859): 234n82, 235n83; Treaty with the Sauk and Fox (1861): 235n83; Treaty with the Seminoles (1866): 233n77; Treaty with the Shawnee (1831): 213; Treaty with the Sioux (1837): 213, 235n84; Treaty with the Stockbridge and Munsee (1856): 234n83; Treaty with the Winnebago (1829): 233n78; Treaty with the Winnebago (1855): 213; Treaty with the Wyandots (1817): 212; Treaty with the Wyandot (1840): 233n78; 1871 suspension of treatymaking with Indians: 12, 213, 235n86, 264, 292n62; *also see* treaties; treatymaking

U.S. 8th Circuit Court of Appeals: 281, 282, 299n136, 299n142

U.S. 9th Circuit Court of Appeals: 299n142

*U.S.S. Adams*: 81

*U.S.S. Boston*: 76, 81, 82, 112n74, 112n75

*U.S.S. Cole*: 359, 394n497

*U.S.S. Peacock*: 77
*U.S.S. Pensacola*: 81
*U.S.S. Portsmouth*: 80
*U.S.S. Tuscarora*: 80
*U.S.S. Vincennes* (sloop of war): 78
*U.S.S. Vincennes* (missile frigate): 359
USSR, *see* Soviet Union
Utah International Corp.: 165
Ute Mountain Reservation: 171
Uzbekis/Uzbekistan: 364

## V

van Dam, Danielle: 370
van Gestel, Allan: 244n153
Vanadium Corp. of America, *see* Union Carbide
    Corp.
Vancouver, Capt. George: 77
Vattel, Emmerich de: 23n9, 36, 38, 42, 47, 55-6,
    57; influence on Lieber Code of: 308
Venne, Sharon H.: 119n209
Vichy France: xvii, xxin12, 141, 240n121
Vienna Convention on the Law of Treaties
    (1969): 56, 71n215; Art. 1 of: 121n238;
    Art. 27 of: 27n70, 31n116, 57; Art. 49 of:
    70n212; Arts. 50-51 of: 70n212; Art. 61
    of: 71n213; Art. 62 § 2 of: 71n221; Art.
    69 of: 71n221
Vietnam/Vietnamese: 67n140, 378n137,
    381n212; "Agent Orange" used in: 339,
    354; and 1954 Geneva Peace Accords:
    378n138; as French colony: 49; as "Indian
    Country": 321; as "Indians": 322; as
    internal colonial state: 52; Batangan
    Peninsula of: 324; "Civic Action" Pgms.
    in: 379n141; civilian death toll among:
    329; ecosystem of: 321, 339; general
    pattern of U.S. atrocities in: 326-7, 333-4;
    Khe Sanh siege in: 379n143; Kien Hoa
    Province in: 326; "Mere Gook Rule"
    (MGR) adopted in: 322, 379n153;
    montagnard people in: 52, 331; My Khe
    Massacre in: 324-5, 326, 327, 345; My Lai
    Massacre in: 322-4, 326, 327, 345;
    387n384; "Operation Speedy Express" in:
    329; Panhandle region of: 321; post-
    World War II U.S. betrayal of: 49; town of
    Ben Tre in: 331; town of Chu Lai in:
    387n384; Truong Son supply route ("Ho
    Chi Minh Trail") and: 382n235; U.S. "free
    fire zones" in: 329; U.S. aerial ordnance
    expended against: 329, 379n143; Truong
    Khanh Massacre in: 325, 326; wartime
    population displacement among: 329

Vietnam Veterans Against the War (VVAW): 337
Villalba, Karla: 118n197
Virgin Islands: as U.S. colony: 19, 66n136
Virginia Colony: 204; College of William and
    Mary in: 237n101; Henrico Academy in:
    237n101
Vitoria (Victoria), Franciscus de: 3, 23n9, 47,
    61n49; influence on Pufendorf: 37; "Just
    War" concept of: 37; on Laws of War: 306

## W

Wagoner, Joseph: 168
Wakatsuki, St. Rep. Richard: 117n168
Wales/Welsh: English conquest/colonization of:
    39
Walker, Deward E.: 244n153
Waller, Maj. Littleton L.T.: 317-8, 324
War of Independence, *see* United States
War of 1812, *see* Great Britain; United States
Waring, SA Gerard: 278, 295n108
Warner, Col. Volney: 270, 273, 291n53
Warren, Shields: 162
Wars of National Liberation: legal protections of:
    118n200
Washburn, Wilcomb E.: 125, 126, 128, 129,
    144n3; as author of *Red Man's Land, White
    Man's Law*: 139
Washington, Pres. George: 5, 306, 320; as "Father
    of His Country": 144n1, 304; as "Town
    Destroyer": 304; diplomacy compared to
    Hitler's: 144n1; orders Sullivan Campaign
    against the Haudenosaunee: 303, 320;
    orders Wayne's campaign against the
    Shawnees: 304
Watkins, Sen. Arthur V.: 138, 139
Wayne, Gen. Anthony ("Mad Anthony"): 5, 304
Wayne, John: 228n38
Webster, Judge William: 281; as FBI director: 281
*Webster's Dictionary*: 255
Weinberger, Sec. of Defense Caspar: as Bechtel
    Corp. vice president: 176; MX missile
    system and: 176, 197n163
Wells Fargo Banking Corp.: 92
Western International Corp.: 92
Western Nuclear Corp.: Sherwood uranium mill
    of: 194m127
Western Shoshones: Duckwater Reservation of:
    175; Timbisha Reservation of: 175; U.S.
    nuclear weapons testing and: 174-6;
    Yomba Reservation of: 175; Yucca Mt.
    nuclear waste repository and: 181
Westmoreland, Gen. William ("Westy"): 321, 327,
    380n174, 383n249; and My Lai Massacre:

322, 323; as head of Military Assistance
Command, Vietnam (MACV): 323
Weyerhauser Corp.: 265
Weyler, Gen. Valeriano: 377n90
Wheeler, Sen. Burton K.: 239n115
Wheeler-Howard Act, *see* Indian Reorganization
Act
Wheelock, Rev. Eleaser: 237n101
White, Justice Edward D.: 14
White Earth Chippewa Reservation: 243n143
"White Indians": phenomenon of: 204-5; policy
towards: 212-3
Whitten, Les: 290n37
Wilcox, Robert W.: 80, 81, 83
Williams, SA Ron: 277, 295n103, 297n122; death
of: 278, 295n108, 296n110, 298n127,
298n128, 298n129, 298n131; funeral of:
296n111
Willingham, Capt. Thomas K.: 325
Wilson, Billy: 294n82
Wilson, George: 291n44
Wilson, Jim: 291n44
Wilson, Gov. Pete: 199n199
Wilson, Richard ("Dickie"): 291n46, 294n91,
295n99; as Pine Ridge tribal president:
269; attempted impeachment of: 269-70;
confrontation with U.S. Marshals of: 274-
5; election fraud committed by: 276, 294-
5n98; forms GOON squads: 269; Giago's
eulogy to: 301n169; misappropriation of
federal funds by: 291n45; nepotism of:
291n44; reservation-wide meeting ban
declared by: 270; signs Sheep Mt. transfer
agreement: 279, 296n114; *also see*
"Guardians of the Oglala Nation"
Wilson, Richard Jr. ("Manny"): 291n44
Wilson, Pres. Woodrow: 47; and declaration of
war on Germany: 63n73; and Ku Klux
Klan: 63n81; as author of *A History of the
American People*: 63n82; as Princeton
history professor: 63n81; 14-Point
Program of: 40, 63n82; white
supremacism of: 43
Wiltse, Capt. G.C.: 82, 112n75, 113n81
Wind River Reservation: 171; Riverton uranium
mill on: 194n127
Winters, Charles David: 294n82
Wirt, Att'ny Gen. William: 7, 10
Wirtz, Capt. Henry: 334, 335
Witt, Indian Claims Comm. Edgar E.: 138,
150n114
Wolf, Bernard: 161
Wong, St. Sen. Francis: 118n185

Wood, SA William: 297n119
Woolworth's Corp.: 252, 253
Work, Sec. of Interior Hubert: 133
World Bank: 94
World Council of Indigenous Peoples: 119n203
World Court, *see* International Court of Justice
World Trade Ctr. (WTC): 360, 369; CIA facility
in: 393n490; fatalities in: 393n489;
occupants of: 393n490; 9-1-1 attack
upon: 358
World War I (First World War): 28n78, 40, 42,
55, 63n73, 385n326
World War II (Second World War): 1, 17, 49, 87,
135, 139, 156, 174, 242n121, 291n46, 326,
369; British/American firebombing of
Dresden during: 333, 378n121; British
firebombing of Hamburg during: 333;
German bombing of Coventry during:
333; German bombing of Rotterdam
during: 333; German bombing of Warsaw
during: 333; German casualties during:
65n110; Malmédy Massacre during: 333;
Soviet casualties during: 65n110;
unrestricted submarine warfare during:
332, 383n262; U.S. aerial ordnance
expended during: 329; U.S. atrocities
committed during: 315-20, 333; U.S.
casualties during: 65n110; U.S. "fire raids"
on Japan during: 320, 378n130; U.S.
nuclear bombings during: 174, 197n160,
320, 378n130; U.S. nuclear weapons
development during: 159
Wounded, Morris: 291n50
Wylie, R.C.: 110n34

**X**

x-rays: 321, 339

**Y**

Yamashita, Gen. Tomoyuki: 333, 383n267
Yemen/Yemenis: al-Qaida cells in: 364; attack on
*U.S.S. Cole* in: 359, 394n497; 2002 oil
tanker bombing in: 403n591
Yellow Thunder, Raymond: 267, 268, 283,
290n28, 290n40
Yellow Thunder Camp (Wincanyan Zi
Tiospaye): 283-4
Young, Lt. Lucien: 76
Young, Phyllis: 272, 300n144
Young Bear, Severt: 267, 291n50
Yugoslavia: as internal colonial state: 1

# Z

Zinn, Howard: 342
Zündel, Ernst: 258n2